LAN	local area network
MAN	metropolitan area network
MD5	Message Digest 5
MIB	management information base
NME	network-management entity
NSAP	network service-access point
OSI	open systems interconnection
OSPF	open shortest path first
PDU	protocol data unit
RFC	request for comments
RMON	remote network monitoring
ROSE	remote-operations-service element
SAP	service-access point
SDU	service data unit
SGMP	simple gateway-monitoring protocol
SMAE	systems-management application entity
SMAP	systems-management application process
SMASE	systems-management application-service element
SMF	systems-management function
SMFA	systems-management functional area
SMI	structure of management information
SMP	simple management protocol
SMTP	simple mail-transfer protocol
SNMP	simple network-management protocol
SNMPv2	simple network-management protocol version 2
TCP	transmission-control protocol
UDP	user datagram protocol
WAN	wide area network

SNMP, SNMPv2, and CMIP

SNMP, SNMPv2, and CMIP

The Practical Guide to Network-Management Standards

William Stallings

ADDISON-WESLEY PUBLISHING COMPANY

Reading, Massachusetts • Menlo Park, California • New York • Don Mills, Ontario
Wokingham, England • Amsterdam • Bonn • Sydney • Singapore • Tokyo • Madrid • San Juan
Paris • Seoul • Milan • Mexico City • Taipei

The publisher offers discounts on this book when ordered in quantity for special sales. For more information, please contact:

Corporate & Professional Publishing Group
Addison-Wesley Publishing Company
One Jacob Way
Reading, Massachusetts 01867

Library of Congress Cataloging-in-Publication Data

Stallings, William.
    SNMP, SNMPv2, and CMIP : the practical guide to network management
standards / William Stallings.
        p.   cm.
    Includes bibliographical references.
    ISBN 0-201-63331-0
    1. Computer networks—Management.   2. Computer network protocols—
Standards.   I. Title.
    TK5105.5.S763   1993
    004.6′2—dc20   92-38220
                                                                          CIP

Cover design by C. Shane Sykes
Cover photo by Dominique Sarraute, The Image Bank
Text design by Carol Keller

ISBN 0-201-63331-0

Text printed on recycled and acid-free paper.

4 5 6 7 8 9 10 CRW 97969594
Fourth printing April 1994

Again, for Tricia

Contents

Preface

The relentless growth in the information-processing needs of organizations has been accompanied by rapid development in computer and data-networking technology to support those needs, and an explosion in the variety of equipment and networks offered by vendors. Gone are the days when an organization would rely on a single vendor and a relatively straightforward architecture to support its needs. The world is no longer divided into the pure mainframe-based, IBM-compatible, centralized environment and the PC-based, single-LAN-type, distributed environment. Today's typical organization has a large and growing but amorphous architecture, with a variety of local area networks (LANs) and wide area networks (WANs), supported by bridges and routers, and a variety of distributed computing services and devices, including PCs, workstations, and servers. And of course, despite over two decades of premature eulogies, the mainframe lives on in countless distributed and a few centralized configurations.

To complicate matters for the system manager, even the basic communications software infrastructure is characterized by diverse and complex choices. The long-awaited open systems interconnection (OSI) set of standards has at last arrived and is making slow but steady progress in the marketplace. But it enters a marketplace already dominated by a well-entrenched set of standards known as the TCP/IP (transmission-control protocol/internet protocol) protocol suite. In the face of these two competing approaches, complicated by proprietary schemes, the system manager must develop a strategy for managing what the organization has now and what it may acquire.

Once the scope of a computing environment extends beyond a single LAN and a few PCs, effective network management is possible only with a set of automated network-management tools. To deal with the multivendor environment of the typical installation, a network-management system is needed that is based on standardized network-management protocols and applications. Unfortunately, here, too, we see two competing approaches evolving. The simple network management protocol (SNMP) was developed to provide a basic, no-frills service for TCP/IP-based environments. Just as TCP/IP now dominates the interoperable communications software market, SNMP dominates the interoperable network-management software market. The alternative approach is a set of standards being developed for use in OSI-based environments, known as OSI systems management. Just as OSI is gradually gaining market share, so, too, OSI systems management should increase in importance over the next few years.

To further complicate matters for the system manager, both SNMP and OSI systems management are "moving targets." A significant revision of SNMP, known as secure SNMP, was issued in 1992. Then, a second-generation facility, originally presented as the simple management protocol (SMP), and now referred to as SNMP version 2 (SNMPv2) was standardized in 1993. SNMPv2 enhances SNMP and secure SNMP with new functionality and is intended for use in both TCP/IP and OSI environments. Meanwhile, OSI systems management continues to evolve, with new standards being published and existing standards being refined.

OBJECTIVE

In order to manage today's systems effectively and plan intelligently for the future use of network-management systems, the system manager needs an understanding of the technology of network management and a thorough grasp of the details of the existing and evolving standards. It is the objective of this book to meet this need.

This book is one of a series of books by the author that provide a comprehensive treatment of computer-communications standards. The series systematically covers all major standards topics, providing the introductory and tutorial text missing from the actual standards. The books function as a primary reference for those who need an understanding of the technology, implementation, design, and application issues that relate to the standards. The books also function as companions to the standards documents for those who need to understand the standards for implementation purposes.

This book provides a comprehensive introduction to network-management standards. Part I is a survey of network-management technology and techniques, to enable the reader to place the various vendor offerings into the context of his or her requirements. Part II presents the SNMP family of standards, including SNMP itself, secure SNMP, and SNMPv2. An important enhancement of SNMP, known as RMON (remote monitoring), is also examined in depth. Part III examines OSI systems management. Throughout, practical issues related to the use of these standards and products based on these standards are examined.

INTENDED AUDIENCE

This tutorial is intended for a broad range of readers interested in network management, including:

- *Students and professionals in data processing and data communications:* This book is intended as a basic tutorial and reference source for this exciting area.

- *Network-management designers and implementers:* This book discusses critical design issues and explores approaches to meeting communication requirements.

- *Network-management system customers and system managers:* This book helps readers understand what features and structures are needed in a network-management facility and provides information about current and evolving standards to enable them to assess a specific vendor's offering.

THE VARIETIES OF SNMP

In August 1988, the specification for SNMP was issued and rapidly became the dominant network management standard. The speed with which SNMP was accepted and the scale of its use caught even its most passionate supporters by surprise. With its widespread use, the deficiencies of SNMP became increasingly apparent; these include both functional deficiencies and a lack of a security facility. To deal with the security requirements, a security enhancement, known as secure SNMP, was published in July 1992 as a proposed standard. That same month, a specification for the simple management protocol (SMP) was published. SMP incorporates, with minor changes, the security features in secure SNMP, and provides functional enhancements to SNMP as well. The proposal was accompanied by four interoperable implementations; two of these implementations are commercial products; the other two are public-domain software.

There was general consensus in the SNMP community that SMP was a good starting place for an open process that would lead to the next generation of SNMP, to be named SNMP version 2 (SNMPv2). Accordingly, SMP was submitted to the standards track process. In the latter part of 1992, there was broad and intense participation in the review of SMP. The result, after several iterations, was a draft set of SNMPv2 specifications that was published in early 1993 as proposed standards.

At the time of this writing (April 1993), the SNMPv2 specification is technically stable. The documents must progress from proposed standards to draft standards to final standards but any technical change at this point is unlikely. This is certainly the hope of the many vendors who have already begun product development.

RELATED MATERIALS

The author has produced other material that may be of interest to students and professionals. *Network Management* (1993; IEEE Computer Society Press, 10662 Los Vaqueros Circle, P.O. Box 3014, Los Alamitos, CA 90720; telephone [714] 821-8380) is a companion to this text and follows the same topical organization. It contains reprints of many of the key references used herein.

The SNMP family of standards is primarily focused on use with TCP/IP-based networks. *Handbook of Computer-Communications Standards, Volume 3: The TCP/IP Protocol Suite, Second Edition* (Macmillan, 1990) provides a detailed treatment of TCP/IP. Similarly, CMIP and the associated OSI network management standards are intended for use with the OSI architecture. Some of the material in this book is adapted from *Networking Standards: A Guide to OSI, ISDN, LAN, and MAN Standards* (Addison-Wesley, 1993) which provides detailed coverage of OSI.

ACKNOWLEDGMENTS

I would especially like to thank three people for their generous assistance. Cheryl Krupczak of Georgia Tech reviewed much of the manuscript with extreme thoroughness; her detailed comments were most helpful. Steve Waldbusser of Carnegie Mellon University provided me with useful insight into the problem of unsupported SNMP MIB objects and provided me with an instructive example of SNMPv2 operation. Finally, the detailed comments of K.K. Ramakrishnan of DEC on the chapter on SNMP RMON resulted in an improved presentation of that complex topic.

Finally, both Vish Narayanan and Gary Wright provided useful reviews of portions of the book.

How to Read This Book

Chapter 1 provides an overview of the concepts used throughout this book and includes a chapter-by-chapter summary. Following this introductory chapter, the book consists of three self-contained parts and four supporting appendixes. The accompanying figure provides a suggested strategy for reading the book.

If you are unfamiliar with network-management concepts or have only a superficial understanding, you should read Part I (Chapters 2 and 3), which provides a basic introduction to the fundamentals of network-management technology.

The remainder of the book deals with the two families of network-management standards, SNMP (simple network management protocol) and OSI (open systems interconnection). Both of these sets of specifications rely heavily on the use of Abstract Syntax Notation One (ASN.1), including the macro facility. The reader not up to speed on this notation should consult Appendix C before proceeding.

Part II (Chapters 4 through 10) deals with SNMP and its enhancements and follow-ons. SNMP was developed for use in a TCP/IP (transmission-control protocol/internet protocol) environment, and the reader unfamiliar with this protocol suite should read Appendix B, which provides an overview. Chapters 4 through 6 cover the basic SNMP standards in detail. Chapter 7 deals with remote monitoring (RMON), which is an important facility that can be provided with SNMP. Chapter 8 covers secure SNMP and Chapters 9 and 10 cover SNMP version 2 (SNMPv2).

Part III deals with OSI systems management. This set of standards relies heavily on the use of object-oriented concepts. The reader unfamiliar with this relatively new technology should consult Appendix D before proceeding. The reader unfamiliar with the basic concepts of OSI architecture should also consult Appendix A, which provides an overview. In addition, the reader who skipped Part II should consider reading Chapters 4 through 7 before reading Part III; many of the mechanisms used in OSI systems management appear in simpler form in SNMP and may be easier to understand if the SNMP versions have been examined first.

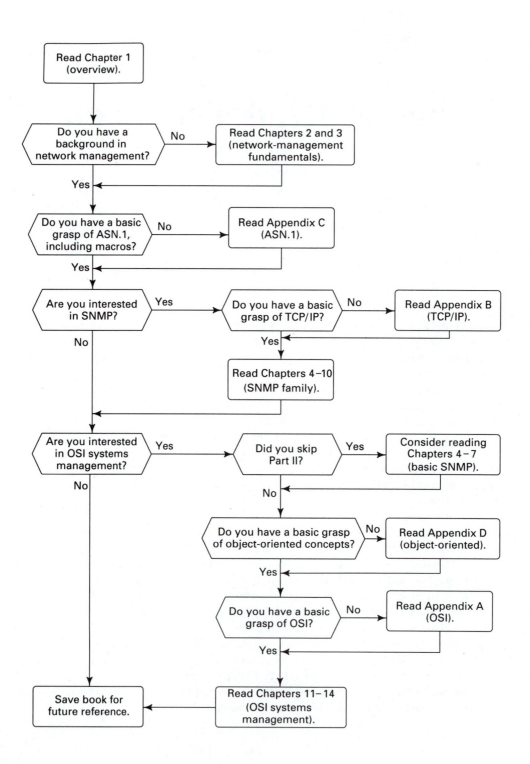

1
Overview

Networks and distributed processing systems are of growing importance and, indeed, have become critical in the business world. Within a given organization, the trend is toward larger, more complex networks supporting more applications and more users. As these networks grow in scale, two facts become painfully evident:

1. The network and its associated resources and distributed applications become indispensable to the organization.
2. More things can go wrong, disabling the network or a portion of the network or degrading performance to an unacceptable level.

A large network cannot be put together and managed by human effort alone. The complexity of such a system dictates the use of automated network-management tools. The urgency of the need for such tools is increased, as is the difficulty of supplying such tools, if the network includes equipment from multiple vendors.

As networked installations become larger, more complex, and more heterogeneous, the cost of network management rises. Figure 1.1, based on a survey among executives of the largest 1,000 U.S. firms, indicates the magnitude of the cost, with over one-quarter of firms spending more than $100,000 on network-management products and one-eighth spending in excess of half a million dollars. An even more impressive result was reported by another survey, this one of 100 of the largest U.S. firms (Horwitt 1992). The survey found that an average of 15 percent of the total information-systems budget is spent on network management, with an average annual expenditure of $1.3 million.

To control costs, standardized tools are needed that can be used across a broad spectrum of product types—including end systems, bridges, routers, and telecommunications equipment—and that can be used in a mixed-vendor environment. In response to this need, two standardization efforts are underway:

1. *SNMP family:* The simple network management protocol (SNMP) actually refers to a set of standards for network management, including a protocol, a database-structure specification,

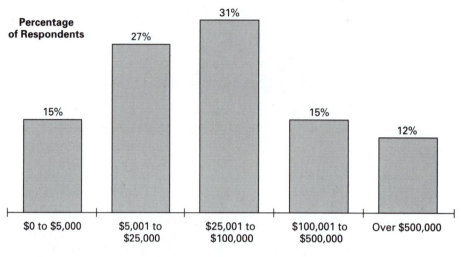

Source: Adapted from Forrester Research, Inc. (May 1992).

Figure 1.1 Company Budgets for Network-Management Products

and a set of data objects. SNMP was adopted as the standard for TCP/IP (transmission-control protocol/internet protocol)–based internets in 1989 and has enjoyed widespread popularity. In 1992, a security enhancement to SNMP was adopted, and an upgrade, known as SNMP version 2 (SNMPv2) was adopted in 1993. The latter is intended to run on OSI (open systems interconnection)–based networks as well as TCP/IP-based networks.

2. *OSI systems management:* This term refers to a large and complex set of standards that define a set of general-purpose network-management applications, a management service and protocol, a database-structure specification, and a set of data objects. This set of international standards is still evolving; as of this writing, some of the standards are final ISO standards, whereas others are still in a draft stage. Because of its complexity and the slow pace of standardization, OSI systems management is only gradually gaining acceptance.

The bulk of this book is devoted to a study of these two approaches to network-management standardization and to some of the practical issues associated with each. The remainder of this chapter, and the next two, provide an overview of network management in general.

1.1   NETWORK-MANAGEMENT REQUIREMENTS

With any design, it is best to begin with a definition of the users' requirements. This is certainly true of an area as complex as network management. One way to do this is to consider the features that are most important to users. Figure 1.2 shows the results of a recent survey. Given the cost of network management and the magnitude of the task, it should be no surprise that ease of use is by far of most critical importance to users.

Another breakdown of users' requirements is provided by Terplan (1992), who lists the following as the principal driving forces justifying an investment in network management:

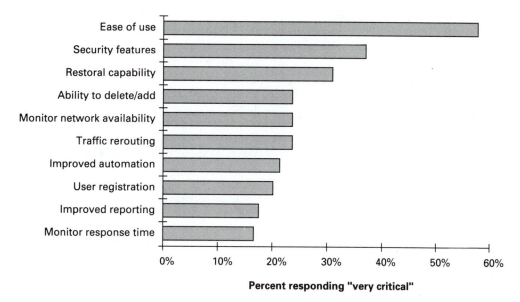

Source: Adapted from International Data Corp. (May 1992).

Figure 1.2 Important Network-Management Features

- *Controlling corporate strategic assets:* Networks and distributed computing resources are increasingly vital resources for most organizations. Without effective control, these resources do not provide the payback that corporate management requires.

- *Controlling complexity:* The continued growth in the number of network components, users, interfaces, protocols, and vendors threatens management with loss of control over what is connected to the network and how network resources are used.

- *Improving service:* Users expect the same or improved service as the organization's information and computing resources grow and become distributed.

- *Balancing various needs:* An organization's information and computing resources must provide a spectrum of users with various applications at given levels of support, with specific requirements in the areas of performance, availability, and security. The network manager must assign and control resources to balance these various needs.

- *Reducing downtime:* As an organization's network resources become more important, minimum availability requirements approach 100 percent. In addition to proper redundant design, network management has an indispensable role to play in ensuring high availability.

- *Controlling costs:* Resource utilization must be monitored and controlled to enable essential user needs to be satisfied at a reasonable cost.

Although such surveys and qualitative statements are useful, and can guide the designer in developing the details of a network-management facility, a functional breakdown of requirements is needed to structure the overall design process. Such a breakdown has been developed by the ISO (International Organization for Standardization) as part of its specification of OSI systems

Table 1.1 OSI Management Functional Areas

Fault management	The facilities that enable the detection, isolation, and correction of abnormal operation of the OSI environment.
Accounting management	The facilities that enable charges to be established for the use of managed objects and costs to be identified for the use of those managed objects.
Configuration and name management	The facilities that exercise control over, identify, collect data from, and provide data to managed objects for the purpose of assisting in providing for continuous operation of interconnection services.
Performance management	The facilities needed to evaluate the behavior of managed objects and the effectiveness of communication activities.
Security management	Address those aspects of OSI security essential to operate OSI network management correctly and to protect managed objects.

management. However, this functional breakdown has found broad acceptance as a useful way of describing the requirements for any network-management system.

Table 1.1 lists the key functional areas of network management as defined by the International Organization for Standardization. Although this functional classification was developed for the OSI environment, it has gained broad acceptance by vendors of both standardized and proprietary network-management systems.

1.1.1 Fault Management

1.1.1.1 Overview

To maintain proper operation of a complex network, care must be taken that systems as a whole, and each essential component individually, are in proper working order. When a fault occurs, it is important, as rapidly as possible, to:

- Determine exactly where the fault is
- Isolate the rest of the network from the failure so that it can continue to function without interference
- Reconfigure or modify the network in such a way as to minimize the impact of operation without the failed component or components
- Repair or replace the failed components to restore the network to its initial state

Central to the definition of fault management is the fundamental concept of a fault. Faults are to be distinguished from errors. A *fault* is an abnormal condition whose repair requires management attention (or action). A fault is usually indicated by failure to operate correctly or by excessive errors. For example, if a communication line is physically cut, no signals can get through. Or a crimp in the cable may cause wild distortions so that there is a persistently high bit-error rate. Certain errors (e.g., a single bit error on a communication line) may occur occasionally and are not normally considered to be faults. It is usually possible to compensate for errors using the error-control mechanisms of the various protocols.

1.1.1.2   User Requirements

Users expect fast and reliable problem resolution. Most end users will tolerate occasional outages. When these infrequent outages do occur, however, users generally expect that they will receive immediate notification and that the problem will be corrected almost immediately. To provide this level of fault resolution requires very rapid and reliable fault-detection and diagnostic-management functions. The impact and duration of faults can also be minimized by the use of redundant components and alternate communication routes, to give the network a degree of "fault tolerance." The fault-management capability itself should be redundant to increase network reliability.

Users expect to be kept informed of the network status, including both scheduled and unscheduled disruptive maintenance. Users expect reassurance of correct network operation through mechanisms that use confidence tests or analyze dumps, logs, alerts, or statistics.

After correcting a fault and restoring a system to its full operational state, the fault-management service must ensure that the problem is truly resolved and that no new problems have been introduced. This requirement is called problem tracking and control.

As with other areas of network management, fault management should have a minimal effect on network performance.

1.1.2   Accounting Management

1.1.2.1   Overview

In many corporate networks, individual divisions or cost centers, or even individual project accounts, are charged for the use of network services. These are internal accounting procedures rather than actual cash transfers, but they are important to the participating users nevertheless. Furthermore, even if no such internal charging is employed, the network manager needs to be able to track the use of network resources by user or user class for a number of reasons, including:

- A user or group of users may be abusing their access privileges and burdening the network at the expense of other users.

- Users may be making inefficient use of the network, and the network manager can assist in changing procedures to improve performance.

- The network manager is in a better position to plan for network growth if user activity is known in sufficient detail.

1.1.2.2   User Requirements

The network manager needs to be able to specify the kinds of accounting information to be recorded at various nodes, the desired interval between sending the recorded information to higher-level management nodes, and the algorithms to be used in calculating the charging. Accounting reports should be generated under network manager control.

In order to limit access to accounting information, the accounting facility must provide the capability to verify users' authorization to access and manipulate that information.

1.1.3   Configuration and Name Management

1.1.3.1   Overview

Modern data-communications networks are composed of individual components and logical sub-systems (e.g., the device driver in an operating system) that can be configured to perform many different applications. The same device, for example, can be configured to act either as a router or as an end-system node or both. Once it is decided how a device is to be used, the configuration manager can choose the appropriate software and set of attributes and values (e.g., a transport-layer retransmission timer) for that device.

Configuration management is concerned with initializing a network and gracefully shutting down part or all of the network. It is also concerned with maintaining, adding, and updating the relationships among components and the status of components themselves during network operation.

1.1.3.2   User Requirements

Start-up and shutdown operations on a network are the specific responsibilities of configuration management. It is often desirable for these operations on certain components to be performed unattended (e.g., starting or shutting down a network-interface unit).

The network manager needs the capability to initially identify the components that comprise the network and to define the desired connectivity of these components. Those who regularly configure a network with the same or a similar set of resource attributes need ways to define and modify default attributes and to load these predefined sets of attributes into the specified network components. The network manager needs the capability to change the connectivity of network components when users' needs change. Reconfiguration of a network is often desired in response to performance evaluation or in support of network upgrade, fault recovery, or security checks.

Users often need, or want, to be informed of the status of network resources and components. Therefore, when changes in configuration occur, users should be notified of these changes. Configuration reports can be generated either on some routine periodic basis or in response to a request for such a report. Before reconfiguration, users often want to inquire about the upcoming status of resources and their attributes.

Network managers usually want only authorized users (operators) to manage and control network operation (e.g., software distribution and updating).

1.1.4   Performance Management

1.1.4.1   Overview

Modern data-communications networks are composed of many and varied components, which must intercommunicate and share data and resources. In some cases, it is critical to the effectiveness of an application that the communication over the network be within certain performance limits.

Performance management of a computer network comprises two broad functional categories—monitoring and controlling. Monitoring is the function that tracks activities on the network. The controlling function enables performance management to make adjustments to improve network performance. Some of the performance issues of concern to the network manager are:

- What is the level of capacity utilization?

- Is there excessive traffic?

- Has throughput been reduced to unacceptable levels?
- Are there bottlenecks?
- Is response time increasing?

To deal with these concerns, the network manager must focus on some initial set of resources to be monitored in order to assess performance levels. This includes associating appropriate metrics and values with relevant network resources as indicators of different levels of performance. For example, what count of retransmissions on a transport connection is considered to be a performance problem requiring attention? Performance management must therefore monitor many resources to provide information for determining network operating level. By collecting this information, analyzing it, and then using the resultant analysis as feedback to the prescribed set of values, the network manager can become more and more adept at recognizing situations indicative of present or impending performance degradation.

1.1.4.2   User Requirements

Before employing a network for a particular application, a user may want to know such things as the average and worst-case response times and the reliability of network services. Thus, performance must be known in sufficient detail to respond to specific user queries.

End users expect network services to be managed in such a way as to consistently afford their applications good response time.

Network managers need performance statistics to help them plan, manage, and maintain large networks. Performance statistics can be used to recognize potential bottlenecks before they cause problems to the end users. Appropriate corrective action can then be taken. This action can take the form of changing routing tables to balance or redistribute traffic load during times of peak use or when a bottleneck is identified by a rapidly growing load in one area. Over the long term, capacity planning based on such performance information can indicate the proper decisions to make—for example, with regard to expansion of lines in that area.

1.1.5   Security Management

1.1.5.1   Overview

Security management is concerned with generating, distributing, and storing encryption keys. Passwords and other authorization or access-control information must be maintained and distributed. Security management is also concerned with monitoring and controlling access to computer networks and access to all or part of the network-management information obtained from the network nodes. Logs are an important security tool, and therefore, security management is very much involved with the collection, storage, and examination of audit records and security logs, as well as with the enabling and disabling of these logging facilities.

1.1.5.2   User Requirements

Security management provides facilities for protection of network resources and user information. Network security facilities should be available to authorized users only. Users want to know that the proper security policies are in force and effective and that the management of security facilities is itself secure.

1.2   NETWORK-MANAGEMENT SYSTEMS

A network-management system is a collection of tools for network monitoring and control that is integrated in the following senses:

- A single operator interface with a powerful but user-friendly set of commands for performing most or all network-management tasks.
- A minimal amount of separate equipment. That is, most of the hardware and software required for network management is incorporated into the existing user equipment.

A network-management system consists of incremental hardware and software additions implemented among existing network components. The software used in accomplishing the network-management tasks resides in the host computers and communications processors (e.g., front-end processors, terminal cluster controllers, bridges, routers). A network-management system is designed to view the entire network as a unified architecture, with addresses and labels assigned to each point and the specific attributes of each element and link known to the system. The active elements of the network provide regular feedback of status information to the network-control center.

1.2.1   Network-Management Configuration

Figure 1.3 suggests the architecture of a network-management system. Each network node contains a collection of software devoted to the network-management task, referred to in the diagram as a network-management entity. Each NME performs the following tasks:

- Collects statistics on communications and network-related activities
- Stores statistics locally
- Responds to commands from the network-control center, including commands to:
  - Transmit collected statistics to the network-control center
  - Change a parameter (e.g., a timer used in a transport protocol)
  - Provide status information (e.g., parameter values, active links)
  - Generate artificial traffic to perform a test

At least one host in the network is designated as the network-control host, or *manager*. In addition to the NME software, the network-control host includes a collection of software called the network-management application. The NMA includes an operator interface to allow an authorized user to manage the network. The NMA responds to user commands by displaying information and/ or by issuing commands to NMEs throughout the network. This communication is carried out using an application-level network-management protocol that employs the communications architecture in the same fashion as any other distributed application.

Each other node in the network that is part of the network-management system includes an NME and, for purposes of network management, is referred to as an *agent*. Agents include end systems that support user applications as well as nodes that provide a communications service, such as front-end processors, cluster controllers, bridges, and routers.

Several observations are in order:

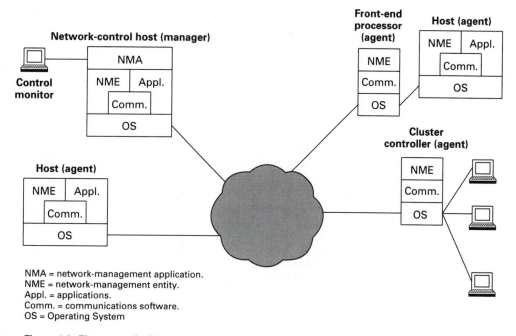

NMA = network-management application.
NME = network-management entity.
Appl. = applications.
Comm. = communications software.
OS = Operating System

Figure 1.3 Elements of a Network-Management System

- Since the network-management software relies on the host operating system and on the communications architecture, most offerings to date are designed for use on a single vendor's equipment. As was mentioned, standards in this area are still evolving. However, recent years have seen the emergence of standardized network-management systems designed to manage a multiple-vendor network.

- As depicted in Figure 1.3, the network-control host communicates with and controls the NMEs in other systems.

- To maintain high availability of the network-management function, two or more network-control hosts are used. In normal operation, one of the centers is idle or simply collecting statistics, while the other is used for control. If the primary network-control host fails, the backup system can be used.

1.2.2   Network-Management-Software Architecture

The actual architecture of the network-management software in a manager or an agent varies greatly, depending on the functionality of the platform and the details of the network-management capability. Figure 1.4, derived from a figure in Feldkhun (1989), presents a generic view of such an architecture. The software can be divided into three broad categories:

1. User presentation software

2. Network-management software

3. Communications and database-support software

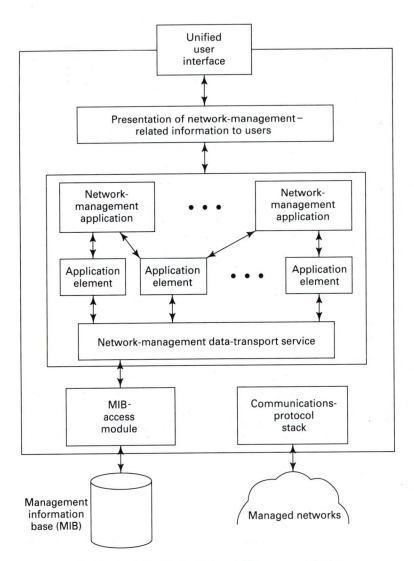

Figure 1.4 Architectural Model of a Network-Management System

1.2.2.1   User Presentation Software

Interaction between a user of network management and the network-management software takes place across a user interface. Such an interface is needed in any manager system, to allow a user to monitor and control the network. It may also be useful to have such an interface in some agent systems for purposes of testing and debugging, and also to allow some parameters to be viewed or set locally.

The key to an effective network-management system is a *unified* user interface. The interface should be the same at any node, regardless of vendor. This allows a user to manage a heterogeneous configuration with a minimum of training.

One danger in any network-management system is information overload. If a configuration is instrumented properly, a tremendous amount of information is available to the network-management user. Presentation tools are needed to organize, summarize, and simplify this information as much as possible. Ideally, there will be an emphasis on graphic presentations over text or tabular outputs.

1.2.2.2 Network-Management Software

The software that specifically provides the network-management application may be very simple, as in the case of SNMP, or very complex, as in the case of OSI systems management. The central box in Figure 1.4 shows a rather complex structure that reflects the architecture of OSI systems management and that is also suggestive of a typical proprietary network-management system.

The network-management software in the figure is organized into three layers. The top layer consists of a collection of network-management applications that provide the services of interest to users. For example, these applications could correspond to the OSI management functional areas: fault management, accounting management, configuration management, performance management, and security. Each application covers a broad area of network management and should exhibit consistent behavior over various types of configurations, although there may be detailed differences depending on the nature of the network facility (e.g., LAN [local area network], WAN [wide area network], T1 multiplexer network).

The small number of network-management applications is supported by a larger number of application elements. These are modules that implement more primitive and more general-purpose network-management functions, such as generating alarms or summarizing data. The application elements implement basic tools that are of use to one or more of the network-management applications. Organizing the software in terms of applications and application elements follows traditional modular design principles and enables a more efficient implementation to be developed based on software reuse.

The lowest level of management-specific software is a network-management data-transport service. This module consists of a network-management protocol used to exchange management information among managers and agents and a service interface to the application elements. Typically, the service interface provides very primitive functions, such as get information, set parameters, and generate notifications.

1.2.2.3 Network-Management–Support Software

To perform its intended functions, network-management software needs access to a local management information base (MIB) and to remote agents and managers.

The local MIB at an agent contains information of use to network management, including information that reflects the configuration and behavior of this node, and parameters that can be used to control the operation of this node. The local MIB at a manager contains such node-specific information as well as summary information about agents under the manager's control. The MIB-access module includes basic file-management software that enables access to the MIB. In addition, the access module may need to convert from the local MIB format to a form that is standardized across the network-management system.

Communication with other nodes (agents and managers) is supported by a communications-protocol stack, such as OSI or the TCP/IP stack. The communications architecture thus supports the network-management protocol, which is at an application level.

1.2.3   Distributed Network Management

The configuration depicted in Figure 1.3 suggests a centralized network-management strategy, with a single network-control center and perhaps a standby center. This is the strategy that has traditionally been favored by both mainframe vendors and information-system executives. A centralized network-management system implies central control. This makes sense in a mainframe-dominated configuration, where the key resources reside in a computer center and service is provided to remote users. The strategy also makes sense to managers responsible for the total information-system assets of an organization. A centralized network-management system enables the manager to maintain control over the entire configuration, balancing resources against needs and optimizing the overall utilization of resources.

But just as the centralized computing model has given way to a distributed computing architecture, with applications shifted from data centers to remote departments, network management is also becoming distributed. The same factors come into play: the proliferation of low-cost, high-power PCs and workstations, the proliferation of departmental LANs, and the need for local control and optimization of distributed applications.

A distributed management system replaces the single network-control center with interoperable workstations located on LANs distributed throughout the enterprise. This strategy gives departmental-level managers, who must watch over downsized applications and PC LANs, with the tools they need to maintain responsive networks, systems, and applications for their local users. To prevent anarchy, a hierarchical architecture is typically used, with the following elements:

- Distributed management stations are given limited access for network monitoring and control, usually defined by the departmental resources they serve.

- One central workstation, with a backup, has global access rights and the ability to manage all network resources. It can also interact with less-enabled management stations to monitor and control their operation.

While maintaining the capacity for central control, the distributed approach offers a number of benefits:

- Network-management traffic overhead is minimized. Much of the traffic is confined to the local environment.

- Distributed management offers greater scalability. Adding management capability is simply a matter of deploying another inexpensive workstation at the desired location.

- The use of multiple, networked stations eliminates the single point of failure that exists with centralized schemes.

Figure 1.5 illustrates the basic structure used for most distributed network-management systems now on the market. Closest to the users are the management clients. These give users access to management services and information and provide an easy-to-use graphic user interface. Depending on access privileges, a client workstation may access one or more management servers. The management servers are the heart of the system. Each server supports a set of management applications and a management information base. They also store common management-data models and route management information to applications and clients. Those devices to be managed that

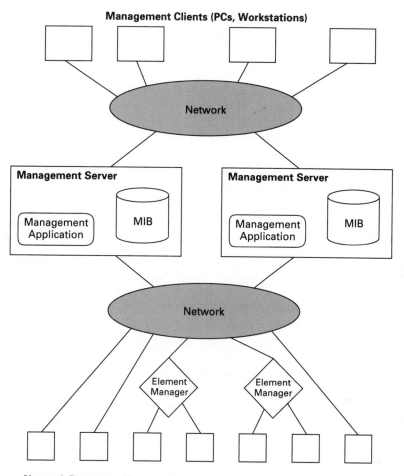

Management Clients (PCs, Workstations)

Network Resources (Servers, Routers, Hosts) with Management Agents

Figure 1.5   Typical Distributed Management-System Architecture

share the same network-management protocol as the management servers contain agent software and are managed directly by one or more management servers. For other devices, management servers can only reach the resources through a vendor-specific element manager, or proxy. The concept of proxy is explored in the next subsection.

The flexibility and scalability of the distributed management model are evident from Figure 1.5. As more resources are added to the configuration, each is equipped with agent software or linked to a proxy. In a centralized system, this growth might eventually overwhelm a central station. But in a distributed system, more management servers and client workstations can be added to cope with the extra resources. Furthermore, the growth of the overall configuration will occur in a structured way (e.g., adding another LAN with a number of attached PCs); the growth of the management system mirrors this underlying resource growth, with servers and clients added where the new resources are located.

1.2.4   Proxies

Figure 1.3 suggests that each component of the configuration that is of management interest includes a network-management entity, with common network-management software across all managers and agents. In an actual configuration, this may not be practical or even possible. For example, the configuration may include older systems that do not support the network-management standards that are being used, small systems that would be unduly burdened by a full-blown NME implementation, or components such as modems and multiplexers that do not support additional software.

To handle such cases, it is common to have one of the agents in the configuration serve as a proxy for one or more other nodes. We will have more to say about proxies in Part II, but for now, we provide a brief introduction to the concept.

When an agent performs in a proxy role, it acts on behalf of one or more other nodes. A network manager that wishes to obtain information from or control the node communicates with the proxy agent. The proxy agent then translates the manager's request into a form appropriate for the target system and uses whatever network-management protocol is appropriate to communicate with the target system. Responses from the target system back to the proxy are similarly translated and passed on to the manager.

Figure 1.6 illustrates a structured architecture that enables a management application to manage a proprietary resource through standard operations and event reports, which are translated by the proxy system into proprietary operations and event reports. In this case, a remote procedure call (RPC) mechanism is used (Aguilar 1991). The RPC mechanism is frequently found with distributed system software and provides a flexible and easy-to-use facility for supporting the proxy function.

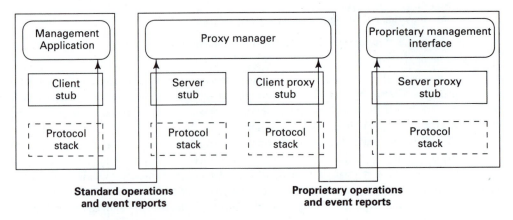

Figure 1.6 Proxy Manager Architecture

1.3   OUTLINE OF THE BOOK

This chapter serves as an introduction to the entire book. A brief synopsis of the remaining chapters follows.

1.3.1   Chapter 2: "Network Monitoring"

Fundamental to network management is the ability to gather information about the status and behavior of the networked configuration, which is the function of network monitoring. Indeed, many network-management systems provide only a network-monitoring capability. This chapter examines the basic architectural and design issues of network monitoring and then looks at three specific areas: performance monitoring, fault monitoring, and accounting monitoring.

1.3.2   Chapter 3: "Network Control"

A complete network-management system will include the capability of controlling a configuration as well as monitoring it. Chapter 3 examines the basic mechanisms of network control and then looks at two specific aspects of network control: configuration control and security control.

1.3.3   Chapter 4: "SNMP Network-Management Concepts"

A network-management framework for TCP/IP–based internets has been developed and standardized for use in conjunction with the TCP/IP protocol suite. The framework includes the simple network-management protocol (SNMP), a structure of management information (SMI), and a management information base (MIB). This chapter provides an overview of the concepts that underlie SNMP and the related standards.

1.3.4   Chapter 5: "SNMP Management Information Base"

Management information accessible via SNMP is maintained in a management information base at each manager and agent node. This chapter summarizes the structure of SNMP management information, which consists of a simple, hierarchical structure of objects. Each object represents some attribute of a managed resource. The chapter then examines MIB-II, which is a structured set of standard objects that includes many of the objects commonly required in an SNMP-based network-management system.

1.3.5   Chapter 6: "Simple Network-Management Protocol (SNMP)"

Chapter 6 examines the basic principles of operation of SNMP. Then, the protocol specification itself is examined in detail. The chapter also discusses the type of transport-level service that may be used to support SNMP and then looks at the MIB objects used to monitor and manage the operation of the protocol itself.

1.3.6   Chapter 7: "Remote Monitoring"

A network-management system is concerned not only with the status and behavior of individual nodes on a network but with the traffic on the network itself. *Remote monitoring* is a term used to refer to the monitoring of a network by one of the nodes on the network, for the purposes of network management. In the context of SNMP, a remote-monitoring (RMON) MIB has been defined. The RMON MIB specifies the information that is to be collected and stored by a remote monitor. The specification also defines the functionality of both the monitor and the manager-monitor interaction.

1.3.7   Chapter 8: "Secure SNMP"

A deficiency of the original SNMP set of specifications is that they contain only a very weak mechanism for enforcing security. To remedy this deficiency, a security enhancement to SNMP has been specified. This chapter summarizes the secure SNMP facility.

1.3.8   Chapter 9: "SNMPv2: Management Information and Protocol"

As the name suggests, SNMP provides a simple facility for network management, one that is easy to implement and should consume minimal processing resources. Many users of SNMP have felt the need for a more powerful and comprehensive facility, without going to the full-blown capability represented by OSI systems management. In response to this need, the version 2 of SNMP (SNMPv2) was developed. SNMPv2 provides the security features of Secure SNMP plus functional enhancements to SNMP. SNMPv2 was actually developed by two separate working groups, one concentrating on management information and protocol issues, and one on security. This chapter examines the management information and protocol aspects of SNMPv2.

1.3.9   Chapter 10: "SNMPv2: Security"

This chapter presents the security features of SNMPv2, emphasizing the differences between this specification and the Secure SNMP specification.

1.3.10   Chapter 11: "OSI Systems-Management Concepts"

A network-management framework for OSI-based networks and internets has been standardized by the ISO (International Organization for Standardization). Within this framework, standards are being developed for systems-management functions, management service and protocols, and a structure of management information. This chapter provides an overview of this framework.

1.3.11   Chapter 12: "OSI Management Information Base"

Chapter 12 summarizes the structure of OSI management information, which makes use of object-oriented design principles. Using the object-oriented concepts of inheritance and containment, complex structures of management objects may be constructed. Each object represents a managed resource, an aspect of a managed resource, or some other element of management information. An object may contain attributes, behaviors, and notifications. This chapter summarizes the principles of the OSI MIB and provides examples of the definition of objects, including a detailed look at objects for the transport layer.

1.3.12   Chapter 13: "CMIS and CMIP"

The foundation of OSI systems-management applications is the common management information service (CMIS), which provides a set of primitive functions, including get and set attributes, create and delete objects, and send an event report. The CMIS is, in turn, implemented by the application-level common management information protocol (CMIP). This chapter describes both CMIS and CMIP.

1.3.13   Chapter 14: "Systems-Management Functions"

Systems-management functions are standardized application elements that make use of CMIS and of each other to provide basic application modules. These, in turn, support broad network-management applications, such as accounting management. Currently, thirteen management functions have been defined; these are described in Chapter 14.

1.3.14   Appendix A: "The Open Systems Interconnection (OSI) Reference Model"

Appendix A summarizes the OSI model, including a discussion of key concepts and a brief description of each of the model's seven layers.

1.3.15   Appendix B: "The TCP/IP Protocol Suite"

Appendix B summarizes the TCP/IP protocol suite, including the protocol architecture and each layer of the architecture.

1.3.16   Appendix C: "Abstract Syntax Notation One (ASN.1)"

ASN.1 is the language used to define the syntax of objects in the management information base for both the SNMP family and OSI systems management. In addition, the syntax of application-level protocol data units for both the SNMP family and OSI systems management is defined using ASN.1. The basic elements of ASN.1 and examples of its use are presented in Appendix C.

1.3.17   Appendix D: "Object-Oriented Design"

Object-oriented design principles play a key role in the OSI structure of management information. Appendix D provides a brief overview.

APPENDIX 1A   How to Keep Up

It is our hope that this book will serve as both a tutorial for learning about the field of network management and a reference that can be returned to for help on specific topics. However, given the rapid changes taking place in both the technology and the standards for this field, no book can hope to stand alone for very long. The reader who is truly interested in this field will therefore need to invest a certain amount of time in keeping up with new developments.

1A.1   PERIODICALS

The International Journal of Network Management, published by John Wiley & Sons (Baffins Lane, Chichester, West Sussex PO191UD, U.K.), provides practical, relatively nontechnical articles on network management, generally from the user's point of view.

Network Management (Circulation Department, P.O. Box 2417, Tulsa, OK 74101) is a trade magazine oriented toward users and customers. It is available free to "qualified" subscribers.

The Simple Times is devoted to the promotion of the simple network-management protocol (SNMP). Each issue includes a refereed technical article, an industry comment, and several featured columns. It is available free of charge via electronic mail in PostScript or MIME (multimedia 822 format); send requests to st-subscriptions@simple-times.org. It is also available free in hard-copy form from most SNMP vendors.

1A.2   ELECTRONIC-MAILING LISTS

A useful way to track developments in a particular area is to join an electronic-mailing list. A mailing list is really nothing more than an alias that has multiple destinations. Mailing lists are usually created to discuss specific topics and provide a useful forum for getting answers to questions. Anyone interested in the particular topic may join that list.

A number of mailing lists are available on the Internet. Anyone directly connected to the Internet, or with indirect connection through such networks as MCImail or Compuserve, can participate in the Internet mailing lists. The general convention for being added to or deleted from mailing list X is to send a message to X-request@host requesting addition or deletion of your name. Once you have been added to a list, you will receive a copy of every message posted to the list. If you wish to ask a question or respond to someone else's question, send a message to X@host. Your message will be posted to the list. As a member of the list, you will yourself receive a copy of the message, which serves as a check that the message was posted.

Mailing lists such as these should not be abused, since excessive messages clog the Internet and the mailbox of every member of the list. On the other hand, don't hesitate to ask even elementary questions that you can't answer yourself with the aid of available documentation. Generally, someone will take the time to answer.

Mailing lists that may be of interest include the following:

- *SNMP mailing list:* discussion of topics related to SNMP. Currently, this is a very active list, covering details of existing SNMP implementations as well as future versions of the protocol, such as SNMPv2. Address: snmp@psi.com.

- *RMON mailing list:* a recently created mailing list devoted to the RMON (remote-monitoring) portion of SNMP. Address: rmonmib@jarthur.claremont.edu.

- *Network-management mailing list:* discussion of general topics related to network management and network operations. Currently, not very active. Address: netops@decwrl.dec.com.

- *ISO mailing list:* discussion of topics related to ISO standards and the open systems interconnection (OSI) model. OSI systems management may be discussed here. Address: iso@nic.ddn.mil.

1A.3 USENET NEWS GROUPS

Another handy way to track developments and get questions answered is USENET. USENET is a collection of electronic bulletin boards that work in much the same way as the Internet mailing lists. If you subscribe to a particular news group, you receive all messages posted to that group, and you may post a message that is available to all subscribers. The differences between USENET and Internet mailing lists have to do with the mechanics of the systems. USENET is actually a distributed network of sites that collect and broadcast news group entries. To access a news group, for read or write, one must have access to a USENET node. Such nodes are accessible over the Internet, and in a variety of other ways.

Relevant news groups:

- *ISO news group:* discussion of topics related to ISO standards and the Open Systems Interconnection (OSI) model. OSI systems management may be discussed here. Address: comp.protocols.iso.

- *SNMP news group:* discussion of topics related to SNMP. Address: comp.protocols.snmp.

If one had to choose between USENET and the Internet mailing lists, the latter are much more important for the topics related to network management. However, it is possible to pick up some useful information via USENET.

1A.4 STANDARDS DOCUMENTS

Extensions to the SNMP capability continue to be developed. These are published as RFCs (requests for comments). Anyone with access to the Internet can keep up by accessing electronic copies of the RFCs via the Internet. A handy and surprisingly inexpensive alternative is to subscribe to the RFC publication service, which provides subscribers with a hard copy of every RFC as it is published. The RFC Subscription Service is available from:

SRI International
Network Information Systems Center
333 Ravenswood Avenue, Room EJ291
Menlo Park, CA 94025
telephone: (415) 859-6387 or (415) 859-3695
fax: (415) 859-6028
E-mail: nisc@nisc.sri.com

The ISO is also very active in producing standards for data communications and networking, including standards related to OSI systems management. A related, and overlapping, set of standards is issued by the CCITT (International Consultative Committee on Telegraphy and Telephony). One convenient source for hard copies of these documents is Omnicom/PPI. This company publishes a bimonthly list entitled *ISO Standards for Open Systems Interconnection and Data Communication.* Each list includes the name, title, number of pages, and date of publication of every ISO standard, draft standard, and working draft related to OSI and data communications; new standards and new editions are highlighted in each list. The same company from time to time publishes lists of new CCITT documents related to OSI and data communications. Both the ISO and CCITT documents can be ordered directly from the company, at the same prices as direct purchase from the standards body. The address:

Omnicom/PPI
7811 Montrose Road
Potomac, MD 20854
telephone: (800)-OMNICOM (666-4266)
fax: (301) 309-3847

1A.5   NETWORK MANAGEMENT FORUM

The Network Management Forum is an independent, incorporated industry consortium of computing and network equipment suppliers, service providers, and users whose goal is the promotion of interoperable, multivendor network-management systems. The forum's activities include:

- Approval and recommendation of specifications based on the most appropriate internationally recognized standards
- The development of support tools, including conformance and interoperability test systems
- The definition of management information structures that can be used to form common, interoperable databases for network-management systems

The most significant achievement of the forum to date was the release in September 1992 of *OMNIPoint* (Open Management Interoperability Point) *1*, a comprehensive set of open standards and specifications for network management. *OMNIPoint 1* is designed as the first of an ongoing series of reference guides for buyers and makers of network-management products and services. It is a set of 97 documents that includes user requirements, procurement and development guides, management information libraries, coexistence plans, regional and consortia standards agreements, application-program interfaces, migration guidelines, testing processes, and other elements.

Although the initial emphasis of the forum was on OSI systems management, its members recognized the reality that, for now, SNMP is the dominant interoperable, multivendor solution. Accordingly, both SNMP and OSI systems management are within the forum's domain of interest.

Membership in the forum ranges from affiliate status, at $1,000 per year, to board membership, at $55,000 plus a commitment of 2.5 staff-years of resources or $140,000 plus a commitment of 1.5 staff-years of resources. The address:

Network Management Forum
40 Morristown Road
Bernardsville, NJ 07924
telephone: U.S.A.: (908) 766-1544
                U.K.: 44-473-288595
fax: (908) 766-5741

Part 1
Network-Management Fundamentals

Network-management functions can be grouped into two categories: network monitoring and network control. Network monitoring is a "read function." It is concerned with observing and analyzing the status and behavior of the configuration and its components. Network control is a "write function." It is concerned with altering the parameters of various components of the configuration and causing those components to perform predefined actions.

Chapter 2 is concerned with network monitoring. Overall architectural considerations for network monitoring are examined first. Then, three of the key areas of network monitoring are examined: performance monitoring, fault monitoring, and accounting monitoring.

Network control is the subject of Chapter 3, which examines two key areas of network control: configuration control and security control.

2
Network Monitoring

The network-monitoring portion of network management is concerned with observing and analyzing the status and behavior of the end systems, intermediate systems, and subnetworks that make up the configuration to be managed.

Chiu and Sudama (1992) suggest that network monitoring consists of three major design areas:

1. *Access to monitored information:* concerned with how to define monitoring information and how to get that information from a resource to a manager

2. *Design of monitoring mechanisms:* concerned with how best to obtain information from resources

3. *Application of monitored information:* concerned with how the monitored information is used in various management functional areas

The first section of this chapter deals with the first two items in the preceding list, by examining some of the general design considerations for a network-monitoring system. The remainder of the chapter deals with network-monitoring applications. Network monitoring encompasses all of the functional areas listed in Table 1.1. In this chapter, we focus on the three functional areas that are generally most important for network monitoring: performance monitoring, fault monitoring, and accounting monitoring.

2.1 NETWORK-MONITORING ARCHITECTURE

Before considering the design of a network-monitoring system, it is best to consider the type of information that is of interest to a network monitor. Then, we can look at the alternatives for configuring the network-monitoring function. Finally, this section addresses the key design issue of the strategy for gathering information.

2.1.1   Network-Monitoring Information

The information that should be available for network monitoring can be classified as follows:

- *Static:* information that characterizes the current configuration and the elements in the current configuration, such as the number and identification of ports on a router. This information will change only infrequently.

- *Dynamic:* information related to events in the network, such as a change of state of a protocol machine or the transmission of a packet on a network.

- *Statistical:* information that may be derived from dynamic information, such as the average number of packets transmitted per unit of time by an end system.

An example of such an information structure, for use in monitoring a real-time system, is suggested in Mazumdar and Lazar (1991). In this scheme, the static database has two major components: a configuration database, with basic information about the computer and networking elements, and a sensor database, with information about sensors used to obtain real-time readings. The dynamic database is primarily concerned with collecting information about the state of various network elements and events detected by the sensors. The statistical database includes useful aggregate measures. Figure 2.1 suggests the relationships among these components.

The nature of the monitored information has implications for where it is collected and stored for purposes of monitoring. Static information is typically generated by the element involved. Thus, a router maintains its own configuration information. This information can be made available directly to a monitor if the element has the appropriate agent software. Alternatively, the information can be made available to a proxy that, in turn, will make it available to a monitor.

Dynamic information, too, is generally collected and stored by the network element responsible for the underlying events. However, if a system is attached to a LAN (local area network), then much of its activity can be observed by another system on the LAN. The term *remote monitor* is used to refer to a device on a LAN that observes all the traffic on the LAN and gathers information about that traffic. For example, the total number of packets issued by an element on a LAN could be recorded by the element itself or by a remote monitor that is listening on the same LAN. Some dynamic information, however, can only be generated by the element itself, such as the current number of network-level connections.

Statistical information can be generated by any system that has access to the underlying dynamic information. The statistical information could be generated back at the network monitor itself. This would require that all the "raw" data be transmitted to the monitor, where they would be analyzed and summarized. If the monitor does not need access to all the raw data, then monitor processing time and network capacity could be saved if the system that holds the dynamic data does the summarization and sends the results to the monitor.

2.1.2   Network-Monitoring Configurations

Figure 2.2, based on a depiction in Chiu and Sudama (1992), illustrates the architecture for network monitoring in functional terms. Figure 2.2, part (a), shows the four major components of a network-monitoring system:

1. *Monitoring application:* the functions of network monitoring that are visible to the user, such as performance monitoring, fault monitoring, and accounting monitoring

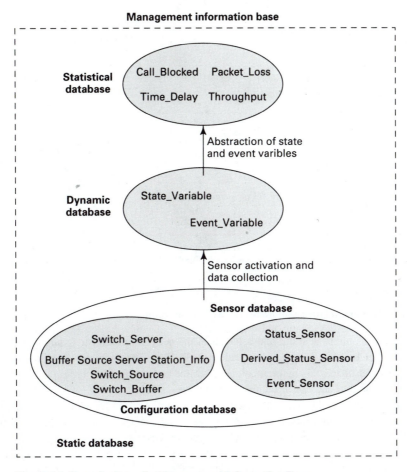

Figure 2.1 Organization of a Management Information Base

2. *Manager function:* the module at the network monitor that performs the basic monitoring function of retrieving information from other elements of the configuration

3. *Agent function:* the module that gathers and records management information for one or more network elements and communicates the information to the monitor

4. *Managed objects:* the management information that represents resources and their activities

It is useful to highlight an additional functional module concerned with statistical information (Figure 2.2, part [b]):

5. *Monitoring agent:* a module that generates summaries and statistical analyses of management information. If remote from the manager, this module acts as an agent and communicates the summarization information to the manager.

These functional modules may be configured in a number of ways. The station that hosts the monitoring application is itself a network element and subject to monitoring. Thus, the network monitor generally includes agent software and a set of managed objects (Figure 2.3, part [a]). In

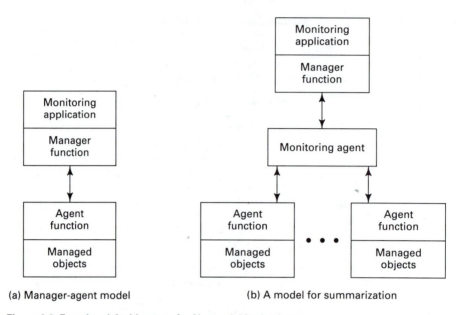

(a) Manager-agent model   (b) A model for summarization

Figure 2.2 Functional Architecture for Network Monitoring

fact, it is vital to monitor the status and behavior of the network monitor to assure that it continues to perform its function and to assess the load on itself and on the network. One key requirement is that the network-management protocol be instrumented to monitor the amount of network-management traffic into and out of the network monitor.

Figure 2.3, part (b), illustrates the most common configuration for monitoring other network elements. This configuration requires that the manager and agent systems share the same network-management protocol and MIB (management information base) syntax and semantics.

A network-monitoring system may also include one or more agents that monitor traffic on a network. These are often referred to as external monitors or remote monitors; the configuration is depicted in Figure 2.3, part (c).

Finally, as was mentioned before, for network elements that do not share a common network-management protocol with the network monitor, a proxy agent is needed (Figure 2.3, part [d]).

2.1.3 Polling and Event Reporting

Information that is useful for purposes of network monitoring is collected and stored by agents and made available to one or more manager systems. Two techniques are used to make the agent information available to the manager: polling and event reporting.

Polling is a request/response interaction between manager and agent. The manager can query any agent (for which it has authorization) and request the values of various information elements; the agent responds with information from its MIB. The request may be specific, listing one or more named variables. A request may also be in the nature of a search, asking the agent to report information matching certain criteria or supply the manager with information about the structure of the MIB at the agent. A manager system may use polling to learn about the configuration it is managing, to periodically obtain an update of conditions, or to investigate an area in detail after

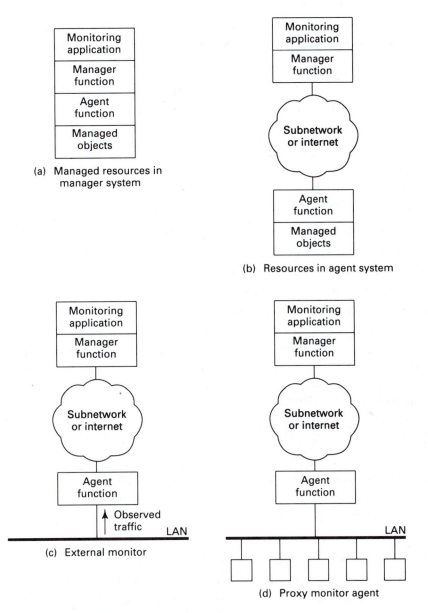

(a) Managed resources in manager system

(b) Resources in agent system

(c) External monitor

(d) Proxy monitor agent

Figure 2.3 Network-Monitoring Configurations

being alerted to a problem. Polling is also used to generate a report on behalf of a user and to respond to specific user queries.

With event reporting, the initiative is with the agent, and the manager is in the role of a listener, waiting for incoming information. An agent may generate a report periodically to give the manager its current status. The reporting period may be preconfigured or set by the manager. An agent may also generate a report when a significant event (e.g., a change of state) or an unusual event (e.g., a fault) occurs. Event reporting is useful for detecting problems as soon as they arise. It is also more efficient than polling for monitoring objects whose states or values change relatively infrequently.

Both polling and event reporting are useful, and a network-monitoring system will typically employ both methods. There is a large disparity in the relative emphasis placed on the two methods in various systems. Telecommunications-management systems have traditionally placed a very high reliance on event reporting. In contrast, the SNMP (simple network-management protocol) approach places very little reliance on event reporting. OSI (open systems interconnection) systems management tends to fall somewhere between these extremes. However, both SNMP and OSI systems management, as well as most proprietary schemes, allow the user considerable latitude in determining the relative emphasis on the two approaches. The choice of emphasis depends on a number of factors, including the following:

- The amount of network traffic generated by each method
- Robustness in critical situations
- The time delay in notifying the network manager
- The amount of processing in managed devices
- The trade-offs of reliable versus unreliable transfer
- The network-monitoring applications being supported
- The contingencies required in case a notifying device fails before sending a report

2.2 PERFORMANCE MONITORING

2.2.1 Performance Indicators

An absolute prerequisite for the management of a communications network is the ability to measure the network's performance. We cannot hope to manage and control a system or an activity unless we can monitor its performance. One of the difficulties facing the network manager involves selecting and using the appropriate indicators to measure the network's performance. Among the problems:

- There are too many indicators in use.
- The meanings of most indicators are not yet clearly understood.
- Some indicators are introduced and supported only by certain manufacturers.
- Most indicators are not suitable for comparison with each other.
- Frequently, the indicators are accurately measured but incorrectly interpreted.
- In many cases, the calculation of indicators takes too much time, and the final results can hardly be used for controlling the environment.

In this subsection, we give some general ideas of the types of indicators that are useful for network management. These fall into two categories: service-oriented measures and efficiency-oriented measures; Table 2.1, based on Terplan (1992), gives a breakdown of major indicators in each category. The principal means of judging that a network is meeting its requirements is that

Table 2.1 Network Performance Indicators

Service-Oriented	
Availability	The percentage of time that a network system, a component, or an application is available for a user.
Response time	How long it takes for a response to appear at a user's terminal after a user action that calls for a response.
Accuracy	The percentage of time that no errors occur in the transmission and delivery of information.
Efficiency-Oriented	
Throughput	The rate at which application-oriented events (e.g., transactions, messages, file transfers) occur.
Utilization	The percentage of the theoretical capacity of a resource (e.g., multiplexer, transmission line, switch) that is being used.

specified service levels are maintained to the satisfaction of the users. Thus, service-oriented indicators are of the highest priority. The manager is also concerned with meeting these requirements at minimum cost—hence, the need for efficiency-oriented measures.

2.2.1.1 Availability

Availability can be expressed as the percentage of time that a network system, a component, or an application is available for a user. Depending on the application, the value of high availability can be significant. For example, the following have been reported: in an airline-reservation network, a one-minute outage may cause \$10,000 in losses; in a banking network, a one-hour outage may introduce losses in the millions of dollars.

Availability is based on the reliability of the individual components of a network. Reliability is the probability that a component will perform its specified function for a specified time under specified conditions. Component failure is usually expressed by the *mean time between failures* (MTBF).

Of more interest to system managers and users is availability, which is the percentage of time that a system or component is available. The availability, A, can be expressed as:

$$A = \frac{\text{MTBF}}{\text{MTBF} + \text{MTTR}},$$

where MTTR is the *mean time to repair* following a failure.

The availability of a system depends on the availability of its individual components plus the system organization. For example, some components may be redundant, such that the failure of just one component does not affect system operation. Or the configuration may be such that the loss of a component results in reduced capability, but the system still functions.

Figure 2.4 shows two simple configurations. In part (a), two components are connected in series, and both must operate properly for the function in question to be available. For example, these might be two modems at opposite ends of a communications link. When two components are connected in series in this fashion, then the availability of the combination is A^2 if the availability

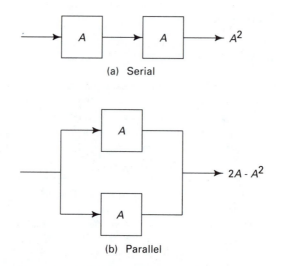

(a) Serial

(b) Parallel

Figure 2.4 Availability of Serial and Parallel Connections

of each component is A. Thus, if the availability of each modem is 0.98, then the availability of the link with the two modems is $0.98 \times 0.98 = 0.96$.[1] Part (b) of the figure shows two devices in parallel. For example, these might be two links connecting a terminal to a host; if one link fails, the other is automatically used for backup. In this case, the dual link is unavailable only if both individual links are unavailable. If the availability of each link is 0.98, then the probability of one of them being unavailable is $1 - 0.98 = 0.02$. The probability of their both being unavailable is $0.02 \times 0.02 = 0.004$. Thus, the availability of the combined unit is $1 - 0.004 = 0.996$.

The availability analysis becomes quite complex as the configurations become more complex and as we take into account not only the availability of the components but also the expected load on the system. As an example, consider a dual-link system, such as just described. The two links are used to connect a multiplexer to a host system. Nonpeak periods account for 40 percent of requests for service, and during those periods, either link can handle the traffic load. During peak periods, both links are required to handle the full load, but one link can handle 80 percent of the peak load. Functional availability for the system can be expressed as:

$$A_f = \text{(capability when 1 link is up)} \times \text{Pr[1 link up]}$$
$$+ \text{(capability when 2 links are up)} \times \text{Pr[2 links up]},$$

where Pr[ ] means "the probability of."

The probability of both links' being up is A^2, where A is the availability of either link. The probability of exactly one processor's being up is $A(1 - A) + (1-A)A = 2A - 2A^2$. Using a value for A of 0.9, then Pr[1 link up] $= 0.9 \times 0.9 = 0.81$, and Pr[2 links up] $= 0.18$. Recalling that one link is sufficient for nonpeak loads, we have:

$$A_f \text{ (nonpeak)} = (1.0)(0.18) + (1.0)(0.81) = 0.99,$$

---

1.   This assumes that the availability of the communications link itself is 1.0. If the link has an availability of, say, 0.99, then the overall availability is $0.99 \times 0.98 \times 0.98 = 0.95$.

and for peak periods,

$$A_f \text{(peak)} = (0.8)(0.18) + (1.0)(0.81) = 0.954.$$

Overall functional availability, then, is

$$A_f = 0.6 \times A_f \text{(peak)} + 0.4 \times A_f \text{(nonpeak)} = 0.9684.$$

Thus, on average, the system can handle about 97 percent of the requests for service.

2.2.1.2 Response Time

Response time is the time it takes a system to react to a given input. In an interactive transaction, it may be defined as the time between the last keystroke by the user and the beginning of the display of a result by the computer. For different types of applications, a slightly different definition is needed. In general, it is the time it takes for the system to respond to a request to perform a particular task.

Ideally, one would like the response time for any application to be short. However, it is almost invariably the case that shorter response time imposes greater cost. This cost comes from two sources:

1. *Computer processing power:* The faster the computer, the shorter the response time. Of course, increased processing power means increased cost.

2. *Competing requirements:* Providing rapid response time for some processes may penalize other processes.

Thus, the value of a given level of response time must be assessed versus the cost of achieving that response time.

Table 2.2, based on Martin (1988), lists six general ranges of response times. Design difficulties are faced when a response time of less than 1 second is required.

That rapid response time is the key to productivity in interactive applications has been confirmed in a number of studies (Shneiderman 1984; Thadhani 1981; Guynes 1988). These studies show that when a computer and a user interact at a pace that ensures that neither has to wait on the other, productivity increases significantly, the cost of the work done on the computer therefore drops, and quality tends to improve. It used to be widely accepted that a relatively slow response time, up to 2 seconds, was acceptable for most interactive applications because the person was thinking about the next task (Miller 1968). However, it now appears that productivity increases as rapid response times are achieved.

The results reported on response time are based on an analysis of on-line transactions. A transaction, which consists of a user command from a terminal and the system's reply, is the fundamental unit of work for on-line system users. It can be divided into two time sequences:

1. *User response time:* the time span between the moment a user receives a complete reply to one command and enters the next command. People often refer to this as *think time*.

2. *System response time:* the time span between the moment the user enters a command and the moment a complete response is displayed on the terminal.

As an example of the effect of reduced system response time, Figure 2.5 shows the results of a study carried out on engineers using a computer-aided design graphics program for the design of integrated-circuit chips and boards (Smith 1983). Each transaction consists of a command by the

Table 2.2 Response-Time Ranges

Greater than 15 seconds

A delay of more than 15 seconds rules out conversational interaction. For certain types of applications, certain types of users may be content to sit at a terminal for more than 15 seconds waiting for the answer to a single simple inquiry. However, for a busy person, captivity for more than 15 seconds seems intolerable. If such delays will occur, the system should be designed so that the user can turn to other activities and request the response at some later time.

Greater than 4 seconds

Delays of more than 4 seconds are generally too long for a conversation requiring the operator to retain information in short-term memory (the operator's memory, not the computer's!). Such delays would be very inhibiting in problem-solving activity and frustrating in data-entry activity. However, after a major closure, delays of from 4 to 15 seconds can be tolerated.

2 to 4 seconds

A delay longer than 2 seconds can be inhibiting to terminal operations demanding a high level of concentration. A wait of 2 to 4 seconds at a terminal can seem surprisingly long when the user is absorbed and emotionally committed to completing what he or she is doing. Again, a delay in this range may be acceptable after a minor closure has occurred.

Less than 2 seconds

When the terminal user has to remember information throughout several responses, the response time must be short. The more detailed the information remembered, the greater the need for response times of less than 2 seconds. For elaborate terminal activities, 2 seconds represents an important response-time limit.

Subsecond response time

Certain types of thought-intensive work, especially with graphics applications, require very short response times to maintain the user's interest and attention for long periods of time.

Decisecond response time

A response to pressing a key and seeing the character displayed on the screen or clicking a screen object with a mouse needs to be almost instantaneous—less than 0.1 second after the action. Interaction with a mouse requires an extremely fast response if the designer is to avoid the use of alien syntax (one with commands, mnemonics punctuation, etc.).

engineer that alters in some way the graphic image being displayed on the screen. The results show that the rate of transactions increases as system response time falls and rises dramatically once system response time falls below 1 second. What is happening is that as the system response time falls, so does the user response time. This has to do with the effects of short-term memory and human attention span.

To measure response time, a number of elements need to be examined. In particular, although it may be possible to directly measure the total response time in a given network environment, this figure alone is of little use in correcting problems or planning for the growth of the network. For these purposes, a detailed breakdown of response time is needed to identify bottlenecks and potential bottlenecks.

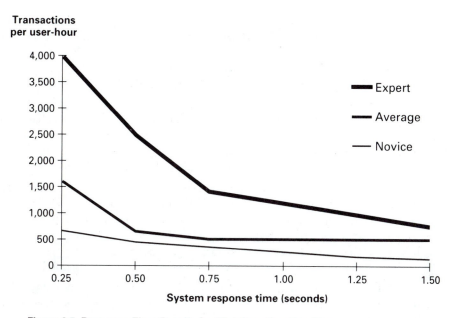

Transactions
per user-hour

Figure 2.5 Response-Time Results for High-Function Graphics

Figure 2.6 illustrates a typical networking situation and indicates the seven elements of response time common to most interactive applications. Each of these elements is one step in the overall path an inquiry takes through a communications configuration, and each element contributes a portion of the overall response time:

$$RT = TI + WI + SI + CPU + WO + SO + TO$$

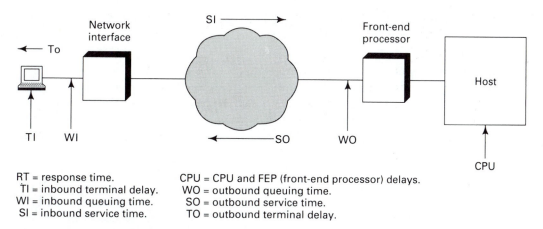

RT = response time.	CPU = CPU and FEP (front-end processor) delays.
TI = inbound terminal delay.	WO = outbound queuing time.
WI = inbound queuing time.	SO = outbound service time.
SI = inbound service time.	TO = outbound terminal delay.

Figure 2.6 Elements of Response Time

1. *Inbound terminal delay:* the delay in getting an inquiry from the terminal to the communications line. By and large, there is no noticeable delay at the terminal itself, so the delay is directly dependent on the transmission rate from terminal to controller. For example, if the data rate on the line is 2,400 bps = 300 characters per second, then the delay is 1/300 = 3.33 milliseconds per character. If the average message length is 100 characters, the delay will be 0.33 second.

2. *Inbound queuing time:* the time required for processing by the controller. The controller is dealing with input from a number of terminals as well as input from the network to be delivered to the terminals. Thus, an arriving message will be placed in a buffer to be served in turn. The busier the controller is, the longer the delay for processing will be.

3. *Inbound service time:* the time to transit the communications link, network, or other communications facility from the controller to the host's front-end processor. This element is itself made up of a number of elements, based on the structure of the communications facility. If the facility is a public packet-switched network, it must be treated as a single element. However, if it is a private network (wide area or local area), leased line, or other user-configured facility, then a breakdown of this element will be needed for network control and planning.

4. *Processing time:* the time the front-end processor, the host processor, the disk drives, and so on at the computer center spend preparing a reply to an inquiry. This element is usually outside the control of the network manager.

5. *Outbound queuing time:* the time a reply spends at a port in the front-end processor waiting to be dispatched to the network or communications line. As with the controller, the front-end processor will have a queue of replies to be serviced, and the delay increases as the number of replies waiting increases.

6. *Outbound service time:* the time to transit the communications facility from the host's front-end processor to the controller.

7. *Outbound terminal delay:* the delay at the terminal itself. Again, this is primarily due to line speed.

Response time is relatively easy to measure and is one of the most important classes of information needed for network management.

2.2.1.3 Accuracy

Accurate transmission of data between user and host or between two hosts is, of course, essential for any network. Because of the built-in error-correction mechanisms in the protocols, such as the data-link and transport protocols, accuracy is generally not a user concern. Nevertheless, it is useful to monitor the rate of errors that must be corrected. This may give an indication of an intermittently faulty line or the existence of a source of noise or interference that should be corrected.

2.2.1.4 Throughput

Throughput is an application-oriented measure. Examples include:

- Number of transactions of a given type during a certain period of time
- Number of customer sessions for a given application during a certain period of time
- Number of calls for a circuit-switched environment

It is useful to track these measures over time to get a feel for projected demand and likely performance trouble spots.

2.2.1.5   Utilization

Utilization is a more fine-grained measure than throughput. It refers to determining the percentage of time that a resource is in use over a given period of time.

Perhaps the most important use of utilization is to search for potential bottlenecks and areas of congestion. The reason this is important is that response time usually increases exponentially as the utilization of a resource increases. This is a well-known result of queuing theory (see Appendix 2A). Because of this exponential behavior, congestion can quickly get out of hand if it is not spotted early and dealt with quickly.

By looking at a profile of which resources are in use at any given time and which are idle, the analyst may be able to find resources that are overcommitted or underutilized and adjust the network accordingly.

As an example, a simple but very effective technique for assessing network efficiency will be given (based on Johnson [1985]). This technique is useful for assessing the capacity of various communication links in a network. The basic idea is to observe differences between planned load and actual load on various links in the network. The planned load is reflected by the capacity, in bits per second, of each individual link. The actual load, of course, is the measured average traffic—again, in bits per second—on each such link. An analogy can be made with a cost-accounting technique that looks at the ratios of actual expenditures to planned expenditures by division within a company. Information regarding significant divergences across divisions is useful because it challenges expectations and raises questions about the accuracy of the budget-planning process in each division.

Consider, for example, the simple network configuration of Figure 2.7, part (a). We will express the load on each channel as the percentage of the total load on the network and the flow on each channel as the percentage of the total flow. Table 2.3 shows the results, and Figure 2.7, part (b), provides a graphic illustration. As we can see, the total capacity of the network provides a comfortable margin over the total load on the network, and of course, no link is carrying a load greater than its capacity. However, by looking at relative capacity and relative loads, we can see that some links are carrying less than a proportionate share of the load and some are carrying more than their share. This indicates an inefficient allocation of resources. By adjusting these ratios, either by redirecting traffic or by changing the relative data rates of the various links, a closer balance between planned and actual load can be achieved. This can result in a reduction in the total required capacity and a more efficient use of resources.

2.2.2   Performance-Monitoring Function

Performance monitoring encompasses three components: performance measurement, which is the actual gathering of statistics about network traffic and timing; performance analysis, which consists of software for reducing and presenting the data; and synthetic-traffic generation, which permits the network to be observed under a controlled load.

Performance measurement is often accomplished by agent modules within the devices on the network (hosts, routers, bridges, etc.). These agents are in a position to observe the amount of traffic into and out of a node; the number of connections (network-level, transport-level, application-level) and the traffic per connection; and other measures that provide a detailed picture

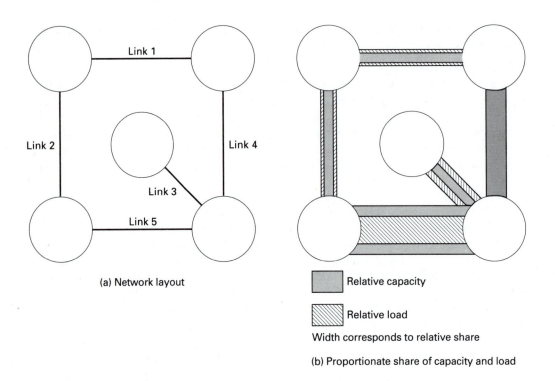

(a) Network layout

Relative capacity

Relative load

Width corresponds to relative share

(b) Proportionate share of capacity and load

Figure 2.7 Simple Efficiency Analysis

of the behavior of that node. Of course, all of this measurement comes at the price of processing resources within the node.

In a shared network, such as a LAN, much of the needed information can be collected by an external or a remote monitor that simply observes the traffic on the network. This arrangement offloads much of the processing requirement from operational nodes to a dedicated system.

Table 2.4 lists the types of measurements reported by one LAN facility (Amer 1982; Amer, Rosenthal, and Toense 1983) and gives some idea of the kinds of measurements that are of interest. These measurements can be used to answer a number of questions. Questions concerning possible errors or inefficiencies include:

Table 2.3 Load and Capacity Analysis for Network Shown in Figure 2.7

	Link 1	Link 2	Link 3	Link 4	Link 5	Total
Load (bps)	3,000	3,000	5,000	4,000	5,000	20,000
Capacity (bps)	4,000	4,000	6,000	8,000	18,000	40,000
Percentage of total load	15	15	25	20	25	100
Percentage of total capacity	10	10	15	20	45	100
Ratio	1.50	1.50	1.67	1.00	0.55	—

Table 2.4 Performance-Measurement Reports

Name	Variables	Description
Host communication matrix	Source × destination	(Number, %) of (packets, data packets, data octets)
Group communication matrix	Source × destination	As above, consolidated into address groups
Packet-type histogram	Packet type	(Number, %) of (packets, original packets) by type
Data-packet-size histogram	Packet size	(Number, %) of data packets by data octet length
Throughput-utilization distribution	Source	(Total octets, data octets) transmitted
Packet-interarrival-time histogram	Interarrival time	Time between consecutive carrier (network busy) signals
Channel-acquisition-delay histogram	Network interface unit (NIU) acquisition delay	(Number, %) of packets delayed at NIU by a given amount
Communication-delay histogram	Packet delay	Time from original packet ready at source to receipt
Collision-count histogram	Number of collisions	Number of packets by number of collisions
Transmission-count histogram	Number of transmissions	Number of packets by transmission attempts

Source: Adapted from Amer (1982) and Amer et. al (1983).

- Is traffic evenly distributed among the network users, or are there source-destination pairs with unusually heavy traffic?

- What is the percentage of each type of packet? Do some packet types occur with unusually high frequency, indicating an error or an inefficient protocol?

- What is the distribution of data-packet sizes?

- What are the channel-acquisition-delay and communication-delay distributions? Are these times excessive?

- Are collisions a factor in getting packets transmitted, indicating possible faulty hardware or protocols?

- What is the channel utilization and throughput?

Questions concerning increasing traffic load and varying packet sizes include:

- What is the effect of traffic load on utilization, throughput, and time delays? When does traffic load start to degrade system performance?

- Defining a stable network as one whose utilization is a nondecreasing function of traffic load, what is the trade-off among stability, throughput, and delay?

- What is the maximum capacity of the channel under normal operating conditions? How many active users are necessary to reach this maximum?

- Do larger packets increase or decrease throughput and delay?

- How does constant packet size affect utilization and delay?

These areas are of interest to the network manager. Other questions of concern have to do with response time and throughput by user class and determining how much growth the network can absorb before certain performance thresholds are crossed.

2.2.3   Statistical versus Exhaustive Measurement

When an agent in a node or an external monitor is monitoring a heavy load of traffic, it may not be practical to collect exhaustive data. For example, in order for an external monitor to construct a matrix that shows accurately the total number of packets in a given time period between each source-destination pair, the monitor would need to capture every packet transmitted on the LAN under observation and read the source and destination address in each packet header. When the LAN is heavily loaded, the monitor simply may not be able to keep up.

The alternative is to treat each parameter as a random variable and sample the traffic stream in order to estimate the value of the random variable. However, care must be taken in employing and interpreting statistical estimation results. Traditional statistical methods were developed for such areas as agriculture and biology, where it can often be assumed that the probabilities of interest are relatively large (typically, 10^{-2} or higher) and that there is independence among observations (where the outcome of one observation indicates nothing about the outcome of another). Neither of these assumptions holds true for data communications, where some events of interest, such as errors, may occur at a rate of 10^{-6} or lower and where clustering or burstiness is commonly observed. The individual responsible for designing sampling functions and for interpreting the results needs to have some familiarity with statistical principles.[2]

2.3   FAULT MONITORING

The objective of fault monitoring is to identify faults as quickly as possible after they happen and to identify their cause so that remedial action may be taken. In this section, we first look at some of the problems inherent in fault monitoring, and then examine key fault monitoring functions.

2.3.1   Problems of Fault Monitoring

In a complex environment, locating and diagnosing faults can be difficult. Dupuy et al. (1989) list the following specific problems that are associated with fault observation and fault isolation. Fault observation must overcome these problems:

- *Unobservable faults:* Certain faults are inherently unobservable through local observation. For example, the existence of a deadlock between cooperating distributed processes may not be observable locally. Other faults may not be observable because the vendor equipment is not instrumented to record the occurrence of a fault.

---

2.   See Appendix 2B for a brief introduction to statistical principles.

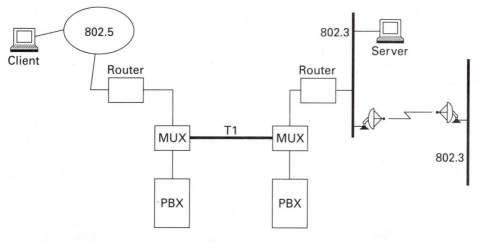

MUX = Multiplexer
PBX = Private Branch Exchange

Figure 2.8 Heterogeneous Network Environment

- *Partially observable faults:* A node failure may be observable, but the observation may be insufficient to pinpoint the problem. For example, a node may be "stuck" due to the failure of some low-level protocol in an attached device.

- *Uncertainty in observation:* Even when detailed observations of faults are possible, there may be uncertainty and even inconsistencies associated with the observations. For example, lack of response from a remote device may mean that the device is stuck, the network is partitioned, congestion caused the response to be delayed, or the local timer is faulty.

Once faults are observed, it is necessary to isolate each fault to a particular component. Problems arise here also, including the following suggested by Fried and Tjong (1990):

- *Multiple potential causes:* When multiple technologies are involved, the potential points of failure and the types of failures increase. This makes it harder to locate the source of a fault. In Figure 2.8, for example, data transmitted between the client workstation and the server must traverse the LAN, router, multiplexer, and transmission subsystems. If connectivity is lost or if error rates are high, the trouble could be due to problems in any one of these subsystems.

- *Too many related observations:* A single failure can affect many active communication paths. The failure of the T1 line in Figure 2.8 will affect all active communication between the token-ring stations and stations on the two Ethernet LANs, as well as voice communication between the PBXs. Furthermore, a failure in one layer of the communications architecture can cause degradations or failures in all the dependent higher layers, as illustrated in Figure 2.9. Thus, a failure in the T1 line will be detected in the routers as a link failure and in the workstations as transport and application failures. Because a single failure may generate many secondary failures, the proliferation of fault-monitoring data that can be generated in this way can obscure the single underlying problem.

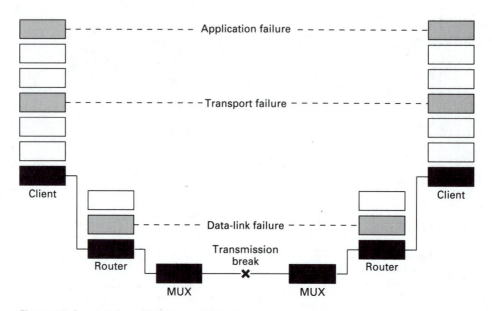

Figure 2.9 Propagation of Failures to Higher Layers

- *Interference between diagnosis and local recovery procedures:* Local recovery procedures may destroy important evidence concerning the nature of the fault, disabling diagnosis.

- *Absence of automated testing tools:* Testing to isolate faults is difficult and costly to administer.

2.3.2   Fault-Monitoring Functions

The first requirement of a fault-monitoring system is that it be able to detect and report faults. At a minimum, a fault-monitoring agent will maintain a log of significant events and errors. These logs or summaries are available to authorized manager systems. Thus, a system that operated primarily by polling would rely on these logs. Typically, the fault-monitoring agent has the capability to independently report errors to one or more managers. To avoid overloading the network, the criteria for issuing a fault report must be reasonably tight.

In addition to reporting known, existing faults, a good fault-monitoring system will be able to anticipate faults. Generally, this involves setting up thresholds and issuing a report when a monitored variable crosses a threshold. For example, if the fraction of transmitted packets that suffers an error exceeds a certain value, this may indicate that a problem is developing along the communications path. If the threshold is set low enough, the network manager may be alerted in time to take action that avoids a major failure in the system.

The fault-monitoring system should also assist in isolating and diagnosing faults. Examples of tests that a fault-monitoring system should have at its command include the following:

- Connectivity test
- Data-integrity test
- Protocol-integrity test

- Data-saturation test

- Connection-saturation test

- Response-time test

- Imaging loopback test

- Function test

- Diagnostic test

Perhaps more than in other areas of network monitoring, an effective user interface is required for fault monitoring. In complex situations, faults will be isolated, diagnosed, and ultimately corrected only by the cooperative effort of a human user and the monitor software.

2.4   ACCOUNTING MONITORING

Accounting monitoring is primarily a matter of keeping track of the usage of network resources by users. The requirements for this function vary widely. In some environments, accounting may be of a quite general nature. For example, an internal accounting system may only be employed to assess the overall usage of resources and to determine what proportion of the cost of each shared resource should be allotted to each department. In other cases, particularly for systems that offer a public service but also for many systems with only internal users, usage must be broken down by account, by project, or even by individual user for the purposes of billing. In this latter case, the information gathered by the monitoring system must be more detailed and more accurate than that required for a general system.

Examples of resources that may be subject to accounting include:

- *Communications facilities:* LANs, WANs, leased lines, dial-up lines, PBX systems

- *Computer hardware:* workstations, servers

- *Software and systems:* applications and utility software in servers, a data center, and end-user sites

- *Services:* includes all commercial communications and information services available to network users

For any given type of resource, and based on the requirements of the organization, accounting data are collected. For example, the following communications-related accounting data might be gathered and maintained on each user:

- *User identification:* provided by the originator of a transaction or a service request

- *Receiver:* identifies the network component to which a connection is made or attempted

- *Number of packets:* count of data transmitted

- *Security level:* identifies the transmission and processing priorities

- *Timestamps:* associated with each principal transmission and processing event (e.g., transaction start and stop times)

- *Network-status codes:* indicate the nature of any errors or malfunctions that are detected

- *Resources used:* indicates which resources are invoked by this transaction or service event

2.5 SUMMARY

Network monitoring is the most fundamental aspect of automated network management. Although many network-management systems, because of lack of security mechanisms, do not include network-control features, all network-management systems include a network-monitoring component.

The purpose of network monitoring is to gather information about the status and behavior of network elements. Information to be gathered includes static information, related to the configuration; dynamic information, related to events in the network; and statistical information, summarized from dynamic information. Typically, each managed device in the network includes an agent module responsible for collecting local management information and transmitting it to one or more management stations. Each management station includes network-management application software plus software for communicating with agents. Information may be collected actively, by means of polling by the management station, or passively, by means of event reporting by the agents.

In the area of performance management, the most important categories of management information are:

- Availability
- Response time
- Accuracy
- Throughput
- Utilization

In the area of fault monitoring, the objective is to identify faults as quickly as possible after they happen and to determine their cause so that remedial action may be taken. The fault-monitoring function is complicated by the fact that, by definition, it is needed at a time when some portion of the network is not functioning properly. Thus, it may be difficult to learn of and identify certain faults.

In the area of accounting management, network monitoring is concerned with gathering usage information to the level of detail required for proper accounting.

APPENDIX 2A Queuing Theory Concepts

Queuing theory is an invaluable tool in performance management. This appendix gives a brief overview of the basic concepts.

2A.1 WHY QUEUING ANALYSIS?

There are many cases in the field of data communications and computer networking when it is important to be able to project the effect of some change in a design: either the load on a system is expected to increase, or a design change is contemplated. For example, an organization supports a number of terminals, personal computers, and workstations on a 4-Mbps token-ring LAN. An additional department in the building is to be cut over onto the network. Can the existing LAN handle the increased workload, or would it be better to provide a second LAN with a bridge between the two? There are other cases in which no facility exists, but on the basis of expected demand, a system design needs to be created. For instance, a department intends to equip all of its personnel with a personal computer and to configure these into a LAN with a file server. Based on experience elsewhere in the company, the load generated by each PC can be estimated.

The concern is system performance. In an interactive or real-time application, often the parameter of concern is response time. In other cases, throughput is the principal issue. In any case, projections of performance are to be made on the basis of existing load information or on the basis of estimated load for a new environment. A number of approaches are possible:

1.   Do an after-the-fact analysis based on actual values.

2.   Make a simple projection by scaling up from existing experience to the expected future environment.

3.   Develop an analytic model based on queuing theory.

4.   Program and run a simulation model.

Option 1—we will wait and see what happens—is no option at all. This leads to unhappy users and to unwise purchases.

Option 2 sounds more promising. The analyst may take the position that it is impossible to project future demand with any degree of certainty. Therefore, it is pointless to attempt some exact modeling procedure. Rather, a rough-and-ready projection will provide ballpark estimates. The problem with this approach is that the behavior of most communications systems is not what one would intuitively expect. If there is an environment in which a shared facility exists (e.g., a network, a transmission line, a time-sharing system), then the performance of that system typically responds in an exponential way to increases in demand.

Figure 2.10 is a typical example. The upper line shows what usually happens to user response time on a shared facility as the load on that facility increases. The load is expressed as a fraction of capacity. Thus, if we are dealing with a router that is capable of processing 1,000 packets per second, then a load of 0.5 represents an input of 500 packets per second, and the response time is the amount of time it takes to retransmit any incoming packet. The lower line is a simple projection[3] based on a knowledge of the behavior of the system up to a load of 0.5. Note that although things appear rosy when the simple projection is made, performance of the system will in fact collapse beyond a load of about 0.8 to 0.9.

Thus, a more exact prediction tool is needed. Option 3 is to make use of an analytic model, which is one that can be expressed as a set of equations that can be solved to yield the desired parameters (response time, throughput, etc.). For networking and communications problems—and indeed, for many practical real-world problems—analytic models based on queuing theory provide a reasonably good fit to reality. The disadvantage of queuing theory is that a number of simplifying assumptions must be made to derive equations for the parameters of interest.

The final approach is a simulation model. Here, given a sufficiently powerful and flexible simulation programming language, the analyst can model reality in great detail and avoid making the many assumptions required of queuing theory. However, in most cases, a simulation model is not needed or at least is not advisable as a first step in the analysis. For one thing, both existing

---

3.   In fact, the lower line is based on fitting a third-order polynomial to the data available up to a load of 0.5.

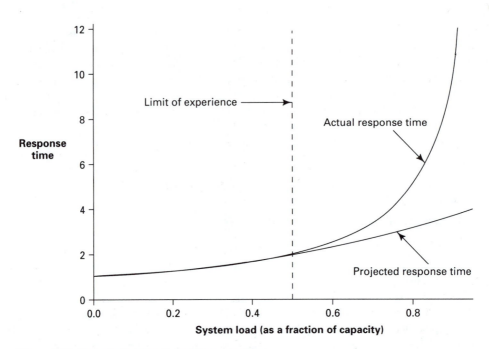

Figure 2.10 Projected versus Actual Response Time

measurements and projections of future load carry with them a certain margin of error. Thus, no matter how good the simulation model, the value of the results is limited by the quality of the input. For another thing, despite the many assumptions required of queuing theory, the results that are produced usually come quite close to those that would be produced by a more careful simulation analysis. Furthermore, a queuing analysis can literally be accomplished in a matter of minutes for a well-defined problem, whereas simulation exercises can take days, weeks, or longer to program and run.

2A.2   SINGLE-SERVER QUEUING MODEL

The most basic queuing system is depicted in Figure 2.11. The central element of the system is a server, which provides some service to items. Items from some population of items arrive at the system to be served. If the server is idle, an item is served immediately. Otherwise, an arriving item joins a waiting line.[4] When the server has completed serving an item, the item departs. If there are items waiting in the queue, one is immediately dispatched to the server.

The figure also illustrates the basic parameters associated with a queuing model. Items arrive at the facility at some average arrival rate (items arriving per second) λ. At any given time, a certain number of items will be waiting in the queue (zero or more); the average number waiting

---

4.   The waiting line is referred to as a queue in some treatments in the literature; it is also common to refer to the entire system as a queue. This latter is to be preferred.

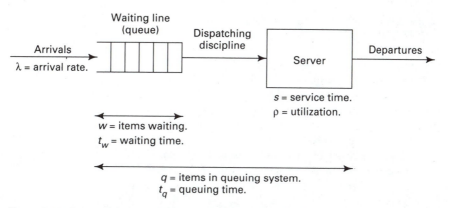

Figure 2.12 · Queuing-System Structure and Parameters for Single-Server Queue

is w, and the mean time that an item must wait is t_w. Note that t_w is averaged over all incoming items, including those that do not wait at all. The server handles incoming items with an average service time s; this is the time interval between the dispatching of an item to the server and the departure of that item from the server. Utilization is the fraction of time ρ that the server is busy, measured over some interval of time. Finally, there are two parameters that apply to the system as a whole. The average number of items in the system, including the item being served (if any) and the items in the queue (if any), is q; and the average time that an item spends in the system, waiting and being served, is t_q.

Table 2.5 provides some equations for single-server queues. Making use of a scaling factor, A, the equations for some of the key output variables are straightforward. Note that the key factor in the scaling parameter is the ratio of the standard deviation of service time to the mean. No other information about the service time is needed. Two special cases are of some interest. When the standard deviation is equal to the mean, the service-time distribution is exponential. This is the simplest case and the easiest one for calculating results. Table 2.5, part (b), shows the simplified versions of equations. The other interesting case is a standard deviation of service time equal to zero—that is, a constant service time. The corresponding equations are shown in Table 2.5, part (c).

Figures 2.12 and 2.13 plot values of average queue size and queuing time versus utilization for three values of σ_s/s. Note that the poorest performance is exhibited by the exponential service time and the best by a constant service time. Usually, one can consider the exponential service time to be a worst case. An analysis based on this assumption will give conservative results.

What value of σ_s/s is one likely to encounter? We can consider four regions:

1. *Zero:* This is the rare case of constant service time. If all transmitted messages are of the same length, they would fit this category.

2. *Ratio less than 1:* Since this ratio is better than the exponential case, using exponential results will give queue sizes and times that are slightly larger than they should be and will therefore be on the safe side. An example of this category might be a data-entry application from a particular form.

3. *Ratio close to 1:* This is the most common occurrence and corresponds to exponential service time. That is, service times are essentially random. Consider the lengths of messages to a

Table 2.5 Formulas for Single-Server Queues

Parameters:

λ = mean number of arrivals per second.

s = mean service time for each arrival.

σ_s = standard deviation of service time.

ρ = utilization; fraction of time the facility is busy.

q = mean number of items in the system (waiting and being served).

t_q = mean time an item spends in the system.

σ_q = standard deviation of number of items in the system.

σ_{tq} = standard deviation of time an item spends in the system.

Assumptions:

1. Poisson arrival rate.
2. Dispatching discipline does not give preference to items based on service times.
3. Formulas for standard deviation assume first-in, first-out dispatching.
4. No items leave the queue (lost calls delayed).

(a) General service times

$$A = \frac{1}{2}\left[1 + \left(\frac{\sigma_s}{s}\right)^2\right] \qquad \text{useful parameter}$$

$$q = \rho + \frac{\rho^2 A}{1-\rho} \qquad\qquad t_q = s + \frac{\rho s A}{1-\rho} \qquad\qquad \rho = \lambda s$$

(b) Exponential service times

$$q = \frac{\rho}{1-\rho}$$

$$t_q = \frac{s}{1-\rho}$$

$$\sigma_q = \frac{\sqrt{\rho}}{1-\rho}$$

$$\sigma_{tq} = \frac{s}{1-\rho}$$

(c) Constant service times

$$q = \frac{\rho^2}{2(1-\rho)} + \rho$$

$$t_q = \frac{s(2-\rho)}{2(1-\rho)}$$

$$\sigma_q = \frac{1}{1-\rho}\sqrt{\rho - \frac{3\rho^2}{2} + \frac{5\rho^3}{6} - \frac{\rho^4}{12}}$$

$$\sigma_{tq} = \frac{s}{1-\rho}\sqrt{\frac{\rho}{3} - \frac{\rho^2}{12}}$$

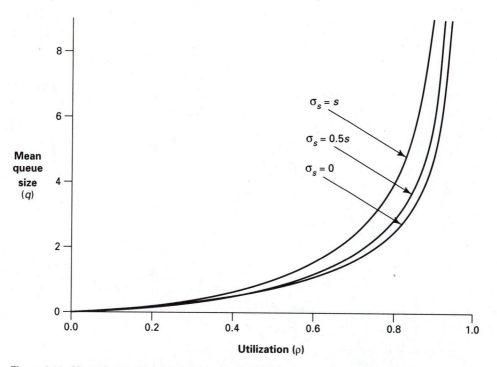

Figure 2.12 Mean Queue Sizes for Single-Server Queue

computer terminal: a full screen might be 1,920 characters, with message sizes varying the full range. Airline reservations, file lookups on inquiries, shared LAN and packet-switching networks are examples of systems that often fit this category.

4. *Ratio greater than 1:* If this is observed, one needs to use the general model and not rely on the exponential model. The most common occurrence of this in a communications system is a bimodal distribution, with a wide spread between the peaks. An example is a system that experiences many short messages, many long messages, and few in between.

Incidentally, the same consideration applies to the arrival rate. For a Poisson arrival rate, the interarrival times are exponential, and the ratio of standard deviation to mean is 1. If the observed ratio is much less than 1, then arrivals tend to be evenly spaced (not much variability), and the Poisson assumption will overestimate queue sizes and delays. On the other hand, if the ratio is greater than 1, then arrivals tend to cluster and congestion becomes more acute.

APPENDIX 2B   Statistical Analysis Concepts

For many parameters of interest to a performance-monitoring system, it is impossible or impractical to measure the parameters by counting all relevant events. In these cases, we need to estimate the values of the parameters; usually, we are interested in the mean and standard deviation.

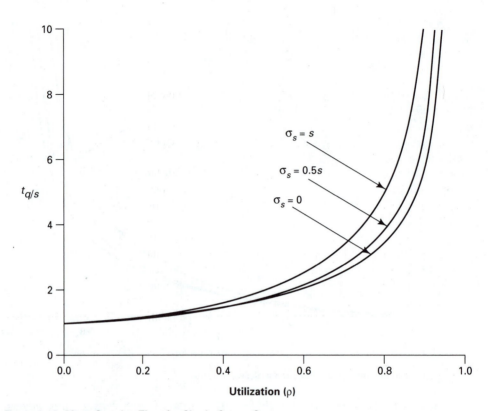

Figure 2.13 Mean Queuing Time for Single-Server Queue

The measurements that are taken are in the form of samples. A particular parameter—for example, the rate of packets generated by a terminal or the size of packets—is estimated by observing some of the packets generated during a period of time.

To estimate a quantity, such as the length of a packet, the following equations can be used:

Sample mean: $\overline{X} = \dfrac{1}{n} \sum_{i=1}^{n} X_i.$

Sample variance: $S^2 = \dfrac{\sum_{i=1}^{n} (X_i - \overline{X})^2}{n - 1}$

$$= \dfrac{n \sum_{i=1}^{n} X_i^2 - \left(\sum_{i=1}^{n} X_i \right)^2}{n(n - 1)}.$$

Sample standard deviation: $S = \sqrt{S^2}.$

Where

n = sample size;
X_i = ith sample.

It is important to note that the sample mean and sample standard deviation are themselves random variables. For example, if you take a sample from some population and calculate the sample mean, and do this a number of times, the calculated values will differ. Thus, we can talk of the mean and standard deviation of the sample mean or even of the entire probability distribution of the sample mean.

It follows that the probabilistic nature of our estimated values is a source of error, known as sampling error. In general, the greater the size of the sample taken, the smaller the standard deviation of the sample mean, and therefore the closer our estimate is likely to be to the actual mean. By making certain reasonable assumptions about the nature of the random variable being tested and the randomness of the sampling procedure, one can in fact determine the probability that a sample mean or sample standard deviation is within a certain distance from the actual mean or standard deviation. This concept is often reported with the results of a sample. For example, it is common for the results of an opinion poll to include a comment such as: "The result is within 5 percent of the true value with a confidence (probability) of 99 percent." The interval around the actual value is known as the confidence interval, and the probability that the sample mean is within that interval is known as the confidence level.

In designing a sampling scheme, we can specify any two of the following three quantities, and the remaining quantity can be determined:

1. Confidence level

2. Sample size

3. Length of confidence interval

It is customary to first specify the confidence level. Then, either the sample size or the length of the confidence interval is specified, and the remaining parameter is calculated. When the budget (amount of resources devoted to sampling) is the more important criterion, the sample size is specified, and the length of the confidence interval is derived from it. Conversely, when the precision of the estimate is the more important criterion, the length of the confidence interval is specified, and the sample size is derived from the interval.

There is, however, another source of error, which is less widely appreciated among nonstatisticians—namely, bias. For example, if an opinion poll is conducted and only members of a certain socioeconomic group are interviewed, the results are not necessarily representative of the entire population. In a communications context, sampling done during one time of day may not reflect the activity at another time of day. If our concern is to design a system that will handle the peak load that is likely to be experienced, then we should observe the traffic during the time of day that is most likely to produce the greatest load.

3
Network Control

The network-control portion of network management is concerned with modifying parameters in, and causing actions to be taken by, the end systems, intermediate systems, and subnetworks that make up the configuration to be managed.

All of the five major functional areas of network management (performance, fault, accounting, configuration, and security) involve both monitoring and control. Traditionally, however, the emphasis in the first three of these areas has been on monitoring, whereas the last two areas are more concerned with control. Hence, Chapter 2 focused on performance, fault, and accounting monitoring. This chapter examines the network-control aspects of configuration management and security management.

3.1 CONFIGURATION CONTROL

Configuration management is concerned with the initialization, maintenance, and shutdown of individual components and logical subsystems within an installation's total configuration of computer and communications resources. Configuration management can dictate the initialization process by identifying and specifying the characteristics of the network components and resources that will constitute the "network." Managed resources include both identifiable physical resources (e.g., a server or a router) and lower-level logical objects (e.g., a transport-layer retransmission timer). Configuration management can specify initial or default values for attributes so that managed resources commence operation in the desired states, possess the proper parameter values, and form the desired relationships with other network components.

While the network is in operation, configuration management is responsible for monitoring the configuration and making changes in response to user commands or in response to other network-management functions. For example, if the performance-monitoring function detects that response time is degrading due to an imbalance in load, configuration management may adjust the configuration to achieve load leveling. Similarly, if fault management detects and isolates a fault, configuration management may alter the configuration to bypass the fault.

Configuration management includes the following functions:

- Defining configuration information.

- Setting and modifying attribute values.

- Defining and modifying relationships.

- Initializing and terminating network operations.

- Distributing software.

- Examining values and relationships.

- Reporting on configuration status.

The final two items in the preceding list are configuration-monitoring functions. A manager station may examine configuration information maintained by an agent station by means of a query/response interaction. An agent may report a change in status to a manager by means of an event report. The remainder of the items on the list are configuration-control functions, and these are the subject of this chapter.

3.1.1 Defining Configuration Information

Configuration information describes the nature and status of resources that are of interest to network management. The configuration information includes a specification of the resources under management and the attributes of those resources. Network resources include physical resources (e.g., end systems, routers, bridges, communications facilities and services, communications media, modems) and logical resources (e.g., timers, counters, virtual circuits). Attributes include, for example, name, address, identification number, states, operational characteristics, software version number, and release level.

Configuration information (indeed, all management information) may be structured in a number of ways:

- A simple structured list of data fields, with each field containing a single value. This is the approach taken by SNMP (simple network-management protocol).

- An object-oriented database. Each element of interest to management is represented by one or more objects. Each object contains attributes whose values reflect the characteristics of the represented element. An object may also contain behaviors, such as notifications to be issued if certain events relating to this element occur. The use of containment and inheritance relationships (see Appendix D) allows relationships among objects to be defined. This is the approach taken by OSI (open systems interconnection) network management.

- A relational database. Individual fields in the database contain values that reflect characteristics of network elements. The structure of the database reflects the relationships among network elements.

Although this information is to be accessible to a manager station, generally, the information is stored near the resource in question, either in an agent node, if the resource is part of that node, or in a proxy node, if the node containing the resource does not support agent software.

The network-control function should enable the user to specify the range and type of values to which the specified resource attributes at a particular agent can be set. The range can be a list of all possible states or the allowed upper and lower limits for parameters and attributes. The type of value allowable for an attribute may be specified as well.

The network-control function should also be able to define new object types or data-element types, depending on the database type. Ideally, it should be possible to define these new objects on-line and to have such objects created at the appropriate agents and proxies. In virtually all systems today, this function is performed off-line, as part of configuring a network element, rather than being possible dynamically.

3.1.2   Setting and Modifying Attribute Values

The configuration-control function should enable a manager station to remotely set and modify attribute values in agents and proxies. There are two limitations on this capability:

1. A manager must be authorized to make the modification of a particular attribute at a particular agent or proxy at a particular time. This is a security concern, addressed in section 3.2.

2. Some attributes reflect the "reality" at a resource and cannot, by their nature, be modified remotely. For example, one item of information could be the number of physical ports on a router. Although each port may be enabled or disabled at any particular time, the actual number of ports can only be changed by a physical action at the router, not by a remote parameter-setting action.

Modification of an attribute will obviously modify the configuration information at the agent or proxy. In general, modifications fall into three categories:

1. *Database update only:* When a manager issues a modify command to an agent, one or more values in the agent's configuration database are changed (if the operation succeeds). In some cases, there is no other immediate response on behalf of the agent. For example, a manager may change contact information (name and address of the person responsible for this resource). The agent responds by updating the appropriate data values and returning an acknowledgment to the manager.

2. *Database update plus resource modification:* In addition to updating values in the configuration database at an agent, a modify command can have an effect on an underlying resource. For example, if the state attribute of a physical port is set to "disabled," then the agent not only updates the state attribute but also disables the port, so that it is no longer in use.

3. *Database update plus action:* In some network-management systems, there are no direct "action commands" available to managers. Rather, there are parameters in the database that, when set, cause the agent to initiate a certain action. For example, a router might maintain a reinitialize parameter in its database. If this parameter is set to TRUE by an authorized manager, the router would go through a reinitialization procedure, which would reinitialize the router and set the parameter to FALSE.

The user should be able to load predefined default attribute values—such as default states, values, and operational characteristics of resources—on a systemwide, individual-node, or individual-layer basis.

3.1.3   Defining and Modifying Relationships

A relationship describes an association, a connection, or a condition that exists between network resources or network components. Examples of relationships are a topology, a hierarchy, a physical or logical connection, or a management domain. A management domain is a set of resources that share a set of common management attributes or a set of common resources that share the same management authority.

Configuration management should allow on-line modification of resources without taking all or part of the network down. The user should be able to add, delete, and modify the relationships among network resources.

One example of the use of relationships is to manage the link-layer connection between LAN (local area network) nodes, at the level of the service-access point (SAP) of logical link control (LLC). An LLC connection can be set up in one of two ways. First, the LLC protocol in one node can issue a connection request to another node, in response to either higher-layer software or a terminal user command; these could be referred to as "switched" connections. Second, a network manager station could set up a fixed, or permanent, LLC connection between two nodes. This connection-setup request would designate the SAP in each node that serves as an end point for the connection. The manager software, under operator command, should also be able to break a connection, permanent or switched. Another useful feature is to be able to designate a backup or an alternate address to be used in case the primary destination fails to respond to a connection request.

3.1.4. Initializing and Terminating Network Operations

Configuration management should include mechanisms to enable users to initialize and close down network or subnetwork operation. Initialization includes verifying that all settable resource attributes and relationships have been properly set; notifying users of any resource, attribute, or relationship still needing to be set; and validating users' initialization commands. For termination, mechanisms are needed to allow users to request retrieval of specified statistics, blocks, or status information before the termination procedures have been completed.

3.1.5 Distributing Software

Configuration management should provide the capability to distribute software throughout the configuration to end systems (hosts, servers, workstations) and intermediate systems (bridges, routers, application-level gateways). This requires facilities to permit software-loading requests, to transmit the specified versions of software, and to update the configuration-tracking systems.

In addition to executable software, the software-distribution function should also encompass tables and other data that drive the behavior of a node. Foremost in this category is the routing table, used by bridges and routers. There may be accounting, performance, or security concerns that require management intervention into routing decisions that cannot be solved by mathematical algorithms alone.

Users need mechanisms to examine, update, and manage different versions of software and routing information. For example, users should be able to specify the loading of different versions of software or routing tables based on particular conditions, such as error rates.

3.2 SECURITY CONTROL

The requirements of *information security* within an organization have undergone two major changes in the last several decades. Prior to the widespread use of data-processing equipment, the security of information felt to be valuable to an organization was provided primarily by physical and administrative means. An example of the former is the use of rugged filing cabinets with a combination lock for storing sensitive documents. An example of the latter is personnel-screening procedures used during the hiring process.

With the introduction of the computer, the need for automated tools for protecting files and other information stored on the computer became evident. This is especially the case for a shared system, such as a time-sharing system, and the need is even more acute for systems that can be accessed over a public telephone or data network. The generic name for the collection of tools designed to protect data and thwart hackers is *computer security*.

The second major change that affects security is the introduction of distributed systems and the use of networks and communications facilities for carrying data between terminal user and computer and between computer and computer. *Network security* measures are needed to protect data during their transmission.

The security-management portion of network management deals with the provision of both computer and network security for the resources under management, including, of course, the network-management system itself. Before examining some of the details of security management, it will be useful to characterize the security threats.

3.2.1   Security Threats

In order to be able to understand the various types of threats to security, we need to have a definition of security requirements. Computer and network security addresses three requirements:

1. *Secrecy:* The information in a computer system must only be accessible for reading by authorized parties. This type of access includes printing, displaying, and other forms of disclosure, including simply revealing the existence of an object.

2. *Integrity:* Computer-system assets must be modifiable only by authorized parties. Modification includes writing, changing, changing status, deleting, and creating.

3. *Availability:* Computer-system assets must be available to authorized parties.

3.2.1.1   Types of Threats

The types of threats to the security of a computer system or network are best characterized by viewing the function of the computer system as that of providing information. In general, there is a flow of information from a source, such as a file or a region of main memory, to a destination, such as another file or a user. This normal flow is depicted in Figure 3.1, part (a). The remainder of the figure shows four general categories of threats:

1. *Interruption:* An asset of the system is destroyed or becomes unavailable or unusable. This is a threat to *availability*. Examples include the destruction of a piece of hardware, such as a hard disk; the cutting of a communication line; or the disabling of the file-management system.

2. *Interception:* An unauthorized party gains access to an asset. This is a threat to *secrecy*. The unauthorized party could be a person, a program, or a computer. Examples include wiretapping to capture data in a network or the illicit copying of files or programs.

3. *Modification:* An unauthorized party not only gains access but tampers with an asset. This is a threat to *integrity*. Examples include changing values in a data file, altering a program so that it performs differently, or modifying the content of messages being transmitted in a network.

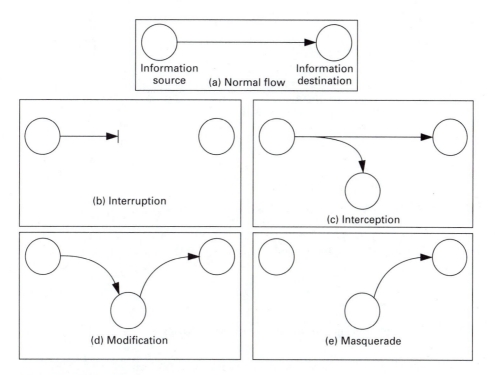

Figure 3.1 Security Threats

4. *Masquerade:* An unauthorized party inserts counterfeit objects into the system. This is also a threat to *integrity*. Examples include the insertion of spurious messages in a network or the addition of records to a file.

The assets of a computer system can be categorized as hardware, software, data, and communication lines and networks. Figure 3.2and Table 3.1 indicate the nature of the threats faced by each category of asset. Let us consider each of these in turn.

3.2.1.2   Threats to Hardware
The main threat to computer-system hardware is in the area of availability. Hardware is the most vulnerable to attack and the least amenable to automated controls. Threats include accidental and deliberate damage to equipment as well as theft. The proliferation of personal computers and workstations and the growing use of local area networks increase the potential for losses in this area. Physical and administrative security measures are needed to deal with these threats.

3.2.1.3   Threats to Software
The operating system, utilities, and application programs are what make computer-system hardware useful to businesses and individuals. Several distinct threats need to be considered.

A key threat to software is availability. Software, especially application software, is surprisingly easy to delete. Software can also be altered or damaged to render it useless. Careful software configuration management, which includes making backups of the most recent version of software, can maintain high availability.

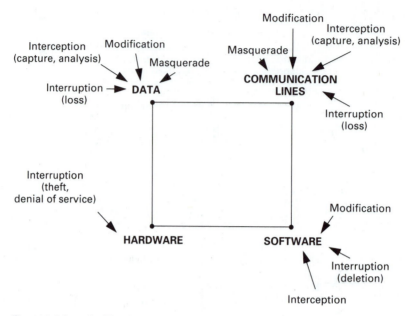

Figure 3.2 Security Threats and Computer-System Assets

A more difficult problem to deal with is software modification that results in a program that still functions but behaves differently than before. Computer viruses and related attacks fall into this category.

A final problem is software secrecy. Although certain countermeasures are available, by and large the problem of unauthorized copying of software has not been solved.

3.2.1.4   Threats to Data

Hardware and software security is typically the concern of either computing-center professionals or individual personal-computer users. A much more widespread problem is data security, which involves files and other forms of data controlled by individuals, groups, and business organizations. Security concerns with respect to data are broad, encompassing availability, secrecy, and integrity.

In the case of availability, the concern is with the destruction of data files, which can occur either accidentally or maliciously.

The obvious concern with respect to secrecy, of course, is the unauthorized reading of data files or databases, and this area has been the subject of perhaps more research and effort than any other area of computer security. A less obvious secrecy threat involves the analysis of data and manifests itself in the use of so-called statistical databases, which provide summary or aggregate information. Presumably, the existence of aggregate information does not threaten the privacy of the individuals involved. However, as the use of statistical databases grows, there is an increasing potential for disclosure of personal information. In essence, characteristics of constituent individuals may be identified through careful analysis. To take a simpleminded example, if one table records the aggregate of the incomes of respondents A, B, C, and D, and another records the aggregate of the incomes of A, B, C, D, and E, the difference between the two aggregates would be the income of E. This problem is exacerbated by the increasing desire to combine data sets. In

Table 3.1 Security Threats and Assets

	Availability	**Secrecy**	**Integrity**
Hardware	Equipment is stolen or disabled, thus denying service.	—	—
Software	Programs are deleted, denying access to users.	An unauthorized copy of software is made.	A working program is modified, either to cause it to fail during execution or to cause it to do some unintended task.
Data	Files are deleted, denying access to users.	An unauthorized read of data is performed. An analysis of statistical data reveals underlying data.	Existing files are modified, or new files are fabricated.
Communication Lines	Messages are destroyed or deleted. Communication lines or networks are rendered unavailable.	Messages are read. The traffic pattern of messages is observed.	Messages are modified, delayed, reordered, or duplicated. False messages are fabricated.

many cases, matching several sets of data for consistency at levels of aggregation appropriate to the problem requires a retreat to elemental units in the process of constructing the necessary aggregates. Thus, the elemental units, which are the subject of privacy concerns, are available at various stages in the processing of data sets.

Finally, data integrity is a major concern in most installations. Modifications to data files can have consequences ranging from minor to disastrous.

3.2.1.5 Threats to Communication Lines and Networks

Communication systems are used to transmit data. Thus, the concerns of availability, security, and integrity that are relevant to data security apply as well to network security. In this context, threats are conveniently categorized as passive or active (Figure 3.3).

Passive threats are in the nature of eavesdropping on or monitoring of the transmissions of an organization. The attacker's goal is to obtain information that is being transmitted. Two types of threats are involved here:

1. *Release of message contents*: This threat is clearly understood by most observers. A telephone conversation, an electronic-mail message, or a transferred file may contain sensitive or confidential information. We would like to prevent the attacker from learning the contents of these transmissions.

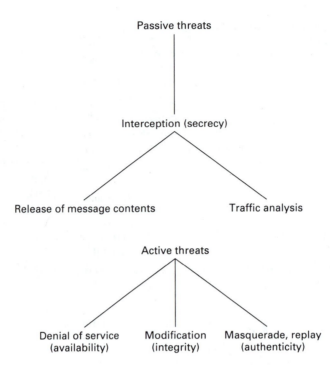

Figure 3.3 Active and Passive Network Security Threats

2. *Traffic analysis:* This threat is more subtle and often less applicable. Suppose that we had a way of masking the contents of messages or other information traffic so that an attacker, even if he or she captured the message, would be unable to extract the information from the message. The common technique for doing this is encryption, discussed at length in Appendixes 8A and 8B. Even if we had such protection in place, it might still be possible for an attacker to observe the pattern of these messages. The attacker can determine the location and identity of communicating hosts and can also observe the frequency and length of messages being exchanged. This information might be useful in guessing the nature of the communication that is taking place.

Passive threats are very difficult to detect, since they do not involve any alteration of the data. However, it is feasible to prevent these attacks from being successful. Thus, the emphasis in dealing with passive threats is on prevention and not detection.

Active threats, the second major category of threat, involve some modification of the data stream or the creation of a false stream. We can subdivide these threats into three categories:

1. *Message-stream modification:* This simply means that some portion of a legitimate message is altered or that messages are delayed, replayed, or reordered, in order to produce an unauthorized effect. For example, a message meaning "Allow John Smith to read confidential file *accounts*" is modified to mean "Allow Fred Brown to read confidential file *accounts*."

2. *Denial of service:* This type of threat prevents or inhibits the normal use or management of communications facilities. This attack may have a specific target; for example, an entity may

suppress all messages directed to a particular destination (e.g., the security-audit service). Another form of service denial is the disruption of an entire network, either by disabling the network or by overloading it with messages so as to degrade performance.

3. *Masquerade:* This occurs when one entity pretends to be a different entity. A masquerade attack usually includes one of the other two forms of active attack. Such an attack can involve, for example, capturing and replaying an authentication sequence.

The characteristics of active threats are the opposite of those of passive threats. Whereas passive attacks are difficult to detect, measures are available to prevent their success. On the other hand, it is quite difficult to absolutely prevent active attacks, since this would require physical protection of all communications facilities and paths at all times. Instead, the goal with respect to active attacks is to detect these attacks and to recover from any disruption or delays they might cause. Because the detection has a deterrent effect, this may also contribute to prevention.

3.2.1.6   Threats to the Network-Management System

Since network management involves a set of applications and databases on various hardware platforms distributed throughout the configuration, all of the threats discussed earlier in this subsection can be considered threats to the network-management system. In addition, three security concerns specific to network management may be cited:

1. *User masquerade:* A user who is not authorized to perform network management functions may attempt to access network-management applications and network-management information.

2. *Network manager masquerade:* A computer system may masquerade as a network manager station (a management server in Figure 1.5).

3. *Interference with manager-agent interchange:* One threat is the observation of manager-agent protocol traffic to extract sensitive management information. More damaging would be the modification of such traffic to disrupt the operation of the agent or the resources it is managing.

3.2.2   Security-Management Functions

The security facility of a system or network of systems consists of a set of security services and mechanisms. It is beyond the scope of this book to describe these services and mechanisms;[1] instead, our focus is on the management of the security facility.

The functions of security management can be grouped into three categories:

1. Maintaining security information
2. Controlling resource access
3. Controlling the encryption process

3.2.2.1   Maintaining Security Information

As with other areas of network management, security management is based on the use of management information exchanges between managers and agents. The same sorts of operations are employed for security management as for other areas of network management; the difference is only

---

1. See Stallings (1993c) for a discussion.

in the nature of the management information involved. Examples of objects appropriate for security management include keys, authentication information, access-right information, and operating parameters of security services and mechanisms.

Security management keeps track of activity, or attempted activity, with these security objects in order to detect and recover from attempted or successful security attacks. This includes the following functions related to the maintenance of security information:

- Event logging
- Monitoring security-audit trails
- Monitoring usage and the users of security-related resources
- Reporting security violations
- Receiving notifications of security violations
- Maintaining and examining security logs
- Maintaining backup copies for all or part of the security-related files
- Maintaining general network user profiles, and usage profiles for specific resources, to permit verification of conformance to designated security profiles

3.2.2.2   Controlling Resource Access

One of the central services of any security facility is access control, which involves authentication and authorization services and the actual decision to grant or refuse access to specific resources. The access-control service is designed to protect a broad range of network resources. Among those resources that are of particular concern for the network-management function are:

- Security codes
- Source-routing and route-recording information
- Directories
- Routing tables
- Alarm threshold levels
- Accounting tables

Security management manages the access-control service by maintaining general network user profiles and usage profiles for specific resources and by setting priorities for access. The security-management function enables the user to create and delete security-related objects, change their attributes or state, and affect the relationships between security-related objects.

3.2.2.3   Controlling the Encryption Process

Security management must be able to encrypt any exchanges between managers and agents, as needed. In addition, security management should facilitate the use of encryption by other network entities. This function involves designating encryption algorithms and providing for key distribution.

3.3 SUMMARY

Network control is concerned with altering parameters of various components of the configuration and causing those components to perform predefined actions.

The area of configuration control encompasses a variety of functions relating to the configuration of network and computing elements. These include initialization, maintenance, and shutdown of individual components and logical subsystems.

In the area of security control, the responsibility of the network-management system is to coordinate and control the security mechanisms built into the configuration of networks and systems under its management control. These security mechanisms are intended to protect user and system resources, including the network-management system itself.

Part 2
The SNMP Family

The simple network management protocol (SNMP) was developed to provide a basic, easily implemented network-management tool for TCP/IP–based environments. The first three chapters of this part cover the basics of SNMP. Chapter 4 introduces the SNMP framework and examines the evolution of SNMP from earlier efforts. Chapter 5 deals with the representation of management information within the SNMP framework; this includes the structure of management information (SMI), which dictates the format of management information, as well as MIB-II (management information base II), which is the current standard database for SNMP management information. Chapter 6 examines the actual protocol specification.

Within the SNMP framework, additional MIBs may be defined to support specific functions. Perhaps the most important, and certainly the most complex, of these is the RMON (remote monitoring) MIB. RMON is examined in Chapter 7.

The most important deficiency in SNMP is its lack of security mechanisms. To correct this deficiency, a major enhancement to SNMP, known as secure SNMP, was recently standardized. This set of standards is examined in Chapter 8.

Chapters 9 and 10 present the second-generation standard for SNMP, known as SNMP version 2 (SNMPv2). Chapter 9 focuses on the functional enhancements that SNMPv2 provides over SNMP and Chapter 10 examines the security features of SNMPv2.

4

SNMP Network-Management Concepts

The term *simple network management protocol* (SNMP) is actually used to refer to a collection of specifications for network management that includes the protocol itself, the definition of a database, and associated concepts. In this chapter, we provide a brief overview of the key concepts of SNMP. The details are developed in the remaining chapters of this part.

4.1 BACKGROUND

The development of SNMP follows a historical pattern similar to the development of the entire TCP/IP (transmission-control protocol/internet protocol) protocol suite, of which it is a part. It is perhaps useful to consider this pattern.

4.1.1 The Origins of TCP/IP

The starting point for TCP/IP[1] goes all the way back to 1969, when the U.S. Department of Defense (DoD) funded, through the Advanced Research Projects Agency, the development of one of the first packet-switching networks, ARPANET. The purpose of ARPANET was to study technologies related to the sharing of computer resources and to spin these technologies off into data networks useful for day-to-day DoD requirements. As ARPANET evolved, it rapidly grew in size to accommodate first dozens and then hundreds of hosts and thousands of terminals. It soon became clear that a major issue was interoperability. With terminals and hosts from many vendors, specialized software needed to be developed to support everything from file transfer to terminal/host interaction. The problem became even greater as ARPANET evolved into the Internet, a collection of wide area networks and local area networks with ARPANET as the core.

---

1. See Appendix B for a brief technical discussion of TCP/IP. A more detailed discussion can be found in Stallings (1990).

To solve the interoperability problem, ARPANET researchers developed a standardized set of protocols, which, by the late 1970s, had evolved into the present TCP/IP protocol suite. These protocols were standardized as official Internet Activities Board (IAB) standards issued as requests for comments (RFCs). Ultimately, the core protocols of the suite were issued as military standards.

TCP/IP met the requirements of the DoD and became standard in DoD procurements. An interesting and generally unexpected development was the growth of the use of TCP/IP in non-military applications. This growth began to take off in the mid-1980s, just at the time when efforts were being made to develop an international consensus around OSI (open systems interconnection). Yet despite OSI, TCP/IP grew rapidly and is today the dominant standardized communications architecture. Although many (perhaps most) observers continue to predict that OSI will ultimately be the foundation for the bulk of interoperable computer communications, the life expectancy of TCP/IP grows with every passing year.

It is natural to ask why these military protocols have found favor in a commercial marketplace that should, on the face of it, prefer international standards. The motivation is much the same as for the DoD: the TCP/IP protocol suite is a mature, working set of protocols that provides inter-operability and a high level of functionality. The international standards have been slow to de-velop—indeed, are still evolving—and have only recently become commercially available. Furthermore, although the OSI protocol suite provides a much richer functionality than TCP/IP, this very richness implies a complexity that has made the implementation of conformant, inter-operable software more difficult than with TCP/IP.

4.1.2   The Origins of TCP/IP Network Management

As TCP/IP was being developed, little thought was given to network management. Initially, vir-tually all of the hosts and subnetworks attached to ARPANET were based in an environment that included systems programmers and protocol designers working on some aspect or another of the ARPANET research. Therefore, management problems could be left to protocol experts, who could tweak the network with the use of some basic tools.

Up through the late 1970s, there were no management protocols as such. The one tool that was effectively used for management was the internet-control message protocol (ICMP). ICMP provides a means for transferring control messages from routers and other hosts to a host, to provide feedback about problems in the environment. ICMP is available on all devices that support IP (internet protocol). From a network-management point of view, the most useful feature of ICMP is the echo/echo-reply message pair. These messages provide a mechanism for testing that com-munication is possible between entities. The recipient of an echo message is obligated to return the contents of that message in an echo-reply message. Another useful pair of messages are timestamp and timestamp reply, which provide a mechanism for sampling the delay characteristics of the network.

These ICMP messages can be used, along with various IP header options such as source routing and record route, to develop simple but powerful management tools. The most notable example of this is the widely used PING (Packet Internet Groper) program. Using ICMP, plus some additional options such as the interval between requests and the number of times to send a request, PING can perform a variety of functions. Examples include determining whether a phys-ical network device can be addressed, verifying that a network can be addressed, and verifying the operation of a server on a host. The PING capability can be used to observe variations in round-

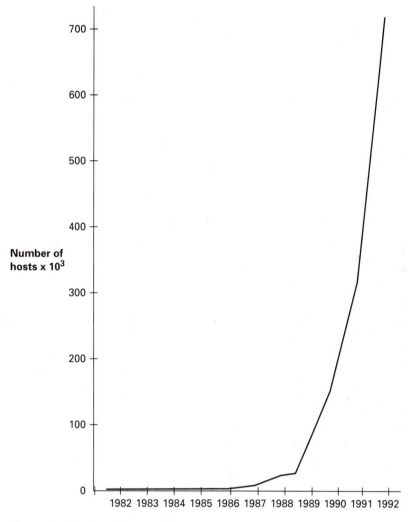

Figure 4.1 Number of Internet Hosts

trip times and in datagram loss rates, which can help to isolate areas of congestion and points of failure.

With some supplemental tools, the PING capability was a satisfactory solution to the network-management requirement for many years. It was only in the late 1980s, when the growth of the Internet became exponential, that attention was focused on the development of a more powerful network-management capability.

Figure 4.1, based on statistics in Lotter (1992), suggests the problem that began to face users of the Internet. The number of hosts attached to the Internet has increased explosively. This growth in sheer size has been accompanied by a growth in complexity. There has been an equally rapid and exponential growth in the number of subnetworks that are part of the Internet and of the number of distinct administrative domains. This latter parameter reflects the number of different entities that have "management" responsibility for part of the Internet.

With the number of hosts on the network in the hundreds of thousands and the number of individual networks in the thousands, it was no longer possible to rely on a small cadre of network experts to solve management problems. What was required was a standardized protocol that would have far more functionality than PING and yet could be easily learned and used by a wide variety of people with network-management responsibilities.

To meet this requirement, various efforts were initiated to develop a network-management protocol. From these efforts, three promising approaches emerged:

1. *High-level entity-management system (HEMS):* This was a generalization of perhaps the first network-management protocol used in the Internet, the host-monitoring protocol (HMP).

2. *Simple network-management protocol (SNMP):* This was an enhanced version of the simple gateway-monitoring protocol (SGMP).

3. *CMIP over TCP/IP (CMOT):* This was an attempt to incorporate, to the maximum extent possible, the protocol (common management information protocol), services, and database structure being standardized by the ISO (International Organization for Standardization) for network management.

In early 1988, the Internet Activities Board reviewed these proposals and approved further development of SNMP as a short-term solution and CMOT as the long-range solution (Cerf 1988). At the time, the line of reasoning was as follows: It was felt that within a reasonable period of time, TCP/IP installations would transition to OSI-based protocols. Thus, there was a reluctance to invest substantial effort in application-level protocols and services on TCP/IP that might soon have to be abandoned. In order to meet immediate needs, SNMP could be developed quickly and provide some basic management tools as well as support the development of an experience base for doing network management. HEMS was more capable than SNMP, but expending extra effort on a dead end seemed unwarranted. Meanwhile, if CMIP could be implemented to run on top of TCP, then it might be possible to deploy CMOT even before the transition to OSI. Then, when the time came to move to OSI, the network-management aspect of the move would require minimal effort.

To further solidify this strategy, the IAB dictated that both SNMP and CMOT use the same database of managed objects. That is, both protocols were to use the same set of monitoring and control variables, in the same formats, within any host, router, bridge, or other managed device. Thus, only a single structure of management information (SMI: the basic format conventions for objects) and a single management information base (MIB: the actual structure, or schema, of the database) would be defined for both protocols. This identity of databases would greatly facilitate transition: only the protocol and supporting software would need to be changed; the actual database would be the same in format and content at the time of transition.

It soon became apparent that this binding of the two protocols at the object level was impractical. In OSI network management, managed objects are seen as sophisticated entities with attributes, associated procedures and notification capabilities, and other complex characteristics associated with object-oriented technology. To keep SNMP simple, it is not designed to work with such sophisticated concepts. In fact, the objects in SNMP are not really objects at all from the point of view of object-oriented technology; rather, objects in SNMP are simply variables with a few basic characteristics, such as data type and whether the variable is read-only or read-write. Accordingly, the IAB relaxed its condition of a common SMI/MIB and allowed SNMP and CMOT development to proceed independently and in parallel (Cerf 1989).

4.1.3   The Emergence of SNMP

With the SNMP developers freed from the constraint of OSI compatibility, progress was rapid and mirrors the history of TCP/IP. SNMP soon became widely available on vendor equipment and flourished within the Internet. In addition, SNMP soon became the standardized management protocol of choice for the general user. Just as TCP/IP has outlasted all predictions of its useful lifetime, so SNMP appears to be around for the long haul, and widespread deployment of OSI network management continues to be delayed. Meanwhile, the CMOT effort languishes.

In the long run, it is still probable that both OSI as a whole and OSI network management will displace TCP/IP and SNMP. Given the massive installed base of TCP/IP and SNMP, that ''long run'' will be many years. In the meantime, as OSI and OSI network management become more widely available and more commonly used, there will be a period of coexistence of the two management schemes. Hence, it is important to have an understanding of both approaches, and hence, both approaches are covered in this book.

4.1.4   The Evolution of SNMP

The ''basic'' SNMP is now in widespread use. Virtually all major vendors of host computers, workstations, bridges, routers, and hubs offer basic SNMP. Work is even progressing on the use of SNMP over OSI and other non-TCP/IP protocol suites. In addition, enhancements to SNMP have been pursued in a number of directions.

Perhaps the most important of these initiatives, so far, is the development of a remote-monitoring (RMON) capability for SNMP. The remote-monitoring specification defines additions to the basic SNMP MIB as well as the functions that exploit the RMON MIB. RMON gives the network manager the ability to monitor subnetworks as a whole rather than just individual devices on the subnetwork. Both vendors and users view RMON as an essential extension to SNMP, and RMON, though relatively new, is already widely deployed. Because of its importance, Chapter 7 is devoted entirely to RMON.

In addition to RMON, other extensions to the basic SNMP MIB have been developed. Some of these are vendor-independent and have to do with standardized network interfaces, such as token ring and FDDI (fiber-distributed data interface). Others are vendor-specific, private extensions to the MIB. In general, these extensions do not add any new technology or concepts to SNMP. Therefore, other than some discussion of the practical issues related to these extensions, they are not covered in this book.

There is a limit to how far SNMP can be extended by simply defining new and more elaborate MIBs. RMON perhaps represents as far as one would want to go in trying to enhance the functionality of SNMP by adding to the semantics of the MIB. However, as SNMP is applied to larger and more sophisticated networks, its deficiencies become more apparent. These deficiencies are in the areas of security and functionality.

Much has been done to remedy these deficiencies. As a first step, a set of three documents defining a security enhancement to SNMP were published in July of 1992 as proposed standards. This enhancement is not compatible with the original SNMP: it requires a change to the outer message header and to a number of the message-handling procedures. However, the format of the protocol data units (PDUs) carried inside an SNMP message that defines the actual protocol operation remained the same, and no new PDUs were added. The intent was to make the transition to a secure version of SNMP as painless as possible. Chapter 8 provides an analysis of these documents.

Unfortunately, the security enhancement was overtaken by events. In the very same month, July of 1992, a proposal for a new version of SNMP, referred to as the Simple Management Protocol (SMP), was submitted by four key contributors to the SNMP effort. At the same time, four interoperable implementations were made available. Two of these implementations are commercial products; the other two are public-domain software. SMP provides both functional and security enhancements to SNMP; in particular SMP adds several new PDUs. The overall message header and security functionality are similar to that of the proposed security enhancement standard.

SMP was accepted as the baseline for defining a second generation of SNMP, known as SNMP version 2 (SNMPv2); no other proposals were submitted. In addition, a consensus emerged with the IETF that a single transition from SNMP to SNMPv2 was desirable. Therefore, the just-completed security enhancements were tabled.

Two working groups were formed to develop the specifications for SNMPv2. One group concentrated on all of the aspects of SNMPv2 other than security, while the other worked on the security features of SNMPv2. The result was a set of 12 documents that was published as proposed standards in early 1993. The documents must progress from proposed standards to draft standards to final standards. It is possible technical changes could be made during this process, but it is not particularly common, and it is likely that the proposed standards will pass through this process with virtually no technical changes. This is certainly the hope of the many vendors who have already begun product development. Chapter 9 covers the non-security aspects of SNMPv2, and Chapter 10 covers the security aspects of SNMPv2.

With the continuing development of and interest in OSI network management, there is some question as to how far the process of extending SNMP can usefully be taken. Given the unwavering commitment to OSI of most governments and some of the major corporations, OSI network management will be widely available within the foreseeable future.

4.1.5 SNMP-Related Standards

The set of specifications that define SNMP and its related functions and databases is comprehensive and growing. Table 4.1 lists the nonobsolete specifications issued in the RFC series as of the time of this writing. The three foundation specifications are:

1. *Structure and Identification of Management Information for TCP/IP-Based Internets (RFC 1155):* describes how managed objects contained in the MIB are defined

2. *Management Information Base for Network Management of TCP/IP-Based Internets: MIB-II (RFC 1213):* describes the managed objects contained in the MIB

3. *Simple Network Management Protocol (RFC 1157):* defines the protocol used to manage these objects

The remaining RFCs define various extensions to the SMI or MIB.

Table 4.1 TCP/IP Network-Management RFCs

RFC	Date	Title
Full Standards		
1155	May 1990	Structure and Identification of Management Information for TCP/IP-Based Internets
1157	May 1990	A Simple Network Management Protocol (SNMP)
1213	March 1991	Management Information Base for Network Management of TCP/IP-Based Internets: MIB-II
Draft Standards		
1212	March 1991	Concise MIB Definitions
Proposed Standards		
1229	May 1991	Extensions to the Generic-Interface MIB
1230	May 1991	IEEE 802.4 Token Bus MIB
1231	May 1991	IEEE 802.5 Token Ring MIB
1232	May 1991	DS1 Interface Type MIB
1233	May 1991	DS3 Interface Type MIB
1239	June 1991	Reassignment of Experimental MIBs to Standard MIBs
1243	July 1991	Appletalk MIB
1253	August 1991	OSPF Version 2 Management Information Base
1269	October 1991	Definitions of Managed Objects for the Border Gateway Protocol (Version 3)
1271	November 1991	Remote Network-Monitoring Management Information Base
1284	December 1991	Definition of Managed Objects for the Ethernet-like Interface Types
1285	January 1992	FDDI Management Information Base
1286	December 1991	Definitions of Managed Objects for Bridges
1289	January 1992	DECnet Phase IV MIB
1304	February 1992	SMDS Interface Protocol (SIP) MIB
1315	April 1992	Management Information Base for Frame Relay DTEs
1316	April 1992	Definitions of Managed Objects for Character Stream Devices
1317	April 1992	Definitions of Managed Objects for RS-232-like Hardware Devices
1318	April 1992	Definitions of Managed Objects for Parallel-Printer-like Hardware Devices
1354	July 1992	IP Forwarding Table MIB

Table 4.1 (*Cont.*)

RFC	Date	Title
		Experimental
1187	October 1990	Bulk Table Retrieval with the SNMP
1227	May 1991	SNMP MUX Protocol and MIB
1228	May 1991	SNMP-DPI: Simple Network Management Protocol Distributed Program Interface
1283	December 1991	SNMP over OSI
		Informational
1215	March 1991	A Convention for Defining Traps for Use with the SNMP
1303	February 1992	A Convention for Describing SNMP-Based Agents

4.2   BASIC CONCEPTS

4.2.1   Network-Management Architecture

The model of network management that is used for TCP/IP network management includes the following key elements:

- Management station

- Management agent

- Management information base (MIB)

- Network-management protocol

The *management station* is typically a stand-alone device but may be a capability implemented on a shared system. In either case, the management station serves as the interface for the human network manager into the network-management system. The management station will have, at minimum:

- A set of management applications for data analysis, fault recovery, and so on

- An interface by which the network manager may monitor and control the network

- The capability of translating the network manager's requirements into the actual monitoring and control of remote elements in the network

- A database of information extracted from the MIBs of all the managed entities in the network

Only the last two elements are the subject of SNMP.

The other active element in the network-management system is the *management agent*. Key platforms—such as hosts, bridges, routers, and hubs—may be equipped with SNMP so that they can be managed from a management station. The management agent responds to requests for information and requests for actions from the management station and may asynchronously provide the management station with important but unsolicited information.

The means by which resources in the network may be managed is to represent these resources as objects. Each object is, essentially, a data variable that represents one aspect of the managed agent. The collection of objects is referred to as a *management information base*. The MIB functions as a collection of access points at the agent for the management station. These objects are standardized across systems of a particular class (e.g., bridges all support the same management objects). A management station performs the monitoring function by retrieving the value of MIB objects. A management station can cause an action to take place at an agent or can change an agent's configuration settings by modifying the value of specific variables.

The management station and agents are linked by a *network-management protocol*. The protocol used for the management of TCP/IP networks is the simple network-management protocol, which includes the following key capabilities:

- *Get:* enables the management station to retrieve the value of objects at the agent
- *Set:* enables the management station to set the value of objects at the agent
- *Trap:* enables an agent to notify the management station of significant events

There are no specific guidelines in the standards as to the number of management stations or the ratio of management stations to agents. In general, it is prudent to have at least two systems capable of performing the management-station function, to provide redundancy in case of failure. The other issue is the practical one of how many agents a single management station can handle. As long as SNMP remains relatively "simple," that number can be quite high—certainly, in the hundreds.

4.2.2   Network-Management-Protocol Architecture

SNMP was designed to be an application-level protocol that is part of the TCP/IP protocol suite. It is intended to operate over the user datagram protocol (UDP).[2] Figure 4.2 suggests the typical configuration of protocols for SNMP. For a stand-alone management station, a manager process controls access to the central MIB at the management station and provides an interface to the network manager. The manager process achieves network management by using SNMP, which is implemented on top of UDP, IP, and the relevant network-dependent protocols (e.g., Ethernet, FDDI, X.25).

Each agent must also implement SNMP, UDP, and IP. In addition, there is an agent process that interprets the SNMP messages and controls the agent's MIB. For an agent device that supports other applications, such as FTP (file transfer protocol), TCP as well as UDP is required.

Figure 4.3 provides a somewhat closer look at the protocol context of SNMP. From a management station, three types of SNMP messages are issued on behalf of a management application: GetRequest, GetNextRequest, and SetRequest. The first two are two variations of the get function. All three messages are acknowledged by the agent in the form of a GetResponse message, which is passed up to the management application. In addition, an agent may issue a Trap message in response to an event that affects the MIB and the underlying managed resources.

---

2.   See Appendix 6B for a brief discussion of UDP.

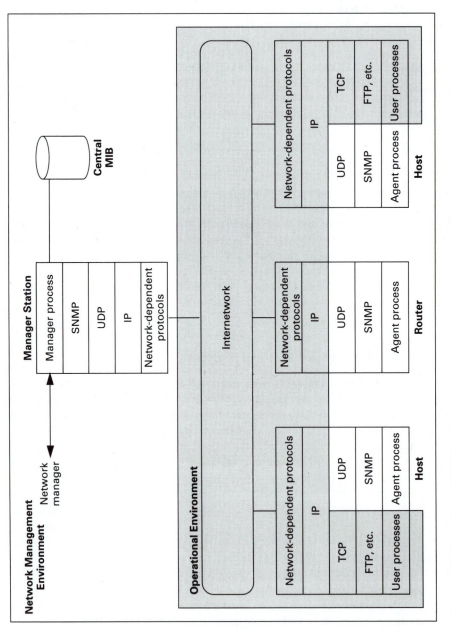

Figure 4.2 Configuration of SNMP

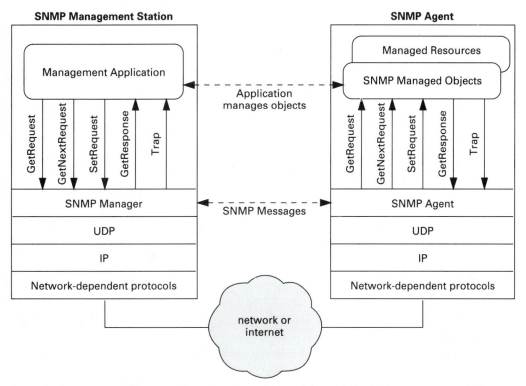

Source: A. Ben=Artzi, A. Chandna, and U. Warrier, "Network Management of TCP = IP Networks: Present and Future," *IEEE Network Magazine* (July 1990).

Figure 4.3 The Role of SNMP

Because SNMP relies on UDP, which is a connectionless protocol, SNMP is itself connectionless. No ongoing connections are maintained between a management station and its agents. Instead, each exchange is a separate transaction between a management station and an agent.

4.2.3 Trap-Directed Polling

If a management station is responsible for a large number of agents, and if each agent maintains a large number of objects, then it becomes impractical for the management station to regularly poll all agents for all of their readable object data. Accordingly, SNMP and the associated MIB are designed to enable the manager to use a technique referred to as trap-directed polling.

The recommended strategy is this: At initialization time, and perhaps at infrequent intervals, such as once a day, a management station can poll all of the agents it knows of for some key information, such as interface characteristics, and perhaps some baseline performance statistics, such as average number of packets sent and received over each interface during a given period of time. Once this baseline is established, the management station refrains from polling. Instead, each agent is responsible for notifying the management station of any unusual event. Examples include the agent's crashing and being rebooted, the failure of a link, or an overload condition as defined

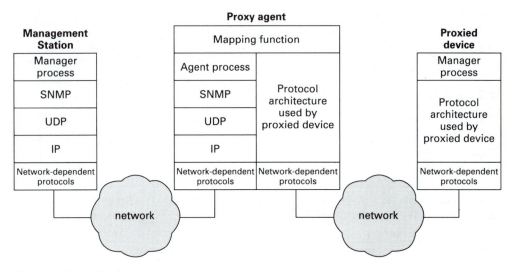

Figure 4.4 Proxy Configuration

by the packet load's crossing some threshold. These events are communicated in SNMP messages known as Traps.

Once a management station is alerted to an exception condition, it may choose to take some action. At this point, the management station may direct polls to the agent reporting the event and perhaps to some nearby agents in order to diagnose any problem and gain more specific information about the exception condition.

Trap-directed polling can result in substantial savings of network capacity and agent processing time. In essence, the network is not made to carry management information that the management station does not need, and agents are not made to respond to frequent requests for uninteresting information.

4.2.4   Proxies

The use of SNMP requires that all agents, as well as management stations, support UDP and IP. This limits direct management to such devices and excludes other devices, such as some bridges and modems, that do not support any part of the TCP/IP protocol suite. Furthermore, there may be numerous small systems (personal computers, workstations, programmable controllers) that do implement TCP/IP to support their applications but for which it is not desirable to add the extra burden of SNMP, agent logic, and MIB maintenance.

To accommodate devices that do not implement SNMP, the concept of proxy was developed. In this scheme, an SNMP agent acts as a proxy for one or more other devices; that is, the SNMP agent acts on behalf of the proxied devices.

Figure 4.4 indicates the type of protocol architecture that is often involved. The management station sends queries concerning a device to its proxy agent. The proxy agent converts each query into the management protocol that is used by the device. When a reply to a query is received by the agent, it passes that reply back to the management station. Similarly, if an event notification of some sort from the device is transmitted to the proxy, the proxy sends that on to the management station in the form of a Trap message.

4.3 SUMMARY

The simple network management protocol was designed to be an easily implemented, basic network-management tool that could be used to meet short-term network-management needs. Because of the slow progress in OSI systems management, SNMP has filled the gap and become the dominant standardized network-management scheme in use today.

The SNMP set of standards provides a framework for the definition of management information and a protocol for the exchange of that information. The SNMP model assumes the existence of managers and agents. A manager is a software module in a management system responsible for managing part or all of the configuration on behalf of network-management applications and users. An agent is a software module in a managed device responsible for maintaining local management information and delivering that information to a manager via SNMP. A management information exchange can be initiated by the manager (polling) or by the agent (trap).

SNMP accommodates the management of devices that do not implement the SNMP software by means of proxies. A proxy is an SNMP agent that maintains information on behalf of one or more non-SNMP devices.

5

SNMP Management Information Base

As with any network-management system, the foundation of a TCP/IP (transmission-control protocol/internet protocol)–based network-management system is a database containing information about the elements to be managed. In both the TCP/IP and OSI (open systems interconnection) environments, the database is referred to as a management information base (MIB). Each resource to be managed is represented by an object. The MIB is a structured collection of such objects. Each node in the system will maintain an MIB that reflects the status of the managed resources at that node. A network-management entity can monitor the resources at that node by reading the values of objects in the MIB and may control the resources at that node by modifying those values.

In order for the MIB to serve the needs of a network-management system, it must meet two objectives:

1. The object or objects used to represent a particular resource must be the same at each node. For example, consider information stored concerning the TCP entity at a node. The total number of connections opened over a period of time consists of active opens and passive opens. The MIB at the node could store any two of the three relevant values (number of active opens, number of passive opens, total number of opens), from which the third could be derived when needed. However, if different nodes select different pairs for storage, it is difficult to write a simple protocol to access the required information. As it happens, the MIB definition for TCP/IP specifies that the active- and passive-open counts be stored.

2. A common scheme for representation must be used to support interoperability.

The second point is addressed by defining a structure of management information (SMI), which we examine in section 5.1. The first point is addressed by defining the objects and the structuring of those objects in the MIB. The remainder of this chapter, after the first section, examines the MIB for SNMP.

This chapter makes use of the ASN.1 notation. The reader not familiar with this notation should first consult Appendix C.

5.1 STRUCTURE OF MANAGEMENT INFORMATION

The structure of management information, which is specified in RFC 1155, defines the general framework within which an MIB can be defined and constructed. The SMI identifies the data types that can be used in the MIB and how resources within the MIB are represented and named. The philosophy behind SMI is to encourage simplicity and extensibility within the MIB. Thus, the MIB can store only simple data types: scalars and two-dimensional arrays of scalars. We will see that SNMP can retrieve only scalars, including individual entries in a table. The SMI does not support the creation or retrieval of complex data structures. This philosophy is in contrast to that used with OSI management, which provides for complex data structures and retrieval modes to support greater functionality.

SMI avoids complex data types to simplify the task of implementation and to enhance interoperability. MIBs will inevitably contain vendor-created data types, and unless tight restrictions are placed on the definition of such data types, interoperability will suffer.

To provide a standardized way of representing management information, the SMI must provide standardized techniques for:

- Defining the structure of a particular MIB
- Defining individual objects, including the syntax and value of each object
- Encoding object values

Let us consider each of these aspects in turn.

5.1.1 MIB Structure

Associated with each type of object in an MIB is an identifier of the ASN.1 type OBJECT IDENTIFIER. The identifier serves to name the object. In addition, because the value associated with the type OBJECT IDENTIFIER is hierarchical, the naming convention also serves to identify the structure of object types.

To summarize from Appendix C, an object identifier is a unique identifier for a particular object type. Its value consists of a sequence of integers. The set of defined objects has a tree structure, with the root of the tree being the object referring to the ASN.1 standard. Starting with the root of the object identifier tree, each object identifier component value identifies an arc in the tree. Starting from the root, there are three nodes at the first level: iso, ccitt, and joint-iso-ccitt. Under the iso node, one subtree is for the use of other organizations, and one of these is the U.S. Department of Defense (dod). RFC 1155 makes the assumption that one subtree under dod will be allocated for administration by the Internet Activities Board (IAB) as follows:

internet OBJECT IDENTIFIER ::= { iso org(3) dod(6) 1 }

This is illustrated in Figure 5.1. Thus, the internet node has the object identifier value of 1.3.6.1. This value serves as the prefix for the nodes at the next lower level of the tree.

As shown, the SMI document defines four nodes under the internet node:

1. *directory:* This subtree is reserved for future use with the OSI directory (X.500).
2. *mgmt:* This subtree is used for objects defined in IAB-approved documents.

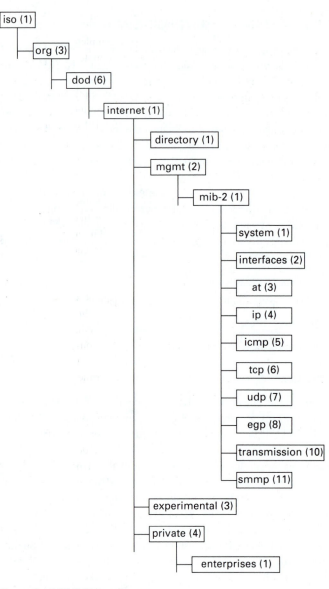

Figure 5.1 MIB-II Object Groups

3. *experimental:* This subtree is used to identify objects used in Internet experiments.

4. *private:* This subtree is used to identify objects defined unilaterally.

The mgmt subtree contains the definitions of management information bases that have been approved by the IAB. At present, two versions of the MIB have been developed: mib-1 and mib-2. The second MIB is an extension of the first. Both are provided with the same object identifier in the subtree, since only one of the MIBs would be present in any configuration.

Additional objects can be defined for an MIB in one of three ways:

1. The mib-2 subtree can be expanded or replaced by a completely new revision (presumably, mib-3). An example of the expansion of mib-2 is the remote network-monitoring MIB, described in Chapter 7.

2. An experimental MIB can be constructed for a particular application. Such objects may subsequently be moved to the mgmt subtree. Examples of these include the various transmission-media MIBs that have been defined, such as the one for IEEE 802.5 token-ring LAN (RFC 1231).

3. Private extensions can be added to the private subtree. One that is documented as an RFC (request for comment) is the MUX (multiplexer) MIB (RFC 1227).

The private subtree currently has only one child node defined, the enterprises node. This portion of the subtree is used to allow vendors to enhance the management of their devices and to share this information with other users and vendors that might need to interoperate with their systems. A branch within the enterprises subtree is allocated to each vendor that registers for an enterprises object identifier.

The division of the internet node into four subtrees provides a strong foundation for the evolution of MIBs. As vendors and other implementers experiment with new objects, they are, in effect, gaining a good deal of practical know-how before these objects are accepted as part of the standardized (mgmt) specification. Thus, the MIB is useful immediately for managing objects that fit within the standardized portion of the MIB and is flexible enough to adapt to changes in technology and product offerings. This evolutionary character mirrors that of the protocols within the TCP/IP suite: all of these protocols underwent extensive experimental use and debugging before being finalized as standard protocols.

5.1.2   Object Syntax

Objects within an SNMP MIB, and the entire MIB structure, are defined using ASN.1. In keeping with the objective of simplicity, only a restricted subset of the elements and features of ASN.1 is used.

5.1.2.1   Universal Types

Within the UNIVERSAL class, only the following data types are permitted to be used to define MIB objects:

- INTEGER (UNIVERSAL 2)
- OCTET STRING (UNIVERSAL 4)
- NULL (UNIVERSAL 5)
- OBJECT IDENTIFIER (UNIVERSAL 6)
- SEQUENCE, SEQUENCE OF (UNIVERSAL 16)

The first four are primitive types that are the basic building blocks of other types of objects. Note that the ENUMERATED type is not included. Therefore, when an enumerated list of integers is to be defined, it must be done with the INTEGER type. There are two conventions associated with the use of enumerations:

1. The value 0 may not be used. This allows for common encoding errors to be caught.

2. Only the enumerated integer values may be used. There is typically one enumerated value labeled ''other,'' or something similar, to handle cases that don't fit under the other enumerated labels.

An object identifier is a unique identifier of an object, consisting of a sequence of integers, known as subidentifiers. The sequence, read from left to right, defines the location of the object in the MIB tree structure. For example, looking at Figure 5.1 and looking ahead to Figure 5.12, the object identifier for the object tcpConnTable is derived as follows:

iso	org	dod	internet	mgmt	mib-2	tcp	tcpConnTable
1	3	6	1	2	1	6	13

This identifier would normally be written as 1.3.6.1.2.1.6.13.

The last item in the preceding list consists of the constructor types SEQUENCE and SEQUENCE OF. These types are used to construct tables, as explained later in this section.

5.1.2.2   Application Types

RFC 1155 lists a number of APPLICATION data types; other types may be defined in future RFCs. The following types are defined:

- *NetworkAddress:* This type is defined using the CHOICE construct, to allow the selection of an address format from one of a number of protocol families. Currently, the only defined address is IpAddress.

- *IpAddress:* a 32-bit address using the format specified in IP.

- *Counter:* a non-negative integer that may be incremented but not decremented. A maximum value of $2^{32} - 1$ (4,294,967,295) is specified; when the counter reaches its maximum, it wraps around and starts increasing again from 0.

- *Gauge:* a non-negative integer that may increase or decrease, with a maximum value of $2^{32} - 1$. If the maximum value is reached, the gauge remains latched at that value until reset.

- *TimeTicks:* a non-negative integer that counts the time in hundredths of a second since some epoch. When an object type is defined in the MIB that uses this type, the definition of the object type identifies the reference epoch.

- *Opaque:* supports the capability to pass arbitrary data. The data are encoded using the OCTET STRING type for transmission. The data themselves may be in any format defined by ASN.1 or some other syntax.

The counter, also known as the rollover counter, is one of the most common types used in defining objects.[1] Typical applications are to count the number of packets or octets sent or received. An alternative type of counter that was considered by the SMI designers is the latch counter, which sticks at its maximum value and must be reset. The latch counter was rejected because of

---

1.   The discussion in the remainder of this subsection is based partly on Partridge and McCloghrie (1990).

the following potential problem. Suppose that more than one management system is allowed access to a particular counter; that is, more than one management system can monitor a device. When a latch counter reaches its maximum and needs to be reset, there are two alternatives:

1. Designate one management system as responsible for latch reset. The problem with this approach is that if that system fails, the counter remains stuck at its latched value.

2. Allow any management system the authority to reset the counter when that system deems it appropriate. The problem here has to do with the time lag involved in communication across a distributed system. Several systems may reset the same counter, resulting in the loss of some information (counts that take place between the arrival of the two resets at the managed object).

With rollover counters, these difficulties are avoided. However, after a rollover counter has wrapped around several times, it is difficult for a management system to know whether a counter value of x means that the quantity observed is x or $(N \times 2^{32}) + x$. The only way around this is for the management station to periodically poll the object to keep track of wraparounds. Because 32-bit counters are used, this should not have to be done very often.

Typically, a gauge is used to measure the current value of some entity, such as the current number of packets stored in a queue. A gauge can also be used to store the difference in the value of some entity from the start to the end of a time interval. This enables a gauge to be used to monitor the rate of change of an entity's value.

The gauge type is referred to as a latched value. There is, unfortunately, some ambiguity concerning the meaning of the word *latch*. It is certainly the case that once a gauge reaches its maximum value, it will not roll over to 0. Rather, if the gauge represents a value that increases beyond the maximum, the gauge remains stuck at its maximum value. If the represented value subsequently falls below the gauge maximum, one of two policies could be adopted:

1. Allow the gauge to decrease so that the gauge always has the same value as the modeled value as long as the modeled value remains in the range of the gauge.

2. Leave the gauge stuck at its maximum value until it is reset by management action.

There is no consensus on the correct interpretation. Thus, the preceding discussion on latched counters does not necessarily apply to latched gauges. If the second interpretation in the preceding list is used, then there is a potential problem of multiple managers being allowed to reset the gauge, as discussed for latched counters. One positive feature of using the second interpretation is that if the latched value is not immediately reset, it tells management stations that some parameter has been exceeded (e.g., maximum queue size).

The timeticks type is a relative timer: time is measured relative to some event (such as startup or reinitialization) within the managed system. Although such values are unambiguous within the managed system, they cannot be directly compared to timer values in other systems. Some designers would have preferred an absolute time value using the standard ASN.1 representation. Unfortunately, most systems running the TCP/IP protocol suite do not support a time-synchronization protocol. Thus, an absolute time type is impractical for SNMP.

One type that is important in the OSI SMI was left out of the SNMP SMI: the threshold type. A threshold is used in the following way: if the threshold value is crossed (in either a positive or negative direction, depending on the definition of the threshold), an event is triggered and an event notification is sent to the management station(s). The SMI designers feared that this capability could lead to *event floods,* in which a managed system's threshold is repeatedly crossed and the system floods the network with numerous event notifications. Such event floods have been experienced on ARPANET and other networks. A particularly deadly kind of event flood is one in which the event is triggered by congestion. The creation of an event flood due to congestion exacerbates the condition being reported! However, we will see that both in the remote monitoring (RMON) MIB (Chapter 7) and in SNMPv2 (Chapter 9), thresholds are used.

5.1.2.3   Defining Objects

A management information base consists of a set of objects. Each object has a type and a value. The object type defines a particular kind of managed object. The definition of an object type is therefore a syntactic description. An object instance is an instantiation of an object type that has been bound to a specific value.

How are we to define objects for inclusion in the MIB? The notation that will be used is ASN.1. As explained in Appendix C, ASN.1 includes a number of predefined UNIVERSAL types and a grammar for defining new types that are derived from existing types. One alternative for defining managed objects would be to define a new type called Object. Then, every object in the MIB would be of this type. This approach is technically possible but would result in unwieldy definitions. We need to allow for a variety of value types, including counters, gauges, etc. In addition, the MIB supports the definition of two-dimensional tables, or arrays, of values.

Because managed objects may contain a variety of information to represent a variety of entities being managed, it makes more sense to define an open-ended set of new types, one for each general category of managed object. This could be done directly in ASN.1. However, this alternative, too, has a drawback. If the only restriction on the definition of a new managed-object type is that the definition be written in ASN.1, we can expect to see considerable variation in the format of object definitions. This variety will make it more difficult for the user or implementer of an MIB to incorporate a variety of object types. More seriously, the use of relatively unstructured object-type definitions complicates the task of using SNMP for interoperable access to managed objects.

A more attractive alternative, and the one employed with SNMP, is to use a macro to define a set of related types used to define managed objects. As explained in Appendix C, a macro definition gives the syntax of a set of related types, whereas a macro instance defines a specific type. Thus, we have the following levels of definition:

- *Macro definition:* defines the legal macro instances; specifies the syntax of a set of related types

- *Macro instance:* an instance generated from a specific macro definition by supplying arguments for the parameters in the macro definition; specifies a particular type

- *Macro instance value:* represents a specific entity with a specific value

The macro used for the SNMP MIBs was initially defined in RFC 1155 (Structure of Management Information) and later expanded in RFC 1212 (Concise MIB Definitions). The RFC 1155 version is used for defining objects in MIB-I. The RFC 1212 version, which includes more information, is used for defining objects in MIB-II and other recent additions to the MIB.

```
IMPORTS   ObjectName,ObjectSyntax FROM RFC-1155-SMI

OBJECT-TYPE MACRO ::=
BEGIN
          TYPE NOTATION ::=    "SYNTAX"     type(TYPE ObjectSyntax)
                               "ACCESS"     Access
                               "STATUS"     Status
                               DescrPart
                               ReferPart
                               IndexPart
                               DefValPart
          VALUE NOTATION ::=value (VALUE ObjectName)

          Access ::="read-only"|"read-write"|"write-only"|"not-accessible"

          Status ::="mandatory"|"optional"|"obsolete"|"deprecated"

          DescrPart ::="DESCRIPTION" value (description DisplayString) | empty

          ReferPart ::="REFERENCE" value (reference DisplayString) | empty

          IndexPart ::="INDEX" "{"IndexTypes"}"

          IndexTypes ::=IndexType | IndexTypes"," IndexType

          IndexType ::=value (indexobject ObjectName)     --if indexobject, use the SYNTAX
                                                          --value of the correspondent
                                                          --OBJECT-TYPE invocation
                              | type (indextype)          --otherwise use named SMI type;
                                                          --must conform to IndexSyntax below

          DefValPart ::="DEFVAL" "{" value (defvalue ObjectSyntax) "}" | empty

          DisplayString ::=OCTET STRING SIZE  (0..255)

END

IndexSyntax ::=CHOICE { number INTEGER (0..MAX),
                        string OCTET STRING,
                        object OBJECT IDENTIFIER,
                        address NetworkAddress,
                        IpAddress IpAddress }
```

Figure 5.2 Macro for Managed Objects (RFC 1212, Mar. 1991)

Figure 5.2 is the definition of the OBJECT-TYPE macro from RFC 1212.[2] The key components are:

- *SYNTAX:* the abstract syntax for the object type. This must resolve to an instance of the
  ObjectSyntax type defined in RFC 1155 (see Figure 5.3). Essentially, the syntax must be
  constructed using the UNIVERSAL types and Applicationwide types allowed in the SMI.

---

2.   Two elements of the definition are not used in MIB-II (ReferPart and DefValPart). They may, however,
be used in other MIB definitions.

```
RFC1155-SMI DEFINITIONS ::= BEGIN

Exports -- EVERYTHING
        internet, directory,mgmt, experimental, private, enterprises, OBJECT-TYPE,
        ObjectName, ObjectSyntax, SimpleSyntax, ApplicationSyntax, NetworkAddress,
        IpAddress, Counter, Gauge, TimeTicks, Opaque;

--the path to the root

internet          OBJECT IDENTIFIER ::= { iso org(3) dod(6) 1 }
directory         OBJECT IDENTIFIER ::= { internet 1 }
mgmt              OBJECT IDENTIFIER ::= { internet 2 }
experimental      OBJECT IDENTIFIER ::= { internet 3 }
private           OBJECT IDENTIFIER ::= { internet 4 }
enterprises       OBJECT IDENTIFIER ::= { private 1 }

--definition of object types

OBJECT-TYPE MACRO::=
BEGIN
     TYPE NOTATION::= "Syntax"    type(TYPE ObjectSyntax)
                            "ACCESS" Access
                            "STATUS" Status
     VALUE NOTATION::= value(VALUE ObjectName)
     Access  ::="read-only"|"read-write"|"write-only"|"not-accessible"
     Status  ::="mandatory"|"optional"|"obsolete"
END

--names of objects in the MIB

ObjectName ::=OBJECT IDENTIFIER

--syntax of objects in the MIB

ObjectSyntax ::= CHOICE { simple SimpleSyntax,

     --note that simple SEQUENCEs are not directly mentioned here to keep things simple
     --(i.e., prevent misuse). However, applicationwide types that are IMPLICITly encoded
     --simple SEQUENCEs may appear in the following CHOICE

                       applicationwide ApplicationSyntax }

SimpleSyntax ::=CHOICE   { number INTEGER,
                          string OCTET STRING,
                          object OBJECT IDENTIFIER,
                          empty NULL }

ApplicationSyntax ::=CHOICE   { address NetworkAddress,
                              counter Counter,
                              gauge Gauge,
                              ticks TimeTicks,
                              arbitrary Opaque
                       --other applicationwide types, as they are defined, will be added here
                              }
--applicationwide types

NetworkAddress ::= CHOICE {internet IpAddress}

IpAddress ::=[APPLICATION 0]                        --in network-byte order
                    IMPLICIT OCTET STRING (SIZE (4))

Counter::=[APPLICATION 1] IMPLICIT INTEGER (0..4294967295)

Gauge ::=[APPLICATION 2] IMPLICIT INTEGER (0..4294967295)

TimeTicks::=[APPLICATION 3] IMPLICIT INTEGER (0..4294967295)

Opaque ::=[APPLICATION 4] OCTET STRING   --arbitrary ASN.1 value, "double-wrapped"
END
```

Figure 5.3 Structure of Management Information (RFC 1155, May 1990)

- *ACCESS:* defines the way in which an instance of the object may be accessed, via SNMP or some other protocol. The access clause specifies the minimum level of support required for that object type. Implementation-specific additions or restrictions to the access are permissible. The options are ''read-only,'' ''read-write,'' ''write-only,'' and ''not-accessible.'' In the latter case, the object's value may be neither read nor set.

- *STATUS:* indicates the implementation support required for this object. Support may be ''mandatory'' or ''optional.'' Alternatively, an object can be specified as ''deprecated.'' A deprecated object is one that must be supported but that will most likely be removed from the next version of the MIB. Finally, the status may be ''obsolete,'' which means that managed nodes need no longer implement this object.

- *DescrPart:* a textual description of the semantics of the object type. This clause is optional.

- *ReferPart:* a textual cross-reference to an object defined in some other MIB module. This clause is optional.

- *IndexPart:* used in defining tables. This clause may be present only if the object type corresponds to a conceptual row. The use of this clause is described later in this subsection.

- *DefValPart:* defines an acceptable default value that may be used when an object instance is created, at the discretion of the agent. This clause is optional.

- *VALUE NOTATION:* indicates the name used to access this object via SNMP.

Because the complete definition of the MIB using the OBJECT-TYPE macro is contained in the MIB documents, and because of the length of such definitions, we will generally refrain from their use. Instead, a more compact representation, based on tree structures and a tabular presentation of object characteristics, is used, as will be seen.

5.1.2.4   Defining Tables

At the present time, the SMI supports only one form of data structuring: a simple two-dimensional table with scalar-valued entries. The definition of tables involves the use of the SEQUENCE and SEQUENCE OF ASN.1 types and the IndexPart of the OBJECT-TYPE macro.

The best way to explain the table-definition convention is by example. Consider the object type tcpConnTable, which, as was mentioned earlier, has the object identifier 1.3.6.1.2.1.6.13. This object contains information about TCP connections maintained by the corresponding managed entity. For each such connection, the following information is stored in the table:

- *State:* the state of the TCP connection. The value of this entry may be one of the 11 TCP states as defined in the standard (see Appendix 5A to this chapter); the value is set by the TCP entity and is changed by the TCP entity to reflect the state of the connection. In addition, the entry may take on the value deleteTCB; this is a value set by a management station, which causes the TCP entity to delete the transmission-control block for this connection, thereby destroying the connection.

- *Local address:* the IP address of this end of the connection.

- *Local port:* the TCP port of this end of the connection.

- *Remote address:* the IP address of the other end of the connection.

- *Remote port:* the TCP port of the other end of the connection.

Before proceeding, it is instructive to note that the tcpConnTable is a part of the MIB and, as such, is maintained by a managed station to provide visibility to the management station of some underlying entity represented by the managed object. In this case, each entry in the tcpConnTable represents the state information stored in the managed station for one connection. As indicated in Appendix 5A, this state information consists of 22 separate items of information for each connection. Only 5 of these items are visible to network management by means of the tcpConnTable. This illustrates SNMP's emphasis on keeping network management simple: only a limited, useful subset of information on a managed entity is contained in the corresponding managed object.

Figure 5.4, taken from RFC 1213, shows the MIB-II specification of tcpConnTable. The technique for defining the table structure, which is invariably followed in all table definitions, is to use the SEQUENCE and SEQUENCE OF constructs as follows:

- The overall table consists of a SEQUENCE OF TcpConnEntry. As discussed in Appendix C, the ASN.1 construct SEQUENCE OF consists of zero or more elements, all of the same type. In this case (and in all other SNMP SMI cases), each element is a row of the table. Thus, a table consists of zero or more rows.

- Each row consists of a SEQUENCE that includes five scalar elements. Again, as discussed in Appendix C, the ASN.1 construct SEQUENCE consists of a fixed number of elements, possibly of more than one type. Although ASN.1 allows any of these elements to be options, the SMI restricts the use of this construct to mandatory elements only. In this case, each row of the table contains elements of type INTEGER, IpAddress, INTEGER (0..65535), IpAddress, INTEGER (0..65535).

Finally, the INDEX component of the entry definition determines which object value(s) will be used to distinguish one row in the table. In TCP, a single socket (IP address, TCP port) may support many connections, but at any one time, there may only be a single connection between any given pair of sockets. Thus, the last four elements in the row are necessary and sufficient to unambiguously distinguish a single row from the table.

Figure 5.5 is an example. In this case, the table contains three rows. The entire table represents a single instance of the object type tcpConnTable. Each row is an instance of the object type tcpConnEntry, for a total of three instances. There are also three instances of each of the scalar elements of the table. Thus, there are three instances of the object type tcpConnState, and so on. In RFC 1212, these scalar objects are referred to as *columnar objects,* emphasizing the fact that each such object corresponds to a number of instances in one column of the table.

The SMI does not permit nesting. That is, it is not allowable to define an element of a table to be another table. This restriction reduces the utility and flexibility of the SMI.

5.1.3   Encoding

Objects in the MIB are encoded using the basic encoding rules (BER) associated with ASN.1 (see Appendix C). Athough not the most compact or efficient form of encoding, BER is a widely used, standardized encoding scheme.

```
tcpConnTable OBJECT-TYPE
        SYNTAX      SEQUENCE OF TcpConnEntry
        ACCESS      not-accessible
        STATUS      mandatory
        DESCRIPTION
                "A table containing TCP connention-specific information."
        ::= { tcp 13 }

tcpConnEntry OBJECT-TYPE
        SYNTAX      TcpConnEntry
        ACCESS      not-accessible
        STATUS      mandatory
        DESCRIPTION
                "Information about a particular current TCP connection.  An object of this type is
                transient, in that it ceases to exist when (or soon after) the connection makes the
                transition to the CLOSED state."
        INDEX       { tcpConnLocalAddress,
                    tcpConnLocalPort,
                    tcpConnRemAddress,
                    tcpConnRemPort }
        ::= { tcpConnTable 1 }


TcpConnEntry ::=SEQUENCE { tcpConnState          INTEGER,
                        tcpConnLocalAddress   IpAddress,
                        tcpConnLocalPort      INTEGER (0..65535),
                        tcpConnRemAddress     IpAddress,
                        tcpConnRemPort        INTEGER (0..65535)}


TcpConnState OBJECT-TYPE
        SYNTAX      INTEGER { closed (1),
                            listen (2),
                            synSent (3),
                            synReceived (4),
                            established (5),
                            finWait1 (6),
                            finWait2 (7),
                            closeWait (8),
                            lastAck (9),
                            closing (10),
                            timeWait (11)
                            deleteTCB (12) }
        ACCESS      read-write
        STATUS      mandatory
        DESCRIPTION
                "The state of this TCP connection.

                The only value which may be set by a management station is deleteTCB(12).
                Accordingly,it is appropriate for an agent to return a 'bad Value' response if a
                management station attempts to set this object to any other value.

                If a management station sets this object to the value deleteTCB(12), then this has the
                effect of deleting the TCB (as defined in RFC 793) of the corresponding connection on
                the managed node, resulting in immediate termination of the connection.


                As an implementation-specific option, a RST segment may be sent from the managed
                node to the other TCP end point (note however that RST segments are not
                sent reliably)."
        ::= { tcpConnEntry 1 }
```

tcpConnLocalAddress OBJECT-TYPE
       SYNTAX   IpAddress
       ACCESS   read-only
       STATUS   mandatory
       DESCRIPTION
              "The local IP address for this TCP connection. In the case of a connection in the listen
                state which is willing to accept connections for any IP interface associated with the
                node, the value 0.0.0.0 is used."
       ::= { tcpConnEntry 2 }

tcpConnLocalPort OBJECT-TYPE
       SYNTAX   INTEGER (0..65535)
       ACCESS   read-only
       STATUS   mandatory
       DESCRIPTION
              "The local port number for this TCP connection."
       ::= { tcpConnEntry 3 }

tcpConnRemAddress OBJECT-TYPE
       SYNTAX   IpAddress
       ACCESS   read-only
       STATUS   mandatory
       DESCRIPTION
              "The remote IP address for this TCP connection."
       ::= { tcpConnEntry 4 }

tcpConnRemPort OBJECT-TYPE
       SYNTAX   INTEGER (0..65535)
       ACCESS   read-only
       STATUS   mandatory
       DESCRIPTION
              "The remote port number for this TCP connection."
       ::= { tcpConnEntry 5 }

Figure 5.4 MIB-II Specification of the TCP Connection Table (RFC 1213, Mar. 1991)

5.2   MIB-II

MIB-II (RFC 1213) defines the second version of the management information base; the first version, MIB-I, was issued as RFC 1156. MIB-II is a superset of MIB-I, with some additional objects and additional groups.

    The following criteria are cited in RFC 1213 for including an object in MIB-II:

- An object needed to be essential for either fault or configuration management.

- Only weak control objects were permitted (by *weak*, it is meant that tampering with them can do only limited damage). This criterion reflects the fact that the current management protocols are not sufficiently secure to do more powerful control operations.

- Evidence of current use and utility was required.

- In MIB-I, an attempt was made to limit the number of objects to about 100 to make it easier for vendors to fully instrument their software. In MIB-II, this limit was raised, given the wide technological base now implementing MIB-I.

- To avoid redundant variables, it was required that no object be included that could be derived from others in the MIB.

tcpConnTable(1.3.6.1.2.1.6.13)

tcpConnState (1.3.6.1.2.1.6.13.1.1)	tcpConnLocalAddress (1.3.6.1.2.1.6.13.1.2)	tcpConnLocalPort (1.3.6.1.2.1.6.13.1.3)	tcpConnRemAddress (1.3.6.1.2.1.6.13.1.4)	tcpConnRemPort (1.3.6.1.2.1.6.13.1.5)	
5	10.0.0.99	12	9.1.2.3	15	tcpConnEntry (1.3.6.1.2.1.6.13.1)
2	0.0.0.0	99	0	0	tcpConnEntry (1.3.6.1.2.1.6.13.1)
3	10.0.0.99	14	89.1.1.42	84	tcpConnEntry (1.3.6.1.2.1.6.13.1)
	◄ INDEX	◄ INDEX	◄ INDEX	◄ INDEX	

Figure 5.5 Instance of a TCP Connection Table

- Implementation-specific objects (e.g., for BSD UNIX) were excluded.

- It was agreed to avoid heavily instrumenting critical sections of code. The general guideline was one counter per critical section per layer.

Since MIB-II contains only objects deemed essential by its designers, none of the objects are optional. As Figure 5.1 shows, the mib-2 object is subdivided into the following groups:

- *system:* overall information about the system

- *interfaces:* information about each of the interfaces from the system to a subnetwork

- *at* (*address translation; deprecated*): describes the address-translation table for internet-to-subnet address mapping

- *ip:* information related to the implementation and execution experience of IP (internet protocol) on this system

- *icmp:* information related to the implementation and execution experience of ICMP (internet-control message protocol) on this system

- *tcp:* information related to the implementation and execution experience of TCP (transmission-control protocol) on this system

- *udp:* information related to the implementation and execution experience of UDP (user datagram protocol) on this system

- *egp:* information related to the implementation and execution experience of EGP (external gateway protocol) on this system

- *transmission:* provides information about the transmission schemes and access protocols at each system interface

- *snmp:* information related to the implementation and execution experience of SNMP (simple network management protocol) on this system

The group organization is a convenience in organizing managed objects according to the function of the underlying managed entities. In addition, it provides guidance for the implementer of managed agents to know which objects they must implement. For MIB-I and MIB-II, the method is as follows: if the semantics of a group is applicable to an implementation, then it must implement all objects in that group. For example, an implementation must include all of the objects in the TCP group if and only if it implements the TCP protocol; thus, a bridge or a router need not implement the TCP group. One exception to this rule is the address translation group, as discussed later in this section.

We examine each of the MIB-II groups in this section, with the exception of the SNMP group, whose discussion is deferred until Chapter 6.

5.2.1   Key to Figures and Tables

Figures 5.6 through 5.14 illustrate the structure of each of the groups. The structure of each group is determined by the tree-structured object identifiers assigned to the members of the group; the figures depict this tree structure. Each table appears as a three-level tree: the name of the table is the top level; the name of each row is the second level; and the name of each scalar table row element is the third level. Those elements that serve as INDEXes are indicated by an arrow.

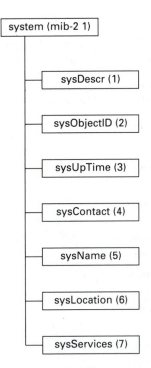

Figure 5.6 MIB-II System Group

Tables 5.1 through 5.8 provide information about the objects in each group. The ACCESS characteristic of an object may be read-only (RO), read-write (RW), write-only (WO), or not-accessible (NA). The STATUS of an object may be mandatory (M) or deprecated (D).

5.2.2   System Group

The system group provides general information about the managed system (Figure 5.6, Table 5.1). The objects in this group are largely self-explanatory, but several comments may be helpful.

The sysServices object has a value that is interpreted as a 7-bit code. Each bit of the code corresponds to a layer in the TCP/IP or OSI architecture, with the least significant bit corresponding to layer 1. If a system offers a service at a particular layer, then the corresponding bit is set. The value can be expressed as

$$\text{sysServices} = \sum_{L \varepsilon S} 2^{L-1},$$

where S = set of numbers of layers for which services are provided. For example a node that is a host offering application services would have a binary value of 1001000, or a decimal value of 72 ($2^{(4-1)} + 2^{(7-1)}$). In the context of the TCP/IP protocol suite, the following layer assignment is used:

Layer	Functionality
1	Physical (e.g., repeaters)
2	Data-link/subnetwork (e.g., bridges)

Table 5.1 MIB-II System Group Objects

Object	Syntax	Access	Status	Description
sysDescr	DisplayString (SIZE (0..255))	RO	M	A description of the entity, such as hardware, operating system, etc.
sysObjectID	OBJECT IDENTIFIER	RO	M	The vendor's authoritative identification of the network-management subsystem contained in the entity
sysUpTime	TimeTicks	RO	M	The time since the network-management portion of the system was last reinitialized
sysContact	DisplayString (SIZE (0..255))	RW	M	The identification and contact information of the contact person for this managed node
sysName	DisplayString (SIZE (0..255))	RW	M	An administratively assigned name for this managed node
sysLocation	DisplayString (SIZE (0..255))	RW	M	The physical location of this node
sysServices	INTEGER (0..127)	RO	M	A value indicating the set of services that this entity primarily offers

3	Internet (e.g., IP routers)
4	End-to-end (e.g., IP hosts)
7	Applications (e.g., mail relays)

The sysUpTime object indicates the amount of time (as counted by the agent) since the network-management portion of the system was last reinitialized. This object can be useful for fault monitoring. A manager can periodically poll each agent for this value. If the current value for an agent is less than the most recent value, then the agent has been restarted since the last poll.

5.2.3 Interfaces Group

The interfaces group contains generic information about the physical interfaces of the entity (Figure 5.7, Table 5.2), including configuration information and statistics on the events occurring at each interface. Each interface is thought of as being attached to a subnetwork, although an interface to a point-to-point link is also allowed. Implementation of this group is mandatory for all systems.

The group includes the object ifNumber, which records the total number of network interfaces, regardless of their current state. The remainder of the group consists of the ifTable, which has one

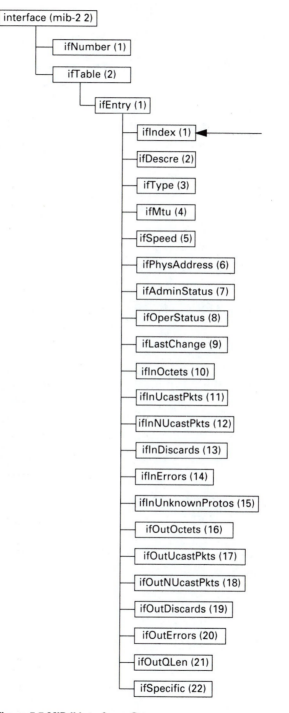

Figure 5.7 MIB-II Interfaces Group

Table 5.2 MIB-II Interfaces Group Objects

Object	Syntax	Access	Status	Description
ifNumber	INTEGER	RO	M	The number of network interfaces
ifTable	SEQUENCE OF IfEntry	NA	M	A list of interface entries
ifEntry	SEQUENCE	NA	M	An interface entry containing objects at the subnetwork layer and below for a particular interface
ifIndex	INTEGER	RO	M	A unique value for each interface
ifDescr	DisplayString (SIZE (0..255))	RO	M	Information about the interface, including name of manufacturer, product name, and version of the hardware interface
ifType	INTEGER	RO	M	Type of interface, distinguished according to the physical/link protocol(s)
ifMtu	INTEGER	RO	M	The size of the largest protocol data unit, in octets, that can be sent/received on the interface
ifSpeed	Gauge	RO	M	An estimate of the interface's current data-rate capacity
ifPhysAddress	PhysAddress	RO	M	The interface's address at the protocol layer immediately below the network layer
ifAdminStatus	INTEGER	RW	M	Desired interface state—up (1), down (2), testing (3)
ifOperStatus	INTEGER	RO	M	Current operational interface state—up (1), down (2), testing (3)
ifLast Change	TimeTicks	RO	M	Value of sysUpTime at the time the interface entered its current operational state
ifInOctets	Counter	RO	M	Total number of octets received on the interface, including framing characters
ifInUcastPkts	Counter	RO	M	Number of subnetwork-unicast packets delivered to a higher-layer protocol
ifInNUcastPkts	Counter	RO	M	Number of nonunicast packets delivered to a higher-layer protocol
ifInDiscards	Counter	RO	M	Number of inbound packets discarded even though no errors had been detected to prevent their being deliverable to a higher-layer protocol (e.g., buffer overflow)
ifInErrors	Counter	RO	M	Number of inbound packets that contained errors preventing them from being deliverable to a higher-layer protocol
ifInUnknownProtos	Counter	RO	M	Number of inbound packets that were discarded because of an unknown or unsupported protocol

Table 5.2 (*Cont.*)

Object	Syntax	Access	Status	Description
ifOutOctets	Counter	RO	M	Total number of octets transmitted on the interface, including framing characters
ifOutUcastPkts	Counter	RO	M	Total number of packets that higher-level protocols requested be transmitted to a subnetwork-unicast address, including those that were discarded or otherwise not sent
ifOutNUcastPkts	Counter	RO	M	Total number of packets that higher-level protocols requested be transmitted to a non-unicast address, including those that were discarded or otherwise not sent
ifOutDiscards	Counter	RO	M	Number of outbound packets discarded even though no errors had been detected to prevent their being transmitted (e.g., buffer overflow)
ifOutErrors	Counter	RO	M	Number of outbound packets that could not be transmitted because of errors
ifOutQLen	Gauge	RO	M	Length of the output packet queue
ifSpecific	OBJECT IDENTIFIER	RO	M	Reference to MIB definitions specific to the particular media being used to realize the interface

row for each interface. The table is indexed by ifIndex, whose value is simply an integer in the range between 1 and the value of ifNumber, with each interface being assigned a unique number.

The object ifType records the type of interface; the following interfaces have been assigned standard numbers in MIB-II:

other (1)	proteon-10Mbit (12)	ppp (23)
regular1822 (2)	proteon-80Mbit (13)	softwareLoopback (24)
hdh1822 (3)	hyperchannel (14)	eon (25)
ddn-x25 (4)	fddi (15)	ethernet-3Mbit (26)
rfc877-x25 (5)	lapb (16)	nsip (27)
ethernet-csmacd (6)	sdlc (17)	slip (28)
iso88023-csmacd (7)	ds1 (18)	ultra (29)
iso88024-tokenBus (8)	e1 (19)	ds3 (30)
iso88025-tokenRing (9)	basicISDN (20)	sip (31)
iso88026-man (10)	primaryISDN (21)	frame-relay (32)
starLan (11)	propPointToPointSerial (22)	

The nature of the physical address, ifPhysAddress, will depend on the type of interface. For example, for all IEEE LANs (local area networks) and MANs (metropolitan area networks) and

FDDI (fiber-distributed data interface), ifPhysAddress contains the value of the MAC (medium-access control) address at that interface.

Two objects in the group relate to the status of the interface. The ifAdminStatus object, which is read-write, enables a manager to specify a desired operational status for the interface. The ifOperStatus object, which is read-only, reflects the actual current operational status of the interface. If both objects have the value down (2), then the interface has been shut off by the manager. If ifAdminStatus has the value up (1) while ifOperStatus has the value down (2), then the interface has failed or been turned off locally.

The object ifSpeed is a read-only gauge that estimates the current capacity of the interface in bits per second. This object is useful in the case of an interface whose capacity can vary as a function of demand or other parameters. More commonly, the value of this object is fixed at the nominal data rate of the interface. For example, for an Ethernet interface, the value will be 10^7, reflecting a data rate of 10 Mbps.

All of the information in the interfaces group is generic and applicable to any type of interface. The MIB may contain additional information specific to a certain type of interface, such as an IEEE 802.5 token ring. The ifSpecific object contains a pointer to another part of the MIB at this node containing the interface-specific managed objects.

The interfaces group contains basic information that is useful as a starting point for any network-management function, such as performance monitoring or fault control. For example, objects in this group can be used to detect congestion, as measured by the total number of octets into or out of the system or the queue length for output. Once congestion has been detected, other group objects can be examined to find out, for example, whether protocol activity at the TCP or IP level might be responsible for the congestion.

5.2.4   Address-Translation Group

The address-translation group consists of a single table (Figure 5.8, Table 5.3). Each row in the table corresponds to one of the physical interfaces of the system. The row provides a mapping from a network address to a physical address. Typically, the network address is the IP address for this system at this interface. The physical address depends on the nature of the subnetwork. For example, if the interface is to a local area network, then the physical address is the MAC address for that interface. If the subnetwork is an X.25 packet-switching network, then the physical address may be an X.121 address.

The table is indexed by atIfIndex, whose value matches that of ifIndex' for one of the entries in the interfaces group. The table is also indexed by network address. The table only contains an entry for each interface that uses a translation table. Some interfaces use an algorithmic method (e.g., DDN-X.25); for these, there is no entry in the table.

This group is deprecated in MIB-II and is included solely for compatibility with MIB-I nodes. In MIB-II, address-translation information is provided within each network protocol group. There are two reasons for this change:

1.   The need to support multiprotocol nodes. When a node supports more than one network-level protocol (e.g., IP and the ISO connectionless network protocol [CLNP]), then more than one network-level address will be associated with each physical interface.

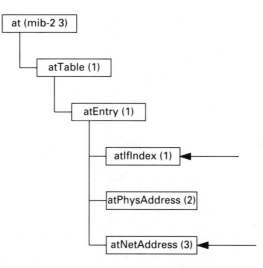

Figure 5.8 MIB-II Address-Translation Group

2. The need for two-way mapping. The address table in the address-translation group is defined to allow mapping to occur only from network address to physical address. Some protocols, such as the ISO end-system to intermediate-system (ES-IS) routing protocol, also require mapping from physical address to network address.

In MIB-II and future MIBs, address tables are located within the appropriate network-level protocol groups. Each group may have one or two such tables to support mapping in both directions. The use of two tables allows for ease of implementation but does not prevent the use of a single internal data structure that is visible via SMI as two tables.

This is a rare example in MIB-II in which duplicate information is found.

Table 5.3 MIB-II Address-Translation Group Objects

Object	Syntax	Access	Status	Description
atTable	SEQUENCE OF AtEntry	NA	D	Contains the NetAddress to physical address equivalent.
atEntry	SEQUENCE	NA	D	Each entry contains one Net-Address to physical address equivalence.
atIfIndex	INTEGER	RW	D	Interface on which this entry is effective.
atPhysAddress	PhysAddress	RW	D	Media-dependent physical address.
atNetAddress	NetAddress	RW	D	The NetAddress (e.g., IP address) corresponding to the media-dependent physical address.

5.2.5   IP Group

The IP group contains information relevant to the implementation and operation of IP at a node (Figure 5.9, Table 5.4). Since IP is implemented in both end systems (hosts) and intermediate systems (routers), not all of the objects in this group are relevant for any given system. Objects that are not relevant have null values.

5.2.5.1   Original Specification

Three tables are included in the IP group. The ipAddrTable contains information relevant to the IP addresses assigned to this entity, with one row for each IP address. Each address is uniquely assigned to a physical interface, indicated by ipAdEntIfIndex, whose value matches that of ifIndex for one of the entries in the interfaces group. This information is useful in monitoring the configuration of the network in terms of IP addresses. Note, however, that the objects in this table are read-only; thus, SNMP cannot be used to change IP addresses. Two of the objects in this table, ipAdEntNetMask and ipAdEntBcastAddr, relate to details of IP addressing, which is explained in Appendix 5B.

The ipRouteTable contains information used for internet routing. The information in the route table is of a relatively general nature and could be extracted from a number of protocol-specific routing tables, such as those for RIP (routing information protocol), OSPF (open shortest path first), and IS-IS (intermediate system to intermediate system). There is one entry for each route presently known to this entity. The table is indexed by ipRouteDest. For each table route, the local interface for the next hop is identified in ipRouteIfIndex, whose value matches that of ifIndex for one of the entries in the interfaces group.

The ipRouteTable information is useful for configuration monitoring and, since the objects in the table are read-write, can be used to control the routing process. In addition, this table can be helpful in fault isolation. For example, if a user is unable to make a connection to a remote host, the fault may lie in inconsistent routing tables among the hosts and routers in the internet.

The ipNetToMediaTable is an address-translation table that provides a correspondence between physical addresses and IP addresses. There is an entry for each interface that does not use an algorithmic mapping technique. The information contained here is the same as that in the address-translation group, with the addition of the object ipNetToMediaType, which indicates the type of mapping used.

In addition to the three tables, there are a number of scalar objects in the IP group that are useful for performance and fault monitoring.

5.2.5.2   IP Forwarding Table

RFC 1354 was issued as a proposed internet standard in July 1992. Its purpose is to fix a problem with the ipRouteTable and to make the routing table more flexible. The intent is to deprecate the ipRouteTable and replace it with the definitions in RFC 1354.

The specific problem that exists with the ipRouteTable is that it is indexed only by ipRouteDest, which is the destination IP address for this route. The description clause of ipRouteDest states that:

> Multiple routes to a single destination can appear in the table, but access to such multiple entries is dependent on the table-access mechanism defined by the network management protocol in use.

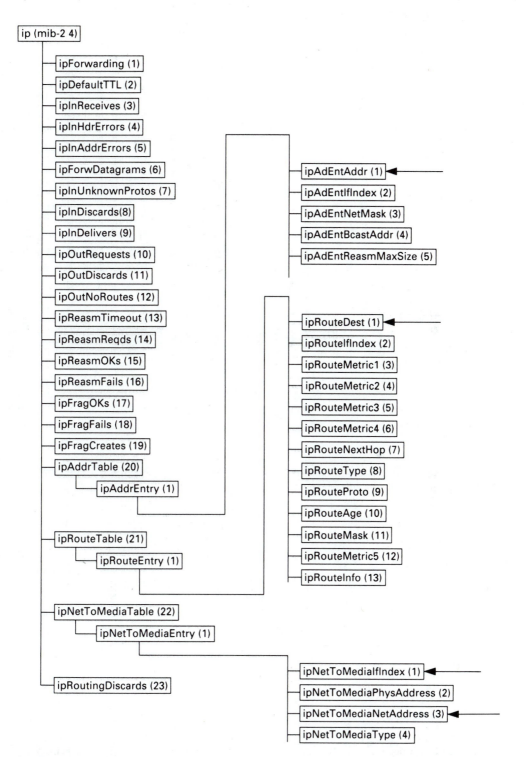

Figure 5.9 MIB-II IP Group

Table 5.4 MIB-II IP Group Objects

Object	Syntax	Access	Status	Description
ipForwarding	INTEGER	RW	M	Acting as IP gateway (1); not acting as IP gateway (2).
ipDefaultTTL	INTEGER	RW	M	Default value inserted into time-to-live field of IP header of datagrams originated at this entity.
ipInReceives	Counter	RO	M	Total number of input datagrams received from interfaces, including those received in error.
ipInHdrErrors	Counter	RO	M	Number of input datagrams discarded due to errors in IP header.
ipInAddrErrors	Counter	RO	M	Number of input datagrams discarded because the IP address in the destination field was not valid to be received at this entity.
ipForwDatagrams	Counter	RO	M	Number of input datagrams for which this entity was not their final IP destination, as a result of which an attempt was made to forward.
ipInUnknownProtos	Counter	RO	M	Number of locally addressed datagrams received successfully but discarded because of an unknown or unsupported protocol.
ipInDiscards	Counter	RO	M	Number of input IP datagrams for which no problems were encountered to prevent their continued processing but that were discarded (e.g., for lack of buffer space).
ipInDelivers	Counter	RO	M	Total number of input datagrams successfully delivered to IP user protocols.
ipOutRequests	Counter	RO	M	Total number of IP datagrams that local IP user protocols supplied to IP in requests for transmission.
ipOutDiscards	Counter	RO	M	Number of output IP datagrams for which no problems were encountered to prevent their continued processing but that were discarded (e.g., for lack of buffer space).
ipOutNoRoutes	Counter	RO	M	Number of IP datagrams discarded because no route could be found.
ipReasmTimeout	INTEGER	RO	M	Maximum number of seconds that received fragments are held awaiting reassembly at this entity.
ipReasmReqds	Counter	RO	M	Number of IP fragments received that needed to be reassembled at this entity.

Name	Type	Access	Status	Description
ipReasmOKs	Counter	RO	M	Number of IP datagrams successfully reassembled.
ipReasmFails	Counter	RO	M	Number of failures detected by the IP reassembly algorithm.
ipFragOK	Counter	RO	M	Number of IP datagrams that have been successfully fragmented at this entity.
ipFragFails	Counter	RO	M	Number of IP datagrams discarded because they needed to be fragmented at this entity but could not be because the don't-fragment flag was set.
ipFragsCreates	Counter	RO	M	Number of IP datagram fragments generated at this entity.
ipAddrTable	SEQUENCE OF IpAddrEntry	NA	M	Table of addressing information relevant to this entity's IP addresses.
ipAddrEntry	SEQUENCE	NA	M	Addressing information for one of this entity's IP addresses.
ipAdEntAddr	IpAddress	RO	M	IP address to which this entry's addressing information pertains.
ipAdEntIfIndex	INTEGER	RO	M	Index value that uniquely identifies the interface to which this entry is applicable.
ipAdEntNetMask	IpAddress	RO	M	Subnet mask associated with the IP address of this entity.
ipAdEntBcastAddr	INTEGER	RO	M	Value of the least-significant bit in the IP broadcast address used for sending datagrams on the logical interface associated with the IP address of this entry.
ipAdEntReasmMaxSize	INTEGER	RO	M	Size of the largest IP datagram that this entity can reassemble from incoming datagrams on this interface.
ipRouteTable	SEQUENCE OF IpRouteEntry	NA	M	This entity's IP routing table.
ipRouteEntry	SEQUENCE	NA	M	A route to a particular destination.
ipRouteDest	IpAddress	RW	M	Destination IP address of this route.
ipRouteIfIndex	INTEGER	RW	M	Index value that uniquely identifies the local interface through which the next hop of this route should be reached.
ipRouteMetric1	INTEGER	RW	M	Primary routing metric for this route.
ipRouteMetric2	INTEGER	RW	M	Alternate routing metric for this route.
ipRouteMetric3	INTEGER	RW	M	Alternate routing metric for this route.
ipRouteMetric4	INTEGER	RW	M	Alternate routing metric for this route.
ipRouteNextHop	IpAddress	RW	M	IP address of next hop of this route.
ipRouteType	INTEGER	RW	M	Other (1), invalid (2), direct (3), indirect (4).
ipRouteProto	INTEGER	RO	M	Other (1), local (2), netmgt (3), icmp (4), egp (5), ggp (6), hello (7), rip (8), is-is (9), es-is (10), ciscoIgrp (11), bbnSpfIgp (12), ospf (13), bgp (14).

Table 5.4 (*Cont.*)

Object	Syntax	Access	Status	Description
ipRouteAge	INTEGER	RW	M	Number of seconds since this route was last updated or verified.
ipRouteMask	IpAddress	RW	M	Mask to be ANDed with destination address before being compared to ipRouteDest.
ipRouteMetric5	INTEGER	RW	M	Alternate routing metric for this route.
ipRouteInfo	OBJECT IDENTIFIER	RO	M	Reference to MIB definitions specific to the routing protocol responsible for this route.
ipNetToMediaTable	SEQUENCE OF IpNetToMediaEntry	NA	M	IP address-translation table used for mapping from IP addresses to physical addresses.
ipNetToMediaEntry	SEQUENCE	NA	M	Each entry contains an IP address to physical address equivalence.
ipNetToMediaIfIndex	INTEGER	RW	M	Interface for which this entry applies.
ipNetToMediaPhysAddress	PhysAddress	RW	M	Media-dependent physical address.
ipNetToMediaNetAddress	IpAddress	RW	M	IP address corresponding to the media-dependent physical address.
ipNetToMediaType	INTEGER	RW	M	Type of mapping: other (1), invalid (2), dynamic (3), static (4).
ipRoutingDiscards	Counter	RO	M	Number of routing entries discarded even though valid.

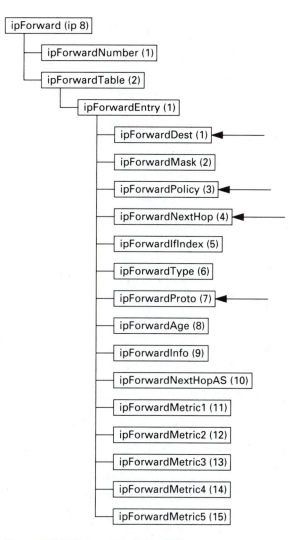

Figure 5.10 IP Forwarding Table MIB

No such mechanism has been approved for SNMP (see section 6.1.3.2 for a discussion). In the absence of such mechanisms, it is only possible to unambiguously define, in the ipRouteTable, a single route to a given destination, even if the routing protocol permits the use of alternate routes for load balancing, reliability, or other reasons.

Figure 5.10 illustrates the structure defined in RFC 1354. At the top level, the object ip-Forward has the object identifier { ip 24 }; thus, it becomes the twenty-fourth object immediately under ip, directly after ipRoutingDiscards.

Underneath ipForward are two objects. The ipForwardNumber object is a read-only gauge that records the number of valid entries in the ipForwardTable. The ipForwardTable defines the routing table that is to replace the ipRouteTable.

Most of the objects in the ipForwardTable correspond to objects in the ipRouteTable, with the same syntax and semantics. The only difference is that the name is prefixed by *ipForward* rather than *ipRoute*. Also, the objects are reorganized for aesthetic reasons. In addition, the following new objects are included in the ipForwardTable:

- *ipForwardPolicy:* indicates the policy used to select among alternate routes to a destination. In the case of the routing of IP datagrams, the policy is based on the IP type-of-service field, which specifies one of eight levels of precedence and a binary value of delay (normal, low), throughput (normal, high), and reliability (normal, high).

- *ipForwardNextHopAS:* the autonomous-system number of the next hop. This value is useful to administrators of regional networks.

The ipRouteTable is indexed only by ipRouteDest. The ipForwardTable is indexed by ipForwardDest, ipForwardProto, ipForwardPolicy, and ipForwardNextHop. Thus, multiple routes can be managed rather than just a single route.

5.2.6 ICMP Group

The ICMP group contains information relevant to the implementation and operation of ICMP at a node (Figure 5.11, Table 5.5). This group consists solely of counters of the various types of ICMP messages sent and received.

5.2.7 TCP Group

The TCP group contains information relevant to the implementation and operation of TCP at a node (Figure 5.12, Table 5.6). The only table that is part of this group is the tcpConnTable, which was discussed earlier in this chapter.

5.2.8 UDP Group

The UDP group contains information relevant to the implementation and operation of UDP (user datagram protocol) at a node (Figure 5.13, Table 5.7). In addition to information about datagrams sent and received, the UDP group includes the udpTable, which contains information about this entity's UDP end points on which a local application is currently accepting datagrams. For each such UDP user, the table contains the user's IP address and UDP port.

5.2.9 EGP Group

The EGP group contains information relevant to the implementation and operation of the external gateway protocol (EGP) at a node (Figure 5.14, Table 5.8). In addition to information about EGP messages sent and received, the EGP group includes the egpNeighTable, which contains information about each of the neighbor gateways known to this entity. The table is indexed by egpNeighAddr, which is the IP address of a neighbor gateway.

5.2.10 Transmission Group

The transmission group is intended to contain objects that provide details about the underlying transmission medium for each interface on a system. Currently, no such objects are defined for MIB-II. However, a number of media-specific definitions have been developed as RFCs (requests for comment) in the experimental portion of the MIB. In time, these definitions will move over to the transmission group. Among the experimental MIBs defined so far are the following:

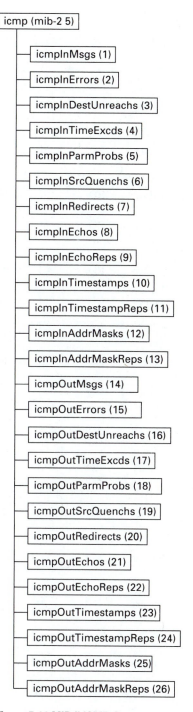

icmp (mib-2 5)

icmpInMsgs (1)

icmpInErrors (2)

icmpInDestUnreachs (3)

icmpInTimeExcds (4)

icmpInParmProbs (5)

icmpInSrcQuenchs (6)

icmpInRedirects (7)

icmpInEchos (8)

icmpInEchoReps (9)

icmpInTimestamps (10)

icmpInTimestampReps (11)

icmpInAddrMasks (12)

icmpInAddrMaskReps (13)

icmpOutMsgs (14)

icmpOutErrors (15)

icmpOutDestUnreachs (16)

icmpOutTimeExcds (17)

icmpOutParmProbs (18)

icmpOutSrcQuenchs (19)

icmpOutRedirects (20)

icmpOutEchos (21)

icmpOutEchoReps (22)

icmpOutTimestamps (23)

icmpOutTimestampReps (24)

icmpOutAddrMasks (25)

icmpOutAddrMaskReps (26)

Figure 5.11 MIB-II ICMP Group

Table 5.5 MIB-II ICMP Group Objects

Object	Syntax	Access	Status	Description
icmpInMsgs	Counter	RO	M	Total number of ICMP messages that the entity received
icmpInErrors	Counter	RO	M	Number of ICMP messages received but determined to have ICMP-specific errors
icmpInDestUnreachs	Counter	RO	M	Number of ICMP destination unreachable messages received
icmpInTimeExcds	Counter	RO	M	Number of ICMP time exceeded messages received
icmpInParmProbs	Counter	RO	M	Number of ICMP parameter problem messages received
icmpInSrcQuenchs	Counter	RO	M	Number of ICMP source quench messages received
icmpInRedirects	Counter	RO	M	Number of ICMP redirect messages received
icmpInEchos	Counter	RO	M	Number of ICMP echo (request) messages received
icmpInEchoReps	Counter	RO	M	Number of ICMP echo-reply messages received
icmpInTimestamps	Counter	RO	M	Number of ICMP timestamp (request) messages received
icmpInTimestampReps	Counter	RO	M	Number of ICMP timestamp (reply) messages received
icmpInAddrMasks	Counter	RO	M	Number of ICMP address mask request messages received
icmpInAddrMaskReps	Counter	RO	M	Number of ICMP address mask reply messages received
icmpOutMsgs	Counter	RO	M	Total number of ICMP messages that the entity attempted to send
icmpOutErrors	Counter	RO	M	Number of ICMP messages that this entity did not send due to problems discovered within ICMP
icmpOutDestUnreachs	Counter	RO	M	Number of ICMP destination unreachable messages sent
icmpOutTimeExcds	Counter	RO	M	Number of ICMP time exceeded messages sent
icmpOutParmProbs	Counter	RO	M	Number of ICMP parameter problem messages sent

Table 5.5 (*Cont.*)

Object	Syntax	Access	Status	Description
icmpOutSrcQuenchs	Counter	RO	M	Number of ICMP source quench messages sent
icmpOutRedirects	Counter	RO	M	Number of ICMP redirect messages sent
icmpOutEchos	Counter	RO	M	Number of ICMP echo (request) messages sent
icmpOutEchoReps	Counter	RO	M	Number of ICMP echo-reply messages sent
icmpOutTimestamps	Counter	RO	M	Number of ICMP timestamp (request) messages sent
icmpOutTimestampReps	Counter	RO	M	Number of ICMP timestamp (reply) messages sent
icmpOutAddrMasks	Counter	RO	M	Number of ICMP address mask request messages sent
icmpOutAddrMaskReps	Counter	RO	M	Number of ICMP address mask reply messages sent

- IEEE 802.4 Token Bus (RFC 1230)
- IEEE 802.5 Token Ring (RFC 1231)
- FDDI (RFC 1285)

Whereas the interfaces group contains generic information that applies to all interfaces, these interface-specific MIBs contain information that relates to a specific type of subnetwork. As an example, let us consider the MIB defined for the IEEE 802.5 token-ring standard. This MIB includes three tables:

1. *Interface table:* contains state and parameter information specific to 802.5 interfaces. Entries include command, which allows a remote network manager to cause the station to set, reset, or close; station status and ring state; ring speed (1, 4, or 16 Mbps); MAC (medium-access control) address of upstream neighbor; and whether or not this station can serve as an active monitor.

2. *Statistics table:* contains 802.5 interface statistics and error counters. These include the counts of various error conditions and counts of various token-control events.

3. *Timer table:* contains the value of 802.5-defined timers.

5.2.11   The Scope of MIB-II

Many users tend to have unrealistic expectations about what can be accomplished with SNMP. A common expectation is that SNMP will enable users to do resource administration and overall system management: Netview types of thing. But the scope of SNMP is limited by the objects available to manage—namely, the MIB. MIB-II essentially supports network monitoring and management from the transport layer down, dealing with how connections get established, how packets

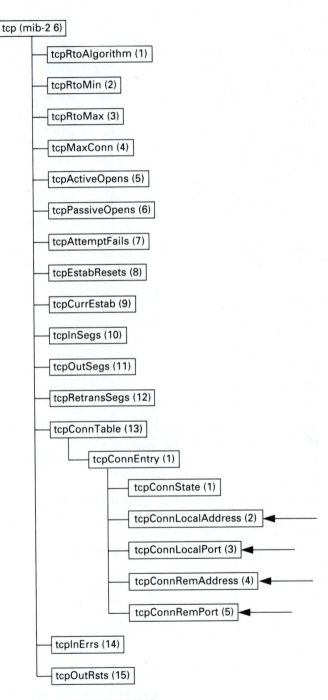

Figure 5.12 MIB-II TCP Group

Table 5.6 MIB-II TCP Group Objects

Object	Syntax	Access	Status	Description
tcpRtoAlgorithm	INTEGER	RO	M	Retransmission time—other (1), constant (2), MIL-STD-1778 (3), Van Jacobson's algorithm (4)
tcpRtoMin	INTEGER	RO	M	Minimum value for the retransmission timer
tcpRtoMax	INTEGER	RO	M	Maximum value for the retransmission timer
tcpMaxConn	INTEGER	RO	M	Limit on total number of TCP connections the entity can support
tcpActiveOpens	Counter	RO	M	Number of active opens that have been supported by this entity
tcpPassiveOpens	Counter	RO	M	Number of passive opens that have been supported by this entity
tcpAttemptFails	Counter	RO	M	Number of failed connection attempts that have occurred at this entity
tcpEstabResets	Counter	RO	M	Number of resets that have occurred at this entity
tcpCurrEstab	Gauge	RO	M	Number of TCP connections for which the current state is either ESTABLISHED or CLOSE-WAIT
tcpInSegs	Counter	RO	M	Total number of segments received, including those received in error
tcpOutSegs	Counter	RO	M	Total number of segments sent, excluding those containing only retransmitted octets
tcpRetransSegs	Counter	RO	M	Total number of retransmitted segments
tcpConnTable	SEQUENCE OF TcpConnEntry	NA	M	Contains TCP connection-specific information
tcpConnEntry	SEQUENCE	NA	M	Information about a particular current TCP connection
tcpConnState	INTEGER	RW	M	Closed (1), listen (2), synSent (3), synReceived (4), established (5), finWait1 (6), finWait2 (7), closeWait (8), lastAck (9), closing (10), timeWait (11), deleteTCB (12)

Table 5.6 (*Cont.*)

Object	Syntax	Access	Status	Description
tcpConnLocalAddress	IpAddress	RO	M	Local IP address for this connection
tcpConnLocalPort	INTEGER	RO	M	Local port number for this connection
tcpConnRemAddress	IpAddress	RO	M	Remote IP address for this connection
tcpConnRemPort	INTEGER	RO	M	Remote port number for this connection
tcpInErrs	Counter	RO	M	Total number of segments received in error
tcpOutRsts	Counter	RO	M	Number of TCP segments sent containing the RST flag

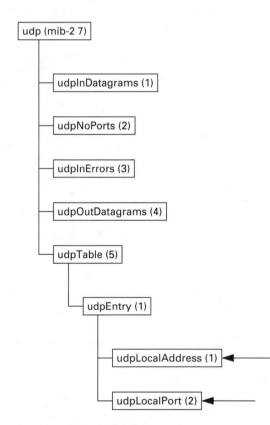

Figure 5.13 MIB-II UDP Group

Table 5.7 MIB-II UDP Group Objects

Object	Syntax	Access	Status	Description
udpInDatagrams	Counter	RO	M	Total number of UDP datagrams delivered to UDP users
udpNoPorts	Counter	RO	M	Total number of received UDP datagrams for which there was no application at the destination port
udpInErrors	Counter	RO	M	Number of received UDP datagrams that could not be delivered for reasons other than the lack of an application at the destination port
udpOutDatagrams	Counter	RO	M	Total number of UDP datagrams sent from this entity
udpTable	SEQUENCE OF UdpEntry	NA	M	Contains UDP listener information
udpEntry	SEQUENCE	NA	M	Information about a particular current UDP listener
udpLocalAddress	IpAddress	RO	M	Local IP address for this UDP listener
udpLocalPort	INTEGER	RO	M	Local port number for this UDP listener

are routed, and similar issues. To manage resources such as mail servers and printers, the MIB will need to be enhanced. Of course, this takes time. What SNMP and MIB-II do provide is a base for gaining experience in doing multivendor network management as well as a limited set of generally useful management features.

5.3 PRACTICAL ISSUES

5.3.1 Measurement

As was discussed in Part I of this book, one of the two key functions of a network-management system is monitoring, which involves measuring certain quantities and reporting the results to a management system. In SNMP, the MIB supports monitoring through the use of scalar values, such as counters and gauges. The risk with SNMP—and indeed, with any network-management scheme—is that the manager will believe reported values that are in fact erroneous.

At first glance, this risk might seem small. For example, consider a device such as a bridge or a router, whose primary function is as an intermediate system that captures and forwards packets going from host to host within an internet. The manager concerned with the sizing of the design (how many bridges or routers, how much throughput each can sustain) will naturally want to monitor the amount of traffic through each bridge or router. What could be more straightforward? Surely any network-management package worth its name would be able to accurately count and

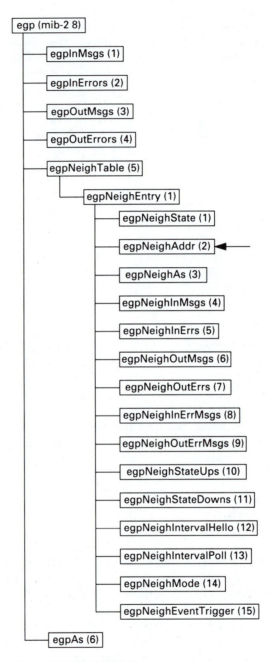

Figure 5.14 MIB-II EGP Group

Table 5.8 MIB-II EGP Group Objects

Object	Syntax	Access	Status	Description
egpInMsgs	Counter	RO	M	Number of EGP messages received without error
egpInErrors	Counter	RO	M	Number of EGP messages received with an error
egpOutMsgs	Counter	RO	M	Total number of locally generated EGP messages
egpOutErrors	Counter	RO	M	Number of locally generated EGP messages not sent due to resource limitations within an EGP entity
egpNeighTable	SEQUENCE OF Egp-NeighEntry	NA	M	The EGP neighbor table
egpNeighEntry	SEQUENCE	NA	M	Information about this entity's relationship with a particular EGP neighbor
egpNeighState	INTEGER	RO	M	Idle (1), acquisition (2), down (3), up (4), cease (5)
egpNeighAddr	IpAddress	RO	M	IP address of this entry's EGP neighbor
egpNeighAs	INTEGER	RO	M	Autonomous system of this EGP peer
egpNeighInMsgs	Counter	RO	M	Number of EGP messages received without error from this EGP peer
egpNeighInErrs	Counter	RO	M	Number of EGP messages received from this EGP peer with an error
egpNeighOutMsgs	Counter	RO	M	Number of locally generated EGP messages to this EGP peer
egpNeighOutErrs	Counter	RO	M	Number of locally generated EGP messages not sent to this EGP peer due to resource limitations within an EGP entity
egpNeighInErrMsgs	Counter	RO	M	Number of EGP-defined error messages received from this EGP peer
egpNeighOutErr-Msgs	Counter	RO	M	Number of EGP-defined error messages sent to this EGP peer
egpNeighStateUps	Counter	RO	M	Number of state transitions to the UP state with this EGP peer

Table 5.8 (*Cont.*)

Object	Syntax	Access	Status	Description
egpNeighState-Downs	Counter	RO	M	Number of state transitions from the UP state to any other state with this EGP peer
egpNeighInterval-Hello	INTEGER	RO	M	Interval between EGP hello command retransmissions
egpNeighInterval-Poll	INTEGER	RO	M	Interval between EGP poll command retransmissions
egpNeighMode	INTEGER	RO	M	Polling mode for this EGP entity—active (1), passive (2)
egpNeighEvent-Trigger	INTEGER	RO	M	Used to control operator-initiated start and stop events—start (1), stop (2)
egpAs	INTEGER	RO	M	Autonomous-system number of this EGP entity

report the total number of packets moving through the device. That is exactly the issue examined by a group of AT&T researchers, in a series of experiments sponsored by the publication *Network World*.

The results of these experiments are somewhat discouraging and, at the very least, serve as a sobering reminder to network managers that one cannot simply believe vendor claims and protocol specifications. It is necessary to verify that the network-management products perform as advertised.

The first experiment that was run was to test various SNMP-managed bridge products (Mier 1991a). The primary objectives were to determine the accuracy of the data collected and reported by the agent entity and the interoperability of the agent with SNMP management stations. In this section, we focus on the first objective and return to the second in Chapter 6.

The test environment was designed to simulate a large user organization's network-management center and was structured to show how the various products could be integrated into an existing SNMP-managed multivendor network. The configuration consisted of two Ethernet LANs with the following key components:

- *Bridge:* The two LANs were connected by a single bridge. Seven different bridge products were tested, each with its own SNMP agent software.

- *Network-management station:* Each experiment was run twice, using two different network-management stations from different vendors. This assured that any anomalous results were the artifact not of the station manager but of the bridge agent.

- *LAN analyzer:* The LAN analyzer generated test packets addressed to off-LAN destinations (MAC and IP addresses) and captured and analyzed messages issued by SNMP agents.

Table 5.9 reports on the results of an experiment to test the accuracy with which bridges count, then report, specific traffic statistics for each interface. The test consisted of a stream of 100 packets generated by the LAN analyzer—88 normal unicast packets ranging in size from 64

Table 5.9 SNMP Bridge Agents Count Differently

Vendor	ifInOctets (1)	Comments	Evaluation	ifInUcastPkts (2)	Comments	Evaluation	ifInErrors (3)	Comments	Evaluation	Overall
A	67,000 to 86,000	Reasonable, but different, values reported from each of 5 tests	Fair	100 (4)	Agent counts SNMP packets and errored packets in total	Excellent	12	Agent reported value accurately	Excellent	Very good
B	66,400 ± 500	Agent reported value accurately and consistently	Excellent	88 (4)	Agent counts only SNMP packets	Excellent	12	Agent reported value accurately	Excellent	Excellent
C	64,700 ± 100	Agent reported value accurately and consistently	Excellent	88 (4)	Agent counts SNMP packets	Excellent	12	Agent reported value accurately	Excellent	Excellent
D	64,900 ± 100	Agent reported value accurately and consistently	Excellent	100 (4)	Agent counts SNMP packets and errored packets in total	Excellent	12	Agent reported value accurately	Excellent	Excellent
E	0	Agent always returns a value of 0 for this object	Poor	0	Agent counts no packets	Poor	0	Agent does not count or report errored packets	Poor	Poor
F	250 to 1,500	Agent apparently counts only SNMP packet traffic	Poor	0 (4)	Agent apparently counts only SNMP packets	Fair	0	Agent does not count or report errored packets	Poor	Poor
G	500 to 1,500	Agent apparently counts only SNMP packet traffic	Poor	0 (4)	Agent apparently counts only SNMP packets	Fair	0	Agent does not count or report errored packets	Poor	Poor

Copyright April 1991 by Network World Inc. Framingham, Mass. Reprinted from *Network World.*

(1) Acceptable response: 64,000 to 68,000 octets. Based on interpretation of MIB standards and reporting requirements by a consensus of experts. A total of 67,640 octets were sent over the LAN in the 100-packet test transmission. However, the acceptable response range takes into account SNMP packets sent to retrieve the values, which added from 500 to 1,500 octets to this count. In addition some agents discounted 12 "errored" packets (total of 2,988 octets), which were included as part of the 100-packet test stream (see Footnote 3 below).

(2) Optimum response: 88 to 100 packets. Per MIB standard, this is the number of packets "delivered to a higher layer protocol." Bridges could technically report 0 (except for SNMP packets, which must be included in this count), but this provides no useful SNMP management information. Errored packets, which are discarded, may legitimately be excluded.

(3) Optimum response: 12 packets. The 100-packet test transmission contains 12 errored packets with misaligned Frame Check Sequences.

(4) After deducting SNMP packets.

to 1,500 octets and 12 packets with intentional frame-check sequence errors. In addition, the management station issued some packets containing SNMP messages to retrieve the data from the agents; these packets were deducted from the reported counts to produce the results shown in the table.

As the table shows, three objects from the interfaces group were tested. Unfortunately, the MIB standard is ambiguous regarding which traffic bridges are supposed to count: it hinges on whether the bridge relay function is considered a higher-layer protocol.[3] Even so, the test results demonstrate that some bridge agents are able to provide an SNMP management station with accurate, consistent counts of packets received, whereas others are not.

The second experiment tested various SNMP-managed IP router products (Mier 1991b). With routers, there is no such ambiguity concerning which packets to count, and so the results are more definitive; those relating to traffic statistics are shown in Tables 5.10 and 5.11. Essentially the same test environment was used, including a LAN analyzer, two different SNMP management stations, and two Ethernets. In this case, the LANs were connected by a router rather than a bridge. Nine different router products were tested, each with its own SNMP agent software.

Again, a test was conducted using objects from the interfaces group; objects from the IP group were also included. The test stream consisted of 245 packets, broken down as follows:

- 120 packets contained IP datagrams with the unicast MAC address of the router, of which:
    - 40 contained the router's IP address.
    - 45 contained a distant IP address with a time-to-live value of zero.
    - 5 contained an invalid IP address.
    - 30 contained a valid distant IP address and a nonzero time-to-live value.
- 65 packets contained a broadcast MAC address that included the router and that should have been delivered to a higher layer within the router.
- 25 packets contained an invalid protocol type in the Ethernet header.
- 35 packets contained an incorrect frame-check sequence.

Table 5.10 shows the results for some of the counters in the interfaces group. Not a single vendor's product reported accurate values for all five counters. Table 5.11 shows the results for counters in the IP group; again, not one vendor's product got all the numbers right. In a few cases, it is possible that the fault lies not with the SNMP agent software but with the entities being managed. For example, five of the routers failed to report datagrams that had expired.[4] This could be because the agent failed to count datagrams that were discarded because they expired, or because the IP entity forwarded expired datagrams. In the latter case, the SNMP agent is a useful tool for detecting faults in other software.

---

3. In most traditional bridge implementations, the relay function is simply picking up frames from one LAN and depositing them on another, and the relay function is viewed as occurring within the MAC layer. However, in the IEEE 802 standards for transparent and source-routing bridges, there is an entity referred to as a *MAC relay entity,* which is, in fact, at a higher layer than, and uses the services of, a *MAC entity.* See Stallings (1993b) for a discussion.

4. The time-to-live parameter in the IP header is used to prevent a datagram's remaining in circulation indefinitely. Each router is supposed to decrement this value prior to forwarding a datagram. If an IP module receives a datagram with a time-to-live value of 0, and it is not addressed to this IP module, the datagram is supposed to be discarded.

Table 5.10 Router SNMP Agent Counts of Interface-Level Traffic

Vendor	ifInOctets (1)	Comments	Evaluation	ifInUcast-Pkts (2)	Comments	Evaluation
1	15,500 ± 500	Consistent count, but low; not clear what traffic was omitted	Fair	145	Apparently adds discarded unknown-protocol packets to count	Good
2	19,000 ± 500	Consistent count within acceptable range	Excellent	145	Apparently adds discarded unknown-protocol packets to count	Good
3	20,000 ± 100	Consistent, accurate count	Excellent	120	Consistent, accurate count	Excellent
4	20,000 ± 100	Consistent, accurate count	Excellent	210	Apparently adds broadcast and unknown-protocol packets to count	Fair
5	20,000 ± 100	Consistent, accurate count	Excellent	180	Apparently adds errored and unknown-protocol packets to count	Fair
6	20,000 ± 100	Consistent, accurate count	Excellent	145	Apparently adds discarded unknown-protocol packets to count	Good
7	19,000 ± 500	Consistent count, but low; not clear what traffic was omitted	Excellent	145	Apparently adds discarded unknown-protocol packets to count	Good
8	14,000 ± 200	Consistent count, but low; not clear what traffic was omitted	Fair	120	Consistent, accurate count	Excellent
9	19,000 ± 500	Consistent count, but low; not clear what traffic was omitted	Excellent	210	Apparently adds broadcast and unknown-protocol packets to count	Fair

(1) The test packet stream delivered a total of 23,290 octets on the LAN. After deducting 12 octets per packet (8 for the preamble and 4 for the Frame Check Sequence, which are stripped off at the physical layer of the receiving LAN adapter and not passed on as part of incoming packet traffic), a net total of 20,350 octets should have been recorded.
(2) The count should be 120: the total of 4 test packet-stream types addressed to the physical address of the router under test, which should have been delivered to higher protocol layers within the router.

Table 5.10 (*Cont.*)

Vendor	ifInNUcast-Pkts (3)	Comments	Evaluation	ifInUnknown Protos (4)	Comments	Evaluation	ifInErrors (5)	Comments	Evaluation
1	65	Consistently correct	Excellent	0	Packets not reported	Poor	35	Consistently correct	Excellent
2	65	Consistently correct	Excellent	0	Packets not reported	Poor	35	Consistently correct	Excellent
3	65	Consistently correct	Excellent	25	Consistently correct	Excellent	0	Packets not reported	Poor
4	0	No count of broadcast packets	Poor	0	Packets not reported	Poor	35	Consistently correct	Excellent
5	65	Consistently correct	Excellent	0	Packets not reported	Poor	35	Consistently correct	Excellent
6	55	Reasonable but incorrect count	Fair	25	Consistently correct	Excellent	0	Packets not reported	Poor
7	65	Consistently correct	Excellent	25	Consistently correct	Excellent	35	Consistently correct	Excellent
8	65	Consistently correct	Excellent	25	Consistently correct	Excellent	0	Packets not reported	Poor
9	0	Consistently correct	Excellent	0	Packets not reported	Poor	35	Consistently correct	Excellent

(3) The count should be 65: the total of 2 test broadcast packet-stream types that should have been delivered to higher protocol layers within the router.

(4) The test packet stream contained 25 packets with an invalid protocol type in the Ethernet header. These could not have been passed to a higher protocol layer within the router and would have been discarded.

(5) Thirty-five packets in the test stream had misaligned Frame Check Sequences.

Table 5.11 Router SNMP Agent Counts of IP Traffic

Vendor	ipInDelivers (1)	Comments	Evaluation	ipInHdr-Errors (2)	Comments	Evaluation	ipOutNo Routes (3)	Comments	Evaluation
1	40	Consistently correct	Excellent	0	Datagrams not counted	Poor	5	Consistently correct	Excellent
2	40	Consistently correct	Excellent	0	Datagrams not counted	Poor	5 or 6	Count was often slightly off	Good
3	20	Consistent but incorrect; unclear what agent counts	Fair	45	Consistent, accurate count	Excellent	5 or 35	Possible configuration problem	Inconclusive
4	40	Consistently correct	Excellent	45	Consistent, accurate count	Excellent	3 or 9	Inaccurate and inconsistent	Fair
5	37	Consistent but slightly low	Good	0	Datagrams not counted	Poor	80	Possible configuration problem	Inconclusive
6	40	Consistently correct	Excellent	45	Consistent, accurate count	Excellent	0	Configuration did not enable count	Inconclusive
7	40	Consistently correct	Excellent	0	Datagrams not counted	Poor	5 or 6	Count was often slightly off	Good
8	0	Datagrams not counted	Poor	0	Datagrams not counted	Poor	5	Consistently correct	Excellent
9	40	Consistently correct	Excellent	45	Consistent, accurate count	Excellent	2	Inaccurate	Fair

Copyright July 1991 by Network World Inc. Framingham, Mass. Reprinted from *Network World.*

(1) Forty of the 245 test-stream packets were addressed to the router's IP address and should have been delivered to the router's IP layer for processing.

(2) Forty-five packets sent to the router and addressed to a destination on a distant subnetwork had a 0 time-to-live value in the IP header. These should have been discarded.

(3) Five packets of the test stream were sent to an invalid network address.

The results of all these tests are clearly cause for concern. These statistics are critical to the network manager. For example, if a router agent fails to report the presence of errored packets, then a serious condition threatening the network could remain unnoticed until a catastrophic failure occurs.

Compared to the OSI network-management scheme, SNMP sacrifices functionality for simplicity. One of the strengths of the SNMP standards is their relative clarity and succinctness. Yet despite this emphasis on simplicity, products from reputable, well-established vendors cannot agree on some of the most basic parameters that a network-management system must measure. Several cautionary observations can be made:

- There is a need for some sort of verification or certification procedure for SNMP/MIB to increase the likelihood of vendor offerings' being "correct."

- In the absence of such certification, the customer/user needs to know that, like any other piece of software, SNMP manager/agent software may contain errors.

- If these are the problems one faces with the relatively simple SNMP, one can imagine the potential for misinformation and miscontrol in OSI network management.[5]

5.3.2 Private MIBs

One of the strengths of the SNMP approach is the way in which the MIB has been designed to accommodate growth and provide flexibility for adding new objects. As was mentioned, private extensions can be added to the private subtree (Figure 5.1). This allows vendors to create objects to manage specific entities on their products and to make those objects visible to a management station. Because of the use of a standardized SMI and a standardized object identifier scheme, it should be possible to manage private objects from a management station of a different vendor. In other words, interoperability should extend to private extensions to the MIB.

With SNMP, a management station can access only the information it knows how to ask for. Recall that this approach was taken in the design of SNMP to prevent the network from being clogged with management information that devices were mindlessly broadcasting. Thus, in order for a management station to be able to manage private MIB objects, the management station must be loaded with the private MIB structure. Otherwise, the management station cannot offer the user the benefits of those private extensions. Of course, loading the private MIB into the management station should present no problem if the management station and the agent station are from the same vendor. The potential for difficulty arises when the two are from different vendors.

Most vendors supply both a text version and a formal description of their MIB extensions. Without the formal description, it would be necessary to type many (perhaps hundreds) of object definitions into the management station. With a formal description, the management station should be able to read an MIB file from disk and compile it into the management station's library of managed objects. One difficulty that occurs is that vendors currently use three different formats to define private MIBs:

---

5. Fortunately, there is a mechanism in place for developing certification/verification procedures for OSI-based standards, based on conformance testing. As of this writing, approved conformance tests for OSI management have not yet been developed but should be forthcoming as the OSI management standards stabilize. See Stallings (1993c) for a description of OSI conformance testing.

1. The original SNMP SMI specification, RFC 1155
2. The newer Concise MIB Format, RFC 1212
3. The OSI SMI specification, described in Part III of this book

Converting from one MIB to another is currently a manual process that requires hours of time on the part of a person knowledgeable in both formats. RFC 1212 provides guidelines for "de-OSIfying" OSI MIBs to the SNMP MIB format and describes the process as "straightforward though tedious."

It is likely that vendors using the SNMP format will all sooner or later convert from RFC 1155 to RFC 1212. Also, an experience base in converting between OSI SMI and SNMP SMI is gradually building up. But another problem is in the actual parsing and compiling of an MIB specification. Despite the fact that MIB objects are defined using formal techniques, different management systems seem to apply different criteria in determining whether a vendor's private MIB is syntactically correct.

For a concrete example of these difficulties, we return to the Bell Labs studies of bridges and routers, reported in Table 5.12. Again, the results are discouraging to the customer/user who believes the "simple" in SNMP. In the case of the bridge products, half of the products equipped with private MIBs produced major problems. In all cases of both bridge and router products, the process was less than smooth.

Again, the conclusions to be drawn from all these tests are that one should be wary of using private SNMP extensions and that greater problems await in OSI systems management. With SNMP, users need to determine how much of the control of SNMP agent products has been embedded in proprietary MIB objects and make sure that the management station they are considering can accommodate such objects.

5.3.3 Limitations of MIB Objects

A network-management system is limited by the capabilities of the network-management protocol and by the objects used to represent the environment to be managed. In Chapter 6, we examine some of the key limitations of SNMP. These limitations are "fundamental," in the sense that the limitations cannot be removed without changing the SNMP specification and subsequently all of the SNMP implementations in a configuration.

The limitations due to an inadequate set of objects in the MIB are less serious. These can be dealt with by adding more objects. However, it is still true that the implementations in a configuration, including both manager and agent, must be enhanced to deal with the new objects. In any case, the standard MIB-II serves as a common base for all implementations, and it is important to recognize that MIB-II does indeed limit the ability to monitor and control a network.

We give one example here, suggested by Masum Hasan at the University of Toronto Computer Systems Research Institute. The example makes use of the configuration shown in Figure 5.15. Suppose that there is substantial traffic to the server from throughout the network, causing a considerable load on router R2 and subnetwork N3, but that the router and network are able to handle this load. Now suppose that a new source of traffic develops between systems on subnetwork N5 and subnetwork N4. This may increase the load on R2 or N3 to unacceptable levels. If we could determine that this increased load is in fact caused by additional N5–N4 traffic, we might be able to design effective countermeasures, such as a new bridge or router linking N4 and N6. However,

Table 5.12 MIB Agent-Manager Compatibility

(a) Bridge Products

Bridge Vendor	Vendor X Management Station		Vendor Y Management Station	
	Able to Load Vendor-Specific MIB on Management Station?	Was Manager Able to Invoke/Access Selected Private MIB Objects?	Able to Load Vendor-Specific MIB on Management Station?	Was Manager Able to Invoke/Access Selected Private MIB Objects?
A	Yes, easily; system adjusted for syntax error in MIB file.	Yes, objects tested worked and provided good data.	Yes, after about one hour (2) but with limited capabilities.	Limited, could only retrieve some object values.
C	Unable to load or to effectively diagnose why not.	Could not be determined.	Yes, after 3 or more hours.	Yes, objects tested worked and provided good data.
D	Yes, after 30 minutes; a minor syntax error was found and corrected.	Could not test, unable to configure bridge or access bridge's SNMP agent (1).	Yes, after about one hour of file reformatting and syntax changes (2).	Could not test, unable to configure bridge or access bridge's SNMP agent (1).
E	Unable to load or to effectively diagnose why not.	Could not be determined.	Yes, after about one hour of file reformatting and syntax changes (2).	Agent returned a value of 0 for most objects tested; other values were questionable.
F	Unable to load or to effectively diagnose why not.	Could not be determined.	Unable to load or to effectively diagnose why not.	Could not be determined.
H	Yes, easily.	Yes, objects tested worked and provided good data.	Yes, after about one hour of file reformatting and syntax changes (2).	Yes, objects tested worked and provided good data.

(1) While vendor's MIB could be loaded in both management systems with relatively minor syntax adjustments, no private MIB objects could be tested because the bridge, containing the SNMP agent, could not be set up and operated with SNMP agent support.
(2) Syntax changes were needed because the Systems Manager requires that MIBs be in the ISO SMI format; most of the submitted MIBs were in SNMP MIB format.

(b) Router Products

	Vendor X Management Station		Vendor Y Management Station	
Router Vendor	**Able to Load Vendor-Specific MIB on Management Station?**	**Was Manager Able to Invoke/Access Selected Private MIB Objects?**	**Able to Load Vendor-Specific MIB on Management Station?**	**Was Manager Able to Invoke/Access Selected Private MIB Objects?**
1	Yes, on first attempt; manager adjusted for a logical error in MIB.	Yes, all objects tested, including sets, worked and provided good data.	Yes, after about an hour; a logical error in MIB had to be corrected before MIB would load.	Yes, all objects tested, including sets, worked and provided good data.
2	Yes, on first attempt.	Some. Agent returned no response for others; a read-write object could not be set.	Yes, on first attempt.	Some. Agent returned no response for others; a read-write object could not be set.
3	Yes, after about an hour; 3 minor syntax corrections were required.	Yes, all objects tested worked and provided good data.	Yes, after about an hour; 5 minor syntax corrections were required.	Yes, all objects tested worked and provided good data.
4	Yes, on first attempt.	Very few to test; private IP objects and not SNMP-accessible.	Yes, after minor format editing required by manager.	Very few to test; private IP objects and not SNMP-accessible.
5	Yes, after about 2 hours; many minor syntax corrections were required.	No. No values were returned by the agent for most of the objects tested.	Yes, after about 2 hours; many minor syntax corrections were required.	No. No values were returned by the agent for most of the objects tested.
6	Yes, in about 10 minutes; 2 minor syntax corrections were required.	Yes, most; however numerous objects were inaccessible because of IP configuration.	Yes, on first attempt, after minor format editing required by manager.	Yes, most; however numerous objects were inaccessible because of IP configuration.
8	After about 2 hours of editing on manager.	Yes, all objects tested, including sets, worked and provided good data.	Yes, after about 2½ hours; numerous corrections required.	Yes, all objects tested, including sets, worked and provided good data.
9	Yes, on first attempt.	Very few to test; private IP objects and not SNMP-accessible.	Yes, on first attempt, after minor format editing required by manager.	Very few to test; private IP objects and not SNMP-accessible.

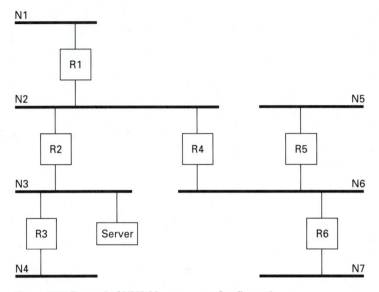

Figure 5.15 Example SNMP Management Configuration

there is no way to determine this using MIB-II objects. For example, if we could examine TCP traffic on a per-connection basis, then we could examine the traffic on connections terminating at N3 hosts and terminating at N4 hosts and determine that the source of the new load on R2 and N3 is due to traffic between N5 and N4. But the MIB-II TCP group (Figure 5.12) does not allow this flow to be measured. All that can be measured at a node is the total TCP traffic in and out, not the per-connection TCP traffic.

The trade-off here is clear: A finer-grained set of MIB objects allows for greater control of the network. The cost is increased storage and processing at the agents and increased SNMP traffic over the network. MIB-II is designed to minimize the burden on systems and networks, which is fine. However, the user must be aware of what is lost by adopting such a strategy.

5.4   SUMMARY

Within the SNMP (simple network management protocol) framework, management information is represented using Abstract Syntax Notation One (ASN.1). A management information base (MIB) consists of a collection of objects organized into groups. Objects hold values that represent managed resources; a group is a unit of conformance.

The structure of management information (SMI) defines the allowable ASN.1 types and the allowable MIB structures. Most objects are scalars; the allowable types are INTEGER, OCTET STRING, NULL, and OBJECT IDENTIFIER. The SEQUENCE and SEQUENCE OF types may be used to construct simple two-dimensional tables of scalar objects. No more elaborate structure is allowed.

The SNMP framework includes the specification of a set of objects that are standardized for use in all implementations. This set, referred to as MIB-II, contains objects in ten groups, most of which deal with a single protocol entity each. Other MIBs may be defined for specific applications and specific vendor products.

APPENDIX 5A   TCP Connection States

In this chapter and Chapter 6, the object tcpConnTable is used as an example. It is instructive to look at the underlying protocol information that is reflected in this managed object. This appendix contains a brief summary. For more detail, see Stallings (1990) or the actual TCP standard.[6]

Since TCP is designed to run over an unreliable network service (specifically, IP), it must contain elaborate mechanisms to deal with lost, duplicated, misordered, and delayed segments. One of these mechanisms defines the procedure for connection establishment:

1. A TCP entity initiates a connection establishment by sending an SYN to the other side.[7]
2. The other side responds with an SYN (synchronize), ACK (acknowledge) sequence.
3. The initiating TCP entity acknowledges the SYN, ACK with an ACK.

The SYN represents a request for connection or a willingness to open a connection. With the procedure just outlined, each side explicitly acknowledges the other side's SYN. This procedure, known as a three-way handshake, prevents a number of problems that could arise if a two-way handshake (SYN followed by ACK) were used.

It could happen that two TCP entities issue an SYN to each other at about the same time. This is allowed, and a connection results. The preceding sequence is modified as follows:

1. A TCP entity initiates a connection establishment by sending an SYN to the other side.
2. The TCP entity receives an SYN from the other side.
3. The TCP entity acknowledges the SYN with an SYN, ACK.
4. The TCP entity receives an ACK from the other side.

A similar three-way handshake is used to close a connection. All of these events can be modeled by a state-transition diagram. Figure 5.16, taken from MIL-STD-1778, shows the TCP state-transition diagram. The upper part of the label on each state-transition shows the input to the

---

6. RFC 793 (Sept. 1981) is the defining document for TCP as used by the Internet Activities Board. MIL-STD-1778 (Oct. 1983), issued by the Defense Communications Agency, is the military standard document used for government procurements of TCP. The latter document is clearer and more comprehensive, and is technically aligned with the RFC definition.

7. Only one type of protocol data unit is employed in TCP, the TCP segment. When the standard refers to issuing an SYN, it means that the sending entity has sent a TCP segment with the SYN bit in the header set to 1.

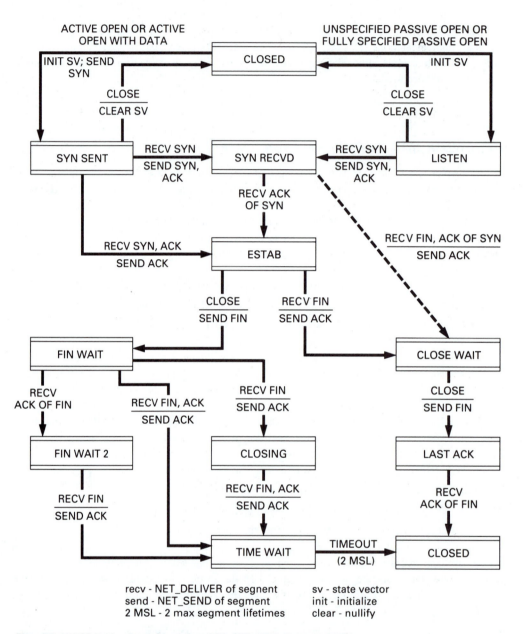

recv - NET_DELIVER of segment   sv - state vector
send - NET_SEND of segment   init - initialize
2 MSL - 2 max segment lifetimes   clear - nullify

Figure 5.16 TCP Entity State Summary (MIL-STD-1778, August, 1983)

TCP entity, which is either a TCP segment from another entity or a service request from a user of this TCP entity. The lower part shows the TCP segment issued by this TCP entity.

To maintain various connections, a TCP entity retains state information about each connection, in what is referred to as a state vector (MIL-STD-1778) or a transmission-control block (RFC 793). The state vector includes the following information:

- *state:* one of the states of the connection.

- *source_address:* IP address of this system.

- *source_port:* port number of the TCP user at this end of the connection.

- *destination_address:* IP address of the system at the other end of the connection.

- *destination_port:* port number of the TCP user at the other end of this connection.

- *lcn:* local connection name; shorthand identifier used in service request and response interaction with the TCP user to refer to this connection.

- *sec:* security label for this connection.

- *sec_ranges:* security structure that specifies the allowed ranges for this connection.

- *original_prec:* precedence level specified by the local TCP user in the open request.

- *actual_prec:* precedence level negotiated at connection opening and used during connection lifetime.

- *ULP_timeout:* longest delay allowed for data delivery before automatic connection termination.

- *ULP_timeout_action:* In the event of a time out, determines whether the connection is terminated or an error is reported to the TCP user.

- *open_mode:* the type of open request issued by the local user (unspecified passive open, fully specified passive open, active open).

- *send_queue:* storage location of data sent by the local user before transmission to the remote TCP. Each data octet is stored with a timestamp indicating its time of entry.

- *send_queue_length:* number of entries in the send queue made up of data and timestamp information.

- *send_push:* an offset from the front of the send queue indicating the end of push data.

- *send_urg:* an offset from the front of the send queue indicating the end of urgent data.

- *recv_queue:* storage location of data received from the remote TCP before delivery to the local user.

- *recv_queue_length:* number of data octets in the receive queue.

- *recv_push:* an offset from the front of the receive queue indicating the end of push data.

- *recv_urg:* an offset from the front of the receive queue indicating the end of urgent data.

- *recv_alloc:* the number of data octets the local TCP user is currently willing to receive.

All of this information is needed to correctly manage the TCP connection. Referring to Figure 5.12, we see that only a small fraction of this information is available to a remote manager via SNMP and the MIB. The advantage of limiting the amount of manager-visible information (indeed, the necessity of doing so) lies in minimizing the complexity of the manager and agent modules, the amount of storage required for the MIB, and the amount of traffic on the network consumed in communicating management information. The disadvantage, of course, is that the management functionality is limited. For example, if a user complains to a network manager that a connection is somehow malfunctioning, the manager has very little information with which to diagnose the

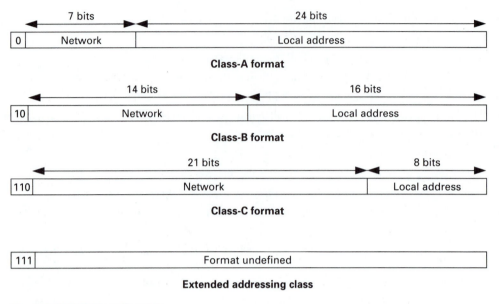

Figure 5.17 IP Address Formats

problem. Worse, the MIB provides no mechanism for representing inactive connections. Thus, if a user reports that a connection has failed, the information that the network manager needs (i.e., concerning the failed connection) is not available.

APPENDIX 5B   IP Addressing

To understand the semantics of several of the objects in the IP (internet protocol) group, it is necessary to understand the conventions for addressing in IP.

5B.1   IP ADDRESS FORMAT

IP makes use of 32-bit addresses. In most cases, the address includes a network identifier and a local address. Typically, the network identifier is the unique identifier of a network in the internet, and the local address is an identifier of a host on a network, with the local address being unique for a particular network. The IP address is coded to allow a variable allocation of bits to specify network and host, as depicted in Figure 5.17. This encoding provides flexibility in assigning addresses to hosts and allows a mix of network sizes in an internet. In particular, the three address classes are best suited to the following conditions:

1. *Class A:* few networks, each with many hosts
2. *Class B:* a medium number of networks, each with a medium number of hosts
3. *Class C:* many networks, each with a few hosts

In a particular environment, it may be best to use addresses all from one class. For example, a corporate internetwork that consists of a large number of departmental local area networks (LANS) may need to use class-C addresses exclusively. However, because of the format of the addresses, it is possible to mix all three classes of addresses on the same internet. A mixture of classes is appropriate for an internet that consists of a few large networks, many small networks, plus some medium-size networks.

The extended address format is used for multicasting. In this format, 29 bits are employed in a flat addressing scheme.

5B.2   SUBNETTING

The typical IP address designates a particular network and a host on that network. This simple scheme has been extended by the concept of ''subnets'' to allow for more flexible addressing in complex configurations.[8] The objective is to allow complex configurations of local area networks within an organization while insulating the overall internet from the need to be aware of a large number of networks.

With ordinary IP addressing, IP addresses have the following structure:

IP-address :: = { <Network-number>, <Local-address> }

When an IP datagram is routed, the source host and each intermediate router except the last router in the path can route solely on the basis of network number. The final router in the path must map the local address into the physical address of a host.

With subnetting, the IP address has the following structure:

IP-address :: = { <Network-number>, <Subnet-number>, <Host-number> }

The interconnected LANs at a site are given the same network number but different subnet numbers. The distinction between subnets is not visible outside the complex of LANs. Instead, routing outside the complex is based solely on network number. Once an IP datagram reaches a router that is on the ''boundary'' of the complex, then routing to the final destination depends on subnet number.

In this structure, the bits allocated to the local address are divided between bits that represent the subnet number and bits that represent the host number. The bit positions containing the subnet number are indicated by a 32-bit subnet mask, which has 1s in the subnet-number bit positions.

5B.3   BROADCAST ADDRESSES

IP addressing includes a capability to transmit datagrams with a broadcast address. Using the notation defined in the previous subsection for IP addresses and the notation ''-1'' to mean a field with all 1 bits, we can define the following formats for broadcasting using class-A, class-B, and class-C address formats:

---

8.   This is one of a number of examples where the terminology used in TCP/IP–related documents differs from that used in OSI–related documents. What are called ''networks'' in the IP addressing scheme are referred to as ''subnetworks'' in the OSI documents. The term *subnet* should not be confused with the OSI term *subnetwork*.

A. { -1, -1 }

   An IP address of all 1s is used for limited broadcast. A datagram with this address is to be delivered to all hosts on the local network or subnetwork but is not transmitted beyond that network.

B. { <Network-number>, -1 }

   This format represents a directed broadcast to a specified network. The datagram is to be delivered to all hosts on that network.

C. { <Network-number>, <Subnet-number>, -1 }

   This format represents a directed broadcast to a specified subnet on a specified network. The datagram is to be delivered to all hosts on that subnet.

   { <Network-number>, -1, -1 }

   This format represents a directed broadcast to all subnets on a specified network. The datagram is to be delivered to all hosts on those subnets.

6
Simple Network Management Protocol (SNMP)

The SNMP specification is contained in RFC 1157. This protocol, obviously, is at the heart of the SNMP management approach. We begin with an examination of this protocol, then look at the SNMP group of MIB-II. Finally, some practical issues are addressed.

6.1 BASIC CONCEPTS

In this section, we examine some of the basic concepts that relate to the operation of the protocol. We begin with a brief summary of the operations supported by SNMP. Then the community feature is examined. The remainder of the section deals with the somewhat complicated issue of how to identify objects and instances of objects, and the ordering imposed by the identification convention.

6.1.1 Operations Supported by SNMP

In SNMP, the only operations that are supported are the alteration or inspection of variables. Specifically, three general-purpose operations may be performed on scalar objects:

1. *Get:* A management station retrieves a scalar-object value from an agent.
2. *Set:* A management station updates a scalar-object value in an agent.
3. *Trap:* An agent sends an unsolicited scalar-object value to a management station.

It is not possible to change the structure of a management information base (MIB) by adding or deleting object instances. Nor is it possible to issue commands for an action to be performed. Furthermore, access is provided only to leaf objects in the object-identifier tree. However, by convention, it is possible to perform operations on simple two-dimensional tables. On the one hand, these restrictions greatly simplify the implementation of SNMP; on the other hand, they do limit the capability of the network-management system.

6.1.2   Communities and Community Names

Network management can be viewed as a distributed application. Like other distributed applications, network management involves the interaction of a number of application entities supported by an application protocol. In the case of SNMP network management, the application entities are the management-station applications and the managed-station (agent) applications that use SNMP, which is the supporting protocol.

SNMP network management has several characteristics not typical of all distributed applications. The application involves a one-to-many relationship between a management station and a set of agents: the management station is able to get and set objects in the agents and is able to receive traps from the agents. Thus, from an operational or a control point of view, the management station ''manages'' a number of agents. There may be a number of management stations, each of which manages all or a subset of the agents in the configuration. These subsets may overlap.

Interestingly, we also need to be able to view SNMP network management as a one-to-many relationship between an agent and a set of management stations. Each agent controls its own local MIB and must be able to control the use of that MIB by a number of management stations. This control has three aspects:

1. *Authentication service:* The agent may wish to limit access to the MIB to authorized management stations.

2. *Access policy:* The agent may wish to give different access privileges to different management stations.

3. *Proxy service:* An agent may act as a proxy to other managed stations. This may involve implementing the authentication service and/or access policy for the other managed systems on the proxy system.

All of these aspects relate to security concerns. In an environment in which responsibility for network components is split, such as among a number of administrative entities, agents need to protect themselves and their MIBs from unwanted/unauthorized access. SNMP, as defined in RFC 1157, provides only a primitive and limited capability for such security—namely, the concept of a community.

An *SNMP community* is a relationship between an SNMP agent and a set of SNMP managers that defines authentication, access-control, and proxy characteristics. The community concept is a local one, defined at the agent. The agent establishes one community for each desired combination of authentication, access-control, and proxy characteristics. Each community is given a community name that is unique (within this agent), and the management stations within that community are provided with, and must employ, the community name in all get and set operations. The agent may establish a number of communities, with overlapping management-station membership.

Since communities are defined locally at the agent, the same name may be used by different agents. This identity of names is irrelevant and does not indicate any similarity between the defined communities. Thus, a management station must keep track of the community name or names that are associated with each of the agents that it wishes to access.

6.1.2.1   Authentication Service

An authentication service is concerned with assuring that a communication is authentic. In the case of an SNMP message, the function of an authentication service would be to assure the recipient that the message is from the source that it claims to be from. SNMP, as defined in RFC 1157, provides for only a trivial authentication scheme. Every message (get or set request) from a management station to an agent includes a community name. This name functions as a password, and the message is assumed to be authentic if the sender knows the password.

With this limited form of authentication, many network managers will be reluctant to allow anything other than network monitoring; that is, get and trap operations. Network control, via a set operation, is clearly a more sensitive area. The community name could be used to trigger an authentication procedure, with the name functioning simply as an initial password-screening device. The authentication procedure could involve the use of encryption/decryption for more secure authentication functions. This is beyond the scope of RFC 1157.

6.1.2.2   Access Policy

By defining a community, an agent limits access to its MIB to a selected set of management stations. By using more than one community, the agent can provide different categories of MIB access to different management stations. This access control has two aspects.

1. *SNMP MIB view:* a subset of the objects within an MIB. Different MIB views may be defined for each community. The set of objects in a view need not belong to a single subtree of the MIB.

2. *SNMP access mode:* an element of the set {READ-ONLY, READ-WRITE}. An access mode is defined for each community.

The combination of an MIB view and an access mode is referred to as an *SNMP community profile.* A community profile therefore consists of a defined subset of the MIB at the agent, plus an access mode for those objects. The SNMP access mode is applied uniformly to all the objects in the MIB view. Thus, if the access mode READ-ONLY is selected, it applies to all the objects in the view and limits management stations' access for this view to read-only operations.

Within a community profile, there are two separate access restrictions that must be reconciled. Recall that the definition of each MIB object includes an ACCESS clause (Figure 5.2). Table 6.1 shows the rules for reconciling an object's ACCESS clause with the SNMP access mode imposed for a particular view. Most of the rules are straightforward. Note, however, that even if an object is declared write-only, it may be possible with SNMP to read that object; this is an implementation-specific matter.

A community profile is associated with each community defined by an agent; the combination of an SNMP community and an SNMP community profile is referred to as an *SNMP access policy.* Figure 6.1 illustrates the various concepts just introduced.

6.1.2.3   Proxy Service

The community concept is also useful in supporting the proxy service. Recall from Chapter 4 that a proxy is an SNMP agent that acts on behalf of other devices. Typically, the other devices are foreign, in the sense that they do not support TCP/IP (transmission-control protocol/internet protocol) and SNMP. In some cases, the proxied system may support SNMP, but the proxy is used to minimize the interaction between the proxied device and network-management systems.

Table 6.1 Relationship between MIB ACCESS Category and
SNMP Access Mode

MIB ACCESS Category	SNMP Access Mode	
	READ-ONLY	**READ-WRITE**
read-only	Available for get and trap operations.	
read-write	Available for get and trap operations.	Available for get, set, and trap operations.
write-only	Available for get and trap operations, but the value is implementation-specific.	Available for get, set, and trap operations, but the value is implementation-specific for get and trap operations.
not-accessible	Unavailable.	

For each device that the proxy system represents, it maintains an SNMP access policy. Thus, the proxy knows which MIB objects can be used to manage the proxied system (the MIB view) and their access mode.

6.1.3   Instance Identification

We have seen that every object in an MIB has a unique object identifier, which is defined by the position of the object in the tree-structured MIB. However, when an access is made to an MIB, via SNMP or some other means, it is a specific instance of an object that is wanted, not an object type.

6.1.3.1   Columnar Objects

For objects that appear in tables, which are referred to as columnar objects, the object identifier alone does not suffice to identify the instance: there is one instance of each object for every row in the table. Therefore, some convention is needed by which a specific instance of an object within

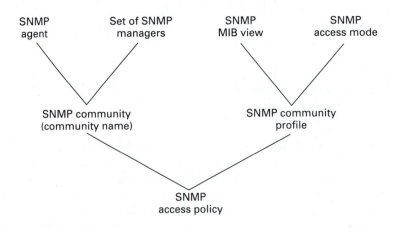

Figure 6.1 Administrative Concepts

a table may be identified. The SMI (structure of management information) document (RFC 1155) states that:

> The means whereby object instances are referenced is not defined in the MIB. Reference to object instances is achieved by a protocol-specific mechanism. It is the responsibility of each management protocol adhering to the SMI to define this mechanism.

Thus, we must turn to the SNMP document for the referencing convention. SNMP actually defines two techniques for identifying a specific object instance: a serial-access technique and a random-access technique. The serial-access technique is based on a lexicographic ordering of objects in the MIB structure (using the get-next operation) and is examined in section 6.2. Here, we consider the random-access technique.

It is relatively easy to deduce the type of referencing convention that must be used. A table consists of a set of zero or more rows. Each row contains the same set of scalar-object types, or columnar objects. Each columnar object has a unique object identifier that is the same in each row. For example, looking back at Figure 5.5, there are three instances of tcpConnState, but all three instances have the same object identifier: 1.3.6.1.2.1.6.13.1.1. Now, as was described in Chapter 5, the values of the INDEX objects of a table are used to distinguish one row from another. Thus, a combination of the object identifier for a columnar object and one set of values of the INDEX objects specifies a particular scalar object in a particular row of the table. In SNMP, the convention used is to concatenate the scalar-object identifier with the values of the INDEX objects, listed in the order in which the INDEX objects appear in the table definition.

As a simple example, consider the ifTable in the interfaces group. There is only one INDEX object, ifIndex, whose value is an integer in the range between 1 and the value of ifNumber, with each interface being assigned a unique number. Now suppose that we want to know the interface type of the second interface of a system. The object identifier of ifType is 1.3.6.1.2.1.2.2.1.3. The value of ifIndex of interest is 2. So the instance identifier for the instance of ifType corresponding to the row containing a value of ifIndex of 2 is 1.3.6.1.2.1.2.2.1.3.2. We have simply added the value of ifIndex as the final subidentifier in the instance identifier.

For a more complicated case, consider the tcpConnTable in the TCP group. As indicated in Figures 5.14 and 5.12, this table has four INDEX objects. Thus, an instance identifier for any of the five columnar objects in the table consists of the object identifier of that object concatenated with the values for a particular row of the four INDEX objects. Table 6.2 shows the instance identifiers for all the columnar objects from Figure 5.5. Note that in forming the instance identifier of an object, it makes no difference whether that object is an INDEX object or not. All instance identifiers for tcpConnTable are of the form

$x.i.$(tcpConnLocalAddress).(tcpConnLocalPort).(tcpConnRemAddress).(tcpConnRemPort)

where

> $x = 1.3.6.1.2.1.6.13.1 =$ object identifier of tcpConnEntry.
> $i =$ the last subidentifier in the object identifier for a columnar object; i.e., its position within the table.

(*name*) = value of object *name*.

More generally, we can describe the convention as follows. Given an object whose object identifier is y, in a table with INDEX objects $i1, i2, \ldots iN$, then the instance identifier for an instance of object y in a particular row is:

$y.(i1).(i2) \ldots (iN)$

Table 6.2 Instance Identifiers for Objects Shown in Figure 5.5

tcpConnState (1.3.6.1.2.1.6.13.1.1)	tcpConnLocalAddress (1.3.6.1.2.1.6.13.1.2)	tcpConnLocalPort (1.3.6.1.2.1.6.13.1.3)	tcpConnRemAddress (1.3.6.1.2.1.6.13.1.4)	tcpConnRemPort (1.3.6.1.2.1.6.13.1.5)
x.1.10.0.0.99.12.9.1.2.3.15	x.2.10.0.0.99.12.9.1.2.3.15	x.3.10.0.0.99.12.9.1.2.3.15	x.4.10.0.0.99.12.9.1.2.3.15	x.5.10.0.0.99.12.9.1.2.3.15
x.1.0.0.0.99.0.0	x.2.0.0.0.99.0.0	x.3.0.0.0.99.0.0	x.4.0.0.0.99.0.0	x.5.0.0.0.99.0.0
x.1.10.0.0.99.14.89.1.1.42.84	x.2.10.0.0.99.14.89.1.1.42.84	x.3.10.0.0.99.14.89.1.1.42.84	x.4.10.0.0.99.14.89.1.1.42.84	x.5.10.0.0.99.14.89.1.1.42.84

x = 1.3.6.1.2.1.6.13.1 = object identifier of tcpConnEntry, which is the tcpConnTable row identifier.

Table 6.3 Instance Identifiers for MIB-II Table Entries

Group	Table	Row Identifier	Object Identifier
Interfaces	ifTable	1.3.6.1.2.1.2.2.1	$x.i.$(ifIndex)
Address translation	atTable	1.3.6.1.2.1.3.1.1	$x.i.$(atIfIndex).(atNetAddress)
IP	ipAddrTable	1.3.6.1.2.1.4.20.1	$x.i.$(ipAdEntAddr)
IP	ipRouteTable	1.3.6.1.2.1.4.21.1	$x.i.$(ipRouteDest)
IP	ipNetToMediaTable	1.3.6.1.2.1.4.22.1	$x.i.$(ipNetToMediaIfIndex).(ipNetToMediaType)
TCP	tcpConnTable	1.3.6.1.2.1.6.13.1	$x.i.$(tcpConnLocalAddress).(tcpConnLocalPort).(tcpConnRemAddress).(tcpConnRemPort)
UDP	udpTable	1.3.6.1.2.1.7.5.1	$x.i.$(udpLocalAddress).(udpLocalPort)
EGP	egpNeighTable	1.3.6.1.2.1.8.5.1	$x.i.$(egpNeighAddr)

x = row identifier (sequence of integers).
i = columnar-object identifier (single integer).
$(\cdot)$ = value of object.

Table 6.3 shows the form of the instance identifier for all the tables in MIB-II.

One detail that must be worked out is exactly how the value of an object instance is converted into one or more subidentifiers. Although this issue is not specifically addressed in the SNMP document (RFC 1157), RFC 1212, which defines the OBJECT-TYPE macro used for MIB-II, includes the following rules for each INDEX object instance:

- *Integer-valued:* a single subidentifier taking the integer value (only valid for non-negative integers).

- *String-valued, fixed-length:* Each octet of the string is encoded as a separate subidentifier, for a total of n subidentifiers for a string of length n octets.

- *String-valued, variable-length:* For a string of length n octets, the first subidentifier is n; this is followed by each octet of the string encoded as a separate subidentifier, for a total of $n + 1$ subidentifiers.

- *Object-identifier-valued:* For an object identifier with n subidentifiers, the first subidentifier is n; this is followed by the value of each subidentifier in order, for a total of $n + 1$ subidentifiers.

- *IpAddress-valued:* four subidentifiers, in the familiar a.b.c.d notation.

6.1.3.2 The Problem of Ambiguous Row References

In RFC 1212, in which the INDEX clause for the OBJECT-TYPE macro is defined, it states that the purpose of the INDEX clause is to list the object or objects whose ''object value(s) will unambiguously distinguish a conceptual row.'' Unfortunately, when the INDEX clause is applied to tables that were originally defined in MIB-I, unambiguous reference is not always possible. For example, the INDEX object for ipRouteTable, in the IP group, is ipRouteDest. However, it is not always the case that only a single route will be stored for any given destination. In this case, two rows will have the same value for ipRouteDest, and the instance-identification scheme just described results in two or more object instances with the same instance identifier.

One way around this problem that has been proposed is to add yet another subidentifier to the instance identifier, under the control of the agent. When two or more rows have the same value(s) of INDEX object(s), the agent designates one such row as primary and appends the subidentifier 1, another row as secondary and appends the subidentifier 2, and so on.

For example, suppose one were interested in the next hop of an entry in the ipRouteTable associated with a destination IP address of 89.1.1.42. Following the rules defined in the preceding subsection, the desired instance identifier is ipRouteNextHop.89.1.1.42. However, if multiple routes have been assigned for the same destination, and the manager is interested in the next hop along the primary route, then the instance identifier would be ipRouteNextHop.89.1.1.42.1.

This proposal has been rejected because of its complexity. For example, either this technique would always have to be used for a particular table, regardless of whether it contained multiple rows with the same index, or the manager would somehow have to discover which references were ambiguous and required the additional subidentifier.

The strategy that has been adopted is to avoid in future defining tables that cannot be unambiguously referenced and to replace (deprecate) existing tables that suffer from such an ambiguity. An example of this strategy is the ipForwardTable, described in subsection 5.2.5.2.

6.1.3.3   Conceptual Table and Row Objects

For table and row objects (e.g., tcpConnTable and tcpConnEntry), no instance identifier is defined. This is because these are not leaf objects and therefore are not accessible by SNMP. In the MIB definition of these objects, their ACCESS characteristic is listed as ''not-accessible.''

6.1.3.4   Scalar Objects

In the case of scalar objects, there is no ambiguity between an object type and an instance of that object; there is only one object instance for each scalar-object type. However, for consistency with the convention for tabular objects, and to distinguish between an object type and an object instance, SNMP dictates that the instance identifier of a nontabular scalar object consist of its object identifier concatenated with 0. For example, Table 6.4 shows the instance identifiers for the nontabular scalar objects in the TCP group.

6.1.4   Lexicographic Ordering

An object identifier is a sequence of integers that reflects a hierarchical or tree structure of the objects in the MIB. Given the tree structure of an MIB, the object identifier for a particular object may be derived by tracing a path from the root to the object.

Because object identifiers are sequences of integers, they exhibit a lexicographic ordering. That ordering can be generated by traversing the tree of object identifiers in the MIB, provided that the child nodes of a parent node are always depicted in ascending numerical order (see Appendix 6A). This ordering extends to object-instance identifiers, since an object-instance identifier is also a sequence of integers.

The reason that an ordering of object and object-instance identifiers is important is this. A network-management station may not know the exact makeup of the MIB view that an agent presents to it. The management station therefore needs some means of searching for and accessing

Table 6.4 Scalar Objects in the TCP Group

Object Name	Object Identifier	Instance Identifier
tcpRtoAlgorithm	1.3.6.1.2.1.6.1	1.3.6.1.2.1.6.1.0
tcpRtoMin	1.3.6.1.2.1.6.2	1.3.6.1.2.1.6.2.0
tcpRtoMax	1.3.6.1.2.1.6.3	1.3.6.1.2.1.6.3.0
tcpMaxConn	1.3.6.1.2.1.6.4	1.3.6.1.2.1.6.4.0
tcpActiveOpens	1.3.6.1.2.1.6.5	1.3.6.1.2.1.6.5.0
tcpPassiveOpens	1.3.6.1.2.1.6.6	1.3.6.1.2.1.6.6.0
tcpAttemptFails	1.3.6.1.2.1.6.7	1.3.6.1.2.1.6.7.0
tcpEstabResets	1.3.6.1.2.1.6.8	1.3.6.1.2.1.6.8.0
tcpCurrEstab	1.3.6.1.2.1.6.9	1.3.6.1.2.1.6.9.0
tcpInSegs	1.3.6.1.2.1.6.10	1.3.6.1.2.1.6.10.0
tcpOutSegs	1.3.6.1.2.1.6.11	1.3.6.1.2.1.6.11.0
tcpRetransSegs	1.3.6.1.2.1.6.12	1.3.6.1.2.1.6.12.0
tcpInErrs	1.3.6.1.2.1.6.14	1.3.6.1.2.1.6.14.0
tcpOutRsts	1.3.6.1.2.1.6.15	1.3.6.1.2.1.6.15.0

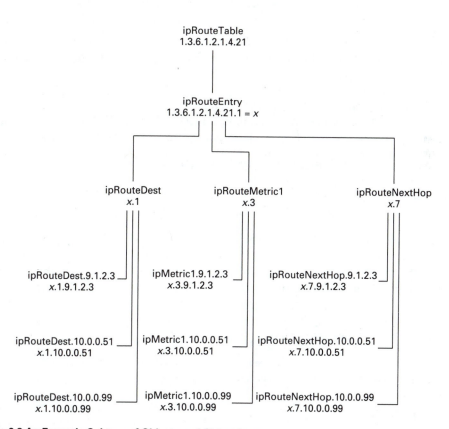

Figure 6.2 An Example Subtree of Objects and Object Instances

Table 6.5 Lexicographic Ordering of Objects and Object Instances in Figure 6.2

Object	Object Identifier	Next Object Instance in Lexicographic Order
ipRouteTable	1.3.6.1.2.1.4.21	1.3.6.1.2.1.4.21.1.1.9.1.2.3
ipRouteEntry	1.3.6.1.2.1.4.21.1	1.3.6.1.2.1.4.21.1.1.9.1.2.3
ipRouteDest	1.3.6.1.2.1.4.21.1.1	1.3.6.1.2.1.4.21.1.1.9.1.2.3
ipRouteDest.9.1.2.3	1.3.6.1.2.1.4.21.1.1.9.1.2.3	1.3.6.1.2.1.4.21.1.1.10.0.0.51
ipRouteDest.10.0.0.51	1.3.6.1.2.1.4.21.1.1.10.0.0.51	1.3.6.1.2.1.4.21.1.1.10.0.0.99
ipRouteDest.10.0.0.99	1.3.6.1.2.1.4.21.1.1.10.0.0.99	1.3.6.1.2.1.4.21.1.3.9.1.2.3
ipRouteMetric1	1.3.6.1.2.1.4.21.1.3	1.3.6.1.2.1.4.21.1.3.9.1.2.3
ipRouteMetric1.9.1.2.3	1.3.6.1.2.1.4.21.1.3.9.1.2.3	1.3.6.1.2.1.4.21.1.3.10.0.0.51
ipRouteMetric1.10.0.0.51	1.3.6.1.2.1.4.21.1.3.10.0.0.51	1.3.6.1.2.1.4.21.1.3.10.0.0.99
ipRouteMetric1.10.0.0.99	1.3.6.1.2.1.4.21.1.3.10.0.0.99	1.3.6.1.2.1.4.21.1.7.9.1.2.3
ipRouteNextHop	1.3.6.1.2.1.4.21.1.7	1.3.6.1.2.1.4.21.1.7.9.1.2.3
ipRouteNextHop.9.1.2.3	1.3.6.1.2.1.4.21.1.7.9.1.2.3	1.3.6.1.2.1.4.21.1.7.10.0.0.51
ipRouteNextHop.10.0.0.51	1.3.6.1.2.1.4.21.1.7.10.0.0.51	1.3.6.1.2.1.4.21.1.7.10.0.0.99
ipRouteNextHop.10.0.0.99	1.3.6.1.2.1.4.21.1.7.10.0.0.99	1.3.6.1.2.1.4.22.1.1.y

objects without specifying them by name. With the use of lexicographic ordering, a management station can, in effect, traverse the structure of an MIB. At any point in the tree, the management station can supply an object or object-instance identifier and ask for the object instance that occurs next in the ordering.

Figure 6.2 illustrates how object-instance identifiers can be seen to be part of the hierarchical ordering of objects. The example shows the ipRouteTable in the MIB-II IP group, as seen through an MIB view that restricts the table to just three entries. The values in the table are as follows:

ipRouteDest	ipRouteMetric1	ipRouteNextHop
9.1.2.3	3	99.0.0.3
10.0.0.51	5	89.1.1.42
10.0.0.99	5	89.1.1.42

Note that the tree is drawn in such a way as to emphasize its logical interpretation as a two-dimensional table.

The lexicographic ordering of the objects and object instances in the table can be seen by simply traversing the tree. The ordering is shown in Table 6.5.

6.2   PROTOCOL SPECIFICATION

In this section we examine the overall message format for SNMP, and then describe each of the protocol data units (PDUs) that can be carried in a message.

6.2.1   SNMP Formats

With SNMP, information is exchanged between a management station and an agent in the form of an SNMP message. Each message includes a version number, indicating the version of SNMP, a

version	community	SNMP PDU

(a) SNMP message

PDU type	request-id	0	0	variable-bindings

(b) GetRequest PDU, GetNextRequest PDU, and SetRequest PDU

PDU type	request-id	error-status	error-index	variable-bindings

(c) GetResponse PDU

PDU type	enterprise	agent-addr	generic-trap	specific-trap	time-stamp	variable-bindings

(d) Trap PDU

name1	value1	name2	value2	• • •	name$n$	value$n$

(e) variable-bindings

Figure 6.3 SNMP Formats

community name to be used for this exchange, and one of five types of protocol data units (PDUs).[1] This structure is depicted informally in Figure 6.3, and the constituent fields are defined in Table 6.6. The ASN.1 definition is reproduced in Figure 6.4. Note that the GetRequest, GetNextRequest, and SetRequest PDUs have the same format as the GetResponse PDU, with the error-status and error-index fields always set to 0. This convention reduces by one the number of different PDU formats that the SNMP entity must deal with.

Note that although a PDU type field is depicted in the illustrations of Figure 6.3, there is no PDU type field defined in the ASN.1 specification. However, each of the five different PDUs is defined as a separate ASN.1 type. Accordingly, since the basic encoding rules (BER) for ASN.1 use a (type, length, value) structure, the type of a PDU appears as an artifact of the BER encoding of the PDU.

6.2.1.1 Transmission of an SNMP Message

In principle, an SNMP entity performs the following actions to transmit one of the five PDU types to another SNMP entity:

1. The PDU is constructed, using the ASN.1 structure defined in RFC 1157.

2. This PDU is then passed to an authentication service, together with the source and destination transport addresses and a community name. The authentication service performs any required transformations for this exchange, such as encryption or the inclusion of an authentication code, and returns the result.

---

1. The terminology chosen by the SNMP developers is unfortunate. It is common practice to designate the overall block of information being transferred as a *protocol data unit*. In the case of SNMP, this term is used to refer to only a portion of the information transferred.

```
RFC1157-SNMP DEFINITIONS ::= BEGIN

IMPORTS
        ObjectName, ObjectSyntax, NetworkAddress, IpAddress, TimeTicks
            FROM RFC1155-SMI;

--top-level message

Message ::= SEQUENCE {version INTEGER {version-1 (0)},  --version-1 for this RFC
                      community OCTET STRING,      --community name
                      data ANY}        --e.g., PDUs if trivial authentication is being used

--protocol data units

PDUs ::= CHOICE {get-request        GetRequest-PDU,
                 get-next-request   GetNextRequest-PDU,
                 get-response       GetResponse-PDU,
                 set-request        SetRequest-PDU,
                 trap               Trap-PDU}

--PDUs

GetRequest-PDU         [0] IMPLICIT PDU
GetNextRequest-PDU     [1] IMPLICIT PDU
GetResponse-PDU        [2] IMPLICIT PDU
SetRequest-PDU         [3] IMPLICIT PDU

PDU ::= SEQUENCE {request-id INTEGER,
                  error-status INTEGER {               --sometimes ignored
                                 noError (0),
                                 tooBig (1),
                                 noSuchName (2),
                                 badValue (3),
                                 readOnly (4),
                                 genError (5)},
                  error-index INTEGER,                 --sometimes ignored
                  variable-binding VarBindList}        --values are sometimes ignored

Trap-PDU ::= [4] IMPLICIT SEQUENCE{
                  enterprise OBJECT IDENTIFIER,        --type of object generating trap,
                                                       --see sysObjectID in RFC1155
                  agent-addr NetworkAddress,           --address of object generating trap
                  generic-trap INTEGER {               --generic trap type
                                 coldStart (0),
                                 warmStart (1),
                                 linkDown (2),
                                 linkUp (3),
                                 authenticationFailure (4),
                                 egpNeighborLoss (5),
                                 enterpriseSpecific (6)},
                  specific-trap INTEGER,               --specific code, present even if
                                                       --generic-trap is not enterpriseSpecific
                  time-stamp TimeTicks,                --time elapsed between the last
                                                       --(re)initialization of the network
                                                       --entity and the generation of the trap
                  variable-bindings VarBindList}       --"interesting" information

--variable binding

VarBind ::= SEQUENCE {name ObjectName,
                      value ObjectSyntax}

VarBindList ::= SEQUENCE OF VarBind

END
```

Figure 6.4 SNMP Formats (RFC 1157)

Table 6.6 SNMP Message Fields

Field	Description
version	SNMP version; RFC 1157 is version 1.
community	A pairing of an SNMP agent with some arbitrary set of SNMP application entities. The name of the community functions as a password to authenticate the SNMP message.
request-id	Used to distinguish among outstanding requests by providing each request with a unique ID.
error-status	Used to indicate that an exception occurred while processing a request. Values are: noError (0), tooBig (1), noSuchName (2), badValue (3), readOnly (4), genErr (5).
error-index	When error-status is non-0, error-index may provide additional information by indicating which variable in a list caused the exception. A variable is an instance of a managed object.
variable-bindings	A list of variable names and corresponding values. In some cases (e.g., GetRequest PDU), the values are null.
enterprise	Type of object generating trap; based on sysObjectID.
agent-addr	Address of object generating trap.
generic-trap	Generic trap type. Values are: coldStart (0), warmStart (1), linkDown (2), linkUp (3), authenticationFailure (4), egpNeighborLoss (5), enterpriseSpecific (6).
specific-trap	Specific trap code.
time-stamp	Time elapsed between the last (re)initialization of the network entity and the generation of the trap; contains the value of sysUpTime.

3. The protocol entity then constructs a message, consisting of a version field, the community name, and the result from step 2.

4. This new ASN.1 object is then encoded, using the basic encoding rules, and passed to the transport service.

In practice, authentication is not typically invoked.

6.2.1.2   Receipt of an SNMP Message
In principle, an SNMP entity performs the following actions upon receipt of an SNMP message:

1. It does a basic syntax check of the message and discards the message if it fails to parse.

2. It verifies the version number and discards the message if there is a mismatch.

3. The protocol entity then passes the user name, the PDU portion of the message, and the source and destination transport addresses (supplied by the transport service that delivered the message) to an authentication service.

   a. If authentication fails, the authentication service signals the SNMP protocol entity, which generates a trap and discards the message.

   b. If authentication succeeds, the authentication service returns a PDU in the form of an ASN.1 object that conforms to the structure defined in RFC 1157.

4. The protocol entity does a basic syntax check of the PDU and discards the PDU if it fails to parse. Otherwise, using the named community, the appropriate SNMP access policy is selected and the PDU is processed accordingly.

In practice, the authentication service merely serves to verify that the community name authorizes receipt of messages from the source SNMP entity.

6.2.1.3   Variable Bindings

All SNMP operations involve access to an object instance. Recall that only leaf objects in the object-identifier tree may be accessed; that is, only scalar objects. However, it is possible in SNMP to group a number of operations of the same type (get, set, trap) into a single message. Thus, if a management station wants to get the values of all the scalar objects in a particular group at a particular agent, it can send a single message requesting all values and get a single response listing all values. This technique can greatly reduce the communications burden of network management.

To implement multiple-object exchanges, all of the SNMP PDUs include a variable-bindings field. This field consists of a sequence of references to object instances, together with the value of those objects. Some PDUs are concerned only with the name of the object instance (e.g., get operations). In this case, the value entries in the variable-bindings field are ignored by the receiving protocol entity. RFC 1157 recommends that in such cases, the sending protocol entity use the ASN.1 value NULL for the value portion of the variable-bindings field.

6.2.2   GetRequest PDU

The GetRequest PDU is issued by an SNMP entity on behalf of a network-management station application. The sending entity includes the following fields in the PDU:

- *PDU type:* indicating that this is a GetRequest PDU.
- *request-id:* The sending entity assigns numbers such that each outstanding request to the same agent is uniquely identified. The request-id enables the SNMP application to correlate incoming responses with outstanding requests. It also enables an SNMP entity to cope with duplicated PDUs generated by an unreliable transport service.
- *variable-bindings:* a list of the object instances whose values are requested.

The receiving SNMP entity responds to a GetRequest PDU with a GetResponse PDU containing the same request-id (Figure 6.5, part [a]). The GetRequest operation is atomic: either all the values are retrieved or none is. If the responding entity is able to provide values for all the variables listed in the incoming variable-bindings list, then the GetResponse PDU includes the variable-bindings field, with a value supplied for each variable. If at least one of the variable values cannot be supplied, then no values are returned. The following error conditions can occur:

- An object named in the variable-bindings field may not match any object identifier in the relevant MIB view, or a named object may be of an aggregate type and therefore not have an associated instance value. In either case, the responding entity returns a GetResponse PDU with an error-status of noSuchName and a value in the error-index field that is the index of the problem object in the variable-bindings field. Thus, if the third variable listed in the incoming variable-bindings field is not available for a get operation, then the error-index field contains a 3.

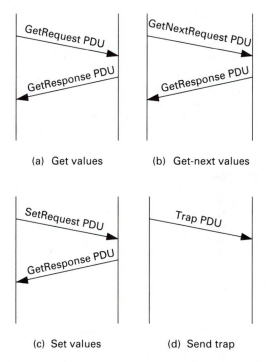

(a) Get values   (b) Get-next values

(c) Set values   (d) Send trap

Figure 6.5 SNMP PDU Sequences

- The responding entity may be able to supply values for all the variables in the list, but the size of the resulting GetResponse PDU may exceed a local limitation. In that case, the responding entity returns a GetResponse PDU with an error-status of tooBig.

- The responding entity may not be able to supply a value for at least one of the objects for some other reason. In that case, the responding entity returns a GetResponse PDU with an error-status of genErr and a value in the error-index field that is the index of the problem object in the variable-bindings field.

This logic is summarized in Figure 6.6.

Keep in mind that SNMP only allows for retrieval of leaf objects in the MIB tree. It is not possible, for example, to retrieve an entire row of a table (e.g., the IP routing table) simply by referencing the entry object (e.g., ipRouteEntry) or to retrieve an entire table simply by referencing the table object (e.g., ipRouteTable). However, a management station can retrieve an entire row of a table at a time simply by including each object instance of the table in the variable-bindings list. For example, for the table shown in Figure 6.2, the management station can retrieve the first row with:

GetRequest (ipRouteDest.9.1.2.3, ipRouteMetric1.9.1.2.3, ipRouteNextHop.9.1.2.3)

The rules for responding to a GetRequest PDU place a burden on the network-management station to be clever in the use of this PDU. If the network-management station requires numerous values, then it is desirable to ask for a large number of values in a single PDU. On the other hand,

```
procedure receive-getrequest;
begin
   if object not available for get then
      issue getresponse (noSuchName, index)
   else if generated PDU too big then
      issue getresponse (tooBig)
   else if value not retrievable for some other reason then
      issue getresponse (genErr, index)
   else    issue getresponse (variablebindings)
end;

procedure receive-getnextrequest;
begin
   if no next object available for get then
      issue getresponse (noSuchName, index)
   else if generated PDU too big then
      issue getresponse (tooBig)
   else if value not retrievable for some other reason then
      issue getresponse (genErr, index)
   else    issue getresponse (variablebindings)
end;

procedure receive-setrequest;
begin
   if object not available for set then
      issue getresponse (noSuchName, index)
   else if inconsistent object value then
      issue getresponse (badValue, index)
   else if generated PDU too big then
      issue getresponse (tooBig)
   else if value not settable for some other reason then
      issue getresponse (genErr, index)
   else    issue getresponse (variablebindings)
end;
```

Figure 6.6 Receipt of SNMP PDUs

if a response is not possible for even one of the objects or if the response to all objects is too big for a single GetResponse PDU, then no information is returned.

One final note about the request-id field. RFC 1157 simply states that request-ids are used to distinguish among outstanding requests, and that a GetResponse must include the same request-id value as the corresponding request PDU. No other use is made of this field in SNMP. For example, the manager is not required to use monotonically increasing values of request-id, which would enable the agent to detect duplicates and replay responses. Thus, the value of this field depends on how it is implemented in SNMP and the use that is made of it by network-management applications that use SNMP.

6.2.3   GetNextRequest PDU

The GetNextRequest PDU is almost identical to the GetRequest PDU. It has the same PDU-exchange pattern (Figure 6.5, part [b]) and the same format (Figure 6.3, part [b]) as the GetRequest PDU. The only difference is the following: In the GetRequest PDU, each variable in the variable-bindings list refers to an object instance whose value is to be returned. In the GetResponse PDU, for each variable, the respondent is to return the value of the object instance that is next in lexi-

Table 6.7 Possible Outcomes of a GetNextRequest PDU

Request	Example Form	Possible Responses	Comment
Object ID of a simple object in MIB	Thing	Value of Thing.0	Object exists in MIB view; value returned.
		Value of next simple object in MIB view (e.g., NextThing.0)	Object does not exist in MIB view; value of lexicographically next object instance returned.
		noSuchName	Object does not exist in MIB view; there is no object instance lexicographically beyond this ID.
Object-instance ID of a simple object in MIB	Thing.0	Value of next simple object in MIB view (e.g., NextThing.0)	Value of lexicographically next object instance returned.
		noSuchName	There is no object instance lexicographically beyond this ID.
Object ID of a table	someTable	Value of first object instance in table	Table exists in MIB view; value of entry in first column, first row returned.
		noSuchName	Object does not exist in MIB view; there is no object instance lexicographically beyond this ID.
Object ID of a table entry	someEntry	Value of first object instance in table	Table exists in MIB view; value of entry in first column, first row returned.
		noSuchName	Object does not exist in MIB view; there is no object instance lexicographically beyond this ID.
Columnar-object ID	Columnar-Thing	Value of first instance of the columnar object (e.g., Columnar-Thing.x)	Table exists in MIB view; value of this columnar object in first row returned.
		noSuchName	Object does not exist in MIB view; there is no object instance lexicographically beyond this ID.
Columnar-object-instance ID	Columnar-Thing.x	Value of next object instance in table	Table exists in MIB view; value of next instance in same column or first instance in next column returned.

Table 6.7 (*Cont.*)

Request	Example Form	Possible Responses	Comment
		Value of first object instance beyond the end of the table	Table exists in MIB view; this object instance is the last in the table, and there is an object instance beyond the end of the table.
		noSuchName	There is no object instance lexicographically beyond this ID.
Object ID that does not match any object in MIB or that corresponds to a subtree		Value of next simple object in MIB view	Object does not exist in MIB view; value of lexicographically next object instance returned.
		noSuchName	Object does not exist in MIB view; there is no object instance lexicographically beyond this ID.

cographic order. Like GetRequest, GetNextRequest is atomic: either all requested values are returned or none is. The logic of GetNextRequest is summarized in Figure 6.6.

Since an agent can only return the value of a simple object instance (and not an aggregate object such as a subtree or a table), the *Next* in GetNextRequest refers to the next object *instance* in lexicographic order, not just the next object. Table 6.5 shows examples of this.

The apparently minor difference between GetRequest and GetNextRequest has tremendous implications. It allows a network-management station to discover the structure of an MIB view dynamically. It also provides an efficient mechanism for searching a table whose entries are unknown. Table 6.7 summarizes the effects that can be achieved using GetNextRequest. We examine its principal uses in the following subsections.

6.2.3.1 Retrieving a Simple Object Value

Suppose that a network-management station wished to retrieve the values of all the simple objects in the UDP (user datagram protocol) group from an agent (see Figure 5.13). The management station could send a GetRequest PDU of the following form:

GetRequest (udpInDatagrams.0, udpNoPorts.0, udpInErrors.0, udpOutDatagrams.0)

If the the MIB view for this community at the agent supported all these objects, then a Get-Response PDU would be returned with the values for all four objects:

GetResponse ((udpInDatagrams.0 = 100), (udpNoPorts.0 = 1), (udpInErrors.0 = 2), (udpOutDatagrams.0 = 200)) where 100, 1, 2, and 200 are the correct values of the four object instances. However, if one of the objects were not supported, then a GetResponse PDU with an error code of noSuchName would be returned, but no values would be returned. In order to assure getting all available values with the GetRequest PDU, the management station would have to issue four separate PDUs.

Now, consider the use of the GetNextRequest PDU:

GetNextRequest (udpInDatagrams, udpNoPorts, udpInErrors, udpOutDatagrams)

In this case, the agent will return the value of the lexicographically next object instance to each identifier in the list. Suppose now that all four objects are supported. The object identifier for udpInDatagrams is 1.3.6.1.2.1.7.1. The next instance identifier in lexicographic order is udpIn-Datagrams.0, or 1.3.6.1.2.1.7.1.0. Similarly, the next instance identifier after updNoPorts is udpNoPorts.0, and so on. Thus, if all values are available, then the agent returns a GetResponse PDU of the form

GetResponse ((udpInDatagrams.0 = 100), (udpNoPorts.0 = 1), (udpInErrors.0 = 2), (udpOutDatagrams.0 = 200))

which is the same as before.

Now, suppose that udpNoPorts is not visible in this view, and the same GetNextRequest PDU is issued. The response is:

GetResponse ((udpInDatagrams.0 = 100), (udpInErrors.0 = 2), (udpInErrors.0 = 2), (udpOutDatagrams.0 = 200))

The identifier for udpNoPorts.0, which is 1.3.6.1.2.1.7.2.0, is not a valid identifier in this MIB view. Therefore, the agent returns the value of the next object instance in order, which, in this case, is 1.3.6.1.2.1.7.3.0 = udpInErrors.0.

In summary, when an agent issues a GetNextRequest PDU with the object identifiers of a set of objects, the result includes the value of the requested object instances for all those object instances that are available. For those that are not, the next object-instance value in order is returned. Clearly, when some object values might be missing, this is a more efficient way to retrieve a set of those values than the use of the GetRequest PDU.

6.2.3.2   Retrieving Unknown Objects

The rules for the use of the GetNextRequest PDU require that the agent retrieve the next object instance that occurs lexicographically after the identifier supplied. There is no requirement that the identifier that is supplied actually represent an actual object or object instance. For example, returning to the UDP group, since udpInDatagrams is a simple object, there is no object whose identifier is udpInDatagrams.2, or 1.3.6.1.2.1.7.1.2. However, if this identifier is supplied to an agent in a GetNextRequest, the agent simply looks for the next valid identifier; it doesn't check the validity of the supplied identifier! Thus, a value is returned for udpNoPorts.0, or 1.3.6.1.2.1.7.2.0.

A management station can therefore use the GetNextRequest PDU to probe an MIB view and discover its structure. In our example, if the management station issues a GetNextRequest (udp), the response will be the GetResponse (udpInDatagrams.0 = 100). The management station learns that the first supported object in this MIB view is udpInDatagrams and obtains the current value of that object at the same time.

6.2.3.3   Accessing Table Values

The GetNextRequest PDU can be used to efficiently search a table. Consider again the example in Figure 6.2. Recall that the table contains three rows with the following values:

ipRouteDest	ipRouteMetric1	ipRouteNextHop
9.1.2.3	3	99.0.0.3
10.0.0.51	5	89.1.1.42
10.0.0.99	5	89.1.1.42

Suppose that the management station wishes to retrieve the entire table and does not currently know any of its contents or even the number of rows in the table. The management station can issue a GetNextRequest with the names of all the columnar objects:

GetNextRequest (ipRouteDest, ipRouteMetric1, ipRouteNextHop)

A review of Figure 6.2 reveals that the agent will respond with the values from the first row of the table:

GetResponse ((ipRouteDest.9.1.2.3 = 9.1.2.3), (ipRouteMetric1.9.1.2.3 = 3),
   (ipRouteNextHop.9.1.2.3 = 99.0.0.3))

The management station can then store these values and retrieve the second row with:

GetNextRequest (ipRouteDest.9.1.2.3, ipRouteMetric1.9.1.2.3, ipRouteNextHop.9.1.2.3)

The SNMP agent responds:

GetResponse ((ipRouteDest.10.0.0.51 = 10.0.0.51), (ipRouteMetric1.10.0.0.51 = 5),
   (ipRouteNextHop.10.0.0.51 = 89.1.1.42))

Then, the following exchange occurs:

GetNextRequest (ipRouteDest.10.0.0.51, ipRouteMetric1.10.0.0.51,
   ipRouteNextHop.10.0.0.51)
GetResponse ((ipRouteDest.10.0.0.99 = 10.0.0.99), (ipRouteMetric1.10.0.0.99 = 5),
   (ipRouteNextHop.10.0.0.99 = 89.1.1.42))

The management station does not know that this is the end of the table and so proceeds with:

GetNextRequest (ipRouteDest.10.0.0.99, ipRouteMetric1.10.0.0.99,
   ipRouteNextHop.10.0.0.99)

However, there are no further rows in the table, so the agent responds with those objects that are next in the lexicographic ordering of objects in this MIB view:

GetResponse ((ipRouteMetric1.9.1.2.3 = 9.1.2.3), (ipRouteNextHop.9.1.2.3 = 3),
   (ipNetToMediaIfIndex.1.3 = 1))

where the example assumes that the next object instance is the one shown in the third entry of the response (see Figure 6.2). Since the object names listed in the response do not match those in the request, this signals the management station that it has reached the end of the routing table.

6.2.4   SetRequest PDU

The SetRequest PDU is issued by an SNMP entity on behalf of a network-management station application. It has the same PDU-exchange pattern (Figure 6.5, part [c]) and the same format as the GetRequest PDU (Figure 6.3, part [b]). The difference is that the SetRequest is used to write an object value rather than read one. Thus, the variable-bindings list in the SetRequest PDU includes both object-instance identifiers and a value to be assigned to each object instance listed.

The receiving SNMP entity responds to a SetRequest PDU with a GetResponse PDU containing the same request-id. The SetRequest operation is atomic: either all the variables are updated or none is. If the responding entity is able to set values for all the variables listed in the incoming variable-bindings list, then the GetResponse PDU includes the variable-bindings field, with a value supplied for each variable. If at least one of the variable values cannot be supplied, then no values are returned, and no values are updated. The same error conditions used in the case of GetRequest may be returned (noSuchName, tooBig, genErr). One other error condition may be reported: badValue. This is returned if the GetRequest contains at least one pairing of variable name and value that is inconsistent. The inconsistency could be in the type, length, or actual value of the supplied value. The logic for SetRequest is summarized in Figure 6.6.

6.2.4.1   Updating a Table

RFC 1157 does not provide any specific guidance on the use of the SetRequest command on columnar objects. In the case of an object that is not an INDEX object, the semantics of the command are obvious. Consider again the example table shown in Figure 6.2. Once again, assume that the following values exist:

ipRouteDest	ipRouteMetric1	ipRouteNextHop
9.1.2.3	3	99.0.0.3
10.0.0.51	5	89.1.1.42
10.0.0.99	5	89.1.1.42

If the management station issues the following:

SetRequest (ipRouteMetric1.9.1.2.3 = 9)

then the appropriate response would be:

GetResponse (ipRouteMetric1.9.1.2.3 = 9)

The effect of this exchange is to update to value of ipRouteMetric1 in the first row.

Now, suppose that the management station wishes to add a new row to the table with values for ipRouteDest, ipRouteMetric1, and ipRouteNextHop of 11.3.3.12, 9, and 91.0.0.5. Then the management station would issue the following:

SetRequest ((ipRouteDest.11.3.3.12 = 11.3.3.12), (ipRouteMetric1.11.3.3.12 = 9),
(ipRouteNextHop.11.3.3.12 = 91.0.0.5))

The columnar object ipRouteDest is the INDEX for the table. The value of ipRouteDest.x is always x, since the value of ipRouteDest is the index value appended to all columnar-object identifiers. Thus, if the *value* of 11.3.3.12 is assigned to the columnar object ipRouteDest, then the *name* of that object is ipRouteDest.11.3.3.12. This is an instance identifier currently unknown to the agent. RFC 1212 indicates three ways in which the agent could handle this request. The agent could:

1. Reject the operation and return a GetResponse with an error-status field of noSuchName.

2. Attempt to accept the operation as requesting the creation of new object instances but find that one of the assigned values is inappropriate due to its syntax or value and return a GetResponse with an error-status field of badValue.

3. Accept the operation and create a new row, resulting in a table with four rows.

In the last case, the agent would return:

> GetResponse ((ipRouteDest.11.3.3.12 = 11.3.3.12), (ipRouteMetric1.11.3.3.12 = 9),
>   (ipRouteNextHop.11.3.3.12 = 91.0.0.5))

SNMP does not dictate whether such a request should be rejected or an attempt should be made to add a new row.

Now, assume the original three-row table and consider the following command:

> SetRequest (ipRouteDest.11.3.3.12 = 11.3.3.12)

There are two ways in which the agent could handle this request. The agent could:

1. Add a new row to the table, resulting in a table with four rows, and supply default values for the columnar objects not listed in the GetRequest.

2. Reject the operation. This would be done if the agent requires that values be supplied for all objects within a row in one SetRequest.

Again, SNMP does not dictate which action will be taken; it is a policy and an implementation matter for the agent.

6.2.4.2   Row Deletion

The set command can also be used to delete a row of a table. In the case of the ipRouteTable, an object value is provided for this purpose. If the management station issues:

> SetRequest (ipRouteType.7.3.5.3 = invalid)

then the appropriate response would be:

> GetResponse (ipRouteDest.7.3.5.3 = invalid)

The effect of this exchange is to logically eliminate the row of the table indexed by an ipRouteDest value of 7.3.5.3. Whether the row is physically deleted from the agent's MIB or simply marked as null is an implementation matter.

Two tables provide a specific columnar object for row deletion. As we have just seen, the ipRouteTable includes an object ipRouteType, one of whose values is "invalid." Similarly, the ipNetToMediaTable includes the object ipNetToMediaType, which may take on the value "invalid." The other tables in MIB-II do not have such a handy device. Table 6.8 indicates what can be done with each table.

6.2.4.3   Performing an Action

SNMP provides no specific mechanism for issuing a command to an agent to perform an action. The only capabilities of SNMP are to read object values and to set object values within an MIB view. However, it is possible to use the set capability to issue a command. An object can be used to represent a command, so that a specific action is taken if the object is set to a specific value.

Table 6.8 Deleting/Nullifying Rows in MIB-II Tables

Group	Table	Relevant Object	Comment
Interfaces	ifTable	ifAdminStatus	This is the only settable object in the table; a value of down (2) makes the interface unusable but does not erase the row.
Address translation	atTable	—	No provision is made for row deletion; however, the entire group is deprecated in MIB-II.
IP	ipAddrTable	—	The entire table is read-only and may not be altered by a management station.
IP	ipRouteTable	ipRouteType	A row is invalidated by setting the value of this object to invalid (2).
IP	ipNetToMediaTable	ipNetToMediaType	A row is invalidated by setting the value of this object to invalid (2).
TCP	tcpConnTable	tcpConnState	The only value that may be set by the management station is deleteTCB (12). This has the effect of deleting the transmission-control block that defines the connection and therefore invalidating the row.
UDP	udpTable	—	The entire table is read-only and may not be altered by a management station.
EGP	egpNeighTable	egpNeighEventTrigger	This is the only settable object in the table; a value of stop (2) causes a non-idle peer to return to the idle state but does not erase the row.

For example, an agent could include a proprietary object reBoot with an initial value of 0; if a management station sets the object's value to 1, the agent system reboots and resets the object value to 0.

6.2.4.4   The Curious Case of readOnly

A close examination of Figure 6.4 reveals that one of the error-status values that may be returned in a GetResponse PDU is readOnly (4). The obvious inference one would make is that this error status should be returned if a set operation is attempted against a read-only object.

Unfortunately, in this case, the obvious inference is wrong, and this has led to some confusion. The definition of the SetRequest PDU in RFC 1157 includes the following rule:

If, for any object named in the variable-bindings field, the object is not available for set operations in the relevant MIB view, then the receiving entity sends to the originator of the received message the GetResponse-PDU of identical form, except that the value of the error-status field is noSuchName, and the value of the error-index field is the index of said object name component in the received message.

This rule is interpreted to mean the following:

- If a set operation is attempted for an object that is not in the MIB view of the manager, return noSuchName.

- If a set operation is attempted for an object that is in the MIB view of the manager but is read-only, return noSuchName.

One can use the line of reasoning that an object that is read-only is not in the MIB view of a manager for purposes of set operations. Two things are ''wrong'' with this rule. First, information is lost: when a manager receives noSuchName in response to a set, the manager must also do a get operation to determine whether the error code refers to a missing object or a read-only object. Second, since the readOnly error code exists, it is clearly confusing not to use it in the obvious circumstances.

The solution to this mystery is that the use of readOnly was omitted in RFC 1157 due to a clerical error. The only occurrence of readOnly in RFC 1157 is in the ASN.1 PDU definitions. Therefore, to be compliant with the standard, one must not use this error code.

The further history of readOnly is worth mentioning. Secure SNMP (RFC 1351), which is a security enhancement to SNMP (described in Chapter 8), makes use of an access-control table in addition to the ACCESS clause in the OBJECT-TYPE macro. The access-control table enables an agent to specify which protocol operations are allowed to a given manager in a given context. If the access-control table dictates that only get and get-next operations are allowed, and an agent receives a set PDU, then the resulting GetResponse includes an error-status value of readOnly. This is true even if the ACCESS clause for the requested object has the value read-write; the access-control entry for the entire MIB view takes precedence over the ACCESS property of the individual object. This policy makes some sense, since for the purposes of this access, all the objects in the MIB view are only available via read-type operations (get, get-next). Nevertheless, it is somewhat misleading, especially since the readOnly code is not used in the original SNMP. Moreover, it gets worse. If for some strange reason, the access-control table dictates that only set operations are allowed (a sort of ''write-only'' access policy), and an attempt is made to perform a get or a get-next, then the resulting GetResponse includes an error-status of readOnly! The rationale for all this is that the desired functionality of secure SNMP could be achieved without changing the ASN.1 definition of the SNMP PDUs.

Finally, there is the simple network management protocol version 2 (SNMPv2). In this specification, there are two new error codes: notWritable, which has the meaning that should have been assigned to readOnly in RFC 1157, but wasn't; and authorizationError, which has the meaning assigned to readOnly in RFC 1351.

Got that?

6.2.5   Trap PDU

The Trap PDU is issued by an SNMP entity on behalf of a network-management agent application. It is used to provide the management station with an asynchronous notification of some significant event. Its format is quite different from that of the other SNMP PDUs. The fields are:

- *PDU type:* indicating that this is a Trap PDU.
- *enterprise:* identifies the network-management subsystem that generated the trap. Its value is taken from sysObjectID in the system group.
- *agent-addr:* the IP address of the object generating the trap.
- *generic-trap:* one of the predefined trap types.
- *specific-trap:* a code that indicates more specifically the nature of the trap.
- *time-stamp:* the time between the last (re)initialization of the network entity that issued the trap and the generation of the trap.
- *variable-bindings:* additional information relating to the trap. The significance of this field is implementation-specific.

The generic-trap field may take on one of seven values:

1. *coldStart (0):* The sending SNMP entity is reinitializing itself such that the agent's configuration or the protocol-entity implementation may be altered. Typically, this is an unexpected restart due to a crash or major fault.

2. *warmStart (1):* The sending SNMP entity is reinitializing itself such that neither the agent's configuration nor the protocol-entity implementation is altered. Typically, this is a routine restart.

3. *linkDown (2):* signals a failure in one of the agent's communications links. The first element in the variable-bindings field is the name and value of the ifIndex instance for the referenced interface.

4. *linkUp (3):* signals that one of the agent's communications links has come up. The first element in the variable-bindings field is the name and value of the ifIndex instance for the referenced interface.

5. *authenticationFailure (4):* signals that the sending protocol entity has received a protocol message that has failed authentication.

6. *egpNeighborLoss (5):* signals that an EGP (external gateway protocol) neighbor for which the sending protocol entity was an EGP peer has been marked down and the peer relationship no longer exists.

7. *enterpriseSpecific (6):* signifies that the sending protocol entity recognizes that some enterprise-specific event has occurred. The specific-trap field indicates the type of trap.

Unlike the GetRequest, GetNextRequest, and SetRequest PDUs, the Trap PDU does not elicit a response from the other side (Figure 6.5, part [d]).

6.3   TRANSPORT-LEVEL SUPPORT

SNMP requires the use of a transport service for the delivery of SNMP messages. The protocol makes no assumptions about whether the underlying service is reliable or unreliable, connectionless or connection-oriented.

6.3.1   Connectionless Transport Service

Most implementations of SNMP are within the TCP/IP architecture and use the user datagram protocol (UDP), which is a connectionless protocol (see Appendix 6B). It is also possible to support SNMP within the OSI (open systems interconnection) architecture using the connectionless transport service (CLTS).

6.3.1.1   UDP Details

UDP segments are transmitted in IP datagrams. The UDP header includes source and destination port fields, enabling application-level protocols such as SNMP to address each other. It also includes an optional checksum that covers the UDP header and user data. If there is a checksum violation, the UDP segment is discarded. No other services are added to IP.

Two port numbers have been assigned for use by SNMP. Agents listen for incoming Get-Request, GetNextRequest, and SetRequest commands on port 161. Management stations listen for incoming Traps on port 162.

6.3.1.2   CLTS Details

As with UDP, the ISO (International Organization for Standardization) connectionless transport service transmits each data unit independently. The connectionless transport protocol data unit includes source and destination transport-service-access points (TSAPs) and an optional checksum.

The TSAP address can be thought of as having two components: a network-layer address and a TSAP identifier, or *selector*. RFC 1283 dictates that agents listen for incoming GetRequest, GetNextRequest, and SetRequest commands on TSAP selector ''snmp,'' and management stations listen for incoming Traps on TSAP selector ''snmp-trap.''

6.3.1.3   Loss of a PDU

Since both UDP and CLTS are unreliable, it is possible for an SNMP message to be lost. SNMP itself has no provision to guarantee delivery. Thus, the burden is on the application that is using SNMP to cope with a lost PDU.

The actions to be taken upon loss of an SNMP message are not covered in the standard. Some commonsense observations can be made. In the case of GetRequest and GetNextRequest, the management station can assume that either the message or the responding GetResponse was lost if there is no response within a certain time period. The management station can repeat the request one or more times, eventually succeeding or giving up and assuming that the agent is either down or cannot be reached. If a unique request-id accompanies each distinct request operation, there is no difficulty if duplicate messages are generated.

In the case of a SetRequest, the recovery should probably involve testing the object with a GetRequest to determine whether or not the set operation was performed. Only if it is determined that the set operation was not performed should a duplicate SetRequest be issued.

Since no acknowledgment is provided in SNMP for traps, there is no easy way to detect the failure to deliver a trap. In SNMP, a trap should be used to provide early warning of a significant event. As a backup, the management station should also periodically poll the agent for the relevant status.

6.3.2   Connection-Oriented Transport Service

SNMP was intended for use over a connectionless transport service. The key reason for this is robustness. Network-management operations become increasingly important as failures and outages of various sorts are experienced. If SNMP relies on the use of a transport connection, then the loss of that connection could impair the effectiveness of SNMP exchanges.

No provision has been made for the use of SNMP over TCP. However, RFC 1283 prescribes conventions for the use of SNMP over the ISO connection-oriented transport service (COTS). In order to issue a GetRequest, GetNextRequest, or SetRequest, the management station must first set up a transport connection to the agent. Once the connection is established, the management station can send requests and receive responses on that connection. If the management station anticipates additional requests to the same agent, it can hold the connection open, thus reducing the overhead associated with connection setup and teardown. The agent may also break the connection if it needs the resources dedicated to managing the connection. Similarly, an agent would need to set up a connection to a management station prior to issuing a Trap.

Although there is a single ISO connection-oriented transport service, this service is supported by five different transport protocols, labeled class 0 through class 4. Class-0 and class-1 transport protocols assume the use of X.25 as the underlying network protocol and further restrict transport connections to be one-to-one with network connections. For these classes, the listening-agent address is the X.25 protocol-ID 03018200, and the listening management-station address is 0301900. For the other three transport classes, the same transport selectors used for CLTS are used for COTS.

6.4   SNMP GROUP

The SNMP group defined as part of MIB-II contains information relevant to the implementation and operation of SNMP (Figure 6.7, Table 6.9). Some of the objects defined in the group are 0-valued in those SNMP implementations that support only SNMP station-management functions or only SNMP agent functions.

With the exception of the last object in the group, all the objects are read-only counters. The snmpEnableAuthenTraps may be set by a management station. It indicates whether the agent is permitted to generate authentication-failure traps. This setting overrides the agent's own configuration information. Thus, it provides a means whereby all authentication-failure traps may be disabled.

6.5   PRACTICAL ISSUES

6.5.1   Differences in SNMP Support

In Chapter 5, we looked at the results of tests conducted on various commercially available SNMP management-station and agent products. The results showed some inconsistencies in the values generated for various MIB objects. Those same tests also looked at the support for SNMP provided by the various products. Unfortunately, the results show some inconsistencies and areas of nonsupport.

Tables 6.10 and 6.11 summarize the key results. One common problem related to the reporting of the medium-access control (MAC) addresses for LAN (local area network) ports. In the

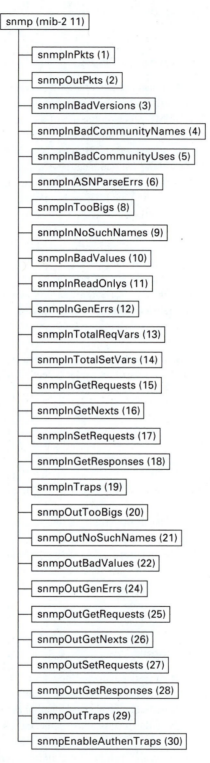

Figure 6.7 MIB-II SNMP Group

Table 6.9 MIB-II SNMP Group Objects

Object	Syntax	Access	Status	Description
snmpInPkts	Counter	RO	M	Total number of messages delivered to the SNMP entity from the transport service
snmpOutPkts	Counter	RO	M	Total number of SNMP messages passed from the SNMP entity to the transport service
snmpInBadVersions	Counter	RO	M	Total number of SNMP messages delivered to the SNMP entity for an unsupported SNMP version
snmpInBadCommunity-Names	Counter	RO	M	Total number of SNMP messages delivered to the SNMP entity that used an SNMP community name not known to the entity
snmpInBadCommunity-Uses	Counter	RO	M	Total number of SNMP messages delivered to the SNMP entity that represented an SNMP operation not allowed by the SNMP community named in the message
snmpInASNParseErrs	Counter	RO	M	Total number of ASN.1 or BER errors encountered when decoding received SNMP messages
snmpInTooBigs	Counter	RO	M	Total number of SNMP PDUs delivered to the SNMP entity for which the value of the error-status field is tooBig
snmpInNoSuchNames	Counter	RO	M	Total number of SNMP PDUs delivered to the SNMP entity for which the value of the error-status field is noSuchName
snmpInBadValues	Counter	RO	M	Total number of SNMP PDUs delivered to the SNMP entity for which the value of the error-status field is badValue
snmpInReadOnlys	Counter	RO	M	Total number of SNMP PDUs delivered to the SNMP entity for which the value of the error-status field is readOnly
snmpInGenErrs	Counter	RO	M	Total number of SNMP PDUs delivered to the SNMP entity for which the value of the error-status field is genErr

Table 6.9 *(Cont.)*

Object	Syntax	Access	Status	Description
snmpInTotalReqVars	Counter	RO	M	Total number of MIB objects retrieved successfully by the SNMP entity as the result of receiving valid SNMP Get-Request and GetNext PDUs
snmpInTotalSetVars	Counter	RO	M	Total number of MIB objects retrieved successfully by the SNMP entity as the result of receiving valid SNMP Set-Request PDUs
snmpInGetRequests	Counter	RO	M	Total number of SNMP Get-Request PDUs accepted and processed by the SNMP entity
snmpInGetNexts	Counter	RO	M	Total number of SNMP Get-Next PDUs accepted and processed by the SNMP entity
snmpInSetRequests	Counter	RO	M	Total number of SNMP Set-Request PDUs accepted and processed by the SNMP entity
snmpInGetResponses	Counter	RO	M	Total number of SNMP Get-Response PDUs accepted and processed by the SNMP entity
snmpInTraps	Counter	RO	M	Total number of SNMP Trap PDUs accepted and processed by the SNMP entity
snmpOutTooBigs	Counter	RO	M	Total number of SNMP PDUs generated by the SNMP entity for which the value of the error-status field is tooBig
snmpOutNoSuchNames	Counter	RO	M	Total number of SNMP PDUs generated by the SNMP entity for which the value of the error-status field is noSuchName
snmpOutBadValues	Counter	RO	M	Total number of SNMP PDUs generated by the SNMP entity for which the value of the error-status field is badValue
snmpOutGenErrs	Counter	RO	M	Total number of SNMP PDUs generated by the SNMP entity for which the value of the error-status field is genErr

Table 6.9 (*Cont.*)

Object	Syntax	Access	Status	Description
snmpOutGetRequests	Counter	RO	M	Total number of SNMP Get-Request PDUs generated by the SNMP entity
snmpOutGetNexts	Counter	RO	M	Total number of SNMP Get-Next PDUs generated by the SNMP entity
snmpOutSetRequests	Counter	RO	M	Total number of SNMP Set-Request PDUs generated by the SNMP entity
snmpOutGetResponses	Counter	RO	M	Total number of SNMP Get-Response PDUs generated by the SNMP entity
snmpOutTraps	Counter	RO	M	Total number of SNMP Trap PDUs generated by the SNMP entity
snmpEnable-AuthenTraps	INTEGER	RW	M	Authentication-failure traps enabled (1) or disabled (2)

configurations tested, all of the physical interfaces were Ethernet ports with 12-byte physical addresses. These addresses are not user-alterable and are fixed in the LAN interface. Clearly, it is important that the agent be able to provide the management station with the correct physical address for each of its interfaces. However, as the tables show, even this simple and basic piece of information is not always reliably reported. A number of the devices reported the same MAC address for all their ports, and one device was unable to report at all.

Another very common problem is limited or nonexistent support for the set command. A number of the vendor products did not support the use of set at all, and others limited it to objects in private MIB extensions. The lack of support for set limits the network-management capability. On the other hand, the basic SNMP specification provides only a password-type feature for security. Until such time as more robust security features are widely implemented, a number of users will be reluctant to allow object values to be remotely set.

For those devices that did support the set command, all could be set up with a community name of ''public,'' which gave any management system unrestricted access to the entire MIB. That is, the MIB view for community name public consists of the entire agent MIB. This is a useful feature; for a first-time SNMP implementation, the user can set all agents and managers to the public name to get some quick experience in the use of the system. The alternative is for the network-management system to be configured with a set of community names, one for each device to be managed.

To test the agents' ability to generate standard SNMP-defined traps, the testers literally pulled the plug on the device's power and then replugged it. The agent should issue a coldStart trap under these conditions. Only two of the bridges and four of the routers were able to generate the correct trap message. Again, this is bad news for the user. If agents cannot be trusted to reliably issue

Table 6.10 Variance in Bridges' SNMP Support

Vendor	Could Manager Obtain the MAC-Layer Ethernet Addresses For All the Bridge's LAN Ports?	Was Manager Able to Remotely Change the Values of SNMP Standards-Specified Read-Write Variables?	Did Bridge Issue the Appropriate SNMP Alarm Message in Response to Power Interruption?
A	Yes.	Agent supported set command for vendor's private-extension MIB objects, but not MIB-I or MIB-II read-write objects.	Agent issued a message, but format was not recognized as the expected coldStart SNMP message.
B	No; agent did not respond to manager's request.	No; unable to set values of MIB-I and MIB-II objects tested.	None within 5 minutes; bridge apparently loses address of manager when power is interrupted.
C	Agent responded with the same MAC address for two different LAN interfaces.	Agent supported set command for vendor's private-extension MIB objects, but not MIB-I or MIB-II read-write objects.	Yes; agent issued correct Trap message within about 20 seconds of power restoral.
D	Agent responded with the same MAC address for two different LAN interfaces.	Some; at least one read-write object was implemented as read-only.	Agent issued a message, but format was not recognized as the expected coldStart SNMP message.
E	Agent responded with the same MAC address for two different LAN interfaces.	No; unable to set values of MIB-I and MIB-II objects tested.	None within 5 minutes.
F	Yes.	Some; at least one read-write object was implemented as read-only.	Yes; agent issued correct Trap message within about 2 minutes of power restoral.
G	Agent responded with the same MAC address for two different LAN interfaces.	No; unable to set values of MIB-I and MIB-II objects tested.	None within 5 minutes.

Source: E. Mier, *"Network World,* Bell Labs Evaluate SNMP on Bridges," *Network World* (Apr. 22, 1991).

Table 6.11 Variance in Routers' SNMP Support

Vendor	Could Manager Obtain Clear SNMP Status, Configuration, and Address Information on Router and All Interfaces?	Was Manager Able to Remotely Change the Values of SNMP Standards-Specified Read-Write Variables?	Did Router Issue the Appropriate SNMP Alarm Message in Response to Power Interruption?
1	Yes. However, textual interface descriptions not explanatory.	Yes, for MIB-I objects and most of the vendor's private MIB objects that were tested.	No. Agent linked a linkUp message after 1.7 minutes rather than the expected coldStart message.
2	Yes. However, interface descriptions (Ethernet 0, 1) don't align with SNMP index numbers (interface 1, 2).	Yes, for MIB-I objects and most of the vendor's private MIB objects that were tested.	Yes; agent issued correct Trap message within about 0.3 minute of power restoral.
3	Yes. However, vendor implements the same physical (MAC-layer) address for different LAN interfaces.	Yes, for MIB-I objects.	No. Agent issued a Trap message, but it contained a format error and was not recognized by managers as the expected trap.
4	Yes.	No; unable to set values of objects tested.	Yes; agent issued correct Trap message within about 1 minute of power restoral.
5	Partially. Operational status of serial link was reported incorrectly.	Yes, for MIB-I objects.	No. Agent issued warmStart and linkUp messages after about 1.5 minutes, but not the expected coldStart message.
6	Yes	No; unable to set values of objects tested.	No. Traps not implemented in this agent.
7	Yes.	Some; at least one read-write object was implemented as read-only.	Yes; agent issued correct Trap message within about 2.1 minutes of power restoral.
8	Yes.	Some; at least one read-write object was implemented as read-only.	Yes; agent issued correct Trap message within about 0.3 minute of power restoral.
9	Yes.	No; unable to set values of objects tested.	Yes; agent issued correct Trap message within about 2.2 minutes of power restoral.

Source: E. Mier, "*Network World*, Bell Labs Test Routers' SNMP Agents," *Network World* (July 1, 1991).

traps, then the trap-directed polling strategy is based on a false premise. The network-management station must either rely more heavily on scheduled polling, which increases network overhead, or suffer a lack of up-to-date knowledge about the network.

6.5.2   Objects Not Supported

The MIB-I and MIB-II specifications dictate that for an implementation to claim support for a group, it must support all the objects in the group. It is certainly permissible for an agent to support only some of the objects in a group, but in that case, the vendor cannot claim that the group is supported.

Unfortunately, a number of vendors have tried to get around this restriction in the following way. If an agent does not count a quantity that is part of a group, it simply returns the static value 0 in response to every get command. This enables the vendor to say that all objects are ''supported,'' since a value is returned for all objects. At first glance, this approach might seem entirely reasonable. If the agent has failed to count a particular event, its count is 0. If the agent never counts that event, its count will always be 0.

The problem with this is that in some circumstances, it may be important for the management station to know whether the count is actually 0 or whether the agent simply isn't doing the counting. Consider the following example, from Steven Waldbusser, one of the key developers of SNMP-related standards:

> As a network manager, I would be very angry if the following happened to me: While debugging a packet loss problem, I inspect ifInErrors on an interface and find that the interface has not received any error packets. Feeling confident of the link layer, I turn my attention up the stack to the network layer and above. Several hours or days later, I learn from my system vendor that ifInErrors is not implemented, but is stating anyway that no errors have been received. If you can't trust your tools to not lie to you, you can't use them effectively. One still needs a healthy dose of skepticism, but if you need to second guess everything you learn, you can't work efficiently (Waldbusser, private communication).

Regardless of whether there is a deliberate attempt to fake out the user and the management station or whether the agent vendor genuinely feels that returning 0 for an unimplemented counter is appropriate, the fact is that this practice can lead to confusion and inefficiency. The correct way to handle this situation is for the agent to return the error code noSuchName and for the vendor to admit that this particular group is not supported.

Since not all vendors are ''doing the right thing,'' the user must beware.

6.5.3   Selection of a Network-Management Station

The discussion earlier in this chapter and in Chapter 5 concerning interoperability highlights the need to be concerned about the degree to which management and agent products conform to the standard and can interoperate with each other. In the case of agent products, one should also be concerned about ease of configuration and the range of MIB support.

For network-management stations, conformance to standards is only a starting point in evaluating products. The network-management station constitutes the user interface to the entire network-management system and should therefore provide a powerful, flexible, and easy-to-use access point for network management. For example, the following list of features that should be included in a network-management station is proposed in Wilkinson and Capen (1992):

- *Extended MIB support:* The full power of SNMP is realized only if the MIB support is open-ended. In particular, a network-management station should be able to load MIB definitions for extended MIBs defined for agent products from other vendors.

- *Intuitive interface:* The interface should make network management as easy and powerful as possible for the user. The use of a graphic window interface should enable the user to open a separate window for each part of the network that he or she wishes to monitor. The interface should be capable of displaying topological and geographic maps of the network. Descriptive, intelligent icons can be used to represent key components such as bridges and routers; when the user clicks on such an icon, the system displays the current status of the device and options for observing and controlling the device.

- *Automatic discovery:* The ideal network-management station, when installed, should be able to discover agents in order to build maps and configure icons.

- *Programmable events:* The user should be able to define the actions to be taken when certain events occur. For example, in the event of a router failure, the management station could change the color of the router's icon or flash the icon, send an E-mail message to the responsible manager, and set off the network troubleshooter's beeper.

- *Advanced network control:* Ideally, the network-management station should perform some predefined functions under certain conditions. For example, an administrator should be able to configure the management station to automatically shut off a bad or suspect hub or isolate an overactive network segment so that the whole network does not suffer. Of course, such features require the use of SNMP set commands. Because of SNMP's weak security, most products limit the scope of the set capability or forbid it altogether.

- *Object-oriented management:* Although the MIB and SMI (structure of management information) specifications of SNMP refer to ''objects,'' SNMP does not use object-oriented technology. However, an object-oriented system can be configured to support SNMP and can easily be upgraded to run multiple management protocols simultaneously.

- *Custom icons:* Descriptive icons are preferable to simple rectangles and circles for displaying network topology and geography. Ideally, the network-management station should enable the user to create custom icons.

6.5.4 Polling Frequency

As we have seen, the traps that are defined by SNMP are few in number. Although it is possible for proprietary traps to be implemented, these may not be understood by a network-management station from another vendor. Thus, virtually all information obtained by the management station is gathered by polling (GetRequest and GetNextRequest). Furthermore, if polling is only done at start-up time and in response to a trap, the management station may have a very out-of-date view of the network. For example, the management station will not be alerted to congestion problems in the network.

It follows that a policy is needed for the frequency with which polling is done by the management station. This, in turn, is related to the size of the network and therefore the number of agents that can be effectively managed by the management station. It is difficult to give guidance in this area, because performance will depend on the processing speed of the management station, the data rate of the various subnetwork segments, the congestion level in the network, and other factors. However, we can provide some simple formulas that give some idea of the scale of what is possible.

To simplify the problem, let us say that the management station can handle only one agent at a time. That is, when the management station polls a particular agent, it does no other work until it is done with that agent. The poll may involve a single get/response transaction or a series of such transactions. We can determine the maximum number of stations that the management station can handle by considering the situation in which the management station is engaged full-time in polling. We have the following equation:

$$N \le \frac{T}{\Delta},$$

where

N = number of agents.

T = desired polling interval; that is, the desired elapsed time between successive polls of the same agent.

Δ = average time required to perform a single poll.

The quantity Δ depends on a number of factors:

- Time to generate a request at the management station
- Network delay from manager to agent
- Processing time at the agent to interpret the message
- Processing time at the agent to generate a response
- Network delay from agent to manager
- Processing time at the manager to receive and interpret the response
- Number of request/response exchanges to obtain all the desired information from an agent

The following example is provided in Ben-Artzi, Chandna, and Warrier (1990). The example consists of a single local area network (LAN), where each managed device is to be polled every 15 minutes (typical at many TCP/IP sites today). Assuming processing times on the order of 50 ms and a network delay of about 1 ms (packet size of 1,000 bytes, no significant network congestion), then Δ is approximately 0.202 sec. Then

$$N \le \frac{(15 \times 60)}{0.202} \approx 4,500.$$

Thus, in this example, a single network manager could support a maximum of 4,500 devices with SNMP-based polling.

In a configuration that includes multiple subnetworks, especially wide area networks (WANs), the network-delay component will be much greater. Typically, data rates are much lower on a WAN than on a LAN, the distances are greater, and there are delays introduced by bridges and routers. A total network delay of half a second would not be unusual. Using this as an example:

$$N \leq \frac{(15 \times 60)}{(4 \times 0.05) + (2 \times 0.5)} = 750,$$

and the number of manageable devices is only 750.

In summary, four critical parameters are involved in these back-of-the-envelope calculations: number of agents, processing time for a request or a response, network delay, and polling interval. If the user can make rough estimates of any three of these, the fourth can be calculated. So for a given network configuration and a known number of agents, the user can determine the minimum polling interval that can be supported. Alternatively, for a given network configuration and a desired polling interval, the user can determine the maximum number of agents that can be managed.

There is, however, yet another factor that must be considered—namely, the load on the network imposed by the polling traffic. For example, one firm with a large Ethernet installation set the polling interval at five minutes and found that this delay was considered too high for responding to network problems (Eckerson 1992). When it changed the polling interval to one second, users complained of slow response time. An interval of 30 seconds turned out to be a reasonable compromise.

6.5.5   Limitations of SNMP

The user who relies on SNMP for network management needs to be aware of its limitations. Ben-Artzi, Chandna, and Warrier (1990) list the following:

- SNMP may not be suitable for the management of truly large networks because of the performance limitations of polling, as just examined. With SNMP, you must send one packet out to get back one packet of information. This type of polling results in large volumes of routine messages and yields problem-response times that may be unacceptable.

- SNMP is not well suited for retrieving large volumes of data, such as an entire routing table.

- SNMP traps are unacknowledged. In the typical case where UDP/IP is used to deliver trap messages, the agent cannot be sure that a critical message has reached the management station.

- The basic SNMP standard provides only trivial authentication. Thus, basic SNMP is better suited for monitoring than for control.

- SNMP does not directly support imperative commands. The only way to trigger an event at an agent is indirectly, by setting an object value. This is a less-flexible and less-powerful scheme than one that would allow some sort of remote procedure call, with parameters, conditions, and status and results to be reported.

- The SNMP MIB model is limited and does not readily support applications that make sophisticated management queries based on object values or types.

- SNMP does not support manager-to-manager communications. For example, there is no mechanism that allows a management system to learn about the devices and networks managed by another management system.

Many of these deficiencies are addressed by OSI network management. Some, however, see this as a case of the cure's being worse than the disease, given the complexity and sheer size of OSI network management. Improvements to SNMP, especially in the area of security, are in the pipeline and are discussed in Chapters 8 and 9. It remains to be seen whether these improvements will have the widespread vendor and customer support of SNMP or whether both vendors and customers will by and large stick with "basic SNMP" until making the big jump to OSI network management.

6.6   SUMMARY

The heart of the SNMP framework is the simple network-management protocol itself. The protocol provides a straightforward, basic mechanism for the exchange of management information between manager and agent.

The basic unit of exchange is the message, which consists of an outer message wrapper and an inner protocol data unit (PDU). The message header includes a community name, which allows the agent to regulate access. For any given community name, the agent may limit access to a subset of objects in its MIB (management information base), known as an MIB view.

Five types of PDUs may be carried in an SNMP message. The GetRequest PDU, issued by a manager, includes a list of one or more object names for which values are requested. The Get-NextRequest PDU is also issued by a manager and includes a list of one or more objects. In this case, for each object named, a value is to be returned for the object that is lexicographically next in the MIB. The SetRequest PDU is issued by a manager to request that the values of one or more objects be altered. For all three of these PDUs, the agent responds with a GetResponse PDU,

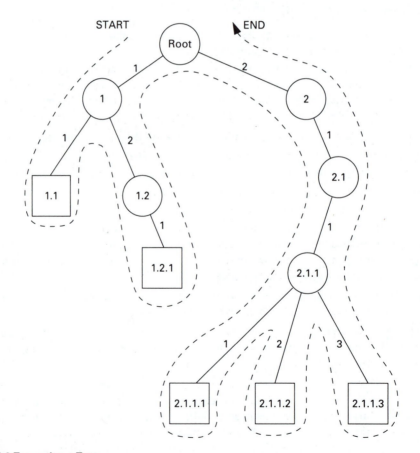

Figure 6.8 Traversing a Tree

which contains the values of the objects in question, or an error-status explaining the failure of the operation.

The final PDU is the Trap, which is issued by an agent to provide information to a manager concerning an event.

SNMP is designed to operate over the connectionless user datagram protocol (UDP). However, SNMP can be implemented to operate over a variety of transport-level protocols.

APPENDIX 6A   Lexicographic Ordering

Given two sequences of non-negative integers $(x_1, x_2, \ldots x_n)$ and $(y_1, y_2, \ldots y_m)$, we can say that $(x_1, x_2, \ldots x_n)$ precedes $(y_1, y_2, \ldots, y_m)$ in lexicographic order if the following conditions are met:

$$[(x_j = y_j \text{ for } 1 \leq j < k) \text{ AND } (x_k < y_k \text{ for } k \leq n, m)]$$
$$\text{OR } [(x_j = y_j \text{ for } 1 \leq j \leq n) \text{ AND } (n < m)]$$

Lexicographic ordering in an object-identifier tree is easily generated. The only restriction is that the tree must be drawn so that the branches under each node are arranged in increasing order left to right. With this convention, the lexicographic order is generated by traversing the tree in what is referred to as a preorder traversal, which is defined recursively as follows:

1. Visit the root.
2. Traverse the subtrees from left to right.

This method of traversal is also known as a depth-first search of the tree. Figure 6.8 illustrates preorder traversal. As can be seen, the nodes of the tree are visited in lexicographic order.

APPENDIX 6B   User Datagram Protocol

In addition to TCP, there is one other transport-level protocol that is in common use as part of the TCP/IP protocol suite: the user datagram protocol (UDP), specified in RFC 768. The UDP provides a connectionless service for application-level procedures. Thus, it enables procedures to send messages to other procedures with a minimum of protocol mechanism. SNMP makes use of UDP.

UDP sits on top of IP. Because it is connectionless, UDP has very little to do. Essentially, it adds a port-addressing capability to IP. This is best seen by examining the UDP header, shown in Figure 6.9.

The header includes a source port and destination port, which identify the sending and receiving users of TCP. For example, port number 161 identifies an SNMP agent, and port number 162 identifies an SNMP manager. The length field contains the length in octets of the entire UDP segment, including header and data. The checksum applies to the entire UDP segment plus a *pseudoheader* prefixed to the UDP header at the time of calculation. The pseudoheader includes the following fields from the IP header: source and destination internet address and protocol. By including the pseudoheader, UDP protects itself from misdelivery by IP. That is, if IP delivers a segment to the wrong host, even if the segment contains no bit errors, the receiving UDP entity

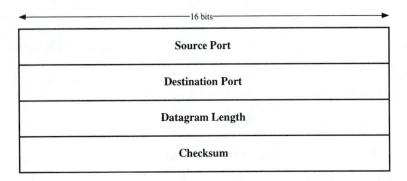

Figure 6.9 UDP Header

will detect the delivery error. If an error is detected, the segment is discarded and no further action is taken.

The checksum field in UDP is optional. If it is not used, it is set to 0. However, it should be pointed out that the IP checksum applies only to the IP header and not to the IP data field, which, in this case, consists of the UDP header and the user data. Thus, if no checksum calculation is performed by UDP, then no check is made on the user data.

7
Remote Network Monitoring

The most important addition to the basic set of SNMP standards—SMI (structure of management information), MIB (management information base), and SNMP—is the remote network-monitoring (RMON) standard, RFC 1271. RMON is a major step forward in internetwork management. It defines a remote-monitoring MIB that supplements MIB-II and provides the network manager with vital information about the internetwork.

For a review of the basic principles of network monitoring, please see Chapter 2.

7.1 BASIC CONCEPTS

With MIB-II, the network manager can obtain information that is purely local to individual devices. Consider a LAN (local area network) with a number of devices on it, each with an SNMP agent. An SNMP manager can learn about the amount of traffic into and out of each device but, with MIB-II, cannot easily learn about the traffic on the LAN as a whole. Devices that traditionally have been employed to study the traffic on a network as a whole are called network monitors; they are also referred to as network analyzers, or probes. Typically, a monitor operates on a LAN in "promiscuous" mode, viewing every packet on the LAN. The monitor can produce summary information, including error statistics, such as a count of undersize packets and the number of collisions; and performance statistics, such as the number of packets delivered per second and the packet-size distribution. The monitor may also store packets or partial packets for later analysis. Filters can be used to limit the number of packets counted or captured, based on packet type or other characteristics of packets.

For the purposes of network management in an internetworked environment, there would typically need to be one monitor per subnetwork. The monitor may be a stand-alone device whose sole purpose is to capture and analyze traffic. In other cases, the monitoring function is performed by a device with other duties, such as a workstation, a server, or a router. For effective network management, these monitors need to communicate with a central network-management station. In this latter context, they are referred to as remote monitors.

7.1.1   RMON Goals

The RMON specification is primarily a definition of an MIB. The effect, however, is to define standard network-monitoring functions and interfaces for communicating between SNMP-based management consoles and remote monitors. In general terms, the RMON capability provides an effective and efficient way to monitor subnetworkwide behavior while reducing the burden both on other agents and on management stations. In addition, RFC 1271 lists the following design goals for RMON:

- *Off-line operation:* It might be desirable or necessary to limit or halt the routine polling of a monitor by a network manager. Limited polling saves on communications costs, especially where dial-up lines may have to be used to reach the monitor. Polling may cease if there is a communications failure or if the manager fails. In general, the monitor should collect fault, performance, and configuration information continuously, even if it is not being polled by a network manager. The monitor simply continues to accumulate statistics that may be retrieved by the manager at a later time. The monitor may also attempt to notify the management station if an exceptional event occurs.

- *Preemptive monitoring:* If the monitor has sufficient resources, and if the practice is not considered too disruptive, the monitor can continuously run diagnostics and log network performance. In the event of a failure somewhere in the internet, the monitor may be able to notify the management station of the failure and provide the management station with information useful in diagnosing the failure.

- *Problem detection and reporting:* Preemptive monitoring involves an active probing of the network and the consumption of network resources to check for error and exception conditions. Alternatively, the monitor can passively (without polling) recognize certain error conditions and other conditions, such as congestion, on the basis of the traffic that it observes. The monitor can be configured to continuously check for such conditions. When one of these conditions occurs, the monitor can log the condition and attempt to notify the management station.

- *Value-added data:* The network monitor can perform analyses specific to the data collected on its subnetwork, thus relieving the management station of this responsibility. For example, the monitor can analyze subnetwork traffic to determine which hosts generate the most traffic or errors on the subnetwork. This type of subnetworkwide information is not otherwise accessible to a network-management station that is not directly attached to the subnetwork.

- *Multiple managers:* An internetworking configuration may have more than one management station in order to achieve reliability, perform different functions (e.g., engineering and operations), and provide management capability to different units within an organization. The monitor can be configured to deal with more than one management station concurrently. The requirements for support of multiple managers are discussed later in this section.

Not all remote monitors may be capable of meeting all these goals, but the RMON specification provides the base for supporting all the goals.

Figure 7.1 is an example configuration for remote monitoring, showing an internet with five subnetworks. The three subnetworks in the lower-left portion of the figure are located in the same building. The other two subnetworks are at two different remote sites. The subnetwork at the top

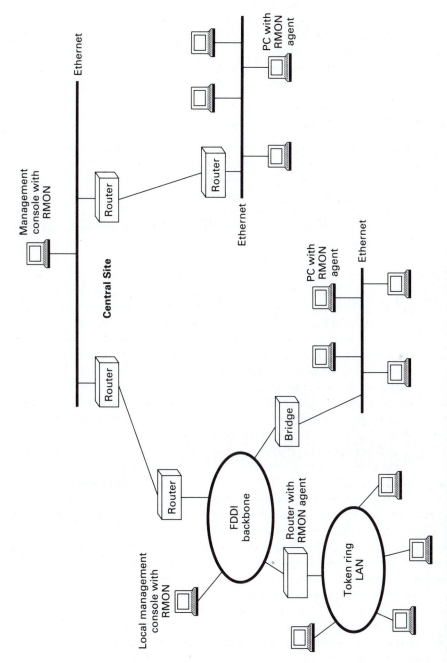

Figure 7.1 Example Configuration Using RMON

of the figure is considered to be the central site. A dedicated management station with RMON management and agent capability is attached to the central LAN. On two of the subnetworks, the RMON agent is implemented in a personal computer, which may be dedicated to remote monitoring or, if the traffic on the subnetwork is light, may perform other functions, such as local network management or a server function. Attached to the FDDI (fiber-distributed data interface) backbone is a second management station with RMON management and agent capability, concerned with management of the networks at that site. Finally, the RMON-agent functions for the token-ring LAN are performed by the router that connects that LAN to the rest of the internet.

7.1.2   Control of Remote Monitors

A remote monitor can be implemented either as a dedicated device or as a function available on a system for which processing and memory resources are specifically dedicated to the monitoring function. With these dedicated resources, a remote monitor is capable of performing more complex functions and a wider range of functions than would be expected of an agent that just supports MIB-II. In order to effectively manage a remote monitor, the RMON MIB contains features that support extensive control from the management station. These features fall into two general categories: configuration and action invocation.

7.1.2.1   Configuration

Typically, a remote monitor will need to be configured for data collection. Configuration dictates the type and form of data to be collected. The way in which this is accommodated by the RMON MIB is as follows. The MIB is organized into a number of functional groups. Within each group, there may be one or more control tables and one or more data tables. A *control table*, which is typically read-write, contains parameters that describe the data in a *data table,* which is typically read-only. So at configuration time, the management station sets the appropriate control parameters to configure the remote monitor to collect the desired data. The parameters are set by adding a new row to the control table or by modifying an existing row. As information is collected according to the parameter settings of a control row, it is stored in rows of the corresponding data table.

Thus, functions to be performed by a monitor are defined and implemented in terms of table rows. For example, a control table may contain objects that specify source of data to be collected, type of data, collection timing, and so on. A single row of the control table, by assigning specific values to the parameters (columnar objects) of the table, defines a specific data-collection function. Associated with that single control row are one or more rows in one or more data tables. The individual control row and its associated data rows are tied together by, in effect, interlocking pointers. The control row includes an index object that can be used to access one or more data rows in one or more data tables; each such data row includes an index that refers to the corresponding control-table row. A number of examples of this structure are illustrated throughout the chapter.

To modify any parameters in a control table, it is necessary to first invalidate the control entry (row). This causes the deletion of that row and the deletion of all associated rows in data tables. The management station can then create a new control row with the modified parameters. The same mechanism is used to simply disable a particular data-collection function. When a row of a control table is deleted, the associated data-table rows are deleted, and the resources used by those rows are reclaimed.

In several cases, there is essentially a one-to-one relationship between the control parameters that define a data-collection function and a single row of objects used to hold collected data. In those cases, the control and data tables are combined into a single table.

7.1.2.2   Action Invocation

As was mentioned in Chapter 6, SNMP provides no specific mechanism for issuing a command to an agent to perform an action. SNMP's only capabilities are to read object values and set object values within an MIB view. However, it is possible to use the SNMP set operation to issue a command. An object can be used to represent a command, so that a specific action is taken if the object is set to a specific value. A number of such objects are included in the RMON MIB. In general, these objects represent states, and an action is performed if the management station changes the state (by changing the value of the object). A request to set an object to its current value does not cause an action to be performed.

7.1.3   Multiple Managers

As Figure 7.1 illustrates, an RMON agent may be subject to management from multiple management stations. Anytime concurrent access is allowed to a resource, there is a potential for conflict and unwanted results. In the case of a shared RMON agent, the following difficulties may arise:

- Concurrent requests for resources could exceed the capability of the monitor to supply those resources.
- A management station could capture and hold monitor resources for a long period of time, preventing their use for other desired management functions by other management stations.
- Resources could be assigned to a management station that crashes without releasing the resources.

To deal with these problems, a combination of avoidance and resolution features is needed. It turns out that a relatively simple feature embedded in the RMON MIB supports these requirements. Associated with each control table is a columnar object that identifies the owner of a particular row of the table and of the associated function. The ownership label can be used in the following ways:

- A management station may recognize resources it owns and no longer needs.
- A network operator can identify the management station that owns a particular resource or function and negotiate for the resource or function to be freed.
- A network operator may have the authority to unilaterally free resources that another network operator has reserved.
- If a management station experiences a reinitialization, it can recognize resources it had reserved in the past and free those it no longer needs.

The RMON specification suggests that the ownership label contain one or more of the following: IP address; management-station name; network manager's name, location, or phone number.

Although the ownership concept is useful, it is important to note that the ownership label does not act as a password or an access-control mechanism. Access control is enforced in SNMP only through the use of the MIB-view mechanism associated with the community name. Thus, if a control table has read-write access, it is available for reading and writing by all management stations for which the table is visible in their MIB view. In general, a row of a control table should only be altered or deleted by its owner and treated as read-only by other management stations. Enforcement of this convention is beyond the scope of SNMP or the RMON specification.

If multiple network managers have access to a control table, some efficiencies can be achieved by sharing. When a management station wishes to utilize a certain function in a monitor, it should first scan the relevant control table to see whether that function, or something close to that function, has already been defined by another management station. In that case, the management station may "share" the function simply by observing the corresponding read-only data rows associated with the control row. However, the management station that owns a control-table row may modify or delete that row at any time. Thus, any management station that shares that row may find the function it desires modified or terminated.

Often, a monitor will be configured with a default set of functions that are set up when the monitor is initialized. The control rows that define these functions are owned by the monitor. By convention, each relevant ownership label is set to a string starting with "monitor." The resources associated with the defined function are therefore owned by the monitor itself. A management station can make use of such functions in a read-only fashion if there is a functional match with the management station's requirements. A management station should not alter or delete a monitor-owned function, except under the direction of the administrator of the monitor, who is often the network administrator.

7.1.4   Table Management

In the SNMP framework, the procedures for adding and deleting table rows are, to say the least, unclear. This lack of clarity has been the source of frequent questions and complaints. The RMON specification includes a set of textual conventions and procedural rules that, while not violating or modifying the SNMP framework, provide a clear and disciplined technique for row addition and deletion. These conventions and procedures are summarized in this subsection.

7.1.4.1   Textual Conventions
Two new data types are defined in the RMON specification. In ASN.1, the definitions appear as follows:

OwnerString :: = DisplayString
EntryStatus :: = INTEGER { valid (1),
                           createRequest (2),
                           underCreation (3),
                           invalid (4) }

Associated with each read-write table (control or combination control/data) in the RMON MIB is an object whose value indicates the owner of that row.[1] This object has the type OwnerString. Recall from the definition of the macro for managed objects (Figure 5.2) that a DisplayString is an

---

1.   The need to specify the management station that owns a row is discussed in subsection 7.1.3.

octet string of from 0 to 255 octets. Thus, *OwnerString* is just a useful mnemonic name for "DisplayString." In all cases, the object name ends in *Owner* and is thus easily identified.

Also associated with each read-write table in the RMON MIB is an object whose value gives the status of the row that contains that object instance. This object has the type EntryStatus and may take one of the four values listed in the ASN.1 definition of that type (valid, createRequest, underCreation, invalid). Objects of type EntryStatus are used in the creation, modification, and deletion of rows, as described in the balance of this subsection. In all cases, the object name ends in *Status* and is thus easily identified.

In the figures that follow, objects of type EntryStatus are indicated by an arrow with an open arrowhead. As in Chapter 5, INDEX objects are indicated by an arrow with a closed arrowhead.

RFC 1271 refers to these definitions as textual conventions. The purpose of these definitions is to enhance the readability of the specification. Objects defined in terms of these definitions are encoded by means of the rules that define the underlying primitive types (INTEGER, OCTET STRING). Thus, no changes to the SMI or SNMP are needed to accommodate the RMON MIB.

Figure 7.2 shows the general structure used for all control and control/data tables in the RMON MIB. The INDEX object defines a unique row in this table. In addition, the INDEX object is used to reference one or more rows in one or more data tables. The characteristics of those data rows are defined by parameters in the control row. In this example, a single such parameter is indicated.

7.1.4.2   Row Addition

The addition of a row to an RMON table by a management station using SNMP is achieved in the same fashion as described in Chapter 6. That is, a SetRequest PDU is issued that includes a list of columnar-object identifiers for the table. Each object identifier is actually an object-instance identifier consisting of the object identifier followed by the instance value for the index or indices for that table. Ideally, the SetRequest variable-bindings list should include all the columnar objects in the table.

When an agent receives such a request, it must check the requested parameter settings to determine whether they are permissible given restrictions defined in the RMON MIB as well as any implementation-specific restrictions, such as lack of resources. If row addition is not possible, a GetResponse with a badValue error status is returned; the error-index field indicates the first field in the variable-bindings list for which the requested setting was invalid.

The RMON MIB supports a mechanism for coping with the problem posed by concurrent table-addition attempts from multiple management stations. The problem occurs if two or more management stations attempt to create a row with the same parameters, including index parameters. To arbitrate this conflict, there is, in effect, a state machine built into the MIB structure defined by the status object. The management station and the agent engage in a multipacket exchange dubbed the "RMON polka" to safely control the construction of the row and prevent other managers from butting in.

The RMON polka consists of the following steps:

1. If a management station attempts to create a new row, and the index-object value or values do not already exist, the row is created with a status-object value of createRequest (2).

2. Immediately after completing the create operation, the agent sets the status-object value to underCreation (3).

```
exampleTable OBJECT-TYPE
    SYNTAX       SEQUENCE OF ExampleEntry
    ACCESS       not-accessible
    STATUS       mandatory
    DESCRIPTION
        "A table containing a list of table entries, or rows."
    ::= {eqroup 1}

exampleEntry OBJECT-TYPE
    SYNTAX       ExampleEntry
    ACCESS       not-accessible
    STATUS       mandatory
    DESCRIPTION
        "Defines the conceptual row for exampleTable."
    INDEX {exampleIndex}
    ::= {exampleTable 1}

ExampleEntry ::= SEQUENCE { exampleIndex      INTEGER (0..65535),
                           exampleParameter   Counter,
                           exampleOwner       OwnerString
                           exampleStatus      INTEGER }

exampleIndex OBJECT-TYPE
    SYNTAX       INTEGER (0..65535)
    ACCESS       read-only
    STATUS       mandatory
    DESCRIPTION
        "The value of this object uniquely identifies this example entry."
    ::= {exampleEntry 1}

exampleParameter OBJECT-TYPE
    SYNTAX       Integer
    ACCESS       read-write
    STATUS       mandatory
    DESCRIPTION
        "The value of this object characterizes data table rows associated with this entry."
    ::= {exampleEntry 2}

exampleOwner OBJECT-TYPE
    SYNTAX       OwnerString
    ACCESS       read-write
    STATUS       mandatory
    DESCRIPTION
        "The entity that configured this entry and is therefore using the resources assigned to it."
    ::= {exampleEntry 3}

exampleStatus OBJECT-TYPE
    SYNTAX       EntryStatus
    ACCESS       read-write
    STATUS       mandatory
    DESCRIPTION
        "The status of this example entry."
    ::= {exampleEntry 4}
```

Figure 7.2 General Structure of an RMON Control Table

3. Rows shall exist in the underCreation (3) state until the management station is finished creating all the rows that it desires for its configuration. At that point, the management station sets the status-object value in each of the created rows to valid (1).

4. If an attempt is made to create a new row, with a createRequest status, and the row already exists, an error is returned.

The effect of these conventions is that if multiple requests are made to create the same conceptual row, only the request received first will succeed, and the others will receive an error.

Another way in which a row could be added to a table is for a management station to activate an existing invalid row by changing the value of the status object from invalid to valid. The danger with this approach is that it may be impossible for the agent to activate that row because at least one of the parameter settings is not currently appropriate. In that case, there is no way for the agent to indicate to the management station which parameter is invalid, since the columnar object was not included in the SetRequest.

7.1.4.3   Row Modification and Deletion

A row is deleted by setting the status-object value for that row to invalid. The owner of the row can therefore delete that row by issuing the appropriate SetRequest PDU. As was previously mentioned, a row may be modified by first invalidating the row and then providing the row with new parameter values.

7.2   THE RMON MIB

The bulk of the RMON specification is devoted to a definition of the RMON management information base. This MIB is now incorporated into MIB-II with a subtree identifier of 16.

7.2.1   RMON MIB Structure

The RMON MIB is divided into nine groups (Figure 7.3):

1. *statistics:* maintains low-level utilization and error statistics for each subnetwork monitored by the agent.

2. *history:* records periodic statistical samples from information available in the statistics group.

3. *alarm:* allows the person at the management console to set a sampling interval and an alarm threshold for any counter or integer recorded by the RMON agent.

4. *host:* contains counters for various types of traffic to and from hosts attached to the subnetwork.

5. *hostTopN:* contains sorted host statistics that report on the hosts that top a list based on some parameter in the host table.

6. *matrix:* shows error and utilization information in matrix form, so the operator can retrieve information for any pair of network addresses.

7. *filter:* allows the monitor to observe packets that match a filter. The monitor may capture all packets that pass the filter or simply record statistics based on such packets.

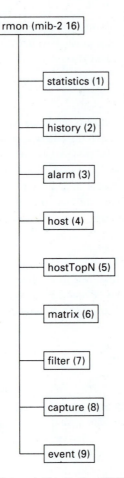

Figure 7.3 Remote Network-Monitoring (RMON) MIB

8. *packet capture:* governs how data are sent to a management console.

9. *event:* a table of all events generated by the RMON agent.

Each group is used to store data and statistics derived from data collected by the monitor. A monitor may have more than one physical interface and hence may be connected to more than one subnetwork. The data stored in each group represent data gathered from one or more of the attached subnetworks, depending on how the monitor is configured for that particular group.

All of the groups in the RMON MIB are optional. However, there are some dependencies:

- The alarm group requires the implementation of the event group.
- The hostTopN group requires the implementation of the host group.
- The packet-capture group requires the implementation of the filter group.

Table 7.1 A Comparison of MIB Coverage

	MIB II	Host MIB	Bridge MIB	Hub MIB	RMON MIB
Interface statistics	✓				
IP, TCP, UDP statistics	✓				
SNMP statistics	✓				
Host job counts		✓			
Host file system information		✓			
Spanning-tree performance			✓		
Wide-area link performance			✓		
Link testing			✓	✓	
Network traffic statistics			✓	✓	✓
Host table of all addresses				✓	✓
Host statistics				✓	✓
Historical data					✓
Alarm thresholds					✓
Configurable statistics					✓
Traffic matrix with all nodes					✓
"Host top N" tables					✓
Packet capture/protocol analysis					✓
Distributed logging of events					✓

Reprinted from May 1992 *Data Communications Magazine.* Copyright (May 1992) McGraw-Hill, Inc. All rights reserved. (Waldbusser, Nair, and Hoerth, 1992).

Table 7.1 compares the data collected by the RMON MIB to those contained in MIB-II and some other standardized MIBs. The remainder of this section provides a brief description of each group.

7.2.2 Statistics Group

The statistics group contains the basic statistics for each monitored subnetwork. The group consists of a single table (Figure 7.4), with one entry (row) for each monitored interface (subnetwork). The statistics are in the form of counters that start from 0 when a valid entry is created.

Currently, this group only contains objects defined for Ethernet interfaces. Future extensions of the MIB will accommodate other types of LANs, including token-ring and FDDI.

Although the purpose of most of the objects in the group is easily deduced from their name, some of the objects warrant explanation:[2]

- *etherStatsIndex:* an integer index for this row.

---

2. In the interests of conserving space, we follow the practice in this chapter of only defining key objects in each table, leaving out objects whose meaning is largely self-explanatory. The reader should consult RFC 1271 for a full list of definitions.

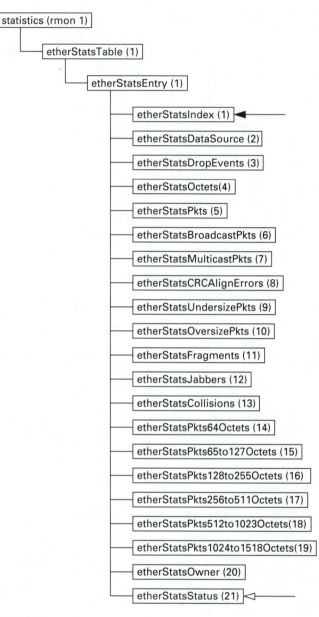

Figure 7.4 RMON Statistics Group

- *etherStatsDataSource:* identifies the interface and hence the Ethernet subnetwork that is the source of the data in this row. The value of this object instance is an object identifier that identifies the instance of ifIndex in the interfaces group of MIB-II that corresponds to this interface. For example, if this row refers to interface number 1, this object would be set to ifIndex.1.

- *etherStatsDropEvents:* a count of the number of events in which packets were dropped by the monitor due to lack of resources. This is not necessarily the actual count of packets dropped but the number of times this condition has been detected.

The statistics group provides useful information about the load on a subnetwork and the overall health of the subnetwork, since various error conditions are counted, such as CRC (cyclic-redundancy check) alignment errors, collisions, and undersize and oversize packets.

Note that this group is used to collect statistics on traffic into the monitor across an interface. It is interesting to compare the objects in this group to the MIB-II interfaces group (Table 5.2), which is concerned with total traffic into and out of an agent's interface. There is some overlap, but the statistics group provides much more detail about Ethernet behavior.

For the statistics group, the functions of control table and data table are combined. The only read-write objects in the table are etherStatsDataSource, etherStatsOwner, and etherStatsStatus. Thus, a management station can request that the monitor gather statistics on one or more of its Ethernet interfaces. The profile of statistics gathered is the same for all interfaces, all of which must be interfaces to Ethernet networks.

7.2.3   History Group

The history group is used to define sampling functions for one or more of the monitor's interfaces. It consists of two tables (Figure 7.5): historyControlTable, which specifies the interface and the details of the sampling function, and etherHistoryTable, which records the data. The latter is a media-specific table for Ethernet; other media-specific data tables may be added in the future.

Each row in the historyControlTable defines a set of samples at a particular sampling interval for a particular interface. Each sample, as it is collected, is stored in a new row of etherHistory-Table. The historyControlTable includes the following columnar objects:

- *historyControlIndex:* an integer that uniquely identifies a row in the historyControlTable. The same integer is also used to identify corresponding rows in the etherHistoryTable.

- *historyControlDataSource:* identifies the interface and hence the Ethernet subnetwork that is the source of the data for samples defined by this row.

- *historyControlBucketsRequested:* the requested number of discrete sampling intervals over which data are to be saved in the part of the media-specific data table associated with this entry. A default value of 50 is assigned to this object if it is not provided by the creator of this row.

- *historyControlBucketsGranted:* the actual number of discrete sampling intervals over which data will be saved. When the associated historyControlBucketsRequested is created or modified, the monitor should set this object as close to the requested value as possible.

- *historyControlInterval:* the interval in seconds over which data are sampled for each bucket. The interval can be set to any number between 1 and 3,600 (1 hour). A default value of 1,800 is assigned to this object if it is not provided by the creator of this row.

The sampling scheme is dictated by historyControlBucketsGranted and historyControlInterval. For example, using the default values, the monitor would take a sample once every 1,800 sec. (30 min.); each sample is stored in a row of etherHistoryTable, and the most recent 50 rows are retained.

The etherHistoryTable includes the following objects:

Figure 7.5 RMON History Group

- *etherHistoryIndex:* the history of which this entry is a part. The history identified by a particular value of this index is the same history as that identified by the same value of historyControlIndex.

- *etherHistorySampleIndex:* an index that uniquely identifies the particular sample that this entry represents among all samples associated with the same row of the historyControlTable. This index starts at 1 and increases by 1 as each new sample is taken.

- *etherHistoryIntervalStart:* the value of sysUpTime (in the MIB-II systems group) at the start of the interval over which this sample was measured.

Figure 7.6 illustrates the relationship between the control table and the data table. Each row of historyControlTable has a unique value of historyControlIndex. No two rows have the same combination of values of historyControlDataSource and historyControlInterval. This means that for any given subnetwork, more than one sampling process can be in effect, but each must have a different sampling period. For example, the specification recommends that there be at least two history-control entries per monitored interface, one with a 30-sec. sampling period and one with a 30-min. sampling period. The shorter period enables the monitor to detect sudden changes in traffic patterns; the longer period enables the steady-state behavior of the interface to be monitored.

For each of the K rows of historyControlTable, there is a set of rows of etherHistory. In the figure, the number of rows of etherHistoryTable associated with control-table row i is B_i. These are the B_i most recent samples for control entry i. The maximum value of B_i is the corresponding value of historyControlBucketsGranted.

The sampling scheme works as follows. The monitor or a management station can define a new "history" that is unique in terms of the interface and the sampling interval. This control-table row is assigned a unique index, starting at 1, by the monitor. Associated with each history (i.e., each row of historyControlTable) is a set of rows of etherHistoryTable. Each row of etherHistoryTable, also called a bucket, holds the statistics gathered during one sampling interval. Thus, etherHistoryPkts is a counter equal to the number of packets (including error packets) received during the corresponding sampling interval. Equivalently, the value of etherHistoryPkts for a given row equals the value of etherStatsPkts at the end of that sampling interval minus the value of etherStatsPkts at the start of that sampling interval.

As each sampling interval occurs, the monitor adds a new row to etherHistoryTable with the same etherHistoryIndex as the other rows for this history and with an etherHistorySampleIndex of 1 more than the value for the row corresponding to the previous sampling interval.

Once the number of rows for a history becomes equal to historyControlBucketsGranted, the set of rows for that history functions as a circular buffer. As each new row is added to the set, the oldest row associated with this history is deleted. Similarly, if the number of rows granted to a history is reduced, by a change in historyControlBucketsRequested and historyControlBuckets-Granted, rows are deleted for that history to match the new granted size. For example, in Figure 7.6, the x oldest entries of etherHistoryTable that have an etherHistoryIndex of 1 have already been discarded, and the y oldest entries of etherHistoryTable that have an etherHistoryIndex of 2 have already been discarded.

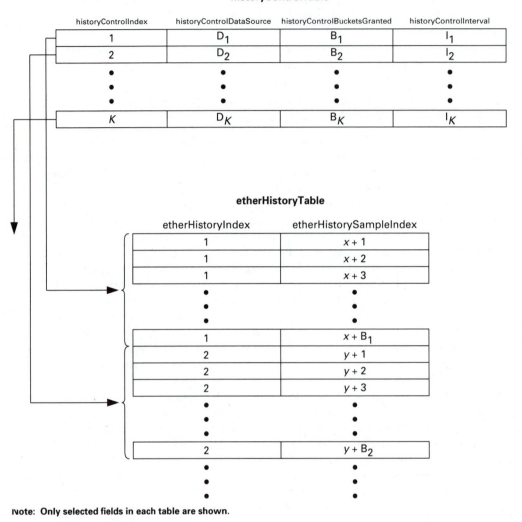

Note: Only selected fields in each table are shown.

Figure 7.6 An Example of History Tables

7.2.4   Alarm Group

The alarm group is used to define a set of thresholds for network performance. If a threshold is crossed in the appropriate direction, an alarm is generated and sent to the central console. For example, an alarm could be generated if there are more than 500 CRC errors (the threshold) in any 5-min. period (the sampling interval).

The alarm group consists of a single table, alarmTable (Figure 7.7). Each entry in the table specifies a particular variable to be monitored, a sampling interval, and threshold parameters. The single entry in the table for that variable using that interval contains the most recent sampled

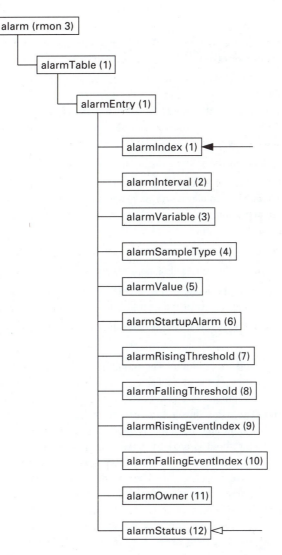

Figure 7.7 RMON Alarm Group

value—that is, the value observed at the end of the last sampling interval. When the current sampling interval is completed, the new value for the sampled variable will be stored and the old value lost.

The alarmTable includes the following objects:

- *alarmIndex:* an integer that uniquely identifies a row in the alarmTable. Each such row specifies a sample at a particular interval for a particular object in the monitor's MIB.

- *alarmInterval:* the interval in seconds over which the data are sampled and compared with the rising and falling thresholds.

- *alarmVariable:* the object identifier of the particular variable in the local MIB to be sampled. The only object types allowed are INTEGER, counter, gauge, and TimeTicks. These are the only object types that resolve to ASN.1 type INTEGER.

- *alarmSampleType:* the method of calculating the value to be compared to the thresholds. If the value of this object is absoluteValue (1), then the value of the selected variable will be compared directly with the thresholds. If the value of this object is deltaValue (2), then the value of the selected variable at the last sample is subtracted from the current value, and the difference is compared with the thresholds.

- *alarmValue:* the value of the statistic during the last sampling period.

- *alarmStartupAlarm:* has the value risingAlarm (1), fallingAlarm (2), or risingOrFallingAlarm (3). This dictates whether an alarm will be generated if the first sample after the row becomes valid is greater than or equal to the risingThreshold, or if the first sample is less than or equal to the fallingThreshold, or both.

- *alarmRisingThreshold:* the rising threshold for the sampled statistic.

- *alarmFallingThreshold:* the falling threshold for the sampled statistic.

- *alarmRisingEventIndex:* the index of the eventEntry that is used when the rising threshold is crossed. The eventTable is part of the event group and is discussed later in this section.

- *alarmFallingEventIndex:* the index of the eventEntry that is used when the falling threshold is crossed.

The alarm scheme works as follows. The monitor or a management station can define a new alarm by creating a new row in the alarmTable. The combination of variable, sampling interval, and threshold parameters is unique to a given row. Two thresholds are provided: a rising threshold and a falling threshold. The rising threshold is crossed if the current sampled value is greater than or equal to the rising threshold and the value at the last sampling interval was less than the threshold. Similarly, a falling threshold is crossed if the current sampled value is less than or equal to the falling threshold and the value at the last sampling interval was greater than the threshold.

Two types of values are calculated for alarms. An absoluteValue is simply the value of an object at the time of sampling, whereas a deltaValue represents the difference in values for the object over two successive sampling periods. This latter value is thus concerned with a rate of change. Note that a counter sampled as an absoluteValue can never cross the falling threshold and will cross the rising threshold at most once. A counter sampled as a deltaValue, or a gauge, can cross both rising and falling thresholds any number of times.

The alarm group defines a mechanism designed to prevent relatively minor alarms from being generated repeatedly. The rules for the generation of rising-alarm events are as follows:

1. If the first sampled value obtained after the row becomes valid is:

    a. less than the rising threshold, then the first time that the sample value becomes greater than or equal to the rising threshold, a rising-alarm event is generated.

    b. greater than or equal to the rising threshold, and if the value of alarmStartupAlarm is risingAlarm (1) or risingOrFallingAlarm (3), then a rising-alarm event is generated.

    c. greater than or equal to the rising threshold, and if the value of alarmStartupAlarm is fallingAlarm (2), then a rising-alarm event is generated the first time that the sample value again becomes greater than or equal to the rising threshold after having fallen below the rising threshold.

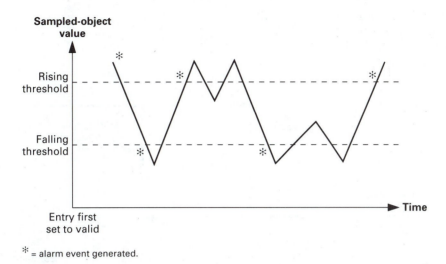

*= alarm event generated.

Figure 7.8 Generation of Alarm Events

2.   After a rising-alarm event is generated, another such event will not be generated until after the sampled value falls below the rising threshold and reaches the falling threshold and then subsequently reaches the rising threshold again.

The rules for the generation of falling-alarm events are the reverse of those just listed.

Figure 7.8 illustrates the mechanism. The example is for an alarm with an alarmStartupAlarm value of risingAlarm or risingOrFallingAlarm. In this example, the first sampling produces a value that exceeds the rising threshold, and a rising-alarm event is generated. Subsequently, the falling threshold and then the rising threshold are crossed, generating two alarm events. Then the fluctuations in the value produce another crossing of the rising threshold; this crossing is not counted as an alarm event, since it does not satisfy the rules spelled out in the preceding list. If those rules were not in force, a value that fluctuated around a threshold could generate many alarms, burdening the monitor.

The mechanism by which small fluctuations are prevented from causing alarms is referred to in the RMON specification as a *hysteresis mechanism*. The term refers to a phenomenon known as relay hysteresis and can be appreciated with the aid of Figure 7.9. We can think of the alarm-generation mechanism as having two states. While in the rising-alarm state, the mechanism will generate a rising alarm when the value of the observed variable reaches or exceeds the rising threshold; while in that state, the mechanism is disabled from generating a falling alarm. Once the rising alarm is generated, the mechanism is in a falling-alarm state and will remain so until the observed variable reaches or falls below the falling threshold. Similarly, while in the falling-alarm state, the mechanism will generate a falling alarm when the value of the observed variable reaches or falls below the falling-alarm threshold; while in that state, the mechanism is disabled from generating a rising alarm.

One final point of interest. The specification recommends that a variable of type deltaValue be sampled with greater precision than indicated by alarmInterval: the delta sample should be taken twice per period, each time comparing the sum of the latest two samples with the threshold. This allows the detection of threshold crossings that span the sampling boundary. It would appear that

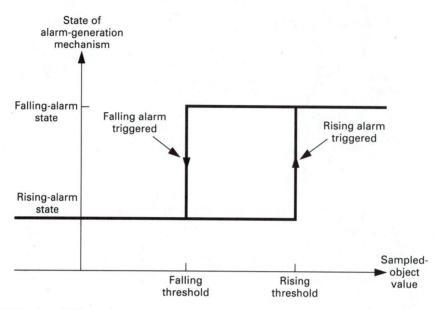

Figure 7.9 Hysteresis Mechanism

a similar mechanism would be desirable for gauge variables sampled by absoluteValue; however, this is not mentioned in the specification.

To appreciate the significance of the double-sampling rule, consider the following sequence of counter values, observed at 10-sec. intervals:

Time	0	10	20
Observed value	0	19	32
Delta value	0	19	13

If the rising threshold is 20, then no alarm is triggered. Now let us observe the same variable at 5-sec. intervals:

Time	0	5	10	15	20
Observed value	0	10	19	30	32
Delta value	0	10	9	11	2

At time = 15, the sum of the last two delta samples is 20, which meets the rising-alarm threshold and triggers a rising-alarm event.

7.2.5   Host Group

The host group is used to gather statistics about specific hosts on the LAN. The monitor learns of new hosts on the LAN by observing the source and destination MAC (medium-access control) addresses in good packets. For each host known to the monitor, a set of statistics is maintained.

As usual, the control table determines for which interfaces (which subnetworks) this function is performed.

The host group consists of three tables: one control table and two data tables (Figure 7.10). The control table, hostControlTable, includes the following objects:

- *hostControlIndex:* an integer that uniquely identifies a row in the hostControlTable. Each row in the control table refers to a unique interface of the monitor (a unique subnetwork). The same integer is also used to identify corresponding rows in the hostTable and the hostTime-Table.

- *hostControlDataSource:* identifies the interface and hence the Ethernet subnetwork that is the source of the data for data-table entries defined by this row.

- *hostControlTableSize:* the number of rows in the hostTable that are associated with this row. It is also the number of rows in the hostTimeTable that are associated with this row. This is a read-only object set by the monitor.

- *hostControlLastDeleteTime:* the value of sysUpTime (in the MIB-II systems group) corresponding to the last time that an entry was deleted from the portion of the hostTable associated with this row. The value is 0 if no deletions have occurred.

The relationship between the hostControlTable and the data table hostTable is straightforward. For each interface specified by a row in the hostControlTable, the hostTable contains one row for each MAC address discovered on that interface. Thus, the number of rows in the hostTable can be expressed as:

$$N = \sum_{i=1}^{K} N_i,$$

where

N = number of rows in the hostTable.
i = value of hostControlIndex.
K = number of rows in the hostControlTable.
N_i = value of hostControlTableSize for row i of the hostControlTable.

For example, Figure 7.11 shows an RMON agent with interfaces to two subnetworks (K = 2). On subnetwork X (interface number 1; hostControlIndex = 1), there are three hosts; therefore, once the monitor has learned of the existence of all three hosts, the corresponding value of hostControlTableSize will reach its maximum value of 3 (N_1 = 3). On subnetwork Y, there are 2 hosts (N_2 = 2).

Each row of the hostTable contains statistical data about the corresponding host. The table as a whole is indexed by the MAC address of the host as well as by the interface index. The table includes the following objects:

- *hostAddress:* the MAC address of this host.

- *hostCreationOrder:* an index that defines the relative ordering of the creation time of hosts captured for a particular hostControlEntry. This index takes on a value between 1 and N_i, where N_i is the value of the associated hostControlTableSize (for row i of the hostControl-Table).

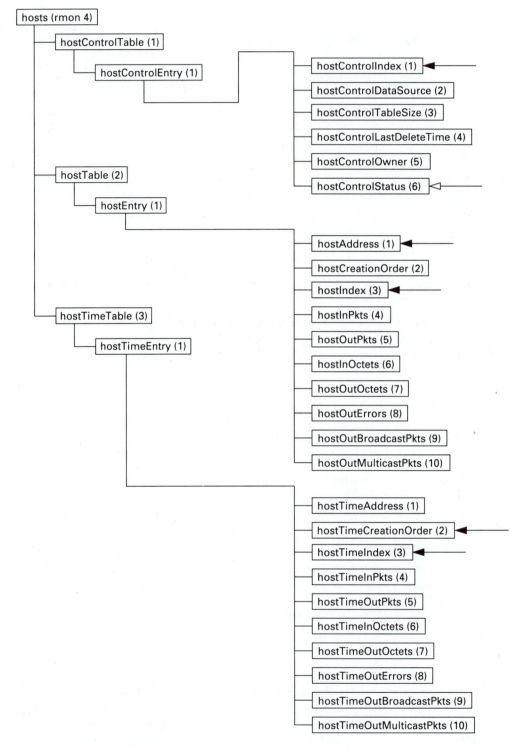

Figure 7.10 RMON Host Group

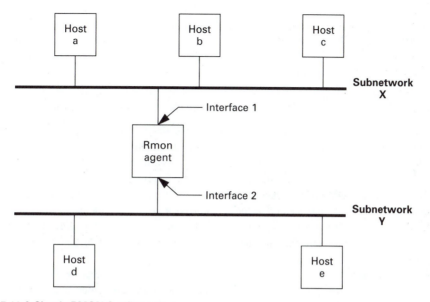

Figure 7.11 A Simple RMON Configuration

- *hostIndex:* the set of collected host statistics of which this entry is a part. The value of this object matches the value of hostControlIndex for one of the rows of the hostControlTable. Thus, all entries in the hostTable with the same value of hostIndex contain statistics for hosts on a single subnetwork.

As can be seen in Figure 7.10, the remaining objects in the hostTable are used to collect basic statistics on traffic into and out of each discovered host.

After a new row is defined in the hostControlTable, the monitor begins to learn MAC addresses on the corresponding interface. Each time a new host is discovered on that interface, a row is added to the hostTable, and the value of hostControlTableSize is incremented by 1. Ideally, the monitor should be able to maintain statistics on all hosts discovered on a subnetwork. However, if the monitor finds itself short of resources, it may delete entries as needed. In that case, the set of rows for that interface functions as a circular buffer. As each new row is added to the set, the oldest row associated with this interface is deleted. The value of hostCreationOrder for each of the existing rows for this interface is decremented by 1, and the new row has a hostCreationOrder value of N_i. This change can potentially cause a problem to a management station if it is "remembering" a host on the basis of its hostCreationOrder number. Therefore, the specification recommends that management stations make use of hostControlLastDeleteTime in the relevant row of the hostControlTable to detect circumstances in which a previous association between a value of hostCreationOrder and a specific row of the hostTable is no longer valid.

The hostTimeTable contains exactly the same information, row by row, as the hostTable but is indexed by the creation order rather than by the host MAC address. This data table has two important uses:

1. The portion of the hostTimeTable associated with a given interface is potentially quite large. The management station can exploit the fact that it knows the size of the portion for each

interface and the size of each row to efficiently pack variables into SNMP GetRequest or GetNextRequest PDUs. Since each row has a unique index that runs from 1 to hostControl-TableSize inclusive, the index values are predictable, and there is no confusion in having multiple packets outstanding.

2. The organization of the hostTimeTable also supports efficient discovery by the management station of new entries for a particular interface without having to download the entire table.

Figure 7.12 illustrates the relationships among the three tables. Each row of the hostControlTable has a unique value of hostControlIndex and a unique value of hostControlDataSource. For each of the K rows of the hostControlTable, there is a set of data rows. These data rows appear in both the hostTable and the hostTimeTable, but with a different ordering for each table.

The host-group specification dictates that there be two logical views of the data: hostTable and hostTimeTable. This does not mean that the monitor must actually implement two separate tables with duplicate information. Depending on the database-management system available at the monitor, it may be possible to store the information only once but provide two logical access methods to the data.

Finally, note that all the information in this group is obtainable directly from each host via MIB-II information in the interfaces group. The reason for using this group instead is that it may not be cost-effective to equip each host on the network with SNMP. Also, the monitor provides a single location of useful information in compact form.

7.2.6   HostTopN Group

The hostTopN group is used to maintain statistics about the set of hosts on one subnetwork that top a list based on some parameter. For example, a list could be maintained of the ten hosts that transmitted the most data during a particular day.

The statistics that are generated for this group are derived from data in the host group. The set of statistics for one host-group object on one interface, or subnetwork, collected during one sampling interval, is referred to as a report. Each report contains the results for only one variable, and that variable represents the amount of change in a host-group object over the sampling interval. Thus, the report lists the hosts on a particular subnetwork with the greatest rate of change in a particular variable.

The hostTopN group consists of one control table and one data table (Figure 7.13). The hostTopNControlTable includes the following fields:

- *hostTopNControlIndex:* an integer that uniquely identifies a row in the hostTopNControlTable. Each row in the control table defines one top-N report prepared for one interface.

- *hostTopNHostIndex:* this value matches a value of hostControlIndex and hostIndex (Figure 7.10). Therefore, this value specifies a particular subnetwork. The top-N report defined by this row of the control table is prepared using the corresponding entries in the hostTable.

- *hostTopNRateBase:* specifies one of seven variables from the hostTable (Figure 7.10); the specified variable is the basis for the hostTopNRate variable in the row of the hostTopNTable defined by this control row. The type of this object is the following:

INTEGER { hostTopNInPkts (1),
         hostTopNOutPkts (2),
         hostTopNInOctets (3),

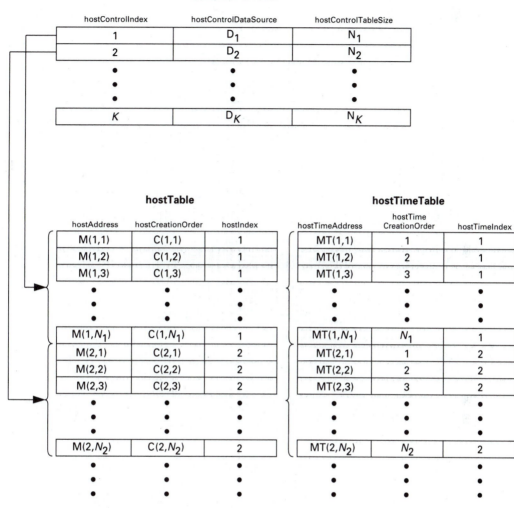

Figure 7.12 An Example of Host Tables

hostTopNOutOctets (4),
hostTopNOutErrors (5),
hostTopNOutBroadcastPkts (6),
hostTopNOutMulticastPkts (7) }

- *hostTopNTimeRemaining:* the number of seconds left in the sampling interval for the report currently being collected.

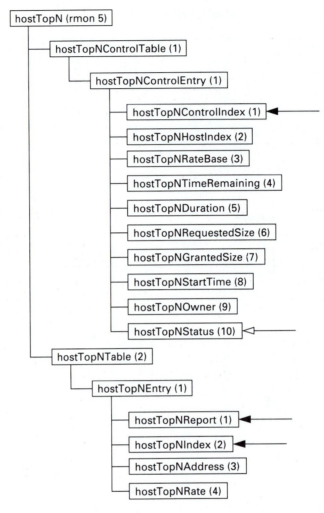

Figure 7.13 RMON HostTopN Group

- *hostTopNDuration:* the sampling interval, in seconds, for this report.

- *hostTopNRequestedSize:* the maximum number of hosts requested for the top-N table for this report.

- *hostTopNGrantedSize:* the maximum number of hosts in the top-N table for this report.

- *hostTopNStartTime:* the value of sysUpTime (in the MIB-II systems group) when this top-N report was last started. In other words, this is the time when the associated hostTopNTime-Remaining object was modified to start the requested report, as explained later in this subsection.

The hostTopNTable includes the following objects:

- *hostTopNReport:* the report of which this entry is a part. The report identified by a particular value of this index is the same report as that identified by the same value of hostTop-NControlIndex.

- *hostTopNIndex:* an index that uniquely identifies one row among all data rows associated with this report. Each row represents a unique host.

- *hostTopNAddress:* the MAC address of this host.

- *hostTopNRate:* the amount of change in the selected variable during this sampling interval. The selected variable is specified by the value of hostTopNRateBase for this report.

The report-preparation process works as follows. To begin, a management station creates a row of the control table to specify a new report. This control entry instructs the monitor to measure the difference between the beginning and ending values of a particular host-group variable over a specified sampling period. The sampling-period value is stored in both hostTopNDuration and hostTopNTimeRemaining. The first value is static; the second value counts the seconds down while the monitor is preparing the report. When hostTopNTimeRemaining reaches 0, the monitor calculates the final results and creates a set of N data rows, indexed by hostTopNIndex, with the top-N hosts listed in decreasing order of the calculated rates.

Once the report is created, it remains as a set of read-only data rows available to the management station. If the management station wishes an additional report for a new time period, it first gets the results of this report and then resets hostTopNTimeRemaining to the value in hostTop-NDuration. This causes the associated data rows to be deleted and a new report to be prepared.

Figure 7.14 illustrates the relationship between the control table and the data table. Each row of the hostTopNControlTable has a unique value of hostTopNControlIndex. The value of host-TopNHostIndex references the relevant row of the hostControlTable in the control group. The value of hostTopNRateBase identifies the host-group variable to be sampled, and hostTop-NGrantedSize indicates how many hosts are to be included in the ranking. For each of the K rows of the hostTopNControlTable, there is a set of rows of the hostTopNTable. Each row in the set of rows gives the MAC address and rate for one host on the subnetwork specified by hostTop-NHostIndex.

7.2.7 Matrix Group

The matrix group is used to record information about the traffic between pairs of hosts on a subnetwork. The information is stored in the form of a matrix. This method of organization is useful for retrieving specific pairwise traffic information, such as finding out which devices are making the most use of a server.

The matrix group consists of three tables: one control table and two data tables (Figure 7.15). The control table, matrixControlTable, includes the following objects:

- *matrixControlIndex:* an integer that uniquely identifies a row in the matrixControlTable. Each row in the control table defines a function that discovers conversations on a particular interface and places statistics about them in the two data tables.

- *matrixControlDataSource:* identifies the interface and hence the subnetwork that is the source of the data in this row.

hostTopNControlTable

hostTopNControlIndex	hostTopNHostIndex	hostTopNRateBase	hostTopNGrantedSize
1	H_1	V_1	N_1
2	H_2	V_2	N_2
•	•	•	•
•	•	•	•
•	•	•	•
K	H_K	V_K	N_K

hostTopNTable

hostTopNReport	hostTopNIndex	hostTopNAddress	hostTopNRate
1	1	$M(1,1)$	$V_1(1)$
1	2	$M(1,2)$	$V_1(2)$
1	3	$M(1,3)$	$V_1(3)$
•	•	•	•
•	•	•	•
•	•	•	•
1	N_1	$M(1,N_1)$	$V_1(N_1)$
2	1	$M(2,1)$	$V_2(1)$
2	2	$M(2,2)$	$V_2(2)$
2	3	$M(2,3)$	$V_2(3)$
•	•	•	•
•	•	•	•
•	•	•	•
2	N_2	$M(2,N_2)$	$V_2(N_2)$
•	•	•	•
•	•	•	•
•	•	•	•

Note: Only selected fields in the control table are shown.

$V_i(j) > V_i(j+1)$.

Figure 7.14 An Example of HostTopN Tables

- *matrixControlTableSize:* the number of rows in the matrixSDTable that are associated with this row. It is also the number of rows in the matrixDSTable that are associated with this row. This is a read-only object set by the monitor.

- *matrixControlLastDeleteTime:* the value of sysUpTime (in the MIB-II systems group) corresponding to the last time that an entry was deleted from the portion of the matrixSDTable and the portion of the matrixDSTable associated with this row. The value is 0 if no deletions have occurred.

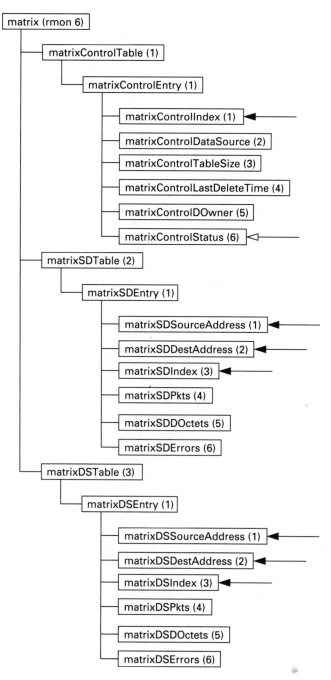

Figure 7.15 RMON Matrix Group

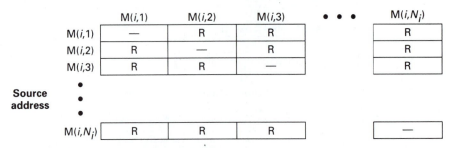

R = row in both matrixSDTable and matrixDSTable.
M(i,j) < M(i, j + 1).

**Figure 7.16 Logical View of the matrixSDTable Rows and the matrixDSTable
Rows Associated with Row *i* of the matrixControlTable**

The matrixSDTable is used to store statistics on traffic from a particular source host to a number of destinations. The table includes the following objects:

- *matrixSDSourceAddress:* the source MAC address.
- *matrixSDDestAddress: the destination MAC address.*
- *matrixSDIndex:* the set of collected matrix statistics of which this row is a part. The set identified by a particular value of this index is the same set as that identified by the same value of matrixControlIndex.

The matrixSDTable is indexed first by matrixSDIndex, then by source address, and then by destination address. The matrixDSTable contains the same information but is indexed first by matrixDSIndex, then by destination address, and then by source address. The interpretation is as follows: Each row of the matrixControlTable identifies a single subnetwork. The matrixSDTable contains two rows for every pair of hosts on that subnetwork that have recently exchanged information: one of the rows reports the traffic in one direction between the two members of the pair; the other row reports the traffic in the opposite direction. The same set of rows also appears in the matrixDSTable. Thus, the management station can easily index the information to find out about the traffic from one host to all others (using the matrixSDTable) or about traffic from all hosts to one particular host (using the matrixDSTable). Figure 7.16 depicts the logical matrix structure that results.

Whenever the monitor detects a new conversation that involves one of the hosts listed in the matrixControlTable, it creates two new rows in both of the data tables. If the limit specified in matrixControlTableSize is reached, then the monitor deletes rows as required. The specification suggests that the monitor delete the least recently used entries first.

Finally, note that, as with the host group, the two data tables in the matrix group contain the same information organized in two different ways. It is permissible to implement this as a single table or as two tables, so long as the logical view presented to the management station is of two data tables.

7.2.8 Filter Group

The filter group provides a means by which a management station can instruct a monitor to observe selected packets on a particular interface (therefore a particular subnetwork). The basic building blocks defined in this group are two kinds of filters: a data filter and a status filter. The *data filter* allows the monitor to screen observed packets on the basis of a bit pattern that a portion of the packet matches (or fails to match); the *status filter* allows the monitor to screen observed packets on the basis of their status (valid, CRC error, etc.). These filters can be combined using logical AND and OR operations to form a complex test to be applied to incoming packets. The stream of packets that pass the test is referred to as a *channel,* and a count of such packets is maintained. In addition, the channel can be configured to generate an event, defined in the event group, when a packet passes through the channel and the channel is in an enabled state. Finally, the packets passing through a channel can be captured if the mechanism is defined in the capture group. The logic defined for a single channel is quite complex. This gives the user enormous flexibility in defining the stream of packets to be counted.

Before examining the structure of the filter group, it is best to present the details of the filter logic and the channel logic.[3]

7.2.8.1 Filter Logic

At the lowest level of the filter logic, a single data filter or status filter defines characteristics of a packet. To begin, let us consider the logic for defining characteristics of a packet, using the following variables:

input	= the incoming portion of a packet to be filtered.
filterPktData	= the bit pattern to be tested for.
filterPktDataMask	= the relevant bits to be tested for.
filterPktDataNotMask	= indicates whether to test for a match or a mismatch.

The actual logical operations are rather complex, and we will approach them step by step. As an initial step, let us suppose that we simply want to test the input against a bit pattern for a match. For example, this could be used to screen for packets with a specific source address. The following expression would hold:

$$(\text{input} \oplus \text{filterPktData}) = 0 \rightarrow \text{match}.$$

In this expression, we take the bitwise exclusive-or of input and filterPktData. The result has a 1 bit only in those positions where input and filterPktData differ. Thus, if the result is all 0s, then there is an exact match. Alternatively, we may wish to test for a mismatch. For example, suppose a LAN consists of a number of workstations and a server; a mismatch test could be used to screen for all packets that did not have the server as a source. The test for a mismatch would be just the opposite of the test for a match:

$$(\text{input} \oplus \text{filterPktData}) \neq 0 \rightarrow \text{mismatch}.$$

---

3. In this discussion, the logical operators AND, OR, NOT, XOR, EQUAL, and NOT-EQUAL are represented by the symbols $\bullet$, $+$, $'$, $\oplus$, $=$, and $\neq$.

So if there is at least one 1 bit in the result, there is a mismatch.

The preceding tests assume that all bits in the input are relevant. There may, however, be some "don't-care" bits, which are not relevant to the filter. For example, we may wish to test for packets with any multicast destination address. Typically, a multicast address is indicated by 1 bit in the address field; the remaining bits of the address field are irrelevant to a test for multicast address. To account for "don't-care" bits, the variable filterPktDataMask is introduced; this variable has a 1 bit in each position that is relevant and 0 bits in those positions considered irrelevant. The tests can be modified as follows:

((input $\oplus$ filterPktData) $\bullet$ filterPktDataMask) $= 0 \rightarrow$ match on relevant bits.
((input $\oplus$ filterPktData) $\bullet$ filterPktDataMask) $\neq 0 \rightarrow$ mismatch on relevant bits.

The XOR operation produces a result that has a 1 bit in every position where there is a mismatch. The AND operation produces a result that has a 1 bit in every *relevant* position where there is a mismatch. If all the resulting bits are 0, then there is an exact match on the relevant bits; if any of the resulting bits is 1, there is a mismatch on the relevant bits.

Finally, we may wish to test for an input that matches in certain relevant bit positions and mismatches in others. For example, one could screen for all packets that had a particular host as a destination (exact match on the DA field) and did not come from the server (mismatch on the SA field). To enable these more complex tests to be performed, filterPktDataNotMask is used. This mask has the following interpretation:

- The 0 bits in filterPktDataNotMask indicate the positions where an exact match is required between the relevant bits of input and filterPktData (all bits match).

- The 1 bits in filterPktDataNotMask indicate the positions where a mismatch is required between the relevant bits of input and filterPktData (at least 1 bit does not match).

For convenience, let us make the following definition:

relevant_bits_different $=$ (input $\oplus$ filterPktData) $\bullet$ filterPktDataMask.

Now, incorporating filterPktDataNotMask into our test for a match, we have:

(relevant_bits_different $\bullet$ filterPktDataNotMask$'$) $= 0 \rightarrow$ successful match.

The test for a mismatch is slightly more complex. If all the bits of filterPktDataNotMask are 0 bits, then no mismatch test is needed.[4] Therefore, the test for a mismatch is as follows:

((relevant_bits_different $\bullet$ filterPktDataNotMask) $\neq 0$) $+$ (filterPktDataNotMask $= 0$) $\rightarrow$
successful mismatch.

The logic for the filter test is summarized in Figure 7.17. The rules can be stated as follows. An incoming packet is to be tested for a bit pattern in a portion of the packet, located at a distance filterPktDataOffset from the start of the packet. The following operations are performed:

---

4.   By the same line of reasoning, if all the bits of filterPktDataNotMask are 1 bits, then no match test is needed. However, in that case, filterPktDataNotMask$'$ is all 0s, and the match test automatically passes: relevant_bits_different $\bullet$ 0 $= 0$.

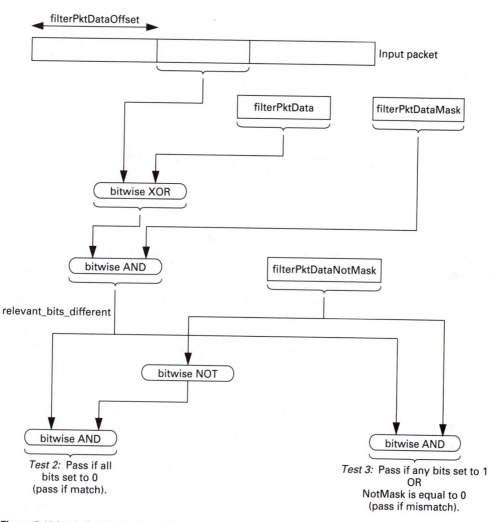

Figure 7.17 Logic for Single Data Filter

1. *Test 1:* As a first test (not shown in the figure), the packet must be long enough so that there are at least as many bits in the packet following the offset as there are bits in filterPktData. If not, the packet fails this filter.

2. *Test 2:* Each bit set to 0 in filterPktDataNotMask indicates a bit position in which the relevant bits of the packet portion should match filterPktData. If there is a match in every desired bit position, then the test is passed; otherwise, the test is failed.

3. *Test 3:* Each bit set to 1 in filterPktDataNotMask indicates a bit position in which the relevant bits of the packet portion should not match filterPktData. In this case, the test is passed if there is a mismatch in at least one desired bit position.

A packet passes this filter if and only if it passes all three tests.

As an example of the use of the filter test, consider that we wish to accept all Ethernet packets that have a destination address of "A5"h (indicates hexadecimal notation) and that do not have a source address of "BB"h. The first 48 bits of the Ethernet packet constitute the destination address, and the next 48 bits of the Ethernet packet constitute the source address. The test can be implemented as follows:

```
filterPktDataOffset   = 0
filterPktData         = "00 00 00 00 00 A5 00 00 00 00 00 BB"h
filterPktDataMask     = "FF FF FF FF FF FF FF FF FF FF FF FF"h
filterPktDataNotMask  = "00 00 00 00 00 00 FF FF FF FF FF FF"h
```

The variable filterPktDataOffset indicates that the pattern matching should start with the first bit of the packet; filterPktData indicates that the pattern of interest consists of "A5"h in the first 48 bits and "BB"h in the second 48 bits; filterPktDataMask indicates that all of the first 96 bits are relevant; and filterPktDataNotMask indicates that the test is for a match on the first 48 bits and a mismatch on the second 48 bits.

The logic for the status filter has the same structure as that for the data filter (Figure 7.17). For the status filter, the reported status of the packet is converted into a bit pattern. This is done as follows: Each error-status condition has a unique integer value, corresponding to a bit position in the status bit pattern. To generate the bit pattern, each error value is raised to a power of 2 and the results added. If there are no error conditions, then the status bit pattern is all 0s. For example, for an Ethernet interface, the following error values are defined:

Bit No.	Error
0	Packet is longer than 1,518 octets.
1	Packet is shorter than 64 octets.
2	Packet experienced a CRC error or an alignment error.

Therefore, an Ethernet fragment would have the status value of 6 ($2^1 + 2^2$).

7.2.8.2   Channel Definition

A channel is defined by a set of filters. For each observed packet, and for each channel, the packet is passed through each of the filters defined for that channel. The way in which these filters are combined to determine whether a packet is accepted for a channel depends on the value of an object associated with the channel, the channelAcceptType. This object has the following syntax:

INTEGER { acceptMatched(1), acceptFailed(2) }

If the value of this object is acceptMatched (1), packets will be accepted for this channel if they pass both the packet-data and packet-status matches of at least one of the associated filters. If the value of this object is acceptFailed (2), packets will be accepted for this channel only if they fail either the packet-data match or the packet-status match of every associated filter.

Figure 7.18 illustrates the logic by which filters are combined for a channel whose accept type is acceptMatched. A filter is passed if both the data filter and the status filter are passed; otherwise, that filter is failed. If we define a pass as a logical 1 and a fail as a logical 0, then the result for a single filter is the AND of the data filter and status filter for that filter. The overall result for a

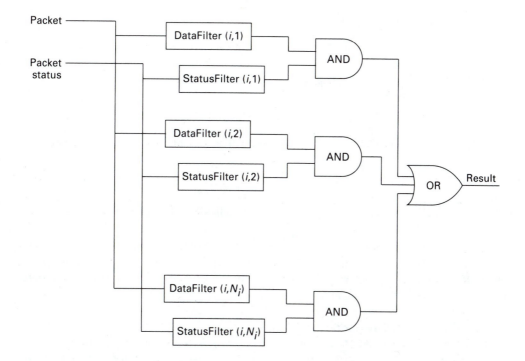

Figure 7.18 Filter Logic for Channel *i* If channelAcceptType = acceptMatched (1)

channel is then the OR of all the filters. Thus, a packet is accepted for a channel if it passes at least one of the associated filter pairs for that channel.

If the accept type for a channel is acceptFailed, then the complement of the function just described is used. That is, a packet is accepted for a channel only if it fails every filter pair for that channel. This would be represented in Figure 7.18 by placing a NOT gate after the OR gate.

7.2.8.3   Channel Operation

The value of channelAcceptType and the set of filters for a channel determine whether a given packet is accepted for a channel or not. If the packet is accepted, then the counter channelMatches is incremented. There are several additional controls associated with the channel: channelData-Control, which determines whether the channel is on or off; channelEventStatus, which indicates whether the channel is enabled to generate an event when a packet is matched; and channel-EventIndex, which specifies an associated event.

If channelDataControl has the value off, then, for this channel, no events may be generated as the result of packet acceptance, and no packets may be captured by the capture group (discussed in the next subsection). If channelDataControl has the value on, then these related actions are possible.

Figure 7.19 summarizes the channel logic. If channelDataControl is on, then an event will be generated if two conditions are met: (1) an event is defined for this channel in channelEventIndex, and (2) channelEventStatus has the value eventReady or eventAlwaysReady. If the event status is eventReady, then each time an event is generated, the event status is changed to eventFired. It

```
procedure packet_data_match;
begin
   if (result = 1 and channelAcceptType = acceptMatched) or
      (result = 0 and channelAcceptType = acceptFailed)
   then begin
      channelMatches := channelMatches +1;
      if channelDataControl = on
      then begin
         if (channelEventStatus ≠ eventFired) and
            (channelEventIndex ≠ 0) then generate_event;
         if (channelEventStatus = eventReady) then channelEventStatus := eventFired
      end;
   end;
end;
```

Figure 7.19 Channel-Operation Logic

then takes a positive action on the part of the management station to re-enable the channel. This mechanism can therefore be used to control the flow of events from a channel to a management station. If the management station is not concerned about flow control, it may set the event status to eventAlwaysReady, where it will remain until explicitly changed.

7.2.8.4   Filter-Group Structure

The filter group consists of two control tables (Figure 7.20). Each row of the channelTable defines a unique channel. Associated with that channel are one or more rows in the filterTable, which define the associated filters.

The channelTable includes the following objects:

- *channelIndex:* an integer that uniquely identifies one row in the channelTable. Each row defines one channel.

- *channelIfIndex:* identifies the monitor interface, and hence the subnetwork, to which the associated filters are applied to allow data into this channel. The value of this object instance is an object identifier that identifies the instance of ifIndex in the interfaces group of MIB-II that corresponds to this interface.

- *channelAcceptType:* controls the action of the filters associated with this channel. If the value of this object is acceptMatched (1), packets will be accepted for this channel if they pass both the packet-data and packet-status matches of at least one of the associated filters. If the value of this object is acceptFailed (2), packets will be accepted for this channel only if they fail either the packet-data match or the packet-status match of every associated filter.

- *channelDataControl:* If this object has the value on (1), then data, status, and events flow through this channel. If this object has the value off (2), data, status, and events do not flow through this channel.

- *channelTurnOnEventIndex:* identifies the event that is configured to turn the associated channelDataControl from off to on when the event is generated. The value of this object identifies an object indexed by eventIndex in the event group. If no such event exists, then no association exists. If no event is intended, this object has the value 0.

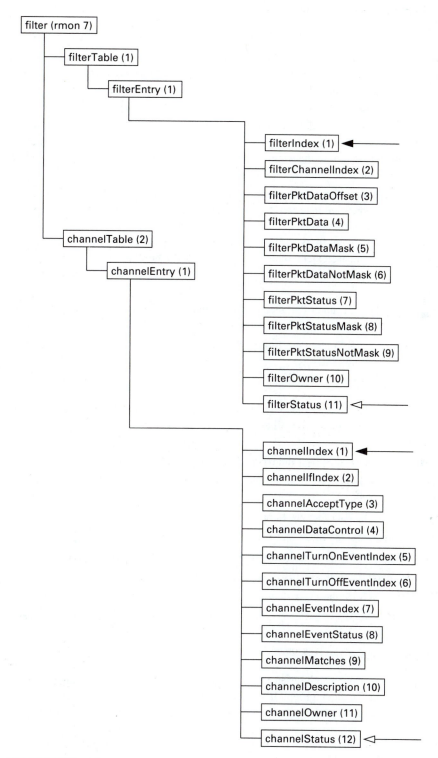

Figure 7.20 RMON Filter Group

- *channelTurnOffEventIndex:* identifies the event that is configured to turn the associated channelDataControl from on to off when the event is generated. The value of this object identifies an object indexed by eventIndex in the event group. If no such event exists, then no association exists. If no event is intended, this object has the value 0.

- *channelEventIndex:* identifies the event that is configured to be generated when the associated channelDataControl is on and a packet is matched. The value of this object identifies an object indexed by eventIndex in the event group. If no such event exists, then no association exists. If no event is intended, this object has the value 0.

- *channelEventStatus:* the event status of this channel. If the channel is configured to generate events when packets are matched, then the value of this object has the following interpretation: When the value is eventReady (1), a single event will be generated for a packet match, after which this object is set to eventFired (2). In the eventFired (2) state, no events are generated. This allows the management station to respond to the notification of an event and then re-enable the object. While the value is eventAlwaysReady (3), every packet match generates an event.

- *channelMatches:* a counter that records the number of packet matches. This counter is updated even when channelDataControl is set to off.

- *channelDescription:* a text description of the channel.

The filterTable includes the following objects:

- *filterIndex:* an integer that uniquely identifies a row in the filterTable. Each such row defines one data filter and one status filter that are to be applied to every packet received on an interface.

- *filterChannelIndex:* identifies the channel of which this filter is a part.

- *filterPktDataOffset:* offset from the beginning of each packet where a match of packet data will be attempted.

- *filterPktData:* the data that are to be matched with the input packet.

- *filterPktDataMask:* the mask that is applied to the match process.

- *filterPktDataNotMask:* the inversion mask that is applied to the match process.

- *filterPktStatus:* the status that is to be matched with the input packet.

- *filterPktStatusMask:* the mask that is applied to the status-match process.

- *filterPktStatusNotMask:* the inversion mask that is applied to the status-match process.

7.2.9 Packet-Capture Group

The packet-capture group can be used to set up a buffering scheme for capturing packets from one of the channels in the filter group. It consists of two tables (Figure 7.21): bufferControlTable, which specifies the details of the buffering function, and captureBufferTable, which buffers the data.

Each row in the bufferControlTable defines one buffer that is used to capture and store packets from one channel. The table includes the following objects:

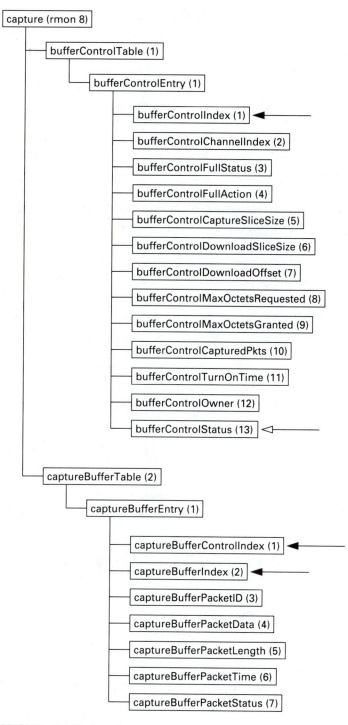

Figure 7.21 RMON Packet-Capture Group

- *bufferControlIndex:* an integer that uniquely identifies a row in the bufferControlTable. The same integer is also used to identify corresponding rows in the captureBufferTable.

- *bufferControlChannelIndex:* identifies the channel that is the source of packets for this row. The value matches that of channelIndex for one row of the channelTable.

- *bufferControlFullStatus:* if the value is spaceAvailable (1), the buffer has room to accept new packets. If the value is full (2), its meaning depends on the value of bufferControlFullAction.

- *bufferControlFullAction:* if the value is lockWhenFull (1), the buffer will accept no more packets after it becomes full. If the value is wrapWhenFull (2), the buffer acts as a circular buffer after it becomes full, deleting enough of the oldest packets to make room for new ones as they arrive.

- *bufferControlCaptureSliceSize:* maximum number of octets of each packet, starting with the beginning of the packet, that will be saved in this capture buffer. If the value is 0, the buffer will save as many octets as possible. The default value is 100.

- *bufferControlDownloadSliceSize:* the maximum number of octets of each packet in this buffer that will be returned in a single SNMP retrieval of that packet.

- *bufferControlDownloadOffset:* the offset of the first octet of each packet in this buffer that will be returned in a single SNMP retrieval of that packet.

- *bufferControlMaxOctetsRequested:* the requested buffer size in octets. A value of -1 requests that the buffer be as large as possible.

- *bufferControlMaxOctetsGranted:* the granted buffer size in octets. This is the maximum number of octets that can be saved, including implementation-specific overhead.

- *bufferControlCapturedPackets:* the number of packets currently in this buffer.

- *bufferControlTurnOnTime:* the value of sysUpTime (in the MIB-II systems group) when this buffer was first turned on.

The data table, captureBufferTable, contains one row for each packet captured. The table includes the following objects:

- *captureBufferControlIndex:* the buffer with which this packet is associated. The buffer identified by a particular value of this index is the same buffer as that identified by the same value of bufferControlIndex.

- *captureBufferIndex:* an index that uniquely identifies this particular packet among all packets associated with the same buffer. This index starts at 1 and increases by 1 as each new packet is captured. Thus, this variable serves as a sequence number for packets in one buffer.

- *captureBufferPacketID:* an index that describes the order of packets that are received on a particular interface. Thus, this variable serves as a sequence number for packets that are captured from one subnetwork, regardless of which buffer or buffers they are stored in.

- *captureBufferPacketData:* the actual packet data stored for this row.

- *captureBufferPacketLength:* the actual length of the packet as received (off the wire). As explained in the following paragraphs, it may be that only a part of the packet is actually stored in this entry.

- *captureBufferPacketTime:* the number of milliseconds that had passed from the time that the buffer was turned on to the time that this packet was captured.

- *captureBufferPacketStatus:* indicates the error status of this packet.

A related set of parameters dictates how much of a packet is stored in the buffer and how much is available for delivery to a management station in one SNMP get or get-next request. For convenience, let's use the following abbreviations:

CS = bufferControlCaptureSliceSize: the maximum number of octets of each packet that will be saved in this capture buffer.

DS = bufferControlDownloadSliceSize: the maximum number of octets of each packet in this buffer that will be returned in an SNMP retrieval of that packet.

DO = bufferControlDownloadOffset: the offset of the first octet of each packet in this buffer that will be returned in an SNMP retrieval of that packet.

PL = captureBufferPacketLength: the actual length of the packet (off the wire).

PDL = length of captureBufferPacketData: the actual packet data stored for this row of captureBufferTable.

The following expression holds:[5]

$$PDL = MIN [PL, CS].$$

This packet (if $PL \geq CS$) or packet slice (if $PL < CS$) is stored as a single OCTET STRING in one row of the captureBufferTable. However, this OCTET STRING may well be longer than will fit in a single SNMP message. The parameters DO and DS provide a tool to retrieve the captured packet in pieces. If you set DO to 0 and DS to 100, then get captureBufferPacketData, you will get octets 0..MIN (PDL-1, 99); then if you set DO to 100, then get captureBufferPacketData, you will get octets 100..MIN(PDL-1, 199); and so on. If the station reads "off the end of the packet," it gets a zero-length string.

Typically, a management station would set DO to 0, DS to 100 or so, then make a complete pass through the table getting PL, the first 100 bytes of the packet, and maybe PacketStatus, etc. Then, the station would set DO to 100 and make another pass through to get more of each packet, and so on until all the captured data for those packets of interest had been retrieved.

Figure 7.22 illustrates the relationship between the control table and the data table. Each row of the bufferControlTable has a unique value of bufferControlIndex. The value of buffer-ControlChannelIndex references the relevant row of the channelTable. For each of the K rows of the bufferControlTable, there is a set of rows of the captureBufferTable, which constitutes the buffer for that control row. In the example, the first buffer either is not full or has just become full, and the second buffer is acting as a circular buffer, storing only the last N_2 packets.

---

5. Unfortunately, the specification is not clear on these relationships. In fact, the definition of capture-BufferPacketData seems to say that PDL = MIN [(PL − DO), (CS − DO), DS]. This is not correct and is not what is intended.

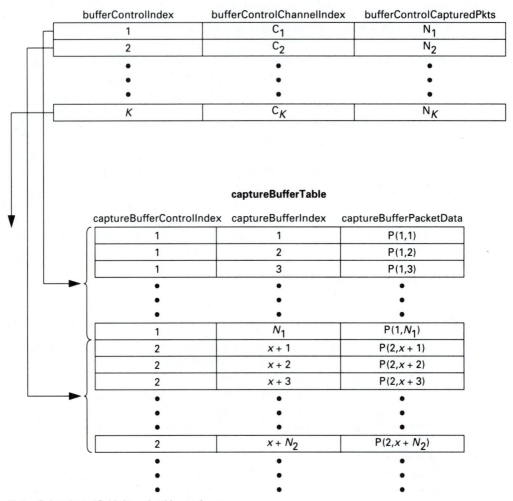

Note: Only selected fields in each table are shown.

Figure 7.22 An Example of Packet-Capture Tables

7.2.10   Event Group

The event group supports the definition of events. An event is triggered by a condition located elsewhere in the MIB, and an event can trigger an action defined elsewhere in the MIB. An event may also cause information to be logged in this group and may cause an SNMP trap message to be issued.

The event group consists of one control table and one data table (Figure 7.23). The control table, eventTable, contains event definitions. Each row of the table contains the parameters that

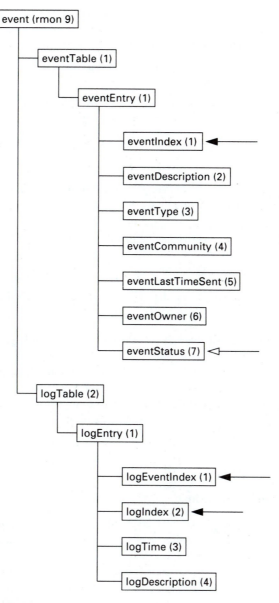

Figure 7.23 RMON Event Group

describe an event to be generated when certain conditions are met. The table includes the following objects:

- *eventIndex:* an integer that uniquely identifies a row in the eventTable. The same integer is also used to identify corresponding rows in the logTable.

- *eventDescription:* a textual description of this event.

- *eventType:* takes on the value none (1), log (2), snmp-trap (3), or log-and-trap (4). In the case of log, an entry is made in the log table for each event. In the case of snmp-trap, an SNMP trap is sent to one or more management stations for each event.

- *eventCommunity:* If an SNMP trap is to be sent, this object specifies the community of management stations to receive the trap.

- *eventLastTimeSent:* the value of sysUpTime (in the MIB-II systems group) at the time this event entry last generated an event.

If an event is to be logged, entries will be created in the associated logTable, which includes the following objects:

- *logEventIndex:* identifies the event that generated this log entry. The value of this index refers to the same event as that identified by the same value of eventIndex.

- *logIndex:* an index that uniquely identifies this particular log entry among all entires associated with the same event type. This index starts at 1 and increases by 1 as each new packet is captured.

- *logTime:* the value of sysUpTime when this log entry was created.

- *logDescription:* an implementation-dependent description of the event that activated this log entry.

The conditions for an event to occur are defined in other RMON groups. One key use of the event group is in conjunction with the alarm group. The alarm group can define rising-threshold and falling-threshold events that are referenced by indexing into the eventTable. Also, the filter group can reference an event that will occur when a packet is captured.

An event that is defined in this group can be used to trigger activity related to another group. For example, an event can trigger turning a channel on or off.

7.3   PRACTICAL ISSUES

7.3.1   Packet-Capture Overload

RMON is so rich that there is the very real danger of overloading the monitor, the internet between the monitor and the management station, and/or the management station. The network manager must avoid the temptation of picking every possible cookie out of the jar.

As an extreme example, the user could set it up so that the management station would retrieve every single packet or even every single packet header in a defined channel. If the internet is moderately busy, this could put quite a stress on one or more of the affected subnetworks. Also, the monitor may not have the speed to capture all these packets while at the same time producing summary information and monitoring alarms. If it does not, the monitor may drop packets or fail to perform one of its other duties adequately.

A preferred alternative is to do as much of the analysis as possible locally, at the monitor, and send much more aggregated results to the management station. Thus, in addition to directly retrieving data from the RMON MIB via SNMP, the user could implement applications on the monitor to do some of the analytical work and then send the results to the management station via file transfer.

The packet-capture feature of RMON can be useful if used intelligently. If, for example, a manager detects a specific problem area in the internet, it may be possible to zero in on a few nodes or a particular protocol as suspects and then, with appropriate filtering, use RMON to gather some raw data for diagnosis. For example, a not-uncommon problem on a network is for all the workstations to begin broadcasting one after another, a phenomenon known as a broadcast storm. Typically, the device that initiated the storm is the malfunctioning device or was triggered by a malfunctioning device. By noting the pattern of the storm, the network manager can usually pin this down. RMON can then be used to capture packets to and from the suspect device, for analysis by the network manager at the management station.

Even if the manager can develop RMON requests with some precision, it is still necessary to be aware of the trade-offs involved. A complex filter will allow the monitor to capture and report a limited amount of data, thus avoiding undue burden on the network. However, complex filters consume quite a bit of processing power at the monitor; if too many filters are defined, the monitor may not be able to keep up. This is especially true if its subnetworks are busy, which is probably the time when one is most interested in monitoring.

7.3.2   Network Inventory

As was just mentioned, it may not be practical or efficient to equip every device on an internet with SNMP. In addition, it may not even be practical or efficient to proxy every device. In that case, RMON provides a handy way to maintain an inventory of all devices on the network that are capable of sending or receiving packets of data (i.e., things like modems would not be included). RMON monitors, by watching traffic on the various subnetworks, can quickly provide an inventory of network devices.

In fact, RMON is useful for this purpose even for SNMP-equipped devices. The SNMP design philosophy discourages agents from initiating communication strictly for the purpose of letting management stations know they exist. Thus, it may be difficult for a management station to determine the identity of all the agents. RMON solves this problem.

7.3.3   Hardware Platform

Any platform that is to be used as an RMON monitor must, of course, support SNMP. In addition, the logic to implement all of the RMON functionality, which is considerable, is added. The choice of platform is wide. It can be a personal computer or workstation dedicated solely to the RMON function. Alternatively, it can be a nondedicated host computer, an interconnect device such as a bridge or router, or even a network-management station.

The choice of dedicated or nondedicated platform will depend on the size and complexity of the given subnetwork. For those subnetworks that have relatively light traffic and do not absolutely require 100 percent uptime, a nondedicated platform may be adequate and would save some money. An example of such a subnetwork is a departmental LAN. For such networks, a good choice for a platform may be an interconnect device, such as a hub or router or bridge. For a high-traffic subnetwork, such as an FDDI backbone, a dedicated platform is almost a necessity.

7.4 SUMMARY

An important addition to the SNMP framework is the RMON (remote network-monitoring) MIB. RMON defines a set of managed objects that are useful for supporting the remote-monitoring function. In addition, the specification of the RMON MIB has the effect of defining a set of functions for remote monitoring. The strength of the RMON approach is that it is compliant with the current SNMP framework; it requires no enhancements to the protocol.

In the context of the RMON MIB, the term *remote monitoring* refers to the use of an agent device connected to a broadcast network to collect statistics concerning traffic on that network. Typically, an agent is only responsible for management information that relates to the agent's device. Without a remote-monitoring function, it is difficult, if not impossible, for a manager to construct a profile of the activity on an individual subnetwork as a whole.

The RMON MIB consists of the following groups:

- *statistics:* maintains low-level utilization and error statistics for each subnetwork monitored by the agent.
- *history:* records periodic statistical samples from information available in the statistics group.
- *alarm:* allows the person at the management console to set a sampling interval and an alarm threshold for any counter or integer recorded by the RMON agent.
- *host:* contains counters for various types of traffic to and from hosts attached to the subnetwork.
- *hostTopN:* contains sorted host statistics that report on the hosts that top a list based on some parameter in the host table.
- *matrix:* shows error and utilization information in matrix form, so the operator can retrieve information for any pair of network addresses.
- *filter:* allows the monitor to observe packets that match a filter. The monitor may capture all packets that pass the filter or simply record statistics based on such packets.
- *packet capture:* governs how data are sent to a management console.
- *event:* a table of all events generated by the RMON agent.

In addition, the RMON MIB defines some useful conventions for row creation and deletion.

8
Secure SNMP

Although SNMP has become the most widely used standardized network-management scheme, it has one major flaw that has inhibited its use: it provides no security facilities. Specifically, there is no capability either to authenticate the source of a management message or to prevent eavesdropping. The existence of the community name in the message header is useless from the standpoint of security. An attacker can observe a message and learn a community name for the target device for subsequent use.

Because of the lack of authentication capability, SNMP is vulnerable to attacks that can modify or disable a network configuration. As a result, many vendors have chosen not to implement the Set command, effectively crippling the management suite by reducing it to a monitoring facility.

A set of RFCs (requests for comment), known informally as secure SNMP (S-SNMP),[1] has been issued to resolve these security problems. Table 8.1 lists these RFCs. The first three, issued in July 1992, provide a security enhancement to SNMP. In addition, S-SNMP makes use of a general-purpose security-related algorithm known as MD5 (Message Digest 5), which was issued as RFC 1321 in April 1992.

Unfortunately, S-SNMP is not compatible with SNMP. The format of the message header is different, and obviously, many of the procedures have been modified. However, the format of the SNMP PDUs (protocol data units) remains the same, and no new PDUs have been added (but see subsection 6.2.4.4 for an interesting consequence of this). Thus, the transition to S-SNMP from SNMP is a manageable effort.

One final point about transition. The security enhancements defined in the S-SNMP documents have been adopted for SNMPv2, described in chapters 9 and 10, with some modifications. SNMPv2 provides both functional and security enhancements to SNMP, whereas S-SNMP provides only security enhancements. Within the Internet Engineering Task Force (IETF), a consensus has emerged that a single transition to the next stage of SNMP evolution is desirable rather than a two-stage

---

1. The designation *S-SNMP* is not ''official'' but is used in this chapter for convenience.

Table 8.1 The Secure SNMP Documents

RFC	Title	Date
1351	SNMP Administrative Model	July 1992
1352	SNMP Security Protocols	July 1992
1353	Definitions of Managed Objects for Administration of SNMP Parties	July 1992
1321	The MD5 Message-Digest Algorithm	April 1992

transition. Since the security aspects of SNMPv2 are not entirely compatible with those of S-SNMP, and since some of the modifications made to those enhancements in SNMPv2 are deemed superior, there is some reluctance to encourage implementation of S-SNMP. However, the immediate security needs of some users may result in deployment of S-SNMP products. In any case, perhaps the best way to understand the substantial changes to SNMP required to provide security is to look first at S-SNMP, which provides a ''pure'' security modification, and then look at SNMPv2, which has an improved but quite similar security facility. That is the approach adopted in this book.

We begin this chapter with an overview of the requirements for security in an SNMP environment and the approach taken in S-SNMP. The next four sections deal with the four RFCs listed in Table 8.1. The appendixes to the chapter summarize key security concepts.

8.1 OVERVIEW

In examining any approach to network and communications security, three concepts must be considered:

1. *Security threat:* any action that compromises the security of information owned by an organization.

2. *Security service:* a communications service that enhances the security of an organization's data-processing systems and information transfers. The service is intended to counter security threats.

3. *Security mechanism:* a communications mechanism that is design to detect, prevent, or recover from a security threat.

In this section, we consider these three concepts from the viewpoint of the objectives of S-SNMP.

8.1.1 Security Threats

To understand the various types of threats to security, we need to have a definition of security requirements. Computer and network security addresses four requirements:

1. *Secrecy:* The information in a computer system and transmitted information must only be accessible for reading by authorized parties. This type of access includes printing, displaying, and other forms of disclosure, including simply revealing the existence of an object.

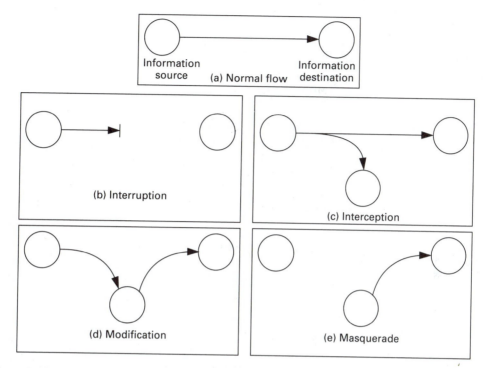

Figure 8.1 Security Threats

2. *Authenticity:* The origin of a message must be correctly identified, with an assurance that the identity is not false.

3. *Integrity:* Computer-system assets and transmitted information must be modifiable only by authorized parties. Modification includes writing, changing, changing status, deleting, and creating.

4. *Availability:* Computer-system assets must be available to authorized parties when needed.

The types of threats to the security of a computer system or network are best characterized by viewing the function of the computer system as that of providing information. In general, there is a flow of information from a source, such as a file or a region of main memory, to a destination, such as another file or a user. This normal flow is depicted in Figure 8.1, part (a). The remainder of the figure shows four general categories of threats:

1. *Interruption:* An asset of the system is destroyed or becomes unavailable or unusable. This is a threat to *availability*. Examples include the destruction of a piece of hardware, such as a hard disk; the cutting of a communication line; or the disabling of the file-management system.

2. *Interception:* An unauthorized party gains access to an asset. This is a threat to *secrecy*. The unauthorized party could be a person, a program, or a computer. Examples include wiretapping to capture data in a network or the illicit copying of files or programs.

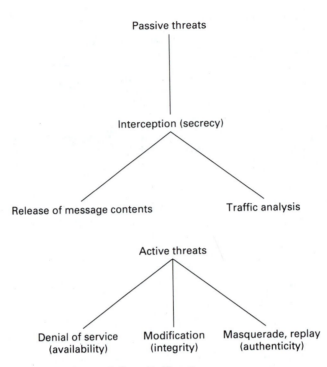

Figure 8.2 Active and Passive Network Security Threats

3. *Modification:* An unauthorized party not only gains access but tampers with an asset. This is a threat to *integrity*. Examples include changing values in a data file, altering a program so that it performs differently, or modifying the content of messages being transmitted in a network.

4. *Masquerade:* An unauthorized party inserts counterfeit objects into the system. This is a threat to *authenticity*. Examples include the insertion of spurious messages in a network or the addition of records to a file.

These threats can usefully be categorized in terms of passive threats and active threats (Figure 8.2).

8.1.1.1   Passive Threats

Passive threats are in the nature of eavesdropping on or monitoring of an organization's transmissions. The attacker's goal is to obtain information that is being transmitted. Two types of threats are involved here: release of message contents and traffic analysis.

The threat of *release of message contents* is clearly understood by most observers. A telephone conversation, an electronic-mail message, or a transferred file may contain sensitive or confidential information. We would like to prevent the attacker from learning the contents of these transmissions.

The second passive threat, *traffic analysis,* is more subtle. Suppose that we had a way of masking the contents of messages or other information traffic so that an attacker, even if he or she captured the message, would be unable to extract the information from the message. The common technique for doing this is encryption, discussed in Appendixes 8A and 8B. Even if we had such protection in place, it might still be possible for an attacker to observe the pattern of these messages. The attacker can determine the location and identity of communicating hosts and can also observe the frequency and length of messages being exchanged. This information might be useful in guessing the nature of the communication that is taking place.

Passive threats are very difficult to detect, since they do not involve any alteration of the data. However, it is feasible to prevent these attacks from being successful. Thus, the emphasis in dealing with passive threats is on prevention rather than detection.

8.1.1.2   Active Threats

The second major category of threat, *active threats,* involve some modification of the data stream or the creation of a false stream. We can subdivide these threats into four categories: masquerade, replay, modification of messages, and denial of service.

A *masquerade* takes place when one entity pretends to be a different entity. A masquerade attack usually includes one of the other forms of active attack. For example, authentication sequences can be captured and replayed after a valid authentication sequence has taken place. This may be done to enable an authorized entity with few privileges to obtain extra privileges by impersonating an entity that has those privileges.

Replay involves the passive capture of a data unit and its subsequent retransmission to produce an unauthorized effect.

Modification of messages simply means that some portion of a legitimate message is altered or that messages are delayed or reordered, in order to produce an unauthorized effect. For example, a message meaning "Allow John Smith to read confidential file *accounts*" is modified to mean "Allow Fred Brown to read confidential file *accounts.*"

The *denial of service* involves preventing or inhibiting the normal use or management of communications facilities. This attack may have a specific target; for example, an entity may suppress all messages directed to a particular destination (e.g., the security-audit service). Another form of service denial is the disruption of an entire network, either by disabling the network or by overloading it with messages so as to degrade performance.

The characteristics of active threats are the opposite of those of passive threats. Whereas passive attacks are difficult to detect, measures are available to prevent their success. On the other hand, it is quite difficult to absolutely prevent active attacks, since this would require physical protection of all communications facilities and paths at all times. Instead, the goal with respect to active attacks is to detect these attacks and to recover from any disruption or delays they might cause. Because the detection has a deterrent effect, this may also contribute to prevention.

8.1.1.3   Threats in the Context of SNMP

The preceding description of security threats can be applied in the SNMP context to identify the specific threats involved in the use of SNMP for network management. The following threats can be identified:

- *Masquerade:* Some entity that is not authorized to perform certain management operations may attempt to perform those operations by assuming the identity of an authorized entity.

- *Modification of information:* An entity may alter an in-transit message generated by an authorized entity in such a way as to effect unauthorized management operations, including the setting of object values. The essence of this threat is that an unauthorized entity could change any management parameter, including those related to configuration, operations, and accounting.

- *Message sequence and timing modification:* SNMP is designed to operate over a connection-less transport protocol. There is a threat that SNMP messages could be reordered, delayed, or replayed (duplicated) to effect unauthorized management operations. For example, a message to reboot a device could be copied and replayed later.

- *Disclosure:* An entity may observe exchanges between a manager and an agent and thereby learn the values of managed objects and learn of notifiable events. For example, the observation of a set command that changes passwords would enable an attacker to learn the new passwords.

- *Denial of service:* An attacker may prevent exchanges between a manager and an agent.

- *Traffic analysis:* An attacker may observe the general pattern of traffic between managers and agents.

S-SNMP is intended to secure against the first four threats in the preceding list, but not the last two. The lack of a counter to the denial-of-service threat may be justified on two grounds: first, denial-of-service attacks are in many cases indistinguishable from the type of network failures with which any viable network-management application must cope as a matter of course; and second, a denial-of-service attack is likely to disrupt all types of exchanges and is a matter for an overall security facility, not one embedded in a network-management protocol.

8.1.2   S-SNMP Security Services

To counter those security threats considered relevant to SNMP, the following security services are provided by S-SNMP:

- *Data integrity:* assures that messages are received as sent, with no duplication, insertion, modification, resequencing, or replays

- *Data-origin authentication:* provides for the corroboration of a message's source

- *Data confidentiality:* assures that information is not made available or disclosed to unauthorized individuals, entities, or processes

The mechanisms used in S-SNMP are such that data-origin authentication and data integrity are both provided by the same set of mechanisms. Thus, the provision of one of these two services implies the provision of the other. Further, both of these services are required to be performed at all times. Data confidentiality is an optional service that may be added to the other two services in a given implementation.

8.1.3   S-SNMP Security Mechanisms

To provide the three security services defined in the preceding list, S-SNMP includes the following mechanisms:

- *Data integrity:* A message-digest algorithm is used to calculate a 128-bit digest over the appropriate portion of an SNMP message. This digest is included with the message to assure that there has been no modification. The message also includes a timestamp whose value is based on the maintenance of loosely synchronized clocks among managers and agents. The recipient of a message uses the timestamp to verify that the message is recent and to determine the proper sequencing of multiple messages. The timestamp can also be used to detect message replay. No protection is provided against unauthorized message destruction. S-SNMP uses the MD5 message-digest algorithm.

- *Data-origin authentication:* The message digest is actually calculated over the appropriate portion of an SNMP message and a secret value prefixed to that message. The value must be known *a priori* to sender and recipient and is not included in the message. The use of the secret value prevents a third party from appending the correct digest to a false message.

- *Data confidentiality:* To provide confidentiality, an appropriate portion of an SNMP message is encrypted using a symmetric encryption algorithm. S-SNMP uses the DES (data-encryption standard) algorithm.

8.2   ADMINISTRATIVE MODEL

S-SNMP is based on a new administrative model for SNMP that replaces the concept of community. Recall that in SNMP, the message header included a community name that could be used by two or more SNMP entities as a sort of unsecured password. To provide for the security services outlined in subsection 8.1.2, two basic changes are needed.

First, instead of a single identifier (community name) that is shared by source and destination, it is essential for secure communication to specifically identify a source and a destination for any exchange. Authentication and message integrity depend on the source: it is the source's responsibility to include information in any message that assures that the origin is authentic, and it is the source's responsibility to perform the required functions to ensure message integrity. However, encryption, which plays a role in both authentication and message confidentiality, depends on the destination. That is, encryption must be done in such a way that only the intended destination can perform the decryption. Finally, access control depends on both source and destination. That is, each destination may have a distinct access policy for each potential source.

Each message must therefore identify both the source and the destination. Furthermore, it is insufficient to equate the source with a sending SNMP entity and the destination with a receiving SNMP entity. Each SNMP entity may behave differently, from a security point of view, depending on the identity of the other SNMP entity involved in an exchange. Put another way, the role of an SNMP entity depends on the context of its operation. The concept of role is captured in S-SNMP as the SNMP party. An SNMP party is defined as an execution context of an SNMP protocol entity. Any protocol entity may include multiple party identities.

Thus, the first major change in moving from SNMP to S-SNMP is the use of two party names (source and destination) instead of a single community name in the message header. The second change is that mechanisms must be employed to secure the message transmission. The mechanisms used depend on whether authentication or privacy or both are required.

We turn now to an examination of the elements of the S-SNMP administrative model. This is followed by several examples.

8.2.1 Elements of the Model

The key elements of the administrative model are SNMP parties, MIB views, and the access control policy. We examine each of these in turn.

8.2.1.1 SNMP Parties

RFC 1351 (July 1992) includes the following definition of an SNMP party:

> A SNMP party is a conceptual, virtual execution context whose operation is restricted (for security or other purposes) to an administratively defined subset of all possible operations of a particular SNMP protocol entity. Whenever a SNMP protocol entity processes a SNMP message, it does so by acting as a SNMP party and is thereby restricted to the set of operations defined for that party. The set of possible operations specified for a SNMP party may be overlapping or disjoint with respect to the sets of other SNMP parties; it may also be a proper or improper subset of all possible operations of the SNMP protocol entity.

Each SNMP protocol entity includes one or more SNMP parties. The essence of a party consists of the following elements:

- A single unique party identity.
- A single authentication protocol and associated parameters by which all SNMP messages originated by this party are authenticated and that provide message integrity. This information relates to the behavior of the party as a source.
- A single privacy protocol and associated parameters by which all protocol messages received by the party are protected. This information relates to the behavior of the party as a destination.
- A single MIB (management information base) view that defines that portion of the local MIB available to this party.
- A logical network location for the party, defined by a transport protocol and transport address.

The elements in the preceding list can be translated into a set of variables that contain all the information needed to completely define a party. Figure 8.3 includes an ASN.1 definition of the required variables. The first five variables contain general information about the party:

1. *partyIdentity:* unique identifier of this party.
2. *partyTDomain:* a transport domain that indicates the transport service used to support SNMP for this party. An example is rfc1351Domain, which specifies SNMP over UDP (user datagram protocol) using SNMP parties.
3. *partyTAddr:* the transport-service address for this party.
4. *partyProxyFor:* identifies another SNMP party or some other management entity, called the proxied entity, for which this party acts as proxy. The value noProxy indicates that this party responds to received management requests by entirely local mechanisms.
5. *partyMaxMessageSize:* the length in octets of the largest SNMP message that this party will accept.

The next seven variables contain values whose significance is specific to the authentication protocol:

```
SnmpParty ::= SEQUENCE {
                        partyIdentity           OBJECT IDENTIFIER,
                        partyTDomain            OBJECT IDENTIFIER,
                        partyTAddr              OCTET STRING,
                        partyProxyFor           OBJECT IDENTIFIER,
                        partyMaxMessageSize     INTEGER,
                        partyAuthProtocol       OBJECT IDENTIFIER,
                        partyAuthClock          INTEGER,
                        partyAuthLastMsg        INTEGER,
                        partyAuthNonce          INTEGER,
                        partyAuthPrivate        OCTET STRING,
                        partyAuthPublic         OCTET STRING,
                        partyAuthLifetime       INTEGER,
                        partyPrivProtocol       OBJECT IDENTIFIER,
                        partyPrivPrivate        OCTET STRING,
                        partyPrivPublic         OCTET STRING  }


AclEntry ::= SEQUENCE {
                        aclTarget               OBJECT IDENTIFIER,
                        aclSubject              OBJECT IDENTIFIER,
                        aclPrivileges           INTEGER  }
```

**Figure 8.3 ASN.1 Definitions for the SNMP Administrative Model
(RFC 1351)**

1. *partyAuthProtocol:* indicates the authentication protocol and mechanism used by this party to authenticate the origin and integrity of its outgoing messages. The value noAuth indicates that messages generated by this party are not authenticated.

2. *partyAuthClock:* represents a current time as kept locally for this party.

3. *partyAuthLastMsg:* a timestamp that represents a local time associated with the most recent authentic message generated by this party.

4. *partyAuthNonce:* represents a monotonically increasing integer associated with the most recent authentic message generated by this party.[2] The nonce associated with a particular message distinguishes it among all others transmitted in the same unit time interval.

5. *partyAuthPrivate:* a secret value needed to support the authentication protocol. It may be a secret value used in a message digest, a conventional-encryption key, or the private key in a public-key encryption scheme.

6. *partyAuthPublic:* represents any public value that may be needed to support the authentication protocol. It may be a public key in a public-key encryption scheme.

7. *partyAuthLifetime:* an administrative upper bound on acceptable delivery delay for messages generated by this party.

The final three variables contain values whose significance is specific to the privacy protocol:

---

2.   The following definitions are useful in understanding the purpose of the nonce component: ''**Nonce:** The present or particular occasion. **Nonce word:** A word occurring, invented, or used just for a particular occasion.'' From *The American Heritage Dictionary of the English Language,* 3d ed. (Boston: Houghton Mifflin, 1992).

1. *partyPrivProtocol:* indicates the privacy protocol and mechanism by which all messages received by this party are protected from disclosure. The value noPriv indicates that messages received by this party are not protected from disclosure.

2. *partyPrivPrivate:* a secret value needed to support the privacy protocol. It may be a conventional-encryption key or the private key in a public-key encryption scheme.

3. *partyPrivPublic:* represents any public value that may be needed to support the privacy protocol. It may be a public key in a public-key encryption scheme.

Several points concerning the preceding list are of interest. First, some but not all of the information in this list should be available to other managers or agents. The way in which this information is organized to permit such access is discussed in section 8.4. Next, note that it is possible to declare that authentication is not used and that privacy is not used. At a minimum, at least one party at each SNMP entity must be configured as noAuth to permit clock synchronization, as explained in section 8.3. In practice, authentication would typically be used for all other parties. With respect to privacy, a privacy protocol may only be used if an authentication protocol is also used.

The current version of S-SNMP requires the use of MD5 for authentication and DES for encryption. The administrative structure permits other selections to be made and is thus more flexible than the current use of that structure. Finally, all of the preceding information is reflected in parameters found in the message header of an SNMP message. The encapsulated PDUs are the same in format and semantics as those defined for the original SNMP.

The administrative model dictates that every SNMP entity maintain a local database that represents all SNMP parties known to it. This includes:

- *Local parties:* the set of parties whose operation is realized by the local SNMP entity; that is, the set of "roles" for this SNMP entity

- *Proxied parties:* the set of parties for proxied entities that this SNMP entity represents

- *Remote parties:* the set of parties whose operation is realized by other SNMP entities with which this SNMP entity is capable of interacting

In addition, every SNMP entity maintains a local database that represents an access-control policy, defining the access privileges accorded to known SNMP parties.

8.2.1.2   MIB View

Recall that the managed objects in a local database can be organized into a hierarchy, or tree, based on the object identifiers of the objects. This local database comprises a subset of all object types defined according to the Internet-standard structure of management information (SMI) and includes object instances whose identifiers conform to the SMI conventions.

For purposes of S-SNMP, the concept of a view subtree is introduced. A view subtree is simply a node in the MIB's naming hierarchy plus all of its subordinate elements. More formally, a view subtree may be defined as the set of all object instances that have a common ASN.1 OBJECT IDENTIFIER prefix to their names. The longest common prefix of all the instances in the subtree is the object identifier of the parent node of that subtree.

Associated with each party is an MIB view, consisting of a set of view subtrees. Each view subtree in the MIB view is specified as being included or excluded. That is, the MIB view either includes or excludes all object instances contained in that subtree. In addition, a view mask is defined in order to reduce the amount of configuration information needed when fine-grained access control is required (e.g., access control at the object-instance level). The conventions for defining view subtrees are examined in section 8.4.

8.2.1.3 Access-Control Policy

Each party has associated with it an MIB view, which defines the local object instances known to that party. The party is configured so that access to the object instances within its MIB view is controlled on the basis of the remote party requesting access. Therefore, an access-control policy consists of three elements:

1. *Target:* an SNMP party performing management operations as requested by the subject party

2. *Subject:* an SNMP party that requests that management operations be performed by the target party

3. *Policy:* the allowable operations, defined in terms of allowable PDUs, that the target will perform on behalf of the subject

This three-part structure is defined in Figure 8.3. The policy is simply a list of the PDUs that may be sent from the subject to the target. For convenience, each PDU is assigned an integer that is a power of 2, so that a policy is represented by the sum of the integers of the allowed PDUs. The assignments are:

Get	1
GetNext	2
GetResponse	4
Set	8
Trap	16

For example, if the subject party is allowed read-only access to the object instances of the target party's MIB view, then the value of the policy is 3 (1 + 2), indicating that Get and GetNext PDUs may be sent.

8.2.2 Application of the Model

Several examples of the administrative model, taken from RFC 1351, are included in this subsection.

8.2.2.1 Nonsecure Minimal Agent Configuration

As the simplest possible example, let us consider the case of a nonsecure agent, which provides neither authentication nor privacy services.

Table 8.2 depicts the administrative information that is known both to the agent and to the manager. For each element of party information, there is one value for the agent and one for the manager. The access-control information includes one set of entries for communication in each direction (agent to manager, manager to agent).

In this example, the agent includes a party with the identifier gracie that operates at UDP port 161 at IP (internet protocol) address 1.2.3.4. The manager includes a party with the identifier george that operates at UDP port 2001 at IP address 1.2.3.5.

Now suppose that the manager party george wishes to retrieve certain object-instance values from the agent party gracie with a Get command. The manager consults the party table and

Table 8.2 Administrative Information for a Nonsecure Minimal Agent

(a) Party Information

partyIdentity	gracie (agent)	george (manager)
partyTDomain	rfc1351Domain	rfc1351Domain
partyTAddr	1.2.3.4, 161	1.2.3.5, 2001
partyProxyFor	noProxy	noProxy
partyAuthProtocol	noAuth	noAuth
partyAuthClock	0	0
partyAuthLastMsg	0	0
partyAuthPrivate	''''	''''
partyAuthPublic	''''	''''
partyAuthLifetime	0	0
partyPrivProtocol	noPriv	noPriv
partyPrivPrivate	''''	''''
partyPrivPublic	''''	''''

(b) Access Information

aclTarget	aclSubject	aclPrivileges
gracie	george	3
george	gracie	20

determines that no authentication protocol is used by george and no privacy protocol is required by gracie. The manager therefore simply constructs an SNMP message that identifies the two parties and contains the Get PDU, and issues it to the agent at the destination-party address (IP address 1.2.3.4, UDP port 161).

When the Get message is received at the agent, the identities of the two parties are extracted from the message header. The agent determines that gracie does not require privacy and therefore assumes that the incoming message is not protected from disclosure and need not be decrypted. The agent then determines that george does not use an authentication protocol and therefore accepts the message as authentic with no further processing.

The agent consults the access information to determine whether george is permitted to issue a Get to gracie. The value of aclPrivileges for george-to-gracie communication is 3, which includes Get and GetNext, so the Get is accepted. Assuming that the requested object instances are in the MIB view, the request is processed in the normal manner and a GetResponse is generated.

The agent determines that no authentication protocol is used by gracie and no privacy protocol is required by george. The agent therefore simply constructs an SNMP message that identifies the two parties and contains the GetResponse PDU, and issues it to george.

When the GetResponse is received at the manager, the identities of the two parties are extracted from the message header. The manager determines that george does not require privacy and therefore assumes that the incoming message is not protected from disclosure and need not be decrypted. The manager then determines that gracie does not use an authentication protocol and

Table 8.3 Administrative Information for a Secure Minimal Agent

(a) Party Information

partyIdentity	ollie (agent)	stan (manager)
partyTDomain	rfc1351Domain	rfc1351Domain
partyTAddr	1.2.3.4, 161	1.2.3.5, 2001
partyProxyFor	noProxy	noProxy
partyAuthProtocol	md5AuthProtocol	md5AuthProtocol
partyAuthClock	0	0
partyAuthLastMsg	0	0
partyAuthPrivate	"01234567891BCDEF"	"GHIJKL0123456789"
partyAuthPublic	""	""
partyAuthLifetime	500	500
partyPrivProtocol	desPrivProtocol	desPrivProtocol
partyPrivPrivate	"MNOPQR0123456789"	"STUVWX0123456789"
partyPrivPublic	""	""

(b) Access Information

aclTarget	aclSubject	aclPrivileges
ollie	stan	3
stan	ollie	20

therefore accepts the message as authentic with no further processing. Finally, the manager consults the access information and determines that gracie may issue GetResponse and Trap PDUs (4 + 16 = 20), and therefore, the manager may accept the incoming GetResponse.

8.2.2.2   Secure Minimal Agent Configuration

Let us now consider a case in which authentication is performed by both manager and agent using the MD5 algorithm and privacy is required by both manager and agent using the DES algorithm. Table 8.3 contains the corresponding information. The table shows the secret value used by the MD5 algorithm and the secret key used by the DES algorithm. Note that different values and keys are used for communication in the two directions. Also note that these values and keys would normally not be printed or displayed for human use but would be maintained in the database in a protected manner for use only by authorized S-SNMP entities.

8.2.2.3   Public-Key Configuration

Finally, let us consider an example in which public-key encryption is used for authentication[3] and in which privacy is not provided. Table 8.4 indicates the administrative information that represents such a configuration. Part (a) is the party information known to the agent; part (b) is the information known to the manager; and part (c) is the common access-control information.

---

3.   See Appendix 8B for a discussion of several techniques for the use of public-key encryption for authentication.

Table 8.4 Administrative Information for a Public-Key Configuration

(a) Party Information for Agent

partyIdentity	ollie (agent)	stan (manager)
partyTDomain	rfc1351Domain	rfc1351Domain
partyTAddr	1.2.3.4, 161	1.2.3.5, 2001
partyProxyFor	noProxy	noProxy
partyAuthProtocol	pkAuthProtocol	pkAuthProtocol
partyAuthClock	0	0
partyAuthLastMsg	0	0
partyAuthPrivate	''0123456789ABCDEF''	''''
partyAuthPublic	''''	''AABBCCDDEEFFGGHH''
partyAuthLifetime	500	500
partyPrivProtocol	noPriv	noPriv
partyPrivPrivate	''''	''''
partyPrivPublic	''''	''''

(b) Party Information for Management Station

partyIdentity	ollie (agent)	stan (manager)
partyTDomain	rfc1351Domain	rfc1351Domain
partyTAddr	1.2.3.4, 161	1.2.3.5, 2001
partyProxyFor	noProxy	noProxy
partyAuthProtocol	pkAuthProtocol	pkAuthProtocol
partyAuthClock	0	0
partyAuthLastMsg	0	0
partyAuthPrivate	''''	''IIJJKKLLMMNNOOPP''
partyAuthPublic	''GHIJKLMNOPQRSTUV''	''''
partyAuthLifetime	500	500
partyPrivProtocol	noPriv	noPriv
partyPrivPrivate	''''	''''
partyPrivPublic	''''	''''

(c) Access Information

aclTarget	aclSubject	aclPrivileges
ollie	stan	3
stan	ollie	20

In this example, the agent's private key is 0123456789ABCDEF, and its public key is GHIJKLMNOPQRSTUV, while the manager's private key is IIJJKKLLMMNNOOPP, and its public key is AABBCCDDEEFFGGHH.

8.3   SECURITY PROTOCOLS

We begin with a look at the overall message format and then examine the associated security protocols.

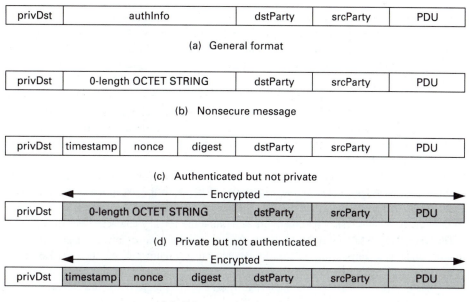

Figure 8.4 S-SNMP Message Formats

8.3.1 S-SNMP Messages

As with SNMP, in S-SNMP, information is exchanged between a management station and an agent in the form of an SNMP message. Each message includes a message header and one of five types of protocol data units; the PDUs for S-SNMP are the same as for SNMP. The message structure is depicted informally in Figure 8.4, and the ASN.1 definition is reproduced in Figure 8.5.

```
SnmpMgmtCom ::= [1] IMPLICIT SEQUENCE {
                    dstParty              OBJECT IDENTIFIER,
                    srcParty              OBJECT IDENTIFIER,
                    pdu                   PDUs }


SnmpAuthMsg ::= [1] IMPLICIT SEQUENCE {
                    authInfo              ANY, --defined by authentication protocol
                    authData              SnmpMgmtCom }


SnmpPrivMsg ::= [1] IMPLICIT SEQUENCE {
                    privDst               OBJECT IDENTIFIER,
                    privData              [1] IMPLICIT OCTET STRING }


AuthInformation::= [1] IMPLICIT SEQUENCE {
                    authTimestamp         INTEGER (0..2147483647),
                    authNonce             INTEGER (0..2147483647),
                    authDigest            OCTET STRING, }
```

Figure 8.5 ASN.1 Definitions for the SNMP Security Protocols (RFC 1352)

The S-SNMP message header consists of four fields. The dstParty and srcParty fields contain the object identifiers of the destination and source parties, respectively. The authInfo field contains information relevant to the authentication protocol. The privDst field repeats the object identifier of the destination party. All four fields are required in all message headers.

Figure 8.4 also provides details of the message header for four different security contexts. If the message is nonsecure (not authenticated and not private), then the authInfo field consists of the ASN.1 encoding of an octet string of zero length. Note that this is not the same as simply omitting the field, due to the ASN.1 encoding. If the message is authenticated but not private, then the authInfo field consists of three subfields, as shown in Figure 8.4, part (c); the significance of these subfields is discussed later in this section.

Parts (d) and (e) of Figure 8.4 show the message format when privacy is provided. In this case, the entire message, including the header and PDU, with the exception of the privDst field, is encrypted. The privDst field must remain unencrypted so that the destination SNMP entity can determine the destination party and therefore determine the privacy characteristics of the message.

The overall S-SNMP framework allows for any combination of privacy and authentication; therefore, under the framework, all the formats shown in Figure 8.4 are allowed. However, the current version of S-SNMP specifically requires the use of authentication when privacy is used. This implies that the message format indicated by part (d) of Figure 8.4 is not allowed.

8.3.1.1   Transmission of an S-SNMP Message

This subsection describes the general procedures followed by an S-SNMP entity for preparing and transmitting SNMP messages, independent of the specific authentication and privacy protocols that may be used. In the next subsection, we look at the specific protocols employed in the current version of S-SNMP.

An SNMP entity performs the following actions to transmit one of the five PDU types to another SNMP entity:

1. An SnmpMgmtCom value (Figure 8.5) is prepared. The dstParty and srcParty values are the object identifiers of the destination and source parties, respectively. The pdu value is constructed using the ASN.1 structure defined in RFC 1157.

2. An SnmpAuthMsg value (Figure 8.5) is prepared. The local database is consulted to determine the authentication protocol and its associated parameters for the sending party. If the authentication protocol for the originating SNMP party is noAuth, then the authInfo value is an OCTET STRING of zero length. Otherwise, the authInfo value is constructed according to the specified authentication protocol. This value is prepended to the SnmpMgmtCom.

3. An SnmpPrivMsg value (Figure 8.5) is prepared. The privDst value is the object identifier of the destination party. The local database is consulted to determine the privacy protocol and its associated parameters for the receiving party. If the privacy protocol for the receiving SNMP party is noPriv, then the privData value is the SnmpAuthMsg value. Otherwise, the privData value is the encrypted value of SnmpAuthMsg.

4. The SnmpPrivMsg is passed to the transport layer using the transport address and transport domain for the receiving party.

Figure 8.6 depicts the transmission procedure in general terms. The details depend on the specific authentication and privacy protocols, if any, that are used.

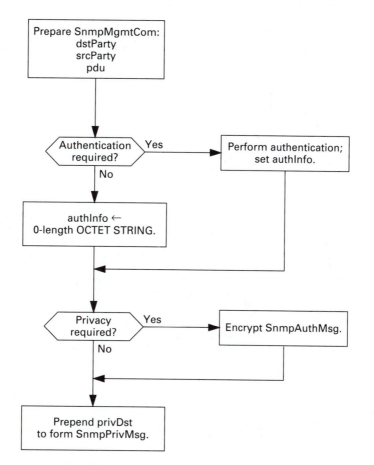

Figure 8.6 Generic Transmission Diagram

8.3.1.2   Reception of an S-SNMP Message

An S-SNMP entity performs the following actions upon reception of an S-SNMP message:

1. If the received message does not match the syntax of a valid SnmpPrivMsg, it is discarded.

2. The local database is consulted for information about the party identified by the privDst value. If the party is not included in the local database, or if the party's transport domain and transport address do not match those of the incoming message, then the message is discarded.

3. If the privacy protocol for the destination SNMP party is other than noPriv, then the privData value is decrypted according to the privacy protocol.

4. If the SnmpAuthMsg does not match the syntax of a valid SnmpAuthMsg, it is discarded. If the dstParty value is not the same as the privDst value, the message is discarded.

5. The local database is consulted for information about the party identified by the srcParty value. If the party is not included in the local database, then the message is discarded.

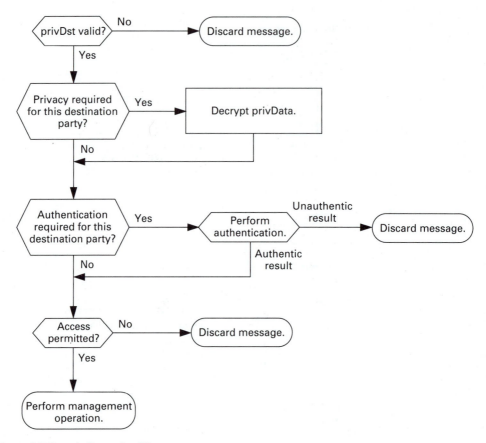

Figure 8.7 Generic Reception Diagram

6. If the authentication protocol for the originating SNMP party is other than noAuth, then the SnmpAuthMsg is evaluated according to the authentication protocol; if the message is evaluated as not authentic, it is discarded.

7. The local database is consulted for information about the access privileges of the originating party with respect to the receiving party. If the received PDU is not allowed, then it is discarded; if the discarded PDU is Get, GetNext, or Set, a response indicating an error is generated.

8. If the proxied party is identified as noProxy, then the management operation indicated by the received PDU is performed by the receiving SNMP entity with respect to the MIB view of the receiving SNMP party. Otherwise, the management operation is performed by the generation of a corresponding request to the proxied party on behalf of the receiving party.

Figure 8.7 depicts the reception procedure in general terms. The details depend on the specific authentication and privacy protocols, if any, that are used.

8.3.2   Digest-Authentication Protocol

The specific authentication mechanism chosen for the current version of S-SNMP is the digest-authentication protocol. It provides for verification of a received message's integrity (i.e., the message received is the message sent) and for authentication of the message's orgin.

In essence, the authentication procedure is as follows. A message digest is computed over the message to be sent (SnmpMgmtCom) prefixed by a secret value, using the MD5 message algorithm. The message, plus the message digest (but not the secret value), is transmitted. On reception, the message digest is recomputed using the incoming message and a local copy of the secret value. If the incoming message digest matches the calculated message digest, the received message is declared authentic. The use of the message digest guarantees integrity, and the use of a secret value guarantees origin authentication.

We now turn to the details of the authentication protocol, considering first transmission and then reception.

8.3.2.1   Generation of an Authenticated S-SNMP Message

Recall from Figure 8.5 that an SnmpAuthMsg includes an authInfo field for authentication. For the digest-authentication protocol, authInfo has the type AuthInformation, which consists of three components:

1. *authTimestamp:* represents the time of generation of this message according to the partyAuthClock (Figure 8.3) of the SNMP party that is the source party. The granularity of the clock, and therefore of this timestamp, is 1 second.

2. *authNonce:* this value is used to permit multiple distinct messages to be sent within the granularity of 1 second. The value of authNonce is a non-negative integer. Successive values for successive messages are values from a monotonically increasing sequence number that is reset for each new authTimestamp value.

3. *authDigest:* represents the digest computed over an appropriate portion of the message, where the message is temporarily prefixed with a secret value for the purpose of computing the digest.

Consider that a message is to be sent from party a on one system to party b on another system. The message-generation process consists of the following steps:

1. The authTimestamp value is set to the current value of partyAuthClock.a; that is, to the value of the party clock for the sending party.

2. If the partyAuthLastMsg.a value is equal to partyAuthClock.a, then the last message sent had the same timestamp as this message. In that case, partyAuthNonce.a is incremented. Otherwise, partyAuthNonce.a is set to 0, and partyAuthLastMsg.a is set to partyAuthClock.a.

3. The authNonce value is set to the current value of partyAuthNonce.a.

4. The authDigest value is temporarily set to the secret value. The message digest is computed over SnmpAuthMsg. The message-digest value is placed in authDigest.

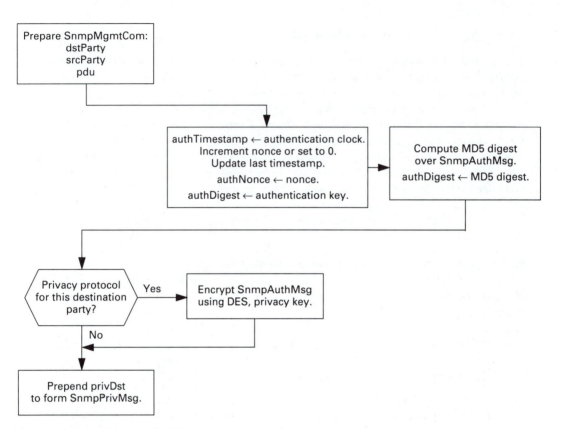

Figure 8.8 Transmission of S-SNMP Message

5.   If a privacy protocol is in use, the resulting SnmpAuthMsg is encrypted.

6.   The destination-party identifier is placed in privDst to form an SnmpPrivMsg.

Figure 8.8 summarizes the procedure.

8.3.2.2   Reception of an Authenticated S-SNMP Message

The procedure to be followed upon reception of an S-SNMP message is somewhat more complex to describe than that for message generation, since various error-checking functions must be taken into account. The procedure is summarized in Figure 8.9. Again, consider that a message is sent from party a on one system to party b on another system. The message-reception process consists of the following steps:

1.   If the privDst value is not valid, the message is discarded.

2.   If a privacy protocol is in use, the privData value is decrypted to obtain the SnmpAuthMsg.

3.   If the ASN.1 type of the authInfo component is not AuthInformation, or if dstParty does not match privDst, or if srcParty is not known, the message is discarded.

4.   If the authTimestamp value does not satisfy the criteria for ordered delivery and timeliness, the message is rejected. The ordered-delivery requirement simply states that messages between

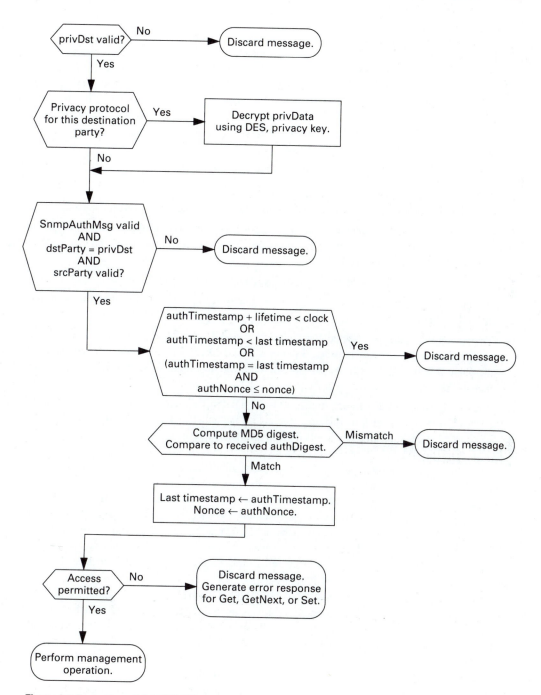

Figure 8.9 Reception of S-SNMP Message

two parties are only accepted in the order in which they were sent; if a message arrives that is "older" than another message that has already arrived, the message is rejected. This ordered-delivery requirement is met if the message timestamp is greater than the timestamp of the preceding message or if the message timestamp is equal to that of the preceding message and the message nonce is greater than that of the preceding message. Using values from the incoming message and from the SnmpParty data for the source party stored at the destination system, the preceding conditions can be expressed as follows. A message is properly sequenced if:

$$(\text{authTimestamp} > \text{partyAuthLastMsg.a})$$

$$\text{OR}$$

$$((\text{authTimestamp} = \text{partyAuthLastMsg.a}) \text{ AND } (\text{authNonce} > \text{partyAuthNonce.a})).$$

The timeliness criterion states that the message must be received within a reasonable period of time that does not exceed an administratively set value. This criterion can be expressed as follows. A message is timely if:

$$\text{partyAuthClock.a} - \text{authTimestamp} \leq \text{partyAuthLifetime.a}.$$

Put another way, the age of the message at the time of receipt must be less than the maximum allowable lifetime.

5. The authDigest value is extracted and temporarily stored. The authDigest value is temporarily set to the secret value. The message digest is computed over SnmpAuthMsg and compared to the value that was stored (the value that arrived in the incoming message). If the two values match, the message is accepted as authentic.

6. The locally stored value of partyAuthLastMsg.a is set to the authTimestamp value. Similarly, partyAuthNonce.a is set to authNonce. Finally, if the authTimestamp exceeds the local value of partyAuthClock.a, the latter is advanced to the authTimestamp value.

The relationship between partyAuthClock, partyAuthLifetime, and authTimestamp is illustrated in Figure 8.10. Part (a) of the figure shows the relationship that exists for a message that is authentic in terms of timeliness. Part (b) shows the case of an unauthentic message. Part (c) illustrates the fact that the timestamp of the incoming message may actually exceed the current value of partyAuthClock for the sending party as maintained at the destination. From a logical point of view, this indicates that a message arrives "before" it is sent. Of course, this logical impossibility is due to a mismatch in clocks. When this condition occurs, the clock at the destination is advanced to equal the incoming timestamp.

The lifetime value for a party should be chosen to be as small as possible given the accuracy of the clocks involved, round-trip communication delays, and the frequency with which clocks are synchronized. If the lifetime value is set too small, authentic messages will be rejected as unauthentic. On the other hand, a large lifetime increases the vulnerability to malicious delays of messages.

It is important to note that the generation of the message depends on the SnmpParty values (Figure 8.3) of the source party that are stored by the sending SNMP entity, where the source party resides, whereas the authentication of the message at the destination depends on the SnmpParty values *for the source party* that are stored at the receiving SNMP entity, where the destination party resides. The values in the two instances of SnmpParty may therefore differ.

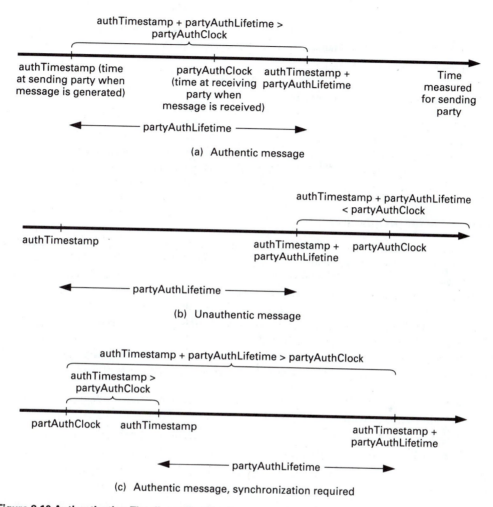

Figure 8.10 Authentication Timeliness Requirement

In terms of the relationship between the two "versions" of SnmpParty for a particular party, we can group the elements into three categories:

1. Those elements that are administratively configured and should therefore always have the same value at both source and destination. These include partyIdentity, partyTDomain, partyTAddr, partyProxyFor, partyMaxMessageSize, partyAuthProtocol, partyAuthPrivate, partyAuth-Lifetime, partyPrivProtocol, partyPrivPrivate, and partyPrivPublic.

2. Those elements whose values are changed at the source when the source party generates a new message and are later updated at the destination when that message arrives. These include partyAuthLastMsg and partyAuthNonce. The value of partyAuthClock may also be updated in this fashion, but this is a "fallback" strategy.

3. The element partyAuthClock. A specific technique is required to maintain a level of synchronization between two different instances of the same clock for the same party. This technique is discussed later in this section.

8.3.3   Symmetric Privacy Protocol

The specific privacy mechanism chosen for the current version of S-SNMP is the symmetric privacy protocol. It provides for protection from disclosure of a received message (i.e., only the intended recipient and the sender are able to read the message). The mechanism for providing such protection is conventional encryption, which requires that the source and destination parties share the same encryption key. The data-encryption standard (DES) is the encryption algorithm used.

8.3.4   Secret Distribution

Associated with each party at each SNMP entity are as many as two secret keys: the secret value used for the MD5 authentication algorithm and the encryption key used for the DES privacy algorithm. Some means is needed for distributing these secret values to local databases to permit communication. Initially, at least some keys must be manually distributed to all management stations and all agents. However, the standard recommends that the process of key distribution be software-controlled to the maximum extent possible. For this purpose, a recommended configuration and key distribution procedure are provided.

The S-SNMP standard recommends that each management station and each agent be initially configured with a minimal set of six parties. At the agent, the set consists of the following:

1. A local SNMP party (an agent party) with no authentication protocol (partyAuthProtocol = noAuth) and no privacy protocol (partyPrivProtocol = noPriv)

2. A remote SNMP party (a manager party) with no authentication protocol (partyAuthProtocol = noAuth) and no privacy protocol (partyPrivProtocol = noPriv)

3. A local SNMP party with the MD5 authentication protocol (partyAuthProtocol = md5AuthProtocol) and no privacy protocol (partyPrivProtocol = noPriv)

4. A remote SNMP party with the MD5 authentication protocol (partyAuthProtocol = md5AuthProtocol) and no privacy protocol (partyPrivProtocol = noPriv)

5. A local SNMP party with the MD5 authentication protocol (partyAuthProtocol = md5AuthProtocol) and the DES privacy protocol (partyPrivProtocol = desPrivProtocol)

6. A remote SNMP party with the MD5 authentication protocol (partyAuthProtocol = md5AuthProtocol) and the DES privacy protocol (partyPrivProtocol = desPrivProtocol)

The corresponding set of information for the six parties is stored at the management station, with the local and remote designations reversed (Figure 8.11). The last two parties in the preceding list can be used to configure all other parties. The following procedure could be used for each agent system:

1. Configure the management station and the agent with the six parties defined in the preceding list.

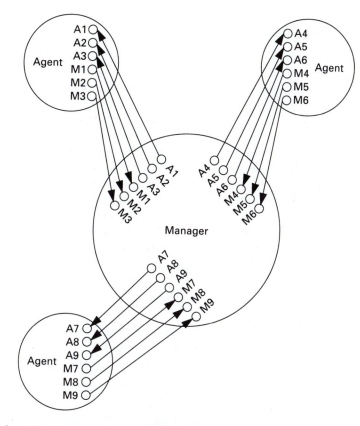

Figure 8.11 Minimal Configuration of Parties for Manager with Three Agents

2. Manually assign secret keys for the parties that use authentication and the parties that use both authentication and privacy.

3. Change the secret keys that were manually configured using an exchange between the two parties that share a privacy protocol.

4. For all new parties to be configured, assign secret keys using an exchange between the original two parties that share a privacy protocol.

5. Periodically change the secret values of each SNMP party in the agent and the corresponding SNMP party in the management station using an exchange between the original two parties that share a privacy protocol.

Initial update or assignment of secret values and subsequent update of secret values is done by means of the authenticated, private exchange of a Set command from the manager and a response from the agent. The frequency with which secrets should be changed is a local administrative matter. In general, the more frequently a secret is used, the more frequently it should be changed.

8.3.5 Clock Synchronization

When a party is first configured, its clock is set to 0 at the same time that secret values are set for the party. Subsequently, every time that a management station updates the secret keys for a party, it also resets the clock to 0. Thus, each time that the secrets are changed, a new epoch begins.

Once a clock has been set, it is incremented once per second for the SNMP entity where the clock is locally stored. That is, each partyAuthClock in a system's MIB, for both local and remote parties, is incremented once per second by that system. There are, however, two "versions" of a party's clock, one stored with the party information at the management station and one stored with the party information at the agent. Thus, there is the potential for drift between the two versions.

The danger in clock drift, or skew, is that it may cause an incorrect result to be produced by the authentication algorithm. To understand the problems caused by clock skew, let us consider the transmission of a message from party a in system A to party b in system B. For the moment, it is irrelevant which party is the manager and which is the agent; the authentication logic is the same in both cases. We introduce the following notation:

$$partyAuthClock.a(A) = \text{the value of partyAuthClock of party a as stored by the SNMP entity at system A.}$$

$$partyAuthClock.a(B) = \text{the value of partyAuthClock of party a as stored by the SNMP entity at system B.}$$

$$partyAuthLifetime.a = \text{the value of partyAuthLifetime of party a as stored by the SNMP entities at system A and system B.}$$

Now, suppose that a message is transmitted from party a to party b. Further suppose that at the time of transmission, $partyAuthClock.a(A) = n$ and that it takes k seconds for the message to be delivered to party b. We can consider three cases:

1. *Case 1:* At the time of transmission, $partyAuthClock.a(B) = n$. There is no clock skew. In this case, the message will be accepted as authentic if the following condition holds:

    authTimestamp + partyAuthLifetime.a > partyAuthClock.a(B)

    or: $n + partyAuthLifetime.a > n + k$

    or: $k < partyAuthLifetime.a$.

    Thus, the message is accepted if the transmission time is less than the allotted lifetime. This is the intended authentication test.

2. *Case 2:* At the time of transmission, $partyAuthClock.a(B) = n + j$. There is a clock skew, with the clock at party b running "faster" than the clock at party a. Put another way, messages from party a will apparently have an "old" timestamp. Using the same derivation as for the preceding case, the authentication test is the following:

    $k < partyAuthLifetime.a - j$.

    Thus, we have made the authentication test tougher and effectively reduced the allowable lifetime. This can lead to a "false rejection." That is, because of the clock skew, a message that should be accepted as authentic may be rejected.

3. *Case 3:* At the time of transmission, $partyAuthClock.a(B) = n - j$. There is a clock skew, with the clock at party b running "slower" than the clock at party a. Now, the authentication test is the following:

    $k < partyAuthLifetime.a + j$.

Thus, we have made the authentication test looser and effectively increased the allowable lifetime. This can lead to a "false acceptance." That is, because of the clock skew, a message that should be rejected as unauthentic may be accepted.

Clearly, then, mechanisms are needed that can correct clock skew. The general strategy must be to advance the clock that is behind, as opposed to decreasing the value of the clock that is ahead. The reason that it is undesirable to decrease the value of the clock that is ahead is that when the value of a party clock is decreased, messages that have been sent with a timestamp value in the range between the new, smaller value and the old, larger value may be replayed.

To avoid the dangers of clock skew, it is the responsibility of the management station to keep the two versions synchronized by advancing the slower clock. For each clock for which it is responsible, the management station periodically checks the two clock values and resynchronizes as necessary. Actually, the synchronization process is applied to pairs of parties that interact. For any pair of parties, four possible conditions can occur that require correction:

1. The manager's version of the agent's clock is greater than the agent's version of the agent's clock.

2. The manager's version of the manager's clock is greater than the agent's version of the manager's clock.

3. The agent's version of the agent's clock is greater than the manager's version of the agent's clock.

4. The agent's version of the manager's clock is greater than the manager's version of the manager's clock.

Returning to the three clock-skew cases listed previously, conditions 2 and 3 equate to case 3. Therefore, these conditions may lead to a false acceptance. Conditions 1 and 4 equate to case 2; therefore, these conditions may lead to a false rejection.

Conditions 2 and 3 are automatically corrected when an authentic message is processed. Recall from the discussion of the digest-authentication protocol that when a message is received, if the authTimestamp exceeds the local value of partyAuthClock, the latter is advanced to the auth-Timestamp value. This rule is referred to as *selective clock acceleration* in the standard. Therefore, when an agent receives a message from a manager, and the authTimestamp in the message exceeds the local value of partyAuthClock for the sending manager party, the clock is advanced and condition 2 is corrected. And when a manager receives a message from an agent, and the auth-Timestamp in the message exceeds the local value of partyAuthClock for the sending agent party, the clock is advanced and condition 3 is corrected.

Because selective clock acceleration corrects conditions 2 and 3, the clock-synchronization procedure does not provide for adjustments in those cases.

To detect and correct conditions 1 and 4, the management station periodically performs the following sequence of steps for every pair of parties:

1. The manager saves the values of partyAuthClock for the two parties agentParty and mgrParty in temporary locations.

2. The manager uses an unauthenticated Get to retrieve the values of partyAuthClock for agentParty and mgrParty from the agent. The retrieval must be unauthenticated, since the manager does not know whether the clocks are synchronized, and an authenticated request may be rejected if synchronization is violated.

3. If the manager's value for the agentParty clock exceeds the agent's value by more than the amount of the communication delay between the two protocol entities, then condition 1 is assumed. To approximate condition 1, the recommended estimate of communication delay is one-half the partyAuthLifetime value for this agentParty. Thus, condition 1 is assumed if:

$$\text{saved\_agent\_clock} - \text{retrieved\_agent\_clock} > \frac{\text{partyAuthLifetime}}{2}.$$

4. If the agent's value for the mgrParty clock exceeds the manager's value, then condition 4 is manifest. Condition 4 is assumed if:

$$\text{retrieved\_manager\_clock} > \text{saved\_manager\_clock}.$$

    If condition 4 is manifest, the manager advances its value of the mgrParty clock to match the agent's value.

5. If condition 1 is manifest, the manager sends an authenticated Set operation to the agent that advances the agent's value of the agentParty clock to equal the manager's value.

6. The manager uses an authenticated Get to retrieve the values of partyAuthClock for agentParty and mgrParty from the agent. The retrieval must be authenticated in order for the manager to verify that the clock values are properly synchronized.

Note that step 4 must be completed before step 5; otherwise, the agent may treat the set message of step 5 as unauthentic.

One final aspect of clock synchronization has to do with the maximum value of a clock. The standard recommends that the maximum value of a clock be set at the maximum potential value of the variable $(2^{32} - 1)$ minus the partyAuthLifetime. When a party's clock reaches this value, it must halt there until reset by the manager. The manager will perform the reset at the same time that it updates the secret keys for the party.

Table 8.5 summarizes the events that cause changes to a party clock.

8.4 MANAGED OBJECTS

The S-SNMP standard includes an MIB to represent SNMP parties, defined in RFC 1353. This MIB is incorporated into MIB-II with subtree identifiers of 20 and 21. The objects in the S-SNMP MIB are organized into four groups:

1. SNMP party public database group

2. SNMP party secrets database group

3. SNMP access-privileges database group

4. MIB-view database group

All four groups are mandatory for those SNMP implementations that realize the security framework and security protocols.

In addition, RFC 1353 defines object identifiers that are used for defining party information. Figure 8.12 contains the ASN.1 definitions provided in RFC 1353, and Figure 8.13 shows the structure of this MIB. Note that each group consists of a single table. The partyPublic group plus

Table 8.5 Changes to partyAuthClock for Party a

Event	Action	Comment
Configuration.	partyAuthClock.a: = 0	When party a is first configured by creating a new row in the partyTable, partyAuthClock.a is initialized to 0.
System clock advances 1 second.	**if** partyAuthClock.a < max_time_value **then** partyAuthClock.a: = partyAuth Clock.a + 1	Clock is automatically incremented once per second until the maximal time value, when it halts.
Clock skew detected by message reception.	**if** authTimestamp > partyAuthClock.a **then** partyAuthClock.a: = auth-Timestamp	This is the selective clock-acceleration mechanism.
Clock skew detected by management query.	partyAuthClock.a in manager (agent) advanced to equal partyAuthClock.a in agent (manager)	Manager uses a set operation to advance one version of the clock to equal another.
Maximal time value reached.	partyAuthClock.a: = 0	When partyAuthClock.a is reset after reaching its maximal time value, the last timestamp and private authentication key are altered as well.
Manager changes secrets.	partyAuthClock.a: = 0	When secrets are changed, the clock is reset.

the object identifiers for defining party information (partyAdmin) are organized under the node snmpParties. The remaining groups are organized under the node snmpSecrets.

8.4.1 SNMP Party Public Database Group

The SNMP party public database group contains public information about SNMP parties; that is, information that is available for access by network-management operations. The group consists of a single table, partyTable, with one entry in the table for each party. An agent must ensure that there is a one-to-one correspondence between entries in this table and entries in the party-SecretsTable. In fact, entries in this table are not directly created by management set operation but are created/deleted as a side effect of the creation/deletion of corresponding entries in the party-SecretsTable.

Each conceptual row in the table includes instances of the following columnar objects:

- *partyIdentity:* unique object identifier of a party. The table is indexed by this columnar object.

- *partyTDomain:* indicates the transport service by which the party receives network-management traffic.

- *partyTAddr:* the transport-service address of the party. For rfc1351Domain, the address is formatted as a 4-octet IP address concatenated with a 2-octet UDP port number.

```
snmpParties       OBJECT IDENTIFIER ::= { mib-2 20 }
partyAdmin        OBJECT IDENTIFIER ::= { snmpParties 1 }
party Public      OBJECT IDENTIFIER ::= { snmpParties 2 }

snmpSecrets       OBJECT IDENTIFIER ::= { mib-2 21 }
partyPrivate      OBJECT IDENTIFIER ::= { snmpSecrets 1 }
partyAccess       OBJECT IDENTIFIER ::= { snmpSecrets 2 }
partyViews        OBJECT IDENTIFIER ::= { snmpSecrets 3 }

--Definitions of Security Protocols

partyProtocols    OBJECT IDENTIFIER ::= { partyAdmin 1 }
noAuth            OBJECT IDENTIFIER ::= { partyProtocols 1 }   --The protocol without authentication
noPriv            OBJECT IDENTIFIER ::= { partyProtocols 3 }   --The protocol without privacy
desPrivProtocol   OBJECT IDENTIFIER ::= { partyProtocols 4 }   --The DES Privacy Protocol
md5AuthProtocol   OBJECT IDENTIFIER ::= { partyProtocols 5 }   --The MD5 Authentication Protocol

--Definitions of Tranport Domains

transportDomains  OBJECT IDENTIFIER ::= { partyAdmin 2 }
rfc1351Domain     OBJECT IDENTIFIER ::= { transportDomains 1 }  --RFC-1351 (SNMP over UDP, using SNMP parties)

--Definitions of Proxy Domains

proxyDomains      OBJECT IDENTIFIER ::= { partyAdmin 3 }
noProxy           OBJECT IDENTIFIER ::= { proxyDomains 2 }   --Local operation

--Definition of Initial Party Identifiers

initialPartyId    OBJECT IDENTIFIER ::= { partyAdmin 4 }
```

Figure 8.12 ASN.1 Definitions for S-SNMP MIB (RFC 1353)

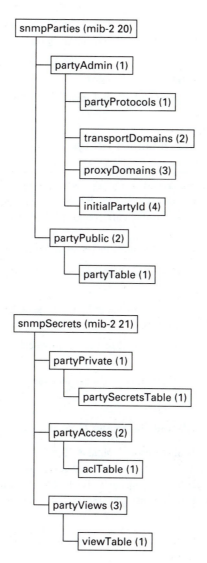

Figure 8.13 S-SNMP MIB Structure

- *partyProxyFor:* object identifier of a proxied entity, if any.

- *partyAuthProtocol:* object identifier of the authentication protocol, if any.

- *partyAuthClock:* a non-negative integer, initialized to 0, with a maximum value of $2^{31} - 1$. This is the local notion of the current time for this party.

- *partyAuthPublic:* a publicly readable value related to the party's authentication protocol.

- *partyAuthLifetime:* a non-negative integer, initialized to 0, with a maximum value of $2^{31} - 1$. This is an upper bound on the lifetime of a message.

- *partyPrivProtocol:* object identifier of the privacy protocol, if any.

- *partyPrivPublic:* a publicly readable value related to the party's privacy protocol.

- *partyMaxMessageSize:* an integer in the range 484 to 65,507 that represents the maximum message length in octets supported by the agent.

- *partyStatus:* takes on the values valid (1) and invalid (2). Indicates the status of the information in this conceptual row.

8.4.2   SNMP Party Secrets Database Group

The SNMP party secrets database group contains secret information about SNMP parties, for which security demands that access be limited to parties that use both authentication and privacy. The group consists of a single table, partySecretsTable, with one entry in the table for each party. An agent must ensure that there is a one-to-one correspondence between entries in this table and entries in the partyTable.

Each conceptual row in the table includes instances of the following columnar objects:

- *partySecretsIdentity:* unique object identifier of a party. The table is indexed by this columnar object.

- *partySecretsAuthPrivate:* an encoding of the party's private authentication key, or value, needed to support the authentication protocol.

- *partySecretsPrivPrivate:* an encoding of the party's private encryption key, needed to support the privacy protocol.

- *partySecretsStatus:* takes on the values valid (1) and invalid (2). Indicates the status of the information in this conceptual row.

8.4.3   SNMP Access-Privileges Database Group

The SNMP access-privileges database group contains objects that allow the SNMP entity itself to be used to configure new SNMP parties or to manipulate the access privileges of existing parties.

The group consists of a single table, aclTable. Each conceptual row in the table lists the access privileges for a particular (target, subject) pair and includes instances of the following columnar objects:

- *aclTarget:* the target SNMP party whose performance of management operations is constrained by this set of access privileges.

- *aclSubject:* the subject SNMP party whose requests for management operations to be performed are constrained by this set of access privileges.

- *aclPrivileges:* an integer in the range 0 to 31 that encodes the access privileges for this (target, subject) pair.

- *aclStatus:* takes on the values valid (1) and invalid (2). Indicates the status of the information in this conceptual row.

8.4.4 MIB-View Database Group

The MIB-view database group contains objects that allow the SNMP entity itself to be used to configure new SNMP parties or to manipulate the MIB views of existing parties.

The group consists of a single table, viewTable. Each conceptual row in the table includes instances of the following columnar objects:

- *viewParty:* the SNMP party whose single MIB view includes or excludes a particular family of view subtrees.
- *viewSubtree:* an object identifier that specifies a view subtree that, in combination with the corresponding instance of viewMask, defines a family of view subtrees.
- *viewStatus:* takes on the values included (1), excluded (2), and invalid (3). Indicates whether the corresponding family of view subtrees defined by viewSubtree and viewMask is included in or excluded from the MIB view or whether this row is invalid.
- *viewMask:* the bit mask that, in combination with the corresponding instance of viewSubtree, defines a family of view subtrees.

The MIB view of party x is defined by the set of entries (rows) in the viewTable that have viewParty = x. Each entry in the table represents a family of view subtrees that, according to the status of the entry, is either included in or excluded from the MIB view for the relevant SNMP party.

8.4.4.1 MIB-View Examples

Perhaps the best way to explain the conventions for defining an MIB view is by first looking at an example. Figure 8.14, part (a), shows MIB views defined for two parties, lucy and ricky.

The lucy group includes all the objects in the subtree defined by the MIB-II object identifier for the system group. That is, all the objects in the system group are included in lucy's MIB view. The next entry for lucy specifies that the subtree identified by { ifEntry 0 2 } is included in the view. Referring back to Figure 5.7, we see that ifEntry defines a conceptual row in ifTable in the interfaces group of MIB-II. This table is indexed by the columnar object ifIndex. Now, the object identifier for ifEntry is 1.3.6.1.2.1.2.2.1, which is derived as follows:

iso	org	dod	internet	mgmt	mib-2	interfaces	ifTable	ifEntry
1	3	6	1	2	1	2	2	1

Recall that the rules for specifying object identifiers for object instances within a table dictate that the identifier consists of the identifier for the columnar object followed by the value of the index variable or variables. In this case, the index variable is ifIndex. So, for example, the object identifier for the columnar object ifType is { ifEntry 3 }, which is 1.3.6.1.2.1.2.2.1.3. An object instance of ifType for interface number 2 (value of ifIndex = 2) is therefore written as:

{ ifEntry 3 2 } = { ifType 2 } = 1.3.6.1.2.1.2.2.1.3.2

Now, there is no such columnar object that can be expressed as { ifEntry 0 } and therefore no object instance that can be expressed as { ifEntry 0 2 }. However, the latter expression can be interpreted to mean "all object instances in the ifTable for which ifIndex = 2"; that is, { ifEntry 0 2 } refers to all object instances related to the second network interface. This interpretation is

Party Identity	Status	Family Name	Family Mask
lucy	include	system	" "h
lucy	include	{ ifEntry 0 2 }	" FFA0"h
lucy	exclude	{ ifSpeed 2 }	" "h
ricky	include	icmp	" "h
ricky	include	{ ifEntry 0 5 }	" FFA0"h
ricky	include	{ ifInOctets 4 }	" "h

(a) MIB views for parties lucy and ricky

Include:
Family name = { ifEntry 0 2 }
Family mask = "FFA0"h

1	3	6	1	2	1	2	2	1	0	2
1	1	1	1	1	1	1	1	1	0	1

Exclude:
Family name = { ifSpeed 2 }
Family mask = ""h

1	3	6	1	2	1	2	2	1	5	2
1	1	1	1	1	1	1	1	1	1	1

(b) MIB view considerations for lucy

Include:
Family name = { ifEntry 0 5 }
Family mask = "FFA0"h

1	3	6	1	2	1	2	2	1	0	5
1	1	1	1	1	1	1	1	1	0	1

Include:
Family name = { ifInOctets 4 }
Family mask = ""h

1	3	6	1	2	1	2	2	1	10	4
1	1	1	1	1	1	1	1	1	1	1

(c) MIB view considerations for ricky

Figure 8.14 An Example of the Use of MIB Views

confirmed by the mask associated with this family name, as shown in Figure 8.14, part (b). The mask has a hexadecimal value of FFA0. Reading from left to right, each bit of the mask is matched against the corresponding subidentifier of the family name. If the mask bit is 1, the subidentifier is used; if the mask bit is 0, then the corresponding subidentifier position is treated as a ''wild card'' in which any value may appear. Thus, it doesn't matter in this case what value of x appears in the expression { ifEntry x 2 }; the mask dictates that all objects with identifiers of the form 1.3.6.1.2.1.2.2.1.x.2 are part of the family of view subtrees defined by this entry.

The next entry in lucy's table has the family name { ifSpeed 2 }. The family mask is a zero-length string. By convention, such a bit mask is extended with 1s to be the same length in bits as the number of subidentifiers in the family name. Thus, there are no wild cards, and this entry identifies the subtree { ifSpeed 2 }. Now, according to the preceding entry, all object instances in the second row of ifTable are included, which would include ifSpeed for the second row. By this entry, ifSpeed for the second row is excluded. When an identifier is included in two or more families, the family name with the greatest number of subidentifiers dominates. If two or more family names have the same number of subidentifiers, then the family name that is lexicographically largest dominates. We have:

{ ifSpeed 2 } = 1.3.6.1.2.1.2.2.1.5.2 > 1.3.6.1.2.1.2.2.1.0.2 = { ifEntry 0 2 }

Therefore, the third entry in Figure 8.14, part (a), takes precedence over the second entry. In summary, the MIB view for lucy consists of the system group plus the conceptual row of ifTable for which ifIndex = 2, with the exception of ifSpeed.

Three entries in the viewTable serve to identify the MIB view for ricky. The first entry specifies that the icmp group of MIB-II is included. The second entry specifies that the conceptual row of ifTable for which ifIndex = 5 is included. Finally, the third entry specifies that the columnar object ifInOctets, from ifTable, for which ifIndex = 4 is included.

8.4.4.2 MIB-View Conventions

The MIB view of a party is defined by the set of entries in the viewTable whose value of viewParty equals the party's object identifier.

Each instance of viewMask contains a bit mask that, in combination with the corresponding instance of viewSubtree, defines a family of view subtrees. Each bit of the mask corresponds to one subidentifier of the object-identifier value of viewSubtree, according to the following conventions:

- The most significant bit of the mask corresponds to the first subidentifier; the second most significant bit of the mask corresponds to the second subidentifier; and so on.

- If there are more bits in the mask than subidentifiers in viewSubtree, the excess least-significant bits of the mask are ignored.

- If there are fewer bits in the mask than subidentifiers in viewSubtree, the mask is extended, from the least-significant side, with 1s to be the required length.

Consider an object instance x with the object identifier $x_1.x_2.x_3 \ldots x_n$, and consider an entry in the viewTable with a viewSubtree value of $v_1.v_2.v_3 \ldots v_k$ and a viewMask value of $m_1m_2m_3 \ldots m_k$. In the notation of the preceding sentence, x_i is the ith subidentifier of x, v_i is the ith subidentifier of viewSubtree, and m_i is the ith bit of viewMask, where viewMask has been adjusted to have the same length as viewSubtree. Object instance x is said to be contained in the family of subtrees defined by an entry in the viewTable if the following conditions are met:

1. $n \geq k$, AND
2. For each subidentifier v_i of viewSubtree, either:

   $m_i = 0$ OR $x_i = v_i$

Finally, to determine whether a specific object instance is included in the MIB view of a particular party, the object identifier x of the object instance is compared to each entry for this party in the viewTable, according to the following rules:

1. If none of the entries matches (x is not contained in the family of subtrees defined by any entry), then x is not in the MIB view.

2. If exactly one of the entries matches, then x is included in, or excluded from, the MIB view according to the value of viewStatus.

3. If more than one of the entries match, then:

   a. If one of the matching entries has a viewSubtree value with more subidentifiers than that of any other matching entry, then that entry determines inclusion or exclusion.

   b. Otherwise, among those entries with the equal, largest number of subidentifiers, the lexicographically greatest instance of viewStatus determines the inclusion or exclusion.

8.4.5   Initial Party Definitions

When devices are installed with an SNMP entity, an initial set of parties needs to be defined for that entity. Among other things, this definition requires the assignment of an unused object identifier for each party.

Recall from subsection 8.3.4 that it is recommended that each SNMP entity be initially configured with six parties organized as three pairs of local and remote parties. RFC 1353 assigns a branch of the naming tree for use in defining these parties. The root of this tree is initialPartyId, defined as follows:

initialPartyId OBJECT IDENTIFIER ::= { partyAdmin 4 }

Table 8.6, part (a), shows the basic party information for the six parties. This is the information that is in the form of object instances indexed by each party identifier. For purposes of this table, it is assumed that the six parties are at IP address a.b.c.d.

The first two parties are the local and remote parties that provide for nonsecure communications, using no authentication protocol and no privacy protocol. The local party is assigned UDP port 161. The port for the remote party is assigned by local administration.

The next two parties share the use of an authentication protocol but no privacy protocol. The protocol used is based on the MD5 digest-authentication algorithm; this is the digest-authentication protocol described in subsection 8.3.2. The initial value of the secret key used by MD5 must be assigned by local administration. A maximum message lifetime of 300 seconds, or 5 minutes, is the default value. This is the window of vulnerability to replay attack.

The final two parties share both an authentication protocol and a privacy protocol. The privacy protocol is the symmetric privacy protocol described in subsection 8.3.3, which uses the DES algorithm. The initial value of the encryption key used by DES must be assigned by local administration.

Table 8.6, part (b), shows the access-control parameters defined for the six initial parties. For the nonsecure pair, just read-only types of operations are allowed. The Set operation is only permitted for authenticated communication.

Table 8.6, part (c), shows the MIB views for the six initial parties. Note that view definitions are only needed for the local agents. For the nonsecure local party, the MIB view includes the MIB-II system group (Figure 5.6) and the snmpParties group, which contains only the public information for the party. Note that the system group is not included in the views of the other two parties. This reflects the fact that the information in the system group is considered public information and therefore can be accessed by an unauthenticated protocol.

Table 8.6 Initial Values of Object Instances for Initial Set of Parties

(a) Party Information

partyIdentity	{ initialPartyId a b c d 1 }	partyIdentity	{ initialPartyId a b c d 2 }
partyTDomain	{ rfc1351Domain }	partyTDomain	{ rfc1351Domain }
partyTAddr	a.b.c.d, 161	partyTAddr	assigned locally
partyProxyFor	{ noProxy }	partyProxyFor	{ noProxy }
partyAuthProtocol	{ noAuth }	partyAuthProtocol	{ noAuth }
partyAuthClock	0	partyAuthClock	0
partySecretsAuthPrivate	''h	partySecretsAuthPrivate	''h
partyAuthPublic	''h	partyAuthPublic	''h
partyAuthLifetime	0	partyAuthLifetime	0
partyPrivProtocol	{ noPriv }	partyPrivProtocol	{ noPriv }
partyPrivPrivate	''h	partyPrivPrivate	''h
partyPrivPublic	''h	partyPrivPublic	''h
partyIdentity	{ initialPartyId a b c d 3 }	partyIdentity	{ initialPartyId a b c d 4 }
partyTDomain	{ rfc1351Domain }	partyTDomain	{ rfc1351Domain }
partyTAddr	a.b.c.d, 161	partyTAddr	assigned locally
partyProxyFor	{ noProxy }	partyProxyFor	{ noProxy }
partyAuthProtocol	{ md5AuthProtocol }	partyAuthProtocol	{ md5AuthProtocol }
partyAuthClock	0	partyAuthClock	0
partySecretsAuthPrivate	assigned locally	partySecretsAuthPrivate	assigned locally
partyAuthPublic	''h	partyAuthPublic	''h
partyAuthLifetime	300	partyAuthLifetime	300
partyPrivProtocol	{ noPriv }	partyPrivProtocol	{ noPriv }
partyPrivPrivate	''h	partyPrivPrivate	''h
partyPrivPublic	''h	partyPrivPublic	''h
partyIdentity	{ initialPartyId a b c d 5 }	partyIdentity	{ initialPartyId a b c d 6 }
partyTDomain	{ rfc1351Domain }	partyTDomain	{ rfc1351Domain }
partyTAddr	a.b.c.d, 161	partyTAddr	assigned locally
partyProxyFor	{ noProxy }	partyProxyFor	{ noProxy }
partyAuthProtocol	{ md5AuthProtocol }	partyAuthProtocol	{ md5AuthProtocol }
partyAuthClock	0	partyAuthClock	0
partySecretsAuthPrivate	assigned locally	partySecretsAuthPrivate	assigned locally
partyAuthPublic	''h	partyAuthPublic	''h
partyAuthLifetime	300	partyAuthLifetime	300
partyPrivProtocol	{ desPrivProtocol }	partyPrivProtocol	{ desPrivProtocol }
partyPrivPrivate	assigned locally	partyPrivPrivate	assigned locally
partyPrivPublic	''h	partyPrivPublic	''h

(b) Access-Control Parameters

aclTarget	{ initialPartyId a b c d 1 }	aclTarget	{ initialPartyId a b c d 2 }
aclSubject	{ initialPartyId a b c d 2 }	aclSubject	{ initialPartyId a b c d 1 }
aclPrivileges	3 (Get & GetNext)	aclPrivileges	20 (GetResponse & Trap)
aclTarget	{ initialPartyId a b c d 3 }	aclTarget	{ initialPartyId a b c d 4 }
aclSubject	{ initialPartyId a b c d 4 }	aclSubject	{ initialPartyId a b c d 3 }

Table 8.6 (*Cont.*)

(b) Access-Control Parameters			
aclPrivileges	11 (Get, GetNext, & Set)	aclPrivileges	20 (GetResponse & Trap)
aclTarget	{ initialPartyId a b c d 5 }	aclTarget	{ initialPartyId a b c d 6 }
aclSubject	{ initialPartyId a b c d 6 }	aclSubject	{ initialPartyId a b c d 5 }
aclPrivileges	11 (Get, GetNext, & Set)	aclPrivileges	20 (GetResponse & Trap)

(c) MIB Views			
viewParty	{ initialPartyId a b c d 1 }	viewParty	{ initialPartyId a b c d 1 }
viewSubtree	{ system }	viewSubtree	{ snmpParties }
viewStatus	{ included }	viewStatus	{ included }
viewMask	{ ''h }	viewMask	{ ''h }
viewParty	{ initialPartyId a b c d 3 }	viewParty	{ initialPartyId a b c d 3 }
viewSubtree	{ internet }	viewSubtree	{ partyPrivate }
viewStatus	{ included }	viewStatus	{ excluded }
viewMask	{ ''h }	viewMask	{ ''h }
viewParty	{ initialPartyId a b c d 5 }		
viewSubtree	{ internet }		
viewStatus	{ included }		
viewMask	{ ''h }		

For the party that includes an authentication protocol but not a privacy protocol, the MIB view includes everything under the internet object (Figure 5.1), which includes MIB-II, but excludes partyPrivate, which contains the secret values. Finally, the party that includes both authentication and privacy protocols includes everything under the internet object.

8.5   THE MD5 MESSAGE-DIGEST ALGORITHM

The MD5 message-digest algorithm (RFC 1321) was developed by Ron Rivest at MIT (the *R* in the RSA [Rivest-Shamir-Adelman] public-key encryption algorithm). The algorithm takes as input a message of arbitrary length and produces as output a 128-bit message digest. The reader unfamiliar with the general application of message digests to message authentication should review Appendix 8B at this point.

Before looking at the details of MD5, it will be useful in understanding the complexity of MD5 to look at two simple examples of hash functions.

8.5.1   Simple Hash Functions

All hash functions operate using the following general principles. The input (message, file, etc.) is viewed as a sequence of *n*-bit blocks and is processed one block at a time in an iterative fashion to produce an *n*-bit hash function.

	Bit 1	Bit 2	• • •	Bit n
Block 1	b_{11}	b_{21}	• • •	b_{n1}
Block 2	b_{12}	b_{22}	• • •	b_{n2}
•	•	•	•	•
•	•	•	•	•
•	•	•	•	•
Block m	b_{1m}	b_{2m}	• • •	b_{nm}
Hash code	c_1	c_2	• • •	c_n

Figure 8.15 Simple Hash Function Using Bitwise XOR

One of the simplest hash functions is to take the bit-by-bit exclusive-or (XOR) of every block. This can be expressed as follows:

$$C_i = b_{i1} \oplus b_{i2} \oplus \ldots \oplus b_{im,}$$

where

C_i = ith bit of the hash code, $1 \le i \le n$.
m = number of n-bit blocks in the input.
b_{ij} = ith bit in jth block.
$\oplus$ = XOR operation.

Figure 8.15 illustrates this operation. Figure 8.16, part (a), is a C program that produces a 128-bit hash code. This type of code produces a simple parity for each bit position and is known as a longitudinal redundancy check. It is reasonably effective for random data as a data-integrity check. Each 128-bit hash value is equally likely. Thus, the probability that a data error will result in an unchanged hash value is 2^{-128}. With more predictably formatted data, the function is less effective. For example, in most normal text files, the high-order bit of each octet is always 0. Therefore, 16 bits in the hash will always be 0, and the effectiveness is reduced to 2^{-112}.

A simple way to improve matters is to perform a 1-bit circular shift, or rotation, on the hash value after each block is processed, as shown in Figure 8.16, part (b). This has the effect of ''randomizing'' the input more completely and overcoming any regularities that appear in the input.

Although the second program provides a good measure of data integrity, it is virtually useless for data security. Consider the following task of a potential attacker: given a hash code, produce a message that yields that hash code. The attacker would simply need to prepare the desired message and then append a 128-bit block that forces the new message plus block to yield the desired hash code.

Thus, we need a hash algorithm that is a much more complex function of the input bits.

8.5.2   MD5-Algorithm Description

The MD5 algorithm produces a 128-bit hash code, or message digest, of an input file. The algorithm—which was designed for speed, simplicity, and compactness on a 32-bit architecture—processes the input in 512-bit blocks.

The algorithm consists of the following five steps:

```
main (int argc, char *argv []) {
    unsigned long hash [4] = (0,0,0,0), data [4] ;
    FILE *fp;
    int i;
    if ((fp == fopen (argv [1], "rb")) != NULL) {
        while ((fread (data, 4,,4, fp) != NULL)
            for (i=0; i<4; i++)
                hash [i]  ^= data [i];
        fclose (fp);
        for (i=0; i<4; i++)
                printf ("%081x", hash [i] );
        printf ("\n") ;
    } }
```

(a)   XOR of every 128-bit block

```
main (int argc, char *argv []) {
    unsigned long hash [4] = (0,0,0,0), data [4] ;
    FILE *fp;
    int i;
    if ((fp == fopen (argv [1], "rb")) != NULL) {
        while ((fread (data, 4,,4, fp) != NULL)
            for (i=0; i<4; i++)
                hash [i]  ^= data [i];  ·
                hash [i] = hash [i]>>1^ hash [i]<<31 ;
                }
        fclose (fp);
        for (i=0; i<4; i++)
                printf ("%081x", hash [i] );
        printf ("\n") ;
    } }
```

(b)   Rolling each longward 1 bit to the right

Source: B. Schneier, "One=Way Hash Functions," *Dr. Dobb's Journal*
(Sept. 1991). Reprinted with permission.

Figure 8.16 Simple Hash Functions

1. *Step 1—append padding bits:* The message is padded so that its length is congruent to 448 modulo 512. That is, the length of the padded message is 64 bits less than an integer multiple of 512 bits. Padding is always added, even if the message is already of the desired length. For example, if the message is 448 bits long, it is padded by 512 bits to a length of 960 bits. Thus, the number of padding bits is in the range of 1 to 512.

   The padding consists of a single 1 bit followed by the necessary number of 0 bits.

2. *Step 2—append length:* A 64-bit representation of the length of the original message (before the padding) is appended to the result of step 1. If the original length is greater than 2^{64}, then only the low-order 64 bits of the length are used. The inclusion of a length value at the end of the message makes a type of attack known as a padding attack more difficult (Tsudick 1992).

   The outcome of the first two steps yields a message that is an integer multiple of 512 bits in length. Equivalently, the result is a multiple of sixteen 32-bit words. Let M[0 . . . N − 1] denote the words of the resulting message, with N being an integer multiple of 16.

Table 8.7 Key Elements of MD5

(a) Truth Table of Logical Functions						
X	Y	Z	F	G	H	I
0	0	0	0	0	0	1
0	0	1	1	0	1	0
0	1	0	0	1	1	0
0	1	1	1	0	0	1
1	0	0	0	0	1	1
1	0	1	0	1	0	1
1	1	0	1	1	0	0
1	1	1	1	1	1	0

(b) Table T, Constructed from the Sine Function

```
T[1]  =D76AA478   T[17]=F61E2562   T[33]=FFFA3942   T[49]=F4292244
T[2]  =E8C7B756   T[18]=C040B340   T[34]=8771F681   T[50]=432AFF97
T[3]  =242070DB   T[19]=265E5A51   T[35]=69D96122   T[51]=AB9423A7
T[4]  =C1BDCEEE   T[20]=E9B6C7AA   T[36]=FDE5380C   T[52]=FC93A039
T[5]  =F57C0FAF   T[21]=D62F105D   T[37]=A4BEEA44   T[53]=655B59C3
T[6]  =4787C62A   T[22]=02441453   T[38]=4BDECFA9   T[54]=8F0CCC92
T[7]  =A8304613   T[23]=D8A1E681   T[39]=F6BB4B60   T[55]=FFEFF47D
T[8]  =FD469501   T[24]=E7D3FBC8   T[40]=BEBFBC70   T[56]=85845DD1
T[9]  =698098D8   T[25]=21E1CDE6   T[41]=289B7EC6   T[57]=6FA87E4F
T[10]=8B44F7AF    T[26]=C33707D6   T[42]=EAA127FA   T[58]=FE2CE6E0
T[11]=FFFF5BB1    T[27]=F4D50D87   T[43]=D4EF3085   T[59]=A3014314
T[12]=895CD7BE    T[28]=455A14ED   T[44]=04881D05   T[60]=4E0811A1
T[13]=6B901122    T[29]=A9E3E905   T[45]=D9D4D039   T[61]=F7537E82
T[14]=FD987193    T[30]=FCEFA3F8   T[46]=E6DB99E5   T[62]=BD3AF235
T[15]=A679438E    T[31]=676F02D9   T[47]=1FA27CF8   T[63]=2AD7D2BB
T[16]=49B40821    T[32]=8D2A4C8A   T[48]=C4AC5665   T[64]=EB86D391
```

3. *Step 3—initialize MD buffer:* A 128-bit buffer is used to hold intermediate and final results of the hash function. The buffer can be represented as four 32-bit registers (A, B, C, D). These registers are initialized to the following hexadecimal values (low-order octets first):

    A = 01 23 45 67
    B = 89 AB CD EF
    C = FE DC BA 98
    D = 76 54 32 10

4. *Step 4—process message in 128-bit (16-word) blocks:* The heart of the algorithm makes use of four functions. Each function takes three 32-bit words as input and produces a 32-bit word as output. Each function performs a set of bitwise logical operations; that is, the nth bit of the output is a function of the nth bit of the three inputs. The functions are:

    $F(X,Y,Z) = X \bullet Y) + (X' \bullet Z)$
    $G(X,Y,Z) = (X \bullet Z) + (Y \bullet Z'),$

$$H(X,Y,Z) = X \oplus Y \oplus Z$$
$$I(X,Y,Z) = Y \oplus (X + Z')$$

where the logical operators AND, OR, NOT, and XOR are represented by the symbols $\bullet$, $+$, $'$, and $\oplus$. Function F is a conditional function: if X, then Y, else Z. Function H produces a parity bit. Table 8.7, part (a), is a truth table of the four functions.

The algorithm also makes use of a 64-element table T[1 . . . 64] constructed from the sine function. The ith element of T, denoted T[i], has the value equal to the integer part of $2^{32} \times abs(sin(i))$, where i is in radians. Since $abs(sin(i))$ is a number between 0 and 1, each element of T is an integer that can be represented in 32 bits. The table provides a "randomized" set of 32-bit patterns, which should eliminate any regularities in the input data. Table 8.7, part (b), lists the values of T.

Figure 8.17, taken from RFC 1321, defines the processing algorithm. The expression (X $<<<$ s) denotes the 32-bit value obtained by performing a circular shift of X left by s bit positions.

5. *Step 5—output:* The message digest produced as output is stored in A, B, C, D.

The MD5 algorithm has the property that every bit of the hash code is a function of every bit in the input. The complex repetition of the basic functions (F, G, H, I) produces codes that are well mixed; that is, it is unlikely that two messages chosen at random, even if they exhibit similar regularities, will have the same hash code. The author of MD5 conjectures that the difficulty of generating two messages with the same MD5 digest is on the order of 2^{64} operations, and the difficulty of generating a message that produces a given digest is on the order of 2^{128} operations.

8.6   SUMMARY

The new security features of SNMP are designed to provide, in essence, three security-related services: privacy, authentication, and access control.

Privacy is the protection of transmitted data from eavesdropping or wiretapping. Privacy requires that the contents of any message be disguised in such a way that only the intended recipient can recover the original message. The specific privacy mechanism chosen for the current version of secure SNMP is the symmetric privacy protocol. It provides for protection from disclosure of a received message (i.e., only the intended recipient, and the sender, are able to read the message). The mechanism for providing such protection is conventional encryption, which requires that the source and destination parties share the same encryption key. The data-encryption standard (DES) is the encryption algorithm used.

A message, file, document, or other collection of data is said to be authentic when it is genuine and came from its alleged source. Message authentication is a procedure that allows communicating parties to verify that received messages are authentic. The two important aspects are to verify that the contents of the message have not been altered and that the source is authentic. We may also wish to verify a message's timeliness (it has not been artificially delayed and replayed) and sequence relative to other messages flowing between two parties. The specific authentication mechanism chosen for the current version of secure SNMP is the MD5 digest authentication protocol. It provides for the verification of the integrity of a received message (i.e., the message received is the message sent), for authentication of the origin of the message, and for the timeliness of message delivery.

```
/* Process each 16-word (512-bit) block. */
For i = 0 to N/16-1 do
    /* Copy block i into X. */
    For j = 0 to 15 do
        Set X[j] to M[i*16+j].
    end /* of loop on j */

    /* Save A as AA, B as BB, C as CC, and D as DD. */
    AA = A
    BB = B
    CC = C
    DD = D
```

/* Round 1. */
/* Let [abcd k s i] denote the operation
?* do the following 16 operations. */

a = b + ((a + F(b,c,d) + X[k] + T[i]) <<<s). */

[ABCD 0 7 1]	[DABC 1 12 2]	[CDAB 2 17 3]	[BCDA 3 22 4]
[ABCD 4 7 5]	[DABC 5 12 6]	[CDAB 6 17 7]	[BCDA 7 22 8]
[ABCD 8 7 9]	[DABC 9 12 10]	[CDAB 10 17 11]	[BCDA 11 22 12]
[ABCD 12 7 13]	[DABC 13 12 14]	[CDAB 14 17 15]	[BCDA 15 22 16]

/* Round 2. */
/* Let [abcd k s i] denote the operation
?* do the following 16 operations. */

a = b + ((a + G(b,c,d) + X[k] + T[i]) <<<s). */

[ABCD 1 5 17]	[DABC 6 9 18]	[CDAB 11 14 19]	[BCDA 0 20 20]
[ABCD 5 5 21]	[DABC 10 9 22]	[CDAB 15 14 23]	[BCDA 4 20 24]
[ABCD 9 5 25]	[DABC 14 9 26]	[CDAB 3 14 27]	[BCDA 8 20 28]
[ABCD 13 5 29]	[DABC 2 9 30]	[CDAB 7 14 31]	[BCDA 12 20 32]

/* Round 3. */
/* Let [abcd k s i] denote the operation
?* do the following 16 operations. */

a = b + ((a + H(b,c,d) + X[k] + T[i]) <<<s). */

[ABCD 5 4 33]	[DABC 8 11 34]	[CDAB 11 16 35]	[BCDA 14 23 36]
[ABCD 1 4 37]	[DABC 4 11 38]	[CDAB 7 16 39]	[BCDA 10 23 40]
[ABCD 13 4 41]	[DABC 0 11 42]	[CDAB 3 16 43]	[BCDA 6 23 44]
[ABCD 9 4 45]	[DABC 12 11 46]	[CDAB 15 16 47]	[BCDA 2 23 48]

/* Round 4. */
/* Let [abcd k s i] denote the operation
?* do the following 16 operations. */

a = b + ((a + I(b,c,d) + X[k] + T[i]) <<<s). */

[ABCD 0 6 49]	[DABC 7 10 50]	[CDAB 14 15 51]	[BCDA 5 21 52]
[ABCD 12 6 53]	[DABC 3 10 54]	[CDAB 10 15 55]	[BCDA 1 21 56]
[ABCD 8 6 57]	[DABC 15 10 58]	[CDAB 6 15 59]	[BCDA 13 21 60]
[ABCD 4 6 61]	[DABC 11 10 62]	[CDAB 2 15 63]	[BCDA 9 21 64]

```
/* Then increment each of the four registers by the value it had before this block was started. */
A = A + AA
B = B + BB
C = C + CC
D = D + DD

end /.* of loop on i */
```

Figure 8.17 Basic MD5 Update Algorithm (RFC 1321)

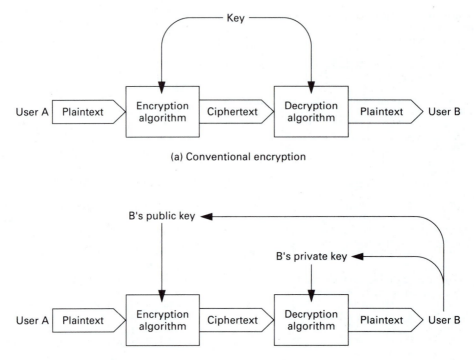

Figure 8.18 Encryption

In the context of network management, the purpose of access control is to ensure that only authorized users have access to a particular management information base and that access to and modification of a particular portion of data are limited to authorized individuals and programs.

APPENDIX 8A   Message Secrecy

This appendix provides a brief overview of two security mechanisms for message secrecy: conventional encryption and public-key encryption.

8A.1   CONVENTIONAL ENCRYPTION

Figure 8.18, part (a), illustrates the conventional encryption process. The original intelligible message, referred to as *plaintext*, is converted into apparently random nonsense, referred to as *ciphertext*. The encryption process consists of an algorithm and a key. The key is a relatively short bit string that controls the algorithm. The algorithm will produce a different output depending on the specific key being used at the time. A minor change in the key results in a radical change to the output of the algorithm.

Once the ciphertext is produced, it is transmitted. Upon reception, the ciphertext can be transformed back to the original plaintext by using a decryption algorithm and the same key that was used for encryption.

The security of conventional encryption depends on several factors. First, the encryption algorithm must be powerful enough so that it is impractical to decrypt a message on the basis of the ciphertext alone. Beyond that, the security of conventional encryption depends on the secrecy of the key, not the secrecy of the algorithm. That is, it is assumed that it is impractical to decrypt a message on the basis of the ciphertext *plus* knowledge of the encryption/decryption algorithm. In other words, we don't need to keep the algorithm secret; we only need to keep the key secret.

This feature of conventional encryption is what makes it feasible for widespread use. The fact that the algorithm need not be kept secret means that manufacturers can, and have, developed low-cost chip implementations of data-encryption algorithms. These chips are widely available and incorporated into a number of products. With the use of conventional encryption, the principal security problem is maintaining the secrecy of the key.

The most widely used encryption scheme is based on the data-encryption standard (DES), adopted in 1977 by the National Bureau of Standards. For DES, data are encrypted in 64-bit blocks using a 56-bit key. Using the key, the 64-bit input is transformed in a series of steps into a 64-bit output. The same steps, with the same key, are used to reverse the encryption.

8A.2 PUBLIC-KEY ENCRYPTION

One of the major difficulties with conventional encryption schemes is the need to distribute the keys in a secure manner. A clever way around this requirement is an encryption scheme that, surprisingly, does not require key distribution. This scheme, known as public-key encryption, is illustrated in Figure 8.18, part (b).

For conventional encryption schemes, the keys used for encryption and decryption are the same. This is not a necessary condition. Instead, it is possible to develop an algorithm that uses one key for encryption and a companion but different key for decryption. Furthermore, it is possible to develop algorithms such that knowledge of the encryption algorithm plus the encryption key is not sufficient to determine the decryption key. Thus, the following technique will work:

1. Each end system in a network generates a pair of keys to be used for encryption and decryption of messages that it will receive.

2. Each system publishes its encryption key by placing it in a public register or file. This is the public key. The companion key is kept private.

3. If A wishes to send a message to B, it encrypts the message using B's public key.

4. When B receives the message, it decrypts it using B's private key. No other recipient can decrypt the message, since only B knows B's private key.

As you can see, public-key encryption solves the key-distribution problem, since there are no keys to distribute! All participants have access to public keys, and private keys are generated locally by each participant and therefore need never be distributed. As long as a system controls its private key, its incoming communication is secure. At any time, a system can change its private key and publish the companion public key to replace its old public key.

Table 8.8 Conventional and Public-Key Encryption

Conventional Encryption	Public-Key Encryption
Needed to work: 1. The same algorithm with the same key can be used for encryption and decryption. 2. The sender and receiver must share the algorithm and the key. **Needed for security:** 1. The key must be kept secret. 2. It must be impossible or at least impractical to decipher a message if no other information is available. 3. Knowledge of the algorithm plus samples of ciphertext must be insufficient to determine the key.	**Needed to work:** 1. One algorithm is used for encryption and decryption with a pair of keys, one for encryption and one for decryption. 2. The sender and receiver must each have one of the matched pair of keys. **Needed for security:** 1. One of the two keys must be kept secret. 2. It must be impossible or at least impractical to decipher a message if no other information is available. 3. Knowledge of the algorithm plus one of the keys plus samples of ciphertext must be insufficient to determine the other key.

A main disadvantage of public-key encryption compared to conventional encryption is that algorithms for the former are much more complex. Thus, for hardware of comparable size and cost, the public-key scheme will provide much lower throughput.

Table 8.8 summarizes some of the important aspects of conventional and public-key encryption.

APPENDIX 8B   *Message Authentication*

Encryption, as described in the preceding appendix, protects against passive attack (eavesdropping). A different requirement is to protect against active attack (falsification of data and transactions). Protection against such attacks is known as message authentication.

A message, file, document, or some other collection of data is said to be authentic when it is genuine and came from its alleged source. Message authentication is a procedure that allows communicating parties to verify that received messages are authentic. The two important aspects are to verify that the contents of the message have not been altered and that the source is authentic. We may also wish to verify a message's timeliness (that it has not been artificially delayed and replayed) and sequence relative to other messages flowing between two parties.

8B.1   AUTHENTICATION USING CONVENTIONAL ENCRYPTION

It is possible to perform authentication simply by using conventional encryption. If we assume that only the sender and receiver share a key (which is as it should be), then only the genuine sender would be able to successfully encrypt a message for the other participant. Furthermore, if the message includes an error-detection code and a sequence number, the receiver is assured that no alterations have been made and that sequencing is proper. If the message also includes a time-stamp, the receiver is assured that the message has not been delayed beyond what would normally be expected for network transit.

8B.2 DIGITAL SIGNATURE USING PUBLIC-KEY ENCRYPTION

Authentication using conventional encryption protects two parties exchanging messages from attack by any third party. However, it does not protect the two parties from each other. Several forms of dispute between the two are possible.

For example, suppose that John sends an authenticated message to Mary, using the scheme shown in Figure 8.18, part (a). Consider the following disputes that could arise:

- Mary may forge a different message and claim that it came from John. Mary would simply have to create a message and encrypt it using the key that John and Mary share.

- John can deny sending the message. Since it is possible for Mary to forge a message, there is no way to prove that John did in fact send the message.

Both these scenarios are of legitimate concern. An example of the first scenario: an electronic funds transfer takes place, and the receiver increases the amount of funds transferred and claims that the larger amount had arrived from the sender. An example of the second scenario: an electronic-mail message contains instructions to a stockbroker for a transaction that subsequently turns out badly. The sender pretends that the message was never sent.

In situations where there is not complete trust between sender and receiver, something more than authentication is needed. The most attractive solution to this problem is the digital signature, which is analogous to the handwritten signature. It must have the following properties:

- It must be possible to verify the author and the date and time of the signature.

- It must be possible to authenticate the contents of the message at the time of the signature.

- The signature must be verifiable by third parties, to resolve disputes.

Thus, the digital-signature function includes the authentication function.

A variety of approaches has been proposed for the digital-signature function. In this section, we look at the use of public-key encryption for providing authentication and digital signature.

Figure 8.19, part (a), illustrates a simple digital-signature scheme using public-key encryption. This scheme exploits an important characteristic of all public-key encryption algorithms: the two keys can be used in either order. That is, one can encrypt with the public key and decrypt with the matching private key, or encrypt with the private key and decrypt with the matching public key. Figure 8.19, part (a), illustrates the latter application. Note what is happening. A prepares a message to B and encrypts it using A's private key before transmitting it. B can decrypt the message using A's public key. Because the message was encrypted using A's private key, only A could have prepared the message. Therefore, the entire encrypted message serves as the signature. In addition, it is impossible to alter the message without access to A's private key, so the message is authenticated.

In the preceding scheme, the entire message is encrypted. Although this validates both author and contents, it would require a great deal of storage. Each document would have to be kept in

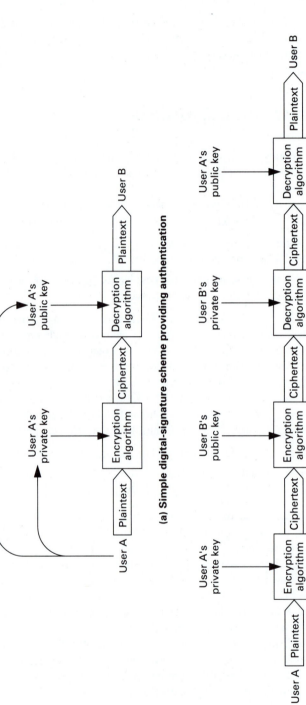

(a) Simple digital-signature scheme providing authentication

(b) Digital-signature scheme providing authentication and secrecy

Figure 8.19 Digital Signature Using Public-Key System

plaintext to be used for practical purposes. A copy would also have to be keyed in ciphertext so the origin and contents could be verified in case of a dispute. A more efficient way of achieving the same results is to encrypt only a portion of the document. A minimal portion would include the sender's name, the receiver's name, a sequence number, and a checksum. If this portion of the message is encrypted with the sender's private key, it serves as a signature that verifies origin, content, and sequencing.

It is important to emphasize that the encryption process just described does not provide secrecy. That is, the message being sent is safe only from alteration, not from eavesdropping. This is obvious in the case of a signature based on a portion of the message, since the rest of the message is transmitted in the clear. Even in the case of complete encryption, as shown in Figure 8.19, part (a), there is no protection of secrecy, since any observer can decrypt the message using the sender's public key.

It is, however, possible to provide both the digital-signature function, which includes authentication, and secrecy by a double use of the public-key scheme. This is illustrated in Figure 8.19, part (b). In this case, we begin, as before, by encrypting a message using the sender's private key. This provides the digital signature. Next, we encrypt again, using the receiver's public key. The final ciphertext can only be decrypted by the intended receiver, who alone possesses the matching private key. Thus, secrecy is provided. The disadvantage of this approach is that the public-key algorithm, which is complex, must be exercised four times rather than two in each communication.

8B.3 MESSAGE AUTHENTICATION WITHOUT MESSAGE ENCRYPTION

We have seen several schemes for message authentication that rely on encryption of the entire message. In this section, we examine several other approaches. In all of these approaches, an authentication tag is generated and appended to each message for transmission. The message itself is not encrypted and can be read at the destination independent of the authentication function at the destination.

Because the approaches discussed in this section do not involve encrypting the message, message secrecy is not provided. Since conventional encryption will provide authentication, and since it is widely used with readily available products, why not simply use such an approach, which provides both secrecy and authentication? Davies and Price (1990) suggest three situations in which message authentication without secrecy is preferable:

1. There are a number of applications in which the same message is broadcast to a number of destinations. For example, notification to users that the network is now unavailable or an alarm signal in a control center. It is cheaper and more reliable to have only one destination responsible for monitoring authenticity. Thus, the message must be broadcast in plaintext with an associated message-authentication tag. The responsible system performs authentication. If a violation occurs, the other destination systems are alerted by a general alarm.

2. Another possible scenario is an exchange in which one side has a heavy load and cannot afford the time to decrypt all incoming messages. Authentication is carried out on a selective basis, with messages being chosen at random for checking.

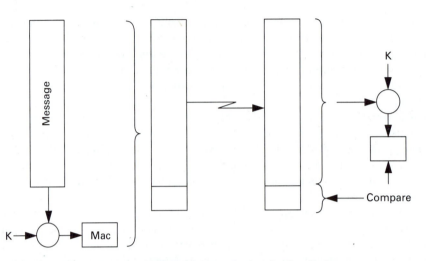

Figure 8.20 Message Authentication Using a Message-Authentication Code

3.   Authentication of a computer program in plaintext is an attractive service. The computer program can be executed without having to decrypt it every time, which would be wasteful of processor resources. However, if a message-authentication tag were attached to the program, it could be checked whenever assurance of the program's integrity is required.

Thus, there is a place for both authentication and encryption in meeting security requirements.

8B.3.1   Message-Authentication Code

One authentication technique involves the use of a secret key to generate a small block of data, known as a message-authentication code, that is appended to the message. This technique assumes that two communicating parties—say, A and B—share a common secret key K_{AB}. When A has a message to send to B, it calculates the message-authentication code (MAC) as a function of the message and the key: $MAC_M = F(K_{AB}, M)$. The message plus code are transmitted to the intended recipient. The recipient performs the same calculation on the received message, using the same secret key, to generate a new message-authentication code. The received code is compared to the calculated code (Figure 8.20). If we assume that only the receiver and the sender know the secret key, and if the received code matches the calculated code, then:

- The receiver is assured that the message has not been altered. If an attacker alters the message but does not alter the code, then the receiver's calculation of the code will differ from the received code. Since the attacker is assumed not to know the secret key, the attacker cannot alter the code to correspond to the alterations in the message.

- The receiver is assured that the message is from the alleged sender. Since no one else knows the secret key, no one else could prepare a message with a proper code.

- If the message includes a sequence number (such as is used with X.25, HDLC [high-level data-link control], TCP [transmission-control protocol], and the ISO [International Organization for Standardization] transport protocol), then the receiver can be assured of the proper sequence, since an attacker cannot successfully alter the sequence number.

A number of algorithms could be used to generate the code. The National Bureau of Standards, in its publication *DES Modes of Operation*, recommends the use of the DES (data-encryption standard) algorithm. This algorithm is used to generate an encrypted version of the message, and the last number of bits of ciphertext are used as the code. A 16- or 32-bit code is typical.

The process just described is similar to encryption. One difference is that the authentication algorithm need not be reversible, as it must for decryption. It turns out that because of the mathematical properties of the authentication function, it is less vulnerable to being broken than encryption.

8B.3.2   One-Way Hash Function

A variation on the message-authentication code that has received much attention recently is the one-way hash function. As with the message-authentication code, a hash function accepts a variable-size message M as input and produces a fixed-size tag H(M), sometimes called a message digest, as output. To authenticate a message, the message digest is sent with the message in such a way that the message digest is authentic.

Figure 8.21 illustrates three ways in which the message digest can be authenticated. The message digest can be encrypted using conventional encryption (part [a]); if it is assumed that only the sender and receiver share the encryption key, then authenticity is assured. The message can also be encrypted using public-key encryption (part [b]). The public-key approach has two advantages: it provides a digital signature as well as message authentication, and it does not require the distribution of keys to communicating parties.

These two approaches have an advantage over approaches that encrypt the entire message in that less computation is required. Nevertheless, there has been interest in developing a technique that avoids encryption altogether. Several reasons for this interest are pointed out in Tsudik (1992):

- Encryption software is quite slow. Even though the amount of data to be encrypted per message is small, there may be a steady stream of messages into and out of a system.

- Encryption hardware costs are non-negligible. Low-cost chip implementations of DES are available, but the cost adds up if all nodes in a network must have this capability.

- Encryption hardware is optimized toward large data sizes. For small blocks of data, a high proportion of the time is spent in initialization/invocation overhead.

- Encryption algorithms may be covered by patents. Some encryption algorithms, such as the RSA public-key algorithm, are patented and must be licensed, adding a cost.

- Encryption algorithms may be subject to export control. This is true of DES.

Figure 8.21, part (c), shows a technique that uses a hash function but no encryption for message authentication. This technique assumes that two communicating parties—say, A and B—share a common secret value S_{AB}. When A has a message to send to B, it calculates the hash function over the concatenation of the secret value and the message: $MD_M = H(S_{AB}\|M)$.[4] It then sends $[M\|MD_M]$ to B. Since B possesses S_{AB}, it can recompute $H(S_{AB}\|M)$ and verify MD_M. Since

---

4. $\|$ denotes concatenation.

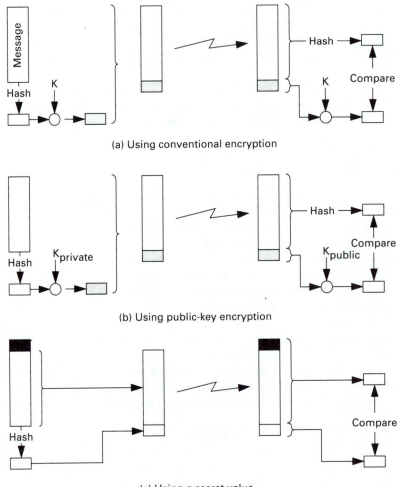

(a) Using conventional encryption

(b) Using public-key encryption

(c) Using a secret value

Figure 8.21 Message Authentication Using a One-Way Hash Function

the secret value itself is not sent, an attacker cannot modify an intercepted message. As long as the secret value remains secret, it is also impossible for an attacker to generate a false message.

This third technique, using a shared secret value, is the one adopted for secure SNMP.

8B.3.3   Hash-Function Requirements

The purpose of a hash function is to produce a "fingerprint" of a file, a message, or some other block of data. To be useful for message authentication, a hash function H must have the following properties, adapted from a list in Nechvatal (1991):

1.   H can be applied to a block of data of any size.

2.   H produces a fixed-length output.

3. H(x) is relatively easy to compute for any given x, making both hardware and software implementations practical.

4. For any given code m, it is computationally infeasible to find x such that $H(x) = m$.

5. For any given block x, it is computationally infeasible to find $y \neq x$ with $H(y) = H(x)$.

6. It is computationally infeasible to find any pair (x, y) such that $H(x) = H(y)$.

The first three properties are requirements for the practical application of a hash function to message authentication.

The fourth property is the "one-way" property: it is easy to generate a code given a message but virtually impossible to generate a message given a code. This property is important if the authentication technique involves the use of a secret value (Figure 8.21, part [c]). The secret value itself is not sent; however, if the hash function is not one-way, an attacker can easily discover the secret value. If the attacker can observe or intercept a transmission, the attacker obtains the message M and the hash code $MD_M = H(S_{AB}\|M)$. The attacker then inverts the hash function to obtain $S_{AB}\|M = H^{-1}(MD_M)$. Since the attacker now has both M and $S_{AB}\|M$, it is a trivial matter to recover S_{AB}.

The fifth property guarantees that an alternative message hashing to the same value as a given message cannot be found. This prevents forgery when an encrypted hash code is used (Figure 8.21, parts [a] and [b]). If this property were not true, an attacker would be capable of the following sequence: first, observe or intercept a message plus its encrypted hash code; second, generate an unencrypted hash code from the message; third, generate an alternate message with the same hash code.

A hash function that satisfies the first five properties in the preceding list is referred to as a weak hash function. If the sixth property is also satisfied, then it is referred to as a strong hash function. The sixth property protects against a sophisticated class of attack known as the birthday attack.[5]

In addition to providing authentication, a message digest also provides data integrity. It performs the same function as a frame-check sequence: if any bits in the message are accidentally altered in transit, the message digest will be in error.

---

5. See Davies and Price (1990) or Nechvatal (1991) for a discussion of birthday attacks.

9
SNMP Version 2 (SNMPv2): Management Information and Protocol

In July 1992, the secure SNMP (simple network management protocol) documents were published as proposed standards. In that same month, the simple management protocol (SMP) was introduced. These two specifications provided the base for developing version 2 of SNMP (SNMPv2). SNMPv2 is intended to remove many of the deficiencies of SNMP and to broaden its applicability to include OSI-based as well as TCP/IP-based networks. This chapter introduces SNMPv2 and then examines the management information and protocol aspects of the standard. The security-related features of SNMPv2 are covered in Chapter 10.

9.1 BACKGROUND

We begin with a short history of the development of SNMPv2, plus a summary of the enhancements to SNMP provided in SNMPv2.

9.1.1 The Development of SNMPv2

The simple network management protocol was originally developed as a stopgap measure to provide a minimal network-management capability. SNMP had two advantages:

1. SNMP, and its associated structure of management information (SMI) and management information base (MIB), is quite simple and therefore can be easily and quickly implemented.

2. SNMP is based on the simple gateway-monitoring protocol (SGMP), for which quite a bit of operational experience had been gained.

By 1988, it became clear that network management was a critical need, both in the short term to deal with the current level of network complexity and in the long term to deal with even more complex environments. Accordingly, a two-track policy was adopted: SNMP would be used to meet immediate network-management needs, and an OSI-based solution would be pursued for long-term needs. The OSI-based solution was CMOT (CMIP [common management information protocol] over TCP/IP), which essentially enabled OSI system-management protocols to operate on top of TCP. This two-track strategy has not worked out, for two reasons:

1. It was initially intended that the SMI and MIB of SNMP be subsets of those for OSI systems management. This would enable a relatively easy transition. However, the complex object-oriented approach of OSI was incompatible with quick deployment of SNMP, and so this linkage was dropped, allowing the SNMP framework to pursue the use of a simple scalar MIB. A result of this decision is to make the transition to OSI more difficult.

2. The development of stable OSI standards for network management, and the subsequent availability of product implementations, has taken much longer than anticipated. This delay opened up a window of opportunity that SNMP filled: SNMP has been implemented by a broad range of vendors and is widely deployed.

There is general agreement that, for many of the large, complex network configurations now becoming common, SNMP is reaching the end of its useful life. There are, and will be for some time, many configurations for which SNMP provides adequate service. However, many users are faced with the choice between an inadequate facility (SNMP) and one that is not yet available (OSI systems management). Accordingly, there has been much interest in "fixing" SNMP to extend its useful lifetime.

One such fix was discussed in Chapter 8. A major deficiency in SNMP is the lack of good security tools. Secure SNMP solves that problem. However, there are other deficiencies, related to performance and functionality, not addressed by secure SNMP. To overcome these deficiencies, SMP was developed.

SMP is the product of four individuals who have each played a major role in the history of SNMP:

1. Jeffrey Case, SNMP Research, Inc., and University of Tennessee
2. Keith McCloghrie, Hughes LAN Systems
3. Marshall Rose, Dover Beach Consulting, Inc.
4. Steven Waldbusser, Carnegie-Mellon University

The SMP proposal was issued in July 1992 as a set of eight documents. These documents are *not* RFCs (requests for comment). They constitute a privately issued proposal to the Internet community for an upgrade to SNMP. The extensions defined in the SMP proposal fall into four categories:

1. *Scope:* SMP is designed to facilitate management of arbitrary resources, not just "network" resources. Thus, SMP can be used for applications management, systems management, and manager-to-manager communication. The SMP framework provides a more concise but more flexible framework for describing information, promoting extensibility. SMP also provides a means for describing both conformance requirements and implementation capabilities.

2. *Size, speed, and efficiency:* SMP remains "simple," to enable the development of small, fast implementations. The major change in this category is the development of a bulk-transfer capability for the efficient exchange of large amounts of management information.

3. *Security and privacy:* SMP incorporates the enhancements found in secure SNMP.

4. *Deployment and compatibility:* SMP is designed to run on top of TCP/IP, OSI, and other communications architectures. SMP is also designed to interoperate with SNMP platforms, using a subset of SMP capabilities.

After the publication of secure SNMP (S-SNMP) and SMP, both in July 1992, a consensus emerged within the Internet community that it was highly desirable to enable users and vendors to make a single transition from the original SNMP to a second-generation SNMP that would include both security and functional enhancements. Accordingly, attempts to develop products based solely on S-SNMP were discouraged, and SMP was accepted as a baseline for beginning the process of defining a new SNMP standard, known as SNMP version 2 (SNMPv2). The original standard is now referred to as SNMPv1.

Two working groups were formed: one to deal with the security aspects of SNMPv2, the other to deal with all other aspects, including protocol and management information. Work officially began on SNMPv2 in October 1992. The charter called for the work to be completed in March 1993. In fact, a more aggressive schedule was followed and work on SNMPv2 was near completion by the end of 1992. The SNMPv2 functional working group completed their work in December 1992, and the SNMPv2 security working group completed their work in February 1993, except for some minor adjustments. The combined effort was then published as a set of proposed Internet Standards.

Table 9.1 lists the 12 documents that constitute the specification for SNMPv2. Given that the specification now totals a hefty 416 pages, some might question the "simple" in SNMPv2. Nevertheless, SNMPv2 does represent a natural progression from SNMPv1 and does retain, to some extent, the characteristics of ease of implementation and clarity of that earlier specification.

SNMPv2 is quite similar to SMP, from whence it developed. SNMPv2 provides a substantial functional enhancement to SNMPv1 and adopts the security enhancements of S-SNMP with some modifications.

If nothing else, the arrival of SNMPv2 has certainly complicated the network-management picture for users. On the one hand, there is the large and growing installed base of SNMP-managed configurations. Many of these users prefer to wait until SNMPv2 goes through IETF's formal standardization process, in case there are changes. Other users wish to respond to their immediate needs by moving quickly to SNMPv2. Still others will wish to retain SNMP as long as possible, eventually migrating to OSI. This fragmentation of the SNMP community leads to interoperability problems. SNMPv2 developers claim to have paved the migration path by basing SNMPv2 largely on SNMP and by providing a "proxy agent" that translates between the two systems. But such a gateway can slow down communications among devices.

On the other hand, there is a growing number of companies, particularly large companies, that are committed to the OSI approach. If SNMPv2 becomes competitive with OSI systems management, this could divide the industry into two camps, inhibiting interoperability.

The ultimate success of SNMPv2 versus OSI systems management is impossible to assess at this point. It seems clear that the telecommunications carriers will provide a major impetus to OSI development, since they are all in the process of developing network-management systems based on the OSI standards. This should drive the multiplexer and PBX (private branch exchange) vendors in the OSI direction. In addition, government support for OSI in the United States, the European Community, and Japan is forcing vendors to develop OSI management products for their

Table 9.1 SNMP Version 2 (SNMPv2) Documents

Introduction to SNMPv2

Provides an overview of version 2 of the Internet-standard Network Management Framework, termed the SNMP version 2 framework (SNMPv2). This framework is derived from the original Internet-standard Network Management Framework (SNMPv1). RFC 1441.

Structure of Management Information for SNMPv2

Defines the subset of Abstract Syntax Notation One (ASN.1) use to define the SNMPv2 MIB. The document also defines the module types and ASN.1 macros used to define the MIB. RFC 1442.

Textual Conventions for SNMPv2

Defines the initial set of textual conventions available to all MIB modules. RFC 1443.

Protocol Operations for SNMPv2

Defines the protocol data units (PDUs) for SNMPv2, and the protocol operations for those PDUs. RFC 1448.

Transport Mappings for SNMPv2

Defines how SNMPv2 maps onto an initial set of transport domains. The mapping onto UDP is the preferred mapping. RFC 1449.

Management Information Base for SNMPv2

Defines managed objects that describe the behavior of an SNMPv2 entity. RFC 1450.

Manager-to-Manager MIB

Defines managed objects that describe the

Manager-to-Manager MIB

behavior of an SNMPv2 entity acting in both a manager role and an agent role. RFC 1451.

Conformance Statements for SNMPv2

Defines the acceptable lower bounds of implementation, and the notation to be used to specify the actual level of implementation achieved. RFC 1444.

SNMPv1/SNMPv2 Coexistence

Describes coexistence between SNMPv2 and SNMPv1. The document covers management information and protocol operations. RFC 1452.

SNMPv2 Administrative Model

Presents an elaboration of the SNMP administrative model. This model provides a unified conceptual basis for administering SNMP protocol entities to support authentication and integrity, privacy, access control, and the cooperation of multiple protocol entities. RFC 1445.

SNMPv2 Security Protocols

Defines protocols to support three data security services: (1) data integrity, (2) data origin authentication, and (3) data confidentiality. RFC 1446.

SNMPv2 Party MIB

Defines a portion of the Management Information Base (MIB) for use with network-management protocols in TCP/IP-based internets. It describes a representation of the SNMP parties as objects, consistent with the SNMP security protocols. RFC 1447.

government customers. On the other hand, computer and data network users already have a large installed SNMP base.

Following the same topical sequence as Table 9.1, the details of SNMPv2 are presented in this chapter and the next.

9.1.2 SNMPv2 Enhancements

Before listing specific enhancements that are part of SNMPv2, we need to note an overall change in the capability provided by SNMPv2. SNMPv2 can support either a highly centralized network-management strategy or a distributed one. In the latter case (e.g., see Figure 1.5), some systems operate both in the role of manager and of agent. In its agent role, such a system will accept commands from a superior management system; these commands may deal with access to information stored locally at the intermediate manager or may require the intermediate manager to provide summary information about agents subordinate to itself. In addition, an intermediate manager can issue trap information to a superior manager.

The key enhancements to SNMP that are provided in SNMPv2 fall into the following categories:

- Structure of management information (SMI)
- Protocol operations
- Manager-to-manager capability
- Security

We briefly summarize these here. The first three items in the preceding list are covered in the remainder of this chapter. A discussion of security is provided in Chapter 10.

The SNMPv2 SMI expands the SNMP SMI in several ways. The macro used to define object types has been expanded to include several new data types and to enhance the documentation associated with an object. A very noticeable change is that a new convention has been provided for creating and deleting conceptual rows in a table. This convention is inspired by the one used in the RMON (remote network monitoring) MIB, but is much more elaborate.

The most noticeable change in protocol operations is the inclusion of two new PDUs. The GetBulkRequest PDU enables the manager to efficiently retrieve large blocks of data. In particular, it is well-suited to retrieving multiple rows in a table. The InformRequest PDU enables one manager to send trap type of information to another.

Two MIBs are defined as part of the SNMPv2 specification. The SNMPv2 MIB contains basic traffic information about the operation of the SNMPv2 protocol; this is analogous to the SNMP group in MIB-II. The SNMPv2 MIB also contains other information related to the configuration of an SNMPv2 manager or agent.

The manager-to-manager (M2M) MIB is specifically provided to support the distributed management architecture. The M2M MIB provides functionality similar to the RMON MIB. In this case, the M2M MIB may be used to allow an intermediate manager to function as a remote monitor of network media traffic. It may also be used to allow an intermediate manager to report on activities at the intermediate manager or at subordinate agents.

Finally, SNMPv2 contains a security capability that is based on that of secure SNMP.

9.2   STRUCTURE OF MANAGEMENT INFORMATION

The structure of management information (SMI) for SNMPv2 is based on the SMI for SNMP. The SNMPv2 SMI provides for more elaborate specification and documentation of managed objects and MIBs. Much of what has been added to the SNMPv2 SMI compared to the SNMP SMI codifies existing practices. The SNMPv2 SMI is nearly a proper superset of the SNMP SMI.

The SNMPv2 SMI is divided into four parts:

1. Object definitions

2. Conceptual tables

3. Notification definitions

4. Information modules

9.2.1   Object Definitions

As with the SNMP SMI, object definitions in the SNMPv2 SMI are used to describe managed objects. The ASN.1 macro OBJECT-TYPE is used to convey the syntax and semantics of all managed objects in a systematic way.

Figure 9.1 reproduces from the SNMPv2 specification the OBJECT-TYPE macro and associated definitions. This macro has the same general structure as the OBJECT-TYPE macro defined in RFC 1155 (SNMP SMI), with refinements in RFC 1212 (Concise MIB Definitions).

Table 9.2 provides a comparison between the macro defined in the SNMPv2 documents and the macro defined for SNMP in RFCs 1155 and 1212. It will only be necessary to comment on the differences.

For both SNMP and SNMPv2, the type of an object may either be simple or application-based. The simple types are quite similar for the two SMIs. One difference is that for SNMPv2, an explicit restriction of integers to 32 bits is provided. The other difference is that enumerated bit-string values are allowed in SNMPv2. These are useful for defining masks and flags.

For application types, the following differences occur. SNMPv2 includes both OSI NSAP (network service-access point) addresses as well as the internet IP address. SNMPv2 includes a 64-bit counter in addition to the 32-bit counter defined in the SNMP SMI. In SNMPv2, both 32-bit and 64-bit counters must always have an access category of read-only. The SNMPv2 specification also states that counters have no defined ''initial'' value, and thus, a single value of a counter has no information content; it is only the difference between two readings of a counter that is significant. SNMPv2 also includes the UInteger type to represent integers in, the range 0 to $2^{32} - 1$.

Both SNMPv2 and SNMP include a 32-bit gauge type. The SNMPv2 standard includes the following statement:

> The value of a Gauge has its maximum value whenever the information being modeled is greater than or equal to that maximum value; if the information being modeled subsequently decreases below the maximum value, the Gauge also decreases.

This removes an ambiguity in the SNMP SMI. RFC 1155 merely states that a gauge latches at its maximum value. The word *latch* is not defined, and it is not specified whether a gauge can decrease after it has attained its maximum value. There had been no agreement within the SNMP community on this point.

```
OBJECT-TYPE MACRO ::= BEGIN

TYPE NOTATION ::= "SYNTAX" type (ObjectSyntax)
                  UnitsPart
                  "MAX-ACCESS" Access
                  "STATUS" Status
                  "DESCRIPTION" Text
                  ReferPart
                  IndexPart
                  DefValPart

VALUE NOTATION ::= value (VALUE ObjectName)

UnitsPart ::= "UNITS" Text | empty

Access ::= "not-accessible" | "read-only" | "read- write" | "read-create"

Status ::= "current" | "deprecated" | "obsolete"

ReferPart ::= "REFERENCE" Text | empty

IndexPart ::= "INDEX" "{" IndexTypes "}" | "AUGMENTS" "{" Entry "}" | empty

IndexTypes ::= IndexType | IndexTypes "," IndexType

IndexType ::= "IMPLIED" Index | Index

Index ::= value (indexobject ObjectName)    --use the SYNTAX value of the correspondent
                                            "OBJECT-TYPE invocation

Entry ::= value (entryobject ObjectName)    --use the INDEX value of the correspondent
                                            --OBJECT-TYPE invocation

DefValPart ::= "DEFVAL" "{" value (Defval ObjectSyntax) "}" | empty

--uses the NVT ASCII character set
Text ::= """"string""""

END
```

Figure 9.1 SNMPv2 Macro for Object Definition

An SNMPv2 OBJECT-TYPE macro includes an optional UNITS clause, which contains a textual definition of the units associated with an object. This clause is useful for any object that represents a measurement in some kind of units. Here is an example of its use, taken from the manager-to-manager MIB:

```
snmpEventNotifyIntervalRequested OBJECT-TYPE
        SYNTAX          Integer32
        UNITS           "seconds"
        MAX-ACCESS      read-create
        STATUS          current
```

objectName ::= OBJECT IDENTIFIER

ObjectSyntax ::= CHOICE { simple   SimpleSyntax,
                    application-wide   ApplicationSyntax }

SimpleSyntax ::= CHOICE {
                    --INTEGERS with a more restrictive range may also be used
                    integer-value   INTEGER (-2147483648..2147483648),
                    string-value   OCTET STRING,
                    objectID-value   OBJECT IDENTIFIER,
                    bit-value   BIT STRING }   --only the enumerated form is allowed

--indistinguishable from INTEGER, but never needs more
--than 32 bits for a two's complement representation
Integer32 ::= [UNIVERSAL 2] IMPLICIT INTEGER (−2147483648..2147483648)

ApplicationSyntax ::= CHOICE { ipAddress-value   IpAddress,
                    counter-value   Counter32,
                    gauge-value   Gauge32,
                    timeticks-value   TimeTicks,
                    arbitrary-value   Opaque,
                    nsapAddress-value   NsapAddress,
                    big-counter-value   Counter64,
                    unsigned-integer-value UInteger32   }

IpAddress ::= [APPLICATION 0] IMPLICIT OCTET STRING (SIZE (4))

Counter32 ::= [APPLICATION 1] IMPLICIT INTEGER (0..4294967295) --this wraps

Gauge32 ::= [APPLICATION 2] IMPLICIT INTEGER (0..4294967295) --this doesn't wrap

--hundredths of seconds since an epoch
TimeTicks ::= [APPLICATION 3] IMPLICIT INTEGER (0..4294967295)

Opaque ::= [APPLICATION 4] IMPLICIT OCTET STRING --for backward-compatibility only

--for OSI NSAP addresses
NsapAddress ::= [APPLICATION 5] IMPLICIT OCTET STRING (SIZE (1 | 4..21))

--for counters that wrap in less than one hour with only 32 bits
Counter64 ::= [APPLICATION 6] IMPLICIT INTEGER (0..18446744073709551615)

UInteger32 ::= [APPLICATION 7] IMPLICIT INTEGER (0..4294967295)

Figure 9.1 SNMPv2 Macro for Object Definition (*Cont.*)

DESCRIPTION
    ''The requested interval for retransmission of Inform PDUs generated on behalf of this entry.

    This variable will be the actual interval used unless the snmpEventNotifyMinInterval is greater than this object, in which case the interval shall be equal to snmpEventNotify-MinInterval.''
DEFVAL { 30 }
::= { snmpEventNotifyEntry 1 }

Table 9.2 A Comparison of the SMI for SNMPv2 and SNMP

SNMPv2	SNMP (RFC 1212)

TYPE NOTATION::= "SYNTAX" type (ObjectSyntax)
ObjectSyntax::= CHOICE { simple SimpleSyntax, application-wide Application Syntax }
SimpleSyntax::= CHOICE {
  integer-value   INTEGER (-2147483648..2147483648),
  string-value   OCTET STRING,
  objectID-value   OBJECT IDENTIFIER,
  bit-value   BIT STRING }
ApplicationSyntax::= CHOICE {
  ipAddress-value   IpAddress,
  counter-value   Counter32,
  gauge-value   Gauge32,
  timeticks-value   TimeTicks,
  arbitrary-value   Opaque,
  nsapAddress-value   NsapAddress,
  big-counter-value   Counter64,
  unsigned-integer-value   UInteger32 }
	TYPE NOTATION::= "SYNTAX" type (ObjectSyntax)
	ObjectSyntax::= CHOICE { simple SimpleSyntax, application-wide Application Syntax }
	SimpleSyntax::= CHOICE {
	  number INTEGER,
	  string OCTET STRING,
	  object OBJECT IDENTIFIER,
	  empty NULL }
	ApplicationSyntax::= CHOICE {
	  internet IpAddress,
	  counter Counter,
	  gauge Gauge,
	  ticks TimeTicks,
	  arbitrary Opaque }

UnitsPart::= "UNITS" Text | empty	
"MAX-ACCESS" Access Access::= "read-only" | "read-write" | "read-create" | "not-accessible"	"ACCESS" Access Access::= "read-only" | "read-write" | "write-only" | "not-accessible"
"STATUS" Status Status::= "current" | "obsolete" | "deprecated"	"STATUS" Status Status::= "mandatory" | "optional" | "obsolete" | "deprecated"
"DESCRIPTION" Text	"DESCRIPTION" value (description DisplayString)
ReferPart::= "REFERENCE" Text | empty	ReferPart::= "REFERENCE" value (reference DisplayString) | empty
IndexPart::= "INDEX" "{" IndexTypes "}" | "AUGMENTS" "{" Entry "}" | empty IndexTypes::= IndexType | IndexTypes "," IndexType IndexType::= "IMPLIED" Index | Index Index::= value (indexobject ObjectName) Entry::= value (entryobject ObjectName)	IndexPart::= "INDEX" "{" IndexTypes "}" IndexTypes::= IndexType | IndexTypes "," IndexType IndexType::= value (indexobject ObjectName)
DefValPart::= "DEFVAL" "{" value (defval ObjectSyntax) "}" | empty	DefValPart::= "DEFVAL" "{" value (defvalue ObjectSyntax) "}" | empty
VALUE NOTATION::= value (VALUE ObjectName)	VALUE NOTATION::= value (VALUE ObjectName)

The SNMPv2 MAX-ACCESS clause is similar to the SNMP ACCESS clause. The prefix *MAX* emphasizes that this is the maximal level of access, independent of any administrative authorization policy. The SNMPv2 definition does not include the write-only category. A new category, read-create, has been added; it is used in connection with conceptual rows, as explained later in this chapter. The four possibilities, ordered from least to greatest capability, are defined as follows:

1. *Not-accessible:* not accessible by a manager for any operation

2. *Read-only:* read access

3. *Read-write:* read access and write access

4. *Read-create:* read access, write access, and create access

The STATUS clause for SNMPv2 does not contain the "optional" or "mandatory" categories defined for SNMP. An object with "current" status is valid for the current standard.

The IndexPart definition for SNMPv2 is more complex than that for SNMP. A discussion of this part is included in the discussion of tables, later in this section.

9.2.2   SNMPv2 Tables

As with SNMP, management operations in SNMPv2 apply only to scalar objects. More complex information can be represented conceptually as a table.

9.2.2.1   Table Definition

A table has zero or more rows, each of which contains one or more scalar objects. In both SNMP and SNMPv2, the following conventions apply.

- A conceptual table has a SYNTAX clause of the form:

    SEQUENCE OF <entry>,

    where <entry> refers to its subordinate conceptual row.

- A conceptual row has a SYNTAX clause of the form:

    SEQUENCE { <type1>, . . . <typeN> },

    where there is one <type> for each columnar object and each <type> is of the form

    <descriptor> <syntax>,

    where <descriptor> is the name of a columnar object and <syntax> has the value of that object's SYNTAX clause. All columnar objects are always present; that is, the DEFAULT and OPTIONAL clauses are not allowed in the SEQUENCE definition.

- Each columnar object is defined in the usual manner with an OBJECT-TYPE macro.

SNMPv2 enhances conventions used in RFC 1212 and in the RMON (remote network-monitoring) specification (RFC 1271) to facilitate row creation, deletion, and access. Essentially, there are two categories of conceptual tables allowed in SNMPv2:

1. *Tables that prohibit row creation and deletion by a manager:* These tables are controlled completely by the agent. The highest level of access allowed on any object is read-write. In many cases, the entire table will consist of read-only objects. This type of table is useful when the number of rows corresponds to a fixed attribute (i.e., the number of physical interfaces) or to a quantity that is controllable only by the agent.

2. *Tables that allow row creation and deletion by a manager:* Such tables may be initialized with no rows, with only the manager causing row creation and deletion. It is also possible for the number of rows in these tables to vary both by manager action and by independent agent action.

Both types of tables provide conventions and facilities for accessing rows in the table by indexing, and we look at this feature first. In addition, tables that allow row creation and deletion have additional features to facilitate these functions; we look at these features next.

9.2.2.2   Table Indexing

In the following discussion, it will be useful to refer to Figure 9.2, which shows a table definition from the SNMPv2 MIB. The table in this case is one that does not permit row creation or deletion.

Each conceptual row definition must include either an INDEX or an AUGMENTS clause, but not both. The INDEX clause defines a *base conceptual row*. The INDEX component of the row definition determines which object value(s) will unambiguously distinguish one row in the table.[1] That is, the INDEX object or objects determine a conceptual-row instance.

The one difference between the SNMPv2 convention for the INDEX clause and the RFC 1212 convention is the optional use of the IMPLIED modifier to an object name in SNMPv2. This modifier comes into play in defining instance identifiers. The rules for constructing the instance identifier of a columnar-object instance are as follows. Given an object whose object identifier is y, in a table with INDEX objects i1, i2, . . . iN, then the instance identifier for an instance of object y in a particular row is:

   y.(i1).(i2). . .(iN),

where each term in parentheses is interpreted as follows:

- *Integer-valued:* a single subidentifier taking the integer value (only valid for non-negative integers).

- *String-valued, fixed-length:* Each octet of the string is encoded as a separate subidentifier, for a total of n subidentifiers for a string of length n octets.

- *String-valued, variable-length preceded by the IMPLIED keyword:* Each octet of the string is encoded as a separate subidentifier, for a total of n subidentifiers for a string of length n octets.

- *String-valued, variable-length not preceded by the IMPLIED keyword:* For a string of length n octets, the first subidentifier is n; this is followed by each octet of the string encoded as a separate subidentifier, for a total of $n + 1$ subidentifiers.

- *Object-identifier-valued:* For an object identifier with n subidentifiers, the first subidentifier is n; this is followed by the value of each subidentifier in order, for a total of $n + 1$ subidentifiers.

- *IpAddress-valued:* Four subidentifiers, in the familiar a.b.c.d notation.

- *NsapAddress-valued:* Each octet of the address value is encoded as a separate subidentifier, for a total of n subidentifiers for an address of length n octets.

---

1. The SNMPv2 document explicitly states that the INDEX objects must be sufficient to unambiguously distinguish a conceptual row. This rule was not always followed in SNMP; see the discussion in subsection 6.1.3.2.

```
snmpORTable OBJECT-TYPE
        SYNTAX          SEQUENCE OF SnmpOREntry
        MAX-ACCESS      not-accessible
        STATUS          current
        DESCRIPTION
            "The (conceptual) table listing the dynamically configurable object resources in an SNMPv2 entity
            acting in an agent role. SNMPv2 entities which do not support dynamically configurable object
            resources will never have any instances of the columnar objects in this table."
        ::= { snmpOR 2 }

snmpOREntry OBJECT-TYPE
        SYNTAX          SnmpOREntry
        MAX-ACCESS      not-accessible
        STATUS          current
        DESCRIPTION
            "An entry (conceptual row) in the snmpORTable."
        INDEX               { snmpORIndex }
        ::= { snmpORTable 1 }

snmpOREntry ::= SEQUENCE  {
                snmpORIndex     Integer32,
                snmpORID        OBJECT IDENTIFIER,
                snmpORDescr     DisplayString }

snmpORIndex OBJECT-TYPE
        SYNTAX          Integer32
        MAX-ACCESS      not-accessible
        STATUS          current
        DESCRIPTION
            "The auxiliary variable used to identify instances of the columnar objects in the snmpORTable."
        ::= { snmpOREntry 1 }

snmpORID OBJECT-TYPE
        SYNTAX          OBJECT IDENTIFIER
        MAX-ACCESS      read-only
        STATUS          current
        DESCRIPTION
            "An authoritative identification of one of the dynamically configurable object resources in an
            SNMPv2 entity acting in an agent role.  This is analogous to the sysObjectID object in MIB-II."
        ::= { snmpOREntry 2 }

snmpORDescr  OBJECT-TYPE
        SYNTAX          DisplayString
        MAX-ACCESS      read-only
        STATUS          current
        DESCRIPTION
            "A textual description of one of the dynamically configurable object resources in an  SNMPv2
            entity acting in an agent role.  This is analogous to the sysDescr object in MIB-II."
        ::= { snmpOREntry 3 }
```

Figure 9.2 An Example of a Table for Which Row Creation and Deletion Are Not Permitted

The IMPLIED keyword enables a small savings in the instance identifier when one of the index objects is a variable-length string. The IMPLIED keyword should only be used when there is no risk of ambiguity. For example, if a table has two index objects, both of which are variable-length strings, at least the first object should be specified without the IMPLIED keyword.

As an alternative to the INDEX clause, a conceptual-row definition may include the AUG-MENTS clause. The object name associated with the AUGMENTS clause must refer to a base conceptual row, and the object that includes the AUGMENTS clause is referred to as a *conceptual-row extension*. In essence, the AUGMENTS feature is designed to increase the number of columns in a table without rewriting the table definition. The scalar objects subordinate to the conceptual-row-extension object become additional columnar objects in the base conceptual row. The resulting table is treated in the same fashion as if it had been defined in a single table definition. Further, it is possible to augment a base conceptual row with multiple conceptual-row extensions.

The AUGMENTS clause is useful in a situation in which there is a core of information that is to be stored in a table and one of several possible extensions to the table depending on the configuration. For example, a vendor can easily specify vendor-specific objects as extensions to a standard MIB table. It should be easier for applications to access these objects than if they were defined as a new, separate table.

Any object that is specified in the INDEX clause of a conceptual row and is also a columnar object of that row is termed an auxiliary object. The MAX-ACCESS clause for newly defined auxiliary objects is not-accessible. This restriction makes sense; consider the possible alternatives:

- *Read:* In order to read any columnar-object instance, it is necessary to know the value of the INDEX object or objects of the row instance; therefore, the only way to read the contents of an auxiliary variable is to already know those contents.

- *Write:* If a manager updates the value of an auxiliary-object instance, the identity of the row is changed. This is not a permissible operation.

- *Create:* The create operation, as explained later in this chapter, involves assigning a value to a columnar-object instance at the time of row-instance creation; this is a task performed by the agent and not the manager.

It is also possible to use an object that is not part of the conceptual row (i.e., not part of the conceptual table) as an index for that conceptual row. In that case, there is no restriction to the not-accessible access category. The DESCRIPTIONS clause for the conceptual row must include a textual explanation of how such objects are used in uniquely identifying a conceptual-row instance.

9.2.2.3   Row Creation and Deletion

Of all the issues addressed in the evolution of SNMPv1 to SNMPv2, none was more controversial, consumed more time, or generated more heat than the issue of row creation and deletion.

Two general strategies were considered:

1. Define two new protocol data units, Create and Delete, to be used for explicit row creation and deletion.

2. Embed the semantics for row creation and deletion into the MIB with a new textual convention called RowStatus. Row creation and deletion is performed using set and get operations, in the manner of the "RMON Polka" described in Section 7.1.4.2.

There are problems with both approaches, both in terms of the complexity of the algorithm and the communications overhead. Ultimately, the second strategy was adopted, and is described in this subsection. In the following discussion, it will be useful to refer to Figure 9.3, which shows a table definition used as an example in the SNMPv2 specification.

A conceptual table may be defined in such a way as to allow the creation of new rows and the deletion of existing rows. Such tables have all of the indexing features described in the preced-

```
evalSlot OBJECT-TYPE
    SYNTAX        INTEGER
    MAX-ACCESS    read-only
    STATUS        current
    DESCRIPTION
        "The index number of the first
        unassigned entry in the evaluation
        table.

        A management station should create
        new entries in the evaluation table
        using this algorithm: first, issue a
        management protocol retrieval
        operation to determine the value of
        evalSlot; and, second, issue a
        management protocol set operation to
        create an instance of the evalStatus
        object setting its value to
        underCreation (1). If this latter
        operation succeeds, then the
        management station may continue
        modifying the instances
        corresponding to the newly created
        conceptual row, without fear of
        collision with other management
        stations."
    ::= { eval 1 }

evalTable OBJECT-TYPE
    SYNTAX        SEQUENCE OF EvalEntry
    MAX-ACCESS    not-accessible
    STATUS        current
    DESCRIPTION
        "The (conceptual) evaluation table."
    ::= { eval 2 }

evalEntry OBJECT-TYPE
    SYNTAX        EvalEntry
    MAX-ACCESS    not-accessible
    STATUS        current
    DESCRIPTION
        "An entry (conceptual row) in the
        evaluation table."
    INDEX            { evalIndex }
    ::= { evalTable 1 }
```

```
EvalEntry ::= SEQUENCE {
        evalIndex    Integer32,
        evalString   OCTET STRING,
        evalValue    Integer32,
        evalStatus   RowStatus }

evalIndex OBJECT-TYPE
    SYNTAX        Integer32
    MAX-ACCESS    not-accessible
    STATUS        current
    DESCRIPTION
        "The auxiliary variable used to
        identify instances of the columnar
        objects in the evaluation table."
    ::= { evalEntry 1 }

evalString OBJECT-TYPE
    SYNTAX        OCTET STRING
    MAX-ACCESS    read-create
    STATUS        current
    DESCRIPTION
        "The string to evaluate."
    ::= { evalEntry 2 }

evalValue OBJECT-TYPE
    SYNTAX        Integer32
    MAX-ACCESS    read-only
    STATUS        current
    DESCRIPTION
        "The value when evalString was last
        executed."
    DEFVAL { 0 }
    ::= { evalEntry 3 }

evalStatus OBJECT-TYPE
    SYNTAX        RowStatus
    MAX-ACCESS    read-create
    STATUS        current
    DESCRIPTION
        "The status column used for creating,
        modifying, and deleting instances of
        the columnar objects in the evaluation
        table."
    DEFVAL { active }
    ::= { evalEntry 4 }
```

Figure 9.3 An Example of a Table for Which Row Creation and Deletion Are Permitted

ing subsection. To support row creation and deletion, there must be one columnar object in the table with a SYNTAX clause value of RowStatus and a MAX-ACCESS clause value of read-create. By convention, this is termed the status column for the conceptual row.

The definition of this textual convention is quite long.[2] However, it does provide a reasonably clear description of the intended use of this convention. It is therefore reproduced in full in Appen-

---

2.   The EntryStatus definition in the RMON specification was about one page long. The RowStatus definition

dix 9A. This appendix should be read before proceeding with the remainder of this subsection. A flowchart that depicts the process of conceptual row creation is shown in Figure 9.4.

A reading of the RowStatus definition shows that two methods are allowed for row creation. They are known as createAndWait and createAndGo. Let us briefly summarize the two methods.

First, consider the createAndWait method. The manager begins by instructing the agent to create a new row with a given instance identifier (index value). If this succeeds, the agent creates the row and assigns values to those objects in the row with default values. If all read-create objects have default values, the row is placed in the notInService state, indicating that the row has been completed but is not active. If some read-create objects do not have default values, the row is placed in the notReady state, indicating that the row cannot be activated because some values are missing. The manager then issues a Get to determine the status of each read-create object in the row. The agent responds with a value for each object that has default values; noSuchInstance for each supported object that has no default value; noSuchObject for each object that is defined in the MIB but which is not supported by this agent. The manager must then use a Set to assign a value to all noSuchInstance objects and may also assign new values to default-value objects. Once all supported columnar objects with a read-create access category have been created, the manager can issue a Set to set the value of the status column to active.

The createAndGo method is simpler, but is restricted in two ways. First, it must be limited to tables whose objects can fit into a single Set or Response PDU. Second, the manager does not automatically learn of default values. The manager begins by selecting an instance identifier. It may then issue a Get PDU to determine which read-create objects are noSuchInstance, or it may already have this information from prior knowledge of the agent. The manager then issues a Set PDU that creates a new row and assigns values to objects in that row. The manager must assign values to all read-create objects that do not have default values and may assign values to read-create objects that do have default values. If the Set operation succeeds, the row is created and put in the active state.

To understand the tradeoffs between the two methods, consider the following checklist of features for row creation, which was constructed by the designers of the RowStatus algorithm:

Mandatory Features:

1. Must handle rows larger than one PDU. For some tables, the number of variables in a row that can be created is so large, a variable-list assignment of all rows will not fit into a single Set PDU.

2. Must allow management station to learn of columns not implemented in agent. An agent may support a particular table but not support some of the objects in that table. It must be possible to create a row for such a table.

3. Must allow management station to learn of columns not accessible in agent. A columnar object with a MAX-ACCESS value of not-accessible can exist, but no value can be set for that object. An example is the INDEX object for the table.

4. Must arbitrate between multiple managers accessing same row. If two managers attempt to create a row with the same instance identifier (i.e., the same value for the INDEX object), the agent must be able to enforce the creation of a single row for one of the managers and inform the other manager to try again with a different INDEX value.

---

originally proposed in the SMP specification ran to two pages. The SNMPv2 RowStatus definition, in all its glory, consumes almost twelve pages in the standard!

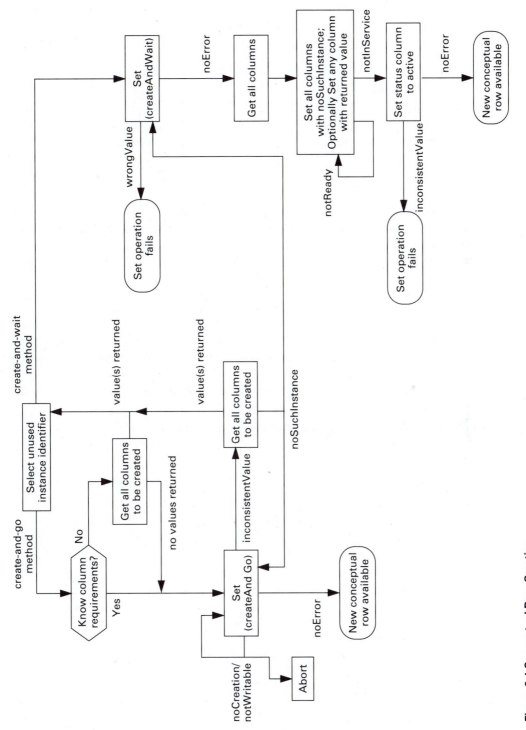

Figure 9.4 Conceptual Row Creation

5. Must protect create operations from reordering.
6. Must allow protocol entity to detect tooBig before create is executed. An agent must not create a row only to discover that it cannot respond properly in a single Response PDU.
7. Must allow read-only and read-create objects to coexist in same row.

Very Important Features

8. Allow simplified agent.
9. Keep protocol entity ignorant of row relationships. The agent should not have to take into account any semantic relationship between rows while performing row creation and deletion.
10. Don't add a new PDU type.

Useful Features

11. Perform operations in one transaction.
12. Allow management station to blindly accept default values for columns it does not care about.
13. Allow management station to learn of agent's default values and optionally override them.
14. Allow agent to choose index when it is arbitrary. For some tables the index has significance (e.g., a table indexed by an IP address). For other tables, the index is simply an arbitrary unique integer.
15. Have agent choose index as part of create operation. This would relieve the manager of the necessity of learning an unused index value before commencing row creation.

Based on this checklist, the two methods can be evaluated as follows:[3]

Feature #	Category	CreateAndWait	CreateAndGo
1	Must	Yes	No
2	Must	Yes	Yes
3	Must	Yes	Yes
4	Must	Yes	Yes
5	Must	Yes	Yes
6	Must	Yes	Yes
7	Must	Yes	Yes
8	Important	No	Yes
9	Important	Yes	Yes
10	Important	Yes	Yes
11	Useful	No	No
12	Useful	Yes	No
13	Useful	Yes	No
14	Useful	Yes	Yes
15	Useful	No	No

---

3. Table provided by Steve Waldbusser.

Table 9.3 Allowable Values of the MAX-ACCESS Clause for Table-Related Objects

(a) Columnar Objects

Object	Table That Permits Row Creation and Deletion	Table That Does Not Permit Row Creation and Deletion
INDEX object (auxiliary)	Not-accessible	Not-accessible
Status object	Read-create	—
Other columnar objects	Read-create or read-only	Read-write or read-only

(b) Noncolumnar Objects Related to the Table

Object	Table That Permits Row Creation and Deletion	Table That Does Not Permit Row Creation and Deletion
Table object	Not-accessible	Not-accessible
Entry (row) object	Not-accessible	Not-accessible
INDEX object (not included in table)	No restriction	No restriction

The createAndWait method places greater burden on the agent, which must be able to maintain conceptual rows in the notInService state. However, it is more powerful than createAndGo and can handle arbitrary row creations. On the other hand, the createAndGo method involves only one or two PDU exchanges and is therefore more efficient in terms of communications resources, management station time, and agent complexity. However, it cannot handle arbitrary row creations. Both options are available and an agent implementor may decide which option to support for each table.

Once we have defined the PDUs for SNMPv2, we return to the topic of row creation in Section 9.3.8 and work through an example.

To delete a conceptual row, a management station issues a set operation that sets the value of the status-column instance to destroy (6). If the operation succeeds, the agent immediately removes the entire conceptual row from the table.

9.2.2.4 Access-Category Restrictions

Table 9.3 summarizes the restrictions on the access category of various objects associated with conceptual tables. Note that the restrictions differ, depending on whether or not the table supports row creation and deletion by management stations.

9.2.3 Notification Definitions

The NOTIFICATION-TYPE macro is used to define the information sent by an SNMPv2 entity when an exceptional event occurs at the entity. Both traps and inform-requests, discussed in Section 9.3, are notifications.

Figure 9.5 shows the NOTIFICATION-TYPE macro. A simple example, taken from the SNMPv2 MIB, is the linkDown trap:

```
NOTIFICATION-TYPE MACRO ::= BEGIN

TYPE NOTATION ::= ObjectsPart
                    "STATUS" Status
                    "DESCRIPTION" Text
                    ReferPart

VALUE NOTATION ::= value (VALUE OBJECT IDENTIFIER)

ObjectsPart ::= "OBJECTS" "{" Objects "}" | empty

Objects ::-= Object | Objects "," Object

Object ::= value (Name ObjectName)

Status ::= "current" | "deprecated" | "obsolete"

ReferPart ::= "REFERENCE" Text | empty

Text ::= """"string""""

END
```

Figure 9.5 Definitions for Notifications

```
linkDown NOTIFICATION-TYPE
    OBJECTS { ifIndex }
    STATUS current
    DESCRIPTION
        "A linkDown trap signifies that the SNMPv2 entity, acting in an agent role, recognizes
        a failure in one of the communication links represented in its configuration."
    :: = { snmpTraps 3 }
```

The optional OBJECTS clause defines the ordered sequence of MIB objects that is contained within every instance of the notification type. The values of these objects are communicated to a manager when a notification occurs. The DESCRIPTION clause contains a textual definition of the semantics of the notification. The optional REFERENCE clause contains a textual cross-reference to an event or a notification defined in some other MIB module. The value of an invocation of the NOTIFICATION-TYPE macro is an object identifier assigned to the notification.

The procedure for issuing a notification using the SNMPv2 is as follows. When an SNMPv2 entity determines that a notification is to be sent, it consults the aclTable (described in Chapter 10) and finds all entries satisfying the following conditions:

- The value of aclSubject refers to this entity.

- The value of aclPrivileges allows for the SNMPv2 Trap PDU (protocol data unit).

- The notification's name is present in the corresponding MIB.

- The object instances associated with this notification, as defined in the OBJECTS clause, are all present in the corresponding MIB view.

For each entry satisfying these conditions, a notification is sent from aclSubject to aclTarget. The PDU includes a variable-bindings list with the following elements:

1. The first variable is sysUpTime.0, as defined in MIB-II.

2. The second variable is SNMPv2TrapOID.0, which is defined in the SNMPv2 MIB and which contains the object identifier of the trap.

3. If the OBJECTS clause is present, then each corresponding object instance is copied in order into the variable-bindings list.

4. The entity may optionally include additional variables.

For the linkDown trap defined earlier in this subsection, the trap event is the discovery of a link failure. The instance of ifIndex corresponding to this link becomes the third variable in the variable-bindings list.

The contents of the aclTable and viewTable determine the way in which trap transmission is configured. For example, an entity could be configured to send all linkDown traps to one particular SNMPv2 entity, and linkDown traps for only certain interfaces to other SNMPv2 entities.

9.2.4   Information Modules

SNMPv2 introduces the concept of an information module, which specifies a group of related definitions. Three kinds of information modules are used:

1. MIB (management information base) modules, which contain definitions of inter-related managed objects, make use of the OBJECT-TYPE and NOTIFICATION-TYPE macros

2. Compliance statements for MIB modules, which make use of the MODULE-COMPLIANCE and OBJECT-GROUP macros

3. Capability statements for agent implementations which make use of the AGENT-CAPABILI-TIES macros

These latter two type modules are discussed in Section 9.7.

Figure 9.6 defines the MODULE-IDENTITY macro. All information modules start with exactly one invocation of the MODULE-IDENTITY macro, which provides contact and revision history. For example, the module identity statement for the main SNMPv2 MIB is as follows:

```
snmpMIB MODULE-IDENTITY
    LAST-UPDATED "9212230000Z"
    ORGANIZATION "IETF SNMPv2 Working Group"
    CONTACT-INFO
        "    Marshall T. Rose

        Postal: Dover Beach Consulting, Inc.
                420 Whisman Court
                Mountain View, CA 94043-2186
                US

        Tel: + 1 415 968 1052
        Fax: + 1 415 968 2510
        E-mail: mrose@dbc.mtview.ca.us"
```

```
MODULE-IDENTITY MACRO ::= BEGIN

TYPE NOTATION ::=      "LAST-UPDATED" value(Update UTCTime)
                       "ORGANIZATION" Text
                       "CONTACT-INFO" Text
                       "DESCRIPTION" Text
                       RevisionPart

VALUE NOTATION ::= value(VALUE OBJECT IDENTIFIER)

RevisionPart ::= Revisions I empty

Revisions ::= Revision I Revisions Revision

Revision ::=     "REVISION" value(Update UTCTime) "DESCRIPTION" Text

  -- uses the NVT ASCII character set
Text ::= """"string""""

END


OBJECT-IDENTITY MACRO ::= BEGIN

TYPE NOTATION ::=      "STATUS" status
                       "DESCRIPTION" Text
                       ReferPart

VALUE NOTATION ::= value(VALUE OBJECT IDENTIFIER)

Status ::= "current" I "obsolete"

ReferPart ::= "REFERENCE" Text I empty

Text ::= """"string""""

END
```

Figure 9.6 SNMPv2 MODULE-IDENTITY and OBJECT-IDENTITY Macros

DESCRIPTION
   ''The MIB module for SNMPv2 entities.''
:: = { snmpModules 1 }

   In addition, SNMPv2 includes the definition of an OBJECT-IDENTITY macro, which is used to document the objects used in an MIB.

9.3   PROTOCOL OPERATIONS

SNMPv2 is an extension of the SNMP. As with SNMP, SNMPv2 PDUs are encapsulated in a message. The SNMPv2 message format is similar to that defined for secure SNMP. That is, the form and meaning of the message header are determined by an administrative framework that defines both authentication and authorization policies. In this section, we will concentrate on the SNMPv2 PDU.

   Three types of access to management information are provided by SNMPv2:

PDU type	request-id	0	0	variable-bindings

(a) GetRequest PDU, GetNextRequest PDU, SetRequest PDU, SNMPv2 Trap PDU, InformRequest PDU

PDU type	request-id	error-status	error-index	variable-bindings

(b) Response PDU

PDU type	request-id	non-repeaters	max-repetitions	variable-bindings

(c) GetBulkRequest PDU

name1	value1	name2	value2	· · ·	name*n*	value*n*

(d) Variable bindings

Figure 9.7 SNMPv2 PDU Formats

1. *Manager-agent request-response:* An SNMPv2 entity acting in a manager role sends a request to an SNMPv2 entity acting in an agent role, and the latter SNMPv2 entity then responds to the request. This type is used to retrieve or modify management information associated with the managed device.

2. *Manager-manager request-response:* An SNMPv2 entity acting in a manager role sends a request to an SNMPv2 entity acting in a manager role, and the latter SNMPv2 entity then responds to the request. This type is used to notify an SNMPv2 entity acting in a manager role of management information associated with another SNMPv2 entity also acting in a manager role.

3. *Agent-manager unconfirmed:* An SNMPv2 entity acting in an agent role sends an unsolicited message, termed a trap, to an SNMPv2 entity acting in a manager role, and no response is returned. This type is used to notify an SNMPv2 entity acting in a manager role of an exceptional event that has resulted in changes to management information associated with the managed device.

Only the second item is new with SNMPv2; the other two types of interaction are found in SNMP.

9.3.1   PDU Formats

The PDU formats for SNMPv2 are depicted informally in Figure 9.7. The ASN.1 definition is reproduced in Figure 9.8. Note that the GetRequest, GetNextRequest, SetRequest, SNMPv2 Trap and InformRequest PDUs have the same format as the Response PDU, with the error-status and error-index fields always set to 0. This convention reduces by one the number of different PDU formats that the SNMPv2 entity must deal with. Also, as with SNMP, there is no PDU type field defined in the ASN.1 specification, but it appears as an artifact of the BER (basic encoding rules) encoding of the PDUs.

```
SNMPv2-PDU DEFINITIONS ::= BEGIN

PDUs ::= CHOICE {get-request        GetRequest-PDU,
                 get-next-request   GetNextRequest-PDU,
                 get-bulk-request   GetBulkRequest-PDU,
                 response           Response-PDU,
                 set-request        SetRequest-PDU,
                 inform-request     InformRequest-PDU,
                 snmpV2-trap        SNMPv2-Trap-PDU }

— —PDUs

GetRequest-PDU      ::=   [0] IMPLICIT PDU
GetNextRequest-PDU  ::=   [1] IMPLICIT PDU
GetBulkRequest-PDU  ::=   [5] IMPLICIT BulkPDU
Response-PDU        ::=   [2] IMPLICIT PDU
SetRequest-PDU      ::=   [3] IMPLICIT PDU
InformRequest-PDU   ::=   [6] IMPLICIT PDU
SNMPv2-Trap-PDU     ::=   [7] IMPLICIT PDU

max-bindings INTEGER ::= 2147483647

PDU ::= SEQUENCE {request-id Integer32,
                  error-status INTEGER {              — — sometimes ignored
                            noError (0),
                            tooBig (1)
                            noSuchName (2),    — — for proxy compatibility
                            badValue (3),      — — for proxy compatibility
                            readOnly (4),      — — for proxy compatibility
                            genError (5),
                            noAccess (6),
                            wrongType (7),
                            wrongLength (8),
                            wrongEncoding (9),
                            wrongValue (10),
                            noCreation (11),
                            inconsistentValue (12),
                            resourceUnavailable (13),
                            commitFailed (14),
                            undoFailed (15),
                            authorizationError (16),
                            notWritable (17),
                            inconsistentName (18) }
                  error-index INTEGER (0..max-bindings),  — — sometimes ignored
                  variable-binding VarBindList   }         — — values are sometimes ignored

BulkPDU ::= SEQUENCE {                             — — MUST be identical in structure to PDU
                  request-id        Integer32,
                  non-repeaters     INTEGER (0..max-bindings),
                  max-repetitions   INTEGER (0..max-bindings),
                  variable-binding  VarBindList   }         — — values are ignored

— — variable binding

VarBind ::= SEQUENCE {name ObjectName,
                  CHOICE {value             ObjectSyntax,
                          unspecified       NULL,          — — in retrieval requests
                                                           — — exceptions in responses
                          noSuchObject [0]   IMPLICIT NULL,
                          noSuchInstance [1] IMPLICIT NULL,
                          endOfMibView [2]   IMPLICIT NULL } }

— — variable-binding list

VarBindList ::= SEQUENCE (SIZE (0..max-bindings)) OF VarBind

END
```

Figure 9.8 SNMPv2 PDU Format Definitions

9.3.2 GetRequest PDU

The SNMPv2 GetRequest PDU is identical to the SNMP GetRequest PDU in format and semantics. The only difference is in the way in which responses are handled. Recall that the SNMP GetRequest operation is atomic: either all the values are retrieved, or none is. If the responding entity is able to provide values for all the variables listed in the incoming variable-bindings list, then the GetResponse PDU includes the variable-bindings list, with a value supplied for each variable. If at least one of the variable values cannot be supplied, then no values are returned; instead, an error response is returned. Thus, in SNMP, a variable-bindings list in a response consists of a sequence of pairs, with each pair consisting of the name of a variable and its associated value.

In contrast, in SNMPv2, a variable-bindings list is prepared even if values cannot be supplied for all variables. If an exception condition related to a variable is found, then the name of that variable is paired with an indication of the exception rather than with a value. In SNMPv2, a Response PDU is constructed by processing each variable in the incoming variable list, according to the following rules:

1. If the variable does not have an OBJECT IDENTIFIER prefix that exactly matches the prefix of any variable accessible by this request, then its value field is set to noSuchObject.

2. Otherwise, if the variable's name does not exactly match the name of a variable accessible by this request, then its value field is set to noSuchInstance.

3. Otherwise, the value field is set to the value of the named variable.

If the processing of a variable name fails for any other reason, then no values are returned. Instead, the responding entity returns a Response PDU with an error status of genErr and a value in the error-index field that is the index of the problem object in the variable-bindings field.

If the size of the message that encapsulates the generated Response PDU exceeds a local limitation or the maximum message size of the request's source party, then the Response PDU is discarded and a new Response PDU is constructed. The new Response PDU has an error status of tooBig, an error index of 0, and an empty variable-bindings field.

A further word needs to be said about alternative 2 in the preceding list. Unless the management station has made an error, the conditions of this alternative will only occur for columnar objects, not for scalar values. Consider the following two cases:

1. A scalar-object type with the object identifier x has an instance identifier x.0. If the variable x.0 appears in a get PDU, the agent first determines whether the object type x is in its MIB. If so, the only instance of that object is x.0, and the appropriate value may be returned.

2. A columnar object with the object identifier y has an instance identifier y.i, where i is a series of one or more subidentifiers containing the values of the index variable for this table. If the variable y.i appears in a get PDU, the agent first determines whether the object type y appears in its MIB. If so, it must then determine whether the row indexed by i exists. If both these conditions are met, then the value of object instance y.i may be returned.

The noSuchInstance code should therefore only be returned in the case of a columnar object for a nonexistent row or a row under creation. This feature is used in row creation, as explained in subsection 9.2.2.3.

The modification of GetRequest to permit partial responses is a significant improvement. In SNMP, if one or more of the variables in a GetRequest are not supported, the agent returns an error message with a status of noSuchName. In order to cope with such an error, either the SNMP manager must return no values to the requesting application, or it must include an algorithm that responds to an error by removing the missing variables, resending the request, and then sending a partial result to the application. It is reported in Waldbusser (1992) that due to the complexity of the code needed to generate a partial response, many management stations do not implement such an algorithm and therefore cannot effectively interoperate with agents that have unimplemented variables. This has given rise to the practice among agent vendors of returning an arbitrary value for unimplemented objects rather than a noSuchName error, a problem discussed in subsection 6.5.2. The provision of partial responses by SNMPv2 agents should eliminate this problem.

9.3.3 GetNextRequest PDU

The SNMPv2 GetNextRequest PDU is identical to the SNMP GetNextRequest PDU in format and semantics. As with the GetRequest PDU, the only difference is that the SNMP GetNextRequest is atomic, whereas the SNMPv2 GetNextRequest processes as many variables as possible.

In SNMPv2, a Response PDU for a GetNextRequest is constructed by processing each variable in the incoming variable list, according to the following rules:

1. The variable (object instance) is located that is next in lexicographic order to the named variable. The resulting variable-binding pair is set to the name and value of the located variable.

2. If no lexicographic successor exists, then the resulting variable-binding pair consists of the name of the variable in the request and a value field set to endOfMibView.

If the processing of any variable fails for any other reason, or if the resulting response is too big, the same procedures as for GetRequest are followed.

As an example (taken from the SNMPv2 specification), consider an SNMPv2 application that wishes to retrieve the media-dependent physical address and the address-mapping type for each entry in the IP net-to-media-address translation table of a particular network element. It also wishes to retrieve the value of sysUpTime at which the mappings existed. Suppose that the table contains three rows with the following values:

Interface Number	Network Address	Physical Address	Type
1	10.0.0.51	00:00:10:01:23:45	Static
1	9.2.3.4	00:00:10:54:32:10	Dynamic
2	10.0.0.15	00:00:10:98:76:54	Dynamic

Suppose that the management station wishes to retrieve the entire table and does not currently know any of its contents or even the number of rows in the table. The management station can issue a GetNextRequest with the names of all the desired columnar objects:

GetNextRequest (sysUpTime, ipNetToMediaPhysAddress, ipNetToMediaType)

The agent responds with the value of sysUpTime and the values from the first row of the table:

Response ((sysUpTime.0 = "123446"),
        (ipNetToMediaPhysAddress.1.9.2.3.4 = "000010543210"),
        (ipNetToMediaType.1.9.2.3.4 = "dynamic"))

The management station can then store these values and retrieve the second row with:

GetNextRequest (sysUpTime, ipNetToMediaPhysAddress.1.9.2.3.4,
    ipNetToMediaType.1.9.2.3.4)

The SNMPv2 agent responds:

Response ((sysUpTime.0 = "123461"),
        (ipNetToMediaPhysAddress.1.10.0.0.51 = "000010012345"),
        (ipNetToMediaType.1.10.0.0.51 = "static"))

Then, the following exchange occurs:

GetNextRequest (sysUpTime, ipNetToMediaPhysAddress.1.10.0.0.51,
    ipNetToMediaType.1.10.0.0.51)
Response ((sysUpTime.0 = "123466"),
        (ipNetToMediaPhysAddress.2.10.0.0.15 = "000010987654"),
        (ipNetToMediaType.2.10.0.0.15 = "dynamic"))

The management station does not know that this is the end of the table and so proceeds with:

GetNextRequest (sysUpTime, ipNetToMediaPhysAddress.2.10.0.0.15,
    ipNetToMediaType.2.10.0.0.15)

However, there are no further rows in the table, so the agent responds with those objects that are next in the lexicographic ordering of objects in this MIB view:

Response ((sysUpTime.0 = "123471"),
        (ipNetToMediaNetAddress.1.9.2.3.4 = "9.2.3.4"),
        (ipRoutingDiscards.0 = "2"))

Since the object names listed in the response do not match those in the request, this signals the management station that it has reached the end of the routing table.

9.3.4 GetBulkRequest PDU

One of the major enhancements provided in SNMPv2 is the GetBulkRequest PDU. The purpose of this PDU is to minimize the number of protocol exchanges required to retrieve a large amount of management information. The GetBulkRequest PDU allows an SNMPv2 manager to request that the response be as large as possible given the constraints on message size.

The GetBulkRequest operation uses the same selection principle as the GetNextRequest operation; that is, selection is always of the next object instance in lexicographic order. The difference is that, with GetBulkRequest, it is possible to specify that multiple lexicographic successors be selected.

In essence, the GetBulkRequest operation works as follows. The GetBulkRequest includes a list of $(N + R)$ variable names in the variable-bindings list. For each of the first N names, retrieval is done in the same fashion as for GetNextRequest. That is, for each variable in the list, the next

name1   name2   • • •   nameN nameN + 1   • • •   nameN + R

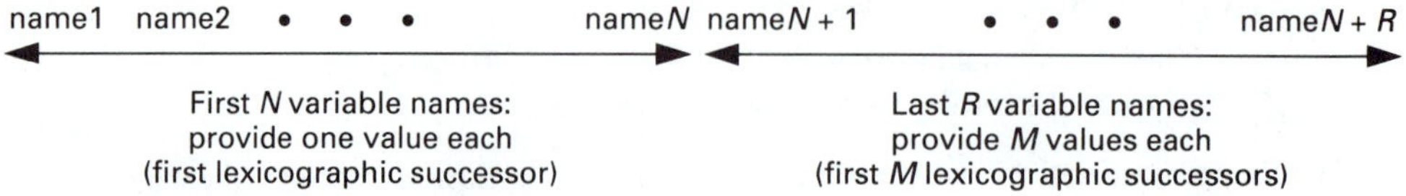

First N variable names:
provide one value each
(first lexicographic successor)

Last R variable names:
provide M values each
(first M lexicographic successors)

Figure 9.9 Interpretation of GetBulkRequest Fields

variable in lexicographic order plus its value is returned; if there is no lexicographic successor, then the named variable and a value of endOfMibView are returned. For each of the last R names, multiple lexicographic successors are returned.

The GetBulkRequest PDU has two fields not found in the other PDUs: nonrepeaters and max-repetitions. The nonrepeaters field specifies the number of variables in the variable-bindings list for which a single lexicographic successor is to be returned. The max-repetitions field specifies the number of lexicographic successors to be returned for the remaining variables in the variable-bindings list. To explain the algorithm, let us define the following:

L = the number of variable names in the variable-bindings field of the GetBulkRequest PDU.

N = the number of variables, starting with the first variable in the variable-bindings field, for which a single lexicographic successor is requested.

R = the number of variables, following the first N variables, for which multiple lexicographic successors are requested.

M = the number of lexicographic successors requested for each of the last R variables.

The following relationships hold:

N = MAX [MIN (nonrepeaters, L), 0].

M = MAX [max-repetitions, 0].

R = $L - N$.

The effect of the MAX operator is that if the value of either nonrepeaters or max-repetitions is less than 0, a value of 0 is substituted. Figure 9.9 illustrates these relationships.

If N is greater than 0, then the first N variables are processed as for GetNextRequest. If R is greater than 0 and M is greater than 0, then for each of the last R variables, its M lexicographic successors are retrieved. That is, for each variable:

1. Obtain the value of the lexicographic successor of the named variable.

2. Obtain the value of the lexicographic successor to the object instance retrieved in the previous step.

3. Obtain the value of the lexicographic successor to the object instance retrieved in the previous step.

4. And so on, until M object instances have been retrieved.

If, at any point in this process, there is no lexicographic successor, then the endOfMibView value is returned, paired with the name of the last lexicographic successor or, if there was no successor, with the name of the variable in the request.

Using these rules, the total number of variable-binding pairs that can be produced is $N + (M \times R)$. The order in which the last $(M \times R)$ of these variable-binding pairs are placed in the Response PDU can be expressed as follows:

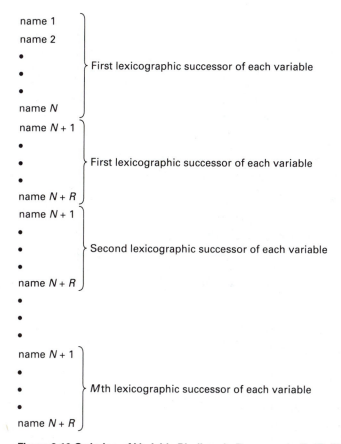

Figure 9.10 Ordering of Variable Bindings in Response to GetBulkRequest

for $i := 1$ **to** M **do**
   for $r := 1$ **to** R **do**
      retrieve ith successor of $(N + r)$th variable

The effect of this definition is that the successors to the last R variables are retrieved row by row rather than retrieving all the successors to the first variable, followed by all the successors to the second variable, and so on. This matches with the way in which conceptual tables are lexico-graphically ordered, so that if the last R values in the GetBulkRequest are columnar objects of the same table, then the Response will return conceptual rows of the table. Figure 9.10 illustrates the ordering.

Three exceptions must be noted. First, if the processing of a variable name fails (either one of the first N or one of the last R) for any reason other than endOfMibView, then no values are returned. Instead, the responding entity returns a Response PDU with an error status of genErr and a value in the error-index field that is the index of the problem object in the variable-bindings field. Second, if the size of the message that encapsulates the generated Response PDU exceeds a local limitation or the maximum message size of the request's source party, then the response is generated with a lesser number of variable-binding pairs. In essence, the Response PDU is constructed by placing variable-binding pairs in the PDU in the proper order until the maximum size is reached. Finally, if, during the iteration depicted earlier in this subsection, all of the variable-binding pairs have a value of endOfMibView, the variable bindings may be truncated at that point.

The example that was used in the discussion of GetNextRequest can be used here to demonstrate the superior efficiency of the GetBulkRequest operation. Let us assume the minimal max-repetitions value that provides an improvement over GetNextRequest—namely, a value of 2. Then, the manager issues:

GetBulkRequest [nonrepeaters = 1, max-repetitions = 2]
        (sysUpTime, ipNetToMediaPhysAddress, ipNetToMediaType)

The agent responds with:

Response ((sysUpTime.0 = ''123446''),
        (ipNetToMediaPhysAddress.1.9.2.3.4 = ''000010543210''),
        (ipNetToMediaType.1.9.2.3.4 = ''dynamic''),
        (ipNetToMediaPhysAddress.1.10.0.0.51 = ''000010012345''),
        (ipNetToMediaType.1.10.0.0.51 = ''static''))

Then, the following exchange occurs:

GetBulkRequest [nonrepeaters = 1, max-repetitions = 2]
        (sysUpTime, ipNetToMediaPhysAddress.1.10.0.0.51,
        ipNetToMediaType.1.10.0.0.51)
Response ((sysUpTime.0 = ''123466''),
        (ipNetToMediaPhysAddress.2.10.0.0.15 = ''000010987654''),
        (ipNetToMediaType.2.10.0.0.15 = ''dynamic''),
        (ipNetToMediaNetAddress.1.9.2.3.4 = ''9.2.3.4''),
        (ipRoutingDiscards.0 = ''2''))

This signals the end of the table.

The GetBulkRequest operation removes one of the major limitations of SNMP, which is its inability to efficiently retrieve large blocks of data. Moreover, the use of this operation can actually enable a reduction in the size of management applications that are supported by the management protocol, realizing further efficiencies. There is no need for the management application to concern itself with some of the details of packaging requests. It need not perform a trial-and-error procedure to determine the optimal number of variable bindings to put in a request PDU. Also, if a request is too big, even for GetBulkRequest, the agent will send back as much data as it can rather than simply sending a tooBig error message. Thus, the manager simply has to retransmit the request for the missing data; it does not have to figure out how to repackage the original request into a series of smaller requests.

9.3.5   SetRequest PDU

The SNMPv2 SetRequest PDU is identical to the SNMP SetRequest PDU in format and semantics. The only difference is in the way in which responses are handled.

First, the responding agent determines the size of a message encapsulating a Response PDU with the same variable-bindings list of names and values. If this size exceeds a local limitation or the maximum message size of the request's source party, a Response PDU is constructed with an error status of tooBig, an error index of 0, and an empty variable-bindings field.

Otherwise, a Response PDU is constructed in which all the fields have the same values as the corresponding fields in the received request, except as indicated later in this subsection.

The variable bindings are conceptually processed in two phases. In the first phase, each variable-binding pair, which constitutes an individual set operation, is validated. If all variable-binding pairs are valid, then each variable is altered in the second phase; that is, each individual set operation is performed in the second phase. Thus, as with SNMP, the SNMPv2 set operation is atomic: either all variables are updated or none is.

9.3.5.1 Validation

The following validations are performed in the first phase on each variable binding (variable name, variable value pair) until they are all successful or until one fails:

1. If the variable is not accessible, then the error status is noAccess.

2. If the variable does not exist and could not ever be created, then the error status is noCreation.

3. If the variable exists but cannot be modified, then the error status is notWritable.

4. If the value specifies a type that is inconsistent with that required for the variable, then the error status is wrongType.

5. If the value specifies a length that is inconsistent with that required for the variable, then the error status is wrongLength.

6. If the value contains an ASN.1 encoding that is inconsistent with that field's ASN.1 tag, then the error status is wrongEncoding.

7. If the value cannot under any circumstances be assigned to the variable, then the error status is wrongValue.

8. If the variable does not exist and can not be created under the present circumstances, then the error status is inconsistentName.

9. If the value could under other circumstances be assigned to the variable but is presently inconsistent, then the error status is inconsistentValue.

10. If the assignment of the value to the variable requires the allocation of a resource that is presently unavailable, then the error status is resourceUnavailable.

11. If the processing of the variable binding fails for a reason other than those just listed, then the error status is genErr.

If any of the preceding conditions is encountered on any of the variables, then a Response PDU is issued with the error-status field set appropriately and the value of the error-index field set to the index of the failed variable binding. The use of a number of different error codes is an improvement over SNMP; it enables a management station to more readily determine the cause of a failed request and take the needed action to solve the problem.

9.3.5.2 Variable Update

If no validation errors are encountered, then an attempt is made to update all the variables in the SetRequest PDU. For each variable in the list, the named variable is created if necessary, and the specified value is assigned to it. If any assignment fails (despite the validation phase), then all assignments are undone, and a Response PDU is issued with an error status of commitFailed and the value of the error-index field set to the index of the failed variable binding. If, however, it is not possible to undo all the assignments, then a Response PDU is issued with an error status of undoFailed and the value of the error-index field set to zero.

9.3.6   SNMPv2 Trap PDU

The SNMPv2 Trap PDU is generated and transmitted by an SNMPv2 entity acting in an agent role when an unusual event occurs. This PDU fulfills the same role as the SNMP Trap PDU, but with a different format. The SNMPv2 Trap PDU uses the same format as all other SNMPv2 PDUs except GetBulkRequest, thus easing the processing task at the receiver.

As with the SNMP Trap PDU, no response is issued to an SNMPv2 Trap PDU.

Section 9.2 describes how the variable-bindings field is constructed and also how the destinations for the PDU are determined.

9.3.7   InformRequest PDU

The InformRequest PDU is sent by an SNMPv2 entity acting in a manager role, on behalf of an application, to another SNMPv2 entity acting in a manager role, to provide management information to an application using the latter entity. This PDU is sent to the destinations specified in the SNMPv2EventNotifyTable, which is defined in the manager-to-manager MIB, or to destinations specified by the requesting application.

The format of the InformRequest PDU is shown in Figure 9.7. The PDU includes a variable-bindings field with the following elements:

1.   The first variable is sysUpTime.0, as defined in MIB-II.

2.   The second variable is SNMPv2EventID.i, which is defined in the manager-to-manager MIB and which contains the object identifier of the event type.

3.   The PDU may optionally include additional variables specified by the requesting application.

When an InformRequest PDU is received, the receiving SNMPv2 entity first determines the size of a message encapsulating a Response PDU with the same values in its request-id, error-status, error-index, and variable-bindings fields as the received InformRequest PDU. If this size exceeds a local limitation or the maximum message size of the request's source party, a Response PDU is constructed with an error status of tooBig, an error index of 0, and an empty variable-bindings field.

If the incoming PDU is not too big, the receiving SNMPv2 entity passes its contents to the destination application and generates a Response PDU with the same values in its request-id and variable-bindings fields as the received InformRequest PDU, with an error-status field of noError, and with a value of 0 in its error-index field.

9.3.8   Table Operations

Having introduced the SNMPv2 protocol operations, we can now return to the topic of SNMPv2 tables. This section provides an example of the use of the various features in SNMPv2 for operating on tables.[4] We first look at the row creation operation, and then examine the implications of augmenting a table.

---

4.   The author is indebted to Steve Waldbusser for providing this example.

```
pingTable OBJECT-TYPE
    SYNTAX    SEQUENCE OF PingEntry
    MAX-ACCESS not-accessible
    STATUS    current
    DESCRIPTION
        "A table of ping request entries."
    ::= { ping 1 }

pingEntry OBJECT-TYPE
    SYNTAX    PingEntry
    MAX-ACCESS not-accessible
    STATUS    current
    DESCRIPTION
        "A ping request entry."
    INDEX { pingIndex }
    ::= { pingTable 1 }

PingEntry ::= SEQUENCE {
            pingIndex        Integer32,
            pingIPAddress    IpAddress,
            pingDelay        Integer32,
            pingsRemaining   Integer32,
            pingsTotal       Integer32,
            pingsReceived    Integer32,
            pingRtt          Integer32,
            pingStatus       RowStatus,
            pingSize         Integer32 }

pingIndex OBJECT-TYPE
    SYNTAX    Integer32
    MAX-ACCESS not-accessible
    STATUS    current
    DESCRIPTION
        "A unique index for each entry."
    ::= { pingEntry 1 }

pingIPAddress OBJECT-TYPE
    SYNTAX    IpAddress
    MAX-ACCESS read-create
    STATUS    current
    DESCRIPTION
        "The IP address to send ICMP echo
        packets to.

        An attempt to modify this object will
        fail with an 'inconsistentValue' error if
        the associated pingStatus object would
        be equal to active(1) both before and
        after the modification attempt."
    ::= { pingEntry 2 }
```

```
pingDelay OBJECT-TYPE
    SYNTAX    Integer32
    MAX-ACCESS read-create
    STATUS    current
    DESCRIPTION
        "The number of milliseconds to delay
        between sending ICMP echo packets.

        An attempt to modify this object will fail
        with an 'inconsistentValue' error if the
        associated pingStatus object would be
        equal to active(1) both before and after
        the modification attempt."
    DEFVAL { 1000 }
    ::= { pingEntry 3 }

pingsRemaining OBJECT-TYPE
    SYNTAX    Integer32
    MAX-ACCESS read-create
    STATUS    current
    DESCRIPTION
        "The number of ICMP echoes left to
        send in this sequence. When this object
        is modified by a management station, a
        new sequence of pings is started,
        possibly aborting a currently running
        sequence. Whenever a sequence is
        started, the value of pingsRemaining is
        loaded into pingsTotal and the
        pingsReceived object is initialized to
        zero."
    DEFVAL { 5 }
    ::= { pingEntry 4 }

pingsTotal OBJECT-TYPE
    SYNTAX    Integer32
    MAX-ACCESS read-only
    STATUS    current
    DESCRIPTION
        "The total number of ICMP echoes to be
        sent in this sequence."
    DEFVAL { 5 }
    ::= { pingEntry 5 }
```

Figure 9.11 Ping Table Example

9.3.8.1   Row Creation

Figure 9.11 defines a table that can be used to provide a remote echo capability at an agent. This capability is part of the internet control message protocol (ICMP), which enables end systems and routers to exchange basic information needed to route internet protocol (IP) datagrams. ICMP is a user of IP (see Appendix B).

pingsReceived OBJECT-TYPE
    SYNTAX   Integer32
    MAX-ACCESS read-only
    STATUS   current
    DESCRIPTION
      "The total number of ICMP echo reply
      packets received in this sequence. The
      success rate may be calculated as:
pingsReceived/(pingsTotal-pingsRemaining)"
    DEFVAL { 0 }
    ::= { pingEntry 6 }

pingRtt OBJECT-TYPE
    SYNTAX   Integer32
    MAX-ACCESS read-only
    STATUS   current
    DESCRIPTION
      "The round trip of the last ICMP
      echo, in milliseconds.

      This object will be created by the agent
      after the first ICMP echo reply in a
      sequence is received. It will only exist
      when this entry is active(1). The agent
      shall delete it if this entry changes from
      the active(1) state."
    ::= { pingEntry 7 }

pingStatus OBJECT-TYPE
    SYNTAX   RowStatus
    MAX-ACCESS read-create
    STATUS   current
    DESCRIPTION
      "The status of this pingEntry. This
      object may not be set to active(1) unless
      the pingIPAddress, pingCount, and
      pingDelay columnar objects exist in this
      row.

      The first ping sequence is started when
      this object is set to active(1)."
    ::= { pingEntry 8 }

pingSize OBJECT-TYPE
    SYNTAX   Integer32
    MAX-ACCESS read-create
    STATUS   current
    DESCRIPTION
      "The size of ICMP echo packets to be
      sent.

      An attempt to modify this object will
      fail with an 'inconsistentValue' error if
      the associated pingStatus object would
      be equal to active(1) both before and
      after the modification attempt."
    DEFVAL { 64 }
    ::= { pingEntry 9 }

Figure 9.11 Ping Table Example (cont.)

Two of the messages that can be sent using ICMP are echo and echo reply. These messages provide a mechanism for testing that communication is possible between entities (end systems and routers). The recipient of an echo message is obligated to return an echo reply message. An identifier and sequence number are associated with the echo message to be matched in the echo reply message. The identifier might be used like a port to identify a particular session and the sequence number might be incremented on each echo request sent. The echo is sometimes referred to as a ping.

Each row of the pingTable corresponds to a particular system that is remote from the agent. A manager can set up a row to instruct an agent to ping another system at regular intervals.

Suppose that this table exists at an agent and currently has only one entry, with the following columnar object values:

Index	IpAddress	Delay	Remaining	Total	Received	Rtt	Status
1	128.2.13.21	1000	0	10	9	3	active

Note that the table does not contain the pingSize object. Let us assume that pingSize was defined in version 2 of this MIB and that this agent has an older version of software.

Now suppose that a manager wishes to add a new row using the createAndWait method. It determines that the next available index is 2, and wishes the new row to have the following values:

Index	IpAddress	Delay	Remaining	Total	Received	Status
2	128.2.13.99	1000	20	20	0	active

To add this entry, the manager begins by issuing a set command:

SetRequest (pingStatus.2 = createAndWait)

If this is successful, the agent responds with:

Response (pingStatus.2 = notInService)

The management station next issues a get request to examine all of the columns in the new conceptual row, except for pingIndex, which is not accessible, and pingsTotal, pingsReceived and pingRtt, which are read-only, and therefore not of interest for row creation.

GetRequest (pingIPAddress.2, pingDelay.2, pingsRemaining.2, pingStatus.2, pingSize.2)

The agent returns:

Response ((pingIPAddress.2 = noSuchInstance), (pingDelay.2 = 1000),
  (pingsRemaining.2 = 5)
  (pingStatus.2 = underModification), (pingSize.2 = noSuchObject))

This response indicates that default values have been assigned to pingDelay, and pingsRemaining. No value has been assigned to pingIPAddress, so this must be assigned by the manager to complete the definition of the table. This makes sense, because this object specifies the target address for the ping operation requested by the manager. Until this value is assigned, the status of the row remains underModification. Finally, the agent does not support the object pingSize.

The manager is happy with the suggested delay, but wants a total count of 20 rather than 5. Therefore, it issues the following:

SetRequest ((pingIPAddress.2 = 128.2.13.99), (pingsRemaining.2 = 20),
  (pingStatus.2 = active))

In summary, the first PDU exchange claimed the row, the second learned of the agent's suggestions and limitations, and the third finalized the parameters and activated the row. In effect, a negotiation has occurred between the management station and the agent.

This example highlights several important features of SNMPv2:

1. Occasionally, an agent will be unable to implement one or more columnar objects in a table. If those objects are mandatory, the agent is non-compliant but still should be able to

interoperate with willing managers. The row creation exchange enables the manager to learn about such objects efficiently.

2.   The agent can often choose a better value for a columnar object than the management station. In effect, the agent suggests the default value as part of the row creation dialogue. If the suggested value is acceptable to the management station, it can leave it alone; otherwise it can set a new value.

9.3.8.2   Augmenting a Table

Figure 9.12 defines an augmentation to the pingTable. This augmentation adds several useful parameters to the table. Let us suppose that the current contents of pingTable are:

```
cmuPingTable OBJECT-TYPE
    SYNTAX  SEQUENCE OF CmuPingEntry
    MAX-ACCESS not-accessible
    STATUS  current
    DESCRIPTION
      "A table of additional ping objects."
    ::= { cmuPing 1 }

cmuPingEntry OBJECT-TYPE
    SYNTAX  CmuPingEntry
    MAX-ACCESS not-accessible
    STATUS  current
    DESCRIPTION
      "Additional ping objects for a ping entry."
    AUGMENTS { pingEntry }
    ::= { cmuPingTable 1 }

cmuPingEntry ::= SEQUENCE {
        cmuPingTotalRtt     Integer32,
        cmuPingsDropped   Integer32 }

cmuPingTotalRtt OBJECT-TYPE
    SYNTAX  Integer32
    MAX-ACCESS  read-only
    STATUS  mandatory
    DESCRIPTION
        "The sum of the round trip times of successful pings received in this sequence. A
        management station may calculate the average round trip time as:
                cmupingTotalRtt / (pingsTotal - pingsRemaining)"
    DEFVAL { 0 }
    ::= { cmuPingEntry 1 }

cmuPingsDropped OBJECT-TYPE
    SYNTAX  Integer32
    MAX-ACCESS  read-only
    STATUS  mandatory
    DESCRIPTION
        "The number of ICMP echo reply packets dropped since this ping sequence was started.
        The success rate may be calculated as:
        pingsReceived / (pingsReceived + pingsDropped)"
    DEFVAL { 0 }
    ::= { cmuPingEntry 2 }
```

Figure 9.12 Augmented Ping Table Example

Index	IpAddress	Delay	Remaining	Total	Received	Rtt	Status
1	128.2.13.21	1000	0	10	9	3	active
2	128.2.13.99	1000	5	20	13	3	active

And that the two entries in pingTable are augmented as follows:

Index	cmuPingTotalRtt	cmuPingsDropped
1	27	1
2	468	2

Now, it is interesting to note that the table is split with respect to the object identifiers. The original pingTable may be part of a standard MIB, while the augmented portion may be part of the enterprises subtree. Thus, a lexicographic walk using the get-next operation will not find the two portions of the table contiguous. A lexicographic walk through the relevant portion of the MIB (as in Figure 6.8) would encounter the following:

```
pingIPAddress.1  =  128.2.13.21
pingIPAddress.2  =  128.2.13.99
pingDelay.1  =  1000
pingDelay.2  =  1000
pingsRemaining.1  =  0
pingsRemaining.2  =  5
[ rest of table. . . ]
[ other tables and other MIBs. . . ]
enterprises.cmu. . .cmuPingTotalRtt.1  =  27
enterprises.cmu. . .cmuPingTotalRtt.2  =  468
enterprises.cmu. . .cmuPingsDropped.1  =  1
enterprises.cmu. . .cmuPingsDropped.2  =  2
```

However, this sort of split table presents no problems to the get-bulk operator. Consider the following request:

```
GetBulkRequest [non-repeaters = 0, max-repetitions = 2]
              (pingIPAddress, pingDelay, pingsRemaining, pingsReceived, pingRtt,
              pingStatus, cmuPingTotalRtt, cmuPingsDropped)
```

The response is:

```
Response ( (pingIPAddress.1 = 128.2.13.21), (pingDelay.1 = 1000),
          (pingsRemaining.1 = 0), (pingsTotal.1 = 10), (pingsReceived.1 = 9),
          (pingRtt.1 = 3), (pingStatus.1 = active), (cmuPingTotalRtt.1 = 27),
          (cmuPingsDropped.1 = 1), (pingIPAddress.2 = 128.2.23.99),
          (pingDelay.2 = 1000), (pingsRemaining.2 = 5), (pingsTotal.2 = 20),
          (pingsReceived.2 = 13), (pingRtt.2 = 3), (pingStatus.2 = active),
          (cmuPingTotalRtt.2 = 468), (cmuPingsDropped.2 = 2) )
```

Thus, the objects in the combined table plus augmented table come back in row order, even though they are retrieved from different parts of the object-identifier hierarchy.

9.4 TRANSPORT MAPPINGS

The SNMPv2 specification includes a discussion of the mapping of SNMPv2 onto various transport-level protocols. The following are included:

- User datagram protocol
- OSI connectionless-mode transport protocol
- Novell internetwork packet exchange (IPX)
- Appletalk

The SNMPv2 specification for transport mappings also spells out the following restrictions on the use of basic encoding rules (BER):

- When encoding the length field, only the definite form is used; the indefinite form is prohibited.
- The primitive form is used to encode the value field whenever possible.
- When a BIT STRING is serialized, all named bits are transferred regardless of their truth value.

9.5 SNMPV2 MANAGEMENT INFORMATION BASE

The SNMPv2 MIB defines objects that describe the behavior of an SNMPv2 entity. This MIB consists of five groups:

1. *SNMPv2 statistics group:* a collection of objects providing basic instrumentation of the SNMPv2 entity.

2. *SNMPv1 statistics group:* a collection of objects providing basic instrumentation of an SNMPv2 entity that also implements SNMPv1.

3. *Object resource group:* a collection of objects allowing an SNMPv2 entity acting in an agent role to describe its dynamically configurable object resources.

4. *Traps group:* a collection of objects that allow the SNMPv2 entity, when acting in an agent role, to be configured to generate SNMPv2-Trap-PDUs.

5. *Set group:* a single object that allows several cooperating SNMPv2 entities, all acting in a manager role, to coordinate their use of the SNMPv2 set operation.

Figure 9.13 illustrates the structure of this MIB. We consider each group in the MIB in turn.

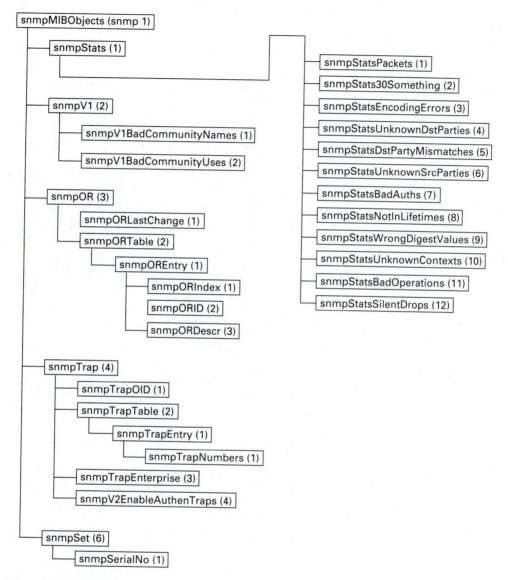

Figure 9.13 SNMPv2 MIB

9.5.1   SNMPv2 Statistics Group

The SNMPv2 statistics group contains some basic traffic information relating to the operation of the SNMPv2 protocol. Table 9.4 lists the objects contained in the group.[5] A comparison with the

5.   The following acronyms are used in Tables 9.4 through 9.9: read-only (RO), read-write (RW), read-create (RC), not-accessible (NA).

Table 9.4 SNMPv2 Statistics Group

Object	Syntax	Access	Description
snmpStatsPackets	Counter32	RO	Total number of packets received by SNMPv2 entity from transport service.
snmpStats30Something	Counter32	RO	Total number of packets that had initial octet value of 30 hex received by SNMPv2 entity that does not support SNMPv1.
snmpStatsEncodingErrors	Counter32	RO	Total number of packets received that were improperly coded or had invalid syntax.
snmpStatsUnknownDstParties	Counter32	RO	Total number of packets received for which the auth-Data.dstParty field was not a known local party.
snmpStatsDstPartyMismatches	Counter32	RO	Total number of packets received for which the auth-Data.dstParty field did not match the privDst field.
snmpStatsUnknownSrcParties	Counter32	RO	Total number of packets received for which the auth-Data.srcParty field was not a known remote party.
snmpStatsBadAuths	Counter32	RO	Total number of packets received that contained an auth-Infor field inconsistent with the authentication protocol associated with the source party.

snmpStatsNotInLifetimes	Counter32	RO	Total number of packets received that were deemed unauthentic due to their authInfo.authSrcTimestamp field being less than the source party's clock plus lifetime.
snmpStatsWrongDigestValues	Counter32	RO	Total number of packets received that were deemed unauthentic due to their authInfo.authDigest field being unequal to the expected digest value.
snmpStatsUnknownContexts	Counter32	RO	Total number of packets received for which the context field was not a known SNMPv2 context.
snmpStatsBadOperations	Counter32	RO	Total number of packets received that were silently dropped because the PDU type not allowed in the aclTable.
snmpStatsSilentDrops	Counter32	RO	Total number of GetRequest, GetNextRequest, GetBulkRequest, SetRequest, and InformRequest PDUs that were silently dropped because the size of a reply containing an alternate Response-PDU with an empty variable-bindings field was greater than either a local constraint or the maximum message size of the request's source party.

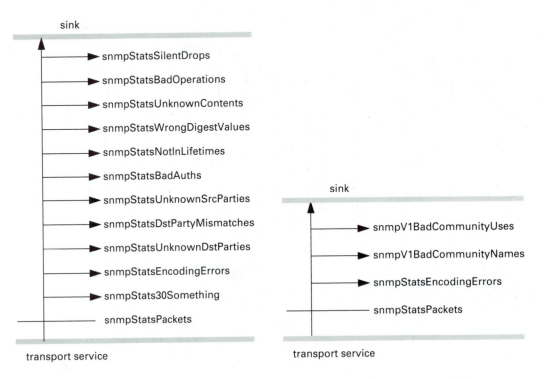

(a) SNMPv2 statistics group   (b) SNMPv1 statistics group

Figure 9.14   SNMPv2 MIB Case Diagrams

MIB-II SNMP group shows that the SNMPv2 group has far fewer parameters. The reason for this is that these detailed statistics aren't essential to debugging real problems and they add quite a bit to the size of an agent. Accordingly, a more streamlined group of objects was adopted. Note that the SNMPv2 statistics group concentrates on counting the number of messages not accepted for various reasons.

With SNMPv2, Case diagrams are used for the first time as part of the official documentation of a standardized MIB. Figure 9.14, part (a) illustrates the Case diagram for this group. See Appendix 9B for an introduction to this tool.

9.5.2   SNMPv1 Statistics Group

The SNMPv2 statistics group contains some basic traffic information relating to the operation of the SNMPv1 protocol at an SNMPv1 entity that also implements SNMPv1. Table 9.5 lists the objects contained in the group. Essentially, this group tracks the number of times SNMPv1 messages are rejected as unauthentic using the SNMPv1 community facility. Figure 9.14, part (b) illustrates the Case diagram for this group.

Table 9.5 SNMPv1 Statistics Group

Object	Syntax	Access	Description
snmpV1BadCommunityNames	Counter32	RO	Total number of SNMPv1 messages delivered to the SNMPv2 entity that used a community name not known to the SNMPv2 entity.
snmpV1BadCommunityUses	Counter32	RO	Total number of SNMPv1 messages delivered to the SNMPv2 entity containing an operation that was not allowed for the community named in the message.

9.5.3   Object Resource Group

The object resource group is used by an SNMPv2 entity acting in an agent role to describe those object resources that it controls that are subject to dynamic configuration by a manager. Table 9.6 lists the objects contained in the group. The group consists of a single scalar object and an object-

Table 9.6 Object Resource Group

Object	Syntax	Access	Description
snmpORLast-Change	TimeStamp	RO	The value of sysUpTime at the time of the most recent change in state or value of any instance of snmpORID.
snmpORTable	SEQUENCE OF SnmpOREntry	NA	Table of dynamically configurable object resources in an SNMPv2 entity acting in an agent role.
snmpOREntry	SEQUENCE	NA	Information on a particular dynamically configurable object resource.
snmpORIndex	Integer32	NA	Integer used as index into snmpORTable.
snmpORID	OBJECT IDENTIFIER	RO	The object ID of this entry. This is analogous to the sysObjectID object in MIB-II.
snmpORDescr	DisplayString	RO	A textual description of the object resource. This is analogous to the sysDescr object in MIB-II.

Table 9.7 Trap Group

Object	Syntax	Access	Description
snmpTrapOID	OBJECT IDENTIFIER	NA	The object ID of the trap currently being sent.
snmpTrapTable	SEQUENCE OF SnmpTrapEntry	NA	Table that keeps track of how many traps have been sent to each SNMPv2 entity.
snmpTrapEntry	SEQUENCE	NA	Information on a particular SNMPv2 entity.
snmpTrapNumbers	Counter32	RO	The number of traps which have been sent to a particular SNMPv2 party, since the last initialization of the SNMPv2 entity, or the creation of the SNMPv2 party, whichever occurred most recently.
snmpTrapEnterprise	OBJECT IDENTIFIER	NA	The object ID of the enterprise associated with the trap currently being sent.
snmpV2EnableAuthen-Traps	TruthValue	RW	Indicates whether the SNMPv2 entity, when acting in an agent role, is permitted to generate authenticationFailure traps.

resource table. The scalar object is snmpORLastChange, which records the value of sysUpTime at the time of the most recent change in state or value of any object instance included in the object-resource table. The object-resource table is a read-only table consisting of one entry for each object resource that can be dynamically configured.

9.5.4   Traps Group

The traps group keeps track of the SNMP-Trap PDUs generated by an agent. Table 9.7 lists the objects contained in the group.

The group consists of three scalar objects and a trap table. The scalar objects are snmp-TrapOID, which is the object identifier of the trap currently being sent; snmpTrapEnterprise, which is the object identifier of the enterprise associated with the trap currently being sent; and snmp-V2EnableAuthenTraps, which provides a means whereby all authenticationFailure traps may be disabled. The snmpTrapOID value occurs as the second varbind of an snmp-Trap-PDU. The snmpTrapEnterprisevalue occurs as the last varbind of an snmp-Trap-PDU. The trap table augments the partyTable defined in Chapter 10. It consists of one columnar object, snmpTrapNumbers, which is the number of traps sent to a particular snmp party.

9.5.5 Set Group

The set group consists, at the present time, of a single object that is used to solve two problems that can occur with the use of the set operation:

1. Multiple set operations on the same MIB object may be issued by a manager, and it may be essential that these operations be performed in the order that they were issued, even if they are re-ordered in transmission.

2. Concurrent use of set operations by multiple managers may result in an inconsistent or inaccurate database.

To see the second problem consider a simple example. Suppose that the value of a MIB object corresponds to the address of a slot in a buffer to be used for collecting data downloaded from a manager using some sort of file transfer protocol. The object's value indicates the next available slot. To use this value, a manager first reads the value, then increments it to the following slot, and then downloads its data. But the following sequence could occur:

1. Manager A gets the object's value, which is x.

2. Manager B gets the same value.

3. Manager A requires y octets of buffer space, and so issues a set to the agent to update the object to a value of x + y.

4. Manager B requires z octets of buffer space, and so issues a set to the agent to update the object to a value of x + z.

5. Both manager A and B are now prepared to send data into the buffer starting at location x.

The result will be that either A will overwrite B's data or vice versa. Furthermore, if z < y and A sends its data after B, not only is B's data overwritten, but part of A's data will be overwritten by the next manager to use the buffer.

This problem, in which the outcome depends on the order in which independent events occur, is referred to as a *race*.[6]

The single object in the set group is defined as follows:

```
snmpSetSerialNo   OBJECT TYPE
    SYNTAX        TestAndIncr
    MAX-ACCESS    read-write
    STATUS        current
    DESCRIPTION
```
"An advisory lock used to allow several cooperating SNMPv2 entities, all acting in a manager role, to coordinate their use of the SNMPv2 set operation.

This object is used for coarse-grain coordination. To achieve fine-grain coordination, one or more similar objects might be defined within each MIB group as appropriate."
```
    ::= { snmpSet 1 }
```

---

6. See (Stallings 92) for a discussion of issues related to distributed concurrent access.

TestAndIncr is a textual convention that has a type of INTEGER $(0..2147483647)$, which is $2^{31} - 1$. The rule for modifying this object is as follows. Suppose that the current value of the object is K, then:

1. If a set operation is received with a value of K, then the value of the object is incremented to $(K + 1)$ mod 2^{31}, and the operation succeeds with the value K being returned.

2. If a set operation is received with a value not equal to K, then the operation fails with an error of ''inconsistentValue''.

Recall that the set operation is performed atomically; that is, if a SetRequest PDU is received, the set operations specified by the variable-bindings are all performed if all operations are valid, or none is performed if at least one operation is invalid. Thus, the snmpSet object can be used in the following way. When a manager wishes to set one or more object values in an agent, it first retrieves the value of the snmpSet object. It then issues a SetRequest PDU whose variable-binding list includes the snmpSet object with its retrieved value. If two or more managers issue SetRequests using the same value of snmpSet, the first to arrive at the agent will succeed (assuming no other problems exist), resulting in an increment of snmpSet; the remaining set operations will fail due to an inconsistent snmpSet value.

As the definition states, this is a coarse-grained coordination technique: if all managers use the snmpSet object, then only one manager at a time can successfully issue a set to an agent, for all objects in the MIB. If a TestAndIncr object is associated with a single group, then concurrency restrictions can be confined to just the objects in that group.

9.6   MANAGER-TO-MANAGER MIB

The manager-to-manager MIB for SNMPv2 consists of a set of objects that describe the behavior of an SNMPv2 entity that acts in a manager role. The MIB consists of two groups:

1. *Alarm group:* a collection of objects allowing the description and configuration of threshold alarms from an SNMPv2 entity acting in a dual role.

2. *Event group:* a collection of objects allowing the description and configuration of events from an SNMPv2 entity acting in a dual role.

Figure 9.15 illustrates the structure of this MIB. This MIB provides essentially a reproduction of the functions addressed by the RMON alarm and event groups (described in Chapter 7), with some useful enhancements.

9.6.1   Alarm Group

The snmpAlarm group in the manager-to-manager MIB serves essentially the same function, in essentially the same way, as the RMON alarm group, defined in Chapter 7.

Table 9.8 lists the objects contained in the group. The snmpAlarm group consists of a single table, the snmpAlarmTable, and a single scalar variable, snmpAlarmNextIndex. The latter object is used to indicate the next available index number of row creation.

The snmpAlarmTable is almost identical to the RMON alarmTable. One difference is that, in addition to being indexed by snmpAlarmIndex, this table is indexed by contextIdentifier from the Party MIB (explained in Chapter 10). This index identifies the context to which sampling queries are directed.

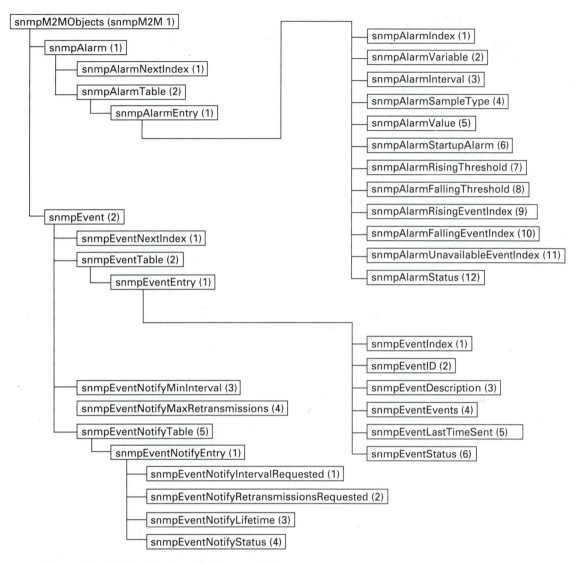

Figure 9.15   SNMPv2 Manager-to-Manager MIB

For an explanation of the functionality of this group, see the discussion of the RMON alarm group in Chapter 7 (subsection 7.2.4).

9.6.2   Event Group

The snmpEvent group in the manager-to-manager MIB is similar to the RMON event group. It supports the definition of events and the configuration of notifications. The snmpEvent group consists of two tables, snmpEventTable and snmpEventNotifyTable, plus associated scalar objects. Table 9.9 lists the objects contained in the group.

Table 9.8 Alarm Group

Object	Syntax	Access	Description
snmpAlarmNextIndex	INTEGER	RO	The index number of the next appropriate unassigned entry in the snmpAlarmTable.
snmpAlarmTable	SEQUENCE OF SnmpAlarmEntry	NA	Table used to define threshold alarms.
snmpAlarmEntry	SEQUENCE	NA	Specifies a diagnostic sample at a particular interval for a particular object on the device.
snmpAlarmIndex	INTEGER	NA	Integer used as index into snmpAlarmTable.
snmpAlarmVariable	Instance Pointer	RC	The object identifier of the particular variable to be sampled. The only object types allowed are INTEGER, counter, gauge, and TimeTicks.
snmpAlarmInterval	Integer32	RC	The interval in seconds over which the data is sampled and compared with the rising and falling thresholds.
snmpAlarmSampleType	INTEGER	RC	The method of calculating the value to be compared to the thresholds. If the value of this object is absoluteValue(1), then the value of the selected variable will be compared directly with the thresholds. If the value of this object is deltaValue(2), then the value of the selected variable at the last sample is subtracted from the current value, and the difference is compared to the thresholds.
snmpAlarmValue	Integer32	RO	The value of the statistic during the last sampling period.
snmpAlarmStartupAlarm	INTEGER	RC	Has the value risingAlarm(1), fallingAlarm(2), or risingOrFallingAlarm(3). This dictates whether an alarm will be generated if the first sample after the

Table 9.8 (*Cont.*)

Object	Syntax	Access	Description
			row becomes valid is greater than or equal to the risingThreshold; or if the first sample is less than or equal to the fallingThreshold; or both.
snmpAlarmRisingThreshold	Integer32	RC	The rising threshold for the sampled statistic.
snmpAlarmFallingThreshold	Integer32	RC	The falling threshold for the sampled statistic.
snmpAlarmRisingEventIndex	INTEGER	RC	The index of the snmpEventEntry that is used when the rising threshold is crossed.
snmpAlarmFallingEventIndex	INTEGER	RC	The index of the snmpEventEntry that is used when the falling threshold is crossed.
snmpAlarmUnavailableEventIndex	INTEGER	RC	The index of the snmpEventEntry that is used when a variable becomes unavailable.
snmpAlarmStatus	RowStatus	RC	The status of a specific row with respect to row creation and deletion.

Each entry in the snmpEventTable defines an event. Some events are triggered by an associated condition in the snmpAlarmTable; others are triggered on behalf of conditions defined in a NOTIFICATION-TYPE macro.

Associated with this table is the scalar object snmpEventNextIndex, which is the index of the next available slot for row creation.

The snmpEventNotifyTable defines notifications that should occur when an associated event is fired. Each entry describes the type and destination for an InformRequest PDU sent for a particular event. The table is indexed by two objects that are not columnar objects of this table: snmpEventIndex identifies the snmpEventEntry that, when triggered, will generate a notification as configured in this entry; partyIdentity identifies the destination party to which a notification will be sent.

Two scalar objects are associated with this table. The snmpEventNotifyMinInterval object defines a minimum interval that the SNMPv2 entity will wait before retransmitting an

Table 9.9 Event Group

Object	Syntax	Access	Description
snmpEventNextIndex	INTEGER	RO	The index number of the next appropriate unassigned entry in the snmpEventTable.
snmpEventTable	SEQUENCE OF SnmpEventEntry	NA	Table that defines the set of events generated on an SNMPv2 entity acting in a dual role.
snmpEventEntry	SEQUENCE	NA	Associates an event type with the notification method and associated parameters.
snmpEventIndex	INTEGER	NA	An integer that uniquely identifies a row in the snmpEventTable.
snmpEventID	OBJECT IDENTIFIER	RC	The object identifier of the event. This variable occurs as the second varbind of an InformRequest-PDU. This object identifier may be defined by a NOTIFICATION-TYPE.
snmpEventDescription	DisplayString	RC	A textual description of this event.
snmpEventEvents	Counter32	RO	The number of events caused by event generators associated with this entry.
snmpEventLastTimeSent	TimeStamp	RO	The value of sysUpTime when this event was last generated.
snmpEventStatus	RowStatus	RC	The status of a specific row with respect to row creation and deletion.
snmpEventNotify MinInterval	Integer32	RO	The minimum interval that the SNMPv2 entity will wait before retransmitting an InformRequest PDU.
snmpEventNotify MaxRetransmissions	Integer32	RO	The maximum number of times that the SNMPv2 entity will retransmit an InformRequest PDU.
snmpEventNotifyTable	SEQUENCE OF snmpEvent NotifyEntry	NA	A list of protocol configuration entries for event notifications from this entity.
snmpEventNotifyEntry	SEQUENCE	NA	A set of parameters that describe the type and destination of InformRequest PDUs sent for a particular event.

Table 9.9 (*Cont.*)

snmpEventNotify IntervalRequested	Integer32	RC	The requested interval for retransmission of InformRequest PDUs generated on behalf of this entry.
snmpEventNotify Retransmissions- Requested	Integer32	RC	The requested number of retransmissions of InformRequest PDUs generated on behalf of this entry.
snmpEventNotifyLifetime	Integer32	RC	The number of seconds this entry shall live until it is put into the underDestruction state. Any management station that is using this entry must periodically refresh this value to ensure continued delivery of events.
snmpEventNotifyStatus	RowStatus	RC	The status of a specific row with respect to row creation and deletion.

InformRequest PDU. If this value is greater than snmpEventNotifyIntervalRequested for a particular table entry, then this value is used instead for that entry.

The snmpEventNotifyMaxRetransmissions object defines the maximum number of times that the SNMPv2 entity will retransmit an InformRequest PDU. If this value is less than snmpEventNotifyRetransmissionsRequested for a particular table entry, then this value is used instead for that entry.

The snmpEventNotifyTable gives notification recipients considerable control over the unsolicited traffic they will receive. It allows them to dictate for which events they will receive notifications as well as the number and rate of retransmissions of InformRequest PDUs by the sending SNMPv2 entity when a response is not returned.

9.7 CONFORMANCE STATEMENTS FOR SNMPv2

The SNMPv2 specification includes a document dealing with conformance. The purpose of the conformance-statements document is to define a notation to be used to specify acceptable lower-bounds of implementation, along with the actual level of implementation achieved.

Three macros are defined in the conformance statements document:

1. OBJECT-GROUP

2. MODULE-COMPLIANCE

3. AGENT-CAPABILITIES

```
OBJECT-GROUP MACRO ::= BEGIN

TYPE NOTATION ::= ObjectsPart
                  "STATUS" Status
                  "DESCRIPTION" Text
                  ReferPart

VALUE NOTATION ::= value (VALUE OBJECT IDENTIFIER)

ObjectsPart ::= "OBJECTS" "{" Objects "}"

Objects ::= Object | Objects "," Object

Object ::= value (object ObjectName)

Status ::= "current" | "obsolete"

ReferPart ::= "REFERENCE" Text | Empty

Text ::= """"string""""

END
```

Figure 9.16 Definitions for Object Groups

9.7.1 OBJECT-GROUP Macro

The OBJECT-GROUP macro is used to specify a grouping of related managed objects. As in the SNMP SMI, a group of managed objects in SNMPv2 is the basic unit of conformance. The OBJECT-GROUP macro provides a systematic means for a vendor to describe its degree of conformance by indicating which groups are implemented.

The SNMPv2 specification clears up an ambiguity in SNMP that was discussed in Section 6.5. The SNMPv2 specification specifies that an object is "implemented" only if a reasonably accurate value can be returned for a read operation. In addition, for writable objects, the implementation must be able to reasonably influence the underlying managed entity in response to a set operation. If an agent cannot implement an object, it must return an error, such as noSuchObject, in response to a protocol operation. The agent is not permitted to return a value for an object that it does not implement.

Figure 9.16 shows the OBJECT-GROUP macro. The OBJECTS clause lists all of the objects in the group that have a MAX-ACCESS clause value of "read-only", "read-write", or "read-create". Thus, objects that have a MAX-ACCESS clause value of "not-accessible" are not included in the OBJECT-GROUP macro. This includes conceptual table, conceptual row, and row index objects. Each of the named objects must be defined with an OBJECT-TYPE macro in the same module as the OBJECT-GROUP module exists. The STATUS clause indicates whether this definition is current or obsolete. The DESCRIPTION clause contains a textual definition of the group, along with a description of any relations to other groups. The value of an invocation of the OBJECT-GROUP macro is an object identifier assigned to the group. The REFERENCE clause may be used to include a textual cross-reference to a group defined in some other information module.

An example of an OBJECT-GROUP definition is that for the SNMPv1 statistics group:

snmpV1Group OBJECT-GROUP
  OBJECTS { snmpV1BadCommunityNames, snmpV1BadCommunityUses }
  STATUS current
  DESCRIPTION
    ''A collection of objects providing basic
    instrumentation of an SNMPv2 entity which also
    implements SNMPv1.''
  :: = { snmpMIBGroups 2 }

9.7.2   MODULE-COMPLIANCE Macro

The MODULE-COMPLIANCE macro specifies a minimum set of requirements with respect to implementation of one or more MIB modules. Figure 9.17 shows the MODULE-COMPLIANCE macro.

    As an example, the compliance statement for the SNMPv2 MIB is:

snmpMIBCompliance MODULE-COMPLIANCE
  STATUS current
  DESCRIPTION
    ''The compliance statement for SNMPv2 entities
    which implement the SNMPv2 MIB.''
  MODULE RFC1213-MIB
    MANDATORY-GROUPS { system }

  MODULE—this module
    MANDATORY-GROUPS { snmpStatsGroup, snmpORGroup,
      snmpTrapGroup, snmpSetGroup }

    GROUP snmpV1Group
    DESCRIPTION
      ''The snmpV1 group is mandatory only for those
      SNMPv2 entities which also implement SNMPv1.''
  :: = { snmpMIBCompliances 1 }

And the compliance statement for the SNMPv2 manager-to-manager MIB is:

snmpM2MCompliance MODULE-COMPLIANCE
  STATUS current
  DESCRIPTION
    ''The compliance statement for SNMPv2 entities
    which implement the Manager-to-Manager MIB.''
  MODULE—this module
    MANDATORY-GROUPS { snmpAlarmGroup, snmpEventGroup }
  :: = { snmpM2MCompliances 1 }

    The MODULE clause is used one or more times to name each module that is included in the compliance requirements. The clause that refers to this module need not include a module name. Other MODULE clauses are identified by their module name and, optionally, their object identifier.

```
MODULE-COMPLIANCE MACRO ::= BEGIN

TYPE NOTATION ::= "STATUS" Status
                  "DESCRIPTION" Text
                  ReferPart
                  ModulePart

VALUE NOTATION ::= value (VALUE OBJECT IDENTIFIER)

Status ::= "current" | "obsolete"

ReferPart ::= "REFERENCE" Text | Empty

ModulePart ::= Modules | empty

Modules ::= Module | Modules Module

Module ::= "MODULE" ModuleName      --name of module
           MandatoryPart
           CompliancePart

ModuleName ::= identifier ModuleIdentifier | empty

ModuleIdentifier ::= value (moduleID OBJECT IDENTIFIER) | empty

MandatoryPart ::= "MANDATORY-GROUPS" "{" Groups "}" | empty

Groups ::= Group | Groups "," Group

Group ::= value (group OBJECT IDENTIFIER)

CompliancePart ::= Compliances | empty

Compliances ::= Compliance | Compliances Compliance

Compliance ::= ComplianceGroup | Object

ComplianceGroup ::= "GROUP" value (Name OBJECT IDENTIFIER)
                    "DESCRIPTION" Text

Object ::= "OBJECT" value (Name ObjectName)
           SyntaxPart
           WriteSyntaxPart
           AccessPart
           "DESCRIPTION" Text
--must be a refinement for object's SYNTAX clause
SyntaxPart ::= "SYNTAX" type (SYNTAX) | empty

--must be a refinement for object's SYNTAX clause
WriteSyntaxPart ::= "WRITE-SYNTAX" type (WriteSYNTAX) | empty

AccessPart ::= "MIN-ACCESS" Access | empty

Access ::= "not-accessible" | "read-only" | "read-write" | "read-create"

Text ::= """"string""""

END
```

Figure 9.17 Definitions for Compliance

Each MODULE section specifies those groups that are mandatory and those that are optional for the implementation. If there is at least one mandatory group, then the MANDATORY-GROUPS clause is included, which lists all of the mandatory groups for the specified module. In order to be compliant with the module, an implementation must implement all objects in all mandatory groups.

For each group that is conditionally mandatory or unconditionally optional, there is a separate GROUP clause. The DESCRIPTION clause is used to specify those conditions under which a group is conditionally mandatory (e.g., if a particular protocol is implemented, or if another group is implemented).

It is also possible, with the OBJECT clause, to specify refinements in the requirements for objects that are in one of the specified groups. For each such object, a separate OBJECT clause is included. Three types of refinements are possible. The first two refinements apply to the syntax of an object when it is read or written. The following refinements are allowed:

- Range: for INTEGER and Gauge32 types, the range of permitted values may be refined by raising the lower-bounds, by reducing the upper-bounds, and/or by reducing the alternative value/range choices.

- Enumeration: for INTEGER and BIT STRING types, the enumeration of named-values may be refined by removing one or more named-values.

- Size: for OCTET STRING types, the size in characters of the value may be refined by raising the lower-bounds, by reducing the upper-bounds, and/or by reducing the alternative size choices.

- Repertoire: for OCTET STRING types, the repertoire of characters in the value may be reduced by further sub-typing.

The third type of refinement possible is in the access category of an object. The MIN-ACCESS clause is used to define a minimal level of access. An implementation is compliant if the level of access it provides is greater than or equal to this minimal level and less than or equal to the level specified in the MAX-ACCESS clause of the object definition.

The value of an invocation of the MODULE-COMPLIANCE macro is an object identifier assigned to the compliance definition.

9.7.3 Capability Definitions

The AGENT-CAPABILITIES macro is used to document the capabilities present in an SNMPv2 protocol entity acting in an agent role. The macro is used to describe the precise level of support that an agent claims with respect to an MIB group. The definition may indicate that some objects have restricted or augmented syntax or access levels. In essence, the capabilities statement specifies refinements or variations with respect to OBJECT-TYPE macros in MIB modules. Note that these refinements and variations are not specified with respect to MODULE-CAPABILITIES macros.

A formal definition of agent capabilities can be useful in promoting and optimizing interoperability. If a management station has the capabilities statement for each of the agents with which it interacts, it can adjust its behavior accordingly to optimize the use of resources: its own, the agent's, and the network's.

Figure 9.18 shows the AGENT-CAPABILITIES macro. The SNMPv2 specification includes the following usage example:

```
AGENT-CAPABILITIES MACRO ::= BEGIN

TYPE NOTATION ::=  "PRODUCT-RELEASE" Text
                   "STATUS" Status
                   "DESCRIPTION" Text
                   ReferPart
                   ModulePart

VALUE NOTATION ::=  --agent's sysObjectID or snmpORID
                    value (VALUE OBJECT IDENTIFIER)

Status ::= "current" | "obsolete"

ReferPart ::= "REFERENCE" Text | Empty

ModulePart ::= Modules | empty

Modules ::= Module | Modules Module

Module ::=  "SUPPORTS" ModuleName
            "INCLUDES" "{" Groups "}"
            VariationPart

ModuleName ::= identifier ModuleIdentifier

ModuleIdentifier ::= value (moduleID OBJECT IDENTIFIER) | empty

Groups ::= Group | Groups "," Group

Group ::= value (Name OBJECT IDENTIFIER)

VariationPart ::= Variations | empty

Variations ::= Variation | Variations Variation

Variations ::=  "VARIATIONS" value (Name Objectname)
                SyntaxPart
                WriteSyntaxPart
                AccessPart
                CreationPart
                DefValPart
                "DESCRIPTION" value (description Text)

SyntaxPart ::= "SYNTAX" type (SYNTAX) | empty

WriteSyntaxPart ::= "WRITE-SYNTAX" type (WriteSYNTAX) | empty

AccessPart ::= "ACCESS" Access | empty

Access ::= "not-implemented" | "read-only" | "read-write" | "read-create" | "write-only"

CreationPart ::= "CREATION-REQUIRES" "{" Cells "}" | empty

Cells ::= Cell | Cells "," Cell

Cell ::= value (Cell ObjectName)

DefValPart ::= "DEFVAL" "{" value (Defval ObjectSyntax) "}" | empty

Text ::= """"string""""

END
```

Figure 9.18 Definitions for Agent Capabilities

```
example-agent AGENT-CAPABILITIES
    PRODUCT-RELEASE              "ACME agent release 1.1 for 4BSD"
    STATUS                      current
    DESCRIPTION                 "ACME agent for 4BSD"

    SUPPORTS                    RFC1213-MIB
      INCLUDES                  { system, interfaces, at, ip, icmp, tcp, udp, snmp }

      VARIATION                 ifAdminStatus
      SYNTAX                    INTEGER { up (1), down (2) }
      DESCRIPTION               "Unable to set test mode on 4BSD"

      VARIATION                 ifOperStatus
      SYNTAX                    INTEGER { up (1), down (2) }
      DESCRIPTION               "Information limited on 4BSD"

      VARIATION                 atEntry
      CREATION-REQUIRES         { atPhysAddress }
      DESCRIPTION               "Address mappings on 4BSD require both protocol and
                                media addresses"

      VARIATION                 ipDefaultTTL
      SYNTAX                    INTEGER {255 . . 255}
      DESCRIPTION               "Hardwired on 4BSD"

      VARIATION                 ipInAddrErrors
      ACCESS                    not-implemented
      DESCRIPTION               "Information not available on 4BSD"

      VARIATION                 ipRouteType
      SYNTAX                    INTEGER { direct (3), indirect (4) }
      WRITE-SYNTAX              INTEGER { invalid (2), direct (3), indirect (4) }
      DESCRIPTION               "Information limited on 4BSD"

      VARIATION                 tcpConnState
      ACCESS                    read-only
      DESCRIPTION               "Unable to set this on 4BSD"

    SUPPORTS                    EVAL-MIB
      INCLUDES                  { functions, expressions }
      VARIATION                 exprEntry
      CREATION-REQUIRES         { evalString }
      DESCRIPTION               "Conceptual row creation supported"

 :: = { acme-agents 1 }
```

The LAST-UPDATED clause contains the date and time that this definition was last altered. The PRODUCT-RELEASE clause contains a textual description of the product release that includes this agent, and the DESCRIPTION clause contains a textual description of this agent. The remainder of the definition includes one section for each MIB module for which the agent claims a complete or partial implementation.

The description of each MIB module begins with a SUPPORTS clause, which names the module. Then the INCLUDES clause specifies the list of MIB groups from this MIB module that the agent claims to implement. Finally, for each supported MIB group, the definition may specify zero or more objects that the agent implements in some variant or refined fashion compared with the OBJECT-TYPE macro definition of the object. For each such object, the following are provided. First the VARIATIONS clause names the object. Then, there may be one or more parts that specify refinements. The SyntaxPart and WriteSyntaxPart have the same semantics as the corresponding parts in the MODULE-COMPLIANCE macro. The AccessPart is used to indicate that the agent provides less than the access level specified in the MAX-ACCESS clause of the object definition. The CreationPart names the columnar objects for a conceptual row to which values must be explicitly assigned, by a management protocol set operation, before the agent will allow the instance of the status column for that row to be set to "active (4)". The DefVal part provides a refined DEFVAL value for the object. The DESCRIPTION clause contains a textual description of the variant or refined implementation.

The value of an invocation of the AGENT-CAPABILITIES macro is an object identifier assigned to the capabilities definition.

In the example given earlier, the agent implements the MIB-II and EVAL-MIB modules. The MIB-II support includes all groups except egp. However, there are syntax refinements on the following objects: ifAdminStatus, ifOperStatus, ipDefaultTTL, and ipRouteType. In the case of ipRouteType, the set of values available for reading is a subset of those available for writing. The ipInAddrErrors object is not implemented, and the tcpConnState object is available only for reading. Finally, in order to create a new row in the atTable, the value of atPhysAddress must be set. The EVAL-MIB support includes all of the objects in the functions and expressions groups, with no refinements. In addition, creation of new instances in the expr table is supported.

9.8   COEXISTENCE WITH SNMP

The SNMPv2 framework is derived from the SNMP framework. It is intended that the evolution from SNMP to SNMPv2 be as smooth as possible. The easiest way to accomplish such an evolution on an existing network is to upgrade the manager systems to support SNMPv2 in a way that allows coexistence of SNMPv2 managers, SNMPv2 agents, and SNMP agents. The SNMPv2 specification provides some guidance for achieving this coexistence, and this section briefly summarizes that guidance.

The issues raised fall into two categories:

1. Management information

2. Protocol operations

9.8.1 Management Information

The SNMPv2 specification notes that the structure of management information (SMI) for SNMPv2 is nearly a proper superset of the SMI for SNMP and that the SNMPv2 approach largely codifies the existing practice for defining MIB modules.

The key design feature of the SNMPv2 SMI, from the point of view of coexistence, is that modules defined using the current SNMP SMI may continue to be used with the SNMPv2 protocol. For the MIB modules to conform to the SNMPv2 SMI, certain changes are necessary. However, it is important to note that these changes are necessary only for conformance to the SNMPv2 SMI but not for interoperability. That is, it is possible for an agent to maintain an SNMP MIB unchanged and still coexist in an SNMPv2-SNMP environment.

The changes required for conformance to SNMPv2 provide a concise summary of the differences between the SNMPv2 and SNMP SMIs. These changes fall into four categories: object definitions, trap definitions, compliance definitions, and capabilities definitions.

9.8.1.1 Object Definitions

The following changes to object definitions are required:

- The IMPORTS statement should reference SNMPv2-SMI instead of RFC1155-SMI and RFC-1212.
- An INTEGER type with no range restriction should be defined as Integer32.
- A Counter type should be defined as Counter32.
- A Gauge type should be defined as Gauge32.
- The ACCESS clause should be replaced with a MAX-ACCESS clause. The same access category should be used unless some other category makes "protocol sense." In particular, the read-create category should be used for object types for which object instances can be created by a set operation.
- Any columnar object used solely for row-instance identification should have an access category of not-accessible.
- STATUS clause values of "mandatory" and "optional" should be replaced by "current" and "obsolete" respectively.
- A DESCRIPTION clause should be added if it is not present.
- For any conceptual row without an INDEX clause, either an INDEX or an AUGMENTS clause should be added.

Other changes that are desirable but not necessary include the following:

- The scheme used for row creation and deletion in SNMP is inconsistent with that used in SNMPv2. It would be desirable to deprecate the columnar objects in SNMP tables that allow row creation and deletion and replace them with objects defined using the SNMPv2 approach.
- For any string-valued object for which there are no bounds on the corresponding OCTET STRING type, bounds could be added.
- Textual conventions can be formally defined using the TEXTUAL-CONVENTIONS macro.
- For any object that represents a measurement in some kind of units, a UNITS clause could be added.

- For any conceptual row that is an extension of another conceptual row, the AUGMENTS clause could be used.

9.8.1.2   Trap Definitions

To update trap definitions, each occurrence of the TRAP-TYPE macro should be mapped into the corresponding NOTIFICATION-TYPE macro as follows:

- The IMPORTS clause should not reference RFC-1215.

- The ENTERPRISE clause should be removed.

- The VARIABLES clause should be renamed the OBJECTS clause.

- In SNMPv2, notifications are assigned object identifiers. These should be incorporated into the object-identifier tree.

9.8.1.3   Compliance Definitions

A MODULE-COMPLIANCE macro should be added to those modules that are ''standard.''

9.8.1.4   Capabilities Definitions

RFC 1303 defines a convention for describing SNMP agents using the MODULE-CONFOR-MANCE macro. To update these definitions, the macro name AGENT-CAPABILITIES should be used. In addition, there is a slight change in the semantics of the CREATION-REQUIRES clause; the clause should be omitted if appropriate.

9.8.2   Protocol Operations

The protocol defined in the SNMPv2 framework is very similar to that of the SNMP framework, using the same PDU formats. The major changes are an extension of the set of PDUs to include the GetBulkRequest PDU and the InformRequest PDU and a change in semantics to allow get operations to provide partial results rather than operate in an atomic manner.

The coexistence strategy deals with two issues: the use of proxy agents and bilingual-manager behavior.

9.8.2.1   Proxy-Agent Behavior

The simplest way to achieve coexistence at the protocol level is to allow existing SNMP agents to remain in place but to reach them from an SNMPv2 manager by means of a proxy agent. An SNMPv2 entity acting in an SNMPv2 agent role can be implemented and configured to act in the role of a proxy agent on behalf of SNMP agents. This would allow conversion between the SNMPv2 and SNMP protocols.

The proxy agent needs to perform two mappings, as illustrated in Figure 9.19. SNMPv2 PDUs coming from an SNMPv2 manager are converted to SNMP PDUs to be sent to an SNMP agent according to the following rules:

- GetRequest, GetNextRequest, and SetRequest PDUs are passed unchanged.

- A GetBulkRequest PDU is converted to a GetNextRequest PDU with the same variable-bindings list. The effect of this mapping is that only the first ''row'' of the max-repetitions portion of the variable-bindings list will be retrieved.

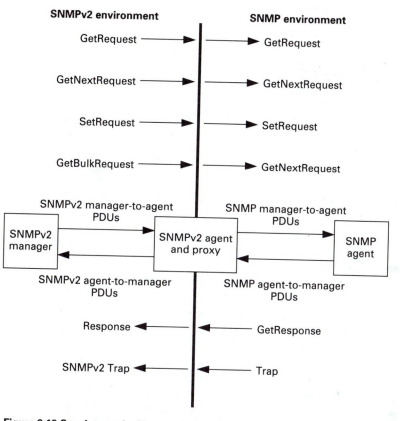

Figure 9.19 Coexistence by Means of Proxy Agent

SNMP PDUs coming from an SNMP agent are converted to SNMPv2 PDUs to be sent to an SNMPv2 agent according to the following rules:

- A GetResponse PDU is passed unchanged. Note that the error-status values of noSuchName, badValue, and readOnly are not used in SNMPv2; however, these values are recognized by an SNMPv2 manager (Figure 9.8) in order to enable it to properly interpret responses from an SNMP agent. In SNMP, if a response would be too big, a GetResponse is returned that includes the variable-bindings field. In SNMPv2, this field is empty. Accordingly, if a Get-Response PDU is received by the proxy agent with an error-status-field value of tooBig, the proxy agent will remove the contents of the variable-bindings field before propagating the response. Also note that an SNMPv2 agent will never generate a response to a GetBulk-Request with an error status of tooBig; instead, the agent returns as many variable-binding pairs as possible. However, the proxy agent will pass a response to a GetBulkRequest with an error status of tooBig.

- A Trap PDU is converted into an SNMPv2 Trap PDU. This is done by prepending two new pairs onto the variable-bindings field: sysUpTime.0 and snmpTrapOID.

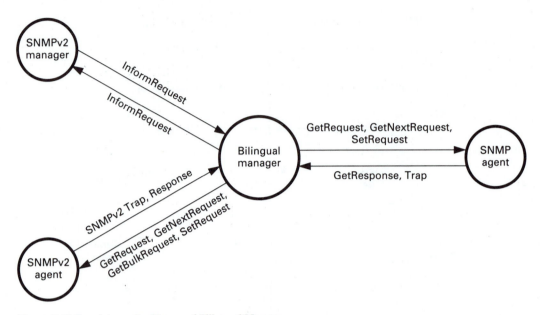

Figure 9.20 Coexistence by Means of Bilingual Manager

9.8.2.2   Bilingual-Manager Behavior

An alternative way to achieve coexistence is to employ management stations that ''speak'' both SNMPv2 and SNMP (Figure 9.20). When a management application needs to contact a protocol entity acting in an agent role, the entity acting in a manager role uses either SNMPv2 or SNMP PDUs based on information in a local database that assigns each correspondent agent to one of the two protocols.

This dual capability in the management station should only be visible at the SNMPv2/SNMP level. Management applications can be written as if they were using only SNMPv2. For communication with SNMP agents, the manager can map operations as if it were acting as a proxy agent.

9.9   SUMMARY

The SNMPv2 framework is a set of specifications for a second-generation SNMP framework. SNMPv2 incorporates the enhancements provided by secure SNMP plus additional functional enhancements to the SNMP framework.

The SNMPv2 SMI provides for more elaborate specification and documentation of managed objects and MIBs. Much of the new material codifies existing SNMP practices. The OBJECT-TYPE macro includes several features not found in the SNMP OBJECT-DEFINITION macro. These include additional ASN.1 types, a UNITS clause, and a more elaborate indexing feature for tables. This latter enhancement provides a systematic and more powerful technique for row creation and deletion. The SNMPv2 SMI also includes new macros for defining object groups, traps, compliance characteristics, and capability characteristics.

There are two major enhancements in the protocol operations for SNMPv2. The GetBulk-Request PDU allows for the retrieval of multiple rows of a table with a single PDU exchange. The

InformRequest PDU enables a manager to transmit management information to another manager. Another change included in SNMPv2 is that the get operations are not atomic; partial results are allowed.

Three MIBs are included in the SNMPv2 specification. The SNMPv2 MIB includes information related to the utilization of the protocol itself. The manager-to-manager MIB includes information relating to alarms and events that result in manager-to-manager exchanges. The party MIB relates to security and is discussed in Chapter 10.

The SNMPv2 specification includes a strategy statement for evolution from SNMP to SNMPv2 by means of a period of coexistence. The three elements of that strategy are as follows:

1. Minor changes to an SNMP MIB are needed to bring it into conformance with the SNMPv2 SMI.

2. A mixed SNMP/SNMPv2 environment can be managed by using a proxy agent that communicates with SNMPv2 managers and SNMP agents or by using bilingual managers.

3. Some changes to secure SNMP are required to conform to the security features of SNMPv2.

APPENDIX 9A   Row-Status Textual Convention

RowStatus :: = TEXTUAL-CONVENTION
STATUS current
DESCRIPTION

"The RowStatus textual convention is used to manage the creation and deletion of conceptual rows, and is used as the value of the SYNTAX clause for the status column of a conceptual row.

The status column has six defined values:

—'active', which indicates that the conceptual row is available for use by the managed device;

—'notInService', which indicates that the conceptual row exists in the agent, but is unavailable for use by the managed device (see NOTE below);

—'notReady', which indicates that the conceptual row exists in the agent, but is missing information necessary in order to be available for use by the managed device;

—'createAndGo', which is supplied by a management station wishing to create a new instance of a conceptual row and to have it available for use by the managed device;

—'createAndWait', which is supplied by a management station wishing to create a new instance of a conceptual row but not to have it available for use by the managed device; and,

—'destroy', which is supplied by a management station wishing to delete all of the instances associated with an existing conceptual row.

Whereas five of the six values (all except 'notReady') may be specified in a management protocol set operation, only three values will be returned in response to a management protocol retrieval operation: 'notReady', 'notInService' or 'active'. That is, when queried, an existing conceptual row has only three states: it is either available for use by the managed device (the status column has value 'active'); it is not available for use by the managed device, though the agent has sufficient information to make it so (the status column has value 'notInService'); or, it is not available for use by the managed device, because the agent lacks sufficient information (the status column has value 'notReady').

NOTE WELL

This textual convention may be used for a MIB table, irrespective of whether the values of that table's conceptual rows are able to be modified while it is active, or whether its conceptual rows must be taken out of service in order to be modified. That is, it is the responsibility of the DESCRIPTION clause of the status column to specify whether the status column must be 'notInService' in order for the value of some other column of the same conceptual row to be modified.

To summarize the effect of having a conceptual row with a status column having a SYNTAX clause value of RowStatus, consider the following state diagram:

STATE

	A status column does not exist	B status column is notReady	C status column is notInService	D status column is active
set status column to createAndGo	noError → D or inconsistentValue	inconsistentValue	inconsistentValue	inconsistentValue
set status column to createAndWait	noError see 1 or wrongValue	inconsistentValue	inconsistentValue	inconsistentValue
set status column to active	inconsistentValue	inconsistentValue or see 2 → D	noError → D	noError → D
set status column to notInService	inconsistentValue	inconsistentValue or see 3 → C	noError → C	noError → C or wrongValue
set status column to destroy	noError → A	noError → A	noError → A	noError → A
set any other column to some value	see 4 → A	noError see 1	noError → C	noError → D

(1) go to B or C, depending on information available to the agent.

(2) if other variable bindings in the same PDU provide values for all columns which are missing but required, then noError is returned and state D is entered.

(3) if other variable bindings in the same PDU provide values for all columns which are missing but required, then noError is returned and state C is entered.

(4) at the discretion of the agent, either noError or inconsistentValue may be returned.

NOTE: other processing of the set request may prevent a noError response from being returned, e.g., wrongValue, noCreation, etc.

Conceptual Row Creation

There are four potential interactions when creating a conceptual row: selecting an instance-identifier which is not in use; creating the conceptual row; initializing any objects for which the agent does not supply a default; and, making the conceptual row available for use by the managed device.

Interaction 1: Selecting an Instance-Identifier

The algorithm used to select an instance-identifier varies for each conceptual row. In some cases, the instance-identifier is semantically significant, e.g., the destination address of a route, and a management station selects the instance-identifier according to the semantics.

In other cases, the instance-identifier is used solely to distinguish conceptual rows, and a management station without specific knowledge of the conceptual row might examine the instances present in order to determine an unused instance-identifier. (This approach may be used, but it is often highly sub-optimal; however, it is also a questionable practice for a naive management station to attempt conceptual row creation.)

Alternately, the MIB module which defines the conceptual row might provide one or more objects which provide assistance in determining an unused instance-identifier. For example, if the conceptual row is indexed by an integer-value, then an object having an integer-valued SYNTAX clause might be defined for such a purpose, allowing a management station to issue a management protocol retrieval operation. In order to avoid unnecessary collisions between competing management stations, 'adjacent' retrievals of this object should be different.

Finally, the management station could select a pseudo-random number to use as the index. In the event that this index was already in use and an inconsistentValue was returned in response to the management protocol set operation, the management station should simply select a new pseudo-random number and retry the operation.

A MIB designer should choose between the two latter algorithms based on the size of the table (and therefore the efficiency of each algorithm). For tables in which a large number of entries are expected, it is recommended that a MIB object be defined that returns an acceptable index for creation. For tables with small numbers of entries, it is recommended that the latter pseudo-random index mechanism be used.

Interaction 2: Creating the Conceptual Row

Once an unused instance-identifier has been selected, the management station determines if it wishes to create and activate the conceptual row in one transaction or in a negotiated set of interactions.

Interaction 2a: Creating and Activating the Conceptual Row

The management station must first determine the column requirements, i.e., it must determine those columns for which it must or must not provide values. Depending on the complexity of the table and the management station's knowledge of the agent's capabilities, this determination can be made locally by the management station. Alternately, the management station issues a management protocol get operation to examine all columns in the conceptual row that it wishes to create. In response, for each column, there are three possible outcomes:

—a value is returned, indicating that some other management station has already created this conceptual row. We return to interaction 1.

—the exception 'noSuchInstance' is returned, indicating that the agent implements the object-type associated with this column, and that this column in at least one conceptual row would be accessible in the MIB view used by the retrieval were it to exist. For those columns to which the agent provides read-create access, the 'noSuchInstance' exception tells the management station that it should supply a value for this column when the conceptual row is to be created.

—the exception 'noSuchObject' is returned, indicating that the agent does not implement the object-type associated with this column or that there is no conceptual row for which this column would be accessible in the MIB view used by the retrieval. As such, the management station cannot issue any management protocol set operations to create an instance of this column.

Once the column requirements have been determined, a management protocol set operation is accordingly issued. This operation also sets the new instance of the status column to 'createAndGo'.

When the agent processes the set operation, it verifies that it has sufficient information to make the conceptual row available for use by the managed device. The information available to the agent is provided by two sources: the management protocol set operation which creates the conceptual row, and, implementation-specific defaults supplied by the agent (note that an agent must provide implementation-specific defaults for at least those objects which it implements as read-only). If there is sufficient information available, then the conceptual row is created, a 'noError' response is returned, the status column is set to 'active', and no further interactions are necessary (i.e., interactions 3 and 4 are skipped). If there is insufficient information, then the conceptual row is not created, and the set operation fails with an error of 'inconsistentValue'. On this error, the management station can issue a management protocol retrieval operation to determine if this was because it failed to specify a value for a required column, or because the selected instance of the status column already existed. In the latter case, we return to interaction 1. In the former case, the management station can re-issue the set operation with the additional information, or begin interaction 2 again using 'createAndWait' in order to negotiate creation of the conceptual row.

NOTE WELL

Regardless of the method used to determine the column requirements, it is possible that the management station might deem a column necessary when, in fact, the agent will not allow that particular columnar instance to be created or written. In this case, the management protocol set operation will fail with an error such as 'noCreation' or 'notWritable'. In this case, the management station decides whether it needs to be able to set a value for that particular columnar instance. If not, the management station re-issues the management protocol set operation, but without setting a value for that particular columnar instance; otherwise, the management station aborts the row creation algorithm.

Interaction 2b: Negotiating the Creation of the Conceptual Row

The management station issues a management protocol set operation which sets the desired instance of the status column to 'createAndWait'. If the agent is unwilling to process a request of this sort, the set operation fails with an error of 'wrongValue'. (As a consequence, such an agent must be prepared to accept a single management protocol set operation, i.e., interaction 2a above, containing all of the columns indicated by its column requirements.) Otherwise, the conceptual row is created, a 'noError' response is returned, and the status column is immediately set to either 'notInService' or 'notReady', depending on whether it has sufficient information to make the conceptual row available for use by the managed device. If there is sufficient information available, then the status column is set to 'notInService'; otherwise, if there is insufficient information, then the status column is set to 'notReady'. Regardless, we proceed to interaction 3.

Interaction 3: Initializing non-defaulted Objects

The management station must now determine the column requirements. It issues a management protocol get operation to examine all columns in the created conceptual row. In the response, for each column, there are three possible outcomes:

—a value is returned, indicating that the agent implements the object-type associated with this column and has sufficient information to provide a value. For those columns to which the agent provides read-create access, a value return tells the management station that it may issue additional management protocol set operations, if it desires, in order to change the value associated with this column.

—the exception 'noSuchInstance' is returned, indicating that the agent implements the object-type associated with this column, and that this column in at least one conceptual row would be accessible in the MIB view used by the retrieval were it to exist. However, the agent does not have sufficient information to provide a value, and until a value is provided, the conceptual row may not be made available for use by the managed device. For those columns to which the agent provides read-create access, the 'noSuchInstance' exception tells the management station that it must issue additional management protocol set operations, in order to provide a value associated with this column.

—the exception 'noSuchObject' is returned, indicating that the agent does not implement the object-type associated with this column or that there is no conceptual row for which this column would be accessible in the MIB view used by the retrieval. As such, the management station cannot issue any management protocol set operations to create an instance of this column.

If the value associated with the status column is 'notReady', then the management station must first deal with all 'noSuchInstance' columns, if any. Having done so, the value of the status column becomes 'notInService', and we proceed to interaction 4.

Interaction 4: Making the Conceptual Row Available

Once the management station is satisfied with the values associated with the columns of the conceptual row, it issues a management protocol set operation to set the status column to 'active'. If the agent has sufficient information to make the conceptual row available for use by the managed device, the management protocol set operation succeeds (a 'noError' response is returned). Otherwise, the management protocol set operation fails with an error of 'inconsistentValue'.

NOTE WELL

A conceptual row having a status column with value 'notInService' or 'notReady' is unavailable to the managed device. As such, it is possible for the managed device to create its own instances during the time between the management protocol set operation which sets the status column to 'createAndWait' and the management protocol set operation which sets the status column to 'active'. In this case, when the management protocol set operation is issued to set the status column to 'active', the values held in the agent supersede those used by the managed device.

If the management station is prevented from setting the status column to 'active' (e.g., due to management station or network failure) the conceptual row will be left in the 'notInService' or 'notReady' state, consuming resources indefinitely. The agent must detect conceptual rows that have been in either state for an abnormally long period of time and remove them. This period of time should be long enough to allow for human response time (including 'think time') between the creation of the conceptual row and the setting of the status to 'active'. It is suggested that this period be approximately 5 minutes in length.

Conceptual Row Suspension

When a conceptual row is 'active', the management station may issue a management protocol set operation which sets the instance of the status column to 'notInService'. If the agent is unwilling to do so, the set operation fails with an error of 'wrongValue'. Otherwise, the conceptual row is taken out of service, and a 'noError' response is returned. It is the responsibility of the DESCRIPTION clause of the status column to indicate under what circumstances the status column should be taken out of service (e.g., in order for the value of some other column of the same conceptual row to be modified).

Conceptual Row Deletion

For deletion of conceptual rows, a management protocol set operation is issued which sets the instance of the status column to 'destroy'. This request may be made regardless of the current value of the status column (e.g., it is possible to delete conceptual rows which are either 'notReady', 'notInService' or 'active'.) If the operation succeeds, then all instances associated with the conceptual row are immediately removed.''

SYNTAX INTEGER {
    —the following two values are states:
    —these values can be read or written
    active(1),
    notInService(2),

    —the following value is a state
    —this value may be read, but not written
    notReady(3),

    —the following three values are
    —actions: these values can be written,
    —but are never read
    createAndGo(4),
    createAndWait(5),
    destroy(6) }

APPENDIX 9B   Case Diagrams

In 1988, the MIB working group, chartered by the Internet Engineering Task Force, began work on MIB-I for SNMP. It was found that it was often difficult to develop clear definitions of the objects needed in the MIB and to make sure that all conditions were represented. Jeffrey Case suggested that the group diagram the flow of packets within individual layers and proposed a diagramming technique that was quickly dubbed Case diagrams (Case 1989). Although these diagrams have been used extensively in the development of MIB-I, MIB-II, and other MIBs, it is

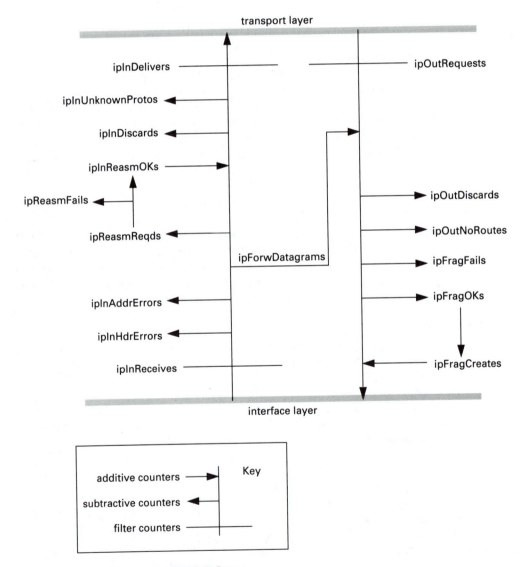

Figure 9.21   Case Diagram for MIB-II IP Group

only with the SNMPv2 MIB that Case diagrams first appear as part of the official documentation of a standardized MIB.

For many MIB groups, the intent is to record the traffic pattern at a particular protocol layer. A key requirement, obviously, is to make sure that every PDU received at a layer or issued from a layer is accounted for, including valid PDUs and errored PDUs with various types of errors. However, it is difficult to determine if all cases are accounted for, and that there are no unnecessary duplications, simply by reading a list of object definitions. It is far easier to determine the correctness and completeness of a group of objects if the flow of PDUs can be depicted in a diagram. The purpose of the Case diagram is to illustrate such flows.

The Case diagram also ensures that all implementations record the same information at the same place in the processing sequence. If the information is recorded in a different sequence, or at different places within the processing of a layer, then the semantics of the corresponding counters may actually differ and the results will not be comparable.

An example will illustrate the use of Case diagrams. Figure 9.21 shows the diagram for the MIB-II IP group. There is a main path in each direction between the layer below (interface layer) and the layer above. A horizontal line cutting across a main path corresponds to a counter that counts all passing PDUs. An arrow leaving the main path indicates an error condition or flow that results in a PDU not continuing on the main path. An arrow into the main path indicates points where additional PDUs are injected into the main path.

Relative position on the diagram is significant. For example, on the inbound side, the diagram indicates that all incoming PDUs are counted (ipInReceives), then those with header errors are counted and discarded (ipInHdrErrors), then those with address errors are counted· and discarded (ipInAddrErrors).

The diagram enables a rather concise depiction of the relationships among various counters. For example, the diagram indicates that PDUs requiring reassembly are removed from the main path. Any resulting reassembled PDUs are returned to the main path, and failed attempts at reassembly are counted.

10
SNMPv2: Security

This chapter completes the examination of SNMPv2 by looking at its security features and functions. The chapter begins with a brief discussion of the context within which these security features were developed. The remainder of the chapter examines the three key areas of SNMPv2 security.

10.1 BACKGROUND

This section provides a brief summary of the history leading to the security features of SNMPv2, and the way in which this chapter presents those features.

10.1.1 The Development of SNMPv2

Chapter 4 presented a history of the evolution of SNMP. Figure 10.1 captures the key milestones in the development of SNMP-related standards. The starting point was the simple gateway-monitoring protocol (SGMP) issued in November 1987. The SGMP provided a straightforward means for monitoring gateways (OSI level 3 routers). When the need for a more general-purpose network management tool was identified, SGMP was taken as the baseline and adapted to produce the simple network management protocol (SNMP) first issued in August 1988. SNMP provided a minimal but powerful set of facilities for monitoring and control of network elements using a straightforward structure of management information (SMI), management information base (MIB), and protocol. One notable deficiency in SNMP was the difficulty of monitoring networks, as opposed to nodes on networks. Remarkably, a quite substantial functional enhancement to SNMP was achieved simply by the definition of a set of standardized management objects, referred to as the remote network monitoring (RMON) MIB, first issued in November 1991. RMON represented the first, and last, major functional enhancement to the first version of SNMP.

Another deficiency in SNMP was the complete lack of security facilities. To remedy this problem, a set of documents referred to as secure SNMP (S-SNMP) was issued as proposed standards in July 1992. In that same month, the simple management protocol (SMP) was issued outside the internet standards structure. SMP provided functional enhancements to SNMP and incorpo-

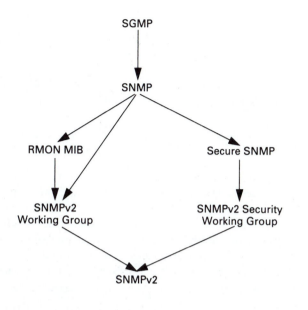

SGMP = simple gateway-monitoring protocol
SNMP = simple network management protocol
RMON MIB = remote network-monitoring management information base
SNMPv2 = SNMP version 2

Figure 10.1   The Evolution of SNMP

rated, with minor modifications, the security enhancements of S-SNMP. SMP also incorporated some of the concepts from RMON, including the specifications of alarms and events, and the use of a status columnar object to facilitate row creation and deletion. SMP was accepted as the baseline for developing a second-generation SNMP, known as SNMP version 2 (SNMPv2). The first generation came to be called SNMPv1.

To produce SNMPv2, two working groups were set up. The SNMPv2 working group was charged with all non-security aspects, including SMI, MIB, protocol, conformance statements, and coexistence strategies with SNMPv1. This work was substantially based on SMP. After many iterations, this working group completed its work in December 1992 and issued a set of nine internet draft documents that were ready to enter the standardization process as proposed internet standards.

The second working group, known as the SNMPv2 security working group, proceeded at a slightly slower pace to develop the security aspects of SNMPv2. This work was substantially based on S-SNMP, as revised for SMP. After many iterations, internet draft documents were produced in January 1993. The draft documents represented broad agreement but some issues were unresolved.

At the time of this writing, the SNMPv2 documents, including the security documents, are proposed internet standards. It is possible that some changes will be made before this portion is published as full internet standards. This chapter provides the latest information available at the time of publication; the reader should consult the standards for any last-minute changes.

10.1.2   Plan of Attack

The material on SNMP security is presented in two chapters:

1. The security enhancements to SNMPv1 (S-SNMP), are presented in Chapter 8, with a detailed discussion of security requirements and the security features designed to meet those requirements.

2. The security features of SNMPv2 are summarized in this chapter. Primarily, this chapter characterizes these features in terms of their differences from S-SNMP.

The alternative to this strategy would be to simply present SNMPv2 security features, including requirements and detailed discussion of algorithms. Instead, the two-chapter approach was adopted for several reasons. To begin, it is useful to focus simply on the security deficiencies of SNMPv1 and how these can be remedied. Then it is instructive to examine the differences between S-SNMP and the security features of SNMPv2. Secure SNMP was designed over a period of three years and provides a coherent, well-thought-out solution to the security deficiencies of SNMPv1. By focusing on the differences between S-SNMP and SNMPv2, we have the opportunity to examine alternative solutions to the same requirements and gain a greater understanding of the rationale for particular techniques.

The remainder of this chapter is organized in accordance with the three documents that constitute the security specification of SNMPv2:

- SNMPv2 Administrative Model
- SNMPv2 Security Protocols
- SNMPv2 Party MIB

10.2   SNMPv2 ADMINISTRATIVE MODEL

The party concept developed in S-SNMP is carried over into SNMPv2 with virtually no change. Figure 10.2 includes an ASN.1 definition of the variables that define an SNMPv2 party. The list of variables is identical to that for S-SNMP, except that SNMPv2 party information does not include partyProxyFor, partyAuthLastMsg, and partyNonce. The absence of the last two variables reflects the lack of an ordered delivery mechanism, which is discussed in Section 10.3. The absence of the partyProxyFor variable is due to the introduction of a new concept in SNMPv2, the context.

We begin this section by looking at the key elements in the SNMPv2 administrative model, and then examine several applications.

10.2.1   MIB View

As in S-SNMP, SNMPv2 includes the concept of the MIB view. A MIB view defines a subset of all the possible MIB objects. The MIB view is defined in terms of a collection of subtrees, with each subtree being included in or excluded from the view. A view subtree is simply a node in the MIB's naming hierarchy plus all of its subordinate elements. See Section 8.4.4 for a detailed description of MIB views.

```
SnmpParty ::= SEQUENCE {
                          partyIdentity              OBJECT IDENTIFIER,
                          partyTDomain               OBJECT IDENTIFIER,
                          partyTAddr                 OCTET STRING,
                          partyMaxMessageSize        INTEGER,
                          partyAuthProtocol          OBJECT IDENTIFIER,
                          partyAuthClock             INTEGER,
                          partyAuthPrivate           OCTET STRING,
                          partyAuthPublic            OCTET STRING,
                          partyAuthLifetime          INTEGER,
                          partyPrivProtocol          OBJECT IDENTIFIER,
                          partyPrivPrivate           OCTET STRING,
                          partyPrivPublic            OCTET STRING }


AclEntry ::= SEQUENCE {
                          aclTarget                  OBJECT IDENTIFIER,
                          aclSubject                 OBJECT IDENTIFIER,
                          aclResources               OBJECT IDENTIFIER,
                          aclPrivileges              INTEGER }
```

Figure 10.2 ASN.1 Definitions for the SNMPv2 Administrative Model

10.2.2 SNMPv2 Contexts

The context is defined in SNMPv2 as follows:

A SNMPv2 context is a collection of managed object resources accessible by a SNMPv2 entity. A SNMPv2 context is accessed either locally or remotely.

A local SNMPv2 context is identified as a MIB view. In this case, an SNMPv2 entity uses local mechanisms to access the management information identified by the SNMPv2 context.

A remote SNMPv2 context is identified as a proxy relationship. In this case, an SNMPv2 entity acts as a proxy agent to access the management information identified by the SNMPv2 context.

The context is a concept that relates both to access control and to MIB views. When a management station interacts with an agent to access management information at the agent, the interaction is between a management party and an agent party, with respect to a chosen context; the access control privileges apply to an MIB view specified for that context. When a management station makes use of an agent as a proxy to access management information that relates to a proxied entity, the interaction is between a management party and an agent party that is acting on behalf of a target entity in the proxied entity. In this case, the access control privileges are expressed in terms of a proxy relationship that applies to this pair of parties and the proxied entity.

The principal motivations for introducing the concept of context are to clarify the relationships involved in accessing management information and to minimize the storage and processing requirements at the agent. To understand these motivations, consider the following progression. In SNMPv1, the community string is used to represent the following security-related information: [1]

---

1. The enumeration in the following two lists is based on an analysis by Marshall Rose.

- The identity of the requesting entity (management station)
- The identity of the performing entity (agent acting for itself or for a proxied entity)
- The identity of the location of the management information to be accessed (agent or proxied entity)
- Authentication information
- Access control information (authorization to perform required operation)
- MIB view information

By lumping all of these concepts into a single variable, flexibility and functionality are lost. Secure SNMP abolished the concept of the community and represented the same security-related information in the following fashion:

- Requesting entity: field in SnmpMgmtCom header
- Performing entity: field in SnmpMgmtCom header
- Location of management information: contextViewIndex object in context table
- Authentication information: partyAuth objects in party table
- Access control information: aclPrivileges object in acl table
- MIB view information: view objects in view table

This is a substantial improvement over SNMPv1. It uncouples various concepts so that values can be assigned to each one separately. However, placing the partyProxyFor object in the party table does result in unnecessarily complex and large tables. In essence, for each proxy relationship there must be a separate party created. The effect of this is felt in the way all of the security-related tables are organized. It should become clear in Section 10.4 that the use of a context allows a more efficient storage of the required information.

10.2.3   Access Control Policy

With the use of a context, an access control policy has four elements, as defined in Figure 10.2:

1. Target: an SNMP party performing management operations as requested by the subject party.
2. Subject: an SNMP party that requests that management operations be performed by the target party.
3. Resources: the management information on which requested management operations may be performed, expressed as a local MIB view or a proxy relationship; this entry is referred to as a context.
4. Privileges: the allowable operations, defined in terms of allowable protocol data units (PDUs), that pertain to a particular context, and that the target is authorized to perform on behalf of the subject.

Thus, the access control policy is determined by three parameters. A subject party requests a management operation of a target party and identifies the context of the request. The context may specify an MIB view local to the target party or may specify a remote proxied entity. For a given pair of subject/target parties, there may be multiple access control policies, one for each context. The context is communicated by the subject to the target in the SNMPv2 message header. This approach eliminates the necessity of defining a unique subject/target party pair for every access control policy, and enables a single target party to perform in a variety of contexts for a given subject party.

The value of the privileges parameter represents the list of SNMPv2 PDUs that may be sent from the subject to the target. The parameter is encoded by assigning an integer value that is a power of two to each PDU. The assignments are:

Get	1
GetNext	2
Response	4
Set	8
—unused	16
Get-Bulk:	32
Inform	64
SNMPv2-Trap	128

10.2.4 Types of Contexts

The concept of context is used to cover a variety of situations. This is best explained with reference to Table 10.1. There are two overall cases, that of a local context and that of a remote context. Let us consider each of these in turn.

10.2.4.1 Local Contexts

In the case where a manager is attempting to directly access management information at an agent, the context is local (to the agent). For the access to take place, some protocol-related information must be shared by the manager and the agent. Specifically, they must share information about the use of this protocol between the given manager party and the given agent party. This is simply the party information defined in Figure 10.2.

Associated with a local context is an MIB view that indicates which management information objects are accessible in this context. Now, if a manager wishes to access information at an agent, it issues a management operation that specifies a source party (at the manager), a destination party (at the agent), and a context. The agent consults the appropriate access control policy (determined by source party, destination party, and context) and determines which operations are permissible. Furthermore, the context references an MIB view that determines which objects are accessible. Knowing the accessible objects and the permissible operations, the agent can respond appropriately.

In the case of a local context, a distinction is made between management information that represents the SNMPv2 entity at the agent and management information that represents some other locally controlled entity, such as a modem or repeater. In both cases, the information is maintained in the MIB at the agent, and the same MIB, access control, and protocol information is required for access.

10.2.4.2 Remote Contexts

The other type of interaction between a manager and an agent is when the agent mediates between a management station and an entity remote to both the manager and the agent. The agent, as a proxy, accesses information at a proxied entity on behalf of the manager.

Two types of proxy relationship are possible:

Table 10.1 Types of Contexts

	Local SNMPv2 Context		Remote SNMPv2 Context	
	SNMPv2 Entity	**Other Local Entity**	**Foreign Proxy Relationship**	**Native Proxy Relationship**
SNMPv2 protocol information required	Party information (SNMPv2 protocol between manager party and agent party)	Party information (SNMPv2 protocol between manager party and agent party)	Party information (SNMPv2 protocol between manager party and proxy agent party	Party information (SNMPv2 protocol between manager party and proxy agent party); Source party, destination party, context (SNMPv2 protocol between proxy agent and proxied agent)
MIB information required	MIB View	MIB View	—	—
Access control information required	aclPrivileges (manager party, agent party, this context)	aclPrivileges (manager party, agent party, this context)	aclPrivileges (manager party, agent party, this context)	aclPrivileges (manager party, proxy agent party, this context); aclPrivileges (proxy agent source party and proxied agent destination, proxy context)

1. When communication between a proxy agent and a logically remote proxied entity is by some means other than SNMPv2, the relationship is called an SNMPv2 foreign proxy relationship. Deployment of foreign proxy relationships is the means whereby otherwise unmanageable devices or portions of an internet may be managed by an SNMPv2 management station.

2. When communication between a proxy agent and a logically remote proxied entity is via SNMPv2, the relationship is called an SNMPv2 native proxy relationship. Deployment of native proxy relationships is the means whereby processing or bandwidth costs may be amortized or shifted, facilitating the construction of large management systems. Native proxy relationships enable the use of distributed management structures such as those discussed in Section 1.2.3 and illustrated in Figure 1.5.

For a foreign proxy relationship, an interaction must still take place between a manager party and an agent party; thus the party information for these two parties must be shared by these two parties. Since no management information local to the agent is accessed, no MIB view is required. Access control information is still needed. For a given foreign proxy relationship, identified by a context, when a manager party issues a request to an agent party, an access control policy indicates which operations are permissible between these two parties for this particular foreign proxy relationship.

For a foreign proxy relationship, no other SNMPv2-related information is required. The proxy agent must have some non-SNMPv2 means of accessing information at the proxied entity. When that information is accessed, it can be returned to the manager party using the context invoked for this exchange.

For a native proxy relationship, all of the information just listed for foreign proxy relationships is required. In addition, since SNMPv2 will be used by the proxy agent to access the proxied agent, additional information is needed. To understand what is needed, consider the following:

1. If a manager wishes to obtain management information from a remote entity by means of a proxy agent, it must issue its request to the proxy agent via SNMPv2. This requires the use of a manager party, a proxy agent party, and a context. The context is sufficient to identify the proxied entity to be accessed.

2. In the case of a native proxy relationship, the proxy agent will assume an SNMPv2 manager role in order to access the proxied agent on behalf of the original manager. For this purpose, a party at the proxy agent must interact with a party at the proxied agent, using some context.

Thus, four parties are involved in a native proxy relationship. The context invoked between manager and proxy agent must enable the proxy agent to determine the two parties and the context to be used between the proxy agent and the proxied agent. The access privileges available for the interaction between the parties at the proxy agent and proxied agent must also be known. The example in Section 10.2.5.2 should make these relationships clearer.

10.2.5   Application of the Model

The SNMPv2 administrative model document includes examples of the application of the model that are essentially the same as those depicted in Tables 8.3 and 8.4. In addition, examples are provided that illustrate the two types of proxy relationships: foreign and native; these are summarized in the remainder of this section.

Table 10.2 Administrative Information for Foreign Proxy Configuration

(a) Party Information Stored at Proxy Agent

Identity	groucho (manager)	chico (proxy agent)	harpo (proxy dst)
Domain	snmpUDPDomain	snmpUDPDomain	acmeMgmtPrtcl
Address	1.2.3.4, 2002	1.2.3.5, 161	0x98765432
Auth Prot	v2md5AuthProtocol	v2md5AuthProtocol	noAuth
Auth Priv Key	"0123456789ABCDEF"	"GHIJKL0123456789"	''
Auth Pub Key	'' ''	'' ''	'' ''
Auth Clock	0	0	0
Auth Lifetime	300	300	0
Priv Prot	noPriv	noPriv	noPriv
Priv Priv Key	'' ''	'' ''	'' ''
Priv Pub Key	'' ''	'' ''	'' ''

(b) Context Information Proxy Agent

Context	Proxy Destination	Proxy Source	Proxy Context
ducksoup	harpo	n/a	n/a

(c) Access Information for Foreign Proxy

Target	Subject	Context	Privileges
chico	groucho	ducksoup	35 (Get, GetNext & GetBulk)
groucho	chico	ducksoup	132 (Response & SNMPv2-Trap)

(d) Party Information Stored at Management Station

Identity	groucho (manager)	chico (proxy agent)
Domain	snmpUDPDomain	snmpUDPDomain
Address	1.2.3.4, 2002	1.2.3.5, 161
Auth Prot	v2md5AuthProtocol	v2md5AuthProtocol
Auth Priv Key	"0123456789ABCDEF"	"GHIJKL0123456789"
Auth Pub Key	'' ''	'' ''
Auth Clock	0	0
Auth Lifetime	300	300
Priv Prot	noPriv	noPriv
Priv Priv Key	'' ''	'' ''
Priv Pub Key	'' ''	'' ''

10.2.5.1 Foreign Proxy Configuration

Table 10.2 depicts the administrative information for a configuration in which a management station party (groucho) communicates with an agent party (chico) using the MD5 authentication algorithm but for which privacy is not required. The two parties communicate to enable groucho to access management information at a proxy destination (harpo) that is part of a proxied entity and does not implement SNMPv2.

Part (a) of the table depicts the party information stored locally at the proxy agent. For this proxy relationship, there is a set of values for the manager, the proxy agent, and the proxy destination. Note that the agent communicates with the proxied entity by means of another management protocol (acmeMgmtPrtcl) and that the proxied entity does not have an internet address.

Part (b) of the table shows context information known to the proxy agent. The table indicates that the context ducksoup refers to a relationship that is satisfied by the party harpo. In the case of a foreign proxy relationship, which this is, the proxy source and proxy context parameters are ignored.

Part (c) of the table indicates the access control policy of the agent and the manager with respect to groucho, chico, and ducksoup. This table is stored at both manager and agent.

Finally, part (d) of the table depicts the party information stored at the management station. Note that the manager has no direct information about harpo. Rather, the management station must know that information about harpo is available in the context ducksoup by means of party chico.

Now suppose that the manager party groucho wishes to interrogate the proprietary device associated with harpo. Groucho can do this by retrieving object instance values from proxy agent chico with a Get command. The manager consults the party table and determines that the MD5 authentication protocol is used by groucho and no privacy protocol is required by chico. The manager therefore constructs an SNMPv2 message that identifies the two parties and the context ducksoup, includes the necessary authentication information, contains the Get PDU, and issues it to the agent at the destination party address (IP address 1.2.3.5, UDP port 161).

When the Get message is received at the agent, the identities of the two parties are extracted from the message header. The agent determines that chico does not require privacy and therefore assumes that the incoming message is not protected from disclosure and need not be decrypted. The agent then determines that groucho use an authentication protocol and therefore uses the authentication information to authenticate the message.

The agent consults the access information to determine if groucho is permitted to issue a Get to chico in the context ducksoup. The corresponding value of aclPrivileges is 35, which includes Get and GetNext, so the Get is accepted.

The agent consults the context information and determines that ducksoup refers to a foreign proxy relationship. The Get request is satisfied by translation into the appropriate operations of the acmeMgmtPrtcl directed at party harpo.

If the required information is returned from harpo, the agent can then construct a corresponding Response PDU. The agent determines that an authentication protocol is used by chico and no privacy protocol is required by groucho. The agent therefore constructs an SNMP message that identifies the two parties and the context, contains authentication information, contains the Response PDU, and issues it to groucho.

When the Response message is received at the manager, the identities of the two parties are extracted from the message header. The manager determines that groucho does not require privacy and therefore assumes that the incoming message is not protected from disclosure and need not be decrypted. The manager then determines that chico uses an authentication protocol and therefore verifies the authentication information in the header. Finally, the manager consults the access information and determines that chico may issue Response PDUs to groucho in context ducksoup and therefore the manager may accept the incoming Response.

Table 10.3 Administrative Information for Native Proxy Configuration

(a) Party Information Stored at Proxy Agent

Identity	groucho (manager)	chico (proxy agent)	harpo (proxy dst)	zeppo (proxy src)
Domain	snmpUDPDomain	snmpUDPDomain	snmpUDPDomain	snmpUDPDomain
Address	1.2.3.4, 2002	1.2.3.5, 161	1.2.3.6, 161	1.2.3.5, 161
Auth Prot	v2md5AuthProtocol	v2md5AuthProtocol	v2md5AuthProtocol	v2md5AuthProtocol
Auth Priv Key	"0123456789ABCDEF"	"GHIJKL0123456789"	"MNOPQR0123456789"	"STUVW0123456789"
Auth Pub Key	""	""	""	""
Auth Clock	0	0	0	0
Auth Lifetime	300	300	300	300
Priv Prot	noPriv	noPriv	noPriv	noPriv
Priv Priv Key	""	""	""	""
Priv Pub Key	""	""	""	""

(b) Context Information Stored at Proxy Agent

Context	Proxy Destination	Proxy Source	Proxy Context
ducksoup	harpo	zeppo	bigstore
bigstore	groucho	chico	ducksoup

(c) Access Information for Native Proxy

Target	Subject	Context	Privileges
chico	groucho	ducksoup	35 (Get, GetNext & GetBulk)
groucho	chico	ducksoup	132 (Response & SNMPv2-Trap)
harpo	zeppo	bigstore	35 (Get, GetNext & GetBulk)
zeppo	harpo	bigstore	132 (Response & SNMPv2-Trap)

10.2.5.2   Native Proxy Configuration

Table 10.3 depicts the administrative information for a configuration which supports SNMPv2 native operations. That is, this configuration allows a management station to access information from a remote agent by means of the mediation of another agent. This last agent is a proxy agent that acts in the role of agent in interacting with the requesting management station and acts in the role of manager in interacting with the responding proxied agent.

Part (a) of the table depicts the party information stored locally at the proxy agent. In this case harpo is at internet address 1.2.3.6. This party can communicate with zeppo, in the proxy agent (at 1.2.3.5); in this case, the SNMPv2 entity at 1.2.3.6 assumes the role of an agent and the SNMPv2 entity at 1.2.3.5 assumes the role of manager.

Part (b) of the table shows context information known to the proxy agent. The table indicates that the context ducksoup refers to a relationship that is satisfied when the party zeppo communicates with the party harpo and references the context bigstore. We can interpret this information as follows. When the manager at 1.2.3.4 wishes to obtain information from 1.2.3.6, it may do so indirectly through the proxy agent at 1.2.3.5. For this purpose, the manager party groucho communicates with the agent party chico in the context ducksoup. The proxy agent can satisfy requests in the context ducksoup, by using the local (to 1.2.3.5) agent zeppo to communicate with the remote agent harpo in the context bigstore.

Part (c) of the table indicates the access control policies relating to ducksoup and bigstore. All of the items in this table are relevant to the proxy agent. Only the ducksoup information is relevant to the manager.

Finally, Table 10.2, part (d) again shows the party information stored at the management station. That is, the management station has the same party information whether the proxy relationship is native or foreign. In both cases, the manager only needs to know the identity of the proxy agent party and the context which refers to the desired remote proxied entity.

10.3   SNMPv2 SECURITY PROTOCOLS

The SNMPv2 security protocols correspond closely to those defined in S-SNMP. The only significant differences between SNMPv2 and S-SNMP are the following:

- SNMPv2 does not employ the ordered delivery mechanism defined in S-SNMP.

- SNMPv2 includes both subject and target party clocks in authenticated messages, to simplify clock synchronization.

- SNMPv2 includes a context parameter in messages, to enable access control.

We examine each of these in turn.

10.3.1   Ordered Delivery Mechanism

Recall from Section 8.3.2.2 that the digest authentication protocol for S-SNMP includes an ordered delivery mechanism. In essence, each message is marked with a timestamp based on a local clock with a granularity of one second. Within the granularity of the clock, messages are marked with a monotonically increasing nonce value. The combination of timestamp and nonce enables a receiving party to determine the relative order in which messages were sent by a sending party and to reject any message that is received out of order.

SNMPv2 does not use the ordered delivery mechanism. As a result:

1. The SNMPv2 message header does not include a nonce value.

2. The SNMPv2 MIB does not need to maintain nonce and last-timestamp values.

The rationale for removing the ordered delivery mechanism is as follows:

1. In most cases, the management protocol is supported by a connectionless transport protocol (e.g., UDP), which does not guarantee ordered delivery. Therefore, messages may arrive out of order due to the normal operation of the network. If such messages are declared unauthentic, there may be considerable network and processing overhead to detect the loss and retransmit the messages. Furthermore, this type of network behavior is more likely to occur at times of high load or in the presence of faults, which are just the times when network management is most needed.

2. There is no security requirement to protect against malicious re-ordering of network management retrieval messages (e.g., get).

3. There is a security requirement to protect against malicious re-ordering of network management set messages. However, this requirement is not confined to set operations between a given pair of parties. The requirement is to protect against malicious re-ordering of set messages issued on behalf of all network managers. Since the S-SNMP ordered delivery mechanism operates only within parties and not across parties, it is not sufficient for this requirement. Further, the use of the SNMPv2 SetSerialNo object, as described in Section 9.5.4, provides the required protection. Thus not only is the S-SNMP ordered delivery mechanism insufficient, it is also unnecessary.

10.3.2   Clock Synchronization Algorithm

The elimination of the nonce value from the message header means, of course, that the definition of the authentication information portion of the header is changed. Since a change is necessary, SNMPv2 introduces an additional change that results in a simplified clock synchronization algorithm. The new definition is as follows:

```
AuthInformation :: = [2] IMPLICIT SEQUENCE {
                      authDigest          OCTET STRING,
                      authDstTimestamp    UInteger 32
                      authSrcTimestamp    UInteger 32 }
```

When a message is transmitted, it includes the value of both the sending and receiving party clocks. Upon message reception, authentication depends on the timeliness of the message with reference to the source timestamp. If the incoming message is authentic, the selective clock acceleration algorithm is applied to both clocks. Figure 10.3 illustrates the use of the two timestamps.

Recall from Section 8.3.5 the conditions that require clock synchronization. For any pair of parties, four possible conditions can occur that require correction:

1. The manager's version of the agent's clock is greater than the agent's version of the agent's clock. This creates the risk of a false rejection of a message from the agent to the manager.

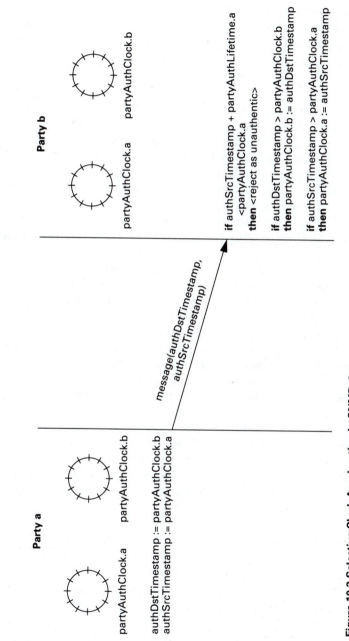

Figure 10.3 Selective Clock Acceleration in SNMPv2

2. The manager's version of the manager's clock is greater than the agent's version of the manager's clock. This creates the risk of a false acceptance of a message from the manager to the agent.

3. The agent's version of the agent's clock is greater than the manager's version of the agent's clock. This creates the risk of a false acceptance of a message from the agent to the manager.

4. The agent's version of the manager's clock is greater than the manager's version of the manager's clock. This creates the risk of a false rejection of a message from the manager to the agent.

Now, let us consider the case in which an agent receives a message from a manager. If the authSrcTimestamp in the message exceeds the agent's value of partyAuthClock for the sending manager party, that clock is advanced and condition two is corrected. If the authDstTimestamp in the message exceeds the agent's value of partyAuthClock for the receiving agent party, the clock is advanced and condition one is corrected. To complete this line of reasoning, consider the case in which a manager receives a message from an agent. If the authSrcTimestamp in the message exceeds the agent's value of partyAuthClock for the sending agent party, the clock is advanced and condition three is corrected. If the authDstTimestamp in the message exceeds the agent's value of partyAuthClock for the receiving manager party, the clock is advanced and condition four is corrected.

At first glance, the effects of selective clock acceleration would appear to eliminate the need for explicit, manager-directed clock synchronization of the type described in Section 8.3.5, since all four clock skew conditions are corrected when messages are exchanged. However, in most cases of manager-agent interaction, the interaction is in the form of a manager request (Get, Get-Next, Get-Bulk, Set) and an agent response (Response). It is intended that the SNMPv2-Trap, which originates at the agent, be used sparingly. If there has been a considerable lapse of time between requests from a particular manager party to a particular agent party, then clock drift may have created condition four with a substantial difference in the two clock values. The result is that any request by the manager will be rejected. If no SNMPv2-Traps are sent by the agent party, and if no action is taken by the manager, then this condition will never be corrected. Accordingly, it remains necessary for the manager to perform clock synchronization on all manager party clocks, but it is not necessary to synchronize agent party clocks. Thus, the clock synchronization algorithm of Section 8.3.5 is simplified as follows: Omit both the retrieval of agent party clock values, and the checking for and correction of condition one. Thus, the clock synchronization algorithm for SNMPv2 can be summarized as follows. The management station periodically performs the following sequence of steps for every pair of parties:

1. The manager saves the value of partyAuthClock for the party mgrParty in a temporary location.

2. The manager uses an unauthenticated Get to retrieve the value of partyAuthClock for mgrParty from the agent. The retrieval must be unauthenticated since the manager does not know if the clocks are synchronized, and an authenticated request may be rejected if synchronization is violated.

3. If the agent's value for the mgrParty clock exceeds the manager's value, then the manager advances its value of the mgrParty clock to match the agent's value.

4. The manager uses an authenticated Get to retrieve the value of partyAuthClock for mgrParty from the agent. The retrieval must be authenticated in order for the manager to verify that the clock values are properly synchronized.

10.3.3   Context Information

One additional change is made to the message header for SNMPv2: the inclusion of a context parameter. Figure 10.4 provides the ASN.1 definition of the message structure used in SNMPv2, and Figure 10.5 informally depicts the structure.

The authentication process can be summarized as follows. Consider that a message is to be sent from party a on one system to party b on another system, using the digest authentication protocol and a privacy protocol. The message generation process consists of the following steps:

1. An SnmpMgmtCom value is constructed with:

    ■ srcParty identifies the originating party
    ■ dstParty identifies the receiving party
    ■ context identifies the desired SNMPv2 context
    ■ pdu represents the desired management operation

2. An SnmpAuthMsg value is constructed with:

    ■ authSrcTimestamp is set to the current value stored locally for partyAuthClock.a.
    ■ authDstTimestamp is set to the current value stored locally for partyAuthClock.b.
    ■ authDigest is temporarily set to the private authentication key of party a. An MD5 digest is computed over the octet sequence representing SnmpAuthMsg. The authDigest component is then set to the computed digest value.

```
SnmpMgmtCom ::= [1] IMPLICIT SEQUENCE {
                    dstParty          OBJECT IDENTIFIER,
                    srcParty          OBJECT IDENTIFIER,
                    context           OBJECT IDENTIFIER,
                    pdu               PDUs }


SnmpAuthMsg ::= [1] IMPLICIT SEQUENCE {
                    authInfo          ANY, —defined by authentication protocol
                    authData          SnmpMgmtCom, }


SnmpPrivMsg ::= [1] IMPLICIT SEQUENCE {
                    privDst           OBJECT IDENTIFIER,
                    privData          [1] IMPLICIT OCTET STRING  }


AuthInformation ::= [2] IMPLICIT SEQUENCE {
                    authDigest        OCTET STRING,
                    authDstTimestamp  UInteger 32,
                    authSrcTimestamp  UInteger 32 }
```

Figure 10.4 ASN.1 Definitions for the SNMPv2 Security Protocols

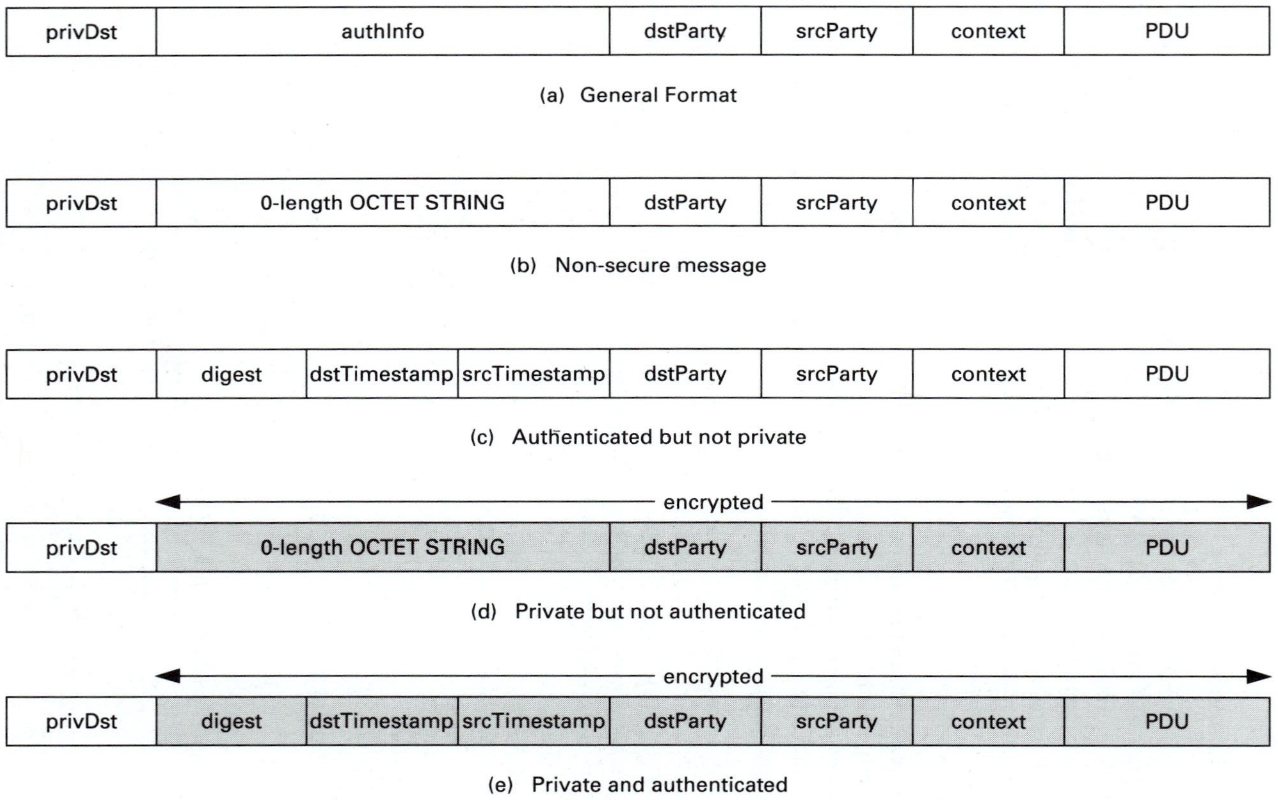

| privDst | authInfo | dstParty | srcParty | context | PDU |

(a) General Format

| privDst | 0-length OCTET STRING | dstParty | srcParty | context | PDU |

(b) Non-secure message

| privDst | digest | dstTimestamp | srcTimestamp | dstParty | srcParty | context | PDU |

(c) Authenticated but not private

←———— encrypted ————→

| privDst | 0-length OCTET STRING | dstParty | srcParty | context | PDU |

(d) Private but not authenticated

←———— encrypted ————→

| privDst | digest | dstTimestamp | srcTimestamp | dstParty | srcParty | context | PDU |

(e) Private and authenticated

Figure 10.5 SMNPv2 Message Formats

3. The resulting SnmpAuthMsg is encrypted.

4. The destination party identifier (party b) is placed in privDst to form an SnmpPrivMsg.

Message reception consists of the following steps:

1. If the privDst value is not valid, the message is discarded.

2. The privData value is decrypted to obtain the SnmpAuthMsg.

3. If the ASN.1 type of the authInfo component is not AuthInformation, or if dstParty does not match privDst, or if srcParty is not known, the message is discarded.

4. If the authSrcTimestamp value does not satisfy the criterion for timeliness the message is rejected. The timeliness criterion states that the message must be received within a reasonable period of time that does not exceed an administratively set value. This criterion can be expressed as follows. A message is timely if:

$$\text{partyAuthClock.a - authSrcTimestamp} \leq \text{partyAuthLifetime.a}$$

Put another way, the age of the message at the time of receipt must be less than the maximum allowable lifetime.

5. The authDigest value is extracted and temporarily stored. The authDigest value is temporarily set to the secret value. The message digest is computed over the modified SnmpAuthMsg and compared to the value that was stored (the value that arrived in the incoming message). If the two values match, the message is accepted as authentic.

6. If the context referenced in the message header is unknown, the message is discarded.

7. The local database is consulted to determine if access privileges permit the requested operation. If so, then:

   - If the authSrcTimestamp value exceeds the locally stored value of partyAuthClock.a, the latter is advanced to the authSrcTimestamp value.
   - If the authDstTimestamp value exceeds the locally stored value of partyAuthClock.b, the latter is advanced to the authSrcTimestamp value.

If a request is successfully received, processing depends on the context. If the context is locally accessible, then the operation is performed with respect to the MIB view identified by the context. If the context is remotely accessible, the operation is performed through the appropriate proxy relationship.

10.4 SNMPv2 PARTY MIB

The party MIB for SNMPv2 is derived from that for S-SNMP. The major changes:

- The S-SNMP party public and party private database groups are combined into a single party database group.
- A new contexts database group is added.
- The access privileges database group is modified to reflect the use of contexts.
- The MIB view database is re-organized for purposes of simplification and efficiency.

In this section, we examine each of these databases in turn and then look at the initial party configurations defined for SNMPv2.

10.4.1   Party Database Group

The party database group contains locally stored information about local and remote parties. Table 10.4 lists the objects in the group.[2] The group consists of a single table. The objects in this table are found in the corresponding tables of S-SNMP, with the following additions:

- partyIndex: this provides a unique integer index to the conceptual row. It makes it easier to provide cross-references from other tables in the party MIB, rather than using the object identifier of the party as the index.

- partyLocal: indicates whether the party is local or remote.

- partyStorageType: indicates how the information is stored.

  A new textual convention is introduced for the partyStorageType:

  StorageType :: = TEXTUAL-CONVENTION
     STATUS current
     DESCRIPTION
        "Describes the memory realization of a conceptual row. A row which is volatile(2) is
           lost upon reboot. A row which is nonVolatile(3) is backed up by stable storage. A row
           which is permanent(4) cannot be changed nor deleted."
     SYNTAX INTEGER {
                            other(1),   —eh?
                            volatile(2),   —e.g., in RAM
                            nonVolatile(3),   —e.g., in NVRAM
                            permanent(4)   —e.g., in ROM }

The motivation for the StorageType convention is to enable an agent to minimize the amount of non-volatile storage that must be dedicated to management information. An example should serve to illustrate the value of this convention: An SNMPv2 station on a LAN is to act as a proxy agent for the other stations on the ring. It should be possible for the proxy agent to dynamically reflect the LAN configuration. The proxy agent can monitor activity on the LAN and build a new party entity for each new station recognized. All of this information is kept in RAM.

10.4.2   Contexts Database Group

This group consists of a single table, with one entry for each context known to this SNMPv2 entity. Table 10.5 lists the objects in this group.

Several definitions come into play in this group. The first is a textual convention for the context syntax:

---

2.   The following acronyms are used in Tables 10.4 through 10.7: read-only (RO), read-write (RW), read-create (RC), not-accessible (NA).

Table 10.4 Party Database Group

Object	Syntax	Access	Description
partyTable	SEQUENCE OF PartyEntry	NA	Table of party information.
partyEntry	SEQUENCE	NA	Information about a particular SNMPv2 party.
partyIdentity	Party	NA	Unique object identifier of a party.
partyIndex	INTEGER	RO	A unique value for each SNMPv2 party used to index this table.
partyTDomain	OBJECT IDENTIFIER	RC	Indicates transport service by which the party receives network management traffic.
partyTAddr	TAddress	RC	The transport service address of the party. For SNMPUDPDomain, the address is formatted as a 4-octet IP address concatenated with a 2-octet UDP port number.
partyMaxMessageSize	INTEGER	RC	An integer in the range 484 to 65,507 that represents the maximum message length in octets that this party will accept.
partyLocal	TruthValue	RC	An indication of whether this party is local to this agent.
partyAuthProtocol	OBJECT IDENTIFIER	RC	Object identifier of the authentication protocol, if any.
partyAuthClock	Clock	RC	A non-negative integer, initialized to zero, with a maximum value of $2^{31} - 1$. This is the local notion of the current time for this party.
partyAuthPrivate	OCTET STRING	RC	An encoding of the party's private authentication key, or value, needed to support the authentication protocol.
partyAuthPublic	OCTET STRING	RC	A publicly readable value related to the party's authentication protocol.
partyAuthLifetime	INTEGER	RC	A non-negative integer, initialized to zero, with a maximum value of $2^{31} - 1$. This is an upper bound on the lifetime of a message in seconds.
partyPrivProtocol	OBJECT IDENTIFIER	RC	Object identifier of the privacy protocol, if any.
partyPrivPrivate	OCTET STRING	RC	An encoding of the party's private encryption key, needed to support the privacy protocol.
partyPrivPublic	OCTET STRING	RC	A publicly-readable value related to the party's privacy protocol.
partyCloneFrom	Party	RC	Identity of a party to clone authentication and privacy parameters from.
partyStorageType	StorageType	RC	The storage type for this conceptual row in the party entry.
partyStatus	RowStatus	RO	The status of this row with respect to row creation and deletion.

Table 10.5 Contexts Database Group

Object	Syntax	Access	Description
contextTable	SEQUENCE OF ContextEntry	NA	Table of context parameters.
contextEntry	SEQUENCE	NA	Information about a particular context.
contextIdentity	Context	NA	A context identifier uniquely identifying a particular SNMPv2 context.
contextIndex	INTEGER	RO	A unique value for each context, used to index this table.
contextLocal	TruthValue	RC	Indicates whether this context is realized by this SNMPv2 entity.
contextViewIndex	INTEGER	RC	If zero, this row refers to a context which identifies a proxy relationship; otherwise, this row refers to a context that identifies a MIB view of a locally accessible entity.
contextLocalEntity	OCTET STRING	RC	If contextViewIndex is greater than zero, this value identifies the local entity whose management information is in the context's MIB view. The empty string indicates that the MIB view contains the entity's own local management information.
contextLocalTime	OBJECT IDENTIFIER	RC	If contextViewIndex is greater than zero, this value identifies the temporal context of the management information in the MIB view.
contextProxyDst-Party	Party	RC	If contextViewIndex is equal to 0, this value identifies a party that is the proxy destination of a proxy relationship.
contextProxySrcParty	Party	RC	If contextViewIndex is equal to 0, this value identifies a party that is the proxy source of a proxy relationship.
contextProxyContext	OBJECT IDENTIFIER	RC	If contextViewIndex is equal to 0, this value identifies the context of a proxy relationship.
contextStorageType	StorageType	RC	The storage type for this conceptual row.
contextStatus	RowStatus	RC	The status of this row with respect to row creation and deletion.

Context :: = TEXTUAL-CONVENTION
   STATUS current
   DESCRIPTION
      "Denotes an SNMPv2 context identifier."
   SYNTAX OBJECT IDENTIFIER

Thus, each context must be provided with an object identifier.

The other important definition is that of temporal domains:

temporalDomains   OBJECT IDENTIFIER ::= { partyAdmin 2 }

—this temporal domain refers to management information at the current time

    currentTime   OBJECT IDENTIFIER ::= { temporalDomains 1 }

—this temporal domain refers to management information
—upon the next re-initialization of the managed device

    restartTime   OBJECT IDENTIFIER ::= { temporalDomains 2 }

—the temporal domain { cacheTime N } refers to management information
—that is cached and guaranteed to be at most N seconds old

    cacheTime   OBJECT IDENTIFIER ::= { temporalDomains 3 }

This enables the agent to store resource information with three different temporal characteristics. Information characterized as currentTime refers to the latest information known to the agent about the relevant resource. Information characterized as restartTime consists of values that will be supplied upon the next re-initialization of the managed device. If the domain is cacheTime, then the agent is using a cache to store frequently accessed values, and guarantees that the values returned will be no more then N seconds old.

For example,[3] the restartTime domain could be used to set the IP addresses used by a workstation when booting (as distinct from the current IP addresses). In contrast, cacheTime.60 domain could be used for a caching proxy agent to consolidate polling activity and protect a network from aggressive polling.

The table accommodates two kinds of entries: those that involve only local information and those that involve a proxy relationship. The kind of entry is determined by contextViewIndex:

- If contextViewIndex has a nonzero value, then the row refers to local information and the value is an index into the view table, thereby specifying the relevant MIB view. In this case contextLocalEntity identifies the local entity whose management information is in the relevant MIB view; the local entity could be the SNMPv2 entity itself (empty string) or some other locally controlled entity (e.g., "Repeater 1"). The value of contextLocalTime identifies the temporal context.

- If contextViewIndex has a zero value, then the row refers to a proxy relationship. In this case contextSrcPartyIndex and contextDstPartyIndex are indexes into the party table for the source and destination parties for this proxy relationship, and contextProxyContext is the identifier of the context.

10.4.3   Access Privileges Database Group

This group consists of a single table, with one entry for each access policy known to this SNMPv2 entity. Table 10.6 lists the objects in this group.

The table has three indexes, all of which are integer values; they identify the subject, target, and context of the access control policy. The policy itself is contained in aclPrivileges.

10.4.4   MIB View Database Group

This group consists of a single table that is used to define MIB views. Note that each context references a single MIB view. Table 10.7 lists the objects in this group.

---

3. These examples are from Marshall Rose.

Table 10.6 Access Privileges Database Group

Object	Syntax	Access	Description
aclTable	SEQUENCE OF AclEntry	NA	Table of access privileges information.
aclEntry	SEQUENCE	NA	Access privileges for a particular subject party when asking a particular party to access a particular context.
aclTarget	INTEGER	NA	The target SNMP party whose performance of management operations is constrained by this set of access privileges.
aclSubject	INTEGER	NA	The subject SNMP party whose requests for management operations to be performed are constrained by this set of access privileges.
aclResources	INTEGER	NA	A context in an access control policy.
aclPrivileges	INTEGER	RC	An integer in the range 0 to 255 that encodes the access privileges for this (target, subject, context) triple.
aclStorageType	StorageType	RC	The storage type for this conceptual row.
aclStatus	RowStatus	RC	The status of this row with respect to row creation and deletion.

This group contains the same information as the corresponding group in S-SNMP, organized somewhat differently. The key elements of information are subtree, mask, and type. A subtree identifies a node in the MIB hierarchy plus all of its subordinate objects. The corresponding mask is used to select a subset or all of the elements of a subtree; the selected elements are referred to as a subtree family. Finally, the corresponding type indicates whether this family is to be included or excluded from an MIB view. For a discussion of the semantics of MIB views, see Section 8.4.4.

The table, viewTable, is used to define a set of MIB views, with each view consisting of one or more subtree families. For this purpose, viewTable is indexed by viewIndex and viewSubtree; all of the entries with the same value of viewIndex constitute a single MIB view. Thus, the table can contain multiple rows for a single view, and the MIB view consists of a collection of included and excluded subtrees. The object contextViewIndex in contextTable may take on a value of viewIndex, which enables a context to point to an MIB view in viewTable.

One final change introduced in SNMPv2 has to do with access-control granularity. In S-SNMP, an agent is capable of enforcing access control down to the level of object instance. In SNMPv2, access control is only required to the level of object type. This relaxation of the granularity requirement is intended to minimize the performance impact of the access-control function.

At this point, now that all of the tables in the party MIB have been introduced, it might be worth summarizing the information involved in a transaction. Consider that a message is sent from a manager to an agent. The message header includes the fields srcParty, dstParty, and context. Therefore:

Table 10.7 MIB View Database Group

Object	Syntax	Access	Description
viewTable	SEQUENCE OF ViewEntry	NA	Table of local MIB views.
viewEntry	SEQUENCE	NA	Information on a particular family of view subtrees included or excluded from a particular party's MIB view.
viewIndex	INTEGER	NA	A unique value for each MIB view.
viewSubtree	OBJECT IDENTIFIER	NA	A MIB Subtree.
viewMask	OCTET STRING	RC	The bit mask which, in combination with the corresponding instance of viewSubtree, defines a family of view subtrees.
viewType	INTEGER	RC	Takes on the values included(1), excluded(2). Indicates whether the corresponding family of view subtrees defined by familySubtree and familyMask is included or excluded from the MIB view.
viewStorageType	StorageType	RC	The storage type for this conceptual row.
viewStatus	RowStatus	RC	The status of this row with respect to row creation and deletion.

- SrcParty defines the manager party
- DstParty defines the agent party
- Context defines who has the required management information
- partyTable defines the authentication parameters for srcParty
- partyTable defines the privacy parameters for dstParty
- contextTable specifies the local MIB view or the remote proxied agent
- aclTable defines access privileges for srcParty to access context via dstParty
- viewTable defines the view visible when srcParty accesses a local context at dstParty

10.4.5 Initial Party Configuration

As with S-SNMP, six initial parties are defined. The first two parties are the local and remote parties that provide for non-secure communications, using no authentication protocol and no privacy protocol. The next two parties share the use of an authentication protocol but no privacy protocol. The final two parties share both an authentication protocol and a privacy protocol.

Table 10.8 shows the information defined for the six initial parties. The party information, shown in part (a) is essentially the same as that defined in S-SNMP.

Table 10.8, part (b) specifies the access control parameters assigned to the initial set of parties. Compare this with Table 8.5, part (b). One difference is that the privileges for each party have been expanded to include the new PDUs in SNMPv2.

Table 10.8 Initial Values of Object Instances for Initial Set of Parties

(a) Party Information

partyIdentity = { initialPartyId a b c d 1 }
partyTDomain = snmpUDPDomain
partyTAddr = a.b.c.d, 161

partyLocal = true (in agent's database)
partyAuthProtocol = noAuth
partyAuthClock = 0
partySecretsAuthPrivate = ''H
partyAuthPublic = ''H
partyAuthLifetime = 0
partyPrivProtocol = noPriv
partyPrivPrivate = ''H
partyPrivPublic = ''H

partyIdentity = { initialPartyId a b c d 2 }
partyTDomain = snmpUDPDomain
partyTAddr = assigned by local administration

partyLocal = false (in agent's database)
partyAuthProtocol = noAuth
partyAuthClock = 0
partySecretsAuthPrivate = ''H
partyAuthPublic = ''H
partyAuthLifetime = 0
partyPrivProtocol = noPriv
partyPrivPrivate = ''H
partyPrivPublic = ''H

partyIdentity = { initialPartyId a b c d 3 }
partyTDomain = snmpUDPDomain
partyTAddr = a.b.c.d, 161

partyLocal = true (in agent's database)
partyAuthProtocol = v2md5AuthProtocol
partyAuthClock = 0
partySecretsAuthPrivate = assigned by
  local administration
partyAuthPublic = ''H
partyAuthLifetime = 300
partyPrivProtocol = noPriv
partyPrivPrivate = ''H
partyPrivPublic = ''H

partyIdentity = { initialPartyId a b c d 4 }
partyTDomain = snmpUDPDomain
partyTAddr = assigned by local administration

partyLocal = false (in agent's database)
partyAuthProtocol = v2md5AuthProtocol
partyAuthClock = 0
partySecretsAuthPrivate = assigned by
  local administration
partyAuthPublic = ''H
partyAuthLifetime = 300
partyPrivProtocol = noPriv
partyPrivPrivate = ''H
partyPrivPublic = ''H

partyIdentity = { initialPartyId a b c d 5 }
partyTDomain = snmpUDPDomain
partyTAddr = a.b.c.d, 161

partyLocal = true (in agent's database)
partyAuthProtocol = v2md5AuthProtocol
partyAuthClock = 0
partySecretsAuthPrivate = assigned by
  local administration
partyAuthPublic = ''H
partyAuthLifetime = 300
partyPrivProtocol = desPrivProtocol
partyPrivPrivate = assigned by local administration
partyPrivPublic = ''H

partyIdentity = { initialPartyId a b c d 6 }
partyTDomain = snmpUDPDomain
partyTAddr = assigned by local administration

partyLocal = false (in agent's database)
partyAuthProtocol = v2md5AuthProtocol
partyAuthClock = 0
partySecretsAuthPrivate = assigned by
  local administration
partyAuthPublic = ''H
partyAuthLifetime = 300
partyPrivProtocol = desPrivProtocol
partyPrivPrivate = assigned by local administration
partyPrivPublic = ''H

Table 10.8 (*Cont.*)

(b) Access Control Parameters

---

aclTarget = 1
aclSubject = 2
aclResources = 1
aclPrivileges = 35 (Get,
  Get-Next & Get-Bulk)
	aclTarget = 2
	aclSubject = 1
	aclResources = 1
	aclPrivileges = 132 (Re-
	  sponse, SNMPv2-Trap)
		aclTarget = 3
		aclSubject = 4
		aclResources = 2
		aclPrivileges = 43 (Get,
		  Get-Next, Set & Get-
		  Bulk)

aclTarget = 4
aclSubject = 3
aclResources = 2
aclPrivileges = 4
  (Response)
	aclTarget = 5
	aclSubject = 6
	aclResources = 2
	aclPrivileges = 43 (Get,
	  Get-Next, Set & Get-
	  Bulk)
		aclTarget = 6
		aclSubject = 5
		aclResources = 2
		aclPrivileges = 4
		  (Response)

(c) Contexts

---

contextIdentity = initialContextId 1 contextLocal = true (in agent's database) contextViewIndex = 1 contextLocalEntity = '' '' contextLocalTime = currentTime contextProxyDstParty = {0.0} contextProxySrcParty = {0,0} contextProxyContext = {0,0}	contextIdentity = initialContextId 2 contextLocal = true (in agent's database) contextViewIndex = 2 contextLocalEntity = '' '' contextLocalTime = currentTime contextProxyDstPartyIndex = {0,0} contextProxySrcPartyIndex = {0,0} contextProxyContext = {0,0}

(d) MIB Views

---

viewIndex	= 1	viewIndex	= 1
viewSubtree	= system	viewSubtree	= snmpStats
viewMask	= ''H	viewMask	= ''H
viewType	= included	viewType	= included
viewIndex	= 1	viewIndex	= 2
viewSubtree	= snmpParties	viewSubtree	= internet
viewMask	= ''H	viewMask	= ''H
viewType	= included	viewType	= included

Table 10.8, part (c) shows that two contexts have been defined for the initial parties. The only difference between these contexts is that they reference different MIB views.

Finally, the MIB views are defined in part (d) of the table.

Combining the information on access control, contexts, and MIB views, we find the following:

- Parties 1 and 2, which engage in non-secure communication, make use of context 1. This context has an MIB view that includes system, snmpStats, and snmpParties.

- Parties 3 and 4, which engage in authenticated communication, and parties 5 and 6, which engage in private, authenticated communication, all make use of context 2. This context has an MIB view that includes everything under the internet object, which includes MIB-II and the SNMPv2 MIBs.

10.5 SUMMARY

The security portion of SNMPv2 is based on S-SNMP and incorporates a number of refinements introduced in SMP. Of these, the most significant are the elimination of the ordered delivery mechanism and the simplification of the clock synchronization algorithm.

In addition, SNMPv2 introduces a new concept, referred to as the context. The use of contexts provides for more efficient storage of access control and MIB view information.

Part 3
OSI Systems Management

The International Organization for Standardization (ISO) and the International Consultative Committee on Telegraphy and Telephony (CCITT) have been working jointly on the development of network management standards for the OSI environment. The result is a massive set of standards referred to as OSI Systems Management.

Chapter 11 introduces the basic concepts of OSI Systems Management, including the overall framework and a functional breakdown. Chapter 12 examines the SMI defined for OSI Systems Management and introduces some specific examples. Chapter 13 covers the Common Management Information Service (CMIS), which provides a basic network-management service to network-management applications, and the Common Management Information Protocol (CMIP), which implements CMIS.

The final chapter in this part, Chapter 14, provides a survey of the systems-management functions so far standardized for OSI Systems Management. These functions are general-purpose application-level tools that can be used to construct specific network-management applications.

11
OSI Systems-Management Concepts

The term *OSI systems management* is actually used to refer to a collection of standards for network management that include a management service and protocol, the definition of a database, and associated concepts. In this chapter, we provide a brief overview of the key concepts of OSI (open systems interconnection) systems management. The details are developed in the remaining chapters of this part.

11.1 THE OSI SYSTEMS-MANAGEMENT STANDARDS

Of all the areas of OSI standardization, the set of standards developed for OSI systems management is the most voluminous and complex. The first standard related to network management issued by the ISO (International Organization for Standardization) was ISO 7498-4, which specifies the management framework for the OSI model. This document dictates that OSI systems management support user requirements for:

- Activities that enable managers to plan, organize, supervise, control, and account for the use of interconnection services

- The ability to respond to changing needs

- Facilities to ensure predictable communications behavior

- Facilities that provide for information protection and for the authentication of sources of and destinations for transmitted data

Subsequently, the ISO has issued a set of standards and draft standards for network management. The CCITT (International Consultative Committee on Telegraphy and Telephony) is the joint sponsor of this effort and has set aside the X.700 series of numbers for these recommendations. Table 11.1 lists the current set of management standards documents. Figure 11.1, from ISO 10040, depicts the relationship among the various documents. The standards fall into five general categories:

Table 11.1 OSI Systems-Management Standards

Title	ISO	CCITT
OSI Management Framework and Overview		
OSI Basic Reference Model Part 4: Management Framework	7498-4	X.700
Systems Management Overview	10040	X.701
CMIS/CMIP		
Common Management Information Service Definition	9595	X.710
Amendment 4: Access Control	9595 DAM 4	X.710
Amendment X: Allomorphism	9595 PDAM X	X.710
Common Management Information Protocol Specification Part 1: Specification	9596-1	X.711
Amendment X: Allomorphism	9596 PDAM X	X.711
Part 2: Protocol Implementation Conformance Statement (PICS) Proforma	9596-2	X.712
Systems-Management Functions		
Part 1: Object Management Function	10164-1	X.730
Part 2: State Management Function	10164-2	X.732
Part 3: Attributes for Representing Relationships	10164-3	X.733
Part 4: Alarm Reporting Function	10164-4	X.734
Part 5: Event Report Management Function	10164-5	X.735
Part 6: Log Control Function	10164-6	X.736
Part 7: Security Alarm Reporting Function	10164-7	X.737
Part 8: Security Audit Trail Function	10164-8	X.740
Part 9: Objects and Attributes for Access Control	10164-9	X.741
Part 10: Accounting Meter Function	10164-10	X.742
Part 11: Workload Monitoring Function	10164-11	X.739
Part 12: Test Management Function	10164-12	
Part 13: Summarization Function	10164-13	
Part 14: Confidence and Diagnostic Test Categories	10164-14	
Accounting Management	SC 21 N 4971	
Part s: Scheduling Function	SC 21 N 6021	
OSI Software Management	SC 21 N 6040	
General Relationship Model	SC 21 N 6041	
Management Domains	SC 21 N 6047	
Management Knowledge	SC 21 N 6048	
Synchronization	SC 21 N 6049	
Performance Management	SC 21 N 6306	
Management Information Model		
Part 1: Management Information Model	10165-1	X.720
Part 2: Definition of Management Information	10165-2	X.721
Part 4: Guidelines for the Definition of Managed Objects	10165-4	X.722
Part 5: Generic Managed Information	10165-5	
Requirements for Implementation Conformance Statement Proformas	10165-6	
Layer Management		
Elements of Management Information Related to OSI Network Layer Standards	10733	
Transport Layer Management	10737	

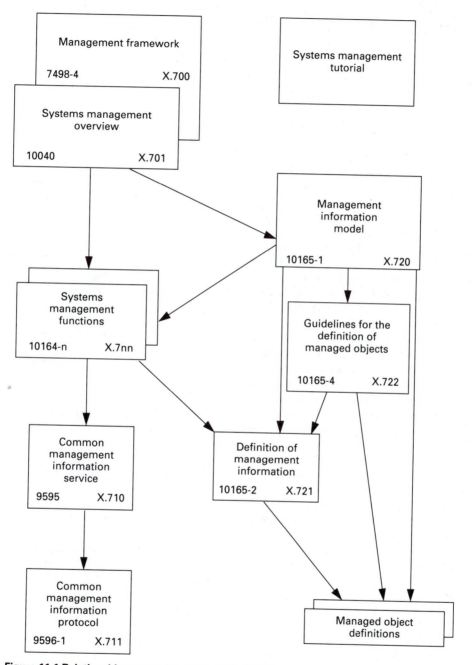

Figure 11.1 Relationship among Standards (ISO 10040)

Table 11.2 A Glossary of Terms for OSI Systems Management

Attribute

A property of a managed object. An attribute has a value.

Common management information service element (CMISE)

An application-service element used to exchange information and commands for the purpose of systems management.

Common management information services

The set of services provided by the common management information service element.

Layer management

Functions related to the management of the *(N)* layer partly performed in the *(N)* layer itself according to the (N)-protocol of the layer and partly performed as a subset of systems management.

Managed object

An abstract representation of a resource on which management operations are performed to enact management of the modeled resource. Examples of modeled resources include a layer entity, a connection, and an item of physical communications equipment.

Management information base

The conceptual repository of management information within an open system. It consists of the set of managed objects, together with their attributes.

Systems management

Functions in the application layer related to the management of various OSI resources and their status across all layers of the OSI architecture.

Systems-management application entity (SMAE)

An application entity whose purpose is systems-management communication.

Systems-management application process (SMAP)

An application process participating in systems management.

Systems-management application-service element (SMASE)

An application-service element providing systems-management services.

Systems-management function

A part of systems-management activities that satisfies a set of logically related user requirements.

Systems-management protocol

An application-layer protocol supporting systems-management services.

Systems-management service

A named set of service primitives that provide a service for use in systems management.

1. *OSI management framework and overview:* includes ISO 7498-4, which provides a general introduction to management concepts, and ISO 10040, which is an overview of the remainder of the documents

2. *CMIS/CMIP:* defines the common management information service (CMIS), which provides OSI management services to management applications, and the common management information protocol (CMIP), which provides the information exchange capability to support CMIS

3. *Systems-management functions:* defines the specific functions that are performed by OSI systems management

4. *Management information model:* defines the management information base (MIB), which contains a representation of all objects within the OSI environment subject to management

5. *Layer management:* defines management information, services, and functions related to specific OSI layers

As in any of the complex subject areas of OSI-related standardization, one key to understanding is to first understand the terminology employed. Table 11.2 provides a glossary of some of the most important terms used in OSI network-management documents. Note especially that the term *systems management* is used for what is generally referred to as network management in non-OSI literature. Furthermore, OSI systems management requires the use of the OSI reference model. Finally, note that OSI systems management is restricted to the management of the OSI components in an OSI environment (not application programs, CD players, toasters, etc.).

11.2 OSI MANAGEMENT FRAMEWORK

An architectural model of an OSI host participating in OSI systems management is shown in Figure 11.2. Key elements of this architecture include:

- *Systems-management application process:* This is the local software within a system that is responsible for executing the systems-management functions within a single system (host, front-end processor, router, etc.). It has access to system parameters and capabilities and can therefore manage all aspects of the system and coordinate with SMAPs on other systems.

- *Systems-management application entity:* This application-level entity is responsible for the exchange of management information with peer SMAEs in other nodes, especially with the system that exercises a network-control-center function. A standardized application-level protocol, common management information protocol, is used for this purpose.

- *Layer-management entity:* Logic is embedded into each layer of the OSI architecture to provide network-management functions specific to that layer.

- *Management information base:* The collection of information at each node pertaining to network management.

Figure 11.3 provides detail concerning the structure of the systems-management application entity. Like any other application-level entity, the SMAE can be logically defined as an interrelated set of application-service elements (ASEs). In this case, two of the elements are ones that have been developed to be generally useful in a variety of applications: the association-control-service element (ACSE) and the remote-operations-service element (ROSE).

Two ASEs that are specific to network management are the common management information service element and the systems-management application-service element. The SMASE provides various services that are available to the network manager and to applications (e.g., SMAP) that implement network-management functions. The SMASE implements basic management functions in the areas of fault management, accounting management, configuration management, performance management, and security management.[1] For those functions that require communication

---

1. An easy way to remember these is the acronym FCAPS, pronounced ''eff-caps.''

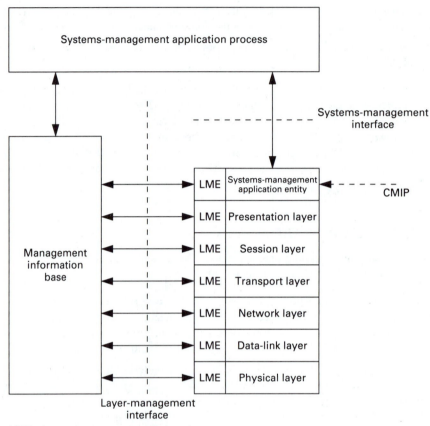

LME = layer-management entity.

Figure 11.2 Architectural Model of OSI Management

with other systems, the SMASE relies on the CMISE. The CMISE provides the collection of basic network-management functions that supports the five functional areas visible to systems managers via the SMASE.

In order to provide systems management of a distributed system, all the elements illustrated in Figures 11.2 and 11.3 must be replicated in a distributed fashion across all the systems that are subject to systems management. Interactions that take place among systems are depicted, in abstract fashion, in Figure 11.4. Management activities are effected through the manipulation of managed objects. Each system contains a number of such objects, each of which is a data structure that corresponds to an actual entity to be managed.

The SMAP in a system is allowed to take on either an agent role or a manager role. The manager role for an SMAP occurs in a system that acts as a network-control center. The agent role for an SMAP occurs in managed systems. The manager issues requests for information and operations commands for execution to the managed systems in the network. In each managed system, the agent interacts with the manager and is responsible for managing the objects within its system.

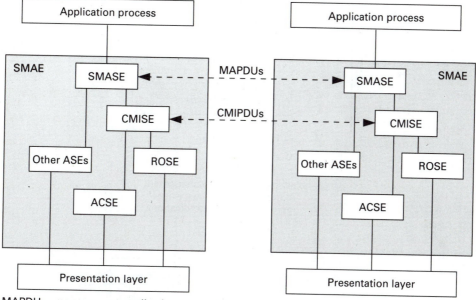

MAPDU = management-application protocol data unit.
CMIPDU = common management information protocol data unit.

Figure 11.3 OSI Management in the Application Layer

The way in which an agent represents and stores the data from which management information is derived is a local matter and not the subject of standardization. A local mapping function is used to map information concerning managed objects into a form that can be stored locally and used by local management software. However, for purposes of interaction with other systems, a standardized form of representation is required. Thus, the local representation must be mapped into a standardized form for agent-manager communication. These concepts are captured in Figure 11.5.

The use of object-oriented principles to define management information is one of the most important ideas in OSI system management. An object is defined by attributes it contains, operations that can be performed on it, notifications it can emit, and its relationships to other objects. While the topic is explored in depth in Chapter 12, it is worth stressing here that objects represent resources and that systems management operations are done directly on objects, not on the resources they represent. Although it may be possible to do other things with or to a resource, only those operations that are defined for the corresponding object are available for systems management.

11.3   OSI MANAGEMENT FUNCTIONAL AREAS

The OSI management documents divide the task of systems management into five functional areas (Table 11.3). These areas, which provide a useful checklist for assessing any network-management offering, were discussed in Chapter 1; some additional comments are provided in this section.

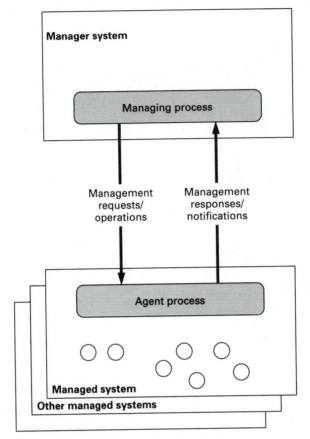

$\bigcirc$ = managed object (may contain other objects).

Figure 11.4 Systems-Management Interactions

11.3.1   Fault Management

OSI fault-management facilities allow network managers to detect problems in the communications network and the OSI environment. These facilities include mechanisms for the detection, isolation, and correction of abnormal operation in any network component or in any of the OSI layers. Fault management provides procedures to:

1.   Detect and report the occurrence of faults. These procedures allow a managed system to notify its manager of the detection of a fault, using a standardized event-reporting protocol.

2.   Log the received event report. This log can then be examined and processed.

3.   Schedule and execute diagnostic tests, trace faults, and initiate correction of faults. These procedures may be invoked as a result of analysis of the event log.

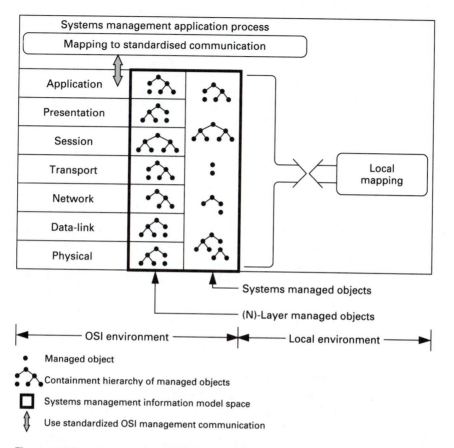

Figure 11.5 Relationship between Information and Communication Aspects of the Systems-Management Model (ISO 10040)

11.3.2 Accounting Management

OSI accounting-management facilities allow a network manager to determine and allocate costs and charges for the use of network resources. Accounting management provides procedures to:

- Inform users of costs incurred, using event-reporting and data-manipulation software.

- Enable accounting limits to be set for the use of managed resources.

- Enable costs to be combined where multiple resources are used to achieve needed communication.

11.3.3 Configuration and Name Management

OSI configuration- and name-management facilities allow network managers to exercise control over the configuration of the network components and OSI layer entities. Configurations may be changed to alleviate congestion, isolate faults, or meet changing user needs. Configuration management provides procedures to:

Table 11.3 OSI Management Functional Areas

Fault management	The facilities that enable the detection, isolation, and correction of abnormal operation of the OSI environment.
Accounting management	The facilities that enable charges to be established for the use of managed objects and costs to be identified for the use of those managed objects.
Configuration and name management	The facilities that exercise control over, identify, collect data from, and provide data to managed objects for the purpose of assisting in providing for continuous operation of interconnection services.
Performance management	The facilities needed to evaluate the behavior of managed objects and the effectiveness of communication activities.
Security management	Addresses those aspects of OSI security essential to operate OSI network management correctly and to protect management information.

- Collect and disseminate data concerning the current state of resources. Locally initiated changes or changes occurring due to unpredicted occurrences are communicated to management facilities by means of standardized protocols.

- Set and modify parameters related to network components and OSI layer software.

- Initialize and close down managed objects.

- Change the configuration.

- Associate names with objects and sets of objects.

11.3.4   Performance Management

OSI performance-management facilities provide the network manager with the ability to monitor and evaluate the performance of system and layer entities. Performance management provides procedures to:

- Collect and disseminate data concerning the current level of performance of resources

- Maintain and examine performance logs for such purposes as planning and analysis

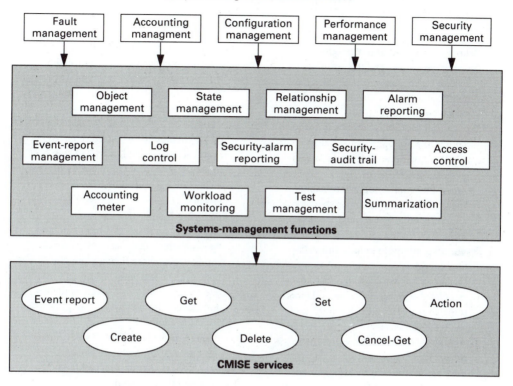

Figure 11.6 Systems-Management Overview

11.3.5 Security Management

OSI security-management facilities allow a network manager to manage those services that provide access protection of communications resources. Security management provides support for the management of:

- Authorization facilities
- Access control
- Encryption and key management
- Authentication
- Security logs

11.4 SYSTEMS-MANAGEMENT FUNCTIONS

The management functional areas defined in the OSI management framework describe broad areas of network-management responsibility. Each of these areas involves the use of specific functions, and there is considerable overlap in these supporting functions. Accordingly, the five functional

Table 11.4 Functional Requirements for OSI Management Functional Areas

Configuration Management

Defining resources and attributes
Specify resources and the attributes associated with a resource. Specify the range and type of values to which the attributes can be set.

Setting and modifying attribute values
Set and modify values of resource attributes. Load predefined default attributes and set clocks.

Defining and modifying relationships
Specify relationships among network resources. Add, delete, and modify relationships on-line.

Examining attribute values and relationships
Locally or remotely examine attributes associated with resources and relationships among resources. Keep track of configuration changes.

Distributing software throughout the network
Provide mechanisms to examine, update, and manage different versions of software and routing information.

Initializing and terminating network operations
Provide facilities to initialize and close down network or subnetwork operation.

Verifying users' authorization
Provide the ability to specify the hierarchy of authorization for performing various configuration functions and the methods used for assigning and validating various levels of authorization.

Reporting configuration status
Notify users of changes in resources and in relationships among resources. The managing system must be able to inform the agent system under what conditions and where configuration-change notifications are to be sent. Users must be able to access configuration reports.

Fault Management

Detecting and reporting faults
Provide mechanisms to allow users to log events and errors, including the specification of logging-filter settings (logging criteria), initialization and stopping of logging, and specification of information to be logged. Define events to be reported, start and stop times for monitoring, and threshold levels when a notification should be given.

Diagnosing faults
Activate predefined tests to determine the location of faults and test network components before they are put on-line. Collect and analyze test data. Request fault-related data, such as dumps and status information.

Correcting faults
Change resource attribute values, take resources down, and put resources back on-line. Request reconfiguration of parts of the network.

Security Management

Controlling access to resources
Grant or restrict access to the entire network or selected critical parts.

Archiving and retrieving security information
Gather and store appropriate information.

Managing and controlling the encryption process
Encrypt security-management communication. Facilitate the user encryption process.

Performance Management

Monitoring performance
Monitor performance-related events, measures, and resources. Specify start and stop times for monitoring. Specify statistical measures to be generated.

Table 11.4 (*Cont.*)

Tuning and controlling performance
Provide mechanisms to execute predefined performance tests and collect test results to diagnose performance problems and determine performance-tuning strategy. Change resource allocation and modify attributes to improve performance.

Evaluating performance tuning
Keep track of tuning results in terms of user-specified criteria.

Reporting on performance monitoring, tuning, and tracking
Generate notifications of abnormal performance changes.

Testing capacity and special conditions
Run tests to determine the potential effects of additional network loading.

Accounting Management

Recording and generating accounting information
Specify the schedule for collecting accounting information. Record and/or collect user-distinguishable accounting information and generate accounting messages.

Specifying accounting information to be collected
Specify what information is to be collected.

Controlling the storage of and access to accounting information
Provide standard procedures for retrieving and storing accounting information and standard ways to name archived files. Control access to accounting information.

Reporting accounting information
Report the degree of resource usage and resource-usage charges at a user-specified level.

Setting and modifying accounting limits
Read, set, and change accounting limits for various groups of users. Change priorities assigned to network users for access to network resources.

Defining accounting metrics
Define standard metrics and accounting information units.

areas are not standardized as such. Rather, a number of specific functions, referred to as *systems-management functions* (SMFs), have been defined. Each SMF standard defines the functionality to support systems-management functional area (SMFA) requirements. A given SMF may support requirements in one or more of the five SMFAs; for example, the event-report management function may be applicable to all SMFAs. Looked at the other way, each SMFA requires several SMFs.

Each of the SMF standards defines the functionality for the SMF and provides a mapping between the services provided by the SMF and CMISE. This relationship is depicted in Figure 11.6. Each of the five management functional areas makes use of one or more of the systems-management functions. Each systems-management function may make use of the services of other SMFs as well as the services of CMISE.

So far, 13 SMFs have been specified. These are:

1. *Object management:* supports the creation and deletion of managed objects and the reading and changing of object attributes. Also specifies notifications to be emitted when the value of an attribute changes.

2. *State management:* specifies a model for how the management state of an object is to be represented. Provides services to support the model.

Table 11.5 Relationship between Management Functional Areas and Systems-Management Functions

	1	2	3	4	5	6	7	8	9	10	11	12	13
Configuration Management													
Defining resources and attributes	✓												
Setting and modifying attribute values			✓										
Defining and modifying relationships			✓										
Examining attribute values and relationships	✓												
Distributing software throughout the network													
Initializing and terminating network operations		✓											
Verifying users' authorization									✓				
Reporting configuration status	✓	✓	✓		✓								
Fault Management													
Detecting and reporting faults				✓		✓							
Diagnosing faults												✓	
Correcting faults	✓	✓											
Security Management													
Controlling access to resources									✓				
Archiving and retrieving security information							✓	✓					
Managing and controlling the encryption process									✓				

Performance Management

	1	2	3	4	5	6	7	8	9	10	11	12	13
Monitoring performance											✓		
Tuning and controlling performance	✓	✓									✓		
Evaluating performance tuning	✓	✓											
Reporting on performance monitoring, tuning, and tracking				✓									
Testing capacity and special conditions												✓	

Accounting Management

	1	2	3	4	5	6	7	8	9	10	11	12	13
Recording and generating accounting information										✓			
Specifying accounting information to be collected										✓			
Controlling storage of and access to accounting information						✓			✓				
Reporting accounting information										✓			
Setting and modifying accounting limits										✓			
Defining accounting metrics										✓			

Code:

1. Object management
2. State management
3. Relationship management
4. Alarm reporting
5. Event-report management
6. Log control
7. Security-alarm reporting
8. Security-audit trail
9. Access control
10. Accounting meter
11. Workload monitoring
12. Test management
13. Summarization

3. *Relationship management:* specifies a model for representing and managing relationships between managed objects. Provides services to support the model.

4. *Alarm reporting:* supports the definition of fault alarms and the notifications used to report them.

5. *Event-report management:* supports the control of event reporting, including the specification of recipients of reports, the definition of reports, and the specification of criteria for generating and distributing reports.

6. *Log control:* supports the creation of logs, the creation and storage of log records, and the specification of criteria for logging.

7. *Security-alarm reporting:* supports the definition of security alarms and the notifications used to report them.

8. *Security-audit trail:* specifies the kinds of event reports that should be contained in a log used for security evaluation.

9. *Access control:* supports the control of access to management information and operations.

10. *Accounting meter:* provides for accounting for the usage of system resources and a mechanism for enforcing accounting limits.

11. *Workload monitoring:* supports the monitoring of attributes of managed objects that relate to the performance of a resource.

12. *Test management:* supports the management of confidence and diagnostic test procedures.

13. *Summarization:* supports the definition of statistical measures to be applied to attributes and the reporting of summarized information.

To see the relationship between SMFAs and SMFs, consider Table 11.4, whose organization is based on Aronoff et al. (1989); it lists key functional requirements in every SMFA. From this, we can derive Table 11.5, which indicates which SMFs provide services to each SMFA.

11.5   SUMMARY

OSI systems management is defined by a large set of standards issued jointly by the ISO and the CCITT. The overall framework for OSI systems management is designed to satisfy network-management requirements in five functional areas: fault management, accounting management, configuration management, performance management, and security management.

To support these five functional areas, OSI includes a number of general-purpose tools known as systems-management functions. Each functional area can be implemented as an application that relies on some subset of the systems-management functions. The functions so far defined include:

- Object management
- State management
- Relationship management
- Alarm reporting
- Event-report management

- Log control
- Security-alarm reporting
- Security-audit trail
- Access control
- Accounting meter
- Workload monitoring
- Test management
- Summarization

These functions, in turn, rely on the common management information service (CMIS) for the basic exchange of management information.

12
OSI Management Information Base

The foundation of any network-management system is a database containing information about the resources and elements to be managed. In OSI (open systems interconnection) systems management, this database is referred to as a management information base (MIB). The general framework within which an MIB can be defined and constructed is referred to as the structure of management information (SMI). The SMI identifies the data types that can be used in the MIB and how resources within the MIB are represented and named.

OSI systems management relies heavily on the concepts of object-oriented design. Each resource that is monitored and controlled by OSI systems management is represented by a managed object. The MIB is a structured collection of such objects. A managed object can be defined for any resource that an organization wishes to monitor and/or control. Examples of hardware resources are switches, workstations, PBXs (private branch exchanges), LAN (local area network) port cards, and multiplexers. Examples of software resources are queuing programs, routing algorithms, and buffer-management routines. Managed objects that refer to resources specific to an individual layer are called (N)-layer managed objects. Managed objects that refer to resources that encompass more than one layer are called system managed objects. Several important points about managed objects need to be kept in mind:

- A managed object is an abstraction that is directly available to the systems-management-function. Some other mechanism, outside the scope of the OSI management standards, maintains the relationship between the managed object and the actual resource.

- A single managed object may represent a single network resource or many resources.

- The same network resource may be represented by a single managed object or by a number of different managed objects, each of which represents a particular aspect of the resource.

- Not all resources need be represented by any managed object. This does not mean that such resources do not exist, only that they are not available for OSI systems management.

- Some managed objects are defined solely for the support of management functions and do not represent resources. Examples include event logs and filters.

This chapter makes use of the ASN.1 notation and of object-oriented concepts. The reader not familiar with these topics should first consult Appendixes C and D, respectively.

12.1   MANAGEMENT INFORMATION MODEL

ISO 10165-1 (X.720) presents a general management information model of OSI systems management information. Specifically, this document:

- Defines the information model of managed objects and their attributes
- Defines the principles of naming managed objects and attributes, so that they can be identified in and accessed by management protocols
- Defines the logical structure of systems-management information—that is, the structure of management information.
- Describes the concept of managed-object classes and the relationships into which they can enter, including inheritance, specialization, allomorphism, and containment

12.1.1   Basic Concepts of the Information Model

A managed object is defined in terms of attributes it possesses, operations that may be performed upon it, notifications that it may issue, and its relationships with other managed objects. In order to structure the definition of an MIB, each managed object is an instance of a managed-object class.[1] A managed-object class is a model or template for managed-object instances that share the same attributes, notifications, and management operations. The definition of a managed-object class, as specified by the template, consists of:

- Attributes visible at the managed-object boundary
- System-management operations that can be applied to the managed object
- Behavior exhibited by the managed object in response to management operations
- Notifications that can be emitted by the managed object
- Conditional packages that can be encapsulated in the managed object
- Position of the managed object in the inheritance hierarchy

The specifications of the OSI SMI and MIB rely heavily on concepts of object-oriented design. This approach allows for new managed-object classes and functions to be added, as needs are identified, in a modular fashion. The object-oriented approach also provides for extensibility of the related protocols and services. It should be kept in mind that the specifications do not dictate that MIBs be implemented using object-oriented database-management systems or object-oriented technology. The only requirement is that the specification of information conveyed between open

---

1.   Throughout this part, the term *managed object* is used to mean an instance of a managed-object class. Occasionally, when it is important to highlight the distinction between an object and an object class, the term *managed-object instance* will be used instead. Also, the qualifier *managed* will often be omitted when there is no ambiguity.

Table 12.1 Key Terms of OSI Structure of Management Information

Term	Common Object-Oriented Term	Definition
Managed object	Object	The OSI management view of a resource within the OSI environment that may be managed through the use of OSI management protocols. Examples include a layer entity, a connection, and an item of physical communications equipment.
Managed-object class	Object class	A named set of managed objects that share the same names, sets of attributes, notifications, and management operations (packages) and that share the same conditions for the presence of those packages.
Attribute	Variable	A property of a managed object. An attribute has a value.
Operation	Message	An operation on a managed object to effect systems management.
Behavior	Method	A description of the way in which managed objects, name binding, attributes, notifications, and actions interact with the actual resources they model and with each other.
Notification	Message	Information emitted by a managed object relating to an event that has occurred within the managed object.
Template	—	A standard format for the documentation of name bindings and managed-object class definitions and their components, such as packages, parameters, attributes, attribute groups, behavior definitions, actions, or notifications.
Encapsulation	Encapsulation	An enclosure relation between a managed object and its attributes, notifications, operations, and behavior. The enclosure relation assures that the managed object can maintain its integrity.
Inheritance	Inheritance	The conceptual mechanism by which attributes, notifications, operations, and behavior are acquired by a subclass from its superclass.
Specialization	Inheriting	The technique of deriving new managed-object classes from an existing class by the addition of new capabilities (such as new attributes and notifications).
Containment	Containment	A structuring relationship for managed-object instances in which the existence of a

Table 12.1 *(Cont.)*

Term	Common Object-Oriented Term	Definition
		managed-object instance is dependent on the existence of a containing managed-object instance.
Allomorphism	Polymorphism	The ability of a managed object of a given class to resemble one or more other object classes.
Package	—	A collection of optional attributes, notifications, operations, and behavior that are either all present or all absent in a managed object. The presence or absence of a package is conditional on the capability of the underlying resource.

systems in systems-management protocols (e.g., CMIP [common management information protocol]) use object-oriented design principles. Table 12.1 defines some of the key terms used in the SMI and relates most of these to the more common object-oriented terminology.

12.1.1.1   Encapsulation

Encapsulation is a fundamental characteristic of an object-oriented system. In the network-management context, encapsulation has the following significance: Each type of resource to be managed in the system is represented by a managed-object class. A specific instance of that resource is represented by a managed-object instance. The management data relating to that resource and the management procedures applicable to that resource are packaged together (encapsulated) in the corresponding object. Management applications have access to the resource, for control and monitoring, only by means of the corresponding object. Furthermore, all operations on the managed object are carried out by means of messages sent to the object. The actual data and procedures encapsulated in the object are protected from the outside world. Thus, encapsulation ensures that the integrity of an object is preserved.

12.1.1.2   Attributes

The actual data elements contained in a managed object are called attributes. Each attribute represents a property of the resource that the object represents, such as the operational characteristics, current state, or conditions of operation. Attributes are most commonly used for monitoring, with the attribute value reflecting the status of the underlying resource. An attribute can also be used for control, with the setting of an attribute value causing a change in the behavior or status of the underlying resource.

The data type of an attribute may be integer, real, Boolean, character string, or some composite type constructed from the basic types. In addition to a data type, each attribute has access rules (read, write, read-write) and rules by which it can be located as the result of a filtered search (matching rules).

An attribute can be a simple scalar variable. Read (get) and write (set, replace) operations are possible on scalar attributes. In addition, an attribute may be set-valued, as defined by the ASN.1

SET-OF construct. Recall that a set-of type is an unordered, variable number (zero or more) of elements, all of one type. In addition to the read and write operations that can be performed on all attributes, operations to add or remove elements from a set-valued attribute are possible.

Within an object class, some of the defined attributes may be grouped together to form a group attribute.[2] The group is merely a convenience that allows the same operation to be performed on all the members of the group with a single operation by applying the operation to the group. The order in which the operation is applied to the group members is not specified.

12.1.1.3   Object Classes and Inheritance

A managed-object class is a template that defines the management operations, attributes, packages, notifications, and behavior included in a particular type of object. All object instances that share these same elements are members of the same class. The individual object instances may differ in the values of their attributes. The class concept is thus a macro-type facility that allows a general type of object to be defined just once and then allows that definition to be reused many times for each actual instance of the object type.

More significantly, the class construct allows for the definition of new object classes in terms of existing classes. This process is referred to as specialization, and a new object class is referred to as a subclass of the class from which it is specialized. The use of the subclass concept has two significant advantages:

1. It allows the development of a class hierarchy, with a subclass, in turn, having its own subclasses. This structure mirrors the actual structure of resources to be modeled in almost every case.

2. The subclass retains characteristics of its superclass, a concept known as inheritance. This minimizes the need to specify characteristics of individual objects.

In the OSI systems-management context, specialization is achieved by extending the characteristics of an object class in one or more of the following ways:

- The addition of new attributes
- The extension or restriction of the range of an existing attribute
- The addition of new operations and notifications
- The addition of arguments to existing operations and notifications
- The extension or restriction of the ranges of arguments to operations and notifications

Unlike a general-purpose object-oriented scheme, OSI systems management does not allow the definition of a subclass by deleting any of the characteristics of its superclass.

As an optional facility, multiple inheritance is allowed. This means that a subclass is specialized from more than one superclass and inherits the operations, attributes, notifications, packages, and behavior from each superclass. Although this allows for the greatest possible reuse of class definitions, it is a difficult design technique to use effectively.

---

2.   As the standard itself points out, this is a somewhat misleading term, and a better term would be *attribute group*.

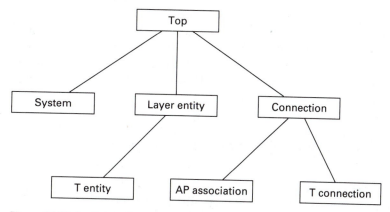

Figure 12.1 Inheritance Example

All object classes ultimately derive from a unique object class referred to as *top*. This is the ultimate superclass, and the other object classes form an inheritance hierarchy with top as the root. Figure 12.1 is an example of a portion of an inheritance hierarchy.

12.1.1.4   Operations

Systems-management operations apply to the attributes of an object or to the managed object as a whole. An operation performed on a managed object can succeed only if the invoking managing system has the access rights necessary to perform the operation, and consistency constraints are not violated.

12.1.1.5   Behavior

A managed object exhibits certain behavioral characteristics, including how the object reacts to operations performed on it and the constraints placed on its behavior.

The behavior of a managed object occurs in response to either external or internal stimuli. External stimuli consist of systems-management operations delivered in the form of CMIP messages. Internal stimuli are events internal to the managed object and its associated resource, such as timers.

All managed-object instances of the same managed-object class exhibit the same behavior. The behavior defines:

- The semantics of the attributes, operations, and notifications
- The response to management operations being invoked on the managed object
- The circumstances under which notifications will be emitted
- The dependencies between values of particular attributes
- The effects of relationships on the participating managed objects

12.1.1.6   Notifications

Managed objects are said to emit notifications when some internal or external occurrence affecting the object is detected. Notifications may be transmitted externally in a protocol or logged. Managing systems may request that some or all of the notifications emitted by a managed object be sent to it. Notifications that are sent to a manager or to a log are contained in an event report.

12.1.1.7   Conditional Packages

A conditional package is a collection of optional attributes, notifications, operations, and behavior that are either all present or all absent in a managed object. The condition under which a package is present is always a condition reflecting the capability of the underlying resource being modeled by the managed object. An example is the set of options of an X.25 protocol machine.

The conditional package is an organizational convenience but is not a construct independent of the managed object that contains it. In particular, operations on attributes that are part of a package are performed on the managed object, not by reference to the package itself.

When a subclass is created, the entire package of attributes, notifications, and so on is inherited by the subclass.

12.1.1.8   Allomorphism

Allomorphism, as defined for OSI systems management, is essentially a special case of the object-oriented concept of polymorphism. Polymorphism provides the ability to hide different implementations behind a common interface. For example, defining a unique *print* method for each kind of document in a system would allow any document to be printed by sending the message *print*, without concern for how that method was actually carried out for a given document.

Similarly, allomorphism provides the ability to implement different objects that present the same interface to management stations. Specifically, allomorphism refers to the ability of an instance of a subclass (called an allomorphic subclass) to resemble the behavior of, or emulate, its superclass (called an allomorphic superclass) as observed by systems-management protocols (e.g., CMIP). A typical use of allomorphism would be to support the evolution of the MIB. A new object can be defined to emulate the behavior of an older, obsolete object, so that a management station could still manage the object in the same way.

The allomorphic concept is defined using the superclass/subclass convention, but with constraints on how the subclass may be derived from the superclass. For example, the range of values of an inherited attribute in the subclass must be a subset of the range in the superset. That is, any value that is acceptable in the subclass must also be acceptable in the superclass.

The allomorphic relationship is indicated by including a set-valued attribute in the subclass that lists all the superclasses that this object imitates. The subclass is said to be "allomorphic to" the superclass.

12.1.2   Principles of Containment and Naming

We have seen that the object-oriented subclass facility allows for the creation of an inheritance hierarchy (Figure 12.1), which reflects the relationship among various types of objects. It is important to realize that this hierarchy simply represents a convenience for defining a variety of object types with a minimum of text. It is also a useful structuring tool in designing objects for an MIB. However, the inheritance hierarchy does not reflect the structure of an actual MIB. This structure is defined using the object-oriented containment facility.

12.1.2.1   The Containment Structure

The containment facility allows one object to "contain" one or more other objects. Containment is achieved by including a reference to the subordinate (contained) object in the superior (containing) object. The reference is in the form of the object identifier of the subordinate object and is stored as the value of an attribute in the superior object. A subordinate managed object may be contained in only one superior managed object, enforcing the condition that the MIB structure be a tree structure.

A containing object may itself be contained in another object, allowing the construction of a tree of arbitrary depth. Thus, the MIB structure can directly model real-world hierarchical structures, such as assembly, subassemblies, components, and directory, files, fields.

12.1.2.2 Naming

Just as we have seen that there is a distinction between the inheritance hierarchy, which defines the relationship among object classes, and the containment hierarchy, which defines the relationship among object instances in the MIB, there is also a distinction between the naming scheme for object classes and that for object instances.

First, consider *object classes*. Each object class registered in the registration tree is identified by a unique object identifier. Each object identifier is a sequence of integers that navigates through the registration tree of assigned identifiers to the managed-object class. This is the same scheme as is used in the SNMP (simple network management protocol) MIB, except, in the case of SNMP, there is no structural difference between object classes and object instances: the same structure is exhibited.

Figure 12.2 shows the top levels of the ISO/CCITT object-identifier tree. As an example of the elaboration of this tree, the OSI Implementers Workshop (OIW) subtree is shown. As part of this workshop, a number of managed-object classes are being defined and registered.

The naming scheme for *object instances* is completely distinct from that for object classes and is dictated by the containment relationship. The naming scheme works as follows:

1. Each managed-object class includes an attribute that is used in naming instances of that object.

2. The *relative distinguished name* of an object instance corresponds to a specific value of the naming attribute. This value must be unique among all objects that are subordinate to the same superior. The actual form of a relative distinguished name is an assertion that an attribute has a particular value—for example, MS-Id = ''BDC,'' where ''MS-Id'' is the name of the attribute and ''BDC'' is the desired value.

3. The *distinguished name* of an object instance is formed as the sequence of relative distinguished names from the root of the containment tree to this object.

Figure 12.3 shows an example of a containment tree. For each object instance, its object-class name and its relative distinguished name are shown. Table 12.2 lists the distinguished name of each object instance.

It is important to note that a managed-object-instance name (the value of the naming attribute) is created when the instance is created. These names do not have to be registered or made public. They do have to be exchanged between interoperating managed systems to permit access to the object. Also, although the naming scheme is based on containment, not all forms of containment are necessarily used for naming. Containment can be used to create pointers between object instances that reflect the structure of the MIB and that go beyond a simple tree structure.

12.1.2.3 The Three Trees of OSI Systems Management

Because the concepts introduced in this subsection are of fundamental importance in OSI systems management, it is worth presenting a summary.

There are three distinct and independent tree structures used in OSI system management:

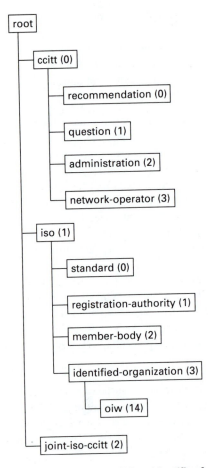

Figure 12.2 Top-Level Object-Identifier Assignments

1. ISO Registration Tree: This is a naming tree where definition of the following are registered

   - managed object classes
   - attribute definitions
   - actions
   - notifications
   - packages

   The registration tree may be thought of as a dictionary or library of "stubs" that can be stuck into new managed object class definitions. Since they are registered they have well-known names and agreed-upon semantics. This is an example of the benefit of re-use available when using object-oriented principles.

2. Inheritance Tree: This tree shows how the definition of object classes is derived from other object classes using object-oriented principles. Inheritance allows for re-use of an object class structure, with refinements to define a related but distinct object class.

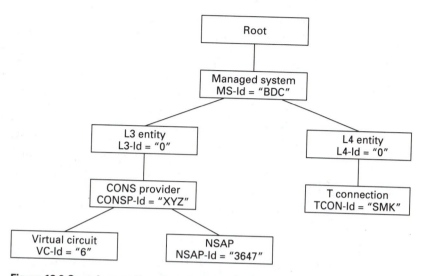

Figure 12.3 Containment Tree, with Relative Distinguished Names

3. Containment Tree: This is the MIB structure. It shows the objects an agent contains and the hierarchy/containment of those objects. This tree is used not only to define the MIB structure but as a means of unambiguously referencing object instances.

It is instructive to compare these structures with the MIB structure used in SNMP. For SNMP, there is a single tree structure, which is the ISO registration tree. This tree serves to define names for objects, as it does for OSI systems management. However, in the case of SNMP, all MIB objects are scalar or tables, and do not include attributes, notifications, and so forth. Therefore, the benefits of re-use that are available for OSI systems management are not available for SNMP. In addition to providing a naming specification, the SNMP tree structure serves to define the SNMP MIB, much as the containment tree does for OSI systems management. The use of groups and tables provide rudimentary structuring tools. However, the structuring capability with OSI containment trees is richer and more flexible.

Table 12.2 Names of Object Instances in Figure 12.3

Relative Distinguished Name	Distinguished Name
Ms-Id = ''BDC''	Ms-Id = ''BDC''
L3-Id = ''0''	Ms-Id = ''BDC,'' L3-Id = ''0''
CONSP-Id = ''XYZ''	Ms-Id = ''BDC,'' L3-Id = ''0,'' CONSP-Id = ''XYZ''
VC-Id = ''6''	Ms-Id = ''BDC,'' L3-Id = ''0,'' CONSP-Id = ''XYZ,'' VC-Id = ''6''
NSAP-Id = ''3647''	Ms-Id = ''BDC,'' L3-Id = ''0,'' CONSP-Id = ''XYZ,'' NSAP-Id = ''3647''
L4-Id = ''0''	Ms-Id = ''BDC,'' L4-Id = ''0''
TCON-Id = ''SMK''	Ms-Id = ''BDC,'' L4-Id = ''0,'' TCON-Id = ''SMK''

Table 12.3 Systems-Management Operations (X.720/DIS 10165-1)

(a) Attribute Oriented Operations

Operation	Scope	Semantics	Behavior
Get attribute value	All attribute types, unless they are defined as not readable.	Read all attribute values or list of attribute values; return values that can be read and indicate an error for values that can not be read.	Return error indications for those attributes that could not be read.
Replace attribute value	Does not apply to group attributes or attributes that are not writable.	Replace the values of specified attributes with supplied values.	Return error indications for those attributes whose values could not be replaced, because the attributes were non-writable.
Replace-with-default value	All attribute types, unless they are defined as not writable.	Replace the value of some attributes with the defaults defined as part of the object class specification.	Return error indication for those attributes whose values could not be replaced, due to attribute not writable, no default defined, or general failure of the replace-with-default request.
Add member	Attributes whose values are sets and whose values are writable.	Add supplied attribute members to the set that currently comprises the attribute's value.	Return error indication for attribute where members could not be added, because attribute is not writable.
Remove member	Attributes whose values are sets and whose values are writable.	Remove from the set that currently comprises the attribute's value those members supplied by the operation.	Return error indication for attribute whose members could not be removed, because attribute is not writable.

(b) Operations that Apply to Managed Objects as a Whole

Operation		
Create	All objects that are creatable as defined by the object class definition.	The create request may specify explicit values for individual attributes and may specify a reference object from which values may be obtained. The managed object class definition may specify initial attribute values. An error indication is provided if the managed object can not be created.
Delete	All managed objects that can be deleted remotely.	Delete the managed object. The operation has analogous effects on the resource, as defined by the managed object class definer.
Action	All managed object classes.	The managed object performs the specified action and indicates the result. Action results and/or error indications are returned.

12.1.3   Systems-Management Operations

The definition of the management information model includes a specification of the operations that may be performed on objects. These operations are performed by a management entity by means of a message sent to the object, using a network-management protocol.

Management operations fall into two categories: those that apply to attributes of an object and those that apply to the object as a whole.

12.1.3.1   Attribute-Oriented Operations

The following operations may be sent to an object to be applied to one or more of its contained attributes:

- Get attribute value

- Replace attribute value

- Set attribute value to default

- Add member to a set-valued attribute

- Remove member from a set-valued attribute

Any operation may request that the same function be performed on a list of attributes. For example, an operation to replace attribute values could specify a list of attributes with the new value for each attribute. An operation may specify that the individual operations are to be performed atomically; that is, either all operations succeed or none is performed. This corresponds to the behavior of SNMP.

If atomic operation is not requested, then the managed object will attempt the individual operation on each attribute in the list of attributes for which the operation is requested. As a result of the operation, the object will report the attribute identifiers and their associated values for those attributes whose values could be operated on and error indications for those attributes that could not be operated on.

Table 12.3, part (a), summarizes the attribute-oriented operations.

12.1.3.2   Object-Oriented Operations

The following operations apply to managed objects as a whole:

- Create

- Delete

- Action

The semantics of these operations are part of the definition of the managed-object class. In particular, the effect of these operations on other related managed objects (e.g., superior or subordinate objects) must be specified.

Table 12.3, part (b), summarizes the object-oriented operations.

12.2   DEFINITION OF MANAGEMENT INFORMATION

ISO 10165-2 (X.720) defines some of the basic object classes, attributes, and notifications that can be used in developing an MIB.

12.2.1   Generic Attributes

Because counting operations are useful in many contexts, ISO/CCITT have defined a set of generic attributes that can be used in defining a variety of specific attributes that relate to counting. Generic attributes can be thought of as attribute types or macros that are refined to construct specific attributes. The specific attribute definition may extend the generic attribute definition to relate the behavior of the attribute to the operation of the resource represented by the managed object, to associate additional parameters with the attribute, or to relate the attribute to other attributes.

Generic attributes fall into two categories: those that relate to counters and those that relate to gauges (Table 12.4).

12.2.1.1   Counters

The counter attribute in OSI systems management is similar to the counter object in the SNMP MIB but is somewhat more flexible. In general, a counter is an abstraction of an underlying counting process. The value of a counter is always a non-negative integer, which may be incremented but not decremented. A maximum value must be specified; when the counter reaches its maximum, it wraps around and starts increasing again from 0.

Two types of counters are defined to meet different management needs. A *nonsettable counter* is not subject to change by management operation but only changes in response to the event or property being counted. This type of counter is suitable for use in a situation in which multiple management stations have access to the counter. Since the counter cannot be set, the management stations cannot interfere with each other with respect to the use of the counter. The *settable counter* can be modified by management operation and is therefore more suitable for use by a single management station.

It is possible to generate one or more notifications based on counter values by using the *counter-threshold* attribute. The basic property of a threshold is that a notification is triggered when the value of the counter first becomes equal to the value defined in the threshold attribute, known as a comparison level. A counter threshold may have a single comparison level as its value. In fact, a counter threshold is set-valued; each value in the set represents a comparison level that triggers a notification. For example, the various comparison levels may represent different degrees of severity of a fault condition, and the notification is triggered whenever the counter value reaches any of the levels. Figure 12.4, part (a), illustrates the use of a set of comparison levels.

In addition, the counter threshold may include an offset. This allows counting intervals to be detected. The offset mechanism works as follows: When the threshold is triggered by the counter value's reaching a comparison level, the comparison level is incremented by the amount of the offset. Thus, a new comparison level is defined, and as the counter continues to increase, it may reach this new level, which triggers a notification and causes the comparison level to once again be incremented by the offset. This process repeats indefinitely. For example, a managed object could be set up to generate a notification after every 100 packets are received by a node. Figure 12.4, part (b), illustrates the use of an offset with a single comparison level. If multiple comparison levels are defined, then each of these will be incremented by the offset when it is crossed by the counter value.

Finally, a notifications on/off switch is associated with the set of thresholds. The counter threshold is activated to send notifications only when the value of this switch is set to on.

As yet, no specific counter attributes applicable to systems management have been standardized. Table 12.5 lists counters useful for layer management that are provided in the standard.

Table 12.4 Definition of Generic Attribute Types (X.721/DIS 10165-2)

(a) Counter-Related Attributes

Attribute Type	Value Type	Inherent Properties	Permitted Operations	Implicit Relations	Specification Properties
Non-settable Counter	Single value	• current value is a non-negative integer • it has a maximum value • counting direction is up, with increment 1 • current value wraps around when it reaches maximum • initial value is 0	• Get	• directly related to a single counter threshold • may trigger a defined event when it wraps	• the internal event that is counted • maximum value • estimated wrap around period, to indicate necessary reading rate
Settable Counter	Single value	• current value is a non-negative integer • it has a maximum value • counting direction is up, with increment 1 • current value wraps around when it reaches maximum • initial value is 0	• Get • Set to arbitrary value (within range) • Set to default	• directly related to a single counter threshold • may trigger a defined event when it wraps or is set	• the internal event that is counted • maximum value • estimated wrap around period, to indicate necessary reading rate
Counter Threshold	Set-valued	• comparison levels are non-negative integers • offset values are non-negative integers • notifications switch is on or off	• Get • Set • Add • Remove	• directly related to a single count • directly related to a defined notification	• count to which it applies • defined notification that may be triggered

(b) Gauge-Related Attributes

Attribute Type	Value Type	Inherent Properties	Permitted Operations	Implicit Relations	Specification Properties
Gauge	Single value	• current value is non-negative integer or real • it has a maximum and minimum value • it may increase or decrease by arbitrary amounts • it does not wrap around	• Get	• directly related to a tide mark or gauge threshold • only one minimum and one maximum tide mark may be applied • only one (possibly multi-level) threshold may be applied • can be used to measure other management information	• the dynamic variable measured • maximum and minimum value
Gauge Threshold	Set-valued	• notifyHigh and notifyLow are integer or real • notifyHigh switch and notifyLow switch are on or off	• Get • Set • Add • Remove	• directly related to a single gauge • directly related to a defined notification	• gauge to which it applies • defined notification that may be triggered
Tide Mark	Set-valued	• associated with a gauge • has a direction (maximum or minimum) • current or former values are integer or real depending on associated gauge	• Get • Set to default	• directly related to a gauge • may be directly related to a defined event that is triggered when the current value changes	• gauge to which it applies • direction (maximum or minimum)

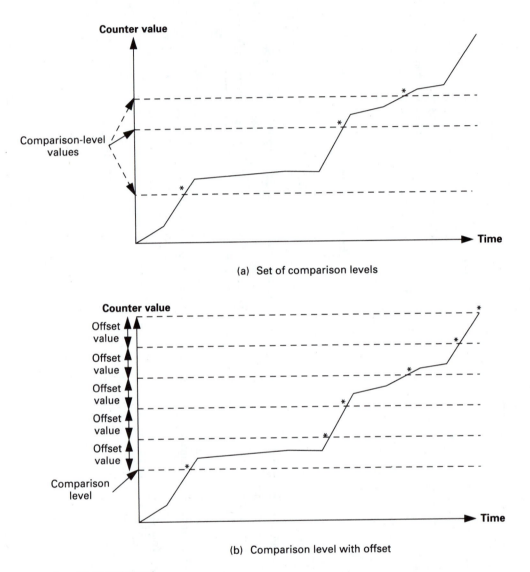

(a) Set of comparison levels

(b) Comparison level with offset

*= notification triggered.

Figure 12.4 Counters and Counter Threshholds

12.2.1.2 Gauges

The gauge attribute in OSI systems management is similar to the gauge object in the SNMP MIB but is somewhat more flexible. In general, a *gauge* is an abstraction of an underlying dynamic variable, such as the number of connections currently open or the rate of change of a traffic counter. The value of a gauge is always a non-negative integer, which may increase or decrease, within a range set by specified maximum and minimum values. Changes that would increase the gauge value above the maximum or decrease it below the minimum leave the value at its maximum

Table 12.5 Suggested Counter Types (X.721/DIS 10165-2)

Counter Type	Definition
Corrupted PDUs Received	The total number of corrupted PDUs received.
Incoming Connection Reject Error	The total number of incoming connection requests which were received by the managed object but rejected due to protocol errors.
Incoming Connection Requests	The total number of incoming connection requests.
Incoming Disconnect	The total number of incoming disconnect requests.
Incoming Disconnect Error	The total number of incoming disconnect requests received by the managed object due to protocol errors.
Incoming Protocol Error	The total number of error report or reset PDUs which were received by the managed object due to protocol errors.
Octets Received	The total number of user data octets received.
Octets Retransmitted Error	The total number of octets retransmitted.
Octets Sent	The total number of user data octets sent.
Outgoing Connection Reject Error	The total number of outgoing connection requests which were sent by the managed object but rejected due to protocol errors.
Outgoing Connection Requests	The total number of outgoing connection requests.
Outgoing Disconnect	The total number of outgoing disconnect requests.
Outgoing Disconnect Error	The total number of outgoing disconnect requests sent by the managed object due to protocol errors.
Outgoing Protocol Error	The total number of error report or reset PDUs which were sent by the managed object due to protocol errors.
PDUs Received	The total number of PDUs received.
PDUs Retransmitted Error	The total number of PDUs retransmitted.
PDUs Sent	The total number of PDUs sent.

or minimum, respectively. The gauge does not lock at its maximum or minimum level. Once the underlying variable exceeds the maximum value of the gauge, the gauge will remain at that maximum value until the underlying variable falls below the maximum value, at which time, the gauge will again begin to track the underlying value. A similar effect occurs with respect to the gauge's minimum value.

A gauge is nonsettable; that is, its value is not subject to change by management operation but only changes in response to changes in the underlying variable.

It is possible to generate notifications based on gauge values by using the *gauge-threshold* attribute. This attribute works in a fashion similar to that of alarm thresholds in the SNMP RMON

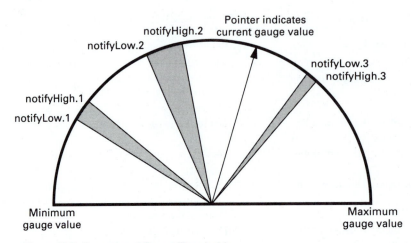

Figure 12.5 Gauges and Gauge Thresholds

(remote network-monitoring) specification. Two types of notification are associated with each threshold. When the threshold is reached or crossed in the positive direction, a notification of that fact is generated. When the threshold is reached or crossed in the negative direction, a notification of that fact is also generated. To avoid the repeated triggering of event notifications when the gauge makes small oscillations around a threshold value, the threshold is specified in pairs: the higher value is used to trigger the positive-going event, and the lower value is used to trigger the negative-going event.

The gauge threshold is set-valued; each member of the set is, in turn, a pair of submembers, notifyLow and notifyHigh. Associated with each of these submembers is an individual notifications on/off switch.

The threshold value for notifyHigh must be greater than or equal to that for notifyLow. The rules for the notifyHigh threshold are as follows:

1. The first time that the gauge value becomes greater than or equal to the notifyHigh threshold, the corresponding event notification is generated.

2. After a notifyHigh event is generated, another such event will not be generated until the gauge value becomes equal to or less than notifyLow.

The rules for the generation of a notifyLow event notification are the converse of the preceding rules.

Figure 12.5 depicts the operation of a gauge with three thresholds. We can view the gauge object as a meter whose value fluctuates between some minimum and maximum values. Once the gauge has crossed a notifyHigh threshold, the corresponding event will not be triggered a second time until the gauge falls through the shaded area to or below the paired notifyLow threshold. The same is true in the opposite direction.

Finally, a tidemark attribute may be associated with a gauge attribute. The tidemark is a mechanism that records the maximum or minimum value reached by a gauge during a measurement period. A tidemark is set-valued with three components: the current value of the tidemark, the value of the tidemark immediately before the last reset, and the last reset time.

Two types of tidemarks are defined: maximum and minimum. The maximum tidemark operates as follows:

1. The tidemark may be reset to the current value of the gauge. Otherwise, the tidemark is read-only.

2. When the tidemark is reset, its value just prior to the reset is saved as its former value, overwriting the former value saved from the next most recent reset.

3. The tidemark changes only in a positive direction in response to changes in the gauge. That is, the tidemark increases only when its gauge increases beyond the current tidemark value. The tidemark does not decrease when its gauge decreases.

The minimum tidemark is the converse of the maximum tidemark.

12.2.2   Specific Attributes

ISO 10165-2 (X.720) also defines a number of specific attributes that are referenced by the systems-management functions of ISO 10164. Unlike the generic attributes discussed in the preceding subsection, specific attributes are fully specified, including an object identifier and a complete ASN.1 definition. These specific attributes are directly usable in the definitions of managed objects without further elaboration.

Table 12.6 lists some of the specific attributes defined in the standard.

12.2.3   Notification Types

ISO 10165-2 (X.720) defines a number of notification types that are applicable to a wide variety of object classes. Each definition includes the following:

- The format of notification data carried in the management protocol (CMIP)
- The behavior of the notification
- The format of the result data carried in the management protocol
- An object-identifier value that uniquely identifies this notification type

Table 12.7 lists the notification types, and the attributes that are found in each one.

12.2.4   Managed-Object Classes

ISO 10165-2 (X.720) also defines a number of object classes that are referenced by the system-management functions of ISO 10164 or that are intended to be used as superclasses for the purpose of inheritance in the definition of object classes in other standards. These defined object classes make use of the attributes and notifications also defined in this standard.

Table 12.8 lists these object classes.

Table 12.6 Specific Attribute Types (X.721/DIS 10165-2)

Events Related	

Name	Description
Additional information	Additional information in notifications
Additional text	Additional textual information in notifications
Attribute identifier list	List of attribute identifiers
Attribute list	List of attribute identifiers and their values
Attribute value change definition	Set of attribute identifiers and their old and new values
Backed-up status	Specifies whether or not a failed object has been backed up
Correlated notifications	A set of notification identifiers that are considered to be correlated to this notification
Event time	Time of the generation of an event
Event type	Type of event
Monitored attributes	A set of attributes and their values at the time of an alarm
Notification identifier	Identifier of an alarm
Perceived severity	Level of severity of an alarm
Probable cause	Probable cause of an alarm
Proposed repair actions	Set of possible repair actions
Relationship change definition	Set of relationship attributes and their old and new values
Security alarm cause	Cause of security alarm
Security alarm detector	Entity that detected security alarm
Security alarm severity	Severity of security alarm
Service provider	Information about the service provider associated with the service request that caused the security alarm
Service user	Information about the service user associated with the service request that caused the security alarm
Source indicator	Indicates the source of the operation that resulted in generating the notification
Specific problems	Identifies refinements to the probable cause
State change definition	Set of state attributes and their old and new values
Threshold info	Information about the threshold that was crossed
Trend indication	Current severity trend in the object

Table 12.6 (*Cont.*)

Used for Naming	
Name	**Description**
Discriminator Id	Names instance of discriminator object class
Log Id	Names instance of log object class
Log record Id	Names instance of log record object class
System Id	Names instance of system object class
System title	Names instance of system object class

States Related	
Name	**Description**
Administrative state	Current administrative state
Alarm status	Set of existing alarm conditions
Availability status	Set of availability status conditions
Control status	Set of control status conditions
Operational state	Current operational state
Procedural status	Status of associated procedure
Standby status	Back-up role
Unknown status	Boolean value to indicate whether state of object is unknown
Usage state	Current usage state
State	Composite state of object

Relationships Related	
Name	**Description**
Back-up object	Object with back-up role to this object
Backed-up object	Object backed up by this object
Member	Set of objects that are members of this object
Owner	Set of objects that are owners of this object
Peer	Object that is peer to this object
Primary	Set of objects acting in a primary role with respect to this object
Provider object	Set of objects providing service to this object
Relationships	Composite relationships of this object
Secondary	Set of objects acting in a secondary role with respect to this object
User	Set of objects using service of this object

12.3   TEMPLATES FOR MANAGED-OBJECT DEFINITION

ISO 10165-1 (X.720) provides guidelines for the format of definitions for managed objects, attributes, packages, and notifications. These guidelines are in the form of templates, which are standard formats to be used in the definitions. The templates are similar to the SNMP MIB ASN.1

Table 12.7 Notification Types (X.721/DIS 10165-2)

Notification Type	Attributes	Report
Attribute value change	sourceIndicator, attributeIdentifierList, attributeValueChangeDefinition, notificationIdentifier, correlatedNotifications, additionalText, additionalInformation	Changes to attributes
Communications alarm	probableCause, specificProblems, perceivedSeverity, backedUpStatus, backUpObject, trendIndication, thresholdInfo, notificationIdentifier, correlatedNotifications, stateChangeDefinition, monitoredAttributes, proposedRepairActions, additionalText, additionalInformation	When object detects a communications error
Environmental alarm	probableCause, specificProblems, perceivedSeverity, backedUpStatus, backUpObject, trendIndication, thresholdInfo, notificationIdentifier, correlatedNotifications, stateChangeDefinition, monitoredAttributes, proposedRepairActions, additionalText, additionalInformation	Problem in the environment
Equipment alarm	probableCause, specificProblems, perceivedSeverity, backedUpStatus, backUpObject, trendIndication, thresholdInfo, notificationIdentifier, correlatedNotifications, stateChangeDefinition, monitoredAttributes, proposedRepairActions, additionalText, additionalInformation	Failure in equipment
Integrity violation	securityAlarmCause, securityAlarmSeverity, securityAlarmDetector, serviceUser, serviceProvider, notificationIdentifier, correlatedNotifications, additionalText, additionalInformation	Potential illegal modification, insertion, or deletion in information flow
Object creation	sourceIndicator, attributeList, notificationIdentifier, correlatedNotifications, additionalText, additionalInformation	Creation of object
Object deletion	sourceIndicator, attributeList, notificationIdentifier, correlatedNotifications, additionalText, additionalInformation	Deletion of object
Operational violation	securityAlarmCause, securityAlarmSeverity, securityAlarmDetector, serviceUser, serviceProvider, notificationIdentifier, correlatedNotifications, additionalText, additionalInformation	Requested service not possible due to unavailability, malfunction, or incorrect invocation
Physical violation	securityAlarmCause, securityAlarmSeverity, securityAlarmDetector, serviceUser,	Potential security attack on physical resource

Table 12.7 (*Cont.*)

Notification Type	Attributes	Report
	serviceProvider, notificationIdentifier, correlatedNotifications, additionalText, additionalInformation	
Processing error alarm	probableCause, specificProblems, perceivedSeverity, backedUpStatus, backUpObject, trendIndication, thresholdInfo, notificationIdentifier, correlatedNotifications, stateChangeDefinition, monitoredAttributes, proposedRepairActions, additionalText, additionalInformation	Processing failure in object
Quality of service alarm	probableCause, specificProblems, perceived-Severity, backedUpStatus, backUpObject, trendIndication, thresholdInfo, notificationIdentifier, correlatedNotifications, stateChangeDefinition, monitoredAttributes, proposedRepairActions, additionalText, additionalInformation	Failure in quality of service of object
Relationship change	sourceIndicator, attributeIdentifierList, relationshipChangeDefinition, notification Identifier, correlatedNotifications, additionalText, additionalInformation	Change in value of relationship attributes
Security service or mechanism violation	securityAlarmCause, securityAlarmSeverity, securityAlarmDetector, serviceUser, serviceProvider, notificationIdentifier, correlatedNotifications, additionalText, additionalInformation	Security attack detected
State change	sourceIndicator, attributeIdentifierList, stateChangeDefinition, notificationIdentifier, correlatedNotifications, additionalText, additionalInformation	Change in state attributes
Time domain violation	securityAlarmCause, securityAlarmSeverity, securityAlarmDetector, serviceUser, serviceProvider, notificationIdentifier, correlatedNotifications, additionalText, additionalInformation	Event has occurred at unexpected or prohibited time

macro definition. The templates summarize the elements that should be included in a definition and the notational tools that are recommended for use in the definition.

The following conventions are used in template definitions:

- Terms in uppercase letters in the template appear in the definition in the same form.

Table 12.8 Object Classes (X.721/DIS 10165-2)

Object Class	Description
Alarm record	Used to define the information stored in the log as a result of receiving alarm reports. Object classes are communicationsAlarm, qualityOfServiceAlarm, processingErrorAlarm, equipmentAlarm, and environmentalAlarm.
Attribute value change record	Used to define the information stored in the log as a result of receiving attribute value change notification.
Discriminator	Used to define the criteria for controlling management services.
Event forwarding discriminator	Used to define the conditions that shall be satisfied by potential event reports before the event report is forwarded to a particular destination.
Event log record	Used to define the information stored in the log as a result of receiving events. This is a superclass from which records for specific event types are derived.
Log	Used to define the criteria for controlling the logging of the information in the management APDUs.
Log record	Used to define the records in a log managed object.
Object creation record	Used to define the information stored in the log as a result of receiving object creation notification.
Object deletion record	Used to define the information stored in the log as a result of receiving object deletion notification.
Object name change record	Used to define the information stored in the log as a result of receiving object name change identification.
Relationship change record	Used to define the information stored in the log as a result of receiving relationship change reports.
State change record	Used to define the information stored in the log as a result of receiving state change reports.
Security alarm report	Used to define the information stored in the log as a result of receiving security alarm reports.
System	Used to represent a set of hardware and software that forms an autonomous whole capable of performing information processing and/or information transfer.
Top	That class of which every other object class is a subclass.

- Terms in lowercase letters in angle brackets are variable names; the actual name is substituted in the definition.

- Terms in square brackets are optional.

- Terms in square brackets followed by an asterisk may appear zero or more times.

12.3.1   Identifier Allocation

Every object, notification, attribute, package, and other element standardized as part of OSI systems management has a unique identifier defined by its position in the tree of identifiers allocated by ISO and CCITT (see Figure 12.2). Figure 12.6 shows a portion of that allocation that is relevant to the OSI systems-management standards. The key nodes in this tree are:

- *Management specification (ms):* All identifier values specified in the OSI systems-management family of standards (Table 11.1) are allocated under this node.

- *Systems-management overview (smo):* allocated to ISO 10040 (X.701).

- *Common management information protocol (cmip):* allocated to ISO 9596-1 (X.711).

- *Systems-management functions (function):* allocated to ISO 10164.

- *Structure of management information (smi):* allocated to ISO 10065.

- *partX:* A number of separate nodes are allocated, one for each part of ISO 10165.

Note also that directly under the joint-iso-ccitt node, there are nodes allocated for layer-management identifiers. Two of these, for the network and transport layers, are shown in the figure.

12.3.2   Attribute Template

The template for defining attributes has the following structure:

```
<attribute-label> ATTRIBUTE
    DERIVED FROM <attribute-label> | WITH ATTRIBUTE SYNTAX type-reference ;
    [MATCHES FOR      qualifier [, qualifier]* ;]
    [BEHAVIOR         <behavior-definition-label> [,<behavior-definition-label>]* ; ]
    [PARAMETER        <parameter-label> [,<parameter-label>]* ; ]
    [REGISTERED AS object-identifier] ;

    supporting productions

    qualifier ->EQUALITY | ORDERING | SUBSTRINGS | SET-COMPARISON | SET-
              INTERSECTION
```

The first entry in the attribute definition is either of two constructs. The DERIVED FROM construct indicates that this attribute definition is derived from another existing definition. If this element is present, then the following rules apply:

1. The set of matching rules consists of the logical OR of any matching rules specified in this attribute definition and those in the referenced attribute from which the new attribute is derived.

2. The behavior is assumed to extend to any derived behavior definitions.

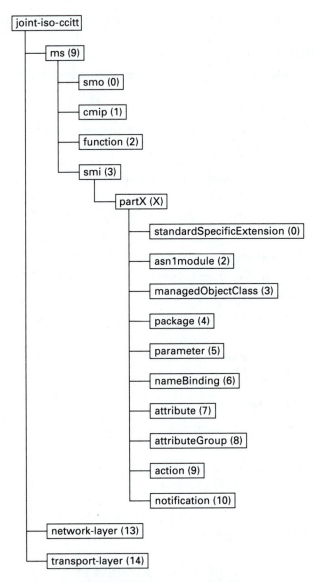

**Figure 12.6 Portion of the Object-Identifier Allocation
under Joint ISO-CCITT Subtree**

If this attribute is not derived from another, then the WITH ATTRIBUTE SYNTAX construct is used to specify the ASN.1 data type.

The MATCHES FOR construct defines the types of tests that may be applied to a value of the attribute. Such tests are used in the filter operation, which is applied to a number of objects; those objects that pass the filter are selected for a management operation. The qualifiers are:

- *EQUALITY:* An attribute value may be tested for equality to a given value.

- *ORDERING:* An attribute value may be tested against a given value to determine which has the greater value.

- *SUBSTRINGS:* An attribute value may be tested for the presence of a substring.

- *SET-COMPARISON:* A set-valued attribute may be tested against a given set value to determine superset/subset relationships.

- *SET-INTERSECTION:* A set-valued attribute may be tested against a given set value to determine whether there is a non-null intersection.

The PARAMETER construct allows the definition of error parameters to be associated with the behavior of the attribute.

An example of the use of the template is the eventTime attribute defined in ISO 10165-2:

eventTime ATTRIBUTE
    WITH ATTRIBUTE SYNTAX Attribute-ASN1Module.EventTime ;
    MATCHES FOR EQUALITY, ORDERING;
    BEHAVIOR timeOrdering
    REGISTERED AS { smi2Attribute ID 13 } ;

    timeOrdering BEHAVIOR DEFINED AS
    ''The year, month, day, hour, minute, and seconds fields are compared in order to determine whether the specified value is greater or less than the value of the attribute. The values for the year, month, day, hour, minute, and seconds are determined from the character string representation and the year value is first compared. If equal the month value is compared and this process is continued if the compared fields are equal'' ;

Note that the BEHAVIOR entry is simply a textual description of the behavior of the managed object; it does not include computer-processable semantics.

As another example, let us consider an attribute definition from CD 10737, which defines transport-layer management:

localSuccessfulConnections ATTRIBUTE
    DERIVED FROM nonWrappingCounter ;
    BEHAVIOR localSuccessfulConnections-B BEHAVIOR DEFINED AS
        The number of transport connections initiated by the local Transport Entity which have reached the Open state ;;
    REGISTERED AS { TLM.aoiLocalSuccessfulConnections (14) } ;

Note that in this case, the behavior definition is embedded in the attribute definition rather than provided as a separate supporting production. Both conventions are permissible. Also, in this case, the attribute data type is defined elsewhere. The attribute data type nonWrappingCounter is simply a counter that does not wrap around.

12.3.3 Package Template

The template for defining packages has the following structure:

```
<package-label> PACKAGE
    [BEHAVIOR            <behavior-definition-label> [,<behavior-definition-label>]* ; ]
    [ATTRIBUTES          <attribute-label> propertylist [,<parameter-label>]*
                         [,<attribute-label> propertylist [,<parameter-label>]* ]* ; ]
    [ATTRIBUTE GROUPS    <group-label> [<attribute-label>]*
                         [<group-label> [<attribute-label>]*]* ; ]
    [ACTIONS             <action-label> [<parameter-label>]*
                         [<action-label> [<parameter-label>]*]* ; ]
    [NOTIFICATIONS       <notification-label> [<parameter-label>]*
                         [<notification-label> [<parameter-label>]*]* ; ]
    [REGISTERED AS object-identifier] ;

    supporting productions

    propertylist -> [REPLACE-WITH-DEFAULT]
                    [DEFAULT VALUE      value-specifier]
                    [INITIAL VALUE      value-specifier]
                    [PERMITTED VALUES type-reference]
                    [REQUIRED VALUES  type-reference]
                    [ GET | REPLACE | GET-REPLACE ]
                    [ ADD | REMOVE | ADD-REMOVE ]
```

The BEHAVIOR construct allows the semantics of the package to be documented. Again, this is a textual description and is not computer-processable. The ATTRIBUTES construct lists all attributes that are part of this package. Associated with each attribute is zero or more properties and zero or more parameters. The properties that may be specified are:

- *REPLACE-WITH-DEFAULT:* The attribute has a default value that may be set by management operation.
- *DEFAULT VALUE:* specifies the default value used when the package is created if no other value is provided.
- *INITIAL VALUE:* a mandatory initial value.
- *PERMITTED VALUES:* restrictions on attribute values, expressed in ASN.1.
- *REQUIRED VALUES:* specifies values that the attribute shall be capable of taking.
- *GET/REPLACE/GET-REPLACE:* operations allowable on single-valued attributes.
- *ADD/REMOVE/ADD-REMOVE:* operations allowable on set-valued attributes.

Similarly, the ACTIONS and NOTIFICATIONS constructs include by reference any actions and notifications that are to be part of the package. Several examples of package definitions are included in the examples of object definitions provided later in this chapter.

12.3.4   Notification Template

The template for defining notifications has the following structure:

```
<notification-label> NOTIFICATION
    [BEHAVIOR          <behavior-definition-label> [,<behavior-definition-label>]* ; ]
    [PARAMETERS        <parameter-label> [,<parameter-label>]* ; ]
    [WITH INFORMATION SYNTAX type-reference
      [AND ATTRIBUTE IDS   <field-name> <attribute-label>
                           [,<field-name> <attribute-label>]* ] ; ]
    [WITH REPLY SYNTAX   type-reference ; ]
    REGISTERED AS object-identifier ;
```

The BEHAVIOR construct defines the behavior of the notification, the data that shall be specified with the notification, the results that the notification may generate, and their meaning. The PARAMETERS construct identifies event information or event-reply parameters, or processing failures associated with the notification type. The WITH INFORMATION SYNTAX construct identifies the ASN.1 data type that describes the structure of the notification information that is carried in the management protocol. Finally, the WITH REPLY SYNTAX construct identifies the ASN.1 data type that describes the structure of the notification-reply information that is carried in the management protocol.

An example of the use of the template is the communicationsAlarm notification defined in ISO 10165-2:

```
communicationsAlarm NOTIFICATION
    BEHAVIOR   communicationsAlarmBehavior;
    WITH INFORMATION SYNTAX Notification-ASN1Module.AlarmInfo
      AND ATTRIBUTE IDS
            probableCause              probableCause,
            specificProblems           specificProblems,
            perceivedSeverity          perceivedSeverity,
            backedUpStatus             backedUpStatus,
            backUpObject               backUpObject,
            trendIndication            trendIndication,
            thresholdInfo              thresholdInfo,
            notificationIdentifier     notificationIdentifier,
            correlatedNotifications    correlatedNotifications,
            stateChangeDefinition      stateChangeDefinition,
            monitoredAttributes        monitoredAttributes,
            proposedRepairActions      proposedRepairActions,
            additionalText             additionalText,
            additionalInformation      additionalInformation;
    REGISTERED AS { smi2Notification 1} ;

communicationsAlarmBehavior
    BEHAVIOR DEFINED AS ''This notification type is used to report when the object detects
      a communications error'' ;
```

Note that each field in the notification is simply given the same name as the attribute from which the field value is obtained.

12.3.5 Managed-Object-Class Template

The template for defining managed-object classes has the following structure:

```
<class-label> MANAGED OBJECT CLASS
    [DERIVED FROM              <class-label>      [,<class-label>]* ; ]
    [CHARACTERIZED BY          <package-label>    [,<package-label>]* ; ]
    [CONDITIONAL PACKAGES      <package-label>    PRESENT IF condition-definition
                               [,<package-label> PRESENT IF condition-definition]* ; ]
    REGISTERED AS object-identifier ;
    supporting productions
```

The DERIVED FROM construct indicates the superclass or superclasses from which this class is inherited. This construct is required in all definitions except for top. Characteristics (attributes, notifications, etc.) that are inherited are not repeated in the definition unless an extension or a modification is made.

The CHARACTERIZED BY construct allows one or more mandatory packages to be included in the object-class definition. The CONDITIONAL PACKAGES construct allows one or more conditional packages to be included.

To illustrate the formalism, we present several object-class definitions. Our first example is the discriminator object class, which is used to define the criteria for controlling management services. The definition is as follows:

```
discriminator MANAGED OBJECT CLASS
    DERIVED FROM top
    CHARACTERIZED BY discriminatorPackage PACKAGE
        BEHAVIOR
        discriminatorBehavior BEHAVIOR
            DEFINED AS "This managed object is used to represent the criteria for controlling
            management services.";;
        ATTRIBUTES
        discriminatorId GET,
        discriminatorConstruct REPLACE-WITH-DEFAULT DEFAULT VALUE
            Attribute-ASN1Module.defaultDiscriminatorConstruct GET-REPLACE,
        administrativeState GET-REPLACE,
        operationalState GET;
        NOTIFICATIONS
        stateChange,
        attributeValueChange,
        objectCreation,
        objectDeletion;;;
    CONDITIONAL PACKAGES
        availabilityStatusPackage PRESENT IF "any of the scheduling packages (duration, weekly,
            scheduling, external) are present",
```

duration PRESENT IF "the discriminator function is scheduled to start at a specified time and stop at either a specified time or function continuously",

dailyScheduling PRESENT IF "both the weekly scheduling package and external scheduler package are not present in an instance and daily scheduling is supported by that instance",

weeklyScheduling PRESENT IF "both the daily scheduling package and external scheduler package are not present in an instance and daily scheduling is supported by that instance",

externalScheduler PRESENT IF "both the daily scheduling package and weekly scheduling package are not present in an instance and external scheduling is supported by that instance";

REGISTERED AS { smi2MObjectClass 3 } ;

This object class includes one mandatory package and five conditional packages. Each attribute that is included indicates the operations that may be performed on that attribute. Finally, note that the four notifications in the mandatory package and the five conditional packages are included by reference; the definition is elsewhere.

Now consider a subclass derived from the discriminator class, the eventForwarding-Discriminator:

eventForwardingDiscriminator MANAGED OBJECT CLASS
  DERIVED FROM discriminator
  CHARACTERIZED BY efdPackage PACKAGE
    BEHAVIOR
    eventForwardingDiscriminatorBehavior BEHAVIOR
    DEFINED AS "This managed object is used to represent the criteria that shall be satisfied by potential event reports before the event report is forwarded to a particular destination.";;
    ATTRIBUTES
    destination GET-REPLACE;;;
  CONDITIONAL PACKAGES
    backUpDestinationListPackage PACKAGE
      ATTRIBUTES
      activeDestination GET,
      backUpDestinationList GET-REPLACE;
      REGISTERED AS {smi2Package 9}; PRESENT IF "the event forwarding discriminator is required to provide a backup for the destination",
    modePackage PACKAGE
      ATTRIBUTES
      confirmedMode GET,
      REGISTERED AS {smi2Package 10}; PRESENT IF "the event forwarding discriminator permits mode for reporting events to be specified by the managing system";
  REGISTERED AS { smi2MObjectClass 4 } ;

This new object class carries over all the characteristics of its superclass. Thus, the amount of detail is greatly reduced. Since a discriminator-type service is commonly used in systems management, it is useful to provide this superclass-subclass structure for the function. Note that in this case, the definition of the conditional packages is included in the object-class definition rather than just providing a reference. However, since each of these packages has a registered identifier, they are available for use elsewhere. Both these object classes are described in greater detail in Chapter 14.

As a final example, let us consider an object-class definition from CD 10737, which defines transport-layer management. One of the definitions is for the managed object class for the connection-oriented transport-protocol machine:

```
comodePM MANAGED OBJECT CLASS
    DERIVED FROM "ISO/IEC 10165-2":top;
    CHARACTERIZED BY comodePM PACKAGE
        ATTRIBUTES
            coPMName DEFAULT VALUE TLM.null-MO-Name-Value
                PERMITTED VALUE TLM.null-MO-Name-Syntax
                REQUIRED VALUE TLM.null-MO-Name-Syntax GET,
            "ISO/IEC 10165-2":octetsSentCounter GET,
            "ISO/IEC 10165-2":octetsReceivedCounter GET,
            "ISO/IEC 10165-2":incomingProtocolErrorsCounter GET,
            openConnections GET
            maxConnections REPLACE-WITH-DEFAULT
                DEFAULT VALUE implementation dependent GET-REPLACE
            localSuccessfulConnections GET,
            remoteSuccessfulConnections GET,
            localUnsuccessfulConnections GET,
            remoteUnsuccessfulConnections GET,
            localErrorDisconnects GET,
            remoteErrorDisconnects GET,
            unassociatedTPDUs GET,
            maxOpenConnections REPLACE-WITH-DEFAULT
                DEFAULT VALUE see attribute behavior GET;
        ATTRIBUTE GROUPS
            TLPMCounters
                openConnections
                localSuccessfulConnections
                remoteSuccessfulConnections
                remoteUnsuccessfulConnections
                localErrorDisconnects
                remoteErrorDisconnects
                unassociatedTPDUs
                maxOpenConnections;;;
    REGISTERED AS { TLM.moe comodePM (4) } ;
```

This managed object contains key parameters for monitoring the operation of a transport-protocol entity in a managed system. Note that a number of the defined attributes are grouped together for convenient access to the counters as a unit.

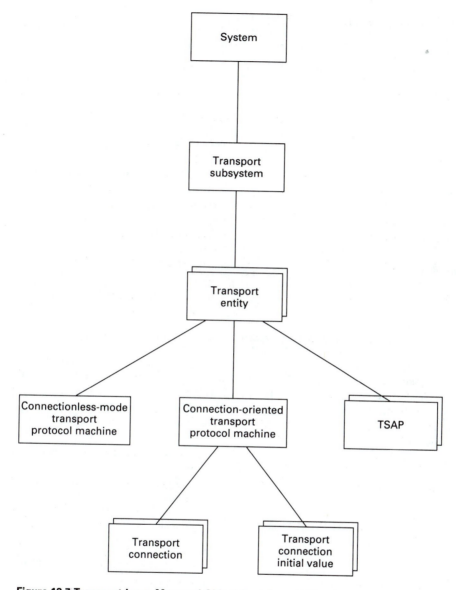

Figure 12.7 Transport-Layer Managed-Object Containment Structure (CD 10737)

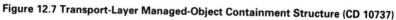

12.4   TRANSPORT-LAYER MANAGEMENT

As an example of the definition of management information, this section gives an overview of CD 10737, which specifies the management information related to the OSI transport layer. The reader may find it useful to compare this specification with the SNMP MIB specification for TCP (transmission-control protocol) and UDP (user datagram protocol).

Table 12.9 Transport Management Objects

Element	Code	Description
		Transport-Subsystem Managed Object
tsName	R	Name of the transport object
		Transport-Entity Managed Object
teName	S	Name of the object
operationalState	R	State of the object
targetNSAP	R/W	NSAP(s) to be used by this transport entity
actualNSAP	R	NSAP(s) actually in use by this transport entity
undecoded NSDUs	C	Number of NSDUs undecoded
checksumErrorsDetected	C	Number of PDUs received with incorrect checksum
protocolErrors	C	Number of TPDUs received with invalid header
communicationsAlarm	N	Notification of a protocol error detected by the local transport entity
		Connectionless-Mode Transport-Protocol-Machine Managed Object
clpMName	S	Name of the object
clChecksumOption	R/W	Enables use/nonuse of the checksum option
octetsSentCounter	C	Number of user data octets sent
octetsReceivedCounter	C	Number of user data octets received
incomingProtocolErrors-Counter	C	Number of protocol errors
undeliverablePDU	C	counter associated with undeliverablePDU notification
communicationsAlarm	N	Issued when a user data PDU cannot be delivered
		Connection-Oriented Transport-Protocol-Machine Managed Object
copMName	S	Name of the object
octetsSentCounter	C	Number of user data octets sent
octetsReceivedCounter	C	Number of user data octets received
incomingProtocolErrors-Counter	C	Number of protocol errors
openConnections	G	Number of transport connections (TCs) currently in open state
maxConnections	R/W	Maximum number of simultaneously open TCs allowed
localSuccessful-Connections	C	Number of locally initiated TCs that have reached open state
remoteSuccessful-Connections	C	Number of remotely initiated TCs that have reached open state

Table 12.9 (*Cont.*)

Element	Code	Description
Connection-Oriented Transport-Protocol-Machine Managed Object		
localUnSuccessful-Connections	C	Number of locally initiated TCs that did not reach open state
remoteUnSuccessful-Connections	C	Number of remotely initiated TCs that did not reach open state
localErrorDisconnects	C	Number of transport disconnects initiated by local entity due to error
remoteErrorDisconnects	C	Number of transport disconnects initiated by remote entity due to error
unassociatedTPDUs	C	Number of TPDUs that could not be associated with a TC
maxOpenConnections	T	Highest number of TCs to simultaneously be in open state
TSAP Managed Object		
tsapName	S	Name of the object; equal to the TSAP name
tsapID	S	Transport selector used to identify this TSAP
userEntityName	S	Name of the managed object for the user entity of this TSAP
Transport-Connection Initial-Value Managed Object		
tcInitialValueName	S	Name of the object
protocolClasses	R/W	The preferred/alternate set of protocol classes that may be stated at connection establishment
extendedFormatOption	R/W	Enables negotiation of extended-format TPDUs
networkExpeditedData-Option	R/W	Enables negotiation of use/nonuse of network expedited-data option
checksumNonuseOption	R/W	Enables negotiation of checksum nonuse
receiptConfirmationOption	R/W	Enables negotiation of network receipt confirmation
implicitFlowControl-Option	R/W	Enables negotiation of nonuse of explicit flow control
initialInactivityTime	R/W	Value for the inactivity timer
initialReassignmentTime	R/W	Value for the reassignment timer
initialRetransmissionTime	R/W	Value for the local retransmission timer
initialWindowTimer	R/W	Value for the window timer
maximumWindow	R/W	Maximum window to be given on the connection
initialMaxTPDUSize	R/W	Maximum TPDU size allowed to be negotiated
initialMaxTransmissions	R/W	Maximum number of transmissions of a TPDU

Table 12.9 (*Cont.*)

Element	Code	Description
		Transport-Connection Managed Object
transportConnectionName	R	Name of the object
protocolClass	R	Transport protocol class being used by the TC
extendedFormat	R	Indicates whether normal or extended TPDU format is used
networkExpeditedData	R	Indicates whether network expedited data is used
checksumNonuse	R	Indicates whether checksums are used
receiptConfirmation	R	Indicates whether network receipt confirmation is used
implicitFlowControl	R	Indicates whether explicit flow control is used
inactivityTime	R	Value of the inactivity timer
acknowledgeTime	R	Value of the local acknowledge timer
reassignmentTime	R	Value of the reassignment timer
retransmissionTime	R	Value of the local retransmission timer
windowTime	R	Value of the window timer
maxTPDUSize	R	Maximum TPDU size that was negotiated
maxTransmissions	R	Maximum number of transmissions used by the TC
localReference	R	Local reference number for this TC
remoteReference	R	Remote reference number for this TC
callingTSelector	R	Calling TSAP-ID specified during connection establishment
calledTSelector	R	Called TSAP-ID specified during connection establishment
callingNSAPAddress	R	Calling NSAP address specified at network-service interface
calledNSAPAddress	R	Called NSAP address specified at network-service interface
respondingNSAPAddress	R	Responding NSAP address specified at network-service interface
connectionDirection	R	Direction of connection (initiated by local or remote entity)
networkConnectionIDs	R	Set of IDs of the NCs that support this TC
pdusSent	C	Number of TPDUs transmitted (excluding retransmissions)
pdusReceived	C	Number of TPDUs received
octetsSentCounter	C	Number of user data octets sent on this TC
octetsReceivedCounter	C	Number of user data octets received on this TC
reassignmentsToNC	C	Number of times the TC has been reassigned to NC

Table 12.9 (*Cont.*)

Element	Code	Description
Transport-Connection Managed Object		
networkDisconnections	C	Number of times the NC has been released
connectionUser	R	Name of object representing user of this TC
objectCreation	N	Notification of creation of this object
objectDeletion	N	Notification of deletion of this object
successfulConnection- Establishment	N	Notification of successful connection establishment (transition to open state)

Code:

R	Read-only attribute		T	Tidemark (read-only) attribute
R/W	Read-write attribute		G	Gauge (read-only) attribute
N	Notification		S	Write attribute when object is created; read attribute after creation
C	Counter (read-only) attribute			

The specification defines seven managed objects that relate to the operation of the transport layer. Figure 12.7 illustrates the containment hierarchy for these objects. Managed objects that can have multiple instances are illustrated as double boxes. The system managed object is a generic object that contains managed objects for specific layers.

Table 12.9 lists the attributes and notifications that are part of each managed object in transport-layer management.

12.4.1 Transport-Subsystem Object

The transport-subsystem object is the umbrella object for all functions of an open system that provide the OSI transport service and are subject to systems-management operation. It serves merely as a container for other managed objects that contain the detailed attributes and notifications that represent the transport operation. Typically, this object is a permanent part of a system's MIB and is neither created nor destroyed.

12.4.2 Transport-Entity Object

One transport-entity object exists for each active transport-protocol entity within the system. Typically, there would be one connection-oriented and one connectionless-mode protocol in use, providing the corresponding transport services.

The details of the management attributes of interest for a given protocol entity are contained in lower-level objects. Each transport-entity object only contains some top-level information about the corresponding transport-protocol entity.

12.4.3 Connectionless-Mode Transport-Protocol-Machine Object

The connectionless-mode transport-protocol-machine object includes management information related to the operation of the connectionless transport-protocol entity in a system. This includes an attribute that may be set by management operation to determine whether or not transport-protocol data units (TPDUs) include the checksum option.

This object also includes a number of counters. These counters, and all of the counters in the transport-layer managed objects, are defined as being of the nonWrappingCounter type. In practice, this simply means that the counters should be represented in such a way that they don't wrap during the lifetime of the management operation.

The object includes one notification, the communicationsAlarm notification, presented earlier. In this case, the alarm is triggered by the undeliverablePDU counter.

12.4.4 Connection-Oriented Transport-Protocol-Machine Object

The connection-oriented transport-protocol-machine object includes management information related to the operation of the connection-oriented transport-protocol entity in a system. The object itself contains overall information about the connections maintained by the transport-protocol entity. Detailed connection-related information is contained in transport-connection objects, with one object per connection.

12.4.5 TSAP Object

One or more TSAP (transport-service-access point) objects are contained in each transport-entity object. There is one TSAP object for each TSAP currently recognized by the corresponding transport-protocol entity.

12.4.6 Transport-Connection Initial-Value Object

A transport-connection initial-value object contains a collection of default values to be used when establishing a connection and creating the corresponding transport-connection object. The values in this object are settable by management operation. One or more of these objects may be contained in the connection-oriented transport-protocol-machine object, and each may be used in the creation of one or more transport connections.

12.4.7 Transport-Connection Object

One transport-connection object exists for each active transport connection (a connection for which a CR (connection request) TPDU has been sent or received and that has not yet been terminated). This object includes a number of read-only attributes that provide information about the status of the connection, including a collection of read-only counters that reflect the traffic on the connection. In addition, three notifications are provided dealing with the creation of this object, successful connection establishment, and the deletion of this object.

12.5 PRACTICAL ISSUES

The OSI MIB standards define a conceptual schema for a database of managed objects. In effect, this is an interface specification for CMIS (common management information service) and the systems-management functions. However, the MIB standards do not specify how an MIB should be implemented.

The implementer and network manager need to be aware that a variety of practical issues are raised in implementing an MIB. Some of these were explored in Part II. In this section, we deal with the important issue of partitioning.

At a minimum, a network-management system will include one central network-management system and some number of managed resources that are represented as managed objects. An important architectural issue that must be addressed during the design of a network-management system is the way in which the management information is distributed across the entire configuration. The following architectural principles are suggested in Bapat (1991):

1. If a network resource can store nonvolatile information (in firmware, internal disk, etc.), then those objects and attributes that deal specifically with this resource should be stored locally.

2. A resource may only be able to store volatile information. This could occur if the resource has no nonvolatile memory (e.g., disk) or if the resource has insufficient capacity, processing or memory, to implement the network-management and database-management software to store management information locally and participate in its retrieval and control by a remote manager. In this case, the relevant management information must be transmitted as it is created to a repository in either a management station or some intermediate system.

3. Systemwide information—such as a directory, networkwide connectivity, high-level security-management functions, historical usage data, and so forth—is most optimally stored in a central database at a management station.

4. If intermediate devices exist—such as bridges, routers, and network-monitoring devices—these may be used in a proxy fashion to store data on behalf of a managed system. This may be more efficient, in both process time and memory use, than storage either in the end resource or in the central management station. It may also reduce network traffic, since the intermediate system can provide only summary information to the network-management station.

5. Reliability and fault-tolerance requirements may dictate that redundant copies of MIB information be stored.

The use of redundancy raises issues of integrity. Consider the situation in which some objects are present in a resource and replicated in a central MIB at the management station. Consistency can be assured by having a well-defined concurrency-control mechanism, which guarantees that, when an update is attempted, all copies of an attribute are updated or none is. This approach requires special features in the operating system or in higher-level support software.[3] Although the techniques for this approach are well known, their use in operating systems is still relatively rare.

The alternative to the use of concurrency control is to declare that temporary windows of inconsistency can be tolerated. If this is the case, then the facilities of OSI systems management can themselves be used for maintaining consistency. Two general approaches are suggested in Klerer and Cohen (1991):

1. *Event-driven shadowing:* To maintain relatively tight synchronization, a notification is sent from the object that is linked to the resource to the object or objects that serve as backups, or shadows, whenever an attribute of the object changes. The object emitting notifications serves as the master copy for that particular resource.

---

3. A discussion of distributed concurrency-control mechanisms can be found in Stallings (1992).

2. *Shadowing via polling:* The shadow instance of an object queries the master instance and updates its own attributes if a change has occurred. This kind of shadowing is more likely to be used when the synchronization need not be as tight (e.g., the collection of billing information).

Both these techniques, of course, add overhead to the network-management system. However, since both make use of network-management facilities, the work in setting up the redundancy is relatively minor.

12.6   SUMMARY

The SMI for OSI systems management uses ASN.1 and object-oriented concepts to define management information. The basic unit of information is the object. An object may include:

- *Attributes:* variables that represent characteristics of managed resources
- *Behaviors:* actions that can be triggered by a manager
- *Notifications:* event reports that can be triggered by defined events

The ASN.1 definition of management information is in the form of object classes. For each object class, actual information is represented as object instances. Thus, there may be more than one object instance in an MIB for a given object class, each with potentially different attribute values.

Two forms of hierarchy lend structure to an MIB. A subclass of an object class can be defined, which inherits the attributes, notifications, and behavior of its superclass. The use of inheritance provides for more efficient definition of object classes. An object instance can be contained in another object instance. The use of containment provides for the definition of data structures within an MIB.

13
CMIS and CMIP

The fundamental function within OSI systems management is the exchange of management information between two entities (manager, agent) by means of a protocol. This functionality within OSI (open systems interconnection) systems management is referred to as the common management information service element (CMISE). As with most areas of functionality within OSI, CMISE is specified in two parts:

1. The interface with a user, specifying the services provided. This is the common management information service (CMIS).

2. The protocol, specifying the protocol data unit (PDU) format and associated procedures. This is the common management information protocol (CMIP).

Figure 13.1 shows the context of CMIS and CMIP. As discussed in section 13.1, the CMIS provides seven services for performing management operations, in the form of service primitives. In addition, CMISE users need to be able to establish associations in order to perform management operations. These latter services are provided by the association-control-service element and are provided by CMISE as a pass-through; there is no CMIP involved. For the management-operation services, the CMISE employs a CMIP to exchange protocol data units. The CMIP, in turn, relies on the services of the remote-operations-service element.[1] Both ACSE and ROSE rely on the presentation service.

13.1   COMMON MANAGEMENT INFORMATION SERVICE

The common management information service defines the services provided for OSI systems management (ISO 9595). These services are invokable by management processes in order to communicate remotely.

---

1.   See Appendixes 13A and 13B for a description of ACSE and ROSE.

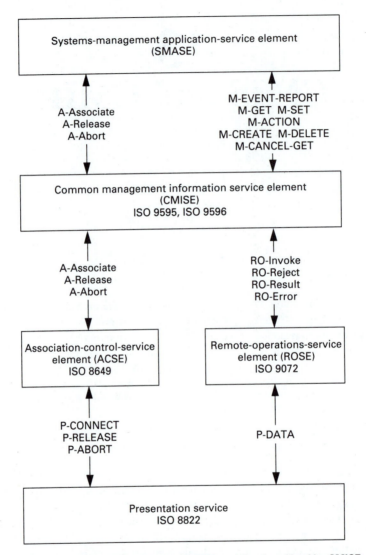

Figure 13.1 Services Provided by CMISE and Services Used by CMISE

The CMIS services are specified in terms of primitives that can be viewed as commands or procedure calls with parameters.[2] These are listed in Table 13.1. The services are of two types: confirmed services require that a remote management process send a response to indicate receipt and success or failure of the requested operation; nonconfirmed services do not provide responses.

Three categories of service are relevant to CMIS:

---

2.   These primitives always include one of four standard modifiers: *request, indication, response, confirm.* The interpretation of these primitives is discussed in Appendix A.

Table 13.1 CMISE Services

(a) Management-Notification Service		
Service	**Type**	**Definition**
M-EVENT-REPORT	Confirmed/nonconfirmed	Reports an event about a managed object to a peer CMISE-service user

(b) Management-Operation Services		
Service	**Type**	**Definition**
M-GET	Confirmed	Requests the retrieval of management information from a peer CMISE-service user
M-SET	Confirmed/nonconfirmed	Requests the modification of management information by a peer CMISE-service user
M-ACTION	Confirmed/nonconfirmed	Requests that a peer CMISE-service user perform an action
M-CREATE	Confirmed	Requests that a peer CMISE-service user create an instance of a managed object
M-DELETE	Confirmed	Requests that a peer CMISE-service user delete an instance of a managed object
M-CANCEL-GET	Confirmed	Requests that a peer CMISE-service user cancel a previously requested and currently outstanding invocation of the M-GET service

1. *Association service:* CMIS users need to establish an application association to communicate. They rely on the association-control-service element for the control of application associations.

2. *Management-notification service:* This service is used to convey management information applicable to a notification. The definition of the notification and the consequent behavior of the communicating entities is dependent on the specification of the managed object that generated the notification and is outside the scope of CMIS.

3. *Management-operation services:* These six services are used to convey management information applicable to systems-management operations. The definition of the operation and the consequent behavior of the communicating entities is dependent on the specification of the managed object at which the operation is directed and is outside the scope of CMIS.

CMIS provides two structuring facilities:

1. Multiple responses to a confirmed operation can be linked to the operation by the use of a linked-identification parameter.

2. Operations can be performed on multiple managed objects, selected to satisfy some criteria and subject to a synchronizing condition.

13.1.1   Linkage

The M-GET, M-SET, M-ACTION, and M-DELETE service primitives can specify operation on multiple objects. When multiple objects are specified in a management request, one response is returned for each object. Some linkage technique is needed to match the multiple responses to the initial request that generated the responses. This linkage is necessary since there may be a number of outstanding requests and incoming responses must be matched to the correct preceding outgoing request.

Linkage is provided by means of the linked-identifier parameter, which appears in each of the response and confirm primitives. The value of the parameter is the same as the invoke identifier that appears in the request and indication primitives. The invoke identifier is a unique identifier assigned to each operation.

13.1.2   Managed-Object Selection

CMIS provides a powerful set of tools that allow a user to select one object or a number of objects to be the subject of a management operation. These facilities are provided as parameters in the M-GET, M-SET, M-ACTION, and M-DELETE service primitives.

Managed-object selection involves three concepts: scoping, filtering, and synchronization.

13.1.2.1   Scoping

Scoping refers to the identification of an object or objects to which a filter is to be applied. Scoping is defined with reference to a specific managed-object instance, referred to as the *base managed object*. The base managed object is the starting point for the selection of one or more objects to which a filter is to be applied. Recall from subsection 12.1.2 that, by the principles of containment and naming, managed objects form a hierarchy, or tree structure. Using the base object as the root, a subtree of the overall object tree is obtained. With this in mind, four specifications of scoping level are possible:

1. The base object alone
2. The *n*th-level subordinates of the base object, with the base object defined as level 0
3. The base object and all its subordinates down to and including the *n*th level
4. The base object and all its subordinates—that is, the entire subtree

Figure 13.2 illustrates these concepts.

13.1.2.2   Filtering

A filter is a Boolean expression, consisting of one or more assertions about the presence or values of attributes in a scoped managed object. Each assertion may be a test for equality, ordering, presence, or set comparison. Attribute-value assertions can require that the following matching rules be met:

- *Equality:* Attribute value is equal to that asserted.
- *Greater or equal:* Attribute value supplied is greater than or equal to the value of the attribute.
- *Less or equal:* Attribute value supplied is less than or equal to the value of the attribute.
- *Present:* Attribute is present.

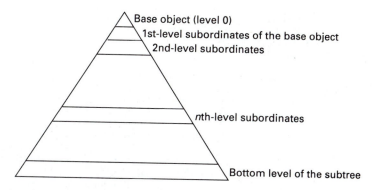

(a) Abstract representation of a containment subtree from a base-object instance

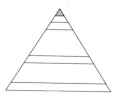

(b) Base object alone

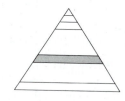

(c) *n*th-level subordinates of the base object

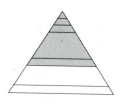

(d) Base object and all its subordinates down through the *n*th level

(e) Entire subtree of the base.object

Figure 13.2 Scoping Alternatives

- *Substrings:* Attribute value includes the specified substrings in the given order.
- *Subset of:* All asserted members are present in the attribute.
- *Superset of:* All members of the attribute are present in the asserted attribute.
- *Non-null-set intersection:* At least one of the asserted members is present in the attribute.

Figure 13.3 is the ASN.1 definition of the CMIS filter parameter. The filter can be a single test, called a filter item, applied to each attribute value to be tested. More complex tests can be made by combining individual filter items, using AND, OR, and NOT.

As example of this notation, consider the following condition to be encoded:

```
CMISFilter ::= Choice { item   [8] FilterItem
                        and    [9] IMPLICIT SET OF CMISFilter,
                        or     [10] IMPLICIT SET OF CMISFilter,
                        not    [11] CMISfilter }

FilterItem ::= CHOICE { equality        [0] IMPLICIT Attribute,
                        substrings      [1] IMPLICIT SEQUENCE OF CHOICE {
                                            initialString [0] IMPLICIT SEQUENCE {
                                                          attributeId   attributeId,
                                                          string        ANY DEFINED BY attributeId },
                                            anyString     [1] IMPLICIT SEQUENCE {
                                                          attributeId   attributeId,
                                                          string        ANY DEFINED BY attributeId },
                                            finalString   [2] IMPLICIT SEQUENCE {
                                                          attributeId   attributeId,
                                                          string        ANY DEFINED BY attributeId }},

                        greaterOrEqual         [2] IMPLICIT Attribute,
                        lessOrEqual            [3] IMPLICIT Attribute,
                        present                [4] AttributeId,
                        subsetOf               [5] IMPLICIT Attribute,
                        supersetOf             [6] IMPLICIT Attribute,
                        nonNullSetIntersection [7] IMPLICIT Attribute }
```

Figure 13.3 ASN.1 Definition of Filtering (ISO 9595)

(objectClass **equal to** protocolEntity)
and (entityId **starts with** ''123'')
and ((severity **not Equal to** minor)
        or (badPduCount **greater than or equal to** 20))

where **boldface** words are operators and plain-type words are variables.
The following value notation represents this condition:

test-filter   CMISFilter :: =
              and {item equality {objectClass, Object-Class protocolEntity},
                       item substrings {initialString {entityID, PrintableString ''123''}},
                       or { not item equality {severity, Severity minor},
                               item lessOrEqual {badPduCount, INTEGER 20}}}

The filter test is applied in the following manner:

1. The filter is applied to every managed object selected by the scope parameter.

2. For each selected object, the filter involves a test of one or more attributes.

3. Assertions about the value of an attribute are evaluated according to the matching rules associated with the attribute syntax. These rules are specified in the MATCHES FOR clause of the attribute template, described in section 12.3.

4. If an attribute-value assertion is present in the filter and that attribute is not present in the object, then the result of that test is FALSE.

5. The object or objects for which the filter test evaluates to TRUE are selected for the application of the operation.

13.1.2.3 Synchronization

The scoping parameter may result in the selection of more than one managed object to be subject to filtering. In turn, if more than one object is scoped, the filtering parameter may result in the selection of more than one object for which the operation is to be performed. The question then arises as to the order in which objects will be processed. Since the order in which object instances are selected by the filter is not specified but is left as a local implementation matter, this order cannot be used.

However, CMIS does include the concept of synchronization. The CMISE-service user may request one of two types of synchronization:

1. *Atomic:* All managed objects selected for the operation are checked to ascertain whether they are able to successfully perform the operation. If one or more managed objects are not able to do so, then none performs it.

2. *Best effort:* All managed objects selected for the operation are requested to perform it.

13.1.3 Management-Notification Service

The only primitive defined for the management-notification service is *M-EVENT-REPORT*. This primitive is used to report a notification to a manager that has requested the notification. Unlike all other management operations, the event report is initiated by the agent process, and the managing process is the responder. The service may be of either the confirmed or nonconfirmed variety.[3]

Table 13.2, part (a), lists the parameters used in the M-EVENT-REPORT primitives, and Table 13.3 provides definitions. The first column in Table 13.2 is a list of the parameter names. The second column indicates which of these parameters are present in the request primitive issued by the source CMIS user to CMIS. These parameters are delivered unchanged to the destination user in a matching indication primitive. If this is a confirmed service, then the destination user responds with a response primitive issued to its CMIS; the third column lists the corresponding parameters. These parameters are delivered unchanged back to the initiating user in a confirm primitive.

Each notification is accompanied by a unique identifier that is provided by the initiating user and delivered to the destination user. The mode parameter indicates whether a response is requested for this notification. The next two parameters specify the class of the object and the specific object instance in which the event occurred. The next three parameters indicate the type of event, the time of its generation, and any information that the invoking user is able to supply about the event.

If a response is requested for this notification, the responding user issues a response primitive with an invoke identifier that matches that of the original request primitive. If the notification was successfully received, then the response may include the current-time and event-reply parameters. The event-reply parameter contains notification-specific information about a notification that is successfully received; when this parameter is included, the event-type parameter is also included.

If a response is requested for the notification and the notification was not successfully received, the response primitive includes the errors parameter. The following errors may be reported (Table 13.4):

---

3. See Appendix A for a discussion of confirmed versus nonconfirmed services.

Table 13.2 CMISE Services and Their Parameters

(a) M-EVENT-REPORT

Parameter Name	Request/ Indication	Response/ Confirm
Invoke identifier	M	M(=)
Mode	M	—
Managed-object class	M	U
Managed-object instance	M	U
Event type	M	C(=)
Event time	U	—
Event information	U	—
Current time	—	U
Event reply	—	C
Errors	—	C

(b) M-GET

Parameter Name	Request/ Indication	Response/ Confirm
Invoke identifier	M	M
Linked identifier	—	C
Base-object class	M	—
Base-object instance	M	—
Scope	U	—
Filter	U	—
Access control	U	—
Synchronization	U	—
Attribute-identifier list	U	—
Managed-object class	—	C
Managed-object instance	—	C
Current time	—	U
Attribute list	—	C
Errors	—	C

(c) M-SET

Parameter Name	Request/ Indication	Response/ Confirm
Invoke identifier	M	M
Linked identifier	—	C
Mode	M	—
Base-object class	M	—
Base-object instance	M	—

(c) M-SET

Parameter Name	Request/ Indication	Response/ Confirm
Scope	U	—
Filter	U	—
Access control	U	—
Synchronization	U	—
Managed-object class	—	C
Managed-object instance	—	C
Modification list	M	—
Attribute list	—	U
Current time	—	U
Errors	—	C

(d) M-ACTION

Parameter Name	Request/ Indication	Response/ Confirm
Invoke identifier	M	M
Linked identifier	—	C
Mode	M	—
Base-object class	M	—
Base-object instance	M	—
Scope	U	—
Filter	U	—
Managed-object class	—	C
Managed-object instance	—	C
Access control	U	—
Synchronization	U	—
Action type	M	C(=)
Action information	U	—
Current time	—	U
Action reply	—	C
Errors	—	C

(e) M-CREATE

Parameter Name	Request/ Indication	Response/ Confirm
Invoke identifier	M	M(=)
Managed-object class	M	U

Table 13.2 (*Cont.*)

(e) M-CREATE

Parameter Name	Request/ Indication	Response/ Confirm
Managed-object instance	U	C
Superior-object instance	U	—
Access control	U	—
Reference-object instance	U	—
Attribute list	U	C
Current time	—	U
Errors	—	C

(f) M-DELETE

Parameter Name	Request/ Indication	Response/ Confirm
Scope	U	—
Filter	U	—
Access control	U	—
Synchronization	U	—
Managed-object class	—	C
Managed-object instance	—	C
Current time	—	U
Errors	—	C

(f) M-DELETE

Parameter Name	Request/ Indication	Response/ Confirm
Invoke identifier	M	M
Linked identifier	—	C
Base-object class	M	—
Base-object instance	M	—

(g) M-CANCEL-GET

Parameter Name	Request/ Indication	Response/ Confirm
Invoke identifier	M	M
Get invoke identifier	M	—
Errors	—	C

M = Mandatory.
(=) = The value of the parameter is equal to the value of the parameter in the column to the left.
U = The use of the parameter is a service-user option.

— = The parameter is not present in the interaction described by the primitive concerned.
C = The parameter is conditional.

- Duplicate invocation
- Invalid argument value
- Mistyped argument
- No such argument
- No such object class
- No such object instance
- Processing failure
- Resource limitation
- Unrecognized operation

Table 13.3 Definition of CMIS Parameters

Access control
Information of unspecified form to be used as input to the access-control functions.

Action information
Specifies extra information when necessary to further define the nature, variations, or operands of the action to be performed.

Action reply
Contains the reply to the action.

Action type
Specifies a particular action that is to be performed.

Attribute-identifier list
A set of attribute identifiers for which the attribute values are to be returned by the performing CMISE-service user.

Attribute list
The set of attribute identifiers and values that are returned by the performing CMISE-service user.

Base-object class
The class of the managed object that is to be used as the starting point for the selection of managed objects to which the filter is to be applied.

Base-object instance
The instance of the managed object that is to be used as the starting point for the selection of managed objects to which the filter is to be applied.

Current time
Time at which the response was generated.

Errors
Error notification for the operation.

Event information
Information that the invoking CMISE-service user is able to supply about the event.

Event reply
Reply to the event report.

Event time
Time of generation of event.

Event type
Type of event being reported.

Filter
Specifies the set of assertions that defines the filter test to be applied to the scoped managed object.

Get invoke identifier
Identifier assigned to the previously requested and currently outstanding M-GET operation.

Invoke identifier
The identifier assigned to this operation.

Linked identifier
If multiple replies are to be sent for this operation, this parameter specifies the identification that is provided by the performing CMISE-service user when those replies are returned. The linked identifier has the same value as that of the invoke identifier provided in the indication primitive.

Managed-object class
The class of the managed object referenced by the primitive.

Managed-object instance
The instance of the managed object referenced by the primitive.

Mode
Requested mode: confirmed or nonconfirmed.

Modification list
A set of attribute-modification specifications.

Reference-object instance
Specifies an existing instance of a managed object, called the reference object, of the same class as the managed object to be created. Attribute values associated with the reference-object instance become the default values for those not specified by the attribute-list parameter.

Scope
Indicates the subtree, rooted at the base managed object, that is to be searched.

Superior-object instance
Identifies the existing managed-object instance that is to be the superior of the new managed-object instance.

Synchronization
Indicates how the invoking CMISE-service user wants this operation synchronized across the selected object instances.

Table 13.4 Definition of CMIS Error Values

Access denied
The requested operation was not performed for reasons pertinent to the security of the open system.

Class-instance conflict
The specified object instance is not a member of the specifed class; for the M-CREATE service, the specified object instance may not be created as a member of the specified class.

Complexity limitation
The requested operation was not performed because a parameter was too complex.

Duplicate invocation
The invoke identifier was used on a previous notification or operation.

Duplicate managed-object instance
The object-instance value supplied for object creation was already registered for a managed object of the specified class.

Get-list error
One or more attribute values were not read for one of the following reasons: access denied, no such attribute.

Invalid argument value
The event-information value specified was out of range or otherwise inappropriate.

Invalid attribute value
An attribute value specified was out of range or otherwise inappropriate.

Invalid filter
The filter parameter contains an invalid assertion or an unrecognized logical operator.

Invalid object instance
The object-instance name specified implied a violation of the naming rules.

Invalid scope
The value of the scope parameter is invalid.

Missing attribute value
A required attribute value was not supplied, and a default value was not available.

Mistyped argument
One of the parameters supplied was not agreed for use when an association was set up between the two CMIS users.

Mistyped operation
The get invoke-identifier parameter did not refer to an M-GET operation.

No such action
The action type specified was not supported.

No such argument
The event information specified was not recognized.

No such attribute
An attribute specified was not recognized.

No such invoke identifier
The get invoke-identifier parameter was not recognized.

No such object class
The class of the specified management object was not recognized.

No such object instance
The instance of the specified management object was not recognized; for the M-CREATE service, the instance of the specified superior management object was not recognized.

No such reference object
The reference object-instance parameter was not recognized.

Processing failure
A general failure in processing the notification or operation was encountered.

Resource limitation
The notification or operation was not processed due to a resource limitation.

Set-list error
One or more attribute values were not modified for one of the following reasons: access denied, invalid attribute value, invalid operator, invalid operation, no such attribute.

Synchronization not supported
The type of synchronization specified is not supported.

Unrecognized operation
The operation is not one of those agreed between the CMIS users.

13.1.4   Management-Operation Services

13.1.4.1   M-GET Service

The M-GET service allows for the retrieval of data from the management information base. One management process, acting in the role of manager, will send a GET request to another management process, acting in an agent role. The request may be for information about a single managed object or a set of managed objects. For each managed object about which information is requested, the value of one, several, or all of its attributes may be requested.

The M-GET service is always a confirmed service. Table 13.2, part (b), lists the parameters used in the M-GET primitives.

In the M-GET.request and indication primitives, the invoke identifier is used to identify this particular request and to enable the corresponding response to be matched. The base-object class and base-object instance identify either the unique managed object that is the subject of this operation or the base object of a subtree.

The scope, filter, and synchronization parameters are used in the following fashion:

- If the scope parameter is absent, the default scope is the base object; otherwise, the scope is that specified by the scope parameter.

- If the filter parameter is absent, all the managed objects included by the scope are selected; otherwise, only those objects in the scope that pass the filter test are selected.

- If the synchronization parameter is absent, best-effort synchronization is performed. If the base object alone is selected, the synchronization parameter is ignored. If the synchronization parameter is present and the scope consists of more than one object, then the synchronization parameter dictates whether best-effort or atomic synchronization is used.

The value of the access-control parameter is unspecified in the current standard but is to be used as input to an access-control function. Finally, the attribute-identifier list contains a set of attribute identifiers for which the attribute values are to be returned. If this parameter is omitted, all attribute identifiers are assumed.

Figure 13.4 illustrates possible responses to a get operation. The first part of the figure indicates the response if the get operation fails. The request is delivered to the target CMIS user in the form of an M-GET.indication primitive with the same parameters as the request primitive. If the CMIS user is unable to perform the operation, it returns an M-GET.response with the same invocation identifier, the class and instance identifiers of the object for which access was attempted, and an error code.

The following errors may be reported (Table 13.4):

- Access denied
- Class-instance conflict
- Complexity limitation
- Duplicate invocation
- Get-list error
- Invalid filter
- Invalid scope

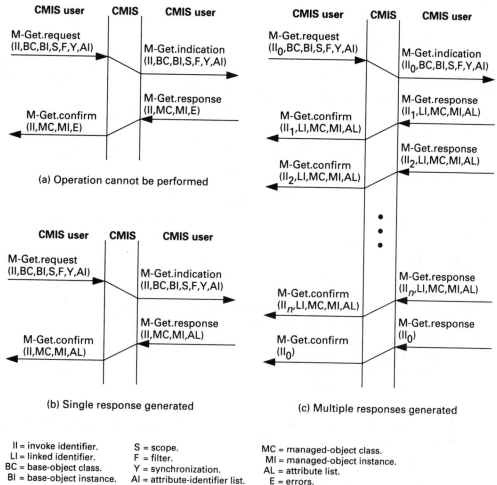

(a) Operation cannot be performed

(b) Single response generated

(c) Multiple responses generated

II = invoke identifier.	S = scope.	MC = managed-object class.
LI = linked identifier.	F = filter.	MI = managed-object instance.
BC = base-object class.	Y = synchronization.	AL = attribute list.
BI = base-object instance.	AI = attribute-identifier list.	E = errors.

Figure 13.4   Time-Sequence Diagrams for M-GET Service

- Mistyped argument
- No such object class
- No such object instance
- Processing failure
- Resource limitation
- Synchronization not supported
- Unrecognized operation

Figure 13.4, part (b), shows the sequence if attribute values from a single object are to be returned and there is a single successful reply. The invoke-identifier parameter in the response primitive matches that of the original request primitive. The managed-object class and instance parameters indicate the object that is the subject of this reply. The attribute list consists of a set of attribute identifiers and their values.

If attribute values from multiple objects are to be returned, there is one successful reply for each object (Figure 13.4, part [c]). In this case, the linked identifier in each response matches the value of the invoke parameter in the corresponding request primitive. Each of the responses has a unique value of its invoke identifier. To mark the end of the linked sequence, there is a final M-GET.response that has an invoke-identifier value equal to that in the initial M-GET.request, no linked identifier, and no attribute list.

There are several possibilities not illustrated in Figure 13.4. In the case of a request for attribute values from a single object, it is possible that some attribute values cannot be returned for one of the reasons indicated in the get-list error parameter (access denied, no such attribute), but that other attribute values can be read and returned. In that case, the sequence of Figure 13.4, part (b), is followed, but the response/confirm primitives include the error parameter as well as the attribute-list parameter. Similarly, when multiple responses are generated (Figure 13.4, part [c]), any of the response/confirm primitives may include a get-list error parameter and an attribute list.

13.1.4.2 M-SET Service

The M-SET service allows for modification of data in the management information base. It is used to change the value or values of one or more attributes in one or more managed objects.

The M-SET service may be either a confirmed or a nonconfirmed service. Table 13.2, part (c), lists the parameters used in the M-SET service.

The following parameters in the M-SET.request and indication primitives have the same meaning as the corresponding parameters in the M-GET service: invoke identifier, base-object class, base-object instance, scope, filter, access control, and synchronization. The mode parameter specifies whether confirmed or nonconfirmed service is requested. The modification list contains a set of attribute-modification specifications, each of which contains:

- *Attribute identifier:* Identifies the attribute or attribute group whose value(s) are to be modified.

- *Attribute value:* Except for the set-to-default option, this parameter lists the value or values to be used in modifying the attribute or attributes.

- *Modify operator:* Specifies one of the following modification functions:
  - *Replace:* Replace current attribute values with those in the attribute-value list.
  - *Add value:* For set-valued attributes, add the specified attribute values to the current set of attribute values. This is a set-union operation; only those values not already in the set are added.
  - *Remove value:* For set-valued attributes, remove those specified values that are currently in the set. If a value is specified that is not in the set, no error occurs.
  - *Set to default:* For a single-valued attribute, the attribute is set to its default value. For a set-valued attribute, the value(s) of the attribute shall be set to the default value(s).

If no operator is specified, the replace operator is assumed.

For the nonconfirmed service, the target CMIS user will simply attempt to perform the requested set operation and will not report either success or failure.

For the confirmed service, the operation of the M-SET service follows the same pattern as that for the M-GET service. As with the M-GET service, multiple responses to an M-SET.request may be generated, and these are returned in a series of M-SET.response primitives using the linked-identifier parameter.

The error parameter is included in a failure notification. The following errors may be reported (Table 13.4):

- Access denied
- Class-instance conflict
- Complexity limitation
- Duplicate invocation
- Invalid filter
- Invalid scope
- Mistyped argument
- No such object class
- No such object instance
- Processing failure
- Resource limitation
- Set-list error
- Synchronization not supported
- Unrecognized operation

Several aspects of the semantics of the M-SET service interact in such a way as to make this a rather complex operation, and so care must be taken in its use. These aspects are:

- Scoping and filtering: scoping and filtering may be used to indicate that the set operation is intended for multiple objects. Note that the collection of objects selected may not have the exact same set of attributes.
- Synchronization: if atomic synchronization is selected, then the set operation will only be performed if it can be successfully performed on all selected objects.
- Partial success within an object: it is possible that some attribute values cannot be modified, for one of the reasons listed in the set list error parameter:
  - access denied: the requested operation was not performed for reasons pertinent to the security of the open system
  - invalid attribute value: the attribute value specified was out of range or otherwise inappropriate
  - invalid operator: the modify operator specified is not recognized
  - invalid operation: the modify operator specified may not be performed on the specified attribute
  - no such attribute: the identifier for the specified attribute was not recognized

If some attribute values cannot be modified, the other attribute values specified in the set operation are modified for this object.

To see the interaction between these three concepts, let us assume that a set request is issued that specifies a number of different attributes in a number of objects. The following strategies may be adopted:

- Objective: perform the set operation on those objects for which the specified set operation can be performed successfully.
  Strategy: specify best-effort synchronization.

- Objective: perform the set operation only on those objects that contain all attributes; it is not necessary that the operation can be performed successfully on all objects.
  Strategy: specify best-effort synchronization; use a filter that includes the *present* assertion for every listed attribute.

- Objective: perform the set operation on all objects only if it can be performed successfully on all objects; it is not necessary that all objects contain all attributes.
  Strategy: specify atomic synchronization.

- Objective: perform the set operation only on those objects that contain all attributes, but only if the operation can be performed successfully on all objects that contain all attributes.
  Strategy: specify atomic synchronization; use a filter that includes the *present* assertion for every listed attribute.

It is instructive to compare the M-SET service with the SNMP set operation. The two are not exactly comparable because of the differences in MIB structures, but we can make the following observations. The SNMP set operation is atomic: it is only performed if it can be performed on all objects specified in the set request. Therefore, the SNMP set appears comparable to M-SET with atomic synchronization. However, remember that an object in SNMP is more comparable to an attribute in OSI systems management than to an object in OSI systems management. The M-SET operation applied to a single object is not atomic: the responding CMIS user will modify those attributes within the object that it is permissible and possible to modify, even if some attributes can not be modified. On the other hand, the M-SET operation applied to multiple objects is not atomic within each selected object but may be either atomic or not atomic across objects, depending on which synchronization alternative is chosen. Furthermore, within CMIS, there is the concept of scoping and filtering, which enables objects to be included or excluded from the set operation on the basis of assertions in the filtering parameter. If an object is selected by the scoping parameter but filtered out by the filtering parameter, that object does not count as unsuccessful in the case of atomic synchronization. Thus, the M-SET operation is considerably more flexible and powerful than the SNMP set operation.

13.1.4.3   M-ACTION Service

The M-ACTION service allows the invocation of a predefined action procedure specified as part of a managed object. The request specifies the type of the action and the input parameters.

The M-ACTION service may be either a confirmed or a nonconfirmed service. Table 13.2, part (d), lists the parameters used in the M-ACTION service.

The following parameters in the M-ACTION.request and indication primitives have the same meaning as the corresponding parameters in the M-SET service: invoke identifier, mode, base-object class, base-object instance, scope, filter, access control, and synchronization. The action-type parameter specifies a particular action to be taken. The action-information parameter, if present, provides additional information about the action requested, including operands, variations, and limitations.

For the nonconfirmed service, the target CMIS user will simply attempt to perform the requested action and will not report either success or failure. For the confirmed service, the operation of the M-ACTION service follows the same pattern as that for the M-GET service. As with the M-GET service, multiple responses to an M-ACTION.request may be generated, and these are returned in a series of M-ACTION.response primitives using the linked-identifier parameter.

The response when a successful action is performed may simply include the managed-object class and instance, confirming that the action has been taken. It may also include the action-type and action-reply parameters, which specify the exact action taken and provide additional information about the result of the action.

The error parameter is included in a failure notification. The following errors may be reported (Table 13.4):

- Access denied
- Class-instance conflict
- Complexity limitation
- Duplicate invocation
- Invalid argument value
- Invalid filter
- Invalid scope
- Mistyped argument
- No such action
- No such argument
- No such object class
- No such object instance
- Processing failure
- Resource limitation
- Synchronization not supported
- Unrecognized operation

13.1.4.4 M-CREATE Service

The M-CREATE primitive is used to create a new instance of an object class. The conditional packages and attribute values that the managed object is to have may be specified as part of the request, or an existing instance can be referenced as a model.

The M-CREATE service is always a confirmed service. Table 13.2, part (e), lists the parameters used in the M-CREATE primitives.

As before, the invoke-identifier parameter in the M-CREATE.request primitive is a unique value assigned to this request. The managed-object-class parameter indicates the object class of the new object instance to be created. In creating a new object, the target CMIS user must assign it an object-instance identifier and must assign values to its attributes. The object-instance identifier may be selected in one of three ways:

1. If the superior-object-instance parameter is present, it identifies the existing managed-object instance in the MIB (management information base) of the target CMIS user that is to be the superior of the new managed-object instance. This is sufficient information to specify the object-instance identifier of the new object instance.

2. If the superior-object-instance parameter is not present, then the managed-object-instance identifier may be present. The value of this parameter is the object-instance identifier that is to be assigned to the new object.

3. If neither of the two parameters just listed is present, then the target CMIS user assigns a value to the identification of the instance.

Values for the attributes of the new object instance may be assigned in one of three ways:

1. If the attribute-list parameter is present, it contains a list of attribute identifiers and values. The corresponding attributes in the new object are assigned these values.

2. If the reference-object-instance parameter is present, it specifies an existing instance of an object of the same class as the object to be created and in the MIB of the target CMIS user. For those attributes not included in the attribute-list parameter, the attribute values of the reference object are assigned to the corresponding attributes in the new object.

3. If the reference-object-instance parameter is not present, those attributes not included in the attribute-list parameter, and for which default values are specified in the definition of the object class, are assigned the default values.

If the requested object is successfully created, the target CMIS user issues an M-CRE-ATE.response without an error field. The managed-object-class parameter may be included. The managed-object-instance parameter must be included if the instance identifier is assigned by the target user; otherwise, its presence is optional. The attribute-list parameter is also optional; when included, it contains a complete list of all the new object's attributes and their values.

The error parameter is included in a failure notification. The following errors may be reported (Table 13.4):

- Access denied
- Class-instance conflict
- Duplicate invocation
- Duplicate managed-object instance
- Invalid attribute value
- Invalid object instance
- Missing attribute value
- Mistyped argument
- No such attribute
- No such object class
- No such object instance
- No such reference object
- Processing failure

- Resource limitation

- Unrecognized operation

13.1.4.5 M-DELETE Service

The M-DELETE service is used to delete one or more objects from the management information base. The M-DELETE service is always a confirmed service. Table 13.2, part (f), lists the parameters used in the M-DELETE primitives.

The parameters used in the M-DELETE.request primitive have the same meaning as the corresponding parameters used in the M-GET service. The request primitive has a unique invoke identifier. It specifies a base object and base-object instance, and may request scoping, filtering, and synchronization, as well as access control. Thus, the request may be for the deletion of a single object or a number of objects.

The operation of the M-DELETE service follows the same pattern as that for the M-GET service. As with the M-GET service, multiple responses to an M-DELETE.request may be generated, one per object, and these are returned in a series of M-DELETE.response primitives using the linked-identifier parameter.

The error parameter is included in a failure notification. The following errors may be reported (Table 13.4):

- Access denied

- Class-instance conflict

- Complexity limitation

- Duplicate invocation

- Invalid filter

- Invalid scope

- Mistyped argument

- No such object class

- No such object instance

- Processing failure

- Resource limitation

- Synchronization not supported

- Unrecognized operation

13.1.4.6 M-CANCEL-GET Service

The M-CANCEL-GET service is used to stop a lengthy GET operation. The reason why only the GET operation may be canceled is that it is difficult to ensure the consistency of the MIB if an operation that alters the MIB is canceled after initiation.

The M-CANCEL-GET service is always a confirmed service. Table 13.2, part (g), lists the parameters used in the M-CANCEL-GET primitives.

The M-CANCEL-GET primitive has only two parameters. The invoke-identifier parameter uniquely identifies this request. The Get-invoke-identifier parameter identifies the M-GET.request that is to be canceled.

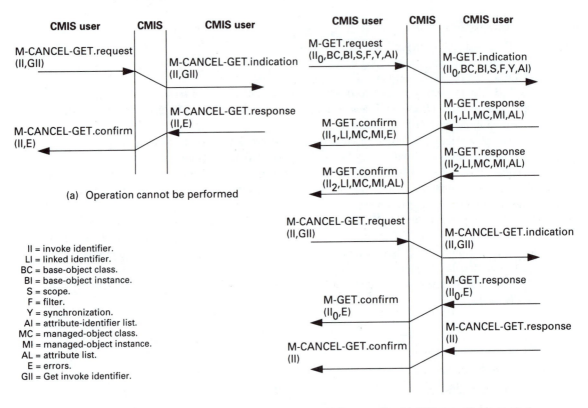

Figure 13.5 Time-Sequence Diagrams for M-CANCEL-GET Service

Figure 13.5 illustrates two possible outcomes of a cancellation request. If the operation cannot be performed, the target user returns an M-CANCEL-GET.response with one of the following error codes (Table 13.4):

- Duplicate invocation
- Mistyped operation
- No such invoke identifier
- Processing failure
- Resource limitation
- Unrecognized operation

If it is able to do so, the target CMIS user cancels the outstanding M-GET operation. It then issues an M-GET.response primitive with the operation-canceled error code and an M-CANCEL-GET.response primitive (Figure 13.5, part [b]).

Table 13.5 CMIS Functional Units

Kernel functional unit
  M-EVENT-REPORT
  M-GET
  M-SET   } Minus linked-identification parameter, scope and synchronization
  M-ACTION } parameters, filter parameter
  M-CREATE
  M-DELETE
Multiple-object-selection functional unit
  Addition of scope and synchronization parameters to kernel functional unit
Filter functional unit
  Addition of filter parameter to kernel functional unit
Multiple-reply functional unit
  Addition of linked-identification parameter to kernel functional unit
Extended-service functional unit
  Presentation-layer services in addition to the P-DATA service
Cancel-Get functional unit
  M-CANCEL-GET

13.1.5 Association Services

For two users to make use of CMIS to perform management operations, they must first establish an application association. For this purpose, CMIS relies on the services of the association-control-service element (ACSE) which is described in Appendix 13A.

There are actually two functions performed by ACSE for CMIS users. The first is to establish an application association that can be used to exchange CMIS-service primitives. Second, at the time of association establishment, the two users agree on which features of CMIS will be used on this association. These features are expressed in terms of functional units.

A functional unit defines a set of capabilities to be supplied by the service. Table 13.5 lists the functional units for CMIS. The default service provided is the kernel functional unit. The kernel functional unit consists of all the CMIS-service primitives except M-CANCEL-GET, with the limitation that multiple responses are not supported and that scoping, synchronization, and filtering are not supported. These limitations apply to the M-GET, M-SET, and M-ACTION services. The two users may negotiate additional functional units to be added to the kernel functional unit for the given association.

An application is established by using the A-ASSOCIATE service of the ACSE. The CMIS user supplies the required parameters when issuing an A-ASSOCIATE.request (see Table 13.9 in Appendix 13A). The ACSE user-information parameter is broken down into three CMIS-specific parts:

1. *Functional units:* This parameter may appear in either the request/indication or the response/confirm primitives and is the list of additional functional units proposed for this association by the issuing user. Only those functional units contained in both lists are added to the kernel functional unit.

2. *Access control:* information of unspecified form to be used for access control.

3. *User information:* application-specific information.

An association may be released by either CMIS user. An orderly release is accomplished with the A-RELEASE service, and an abrupt release is accomplished with the A-ABORT service.

13.2   COMMON MANAGEMENT INFORMATION PROTOCOL

While the common management information service (CMIS) defines the services for management operations, the common management information protocol (CMIP) defines procedures for the transmission of management information and defines the syntax for the management service of CMIS. CMIP is defined in terms of CMIP protocol data units that are exchanged between peer common management information service elements (CMISEs) to carry out the CMIS service.

13.2.1   CMIP Operation

To understand the operation of CMIP, we need to see it in context with the CMISE-service user and the services that CMISE relies on. Figure 13.1 shows this relationship. As discussed in section 13.1, the CMIS provides seven services for performing management operations, in the form of service primitives. In addition, CMISE users need to be able to establish associations in order to perform management operations. These latter services are provided by the association-control-service element (ACSE) and are provided by CMISE as a pass-through; there is no CMIP involved. For the management-operation services, the CMISE employs a CMIP to exchange PDUs. The CMIP, in turn, relies on the services of the remote-operations-service element (ROSE). Both ACSE and ROSE rely on the presentation service.

Table 13.6 lists the 11 PDUs that make up the CMIP. There are up to three types of information carried in each data unit. The arguments entry defines the arguments, or parameters, carried in the data unit that are derived from the triggering CMISE-service primitive. The results and errors entries contain information from the performing entity about the result of the systems-management operation. These values are derived from the CMISE response primitive.

Table 13.7 shows the mapping between the CMIS primitives and the CMIP data units. Note that in carrying the response to M-GET, M-SET, M-ACTION, and M-DELETE service primitives, the CMIP data unit, in addition to its other parameters, includes a linked-Id parameter, in order to link multiple responses to the invoking operation that caused them. This linkage facility is discussed in section 13.1.

As an example of the use of CMIP to implement a CMIS service, Figure 13.6 illustrates the M-GET service. Implementations of the other services exhibit similar behavior. The following sequence of events occurs:

1. An M-GET.request primitive is received from a CMISE user. The parameters in the primitive distinguish this operation from others supported by CMISE, provide information about the managed object, and provide other relevant information. The request is handled by the common management information protocol machine (CMIPM).

2. The CMIPM constructs an m-Get application-protocol data unit (APDU) that contains the parameters in the M-GET.request primitive.

3. The CMIPM uses the RO-INVOKE.request service of the ROSE to send the APDU to the destination.

4. The ROSE delivers the APDU to the responding CMIPM in an RO-INVOKE.indication.

5. If the data unit is acceptable, the CMIPM issues an M-GET.indication to the destination CMISE user, containing the parameters from the original request primitive. This directs the peer service user to perform the requested GET operation and report the results.

6. The responding CMISE user issues an M-GET.response primitive to the responding CMIPM. The parameters in the primitive distinguish this operation from others supported by CMISE, provide the requested information from the managed object, and provide other relevant information. If this operation fails, the primitive includes an error parameter to describe the nature of the error.

7. The responding CMIPM constructs an m-Get APDU that contains the parameters in the M-GET.response primitive.

8. If the operation is successful, the CMIPM uses the RO-RESULT.request service of the ROSE to send the APDU back to the initiating system.

9. The ROSE delivers the APDU to the initiating CMIPM in an RO-RESULT.indication.

10. The CMIPM issues an M-GET.confirmation to the initiating CMISE user.

Figure 13.7, part (a), illustrates the sequence of events in terms of service primitives and APDUs. The figure also illustrates other possible outcomes of an M-GET.request. If the operation fails, the m-Get includes the error parameter obtained from the responding CMISE user, and the m-Get APDU is sent using the RO-ERROR service. Table 13.6 lists the possible error-parameter values for all the CMIP APDUs.

If the arriving APDU from the requesting system is in error, then no indication is given to the destination CMISE user. Instead, the responding CMIPM issues an m-Get APDU using the RO-REJECT service.

Finally, if the M-GET operation specifies more than one managed object, each operation in the responding CSIME user results in the issuance of a separate M-GET.response. Each response includes the linked-Id parameter except the last. For each intermediate response, the responding CMIPM issues an m-Linked-Reply APDU using the RO-INVOKE service.

13.2.2 Use of ROSE

CMIP makes use of ROSE to transfer CMIP PDUs; see Appendix 13B for a discussion of ROSE. The following rules apply to the use of ROSE:

1. CMIP always uses ROSE association class 3. Both the association initiator and the association responder can invoke operations.

2. For confirmed CMIS operations, CMIP makes use of ROSE operation class 1 or class 2. That is, the reporting mode is to return a result for both success or failure, and the operation mode may be either synchronous (invoker requires a reply before invoking another operation) or asynchronous (invoker may invoke further operations without awaiting a reply). The choice of operation class is a local matter.

Table 13.6 CMIP Data Units

CMIP Data Unit	Arguments	Results	Errors
m-EventReport	managedObjectClass, managedObjectInstance, eventTime, eventType, eventInfo	—	—
m-EventReport-Confirmed	managedObjectClass, managedObjectInstance, eventTime, eventType, eventInfo	managedObjectClass, managedObjectInstance, currentTime, eventReply	invalidArgumentValue, noSuchArgument, noSuchEventType, noSuchObjectClass, noSuchObjectInstance, processingFailure
m-Get	baseManagedObjectClass, baseManagedObjectInstance, accessControl, synchronization, scope, filter, attributeIdList	managedObjectClass, managedObjectInstance, currentTime, attributeList	accessDenied, classInstanceConflict, complexityLimitation, getListError, invalidFilter, invalidScope, noSuchObjectClass, noSuchObject-Instance, operationCanceled, processingFailure, syncNotSupported
m-Linked-Reply	getResult, getListError, setResult, setListError, actionResult, processingFailure, deleteResult, actionError, deleteError	—	—
m-Set	baseManagedObjectClass, baseManagedObjectInstance, accessControl, synchronization, scope, filter, modificationList	—	—
m-Set-Confirmed	baseManagedObjectClass, baseManagedObjectInstance, accessControl, synchronization, scope, filter, modificationList	managedObjectClass, managedObjectInstance, currentTime, attributeList	—

Service	Parameters	Reply	Errors
m-Action	baseManagedObjectClass, baseManagedObjectInstance, accessControl, synchronization, scope, filter, actionInfo	—	
m-Action-Confirmed	baseManagedObjectClass, baseManagedObjectInstance, accessControl, synchronization, scope, filter, actionInfo	managedObjectClass, managedObjectInstance, currentTime, actionReply	accessDenied, classInstanceConflict, complexityLimitation, invalidScope, invalidArgumentValue, invalidFilter, noSuchAction, noSuchArgument, noSuchObjectClass, noSuchObjectInstance, processingFailure, syncNotSupported
m-Create	managedObjectClass, objectInstance, accessControl, referenceObjectInstance, attributeList	managedObjectClass, managedObjectInstance, currentTime, attributeList	accessDenied, classInstanceConflict, duplicateManagedObjectInstance, invalidAttributeValue, invalidObjectInstance, missingAttributeValue, noSuchAttribute, noSuchObjectClass, noSuchObjectInstance, noSuchReferenceObject, processingFailure
m-Delete	baseManagedObjectClass, baseManagedObjectInstance, accessControl, synchronization, scope, filter	managedObjectClass, managedObjectInstance, currentTime	accessDenied, classInstanceConflict, complexityLimitation, invalidFilter, invalidScope, noSuchObjectClass, noSuchObjectInstance, processingFailure, syncNotSupported
m-Cancel-Get-Confirmed	getInvokedId	—	mistypedOperation, noSuchInvokeId, processingFailure

Table 13.7 Correspondence between CMISE Primitives and CMIP Data Units

CMIS Primitive	Mode	Linked-Id	CMIP Data Unit
M-EVENT-REPORT request/indication	Nonconfirmed	Not applicable	m-EventReport
M-EVENT-REPORT request/indication	Confirmed	Not applicable	m-EventReport-Confirmed
M-EVENT-REPORT response/confirm	Not applicable	Not applicable	m-EventReport-Confirmed
M-GET request/indication	Confirmed	Not applicable	m-Get
M-GET response/confirm	Not applicable	Absent	m-Get
M-GET response/confirm	Not applicable	Present	m-Linked-Reply
M-SET request/indication	Nonconfirmed	Not applicable	m-Set
M-SET request/indication	Confirmed	Not applicable	m-Set-Confirmed
M-SET response/confirm	Not applicable	Absent	m-Set-Confirmed
M-SET response/confirm	Not applicable	Present	m-Linked-Reply
M-ACTION request/indication	Nonconfirmed	Not applicable	m-Action
M-ACTION request/indication	Confirmed	Not applicable	m-Action-Confirmed
M-ACTION response/confirm	Not applicable	Absent	m-Action-Confirmed
M-ACTION response/confirm	Not applicable	Present	m-Linked-Reply
M-CREATE request/indication	Confirmed	Not applicable	m-Create
M-CREATE response/confirm	Not applicable	Not applicable	m-Create
M-DELETE request/indication	Confirmed	Not applicable	m-Delete
M-DELETE response/confirm	Not applicable	Absent	m-Delete
M-DELETE response/confirm	Not applicable	Present	m-Linked-Reply
M-CANCEL-GET request/indication	Confirmed	Not applicable	m-Cancel-Get-Confirmed
M-CANCEL-GET response/confirm	Not applicable	Not applicable	m-Cancel-Get-Confirmed

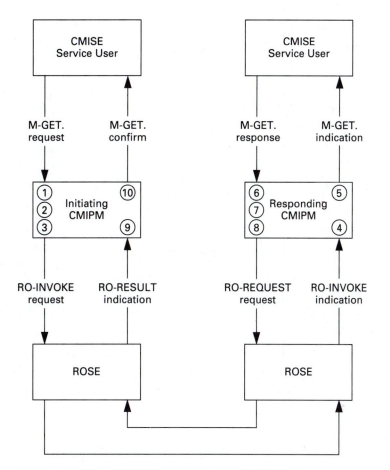

Based on: U. Black, *OSI: A Model for Computer Communications Standards* (Englewood Cliffs, N.J.: Prentice-Hall, 1991).

Figure 13.6 CMIP GET Operation

3. For unconfirmed CMIS operations, ROSE operation class 5 is used (no reply, asynchronous operation).

As an example of the definition of the CMIP operations, Figure 13.8 shows the definition of the m-Get operation using the ASN.1 remote-operations notation. For the sake of brevity, only one of the error definitions is shown.

13.3 PRACTICAL ISSUES

13.3.1 Performance

Three competing requirements for a network-management system can be stated:

1. It should not seriously degrade the network operation it is intended to maintain.

2. Its decisions must be made and its control actions taken quickly before network conditions

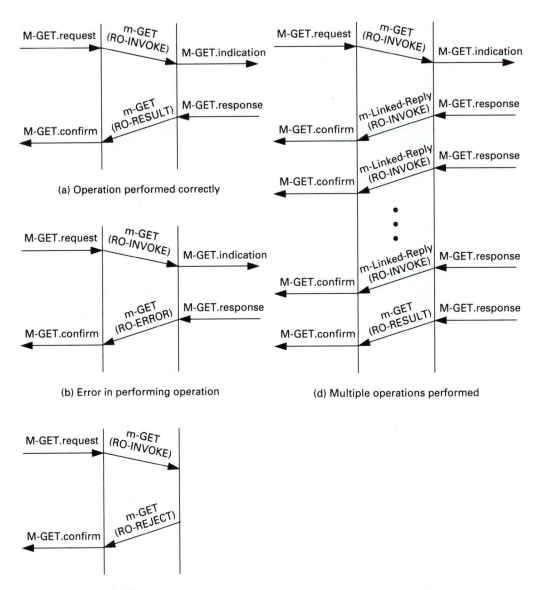

Figure 13.7   CMIP Support of the M-GET Service

significantly change (otherwise, instability may arise in the measurement/control-action feedback loop).

3.   It should provide a rich set of services to handle a wide range of network-management functions and to provide detailed monitoring and control.

```
m-Get  OPERATION
       ARGUMENT    GetArgument
       RESULT      GetResult
       ERRORS  {   accessDenied, classInstanceConflict, complexityLimitation, getListError, invalidFilter, invalidScope,
                   noSuchObjectClass, noSuchObjectInstance, operationCanceled, processingFailure, syncNotSupported }
       LINKED  {   m-Linked-Reply }

GetArgument ::= SEQUENCE { COMPONENTS OF  BaseManagedObjectId,
                          accessControl       [5] AccessControl OPTIONAL,
                          synchronization     [6] IMPLICIT CMISSync DEFAULT bestEffort,
                          scope               [7] Scope DEFAULT baseObject,
                          filter                  CMISFilter DEFAULT and { },
                          attributeIdList     [12] IMPLICIT SET OF AttributeId OPTIONAL }

BaseManagedObjectId ::= SEQUENCE { baseManagedObjectClass      ObjectClass,
                                   baseManagedObjectInstance   ObjectInstance }

AccessControl ::= EXTERNAL

CMISSync ::= ENUMERATED { bestEffort (0), atomic (1) }

Scope ::= CHOICE { INTEGER { baseObject (0), firstLevelOnly (1), wholeSubtree (2) }
                   individualLevels  [1] IMPLICIT INTEGER,
                   baseToNthLevel   [2] IMPLICIT INTEGER }

GetResult ::= SEQUENCE { managedObjectClass        ObjectClass OPTIONAL,
                         managedObjectInstance     ObjectInstance OPTIONAL,
                         currentTime           [5] IMPLICIT GeneralizedTime OPTIONAL,
                         attributeList         [6] IMPLICIT SET OF attribute OPTIONAL }

classInstanceConflict ERROR
       PARAMETER BaseManagedObjectId
       ::= localValue 20
```

Figure 13.8 ASN.1 Definition of m-Get APDU (ISO 9596)

The first requirement implies that network bandwidth and computing resources be conserved. A useful rule of thumb that has been suggested by a number of designers is that the absolute maximum allowable bandwidth consumption by management operations should be 5 percent (Aronoff et al. 1989). On the other hand, the need for timely action implies that a significant amount of management information be exchanged on a regular basis. Furthermore, the need for a feature-rich network-management service also implies that a lot of management information will be generated.

These issues must be dealt with in any network-management system but become particularly acute in the case of OSI systems management. Three interrelated reasons can be cited:

1. OSI systems management offers a broad range of functions and services. If the user takes advantage of these services, the results are sizable implementations at each node and a lot of network traffic.

2. The OSI MIB (management information base) is large and complex. The individual unit of management is the object, which may include attributes, notifications, and actions. There may be many such objects in a large structure, including objects closely tied to resources, as well as those related to management functions, such as logs, summarization objects, and so forth.

3. CMIP PDUs tend to be large because of the use of BER (basic encoding rules) encoding. Although data encoded using BER are machine-independent, they are usually not as compact as machine-dependent representations. Furthermore, CMIP uses the seven-layer OSI architecture, resulting in substantial blocks of data for individual exchanges.

One technique for reducing CMIP traffic is to employ a hierarchy of managers. Local managers can be used to manage small LAN (local area network) segments and convey summary information to more global managers. This reduces overall traffic, since most of the management messages are confined to those network segments where they are needed. A global manager could control local systems by setting parameters in local managers, which then forward these settings to one or more local systems.

Another way to limit CMIP traffic is to be efficient in accessing objects. For example, to access a single object instance, object-class and object-instance identifiers must be supplied, each of which may be a long string of integers. Thus, a rather large PDU may be required to access a single small counter (e.g., a 32-bit counter). If many counters must be interrogated, considerable bandwidth would be consumed. However, if the MIB is properly organized, the scoping and filtering facility of CMIS can be employed so that a reference to a single base object results in access to a number of counters simultaneously.

A third way to reduce network traffic is to streamline the protocol architecture supporting CMIP. This raises issues beyond those related to performance and is dealt with in the next subsection.

13.3.2   Protocol Architecture

The OSI management framework document, ISO 7498–4, has the following to say about support for OSI management:

1. An open system must have sufficient functionality at all seven layers to support a management application before that application can be accessed by another system.
2. When sufficient 7-layer functionality does not exist, layer management functionality can be employed between open systems if the support for those layers is provided.

Let us briefly consider the second point first. This says that layer-management entities may convey management information directly between peers without employing the application layer, including CMIS, for the transfer of that information. This approach, although not nearly as general as CMIS/CMIP, might be employed on local network segments to reduce overhead. This capability also adds robustness to the design. For example, if upper-layer communications were disrupted, systems management would probably cease to function, but management at a lower layer might be able to resolve the problem.

The other point is perhaps a more important one. There are two concerns here:

1. It is desirable to run network-management applications on intermediate systems, such as bridges and routers, without requiring these devices to implement a full-blown seven-layer architecture.
2. Even on end systems with full OSI support, it would be desirable to streamline the lower layers as much as possible to reduce processing and communications overhead.

Keep in mind that these are not just academic architectural design puzzles. These are concrete issues that need to be resolved to enable practical, efficient implementation of OSI management.

A way to address the concerns in the preceding list is to somehow streamline the OSI architecture. Fortunately, an effort in this direction is underway. Recognizing that TCP/IP (transmission-control protocol/internet protocol) is continuing to gain acceptance and that users are growing impatient with the slow pace of OSI deployment, OSI standards developers are working on a slimmed-down version of the seven-layer OSI stack (Eckerson and Messmer 1992). This minimal OSI stack, referred to as the *skinny stack,* specifies a narrow subset of the session, presentation, and application layers that can run on top of either TCP or the OSI transport layer. The skinny stack would make it easier for users to migrate from TCP/IP to OSI and would make it easier to support applications such as CMIS on bridges and routers.

The skinny stack is well suited to the support of CMIP. CMIP requires the use of ACSE and ROSE, which, in turn, require only minimal services from the presentation and session layers.

13.4   SUMMARY

The common management information service (CMIS) provides a basic service for the exchange of management information between systems-management functions. CMIS consists of the following service primitives:

- *M-EVENT-REPORT:* Used to report a notification to a manager that has requested notification.
- *M-GET:* Used by a manager to retrieve management information from an agent.
- *M-SET:* Used by a manager to modify management information in an agent.
- *M-ACTION:* Used to invoke a predefined action procedure specified as part of a managed object. The request specifies the type of the action and the input parameters.

- *M-CREATE:* Used to create a new instance of an object class.

- *M-DELETE:* Used to delete one or more objects.

- *M-CANCEL-GET:* Used to terminate a lengthy GET operation.

The M-GET, M-ACTION, and M-DELETE service primitives, which are primitives that can specify operations on multiple objects, include a linkage parameter to provide for multiple replies to a single request. Although the M-SET primitive also allows specification of multiple objects, it does not support linked replies. For all four of these primitives, a powerful set of tools is provided for object selection. These tools fall into three categories:

1. *Scoping:* identifies the object or objects to which a filter is to be applied. Scoping is based on the containment structure of the MIB.

2. *Filtering:* consists of a Boolean expression with one or more assertions about the presence or values of attributes in a scoped object.

3. *Synchronization:* specifies whether the operation is to be atomic (all selected objects are processed or none is) or best effort (as many objects as possible are processed).

The common management information protocol (CMIP) supports CMIS. CMIP consists of a set of PDUs onto which the CMIS primitives are mapped. CMIP, in turn, makes use of ASCE (association-control-service element), ROSE (remote-operations-service element), and the presentation service.

APPENDIX 13A   Association-Control-Service Element

One set of services that is a common requirement of almost all applications is that of establishing, maintaining, and terminating connections between application entities. Accordingly, service (ISO 8649, X.217) and protocol (ISO 8650, X.227) standards for an association-control-service element (ACSE) have been developed.

The discussion in this appendix makes reference to concepts from the presentation and session layers. If the reader is unfamiliar with these concepts, see Stallings (1993c).

13A.1   BASIC CONCEPTS

Two concepts are essential to an understanding of the association-control facility: application association and application context; these are defined in Table 13.8. The concept of *application association* needs to be contrasted with that of presentation connection. The application association and the presentation connection are actually two different aspects of the same thing—namely, the relationship that exists between two application entities that are performing a shared task. From the point of view of the connection mechanisms needed to support information exchange, the relationship is a presentation connection. The presentation connection provides a *pipe* for the transfer of abstract data values with no constraints on the way these values are used. From the point of view of the information exchange itself, the relationship is an application association, which supports agreed procedures and shared semantics for the use of the corresponding presentation connection.

Table 13.8 Application-Layer Terms (ISO 7498, ISO 8649, ISO 9545)

Application Association

A cooperative relationship between two application entities formed by the exchange of application protocol control information through their use of presentation services.

Application Context

A set of rules shared in common by two application entity invocations in order to enable their cooperative operation. An application association has only one application context.

Application Entity Invocation

A specific utilization of part or all of the capabilities of a given application-entity in support of the communication requirements of an application-process-invocation.

Application Process Invocation

A specific utilization of part or all of the capabilities of a given application-process in support of a specific occasion of information processing.

Application Process

A set of resources, including processing resources, within a real open system that may be used to perform a particular information processing activity.

Application Service Element

A part of an application entity which provides an OSI environment capability, using underlying services where appropriate.

Application Entity

The aspects of an application process pertinent to OSI.

The application association supports the meaningful cooperative exchange between application entities within a defined *application context*. An application context is a mutually agreeable relationship between application entities in different open systems. The relationship exists for a period of time during which a cooperative task is performed. The relationship includes an agreement as to which application-service elements (ASEs) will be employed and the options and procedures related to those ASEs.

13A.2 ASSOCIATION-CONTROL SERVICE

Table 13.9 lists the primitives and parameters for the ACSE service. The purpose of this service is to provide for the establishment and termination of application associations. Note that many of the parameters provided by a user are not used directly by the application-association service but are mapped directly into parameters for the presentation or session service.

The A-ASSOCIATE service is used to set up an application association. A one-to-one correspondence exists between an application association and a presentation connection and, therefore, between an application association and a session connection. The A-ASSOCIATE primitives are supported by the P-CONNECT primitives. The added value of the association-control service is represented by those parameters that are carried in APDUs and not mapped onto the lower layers:

- Application-context name
- Calling, called, and responding application-process (AP) titles
- Calling, called, and responding application-entity (AE) qualifiers

Table 13.9 Association-Control-Service Primitives and Parameters

Primitive	Parameters Carried in APDU	Parameters Mapped Directly to Presentation Service	Parameters Mapped Directly to Session Service
A-ASSOCIATE.request	application-context name, calling AP title, calling AE qualifier, calling AP invocation-identifier, calling AE invocation-identifier, called AP title, called AE qualifier, called AP invocation-identifier, called AE invocation-identifier, user information	mode, calling presentation address, called presentation address, presentation-context definition list, default presentation-context name, presentation requirements	quality of service, session requirements, serial number, token assignment, session-connection identifier
A-ASSOCIATE.indication	application-context name, calling AP title, calling AE qualifier, calling AP invocation-identifier, calling AE invocation-identifier, called AP title, called AE qualifier, called AP invocation-identifier, called AE invocation-identifier, user information	mode, calling presentation address, called presentation address, presentation-context definition list, presentation-context definition result list, default presentation-context name, presentation requirements	quality of service, session requirements, serial number, token assignment, session-connection identifier

Primitive	Parameters		
A-ASSOCIATE.response	application-context name, responding AP title, responding AE qualifier, responding AP invocation-identifier, responding AE invocation-identifier, user information, result, diagnostic	responding presentation address, presentation-context definition result list, default presentation-context result, presentation requirements	quality of service, session requirements, serial number, token assignment, session-connection identifier
A-ASSOCIATE.confirm	application-context name, responding AP title, responding AE qualifier, responding AP invocation-identifier, responding AE invocation-identifier, user information, result, result source, diagnostic	responding presentation address, presentation-context definition result list, default presentation-context result, presentation requirements	quality of service, session requirements, serial number, token assignment, session-connection identifier
A-RELEASE.request/indication	reason, user information		
A-RELEASE.response/confirm	reason, user information, result		
A-ABORT.request	user information		
A-ABORT.indication	abort source, user information		
A-P-ABORT.indication	provider reason		

- Calling, called, and responding AP invocation-identifiers
- Calling, called, and responding AE invocation-identifiers
- User information
- Result, result source
- Diagnostic

Application-context names identify the context; the responder may propose a different application context than the requester. The result of this negotiation is not defined in the standard but is application-specific. Names may be assigned to application contexts by standards organizations as part of the application-layer standards.

The next four bulleted entries are parameters that unambiguously identify application processes, application entities, and the invocations of application processes and entities (see Table 13.8).

Either the requester or the accepter may optionally include user information. Its meaning depends on the application context that accompanies the primitive.

The result parameter indicates the result of using the A-ASSOCIATE service and takes one of the following values:

- Accepted
- Rejected (permanent)
- Rejected (transient)

If the association is accepted, then an application association is created simultaneously with the underlying presentation and session connections.

The result-source parameter indicates that the result is provided by either the responding ACSE user, ACSE, or the presentation-service provider.

The diagnostic parameter is only used if the result parameter has the value rejected (permanent) or rejected (transient). If the result-source parameter has the value ACSE service provider, then the diagnostic parameter takes on one of the following values:

- No reason given
- No common ACSE version

If the result-source parameter has the value ACSE service user, then the diagnostic parameter takes on one of the following values:

- No reason given
- Application-context name not supported
- Calling AP title not recognized
- Calling AE qualifier not recognized
- Calling AP invocation-identifier not recognized
- Calling AE invocation-identifier not recognized
- Called AP title not recognized
- Called AE qualifier not recognized

- Called AP invocation-identifier not recognized
- Called AE invocation-identifier not recognized

Of the A-ASSOCIATE parameters, only the application-context name, the result, and the result-source parameters are mandatory. The others may be set by prior agreement to simplify implementation.

The A-RELEASE service is used for the orderly release of an association. If the session negotiated-release functional unit was selected for the association, the responder may respond negatively, thus causing the unsuccessful completion of the release service and the continuation of the association. For the request and indication primitives, the reason parameter takes on one of the following values: normal, urgent, or user-defined. For the response and confirm primitives, it takes on one of the following values: normal, not finished, or user-defined. The result parameter indicates acceptance or rejection of the release request. If the release is successful, then the application association is released simultaneously with the underlying presentation and session connections.

The A-ABORT and A-P-ABORT services cause the termination of the application association simultaneously with the underlying presentation and session connections. With A-ABORT, the abort-source parameter indicates that the abort was initiated by either the ACSE or the other service user. With A-P-ABORT, the provider-reason parameter is mapped directly from the P-P-ABORT service.

APPENDIX 13B Remote-Operations-Service Element

Though not as universally employed as the ACSE (association-control-service element), the remote-operations-service element (ROSE) is one of the most widely used of the general-purpose application-service entities. ROSE is intended to support interactive types of applications, which are characterized by a request by one application for another application to perform some operation. In the programming field, a common example of this mechanism is the remote procedure call.

13B.1 PRINCIPLES

The basic service provided by ROSE is the facility for invoking an operation on a remote open system. The application entity (AE) invoking the operation issues a request to the peer AE, specifying a particular operation to be performed. The other AE attempts to perform the operation and may report the outcome of the attempt. The interchange between the two entities is carried out in the context of an application association.

13B.1.1 Operation Class

Operations invoked by one application entity (*the invoker*) are performed by the other application entity (*the performer*). The interaction between two entities that results in an operation's being attempted is characterized by an operation class, which is agreed between the two entities for each separate invocation. The operation class is defined by two characteristics of the interchange: the

Table 13.10 ROSE Operation Classes

		Operation Mode	
		Synchronous	**Asynchronous**
Reporting Mode	If success, return result reply. If failure, return error reply.	Operation class 1	Operation class 2
	If success, no reply. If failure, return error reply.		Operation class 3
	If success, return result reply. If failure, no reply.		Operation class 4
	If success, no reply. If failure, no reply.		Operation class 5

reporting behavior of the AE attempting the operation and whether the interchange is synchronous or asynchronous (Table 13.10).

The performing AE may observe one of four types of reporting behavior:

1. Always report a result, whether it is success or failure.

2. Only report a failure.

3. Only report a success.

4. Do not report the result.

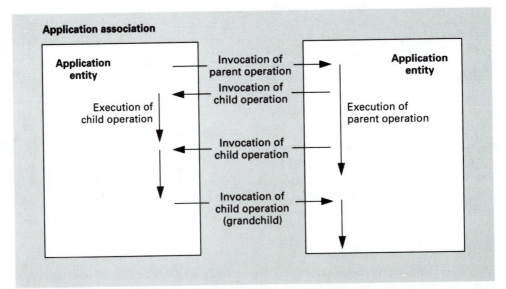

Figure 13.9 Linked Operations

If a result, success or failure, is always reported, then the invoking AE has the option of waiting or not waiting for a report before continuing. With synchronous operation, the invoker requires a reply from the performer before invoking another operation. With asynchronous operation, the invoker may continue to invoke further operations without awaiting a reply.

13B.1.2 Association Class

ROSE may be used by two application entities that share an application association to invoke one or more operations. The AE that initiates an application association (by issuing an A-ASSOCI-ATE.request to ACSE) is called the *association initiator,* whereas the AE that responds to the request is called the *association responder.* The two AEs must agree on one of three association classes that will hold for the life of the association:

1. *Association class 1:* Only the association initiator can invoke operations.

2. *Association class 2:* Only the association responder can invoke operations.

3. *Association class 3:* Both the association initiator and the association responder can invoke operations.

The association class is an attribute of an application context and must be selected at the time that the association is set up using ACSE.

When association class 3 is selected, it is possible to group operations into a set of linked operations, which is formed by one parent operation and one or more child operations. The sequence is as follows:

1. One AE invokes an operation on the peer AE, referred to as the parent operation.

2. The performer of the parent operation may invoke zero, one, or more child operations during the execution of the parent operation. Thus, each of these child operations is performed by the AE that is the invoker of the corresponding parent operation.

3. Each child operation may, in turn, function as a parent operation to trigger zero, one, or more child operations in a recursive fashion.

Figure 13.9 illustrates the concept of linked operations.

13B.2 REMOTE-OPERATIONS-SERVICE DEFINITION

The remote-operations service is defined in X.219 and ISO 9072-1. Table 13.11 lists the remote-operations-service primitives and parameters. The RO-INVOKE primitive is used for the invoker to request an operation of the performer. The parameters of this primitive are:

- *Operation value:* This identifies the operation to be performed. The identity and nature of the operation are beyond the scope of ROSE and must be agreed between the two application entities.

- *Operation class:* indicates one of the five operation classes (Table 13.10).

- *Argument:* the argument or list of arguments that accompany the operation. Again, the nature of these arguments is beyond the scope of ROSE.

Table 13.11 Remote-Operations-Service Primitives and Parameters

RO-INVOKE.request (operation value, operation class, argument, invoke ID, linked ID, priority)

RO-INVOKE.indication (operation value, argument, invoke ID, linked ID)

RO-RESULT.request (operation value, result, invoke ID, priority)

RO-RESULT.indication (operation value, result, invoke ID)

RO-ERROR.request (error value, error parameter, invoke ID, priority)

RO-ERROR.indication (error value, error parameter, invoke ID)

RO-REJECT-U.request (reject reason, invoke ID, priority)

RO-REJECT-U.indication (reject reason, invoke ID)

RO-REJECT-P.indication (invoke ID, returned parameters, reject reason)

- *Invoke ID:* identifies the request of an RO-INVOKE service and is subsequently used to correlate this request with the corresponding replies. This parameter is needed for asynchronous operation.

- *Linked ID:* If this parameter is present, the invoked operation is a child operation and the parameter is the invoke ID of the linked parent operation.

- *Priority:* identifies the priority of the transfer of the corresponding APDU (application-protocol data unit) relative to other APDUs to be exchanged between the AEs.

The RO-RESULT primitives are used to provide a reply in the event of a successful operation. The result parameter provides information concerning a successfully performed operation and is beyond the scope of ROSE.

The RO-ERROR primitives are used to provide a reply in the event of an unsuccessfully performed operation. The error-value parameter indicates the type of error, and the error parameter provides additional information about the error. Both parameters are beyond the scope of ROSE.

The RO-REJECT-U service is used by a ROSE user to reject a request (RO-INVOKE) if the user has detected a problem. It may also be used to reject a reply (RO-RESULT, RO-ERROR). Table 13.12 lists the values of the reject-reason parameter.

13B.3   REMOTE-OPERATIONS NOTATION

As we have seen, ROSE provides a general-purpose remote-operations service that can be used by a number of application-service elements. Thus, the user of an ASE makes direct use of the services of that ASE and indirect use of the services of ROSE.

Figure 13.10 depicts the structure of these interactions. The ASE user can invoke an operation by issuing a request primitive to the ASE. For example, a CMISE user may issue an M-GET.request. In the figure, a generic OPERATION.request is used. Associated with each OPERATION.request are a number of parameters. Most of these are of interest only to the peer ASE user, but some of these parameters are needed by ROSE. Examples of the latter include invoke identifier and linked

Table 13.12 Values of the Reject-Reason Parameter for the Remote-Operations Service

(a) ROSE-User Reject of an RO-INVOKE

Parameter Value	Interpretation
Duplicate invocation	Invoke-ID parameter is inconsistent or conflicts with outstanding IDs.
Unrecognized operation	Operation is not one of those agreed between the ROSE users.
Mistyped argument	Type of the operation argument is not that agreed between the ROSE users.
Resource limitation	Performer is unable to perform the invoked operation due to resource limitation.
Initiator releasing	Association initiator is not willing to perform the invoked operation because it is about to attempt to release the application association.
Unrecognized linked ID	No operation with an invoke ID equal to the specified linked ID is in progress.
Linked response unexpected	Invoked operation referred to by the linked ID is not a parent operation.
Unexpected child operation	Invoked child operation is not one that the invoked parent operation referred to by the linked ID allows.

(b) ROSE-User Reject of an RO-RESULT

Parameter Value	Interpretation
Unrecognized invocation	No operation with the specified invoke ID is in progress.
Result response unexpected	Invoked operation does not report a result.
Mistyped result	Type of the result parameter is not that agreed between the ROSE users.

(c) ROSE-User Reject of an RO-ERROR

Parameter Value	Interpretation
Unrecognized invocation	No operation with the specified invoke ID is in progress.
Error response unexpected	Invoked operation does not report a failure.
Unrecognized error	Reported error is not one of those agreed between the ROSE users.
Unexpected error	Reported error is not one that the invoked operation may report.
Mistyped parameter	Type of the error parameter is not that agreed between the ROSE users.

(d) ROSE-Provider Reject of an APDU

Parameter Value	Interpretation
Unrecognized APDU	Type of the APDU is not one of the four defined for the ROSE protocol.
Mistyped APDU	Structure of the APDU does not conform to the ROSE protocol.
Badly structured APDU	Structure of the APDU does not conform to the standard notation and encoding.

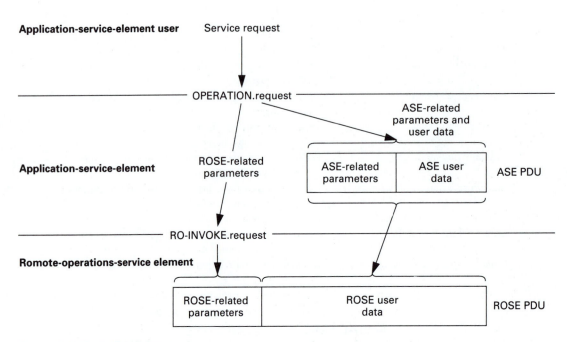

Figure 13.10 Use of ROSE Services

identifier. Accordingly, those parameters needed by ROSE are passed down to ROSE as parameters in the ROSE-service request. The remaining parameters are used by the ASE to construct an ASE protocol data unit. For example, in the case of M-GET.request, the invoke-identifier argument is passed down to ROSE as the invoke-ID argument of the RO-INVOKE.request. The remaining M-GET arguments (base-object class, etc.) are used by CMISE to construct a CMIP protocol data unit. This entire PDU is transparent to ROSE and is passed to ROSE as user data, which are the arguments parameter of the RO-INVOKE.request.

This same pattern is repeated for all ASE-service primitives and all ROSE-service primitives: Some of the parameters in the ASE-service primitive are mapped directly into parameters of a ROSE-service primitive. The remaining parameters are used by the ASE to construct an ASE PDU, which is passed down to ROSE as user data.

Because this pattern is consistent across all ASEs that use ROSE, it is convenient to provide a formal descriptive technique to define the mapping of ASE-service primitives to ROSE-service primitives. Such a technique has been developed. It is referred to as remote-operations notation and is in the form of a set of ASN.1 macros.

Figure 13.11 shows the two macros that are of relevance to CMISE: the OPERATION macro and the ERROR macro.

The OPERATION macro is used to specify a remote operation. The TYPE NOTATION and VALUE NOTATION clauses serve to identify the operation and need not be present. The operation may be accompanied by an argument, specified in the Argument clause. If the operation reports a successful outcome, the Result clause specifies that result. If the operation reports a failure, the

```
OPERATION MACRO ::=

BEGIN

TYPE NOTATION        ::=  ArgumentResultErrorsLinkedOperations

VALUE NOTATION       ::=  value (VALUE CHOICE {
                                    localValue  INTEGER,
                                    globalValue OBJECT IDENTIFIER})

Argument             ::=  "ARGUMENT" NamedType I empty

Result               ::=  "RESULT" ResultType I empty

ResultType           ::=  NamedType I empty

Errors               ::=  "ERRORS" "{"ErrorNames"}" I empty

LinkedOperations     ::=  "LINKED" "{"LinkedOperationsNames"}" I empty

ErrorNames           ::=  ErrorList I empty

ErrorList            ::=  Error I ErrorList "," Error

Error                ::=  value (ERROR)              --shall reference an error value
                          I type  --shall reference an error type if no error value is specified

LinkedOperation-     ::=  OperationList I empty
Names

OperationList        ::=  Operation I OperationList "," Operation

Operation            ::=  value (OPERATION)              --shall reference an operation value
                          I type  --shall reference an operation type if no operation value is specified

NamedType            ::=  identifier type I type

END

ERRORMACRO ::=

BEGIN

TYPE NOTATION        ::=  Parameter

VALUE NOTATION       ::=  value (VALUE CHOICE {
                                    localValue  INTEGER,
                                    globalValue OBJECT INDENTIFIER})

Parameter            ::=  "PARAMETER" NamedType I empty

NamedType            ::=  identifier type I type

END
```

Figure 13.11   Formal Definintion of Remote-Operations Data Types (x.249)

Errors clause specifies that result. If the operation is the parent operation of a set of linked operations, the LinkedOperations clause references the child operations.

The ERROR macro is used to specify an error that occurs during the execution of an operation. Each error item has a value that acts as a code that identifies the error. In addition, the error may be accompanied by a parameter that provides additional information about the error.

14
Systems-Management
Functions

A set of standards has been issued under the general category *systems-management functions* (SMF). The SMFs have been defined to provide the functionality specified in the five systems management functional areas (SMFAs) in order to avoid duplication of functions in the five areas. A given SMF may support requirements in one or more of the five SMFAs; for example, the event-report-management function may be applicable to all SMFAs. Looked at the other way, each SMFA requires several SMFs.

Each of the SMF standards defines the functionality for the SMF and provides a mapping between the services provided by the SMF and CMIS (common management information service). This relationship is depicted in Figure 11.6. Looked at another way, each SMF provides a certain category of access to management information for one or more SMFAs. In this chapter, we summarize the SMFs that are currently defined.

The SMFs are related to each other in complex ways. Table 14.1 shows that some of the SMFs use some of the services of CMISE (common management information service element) directly. For many operations, the object-management function acts as an intermediary, with the other SMFs using the object-management function to gain access to CMISE services.

14.1 OBJECT-MANAGEMENT FUNCTION

ISO 10164-1/X.730 specifies the object-management function. Object management specifies how to create, delete, examine, and change the values of attributes of existing objects. It also specifies the notifications to be sent when the value of an attribute changes.

The object-management function is the most fundamental of all the systems-management functions. In essence, systems management deals with the management of managed objects. Each object represents some entity in the environment over which management control is desired. However, the actual mapping between real objects and their abstract representation as managed objects is beyond the scope of the standards. All that can be observed and controlled through systems management are the managed objects and their attributes.

Table 14.1 Use of CMISE Services by Systems-Management Functions

	M-EVENT-Report	M-GET	M-SET	M-ACTION	M-CREATE	M-DELETE
Object management	√	√	√	√	√	√
State management	√					
Relationship management	√					
Alarm reporting	√					
Event-report management						
Log control						
Security-alarm reporting	√					
Security-audit trail	√					
Access-control management						
Accounting meter	√			√		
Workload monitoring						
Test management	√			√		
Summarization	√			√		

Managed objects can be created and deleted, and values of their attributes can be changed, in one of three distinct ways:

1. Through configuration processes in the local system environment that are outside the scope of OSI (open systems interconnection)

2. Through (N)-layer operation of the (N)-layer-management entity of an open system

3. Through the object-management function as part of the OSI systems-management services

The last method is dealt with in X.730/ISO 10164-1.

Table 14.2 lists the nine services provided by the object-management function.

14.1.1   Pass-Through Services

Six of the object-management services are referred to as pass-through services. These services do not require any independent functionality in the object-management-function module. Rather, requests from higher layers are simply mapped into requests to the common management information service. The mapping is as follows:

Object-Management-Function-Service Primitive	CMIS Service Primitive
PT-CREATE	M-CREATE
PT-DELETE	M-DELETE

Table 14.2 Services Provided by the Object-Management Function

	(a) Pass-Through Services
PT-CREATE	Used to request that a peer service user create a new managed object, complete with its identification and the values of its associated management information, and simultaneously register its identification.
PT-DELETE	Used to request that a peer service user delete a managed object and deregister its identification.
PT-ACTION	Used to request that a peer service user perform an action on one or more managed objects.
PT-SET	Used to request the modification of attribute values by a peer service user.
PT-GET	Used to retrieve attribute values from a peer service user.
PT-EVENT-REPORT	Used to report an event to a peer service user.
	(b) Direct Services
Object-creation reporting	Allows an open system to keep other open systems aware of the creation of new managed objects, so that those other open systems can address and manage newly created objects.
Object-deletion reporting	Allows an open system to keep other open systems aware of the deletion of existing managed objects, because those other open systems can no longer manage the deleted objects.
Attribute-value-change reporting	Allows an open system to keep other open systems aware of changes in attributes of managed objects.

PT-ACTION	M-ACTION
PT-SET	M-SET
PT-GET	M-GET
PT-EVENT-REPORT	M-EVENT-REPORT

Table 14.3 shows the relationship of these services to underlying object-management operations as defined in the structure of management information (SMI).

14.1.2 Direct Services

The remaining three services involve the use of the M-EVENT-REPORT CMIS service but add value to that service. Each of these services involves notifying a higher layer of an event: object creation, object deletion, or attribute-value change. Each primitive passes information that identifies the object and the change and indicates the source of the change. Possible sources of an event occurrence are:

- *Internal resource:* The event was effected through the internal operation of the resource that is represented by this managed object.

Table 14.3 Mapping of Pass-Through Services

SMI Operation	Pass-Through Service	CMISE Service
Get attribute value	PT-GET	M-GET
Replace attribute value	PT-SET	M-SET
Replace with default value	PT-SET	M-SET
Add member	PT-SET	M-SET
Remove member	PT-SET	M-SET
Notification	PT-EVENT-REPORT	M-EVENT-REPORT
Create	PT-CREATE	M-CREATE
Delete	PT-DELETE	M-DELETE
Action	PT-ACTION	M-ACTION

- *Local open system:* The event was effected by a create request from a higher layer that was initiated within the same open system.

- *Remote open system:* The event was effected by a create request from a higher layer that was initiated from another open system.

- *Unknown:* The cause of the event is unknown.

Table 14.4 shows the event-information parameter that is provided by the user to the object-management service and is, in turn, provided to the M-EVENT-REPORT service.

Table 14.4 Event Information Provided in Request/Indication Primitives of Direct Service

Object-Creation Reporting		Attribute-Value-Change Reporting	
Source indicator	U	Source indicator	U
Attribute list	U	Attribute-identifier list	U
Notification identifier	U	Attribute-value-change definition	
Correlated notifications	U	Attribute identifier	M
Additional text	U	Old attribute value	U
Additional information	U	New attribute value	M
Object-Deletion Reporting		Notification identifier	U
		Correlated notifications	U
Source indicator	U	Additional text	U
Attribute list	U	Additional information	U
Notification identifier	U		
Correlated notifications	U		
Additional text	U		
Additional information	U		

M = The parameter is mandatory.
U = The use of the parameter is a service-user option.

14.2   STATE-MANAGEMENT FUNCTION

X.731/ISO 10164-2 specifies a model for how the management state of an object is to be represented. The model allows the OSI management user to monitor the past state of managed objects and receive notices in response to changes in the state of managed objects. Services are defined for monitoring operability and usage of system resources and for administratively restricting their availability.

14.2.1   State Attributes

The management state of a managed object represents the instantaneous condition of availability and operability of the associated resource from the point of view of management. Different classes of managed objects may have different attributes that are relevant to the monitoring and operation of the associated resource. However, the management state is expected to be common to a large number of resources and has therefore been standardized in X.731/ISO 10164-2. The state-management function provides services for inquiring about and changing the management state and for reporting changes in management state that occur through some cause other than the state-management function.

Three state diagrams are defined in the standard, corresponding to the three primary factors that affect the management state of an object:

1. *Operability:* whether or not the resource is installed and operational
2. *Usage:* whether or not the resource is actively in use at a specific instant and, if so, whether or not it has spare capacity for additional users at that instant
3. *Administration:* whether or not an object may be used.

In each of these areas, there is a state attribute whose value is the current state of the object with respect to that area. These attributes are summarized in Table 14.5.

For operability, the operational-state attribute takes on two values (Figure 14.1, part [a]): disabled and enabled. The state of the object is determined by the natural operation of the resource. Therefore, this attribute cannot be set by management but is read-only in nature.

The usage-state attribute has four possible state values (Figure 14.1, part [b]): idle, active, busy, and unknown. A resource is said to be *in use* when it has received one or more requests for service that it has not yet completed or otherwise discharged or when some part of its capacity has been allocated, and not yet retrieved, as a result of a previous service request. Two states are needed to describe the concept of *in use*. If the object is in use but is able to accommodate one or more additional users, it is in the active state. If the object is in use and can accommodate no more additional users, then it is in the busy state. Thus, an object that can accommodate only one user does not exhibit the active state, and an object that can accommodate an unlimited number of users does not exhibit the busy state.

The usage-state diagram shows that the state of the object can change with the addition or deletion of a user and with a capacity increase (CI) or capacity decrease (CD). As with the operational state, the usage state is determined by the operation of the resource, and therefore, the usage-state attribute is read-only.

Table 14.5 State Attributes

Type	Description	Access
Operational		
Disabled	Resource is totally inoperable and unable to provide service to the user(s).	Read-only
Enabled	Resource is partially or fully operable and available for use.	Read-only
Usage		
Idle	Resource is not currently in use.	Read-only
Active	Resource is in use and has sufficient spare operating capacity to provide for additional users simultaneously.	Read-only
Busy	Resource is in use but has no spare operating capacity to provide for additional users at this instant.	Read-only
Administrative		
Locked	Resource is administratively prohibited from performing services for its users.	Read-write
Shutting down	Use of resource is administratively permitted to existing instances of use only. While the system remains in this state, the manager may at any time cause the managed object to revert to the unlocked state.	Read-write
Unlocked	Resource is administratively permitted to perform services for its users. This is independent of its inherent operability.	Read-write

The administrative-state attribute has three possible state values (Figure 14.1, part [c]): unlocked, locked, and shutting down. This state is under the control of management and allows a management user to lock or unlock access to a resource for purposes of enforcing a concurrency discipline. When a resource is locked, the resource is administratively prohibited from performing services for its users. If the resource can be locked gracefully, then locking involves the act of shutting down. When the shutting-down service is invoked, the resource will only be locked if there are no current users. If there is one or more current users, the resource enters the shutting-down state, which denies access to new users. As soon as the last user quits, the object's state becomes locked. If the resource can only be locked abruptly, then there is no shutting-down state.

Figure 14.2 shows the combined state diagram, indicating the relationships among the various states. The possible combinations have the following interpretations:

- *Disabled, idle, locked:* The resource is inoperable and is providing no service to users. It is also administratively locked. For the resource to become available for use, some corrective action is required, and the resource must also be administratively unlocked.

- *Enabled, idle, locked:* The resource is operable but is providing no service to users and is administratively locked. To become available for use, the resource must be unlocked.

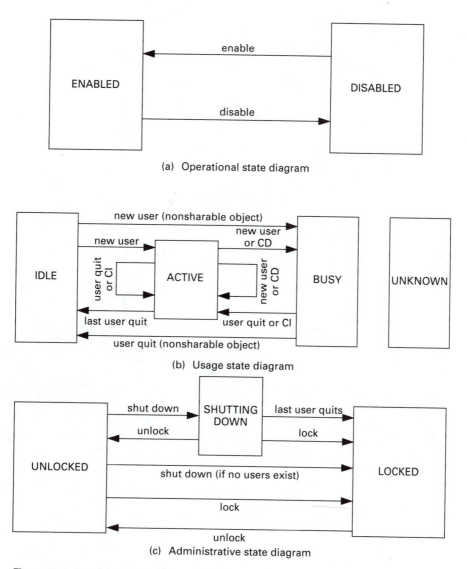

(a) Operational state diagram

(b) Usage state diagram

(c) Administrative state diagram

Figure 14.1 Individual State Diagrams (ISO 10164-2)

- *Enabled, active, shutting down:* The resource is operable, but usage is restricted to current users. The resource can be made available to additional users only if it is administratively changed to unlocked. Otherwise, when all current users terminate, the resource will transition to the enabled, idle, locked state.

- *Enabled, busy, shutting down:* The resource is operable, but usage is restricted to current users. In addition, the resource has no spare capacity for more users. The resource can be made available to additional users only if it is administratively changed to unlocked and if one

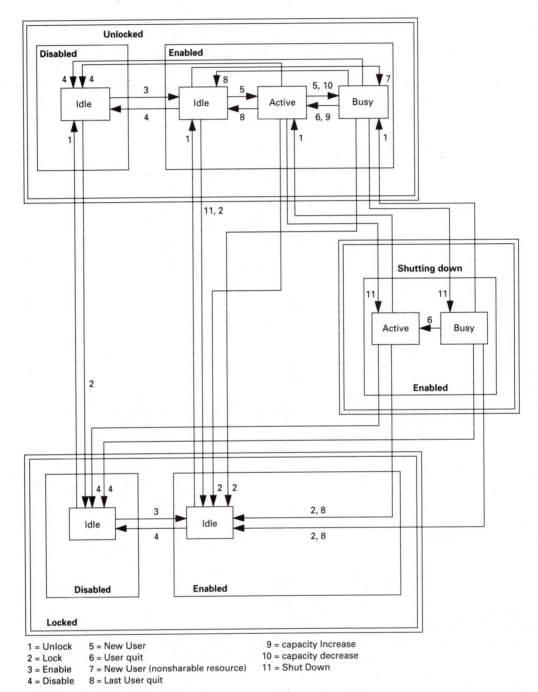

Figure 14.2 Combined State Diagram (ISO 10164-2)

Table 14.6 Standby-Status Conditions

Standby Status	Operational State	Administrative State	Procedural Status	Availability Status
Hot standby	Enabled	Unlocked	—	Off-line
Cold standby	Enabled or disabled	Unlocked or locked	Not initialized or initialization required	Off-line
Providing service	Enabled	Unlocked	—	On-line

or more current users terminate. If an administrative change is not made, when all current users terminate, the resource will transition to the enabled, idle, locked state.

- *Disabled, idle, unlocked:* The resource is inoperable and is providing no service to users. For the resource to become available for use, some corrective action is required.

- *Enabled, idle, unlocked:* The resource is available but is currently not providing service to any user.

- *Enabled, active, unlocked:* The resource is available and is currently providing service to users.

- *Enabled, busy, unlocked:* The resource is operable and is currently providing service to users but has no spare capacity for more users.

14.2.2   Status Attributes

In addition to the state attributes, there are status attributes that provide additional, more detailed, information about the state of a resource. The following status attributes are defined in the standard:

- *Alarm status:* provides an indication of the presence of various alarms related to the resource.

- *Procedural status:* supported only by those object classes that represent some procedure (e.g., a test process) that progresses through a sequence of phases. For certain object classes, the procedure may be required to reach a certain phase in order for the resource to be operational and available for use.

- *Availability status:* provides additional information about the operational state of the resource.

- *Control status:* provides additional information about the administrative state of the resource.

- *Standby status:* provides additional information when the backup relationship role exists. Table 14.6 illustrates the dependencies between this attribute and several of the state and status attributes.

- *Unknown status:* indicates whether the state of the resource is known or unknown. When the value of this attribute is true, the value of the state attributes may not reflect the actual state of the resource.

Table 14.7 lists the possible values of each status attribute. For all the set-valued attributes, when the value of the attribute is an empty set, this implies that none of the allowable status

Table 14.7 Status Attributes

Attribute	Type	Access	Values
Alarm status	Set-valued	Read-write	Under repair: Resource is currently being repaired.
			Critical: One or more critical alarms indicating a fault has been detected and not cleared.
			Major: One or more major alarms indicating a fault has been detected and not cleared.
			Minor: One or more minor alarms indicating a fault has been detected and not cleared.
			Alarm outstanding: One or more alarms indicating a fault has been detected.
Procedural status	Set-valued	Read-only	Initialization required: Initialization invoked by manager required, and initialization procedure has not been initiated.
			Not initialized: Initialization invoked autonomously required, and initialization procedure has not been initiated.
			Initializing: Initialization procedure has been initiated but is not yet complete.
			Reporting: Resource has completed some processing operation and is notifying the results.
			Terminating: Resource is in a termination phase.
Availability status	Set-valued	Read-only	In test: Resource is undergoing a test procedure.
			Failed: Resource has an internal fault that prevents it from operating.
			Power off: Resource requires power to be applied and is not powered on.
			Off-line: Resource requires a routine operation to be performed to place it on-line and make it available for use.
			Off duty: Resource has been made inactive by an internal control

Table 14.7 (*Cont.*)

Attribute	Type	Access	Values
			process using a predetermined time schedule.
			Dependency: Resource cannot operate because some other resource is unavailable.
			Degraded: Service available from resource is degraded in some respect.
			Not installed: Resource is not present or is incomplete.
			Log full: Log-full condition exists.
Control status	Set-valued	Read-write	Subject to test: Resource is available to normal users, but tests may be conducted on it.
			Part of services locked: Part of a service is administratively restricted.
			Reserved for test: Resource is unavailable because it is undergoing a test procedure.
			Suspended: Service is administratively suspended to users of resource.
Standby status	Single-valued	Read-only	Hot standby: Resource is operating in synchronism with another resource that is to be backed up.
			Cold standby: Resource is to back up another resource but is not synchronized with it.
			Providing service: Resource is providing service and backing up another resource.
Unknown status	Boolean	Read-only	True: State of resource is unknown.
			False: State of resource is known.

conditions is present. In the case of the procedural-status attribute, if the value is an empty set, the managed object is ready and the initialization is complete.

For the single-valued attributes (standby-status attribute, unknown-status attribute), of course, only one value at a time is possible.

14.2.3 State-Management Services

The state-management function is intended to provide the following services:

- Reporting changes in the state attributes
- Reading the state attributes
- Changing the state attributes

Currently, only the state-change-reporting service has been defined. For reading and changing attributes, the services of the object-management function are used.

The state-change-reporting service uses the CMIS primitive M-EVENT-REPORT (Table 13.2, part [a]). The event-type parameter in the request primitive has the value *state change*. The event-information parameter that is provided by the user to the state-management service and is, in turn, provided to the M-EVENT-REPORT service contains the following elements:

Source indicator	U
Attribute-identifier list	U
State-change definition	
Attribute identifier	M
Old attribute value	U
New attribute value	M
Notification identifier	U
Correlated notifications	U
Additional text	U
Additional information	U

The source indicator specifies whether the state-attribute-value change was effected through the internal operation of the resource or by management operation.

14.3   RELATIONSHIP-MANAGEMENT FUNCTION

X.732/ISO 10164-3 models and identifies types of relationships that can exist among managed objects representing different parts of a system. Services are defined for establishing, examining, and monitoring the relationships among objects and therefore for observing how the operation of one part of a system depends on other parts.

In general, a relationship is a set of rules that describes how the operation of one managed object affects the operation of another managed object. For example, two managed objects may have a relationship in which one is activated in the event that the other fails as a result of a fault-management diagnostic.

14.3.1   Relationship Model

Relationships are defined by relationship attributes. For each particular type of relationship, called a *role,* there is a separate relationship attribute. A managed object may have multiple instances of any particular type of relationship. A relationship attribute is a set-valued attribute whose values are the names of other managed objects with which an object has a relationship. The use of sets supports one-to-one, one-to-many, many-to-one, and many-to-many relationships.

Figure 14.3, part (a) illustrates several concepts of the relationship model. A direct relationship exists between two objects if some portion of the management information associated with

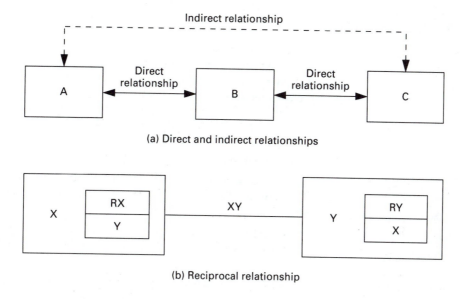

(a) Direct and indirect relationships

(b) Reciprocal relationship

(c) Relationship roles

Figure 14.3 Model for Relationship Attributes

one managed object explicitly identifies the other managed object. An indirect relationship exists if the relationship can be deduced from the concatenation of two or more direct relationships.

Three categories of relationships are recognized by OSI management:

1. *Containment relationship:* This is a structuring relationship in which the existence of a managed object is dependent on the existence of a containing managed object.

2. *Reciprocal relationship:* This is a binding between two objects. To represent the relationship, each object includes an attribute whose value is the name of the other object.

3. *One-way relationship:* This is an asymmetric relationship between two objects in which the relationship is expressed in the value of the relationship attribute of only one member of the pair.

Figure 14.3, part (b), illustrates a reciprocal one-to-one relationship. The two objects, X and Y, have a direct reciprocal relationship XY that is expressed by the existence of the name of object Y as a value of X's relationship attribute RX and by the existence of the name of object X as a value of Y's relationship attribute RY.

14.3.2   Relationship Type

The relationship type, which is implied by the name of the relationship attribute, describes the nature of the relationship between two or more objects. The relationship role describes the part played by each object that is in a particular relationship type. The following list describes relationship types and their corresponding relationship roles:

- *Service relationship:* This is an asymmetric relationship in which one of a pair of objects has the provider role and the other has the user role (Figure 14.3, part [c]).

- *Peer relationship:* This is a symmetric relationship between peers.

- *Fallback relationship:* This is an asymmetric relationship denoting that the second of a pair of managed objects (secondary role) is capable of service as a fallback or "next preferred choice" to the first managed object (primary role).

- *Backup relationship:* This is an asymmetric relationship in which the object in the backup role is providing backup to the object in the backed-up role. The backed-up object is in the disabled state, defined earlier.

- *Group relationship:* This is a relationship between two objects in which one object (the member role) belongs to a group represented by the other object (the owner role).

14.3.3   Relationship-Management Services

When performing an operation on a relationship attribute, the relationship management function provides a pass-through service to the PT-GET and PT-SET services of the object-management function.

The relationship-change-reporting service allows a user in the agent role to report the changes in values of managed-object relationship attributes. The service uses the CMIS primitive M-EVENT-REPORT (Table 13.2, part [a]). The event-type parameter in the request primitive has the value *relationship change*. The event-information parameter that is provided by the user to the relationship-change-reporting service and is, in turn, provided to the M-EVENT-REPORT service contains the following elements:

Source indicator	U
Attribute-identifier list	U
Relationship-change definition	
Attribute identifier	M
Old attribute value	U
New attribute value	M
Notification identifier	U
Correlated notifications	U
Additional text	U
Additional information	U

The source indicator specifies whether the relationship attribute-value change was effected through the internal operation of the resource or by management operation. Table 14.8 lists the relationship-change attributes.

Table 14.8 Generic Relationship Attributes

Attribute	Type	Access	Description
providerObject	Set-valued	Read-write	Identifies one or more objects acting in a service-provider role with respect to this object and the order of priority in which they do so.
userObject	Set-valued	Read-write	Identifies one or more objects acting in a service-user role with respect to this object and the order of priority in which they do so.
peer	Single-valued	Read-only	Identifies one other object that acts in the peer role with respect to this object.
primary	Set-valued	Read-write	Identifies one or more objects acting in a primary role with respect to this object and the order of priority in which they do so.
secondary	Set-valued	Read-write	Identifies one or more objects acting in a secondary role with respect to this object and the order of priority in which they do so.
backUpObject	Single-valued	Read-only	Identifies one other object that acts in the backup role with respect to this object.
backedUpObject	Single-valued	Read-only	Identifies one other object that acts in the backed-up role with respect to this object.
member	Set-valued	Read-write	Identifies one or more objects acting in a member role with respect to this object and the order of priority in which they do so.
owner	Set-valued	Read-write	Identifies one or more objects acting in an owner role with respect to this object and the order of priority in which they do so.
relationships	—	—	An empty attribute group that provides a means of referring to the collection of all relationship attributes of an object.

14.4 ALARM-REPORTING FUNCTION

X.733/ISO 10164-4 models alarm reporting. It specifies generic alarm notifications (events), together with their parameters and semantics. These notifications are associated primarily with fault management. The information provided includes error types, probable causes, and measures of severity. This type of functionality is essential in an environment with multiple open systems and multiple networks, where there is a requirement to locate the source of a fault.

14.4.1   Alarm Definition

Alarms are specific types of notifications concerning detected faults or abnormal conditions. The standard does not dictate the information that must be included in the alarm. Rather, the managed-object designer is encouraged to include in alarms information that will help with understanding the cause of the potentially abnormal situation and information related to side effects. An example of such diagnostic information is the current and past values of the configuration-management state of the object. The standard does provide a common set of notification types, with standardized parameters and parameter definitions, independent of particular managed objects. These elements are available to the managed-object designer but may be supplemented by object-specific information.

Five basic categories of alarms are defined:

1. *Communications:* used to report when an object detects a communications error. It is principally associated with the procedures and/or processes required to convey information from one point to another.

2. *Quality of service:* used to report a failure or degradation in the quality of service of an object.

3. *Processing:* used to report processing failure in a managed object.

4. *Equipment:* used to report equipment failure.

5. *Environmental:* used to report a problem in the environment. It is principally associated with a condition relating to an enclosure in which the equipment resides.

Each of these notification alarms is defined in X.721/ISO 10165-2. One example, the communicationsAlarm notification, was presented in section 12.3. All the notifications include the following attributes:

- *probableCause:* provides further qualification as to the probable cause of the alarm. Table 14.9 lists the probable causes that have been defined.

- *specificProblems:* provides further refinements to the probable cause of the error.

- *perceivedSeverity:* an indication of the degree to which the capability of the object has been affected. The ability to categorize alarms by severity helps the network manager decide quickly which alarms require an immediate response and which ones can wait. In order of decreasing severity, six levels are defined:

    1. *Critical:* indicates that a service-affecting condition has occurred and an immediate corrective action is required. An example of this condition is when a resource defined by a managed object has gone out of service and that resource is required.

    2. *Major:* indicates that a service-affecting condition has developed and an urgent corrective action is required. An example of this condition is when a severe degradation in the capability of an object has occurred and the object needs to be restored to full capability.

    3. *Minor:* indicates that a non–service-affecting fault condition has developed and corrective action should be taken in order to prevent a more serious fault.

Table 14.9 Probable Causes Defined by the Alarm-Reporting Function

Loss of signal	Software error	Processor problem
Framing error	Out of memory	High/low ambient temperature
Local transmission error	Underlying resource	High/low humidity
Remote transmission error	unavailable	Intrusion detection
Call-establishment error	Power problem	Heating/cooling-system
Degraded signal	Timing problem	failure
Response time excessive	Trunk-card problem	Ventilation-system failure
Queue size excessive	Line-card problem	Fire
Bandwidth reduced	Terminal problem	Flood
Retransmission rate excessive	External-interface-device	Toxic gas
Threshold crossed	problem	High/low pressure
Storage-capacity problem	Dataset problem	Air-compressor failure
Version mismatch	Multiplexor problem	Pump failure
Corrupt data	Receiver failure	Engine failure
CPU-cycles limit exceeded	Transmitter failure	Fuel problem
	Smoke detection	
	Enclosure door open	

4. *Warning:* indicates the detection of a potential or an impending service-affecting fault, before any significant effects have been felt. Action should be taken to further diagnose (if necessary) and correct the problem in order to prevent it from becoming a more serious service-affecting fault.

5. *Indeterminate:* indicates that the severity level of the service-affecting condition cannot be determined.

6. *Cleared:* indicates the clearing of one or more previously reported alarms. This alarm clears all alarms for this managed object that have the same alarm type, probable cause, and specific problems (if given).

- *backedUpStatus:* a Boolean parameter that specifies whether the failed object has been backed up. If so, the services to the user have not been disrupted.

- *backUpObject:* the object instance that is providing backup services.

- *trendIndication:* if present, indicates that in addition to this current alarm, one or more outstanding alarms have not been cleared. The attribute has three possible values:

  1. *More severe:* The current alarm has a higher perceivedSeverity than any outstanding alarm.

  2. *No change:* The perceivedSeverity of the current alarm is the same as that of the highest outstanding alarm.

  3. *Less severe:* The current alarm has a lower perceivedSeverity than any outstanding alarm.

- *thresholdInfo:* included when the alarm is the result of crossing a threshold. It consists of four subparameters:

1. *Triggered threshold:* threshold attribute that caused the notification
2. *Threshold level:* threshold value (counter) or pair of threshold values (gauge) that have been crossed
3. *Observed value:* value of the gauge or counter that crossed the threshold
4. *Arm time:* for a gauge threshold, the time after the previous threshold crossing at which the paired value was crossed, again permitting notification of a threshold crossing; for a counter threshold, the time of last initialization (or wrap back to zero)

-   *notificationIdentifier:* an identifier of this alarm that may be carried in the correlated-Notifications attribute of a future alarm.

-   *correlatedNotifications:* a set of notification identifiers to which this alarm is considered to be correlated.

-   *stateChangeDefinition:* included when there is a state transition. It consists of two subparameters: the state of the object at the time the alarm occurred and the current state of the object.

-   *monitoredAttributes:* identifies one or more attributes of the object and their values at the time of the alarm.

-   *proposedRepairActions:* an enumeration of possible solutions.

-   *additionalText:* a free-form text description of the problem being reported.

-   *additionalInformation:* a set of additional information.

14.4.2   Alarm-Reporting Service

The alarm-reporting service enables one user to notify another user of an alarm detected in a managed object. The originating user specifies whether or not a reply is required.

The service uses the CMIS primitive M-EVENT-REPORT (Table 13.2, part [a]). The event-type parameter in the request primitive indicates the type of alarm. The alarm-information parameter that is provided by the user to the alarm-reporting service, and is, in turn, provided to the M-EVENT-REPORT service, contains the following elements:

Probable cause	M
Specific problems	U
Perceived severity	M
Backed-up status	U
Backup object instance	C[1]
Trend indication	U
Threshold information	C
Notification identifier	U
Correlated notifications	U
Generic state change	C
Monitored attributes	U

---

1. C = Conditional

Proposed repair actions   U
Problem text   U
Problem data   U

14.4.3 Alarm Record

One result of the generation of an alarm notification may be the production of an alarm record that is stored in a log (the log-control function is defined in section 14.6) on the system that receives the notification. The alarm record has the following structure:

alarmRecord MANAGED OBJECT CLASS
  DERIVED FROM eventLogRecord
  CHARACTERIZED BY alarmRecordPackage PACKAGE
    BEHAVIOR
    AlarmRecordBehavior BEHAVIOR
      DEFINED AS ''This managed object is used to represent logged information that re-
      sulted from alarm notifications or event reports'';;
    ATTRIBUTES
    probableCause GET,
    perceivedSeverity GET;;
  CONDITIONAL PACKAGES
    specificProblemsPackage PACKAGE
      ATTRIBUTES specificProblems GET;
      REGISTERED AS {smi2Package 1}; PRESENT IF ''the specificProblems parameter is
        present in the alarm notification or event report corresponding to the instance of
        alarm record'',
    backedUpStatusPackage PACKAGE
      ATTRIBUTES backedUpStatus GET;
      REGISTERED AS {smi2Package 2}; PRESENT IF ''the backedUpStatus attribute has
        a value TRUE and the backedUpStatus parameter is present in the alarm notification
        or event report corresponding to the instance of alarm record'',
    backUpObjectPackage PACKAGE
      ATTRIBUTES backUpObject GET;
      REGISTERED AS {smi2Package 3}; PRESENT IF ''BackUpObject parameter is pres-
        ent in the alarm notification or event report corresponding to the instance of alarm
        record'',
    trendIndicationPackage PACKAGE
      ATTRIBUTES trendIndication GET;
      REGISTERED AS {smi2Package 4}; PRESENT IF ''the trendIndication parameter is
        present in the alarm notification or event report corresponding to the instance of
        alarm record'',
    thresholdInfoPackage PACKAGE
      ATTRIBUTES thresholdInfo GET;
      REGISTERED AS {smi2Package 5}; PRESENT IF ''the value for probableCause at-
        tribute is thresholdCrossed'',
    stateChangeDefinitionPackage PACKAGE

ATTRIBUTES stateChangeDefinition GET;

REGISTERED AS {smi2Package 6}; PRESENT IF "there is a state transition for the states defined in State Management Function, corresponding to the alarm type specified in the alarm record",

monitoredAttributesPackage PACKAGE

ATTRIBUTES monitoredAttributes GET;

REGISTERED AS {smi2Package 7}; PRESENT IF "the monitoredAttributes parameter is present in the alarm notification or event report corresponding to the instance of alarm record",

proposedRepairActionsPackage PACKAGE

ATTRIBUTES proposedRepairActions GET;

REGISTERED AS {smi2Package 8}; PRESENT IF "the proposedRepairActions parameter is present in the alarm notification or event report corresponding to the instance of alarm record",

REGISTERED AS {smi2MObjectClass 1};

14.5   EVENT-REPORT-MANAGEMENT FUNCTION

X.734/ISO 10164-5 provides a model for the control of event reporting. The event-report-management function allows a manager to control the transmission of event reports from managed objects independently of the definition of those managed object. Interestingly, the means by which reports from objects are controlled is the definition of additional objects, called event-forwarding discriminators. A discriminator is a managed object that allows a system to control management operations relating to other objects; an event-forwarding discriminator is one that acts on potential event reports. In effect, a filter can be defined that specifies the events that are to be reported.

The event-report-management function enables the user to control the selection of events and their distribution to manager-specifiable destinations. It enables the user to create an event-forwarding-discriminator managed object that defines manager-creatable/selectable criteria by which managed-object notification may be conveyed remotely as event reports, as well as time periods during which such event-forwarding discrimination can occur. Finally, the function enables the user to suspend and resume event reporting on a per-destination basis.

This function can play a key role in controlling the flow of management information. It is particularly important in WAN (wide area network) environments that have a limited bandwidth and in other real-time or bandwidth-constrained environments. As an example of its use, the network manager can specify which information can be exchanged between a managing process and individual agent processes (Figure 11.4).

The standard lists the following requirements to be met by the event-report-management function:

- The definition of a flexible event-report-control service that will allow systems to select which event reports are to be sent to particular managing systems.

- Specification of the destinations (e.g., the identities of managing systems) to which event reports are to be sent; one such possible destination is the local system.

- Specification of a mechanism to control the forwarding of event reports—for example, by suspending and resuming their forwarding.

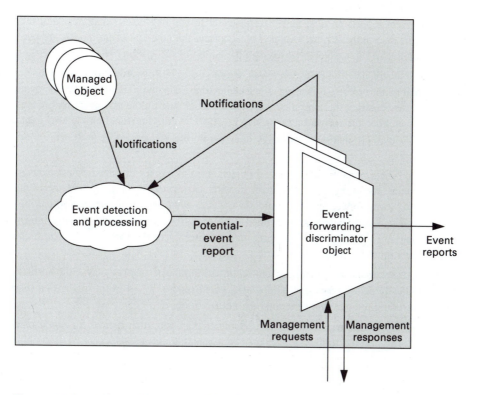

Figure 14.4 Event-Report-Management Model

- The ability for an external managing system to modify the conditions used in the reporting of events.

- The ability to designate a backup location to which event reports can be sent if the primary location is not available.

14.5.1   Event-Report-Management Model

Figure 14.4 illustrates the event-report-management model, which describes the conceptual components that provide for remote event reporting and local processing of potential events and describes the message flows for the control messages, event-reporting messages, and retrieval messages. The model behaves as follows:

1. At least one managed object in the managed system is capable of generating notifications that may be forwarded within an event report. Notifications are issued by managed objects when events occur.

2. An event-detection and processing module receives the locally generated notifications and forms potential event reports. Potential event reports contain all the information in the notification, plus information added by the detection and processing module, such as event time, object class, and instance.

3. Potential event reports are distributed to all event-forwarding discriminators within the local system. The discriminators are managed objects, and the potential event reports are perceived as a discriminator-input object that triggers the action of the discriminator object.

4. The discriminator determines which event reports are to be forwarded to a particular destination as real event reports, following a particular time schedule. The discriminator contains a discriminator construct that specifies the characteristics that a potential event report must satisfy to be eligible for forwarding; this is, in effect, a filtering function. It also contains a scheduling capability that determines the intervals during which event reports will be selected for forwarding.

5. Event-report discriminators are managed objects and, like other managed objects, have states and attributes. Event-report management provides a service for reading and modifying the attributes of event-forwarding discriminators. Thus, event-report discrimination can be initiated, terminated, suspended, and resumed. The specific scheduling and filtering information can be read and modified. Event reports may be directed to the local system, the requesting system, or a third system.

6. Also like other managed objects, event-report-discriminator objects may emit notifications. These notifications are processed as potential event reports by all event-forwarding discriminators, including the one that generated the notification.

The discriminator construct consists of a Boolean expression that defines the event or events to be reported. Tests on the following attributes of a potential event report may be specified:

- Managed-object class

- Managed-object instance

- Event type

- Event-type specific attributes—e.g., for fault-related events, such attributes as severity, backed-up status, and probable cause

    The scheduling attributes include the following:

- *Start time:* defines the date and time at which the discriminator enters the phase of periodic behavior.

- *Stop time:* defines the date and time at which the discriminator stops exhibiting periodic behavior. If scheduling attributes are present, event reports are only issued between the start and stop times while the discriminator is unlocked.

- *Week mask:* This defaults to "always on." Otherwise, the week mask specifies the days of the week and a list of the time intervals during the day when the discriminator is active.

14.5.2   Discriminator Objects

The discriminator superclass and eventForwardingDiscriminator class were presented in Chapter 12. For convenience, these definitions are reproduced here, together with a discussion of each.

14.5.2.1   Discriminator-Object Superclass

The discriminator-object class specifies conditions that must be satisfied prior to allowing the associated discriminator-input object to proceed. These conditions, which are common to all types of discriminators, include:

- Identification of a scheduling package that determines when a function will be performed
- The criteria for discrimination
- The administrative and operational state of the discriminator

This class serves as a basic superclass, which may be refined into subclasses to specify management-support-object classes that allow the control of various systems-management functions. Each subclass includes conditions that are unique to the specific function being performed. The discriminator is defined in X.721/ISO 10165-2 as follows:

```
discriminator MANAGED OBJECT CLASS
    DERIVED FROM top
    CHARACTERIZED BY discriminatorPackage PACKAGE
        BEHAVIOR
        discriminatorBehavior BEHAVIOR
            DEFINED AS "This managed object is used to represent the criteria for controlling
            management services.";;
        ATTRIBUTES
        discriminatorId GET,
        discriminatorConstruct REPLACE-WITH-DEFAULT DEFAULT VALUE
            Attribute-ASN1Module.defaultDiscriminatorConstruct GET-REPLACE,
        administrativeState GET-REPLACE,
        operationalState GET;
        NOTIFICATIONS
        stateChange,
        attributeValueChange,
        objectCreation,
        objectDeletion;;;
    CONDITIONAL PACKAGES
        availabilityStatusPackage PRESENT IF "any of the scheduling packages (duration, weekly,
            scheduling, external) are present",
        duration PRESENT IF "the discriminator function is scheduled to start at a specified time
            and stop at either a specified time or function continuously",
        dailyScheduling PRESENT IF "both the weekly scheduling package and external sched-
            uler package are not present in an instance and daily scheduling is supported by that
            instance",
        weeklyScheduling PRESENT IF "both the daily scheduling package and external sched-
            uler package are not present in an instance and weekly scheduling is supported by that
            instance",
        externalScheduler PRESENT IF "both the daily scheduling package and weekly sched-
            uling package are not present in an instance and external scheduling is supported by
            that instance";
    REGISTERED AS { smi2MObjectClass 3 } ;
```

The discriminator-object class includes one mandatory package, the discriminatorPackage, which contains four attributes:

1. *discriminatorId:* used to uniquely identify the instance of the discriminator-object class.

2. *discriminatorConstruct:* specifies tests on the information that is to be processed by the discriminator. This is essentially a filtering mechanism that acts on attributes of discriminator-input objects. It is a set of one or more assertions about the presence or values of attributes. If there are multiple assertions, these form logical expressions using AND, OR, and NOT operators. The syntax of this construct is in fact identical to that of the CMISFilter (Figure 13.3).

3. *administrativeState:* is either locked or unlocked. This attribute may be changed by management operation.

4. *operationalState:* is either enabled or disabled. The discriminator object processes input objects only while in the enabled state.

If the discriminator construct evaluates to TRUE, and the discriminator is in the unlocked and enabled states, then the discriminator-input object passes the discriminator and will be processed further. The processing to be performed depends on the semantics of the subclass.

The discriminator-object class definition also includes a number of conditional packages relating to scheduling. The scheduling packages provide discriminators with the ability to automatically switch between an on-duty status (reporting on) and an off-duty status (reporting off). If any of the scheduling packages are present, the availabilityStatusPackage is also present. It contains a single attribute that indicates whether the discriminator is on-duty or off-duty. The scheduling packages are:

- *duration:* includes startTime and stopTime attributes, which are settable by management operation.

- *dailyScheduling:* provides scheduling with a period of 24 hours. The intervalsOfDay is a list of intervals (start time, stop time) for which the discriminator will be on-duty. The same intervals are used each day.

- *weeklyScheduling:* provides scheduling with a period of one week. The package includes a list of the days of the week and the intervals within each day during which the discriminator is on-duty.

- *externalScheduler:* the name of a scheduling object that controls the schedule for this discriminator.

14.5.2.2   eventForwardingDiscriminator Object Class

The eventForwardingDiscriminator is a subclass derived from the discriminator class and is defined as follows:

```
eventForwardingDiscriminator MANAGED OBJECT CLASS
    DERIVED FROM discriminator
    CHARACTERIZED BY efdPackage PACKAGE
      BEHAVIOR
      eventForwardingDiscriminatorBehavior BEHAVIOR
      DEFINED AS "This managed object is used to represent the criteria that shall be satisfied
          by potential event reports before the event report is forwarded to a particular destina-
          tion.";;
```

```
ATTRIBUTES
  destination GET-REPLACE;;;
CONDITIONAL PACKAGES
  backUpDestinationListPackage PACKAGE
    ATTRIBUTES
    activeDestination GET,
    backUpDestinationList GET-REPLACE;
    REGISTERED AS {smi2Package 9}; PRESENT IF "the event forwarding discriminator
      is required to provide a backup for the destination",
  modePackage PACKAGE
    ATTRIBUTES
    confirmedMode GET,
    REGISTERED AS {smi2Package 10}; PRESENT IF "the event forwarding discrimi-
      nator permits mode for reporting events to be specified by the managing system";
  REGISTERED AS { smi2MObjectClass 4 } ;
```

This new object class carries over all the characteristics of its superclass. It includes a desti-nation attribute, which indicates the address of the primary application entity (AE) to which the discriminator forwards events. This usually indicates an application in the managing system, but it may also indicate a local application or log. Conditionally, the object may include a backup-DestinationListPackage, which is a list, in priority order, of AEs that may be used as an event destination if the primary address fails. Another conditional package, the modePackage, can be used to indicate whether the managing system can specify the mode for reporting events (confirmed or nonconfirmed).

14.5.2.3 Discriminator Function

It is important to understand the distinction between the discriminatorConstruct attribute and the discriminator managed-object class. Consider the following definitions from ISO 10164-5:

A discriminator is a management support object that allows a system to select manage-ment operations and event reports relating to other managed objects.

A discriminator contains a discriminator construct that is a filtering mechanism that acts on attributes of discriminator input objects. A discriminator construct is a set of one or more assertions about the presence or values of attributes.

The functioning of the discriminator construct depends on the management state of the dis-criminator object, as follows:

- If the discriminator object is created without the availabilityStatusPackage, then the manager cannot change the time when the object is available, and the discriminator is assumed to always be available (i.e., availability status is "on-duty").

- If the discriminator construct evaluates to TRUE, and the discriminator object is in the Un-locked and Enabled states, and the availability status is not "off-duty", then the discriminator input object passes the discriminator and will be processed further. The processing to be performed depends on the precise semantics of the discriminator subclass (for example, the eventForwardingDiscriminator).

- If the discriminator is in the Locked or Disabled states or has the "off-duty" availability status, then discriminator input objects will not be processed by that discriminator.

A discriminator object is set up as an intermediate point between a source of information and one or more destinations, much like a gate that must be passed. A discriminator object acts like a sieve, or filter, in order to discriminate, or limit, the volume of notifications sent, information logged, or the performance of some other operation. A discriminator object is a support object that acts like a border guard that won't let information pass through the gate unless it meets certain criteria. The criteria are defined by the value of the discriminatorConstruct attribute. Also, a guard can be told to be off duty during certain time intervals, during which nothing can pass through the gate.

The key features of a discriminator object are that it includes a discriminatorConstruct attribute and that it is defined as an intermediate point for the delivery of information. Not all specific discriminator object classes are subclasses of the general discriminator object class defined in X.72/ISO 10165-2. For example, the log object class, described in Section 14.6.1, is a discriminator but is not a subclass of the discriminator object class.

14.5.3   Event-Report-Management Services

The event-report-management function provides the following services to users:

- Creation of a discriminator

- Deletion of a discriminator

- Modification of discriminator attributes

- Suspension of the discriminator activity

- Resumption of the discriminator activity

Discriminator creation makes use of the PT-CREATE service of the object-management function. Discriminator deletion makes use of the PT-DELETE service. The remaining event-report-management services make use of the PT-SET service.

14.6   LOG-CONTROL FUNCTION

X.735/ISO 10164-6 specifies a model for how event logs can be controlled. A filter can be defined that specifies the events that are to be placed in the log. As with the event-report-management function, the log-control function provides for logging according to manager-settable schedules and manager-creatable logging criteria. The standard states that the following requirements are to be satisfied by the log-control function:

- Definition of a flexible log-control service that allows selection of records to be logged

- Ability for an external system to modify the criteria used in logging records

- Ability for an external system to determine whether the logging characteristics were modified or whether logs have been lost

- Specification of a mechanism to control the time during which logging occurs

- Ability for an external system to retrieve and delete log records

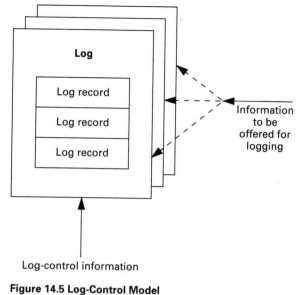

Figure 14.5 Log-Control Model

- Ability for an external system to create and delete logs

Figures 14.5 and 14.6 depict a model of the log-control function. Each log consists of a set of records, one for each event logged. Information to be logged is derived from received event reports provided by the event-report function, incoming CMIP (common management information protocol) PDUs (protocol data units), and internal events. The internal events are in the form of notifications that trigger the log-preprocessing function. This function, in turn, generates potential log reports, which are distributed to all local log objects. All arriving reports are subjected to a discriminator function to determine whether there is a match for storing. Those reports that are accepted are transformed into records. Records in a log are stored in order of arrival, and record identifiers are assigned in numerical sequence.

Each log is a managed object. Table 14.10 lists the attributes of the log-object class. The key attributes that dictate the operation of the log are the scheduling information and the discriminator construct. The scheduling information dictates when the log is available to add new records. When information is presented for logging during the time that the log is available, a new record is added only if the information passes the discriminator-construct test.

To accommodate various levels of complexity in scheduling logging activity periods, three conditional packages that are related to scheduling are defined for logging.

14.6.1 Log Structure

The log managed object is used to define the criteria for controlling the logging of information. The log-object class is defined in X.721/ISO 10165-2 as follows:

```
log MANAGED OBJECT CLASS
    DERIVED FROM top
    CHARACTERIZED BY logPackage PACKAGE
```

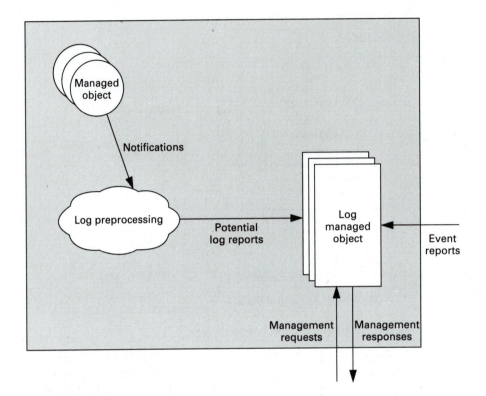

Figure 14.6 Log-Management Model

BEHAVIOR
logBehavior BEHAVIOR
   DEFINED AS "This managed object is used to store incoming event reports and local
   system notifications.";;
ATTRIBUTES
logId GET,
discriminatorConstruct GET-REPLACE,
administrativeState GET-REPLACE,
operationalState GET;
availabilityStatus PERMITTED VALUES Attribute-ASN1Module.LogAvailability
   REQUIRED VALUES Attribute-ASN1Module.UnscheduledLogAvailability GET,
logFullAction GET-REPLACE;
NOTIFICATIONS
objectCreation,
objectDeletion,
attributeValueChange,
stateChange,
processingErrorAlarm;;;

Table 14.10 Log-Object Class Attributes

Attribute	Description
Log ID	Used to uniquely identify an instance of a log.
State	The administrative, operational, and usage states of the log.
Scheduling information	A description of the time during which logging is active.
Discriminator construct	A description of the type of information to be logged.
Maximum log size	The maximum size of the log in octets. When this attribute is set to 0, the log size is indeterminate.
Current log size	The current size of the log in octets.
Number of records	The number of records currently in the log.
Log-full action	The behavior of the log when its maximum capacity is reached. Options are: wrap (the earliest set of records in the log will be deleted to make room for new records) and halt (no more records will be logged).
Capacity-alarm threshold	Defined as percentages of the maximum log size. Used to generate events that will indicate that various levels of the log-full condition have been approached.
Notifications	Generated when the log is created, deleted, suspended, resumed, and modified.

CONDITIONAL PACKAGES
   finiteLogSizePackage PACKAGE
      ATTRIBUTES
     maxLogSize GET-REPLACE,
     currentLogSize GET,
     numberOfRecords GET;
     REGISTERED AS {smi2Package 12}; PRESENT IF ''an instance supports it'',
   logAlarmPackage PACKAGE
      ATTRIBUTES
     capacityAlarmThreshold GET-REPLACE ADD-REMOVE;
     REGISTERED AS {smi2Package 13}; PRESENT IF ''a log is of finite size and halts
      logging when the availability status has the log full value.'',
  availabilityStatusPackage PRESENT IF ''any of the scheduling packages (duration, weekly,
    scheduling, external) are present'',
   duration PRESENT IF ''the logging function is scheduled to start at a specified time and
    stop at either a specified time or function continuously'',
   dailyScheduling PRESENT IF ''both the weekly scheduling package and external sched-
    uler package are not present in an instance and daily scheduling is supported by that
    instance'',
   weeklyScheduling PRESENT IF ''both the daily scheduling package and external sched-
    uler package are not present in an instance and weekly scheduling is supported by that
    instance'',

externalScheduler PRESENT IF "both the daily scheduling package and weekly scheduling package are not present in an instance and external scheduling is supported by that instance";
REGISTERED AS { smi2MObjectClass 6 } ;

The log-object class includes one mandatory package, the logPackage, which contains the following attributes:

- *logId:* used to uniquely identify the instance of the log-object class.

- *discriminatorConstruct:* specifies tests on the record that is to be logged. The record is logged only if it passes the discriminator-construct test.

- *administrativeState:* takes on the following values: unlocked, (the log is available for both logging and retrieval of records), or locked (the log is unavailable for both retrieval and creation of new records).

- *operationalState:* takes on the following values: enabled (the log has been created and is ready for use), or disabled, (the log is inoperable for operational reasons).

- *availabilityStatus:* qualifies the operational state of the log. The attribute may indicate a log-full condition.

- *logFullAction:* takes on the following values: wrap (the earliest set of records in the log will be deleted to make room for new records), or halt (no more records will be logged).

The log-object class includes a number of conditional packages. The finiteLogSize package is present if the size of the log is bounded. The package includes the maxLogSize in octets, the currentLogSize in octets, and the numberOfRecords contained in the log. If the log is of finite size, the logAlarmPackage defines the thresholds, each specified as a percentage of maxLogSize, at which an event will be generated to indicate that a log-full or log-wrap condition is approaching.

The remaining conditional packages have to do with scheduling the logging activity and have the same interpretation as for the discriminator-object class.

14.6.2   Log Records

Log records are managed objects that represent the actual information stored in logs. The logRecord object class serves as a superclass for other record classes that define the detailed information to be logged.

The logRecord object class is defined in X.721/ISO 10165-2 as follows:

logRecord MANAGED OBJECT CLASS
  DERIVED FROM top;
  CHARACTERIZED BY logRecordPackage PACKAGE
    BEHAVIOR
    logRecordBehavior BEHAVIOR
      DEFINED AS "This managed object represents information stored in the logs.";;
    ATTRIBUTES
    logRecordId GET,
    loggingTime GET;;;
  REGISTERED AS { smi2MObjectClass 7 } ;

Log records are created as a result of the receipt of an event report or as a side effect of some management operation. They cannot be directly created by explicit management operation, and all of their attributes are read-only. The logRecordId is an integer unique within the scope of the log; these IDs are assigned sequentially.

As an example of a subclass that defines a log record more specifically, consider the event-LogRecord:

```
eventLogRecord MANAGED OBJECT CLASS
  DERIVED FROM logRecord;
  CHARACTERIZED BY eventLogRecordPackage PACKAGE
    BEHAVIOR
    eventLogRecordBehavior BEHAVIOR
      DEFINED AS ''This managed object represents the information stored in the log as a
      result of receiving notifications of incoming event reports.'';;
    ATTRIBUTES
    managedObjectClass GET,
    managedObjectInstance GET,
    eventType GET;;;
  CONDITIONAL PACKAGES
    eventTimePackage PACKAGE
      ATTRIBUTES
      eventTime GET;
      REGISTERED AS {smi2Package 11}; PRESENT IF ''the eventTime parameter was
        present in the received event report.'',
    notificationIdentifierPackage PRESENT IF ''the notificationIdentifier parameter is present
      in the notification or event report corresponding to the instance of an event record or
      an instance of its subclasses'',
    correlatedNotificationPackage PRESENT IF ''the correlatedNotification parameter is pres-
      ent in the notification or event report corresponding to the instance of an event record
      or an instance of its subclasses'',
    additionalTextPackage PRESENT IF ''the additionalText parameter is present in the no-
      tification or event report corresponding to the instance of an event record or an instance
      of its subclasses'',
    additionalInformationPackage PRESENT IF ''the additionalInformation parameter is pres-
      ent in the notification or event report corresponding to the instance of an event record
      or an instance of its subclasses'',
    REGISTERED AS { smi2MObjectClass 5 } ;
```

14.6.3   Log-Control Services

The log-control function provides the following services to users:

- *Creation of a log:* uses the PT-CREATE service
- *Deletion of a log:* uses the PT-DELETE service
- *Modification of log attributes:* uses the PT-SET service
- *Suspension of the log activity:* uses the PT-SET service

- *Deletion of log records:* uses the PT-DELETE service
- *Retrieval of log records:* uses the PT-GET service
- *Resumption of the log activity:* uses the PT-SET service

14.7   SECURITY-ALARM-REPORTING FUNCTION

X.736/ISO 10164-7 models the reporting of security-related events and misoperations in security services and mechanisms. It specifies generic security-alarm notifications, together with their parameters and semantics. It provides services for creating, deleting, and modifying event-forwarding discriminators for controlling the selection of security alarms and their distribution to manager-specifiable destinations.

The basic requirement that this function is intended to satisfy is the need to alert management users whenever an event indicating an attack or a potential attack on system security has been detected.

14.7.1   Security Alarms

Security-related events are selected by an event-forwarding discriminator that sends them to a requesting security-management user through the use of the CMIS M-EVENT-REPORT service. These events, known as security alarms, carry a standard set of information as presented by the affected managed object.

Five types of security alarms are supported:

1. *Integrity violation:* an indication that a potential interruption in information flow has occurred, such that information may have been illegally modified, inserted, or deleted

2. *Operational violation:* an indication that the provision of the requested service was not possible due to the unavailability, malfunction, or incorrect invocation of the service

3. *Physical violation:* an indication that a breach of the physical resource has been detected

4. *Security-service or mechanism violation:* an indication that a security attack has been detected by a security service or mechanism

5. *Time-domain violation:* an indication that an event has occurred outside the permitted time period

Table 14.11 lists possible causes for each security-alarm type that has been defined, and Table 14.12 provides a definition for each cause.

14.7.2   Security-Alarm-Reporting Service

The security-alarm-reporting service allows a user in the agent role to report security alarms. The service uses the CMIS primitive M-EVENT-REPORT (Table 13.2, part [a]). The event-type parameter in the request primitive defines the type of security-alarm report (Table 14.11). The event-information parameter is provided by the user to the security-alarm-reporting service and is, in turn, provided to the M-EVENT-REPORT service; Table 14.13 lists the subparameters of this parameter.

Table 14.11 Security-Alarm Types and Causes

Security-Alarm Type	Security-Alarm Causes
Integrity violation	Duplicate information
	Information missing
	Information modification detected
	Information out of sequence
	Unexpected information
Operational violation	Denial of service
	Out of service
	Procedural error
	Other reason
Physical violation	Cable tamper
	Intrusion detection
	Unspecified reason
Security-service or mechanism violation	Authentication failure
	Breach of confidentiality
	Unauthorized access attempt
	Other reason
Time-domain violation	Delayed information
	Key expired
	Out-of-hours activity

14.8 SECURITY-AUDIT-TRAIL FUNCTION

X.740/ISO 10164-8 specifies the kinds of event reports that should be contained in a log that is to be used for evaluating the security of an open system as well as the performance of security mechanisms. Security-audit trails can be used to look for security attacks that are not detectable as they occur. This function is an extension of the log-control function.

The types of security-related events that may be subject to security auditing include:

- Connections
- Disconnections
- Security-mechanism utilization
- Management operations
- Usage accounting

The security-audit-trail-function also provides the ability to control the security-audit-trail logging mechanism.

The security-audit-trail service uses the CMIS primitive M-EVENT-REPORT (Table 13.2, part [a]). The event-type parameter in the request primitive indicates the type of security-audit-trail report and may take one of two values:

1. *Service report:* an indication of an event appertaining to the provision, denial, or recovery of a service

Table 14.12 Explanation of Security-Alarm Causes

Authentication failure

An indication that an attempt to authenticate a user was unsuccessful.

Breach of confidentiality

An indication that information may have been read by an unauthorized user.

Cable tamper

An indication that a physical violation of a communications medium has occurred.

Delayed information

An indication that information has been received later than expected.

Denial of service

An indication that a valid request for service has been prevented or disallowed.

Duplicate information

An indication that an item of information has been received more than once and therefore may be a replay attack.

Information missing

An indication that expected information has not been received.

Information modification detected

An indication—for example, by a data-integrity mechanism—that information has been modified.

Information out of sequence

An indication that information has been received in an incorrect sequence.

Intrusion detection

An indication that either the site on which the identified equipment is located may have been illegally entered or the equipment itself has been violated.

Key expired

An indication that an out-of-date encipherment key has been presented or used.

Nonrepudiation failure

An indication that communication has been prevented or halted due to a failure or an unavailability of a nonrepudiation service.

Out-of-hours activity

An indication that resource utilization has occurred at an unexpected time.

Out of service

An indication that a valid request for service could not be satisfied due to the unavailability of the service provider.

Procedural error

An indication that an incorrect procedure has been used in invoking a service.

Unauthorized access attempt

An indication that an access-control mechanism has detected an illegal attempt to access a resource.

Unexpected information

An indication that information that was not expected has been received.

Unspecified reason

An indication that an unspecified security-related event has occurred.

---

2. *Usage report:* an indication of a record that contains information of a statistical nature

The event-information parameter that is provided by the user to the security-audit-trail service and is, in turn, provided to the M-EVENT-REPORT service contains the following elements:

Service-report cause	C
Notification identifier	U
Correlated notifications	U
Additional text	U
Additional information	U

Table 14.13 Event Information for the Security-Alarm-Reporting Service

Parameter	Use	Description
Security-alarm cause	M	Indicates one of the causes defined for this alarm type.
Security-alarm severity	M	Indicates indeterminate, critical, major, or minor.
Security-alarm detector	M	Identifies the detector of the security alarm.
Service user	M	Identifies the service user whose request for service led to the generation of the security alarm.
Service provider	M	Identifies the intended provider of the service that led to the generation of the security alarm.
Notification identifier	U	Identifies this notification.
Correlated notifications	U	Lists other notifications that are associated with this notification.
Additional text	U	Allows for the inclusion of a free-form text description relevant to the security alarm.
Additional information	U	Allows for the inclusion of additional information relevant to the security alarm.

The service-report-cause parameter may take one of the following values:

- *Request for service:* The notification has been generated because of a request for the provision of service.

- *Denial of service:* The notification has been generated because a request for service has been denied.

- *Response from service:* The notification has been generated because a request for service has been satisfied.

- *Service failure:* The notification has been generated because an abnormal condition that caused the service to fail has been detected during the provision of a service.

- *Service recovery:* The notification has been generated because a service has recovered from an abnormal condition.

- *Other reason:* The notification has been generated for reasons other than those just listed.

14.9 ACCESS-CONTROL-MANAGEMENT FUNCTION

X.741/ISO 10164-9 specifies a model for controlling access to management information and operations. It specifies managed objects and attributes to be used to grant or deny access according to the access control policy represented by this access-control-management information.

Various levels of access control may be required. Some users may be given read and write access to specific attributes, whereas other users may have only read access or no access. Access

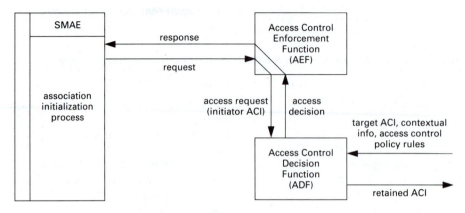

(a) Access control for a management association

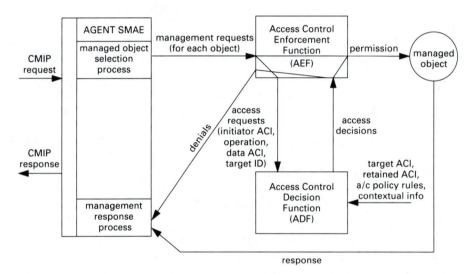

(b) Access control for management operations

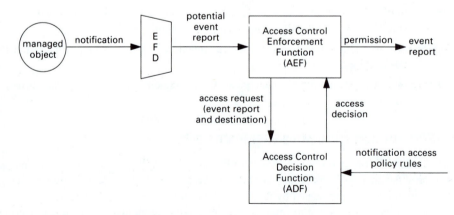

(c) Access-control for a management notification

Figure 14.7 Access-Control Model

control must prevent management notifications from being sent to unauthorized recipients, prevent unauthorized initiators from having access to management operations, and protect management information from unauthorized disclosure.

14.9.1   Access-Control Model

Figure 14.7 depicts the access-control model. A request for access to an object is validated by an access-control function that may grant or deny access according to an access-control policy. The access control policy for a given object is in fact represented by an access control object associated with the given object. Figure 14.7, part (a), shows the access-control aspects of establishing a management association, which is a logical connection at the application level. The association process passes the request to the access-control-enforcement function, which, in turn, passes the access-control information (ACI) to the access-control-decision function. The ADF compares the subject ACI to ACI related to the target and examines contextual information (address of the requester, time of day, etc.) and the relevant access-control-policy rules. The access decision is sent back to the AEF. If the decision is to grant access, the ACI is retained for future decisions.

Figure 14.7, part (b), provides an example of the access-control aspects of management operations. A request for access to a managed object triggered by a CMIP action results in a management request to the AEF. To enable the ADF to make a decision, the AEF passes it the required information: the ACI of the initiator, the management operation (action, create, delete, get, or set), ACI related to the data, and the identification of the target (object class and instance, action identifier, attribute identifiers). The ADF examines the retained ACI for the association that generated the request, as well as the target ACI, contextual information, and access-control-policy rules to make a decision. If permission is granted, the AEF allows the management request to be presented to the managed object.

Figure 14.7, part (c), provides an example of the access-control aspects of a management notification. A notification is issued by a managed object and passed to an event-forwarding discriminator. If the notification passes the discriminator filter, a potential event report is generated and sent to the AEF. To enable the ADF to make a decision, the AEF passes it the required information. This information consists of the event report itself and the intended destination for the report. The ADF examines this information and the notification access-policy rules. If permission is granted, the AEF allows the event report to be issued.

14.9.2   Access-Control Mechanisms

The access-control-management function supports the use of three different categories of access-control mechanisms, as defined in ISO 10181-3: access-control lists, capability tickets, and security labels.

To explain the difference between the first two categories, consider the concept of an access matrix (Figure 14.8). The basic elements in the matrix are:

- *Initiator:* an entity capable of accessing targets. Generally, the concept of initiator equates with that of user. Any user or application actually gains access to a target by means of a process that represents that user or application.

- *Target:* anything to which access is controlled. Examples include files, portions of files, programs, and segments of memory. In particular, in the context of systems management, managed objects are the entities to which access is attempted.

	Target1	**Target2**	• • •	**Targetn**
Initiator1	Read Execute	Read Write		
Initiator2				Read
• • •				

(a) Access matrix

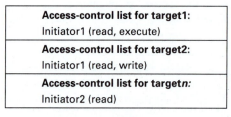

Access-control list for target1:
Initiator1 (read, execute)

Access-control list for target2:
Initiator1 (read, write)

Access-control list for targetn:
Initiator2 (read)

(b) Access-control list

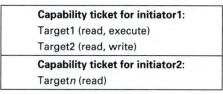

Capability ticket for initiator1:
Target1 (read, execute)
Target2 (read, write)

Capability ticket for initiator2:
Targetn (read)

(c) Capability ticket

Figure 14.8 Access-Control Structures

- *Access right:* the way in which a target is accessed by an initiator. Examples are read, write, and execute.

One axis of the matrix consists of identified initiators that may attempt data access. Typically, this list will consist of individual users or user groups, although access could be controlled for terminals, hosts, or applications instead of or in addition to users. The other axis lists the targets that may be accessed. Each entry in the matrix indicates the access rights of that initiator for that target.

In practice, an access matrix is usually sparse and is implemented by decomposition in one of two ways. The matrix may be decomposed by columns, yielding *access-control lists* (Figure 14.8, part [b]). Thus, for each target, an access-control list lists users and their permitted access rights. The access-control list may contain a default, or public, entry. This allows users that are not explicitly listed as having special rights to have a restricted default set of rights. Elements of the list may include individual users as well as groups of users.

Decomposition by rows yields *capability tickets* (Figure 14.8, part [c]). A capability ticket specifies authorized targets and operations for a user. Each user has a number of tickets and may be authorized to loan or give them to others. Because tickets may be dispersed around the system, they present a greater security problem than access-control lists.

The third category of access-control mechanism is based on the use of *security labels*. In this scheme, each target has a classification level, and each initiator has a clearance level. This scheme is commonly used in military and intelligence applications, with the levels identified as confidential, secret, top-secret, and so forth. In this scheme, there must be an access-control policy that dictates the required clearance level for access to a given classification level.

The most common set of rules used with security labels is referred to as multilevel security, and it consists of the following:

- *No read up:* A subject can only read an object of less or equal security level. This is referred to in the literature as the simple security property.

- *No write down:* A subject can only write into an object of greater or equal security level. This is referred to in the literature as the *-property[2] (pronounced *star property*).

The no-write-down policy often strikes the first-time reader as the opposite of what is wanted. Some thought should convince you, however, that this policy is in fact a desirable security policy. Consider the case of an individual with Secret security clearance. Such an individual may possess a document labeled with a Secret security classification. Now consider the following actions:

1. The individual places a copy of the document in a filing cabinet labeled Secret. Obviously this should be allowed.

2. The individual places a copy of the document in a filing cabinet labeled Unclassified. This is equivalent to "writing down" information. It should be equally obvious that this should not be allowed either. If a Secret document is placed in an Unclassified filing cabinet, other individuals without the proper security clearance will have access to the Secret document.

3. The individual places a copy of the document in a Top Secret filing cabinet. This is equivalent to "writing up" information. Since the document is labeled Secret, there is no security violation in placing it in a Top Secret filing cabinet. Anyone who is authorized to open a Top Secret filing cabinet is certainly cleared to read Secret documents.

14.9.3 Access-Control Objects

One design goal for the access-control-management function is to separate the elements of management information from the specification of mechanisms to be used to protect the management information. To achieve this goal, the access-control information is modeled as a set of managed objects. These managed objects are used by the access-control mechanism in a system to regulate access to its management information.

Three classes of managed objects are used for the access-control-management function:

---

2. The "*" does not stand for anything. No one could think of an appropriate name for the property during the writing of the first report on the model. The asterisk was a dummy character entered in the draft so that a text editor could rapidly find and replace all instances of its use once the property was named. No name was ever devised, and so the report was published with the "*" intact.

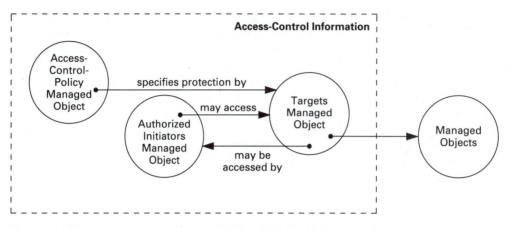

Figure 14.9 Relationships among Managed Objects (ISO 10164-9)

1. Access-control-policy objects
2. Targets objects
3. Authorized-initiators objects

Figure 14.9 illustrates the relationship of these objects to each other and to the management information objects to be protected. Table 14.14 lists the attributes of these objects.

To understand the three classes of security-related objects and their relationships, we need two definitions:

1. *Security policy:* a set of criteria, or rules, for the provision of security services
2. *Security domain:* a set of elements under a given security policy administered by a single authority for some specific classes of security-relevant activity

Each managed open system has at least one domain. A system may have more than one domain to describe security for different sets of elements. Examples of elements within a security domain include:[3]

- OSI (*N*)-layer connections
- Operations relating to a specific management function (e.g., authentication)
- Nonrepudiation operations involving a notary

The security policy defines what is meant by security within the domain, the security rules for the elements within the domain, and the classes of activity to which the rules apply.

With these concepts in mind, we can provide a brief definition of each of the three classes of managed objects that are used for the access control management functions listed earlier. This is followed by a more detailed discussion of each.

There is a single access-control-policy object associated with each security domain. This object identifies the rules and types of access-control mechanisms applicable within the domain. The

---

3. For more detail on OSI security, see Stallings (1993c).

domain is specified in terms of a set of targets objects contained within the access-control-policy object. Each targets object identifies managed objects to which access control applies and specifies the initiators that access the protected objects by pointing to the list of authorized initiators (the authorized-initiators object). The set of targets objects contained within an access-control-policy object defines the set of objects that fall under the corresponding security domain.

The access-control-policy object also contains a set of authorized-initiator objects. Each authorized-initiator object identifies the access rights of a set of initiators and contains pointers to the list of targets they may access.

Thus, the overall structure allows for the identification of both the targets that particular initiators may access and which initiators may access particular targets, all within a specific security domain with a specific security policy.

14.9.3.1 Access-Control-Policy Object
On a given system, a security domain is represented by a single access-control-policy object, which may contain the following information:

- Access rules that define the access-control policies for the establishment of management associations, for the control of management notifications, and for the execution of operations on managed objects
- The name of the security domain
- The identity of the security-domain authority
- Validity information—for example, the period during which access is valid
- Protection information

The association access policy defines the access-control rules for both initiators and responders in association establishment. It specifies the mechanisms that must be employed by the initiator and the restrictions to be used by the responder. For example, the responder may restrict access on the basis of the identity of the application entity that is requesting the association.

Similarly, the notification access policy defines the access restrictions that are to be applied before forwarding an event report or storing a log entry. Finally, the object access policy defines the access restrictions to be applied for access to particular objects.

In all these cases, the policy specifies the kind of access controls that may be applied. The specific access controls are defined in the targets objects.

14.9.3.2 Targets Object
The targets object includes the following information:

- Sets of managed objects selected by name, containment, or filtering
- The operations that may be performed on those managed objects
- The initiators that are authorized to request those operations

14.9.3.3 Authorized-Initiators Object
The authorized-initiators object is used to specify authorized initiators, which may be identified by:

- *Capability:* Initiators are not specifically identified. Possession of a particular capability enables an initiator to obtain certain access rights.

Table 14.14 Access-Control Attributes

Access-Control-Policy Object	Targets Object	Authorized Initiators	Attribute	Description
		C	Access-control list	List of names for a security policy based on an access-control list.
M			Access-control-policy object name	Instance name of the access-control-policy object.
M			Association access policy	Set of access-control rules that are applied to association control.
		C	Authentication information	Authentication requirements to be applied to initiators that request the establishment of management associations or that request access to specified targets.
		M	Authorized-initiators object name	Instance name of the authorized-initiators object.
		C	Capability	A capability that applies to elements of management information for a security policy based on capabilities.
C	C	C	Cryptographic algorithm	Identifies the registered algorithm used to encrypt access-control information.
C	C	C	Cryptographic checksum	Value of the checksum that was generated by the use of the cryptographic algorithm on the access-control information. It can be used to verify that the access-control information has not been altered.
	M		Initiator list	List of instance names of authorized-initiator objects. Used to associate lists of initiators with the targets and operations that they are allowed to access.
M			Notification access policy	Rules to be applied to the output of event-forwarding discriminators to prevent the unauthorized forwarding of event reports and to prevent the unauthorized storage of log records.

	Attribute	Description	
M	Object access policy	Rules to be applied when determining access to objects. Permissions and denials can be specified for the protection of objects, individual actions, attributes, and values of set-valued attributes.	M
C	Object list	Set of identifiers of all objects specified by the selected objects attribute.	C
M	Operations	Set of operations that may be performed on the associated set of objects by the associated authorized initiators.	M
C	Security domain	Name of the security domain and identifier of the security-domain authority.	C
	Security label	A label that can be associated with an initiator or with management information. Used for a security policy based on security labels.	C
M	Selected objects	Set of managed objects to which the associated access controls are to be applied. Set may be specified as individual objects, classes, or subtrees. Selection may be refined by the use of filters.	M
M	Targets list	Set of instance names of targets objects. Used to identify those sets of objects to which particular access controls are to be applied.	M
M	Targets object name	Instance name of a targets managed object.	M
C	Time of creation	Time at which the access-control information was created.	C
C	Valid from	Time at which the access-control information becomes valid.	C
C	Valid until	Time at which the access-control information no longer applies.	C

M = attribute that is part of a mandatory package for this object.
C = attribute that is part of a conditional package for this object.

Table 14.15 Accounting-Meter-Function Terminology

Term	Definition
Accounting meter	The abstraction of activities, monitoring the utilization of resources, for the purpose of accounting and controlling the recording of accounting data.
Accounting meter control	Accounting meter functionality dedicated to controlling the activities of gathering and providing data concerning the utilization of resources.
Accounting meter control object	A managed object dedicated to the control of accounting management.
Accounting meter data	Data that accounts for the use of a resource and from which accounting records may be derived.
Accounting meter data object	A managed object dedicated to the provision of management data.
Accounting record object	A data item containing accounting information relating to a specific period of resource utilization by a specific user.

- *Label:* Initiators are not specifically identified. An initiator provides evidence of permission to access management information on the basis of the value of a security label.

- *Identity:* Initiators are identified by individual, anonymous, or group names. In this case, the object includes an access-control list.

14.10   ACCOUNTING-METER FUNCTION

X.742/ISO 10164-10 specifies a model for accounting for the usage of system resources and a mechanism for enforcing account limits. The standard defines account meters and logs and specifies services for retrieving, reporting, and recording resource-usage data and for selecting which usage data are to be collected and under what conditions they are to be reported. Table 14.15 lists the terminology employed in the standard.

An accounting meter is an abstraction that represents the accounting-management function. There are two aspects to this function:

1.   Control of the reporting of data associated with the usage of a resource

2.   The specifics of the recorded data

To provide visibility of both aspects, three types of management-support objects are defined: accounting-meter-control object, accounting-meter-data object, and accounting-record object.

14.10.1   Accounting-Meter-Control Object

The accounting-meter-control object specifies the rules for the collection of accounting data as they relate to specific resources and their utilization. Accounting-management control allows a managing system to:

- Collect resource-usage data from a resource and enable and disable the collection through operations upon an accounting-meter-control object

- Select, within the constraints imposed by a particular managed-object class, which resource-usage data are to be collected and under what circumstances they are to be reported

In order to collect resource-utilization data for one managed object or a set of managed objects, an accounting-meter-control object that specifies such collection must exist. The accounting-meter-control object can be generated as part of the creation of the resource-object instance, or it can be generated later, in response to a management request for the accounting function.

The ASN.1 definition of the accounting-meter-object class is as follows:

```
accountingMeterControlObject MANAGED OBJECT CLASS
    DERIVED FROM "ISO10165-2":top
    CHARACTERIZED BY meter-control-info PACKAGE
    BEHAVIOR
    AMControlBehavior BEHAVIOR
        DEFINED AS "When an instance of accounting meter control has been created to
        account for usage of a named resource, it controls the behavior of related instances of
        accounting meter data through its recording-triggers and reporting-triggers attributes.
        These identify the internal events which will cause a unit-of-usage to be recorded within
        a controlled instance of accounting meter data and cause accountingRecord notification
        to be generated respectively. When the named resource requires no further accounting
        and there are no more instances of usage, the instance of account meter control may be
        deleted";;
    ATTRIBUTES
    control-object-id        GET,
    units-of-usage           GET,
    recording-triggers       GET-REPLACE, ADD-REMOVE,
    reporting-triggers       GET-REPLACE, ADD-REMOVE;;
CONDITIONAL PACKAGES
    accounting-Meter-Actions PACKAGE
        ACTIONS              start,
                             suspend,
                             resume;
        NOTIFICATIONS        accountingStarted,
                             accountingSuspended,
                             accountingResumed,
                             "ISO10165-2":objectCreation,
                             "ISO10165-2":objectDeletion;
    REGISTERED AS {joint-iso-ccitt ms(9) function(2) part10(10) package(4) 1};
        PRESENT IF "the Specific problems parameter is present in the alarm notification
        or event report corresponding to the instance of alarm record",
    REGISTERED AS {joint-iso-ccitt ms(9) function(2) part10(10) managedObjectClass(3) 1};
```

The attributes of an accounting-meter-control object are:

- *Control-object ID:* identifies this object instance.

- *Units of usage:* specify the type of accounting unit being used. Possible units include SDUs (service data units), PDUs (protocol data units), seconds, minutes, bits, octets, characters, and blocks.

- *Recording triggers:* specify occurrences causing an update to the accounting-meter data. Events may be of three types: periodically scheduled, induced as a result of accounting-meter actions (e.g., upon the resumption of accounting for usage), and induced as a result of an identified stimulus (e.g., completion of a service request).

- *Reporting triggers:* specify occurrences causing the accounting-meter-data object to emit an accounting-record notification.

The conditional accounting-Meter-Actions package is included when the resource supports explicit actions upon a control object and related data objects. The start-metering action allows a manager to start or restart accounting. The effect of a start or restart is to initialize accounting-usage parameters for related data objects and to set the meter condition to running. The suspend-metering action causes current usage values to be held and suspends metering. This allows the manager to retrieve specific usage values. The resume-metering action resumes the accounting without reinitializing accounting-usage parameters.

14.10.2 Accounting-Meter-Data Object

Resource-usage data represent the use made of a resource by a user of that resource. An accounting-meter-data object contains information identifying the user of the resource and a measure of the quantity used, together with qualifying data.

The ASN.1 definition of the accounting-meter-object class is as follows:

```
accountingMeterDataObject MANAGED OBJECT CLASS
    DERIVED FROM ''ISO10165-2'':top
    CHARACTERIZED BY meter-data-info PACKAGE
        ATTRIBUTES
        data-object-id      GET,
        requester-id        GET,
        responder-id        GET,
        subscriber-id       GET,
        meter-info          GET,
        data-errors         GET;
        NOTIFICATIONS    accountingRecord
                         ''ISO10165-2'':objectCreation,
                         ''ISO10165-2'':objectDeletion;;;
    CONDITIONAL PACKAGES
    meter-time-info PACKAGE
        ATTRIBUTES
        usage-start-time    GET,
        usage-meter-time    GET;
        REGISTERED AS {joint-iso-ccitt ms(9) function(2) part10(10) package(4) 2};
            PRESENT IF ''the accountable resource supports timing information'',
        data-meter-condition PACKAGE
```

ATTRIBUTES   data-object-conditionGET;
REGISTERED AS {joint-iso-ccitt ms(9) function(2) part10(10) package(4) 3};
        PRESENT IF "the accountable resource supports explicit actions upon the control
        object and related data objects",
REGISTERED AS {joint-iso-ccitt ms(9) function(2) part10(10) managedObjectClass(3) 2};

The mandatory attributes of an accounting-meter-data object are:

- *Data-object ID:* identifies this object instance.

- *Requester ID:* indicates the user of the service provided.

- *Responder ID:* indicates the service provider.

- *Subscriber ID:* indicates the subscriber having a contract with the authority providing the resource that is subject to accounting metering on behalf of the identified requester.

- *Meter info:* provides accounting data relating to the specific usage of a resource. Its parameters are unit, which defines the class of unit used to measure usage; usage, which is the amount of units used; and tariff, which defines tariff-related information.

- *Data errors:* indicates whether the usage data are believed to be in error.

The conditional meter-time-info package provides timing information. The usage-start-time parameter provides the time at which accounting started. The usage-meter-time parameter indicates whether the time is the current time (metering is still taking place) or the time at which metering was stopped.

The conditional data-meter-condition package includes the data-object-condition attribute, which indicates whether the meter is running or suspended.

14.10.3 Accounting-Record Object

The data contained in accounting records may be derived either as a result of reading accounting data from an accounting-meter-data object or as a result of notifications generated by instances of accounting-meter data. They are logged according to the discriminator construct used by a log that contains accounting records.

14.10.4 Accounting-Meter Service

During the lifetime of an accounting-meter-control object and its related accounting-meter-data objects, attributes of these objects may be read and, if permissible, modified using the pass-through services of object management. In addition, the accounting-meter function makes direct use of CMIS for the following services:

- Accounting-meter-action service

- Accounting-meter-control-notification service

- Accounting-meter-data-record-notification service

The *accounting-meter-action service* is invoked by a user of the accounting-meter function to trigger an action on the part of a peer user. On receipt of a user request, the accounting-meter-action service makes use of the CMIS M-ACTION service to transmit the request (Table 13.2, part

[d]). The mode parameter is always confirmed, requesting either an action response or an error response. The action type is one of three values: start, suspend, resume.

When an accounting-meter-control object generates an event to provide data related to actions, it may communicate this information using the CMIS M-EVENT-REPORT service (Table 13.2, part [a]). The *accounting-meter-control-notification service* delivers the information to the intended destination user. The event-information parameter that is provided by the user to the accounting-meter-control-notification service and is, in turn, provided to the M-EVENT-REPORT service contains the following elements:

Action response	M
Units of usage	U
Recording triggers	U
Reporting triggers	U

When an accounting-meter-data object generates an event to provide data upon the usage of resources, it may communicate this information using the CMIS M-EVENT-REPORT service (Table 13.2, part [a]). The *accounting-meter-data-record-notification service* delivers the information to the intended destination user. The event-information parameter that is provided by the user to the accounting-meter-data-record-notification service and is, in turn, provided to the M-EVENT-REPORT service contains the following elements:

Notification cause	M
Requester ID	M
Responder ID	M
Provider ID	M
Subscriber ID	M
Meter information	M
Data errors	M
Usage-start time	U
Usage-meter time	U
Data-object condition	U
Extension	U

14.11 WORKLOAD-MONITORING FUNCTION

X.739/ISO 10164-11 specifies a model for monitoring the attributes of managed objects. It defines managed objects that can report events based on the values of counters and gauges that reflect system performance. Services are provided for initiating, terminating, suspending, resuming, and modifying workload monitoring. A key use of workload monitoring is to recognize potential resource-overload situations, which is an important fault-prevention function.

Table 14.16 lists the terminology employed in the standard. A key concept is that of capacity, which is the amount of a resource that can be supplied to users, consisting of already-allocated capacity and available capacity. The systems manager is concerned with monitoring the level of demand on the capacity of various resources. To support this requirement, the workload-monitoring function provides a service that can be characterized along several dimensions:

Table 14.16 Workload-Monitoring-Function Terminology

Term	Definition
Capacity	Current amount of resources available to serve users, including resources already allocated for use, as well as resources available for future allocation.
Resource Utilization	The amount of capacity in use. It can be measured as instantaneous (amount in use at a point in time) or an estimate of the mean (mean resource utilization calculated over a period of time).
Resource Rejection Rate	An estimate of the mean amount of service requests rejected per unit time, calculated over a period of time.
Resource Request Rate	An estimate of the mean amount of service requests per unit time, calculated over a period of time.
Severe Threshold	Indicates that a gauge value is close to or at capacity (for resource utilization) or that maximum acceptable rate (for rejection rate or request rate) has been met or exceeded.
Severe Clear Threshold	Indicates that the severe condition has cleared.
Early Warning Threshold	Indicates that a gauge value is approaching capacity (for resource utilization) or the maximum rate (for rejection rate or request rate).
Early Warning Clear Threshold	Indicates that the early warning condition has cleared.
Gauge	An attribute whose value represents a dynamic variable in the system. The value of the gauge may be incremented or decremented. Changes that would take the gauge beyond its maximum or minimum leave the gauge value at its maximum or minimum respectively.
Counter	An attribute whose integer value is associated with some internal event. The value is incremented by 1 when the event occurs. When it reaches its maximum value, it wraps around to 0.
Metric Object	A managed object that contains at least one attribute whose value is calculated from values of attributes observed in other managed objects.
Gauge Monitor Metric Object	Used for generating notifications based on the thresholds of a gauge for resource utilization, rejection rate, or request rate.
Mean Monitor Metric Object	Used for generating notifications related to a time averaged value of the resource utilization, rejection rate, or request rate.

- *Resource-usage model:* resource utilization, resource-rejection rate, and resource-request rate
- *Managed-object attribute:* settable counter, nonsettable counter, and gauge
- *Metric object:* gauge-monitor metric object and mean-monitor metric object

Three models are defined to fulfill resource-usage-monitoring requirements. *Resource utilization* provides for monitoring the current demand on capacity. The *resource-rejection rate* measures the rate at which resource requests are rejected due to overload. The *resource-request rate* is a measure of the demand on the resource. The workload-monitoring function enables managers to use one or more of these models to meet their requirements. If more than one model is used in monitoring a single resource, there is a relationship among the parameters measured. Figure 14.10 suggests the relationship among the three concepts for the same hypothetical resource.

Another dimension of the workload monitoring function has to do with the nature of the attribute that reflects the performance of a resource. A *counter* is a management abstraction of an underlying counting process. Two types of counters are modeled to meet different needs. A nonsettable (simple) counter is not subject to change by management operation. It simply counts from 0 to some maximum value and then wraps around and begins again at 0. A settable counter exhibits the same behavior as a simple counter, but in addition, its value may be reset by management action. This allows management to reinitialize some resource and begin counting again from 0. Some examples of counters suggested in the ISO (International Organization for Standardization) documents were listed in Table 12.5.

A *gauge* is a management abstraction of an underlying dynamic variable. Examples are the number of logical connections currently operated by a protocol machine or the rate of change of a traffic counter. As the dynamic variable changes, the gauge value increases and decreases.

14.11.1 Metric-Monitoring Process

The basic process provided by the workload-monitoring function can be divided into the following steps:

1. *Data capture:* Data are extracted from the observed objects. This is the basic monitoring function. Observation values are computed by sampling attribute values at intervals specified by the granularity period.

2. *Data conversion:* If there is an interest in observing the rate of change of a counter, then a conditional counter-difference package is included to convert a counter to a gauge. Typically, this is done by taking the difference in counter values over a fixed period of time and repeating the calculation periodically.

3. *Data enhancement:* To find trends within the data, a data-enhancement algorithm may be used to smooth the observed data. The results are stored in a gauge.

4. *Data analysis:* The calculated gauge values may be compared with thresholds to trigger alarms.

14.11.2 Monitor Objects

The workload-monitoring function makes use of a number of managed objects to store statistics on the resources being monitored. Each object, called a metric object, can monitor any of the three performance-related resource attributes (simple counter, settable counter, gauge) and can support

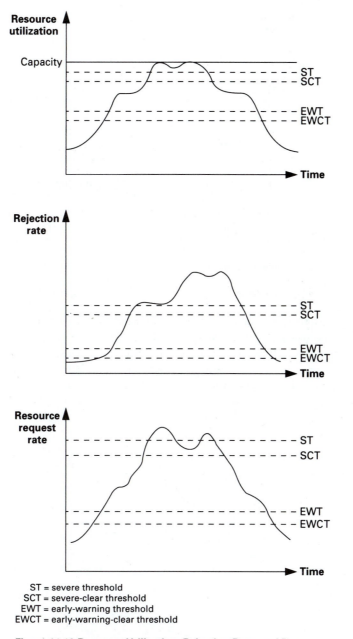

ST = severe threshold
SCT = severe-clear threshold
EWT = early-warning threshold
EWCT = early-warning-clear threshold

Figure 14.10 Resource Utilization, Rejection Rate, and Resource-Request Rate (ISO 10164-11)

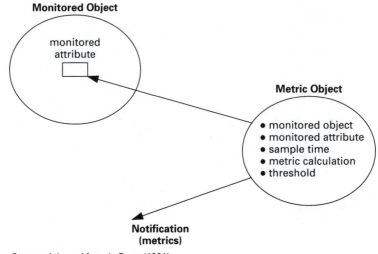

Source: Adapted from LaBarre (1991).

Figure 14.11 Metric Objects

any of the three performance models (resource utilization, resource-rejection rate, resource-request rate). A general depiction of the relationship between metric objects and monitored objects is provided in Figure 14.11. These objects share a number of attributes, and so the object classes have been defined in an inheritance hierarchy, as shown in Figure 14.12. Figure 14.13 provides the ASN.1 definition of each object, while Figure 14.14 defines the associated packages.

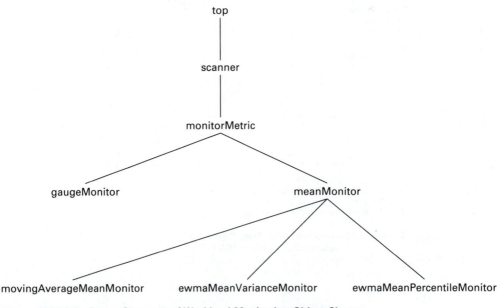

Figure 14.12 Inheritance Structure of Workload-Monitoring-Object Classes

```
monitorMetric MANAGED OBJECT CLASS
    DERIVED FROM scanner;
    CHARACTERIZED BY monitorMetricPackage PACKAGE
    BEHAVIOR DEFINITIONS
    monitorMetricBehavior BEHAVIOR DEFINED AS see clause 8.2.1.1;;
    ATTRIBUTES
        observedObjectInstance          GET,
        observedAttributeId             GET,
        derivedGauge                    GET-REPLACE,
    NOTIFICATIONS
        objectCreation, objectDeletion, stateChange, attributeValueChange;;
    CONDITIONAL PACKAGES
        counterDifferencePackage PRESENT IF data conversion exists;
        derGaugeTimestampPackage PRESENT IF object instance supports timestamping
            associated with updating the derived Gauge;;
    REGISTERED AS { managedObjectClass ?? }

gaugeMonitor MANAGED OBJECT CLASS
    DERIVED FROM monitorMetric;
    CHARACTERIZED BY gaugeMonitorPackage PACKAGE
    BEHAVIOR DEFINITIONS
    gaugeMonitorBehavior BEHAVIOR DEFINED AS see clause 8.2.2.1;;
    ATTRIBUTES
        severityIndicatingGaugeThreshold    GET-REPLACE, ADD-REMOVE;
    NOTIFICATIONS
        qualityOfServiceAlarm;;
    CONDITIONAL PACKAGES
        specificProblemIndication PRESENT IF specific problem indication behavior is
            implemented in the instance;;;
    REGISTERED AS { managedObjectClass ?? }

meanMonitor MANAGED OBJECT CLASS
    DERIVED FROM monitorMetric;
    CHARACTERIZED BY meanMonitorPackage PACKAGE
    BEHAVIOR DEFINITIONS
    meanMonitorBehavior BEHAVIOR DEFINED AS see clause 8.2.3.1;;
    ATTRIBUTES
        estimateOfMean                      GET-REPLACE,
        severityIndicatingGaugeThreshold    GET-REPLACE, ADD-REMOVE;
    NOTIFICATIONS
        qualityOfServiceAlarm;;
    CONDITIONAL PACKAGES
        specificProblemIndication PRESENT IF specific problem indication behavior is
            implemented in the instance;;;
    REGISTERED AS { managedObjectClass ?? }
```

Figure 14.13 Metric Objects (ISO 10164-11)

Note that all the workload-monitoring objects are descended from the scanner object. This is a basic statistics-gathering object described in section 14.13.

Within the set of definitions provided by the workload-monitoring function, the topmost object is the monitorMetric object. The mandatory attributes included in this object are the identity of the managed object under observation and the attribute within that object that is under observation. Thus, a given metric object captures data from a single attribute. The derivedGauge attribute contains the most recent observation and is derived from the managed-object attribute according to the following rules:

```
movingAverageMeanMonitor MANAGED OBJECT CLASS
     DERIVED FROM meanMonitor;
     CHARACTERIZED BY movingAverageMeanMonitorPackage PACKAGE
     BEHAVIOR DEFINITIONS
     movingAverageMeanMonitorBehavior BEHAVIOR DEFINED AS see clause 8.2.6.1;;
     CONDITIONAL PACKAGES
          ewmaGaugeMean PRESENT IF the uwmaGaugeMean package is not present,
          uwmaGaugeMean PRESENT IF the ewmaGaugeMean package is not present,
          incrementingTimeConstant PRESENT IF either the uwmaGaugeMean or ewmaGaugeMean
               package is present and incrementingTimeConstant is supported;;;
REGISTERED AS { managedObjectClass ?? }

ewmaMeanVarianceMonitor MANAGED OBJECT CLASS
     DERIVED FROM meanMonitor;
     CHARACTERIZED BY ewmaMeanVarianceMon PACKAGE
     BEHAVIOR DEFINITIONS
     ewmaMeanVarianceMonitorBehavior BEHAVIOR DEFINED AS see clause 8.2.4.1;;
     ewmaGaugeMeanBehavior BEHAVIOR DEFINED AS see clause B.2.1;;
     ewmaGaugeVarBehavior BEHAVIOR DEFINED AS see clause 8.2.3;;
     ATTRIBUTES
          timeConstant2    GET-REPLACE,
          estimOfVariance   GET-REPLACE;
REGISTERED AS { managedObjectClass ?? }

ewmaMeanPercentileMonitor MANAGED OBJECT CLASS
     DERIVED FROM meanMonitor;
     CHARACTERIZED BY ewmaMeanPctMon PACKAGE
     BEHAVIOR DEFINITIONS
     ewmaMeanPctMonitorBehavior BEHAVIOR DEFINED AS see clause 8.2.5.1;;
     ewmaGaugeMeanBehavior BEHAVIOR DEFINED AS see clause B.2.1;;
     ewmaGaugePctBehavior BEHAVIOR DEFINED AS see clause B.2.4;;
     ATTRIBUTES
          timeConstant2                         GET-REPLACE,
          estimOfLargest                        GET-REPLACE,
          estimOfSmallest                       GET-REPLACE,
          estimOfMedian                         GET-REPLACE,
          estimOf100-PCTPctile                  GET-REPLACE,
          estimOfPCTPctile                      GET-REPLACE,
          numberOfReplications                  GET-REPLACE,
          timeBetweenReplications               GET-REPLACE,
REGISTERED AS { managedObjectClass ?? }
```

Figure 14.13 Metric Objects (continued)

- If the attribute is a gauge, the derivedGauge value is simply the last observed gauge value.

- If the attribute is a simple counter, the derivedGauge value is the difference between successive observations of the counter.

- If the attribute is a settable counter, the derivedGauge value is the value of the counter just prior to its last reset.

For the simple counter, the gauge-value calculation must take into account the wraparound feature of counters. Thus, the gauge value is defined as follows:

$$V(t) = [\text{counter}(t) - \text{counter}(t - DT) + \text{CWV}] \text{ modulo CWV},$$

where

```
configurablePctPackage PACKAGE
    ATTRIBUTES confPCT GET-REPLACE;;
REGISTERED AS { package ?? }

counterDifference PACKAGE
    BEHAVIOR DEFINITIONS
    counterDifferenceBehavior DEFINED AS see clause 8.3.1.1;;
    ATTRIBUTES counterTMinusDT GET-REPLACE;;
REGISTERED AS { package ?? }

derGaugeTimestampPackage PACKAGE
    ATTRIBUTES derivedGaugeTimestamp GET;;
REGISTERED AS { package ?? }

ewmaGaugeMean PACKAGE
    BEHAVIOR DEFINITIONS ewmaGaugeMeanBehavior;
REGISTERED AS { package ?? }

incrementingTimeConstant PACKAGE
    BEHAVIOR DEFINITIONS
    incrementingTimeConstantBehavior DEFINED AS see clause 8.3.2.1;;
    ATTRIBUTES incrementingFactor GET-REPLACE;;
REGISTERED AS { package ?? }

specificProblemIndication PACKAGE
    BEHAVIOR DEFINITIONS
    Included if specific problem Indication is wanted in the metric object instance;
    ATTRIBUTES specificproblemIndicator GET-REPLACE;;
REGISTERED AS { package ?? }

uwmaGaugeMean PACKAGE
    BEHAVIOR DEFINITIONS uwmaGaugeMeanBehavior;
REGISTERED AS { package ?? }
```

Figure 14.14 Package Definitions

$V(t)$	= derived gauge value.
counter(t)	= value of the counter at current time t.
counter($t - DT$)	= previous value of the counter, at time $t - DT$.
DT	= sampling interval.
CWV	= modulus of the counter

14.11.2.1 Gauge-Monitor Metric Object

The gaugeMonitor object simply provides a gauge derived from the counter or gauge under observation. A generic model of a gauge used for workload monitoring is illustrated in Figure 14.15. The gauge can theoretically take on any value between 0 and the upper limit of the gauge variable. For a specific resource attribute, the maximum value it can take on is the capacity of the resource. Associated with the gauge metric object are two pairs of thresholds, which are used to trigger notifications (see Chapter 12 for a discussion of gauge-threshold attributes). The severe threshold indicates that the resource being monitored is at or near capacity; this might trigger some urgent action. The early-warning threshold indicates that the resource being monitored is approaching capacity; this might trigger some countermeasure to avoid saturation. The current ASN.1 definition of the object does not show the early-warning threshold, although the text lists it as an optional attribute.

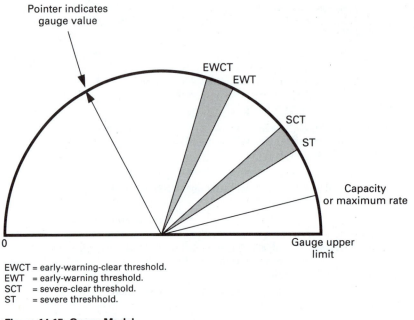

EWCT = early-warning-clear threshold.
EWT = early-warning threshold.
SCT   = severe-clear threshold.
ST   = severe threshhold.

Figure 14.15 Gauge Model

Two types of notification are associated with each threshold. When the threshold is reached or crossed in the positive direction, a notification that the condition exists is sent out. When the threshold is reached or crossed in the negative direction, a notification that the condition has cleared is sent out. To avoid the repeated triggering of event notifications when the gauge makes small oscillations around a threshold value, the threshold is specified in pairs: the higher value is used to trigger the positive-going event, and the lower value is used to trigger the negative-going event. Figure 14.10 illustrates the use of these thresholds for the three monitoring models.

14.11.2.2   Mean-Monitor Metric Objects

The mean-monitor metric objects may be used for generating notifications related to a time-averaged value of the resource utilization. As with the gauge monitor, the mean monitor derives a value from a counter or gauge using the rules just outlined. The difference here is that this derived value is then used as input to a calculation for estimating a mean value. Again, thresholds are used to trigger notifications.

There are three types of mean-monitor metric objects (Figure 14.12). The *movingAverage-MeanMonitor* object is the simplest, providing only an estimate of the mean. The object specifies one of two techniques for calculating the estimated mean:

1. Uniformly weighted moving average (uwma)

2. Exponentially weighted moving average (ewma)

With uwma, each observation over an extended period is given equal weight, and an average value is computed. The formula is:

$$\sim V(t) = \frac{1}{N} \sum_{i=0}^{N-1} V(t - (i \times DT)),$$

where

$V(t)$	= derived gauge value at time t.
$V(t - (i \times DT))$	= derived gauge value at time $t - (i \times DT)$.
$\sim Vt)$	= estimate of the mean of $V(t)$ at time t.
DT	= time between successive observations of $V(t)$.

This value is commonly referred to as the *sample mean*. Note that this formulation gives equal weight to each instance. Furthermore, it requires that the last N values be saved for the calculation. Typically, we would like to give greater weight to more recent instances, since these are more likely to reflect future behavior. Thus, a common technique for predicting a future value on the basis of a time series of past values is to use an *exponential average:*

$$\sim V(t + DT) = \alpha \times V(t + DT) + (1 - \alpha) \times (\sim V(t))$$

By using a constant value of α, independent of the number of past observations, we have a circumstance in which all past values are considered, but the more distant ones have less weight. To see this more clearly, consider the following expansion:

$$\sim V(n \times DT) = \alpha V(n \times DT) + (1 - \alpha)\alpha V((n - 1) \times DT) + \ldots +$$
$$(1 - \alpha)^i \alpha V((n - i) \times DT)$$
$$+ \ldots + (1 - \alpha)^n \sim V(0)$$

Since both α and $(1 - \alpha)$ are less than 1, each successive term in the preceding equation is smaller. The size of the coefficient as a function of its position in the expansion is shown in Figure 14.16. Figure 14.17 compares unweighted averaging with exponential averaging (using two values of α and assuming that the unweighted average covers at least the last 20 observations). In both cases, we start out with an estimate of $\sim V(0) = 0$. Note that exponential averaging tracks changes in attribute values faster than does simple averaging.

The *ewmaMeanVarianceMonitor* object provides estimates of the mean and variance of a derived gauge. The estimate of the mean uses the exponentially weighted moving average algorithm. The estimate of the variance is also calculated using an exponential algorithm. To understand the formulation, first consider the unweighted estimate of variance, commonly referred to as the sample variance:

$$\sim S(t) = \frac{1}{N-1} \sum_{i=0}^{N-1} [V(t) - \sim V(t)]^2$$

where $\sim S(t)$ = estimate of variance at time t.

The exponential average of the variance, which is the algorithm used in the ewmaMean-VarianceMontior object, is as follows:

$$\sim S(t) = \alpha \times [V(t) - \sim V(t)]^2 + (1 - \alpha) \times (\sim S(t - DT)),$$

where

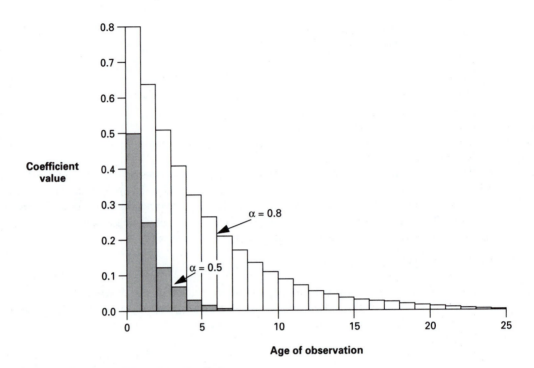

Figure 14.16 Exponential Smoothing Coefficients

DT = time between observations.

$T2$ = time constant for calculating variance, constrained to be a positive value greater than DT.

α = weighting factor $= \dfrac{DT}{T2}$.

The *ewmaMeanPercentileMonitor* object provides estimates of the mean, median, nth percentile, 100-nth percentile, largest, and smallest values of a derived gauge. The n in the nth percentile is a positive integer from 1 to 49 inclusive. All these quantities are calculated using exponential averaging.

14.12 TEST-MANAGEMENT FUNCTION

ISO 10164-12 specifies a model for managing confidence- and diagnostic-test procedures. It defines managed-object classes that are used to control the tests, which may be conducted either interactively or asynchronously, with results to be reported later.

The test-management function provides options for testing along several dimensions:

- Synchronous versus asynchronous test
- Solicited versus unsolicited report
- Implicit versus explicit termination

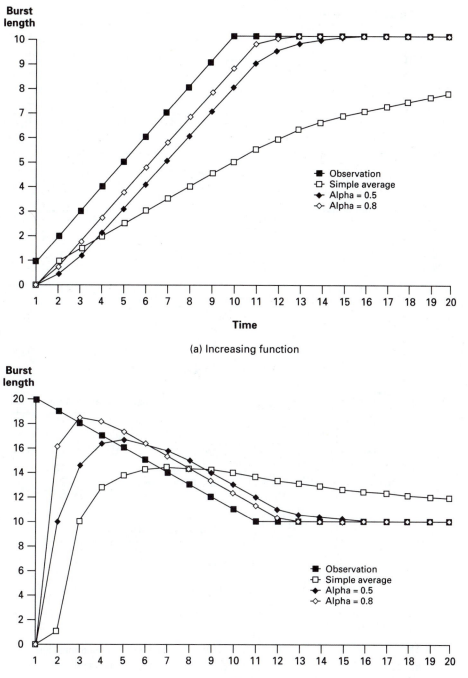

(a) Increasing function

(b) Decreasing function

Figure 14.17   Use of Exponential Averaging

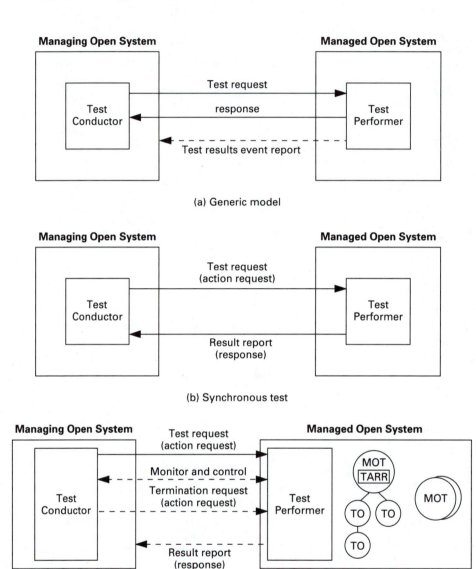

(a) Generic model

(b) Synchronous test

(c) Asynchronous test

Figure 14.18 Test-Management-Function Model (ISO 10164-12)

14.12.1   Test Model

Figure 14.18, part (a), presents a general model of the test-management function. The managing system initiates a test on a remote open system by means of an exchange between application processes. An application process in the managing system, the test conductor, issues a test request to an application process in the managed system, the test performer. Each test involves some action on the managed system, making use of managed objects. In general, a configuration must be set up and a test workload processed. There may also be a need to indicate the scheduling of the test and the reporting of results. The test request may provoke a response, which either includes the test results or which simply acknowledges agreement to perform the test. In the latter case, the test results may be issued at a later time in the form of an event report.

Tests may be defined as being synchronous or asynchronous. In a synchronous test (Figure 14.18, part [b]), the final results of the test are returned in the response to the test initiation operation.

An asynchronous test is one in which the final results of the test are to be made available by some further management operation or via notification. Figure 14.18, part (c), illustrates an asynchronous test and indicates the key elements of the asynchronous-test model:

- *Test-action-request receiver (TARR):* refers to the ability of a managed object to act upon a test request. A managed object with TARR functionality may create an instance of a particular test-object class, representing a particular test invocation.

- *Test object (TO):* object required for the control and monitoring of tests and for the emission of notifications pertaining to tests. The TO holds state information and may hold intermediate and unreported test results.

- *Managed object under test (MOT):* an object that provides a management view of the subjects of tests.

14.12.1.1   Reporting of Test Results

For a synchronous test, the results of the test are reported in the confirmation to the test request. For an asynchronous test, the results may be reported in a solicited or an unsolicited manner. A solicited test result is reported when the test conductor issues a report request to a test object. An unsolicited test result is issued by a test object as a notification.

14.12.1.2   Test Termination

A test may be terminated in one of two ways: implicit and explicit. An explicit test termination occurs when the test conductor requests termination; this occurs for asynchronous tests. The termination may occur whether or not the test is completed. Upon receipt of a test-termination request, the test performer shall terminate the test in progress, perform any necessary cleanup, return available results in test-result reports, and acknowledge the termination request. A test conductor may also request an abnormal, or aborted, test termination by requesting deletion of the test objects participating in the test. In this case, the test performer terminates the test without issuing any additional test-result reports.

Implicit, or spontaneous, termination occurs in synchronous tests upon the fulfillment of predefined criteria, including completion of the test and error conditions.

14.12.2   Test-Management Services

The test-management function provides the following services:

- *Retrieving test-object attributes:* uses the PT-GET service
- *Modifying test-object attributes:* uses the PT-SET service
- *Aborting asynchronous tests:* uses the PT-DELETE service to delete the test objects that constitute the asynchronous test

- *Test request asynchronous service:* uses the M-ACTION service to cause the remote user to create the required test objects

- *Test request synchronous service:* uses the M-ACTION service to cause the remote user to perform the test and report the results

- *Test-suspend/resume service:* uses the M-ACTION service to suspend/resume an asynchronous test

- *Test-termination service:* uses the M-ACTION service to terminate an asynchronous test

- *Test-result service:* uses the M-EVENT-REPORT service to report asynchronous-test results

- *Scheduling-conflict service:* uses the M-EVENT-REPORT service to report a test-schedule conflict

14.13   SUMMARIZATION FUNCTION

ISO 10164-13 defines a model and managed-object classes used to summarize and apply statistical analysis to management information. The summarization of attribute values includes specific object instances across time (time averages) and a set of object instances at a particular time (ensemble averages). Services include specifying management objects and attributes that are to be included in summary reports, scheduling observations upon these objects and attributes, and scheduling summary reports.

The summarization function involves extracting information from managed objects and placing it in a summarization object. Information may be obtained from the attributes of managed objects representing underlying resources, metric objects, and log records. The summarization object specifies an algorithm to be used to calculate summary information from the observed attributes. Figure 14.19 depicts the summarization function.

All summarization functions are based on the concept of a scanner. Scanning is a sampling process of observing attribute values at specified points in time. A summarization object may be defined as one of three types of scanners:

1. *Homogeneous scanner:* scans a common set of attribute types across a selected set of object instances to calculate ensemble and time statistics

2. *Heterogeneous scanner:* collects statistics from a set of different attributes collected from different managed objects

3. *Heterogeneous buffered scanner:* the same as a heterogeneous scanner but includes the ability to buffer results so that the results of multiple periods can be reported together

14.13.1   Summarization-Function Objects

The various object classes defined for the summarization function are related to each other in an inheritance hierarchy, as illustrated in Figure 14.20. Most of the objects are descended from the scanner object, which has the following ASN.1 definition:

```
scanner MANAGED OBJECT CLASS
    DERIVED FROM "Rec. X.721 | ISO/IEC 10165-2: top;"
    CHARACTERIZED BY scannerPackage PACKAGE
```

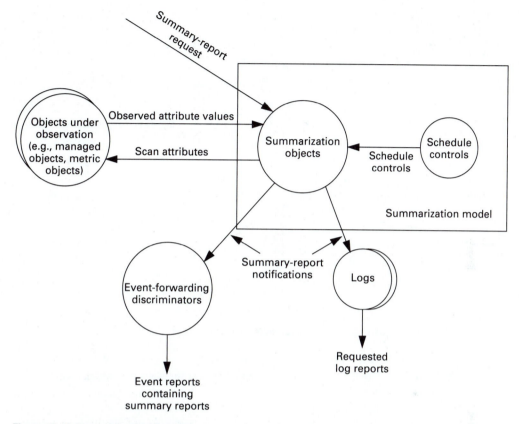

Figure 14.19 Summarization Function

BEHAVIOR
scannerBehavior BEHAVIOR
   DEFINED AS ''see 8.1.1.3'';;
ATTRIBUTES
scannerId GET,
''Rec. X.721 | ISO/IEC 10165-2: administrativeState GET-REPLACE,''
granularityPeriod GET-REPLACE,
''Rec. X.721 | ISO/IEC 10165-2: operationalState GET;;;''
CONDITIONAL PACKAGES
   ''Rec. X.721 | ISO/IEC 10165-2: availabilityStatusPackage''
     PRESENT IF ''the managed object can be scheduled'',
   ''Rec. X.721 | ISO/IEC 10165-2: durationPackage''
     PRESENT IF ''the scanning function is to be enabled between specified start and stop
       times'',
   ''Rec. X.721 | ISO/IEC 10165-2: dailyScheduling''
     PRESENT IF ''daily scheduling is supported and the weekly or external scheduling
       package is not present'',

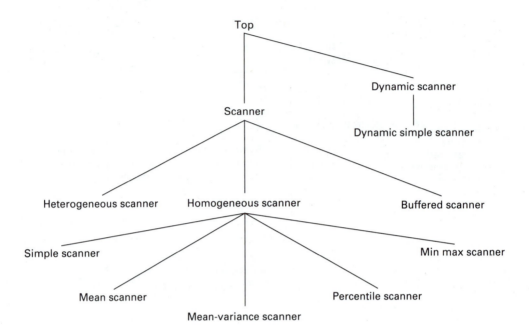

Figure 14.20 Inheritance Structure of Summarization-Object Classes

       ''Rec. X.721 | ISO/IEC 10165-2: weeklyScheduling''

        PRESENT IF ''weekly scheduling is supported and the daily or external scheduling package is not present'',

       ''Rec. X.721 | ISO/IEC 10165-2: externalScheduler''

        PRESENT IF ''reference to external scheduler is supported and the daily or weekly scheduling package is not present'',

      granularityPeriodSynchronizationPackage

        PRESENT IF ''configurable agent internal synchronization of granularity period is supported'',

      configurationEventReportingPackage

        PRESENT IF ''configuration event reporting is supported'',

     REGISTERED AS {summarizationMObjectClass ???};

The scanner-object class is a superclass from which other summarization objects with the capability to emit summary reports are derived. We have also seen that metric-monitoring objects are derived from this superclass. This object defines facilities for periodically sampling the values of a specified set of attributes within specified managed objects.

A managed object of this class represents the ability to retrieve values of attributes of other objects and produce summary information from those values. Observed attributes are retrieved during a scan that is initiated periodically, at the end of each granularity period.

14.13.1.1   Homogeneous Scanners

Homogeneous scanners observe a set of attributes that are common across a number of object instances. The object instances selected for observation are identified by a list or by scoping and filtering. The attributes to be observed in all selected object instances are identified by a list.

The following types of scanner objects are defined:

- *Simple scanner:* reports the values of the scanned attributes
- *Mean scanner:* reports the values and sample means of the scanned attributes
- *Mean-variance scanner:* reports the values and sample variances of the scanned attributes
- *Percentile scanner:* reports the values and sample percentiles of the scanned attributes
- *Min max scanner:* reports the values and minimum and maximum of the scanned attributes

14.13.1.2   Heterogeneous Scanner

The heterogeneous scanner reports, at the end of each granularity period, the sampled values of a set of attributes collected from managed objects. The object includes an observation-identifier-list parameter, which is a set of object classes, object instances, and associated attribute identifiers. The attributes selected for observation may be different in different object instances. The results are reported by pairing attribute values with attribute instance-identifiers.

14.13.1.3   Buffered Scanner

The buffered-scanner object behaves in a manner similar to the heterogeneous scanner. However, instead of reporting at the end of each granularity period, it retains the scanned attribute values and reports these according to a report period specified independently of the granularity period.

14.13.1.4   Dynamic Scanner

A dynamic scanner is one that is activated by an action request to observe specified attributes and return results. The only dynamic scanner defined so far is the dynamic simple scanner, which simply returns the observed values.

14.13.2   Summarization-Function Services

The following services are provided by the summarization function:

- *Modification and retrieval:* uses the PT-CREATE, PT-DELETE, and PT-SET services to create, delete, and modify summarization objects
- *Scan-report service:* uses the M-EVENT-REPORT service to report a scan
- *Statistical report service:* uses the M-EVENT-REPORT service to provide a statistical report
- *Buffered-scan-report service:* uses the M-EVENT-REPORT service to provide a buffered-scan report
- *Action services:* use the M-ACTION service to stimulate reporting of retained values in buffers, a dynamic-scan report, or a partial scan or statistical report

14.14   PRACTICAL ISSUES

14.14.1   Management by Exception

Many current network-management systems overload network operators with raw data that are redundant and difficult to assimilate for effective monitoring and control. Typically, such systems are based on regular polling for large volumes of data. Such an approach overloads both the network communications capacity and the management station processing capacity, to say nothing of the human operator's management capacity.

Although it is true that OSI systems management provides an almost overwhelmingly complex set of management information and management functions, these can be used intelligently to ease the burden on the network, the network-management station, and the network operator. Essentially, the strategy should be similar to the trap-directed polling concept, discussed in Chapter 4.

This approach is often called management by exception; LaBarre (1991) lists the key elements of the strategy:

1. Use infrequent polling to determine connectivity between managed systems and the management stations. Such polling could be done using efficient lower-layer protocol facilities, such as network-layer echo. Alternatively, some simple queries via the object-management function could be used.

2. Maintain information about the network configuration, fault history, and "normal" levels of component and system performance as indicated by metrics derived from raw-data sample measurements made at the managed system. The log-control, workload-monitoring, and summarization functions can be used to set up the appropriate MIB (management information base) objects.

3. Transfer information—not raw data—from managed systems to the manager station in the form of timely event reports containing notifications about significant occurrences in the network. Alarm-reporting and event-report management support this function, as well as notifications defined in the workload-monitoring and summarization functions.

4. Use the timely exception reports (event reports) about faults, configuration changes, and deviations from "normal" or desired performance—along with information about the network configuration, fault history, and "normal" component and system performance levels—to diagnose problems and make decisions to effect control actions. One such decision may be to request additional information from the affected devices to assist in the decision process.

The MIB provides, potentially, an abundance of information, and the set of systems-management functions provides an abundance of functionality for performing network management. To make OSI management manageable, it is essential to employ a manageable number of functions on a manageable MIB. A practical approach is to rely heavily on management by exception and to begin with a modest number of objects (a small MIB) and a modest amount of functionality. Then, as both the configuration and the expertise of the staff grow, the network-management system can gradually be expanded.

14.14.2 Interoperability

We saw that interoperability problems exist with SNMP (simple network-management protocol), in terms of both the management protocol (section 6.5) and the MIB (section 5.3). One can imagine that these problems will be even more apparent in the OSI scheme, with a more complex protocol and a far more complex MIB structure.

On the other hand, the OSI systems-management scheme provides a rich functionality and an extensive MIB capability. For the network manager who needs more capability than is available in the SNMP family, OSI has appeal, compared to designing and implementing ad hoc capabilities.

The best advice is to be aware of other users' experience with the standards and with specific products and be prepared to start in a modest fashion.

Another consideration is the fact that OSI systems management continues to evolve. Thus, future releases of OSI-based network-management products will exhibit capabilities not found in systems procured earlier. The standards will evolve in a direction that is backward-compatible, but the network manager needs to be aware that there will come a time when the configuration will include equipment representing various incarnations of the standards, limiting the ability to make full use of the latest version of OSI systems management.

14.15 SUMMARY

A set of systems-management functions (SMFs) has been defined within OSI systems management. Each SMF provides a general-purpose, application-level functionality. The SMFs serve as building blocks for constructing applications for the five systems-management functional areas (SMFAs). The following SMFs have been defined:

- *Object management:* provides basic services for object manipulation; these map more or less directly onto CMIS services.

- *State management:* used to monitor the past state of managed objects, receive notices in response to changes in the state of managed objects, and administratively alter the state of managed objects.

- *Relationship management:* used for establishing, examining, and monitoring the relationships among objects.

- *Alarm reporting:* specifies generic alarm notifications, together with their parameters and semantics.

- *Event-report management:* enables a manager to control the transmission of event reports from managed objects independently of the definition of those managed objects.

- *Log control:* provides for logging according to manager-settable schedules and manager-creatable logging criteria.

- *Security-alarm reporting:* provides services for creating, deleting, and modifying event-forwarding discriminators for controlling the selection of security alarms and their distribution to manager-specifiable destinations.

- *Security-audit trail:* specifies the kinds of event reports that should be contained in a log that is to be used for evaluating the security of an open system.

- *Access-control management:* specifies managed objects and attributes to be used to grant or deny access according to the access-control policy represented by this access-control-management information.

- *Accounting meter:* provides services for retrieving, reporting, and recording resource-usage data and for selecting which usage data are to be collected and under what conditions they are to be reported.

- *Workload monitoring:* provides services for initiating, terminating, suspending, resuming, and modifying workload-monitoring functions.

- *Test management:* defines managed-object classes that are to be used to control confidence and diagnostic tests.
- *Summarization:* provides services for specifying management objects and attributes that are to be included in summary reports, scheduling observations upon these objects and attributes, and scheduling summary reports.

Appendix A
The Open Systems
Interconnection (OSI)
Reference Model

Throughout this book, reference is made to both the concepts and the specifics of the open systems interconnection reference model. For the reader unfamiliar with the OSI model, this appendix provides a brief overview. Greater detail can be found in Stallings (1993c) or Stallings (1994).

A.1 CONCEPTS

With the widespread use of communications networks and distributed computing, standards are needed to promote interoperability among vendor equipment and to encourage economies of scale. Because of the complexity of the communications task, no single standard will suffice. Rather, the functions should be broken down into more manageable parts and organized as a communications architecture. The architecture would then form the framework for standardization.

This line of reasoning led the ISO (International Organization for Standardization) in 1977 to establish a subcommittee to develop such an architecture. The result was the open systems interconnection reference model. Although the essential elements of the model were in place quickly, the final ISO standard, ISO 7498, was not published until 1984. A technically compatible version was issued by the CCITT (International Consultative Committee on Telegraphy and Telephony) as X.200.

Table A.1, excerpted from ISO 7498, summarizes the purpose of the model. Note that the emphasis is on developing a framework within which standards can be developed. Thus, we can view OSI as a master plan for all networking standards.

A.1.1 The Concept of Open Systems

Open systems interconnection is based on the concept of cooperating distributed applications. In the OSI model, a system consists of a computer, all of its software, and any peripheral devices attached to it, including terminals. A distributed application is any activity that involves the exchange of information between two open systems. Here are some examples of such activities:

Table A.1 Purpose of the OSI Model Standard (ISO 7498)

The purpose of this International Standard Reference Model of Open Systems Interconnection is to provide a common basis for the coordination of standards development for the purpose of systems interconnection, while allowing existing standards to be placed into perspective within the overall Reference Model.

The term Open Systems Interconnection (OSI) qualifies standards for the exchange of information among systems that are ''open'' to one another for this purpose by virtue of their mutual use of the applicable standards.

The fact that a system is open does not imply any particular systems implementation, technology or means of interconnection, but refers to the mutual recognition and support of the applicable standards.

It is also the purpose of this International Standard to identify areas for developing or improving standards, and to provide a common reference for maintaining consistency of all related standards. It is not the intent of this International Standard either to serve as an implementation specification, or to be a basis for appraising the conformance of actual implementations, or to provide a sufficient level of detail to define precisely the services and protocols of the interconnection architecture. Rather, this International Standard provides a conceptual and functional framework which allows international teams of experts to work productively and independently on the development of standards for each layer of the Reference Model of OSI.

- A user at a terminal on one computer is logged onto an application such as transaction processing on another computer.

- A file-management program on one computer transfers a file to a file-management program on another computer.

- A user sends an electronic-mail message to a user on another computer.

- A process-control program sends a control signal to a robot.

OSI is concerned with the exchange of information between a pair of open systems and not with the internal functioning of each individual system. Specifically, it is concerned with the capability of systems to cooperate in exchanging information and accomplishing tasks.

The objective of the OSI effort is to define a set of standards that will enable open systems located anywhere in the world to cooperate by being interconnected through some standardized communications facility and by executing standardized OSI protocols.

An open system may be implemented in any way, provided that it conforms to a minimal set of standards that allows communication to be achieved with other open systems. An open system consists of a number of applications, an operating system, and system software such as a database-management system and a terminal-handling package. It also includes the communications software that turns a closed system into an open system. Different manufacturers will implement open systems in different ways, in order to achieve a product identity that will increase their market share or create a new market. However, virtually all manufacturers are now committed to providing communications software that behaves in conformance with OSI in order to provide their customers with the ability to communicate with other open systems.

Table A.2 Principles Used in Defining the OSI Layers (ISO 7498, 1984)

1. Do not create so many layers as to make the system engineering task of describing and integrating the layers more difficult than necessary.
2. Create a boundary at a point where the description of services can be small and the number of interactions across the boundary are minimized.
3. Create separate layers to handle functions that are manifestly different in the process performed or the technology involved.
4. Collect similar functions into the same layer.
5. Select boundaries at a point which past experience has demonstrated to be successful.
6. Create a layer of easily localized functions so that the layer could be totally redesigned and its protocols changed in a major way to take advantage of new advances in architecture, hardware or software technology without changing the services expected from and provided to the adjacent layers.
7. Create a boundary where it may be useful at some point in time to have the corresponding interface standardized.*
8. Create a layer where there is a need for a different level of abstraction in the handling of data, for example morphology, syntax, semantic.
9. Allow changes of functions or protocols to be made within a layer without affecting other layers.
10. Create for each layer boundaries with its upper and lower layer only.

Similar principles have been applied to sublayering:

11. Create further subgrouping and organization of functions to form sublayers within a layer in cases where distinct communication services need it.
12. Create, where needed, two or more sublayers with a common, and therefore minimal functionality to allow interface operation with adjacent layers.
13. Allow by-passing of sublayers.

---

* The advantages and drawbacks of standardizing internal interfaces within open systems are not considered in this international standard. In particular, mention of, or reference to, principle 7 should not be taken to imply usefulness of standards for such internal interfaces.

It is important to note that OSI per se does not require interfaces within open systems to be standardized. Moreover, whenever standards for such interfaces are defined, adherence to such internal-interface standards can in no way be considered as a condition of openness.

A.1.2   The Model

A widely accepted structuring technique, and the one chosen by the ISO, is layering. The communications functions are partitioned into a hierarchical set of layers. Each layer performs a related subset of the functions required to communicate with another system. It provides services to the next higher layer and relies on the next lower layer both to perform more primitive functions and to conceal the details of those functions. Ideally, the layers should be defined so that changes in one layer do not require changes in the other layers. Thus, we have decomposed one problem into a number of more manageable subproblems.

The ISO's task was to define a set of layers and the services performed by each layer. The partitioning should group functions logically and should have enough layers to make each layer manageably small but should not have so many layers that the processing overhead imposed by the

Table A.3 The OSI Layers

Layer	Definition
1 Physical	Concerned with transmission of unstructured bit stream over physical link; involves such parameters as signal voltage swing and bit duration; deals with the mechanical, electrical, and procedural characteristics needed to establish, maintain, and deactivate the physical link.
2 Data link	Provides for the reliable transfer of data across the physical link; sends blocks of data (frames) with the necessary synchronization, error control, and flow control.
3 Network	Provides upper layers with independence from the data-transmission and switching technologies used to connect systems; responsible for establishing, maintaining, and terminating connections across networks.
4 Transport	Provides reliable, transparent transfer of data between end points; provides end-to-end error recovery and flow control.
5 Session	Provides the control structure for communication between applications; establishes, manages, and terminates connections (sessions) between cooperating applications.
6 Presentation	Performs generally useful transformations on data to provide a standardized application interface and to provide common communications services; examples include encryption, text compression, and reformatting.
7 Application	Provides services to the users of the OSI environment; examples include transaction server, file-transfer protocol, and network management.

collection of layers is burdensome. The principles that guided the design effort are summarized in Table A.2. The resulting reference model has seven layers, which are listed with a brief definition in Table A.3. Table A.4 provides the ISO's justification for the selection of these layers.

Figure A.1 illustrates the OSI architecture. Each system contains the seven layers. Communication is between applications in the two computers, labeled application X and application Y in the figure. If application X wishes to send a message to application Y, it invokes the application layer (layer 7). Layer 7 establishes a peer relationship with layer 7 of the target computer, using a layer-7 protocol (application protocol). This protocol requires services from layer 6, so the two layer-6 entities use a protocol of their own, and so on down to the physical layer, which actually transmits bits over a transmission medium.

Note that there is no direct communication between peer layers except at the physical layer. That is, above the physical layer, each protocol entity sends data down to the next lower layer to get the data across to its peer entity. Even at the physical layer, the OSI model does not stipulate that two systems be directly connected. For example, a packet-switched or circuit-switched network may be used to provide the communication link. This point should become clearer later in this appendix, when we discuss the network layer.

Table A.4 Justification of the OSI Layers (ISO 7498, 1984)

1. It is essential that the architecture permits usage of a realistic variety of physical media for interconnection with different control procedures (for example V.24, V.25, etc.). Application of principles 3, 5, and 8 (Table A.2) leads to identification of a **Physical Layer** as the lowest layer in the architecture.

2. Some physical communication media (for example telephone line) require specific techniques to be used in order to transmit data between systems despite a relatively high error rate (i.e., an error rate not acceptable for the great majority of applications). These specific techniques are used in data-link control procedures which have been studied and standardized for a number of years. It must also be recognized that new physical communication media (for example fiber optics) will require different data-link control procedures. Application of principles 3, 5, and 8 leads to identification of a **Data Link Layer** on top of the Physical Layer in the architecture.

3. In the open systems architecture, some open systems will act as the final destination of data. Some open systems may act only as intermediate nodes (forwarding data to other systems). Application of principles 3, 5, and 7 leads to identification of a **Network Layer** on top of the data link layer. Network oriented protocols such as routing, for example, will be grouped in this layer. Thus, the Network Layer will provide a connection path (network-connection) between a pair of transport entities; including the case where intermediate nodes are involved.

4. Control of data transportation from source end open system to destination end open system (which is not performed in intermediate nodes) is the last function to be performed in order to provide the totality of the transport service. Thus, the upper layer in the transport service part of the architecture is the **Transport Layer,** on top of the Network Layer. This Transport Layer relieves higher layer entities from any concern with the transportation of data between them.

5. There is a need to organize and synchronize dialogue, and to manage the exchange of data. Application of principles 3 and 4 leads to the identification of a **Session Layer** on top of the Transport Layer.

6. The remaining set of general interest functions are those related to representation and manipulation of structured data for the benefit of application programs. Application of principles 3 and 4 leads to the identification of a **Presentation Layer** on top of the Session Layer.

7. Finally, there are applications consisting of application processes which perform information processing. An aspect of these application processes and the protocols by which they communicate comprise the **Application Layer** as the highest layer of the architecture.

Some useful OSI terminology is illustrated in Figure A.2. For simplicity, any layer is referred to as the (N) layer, and names of constructs associated with that layer are also preceded by "(N)." Within a system, there is one or more active entities in each layer. An (N) entity implements functions of the (N) layer and also the protocol for communicating with (N) entities in other systems. An example of an entity is a process in a multiprogrammed or multitasking system. There

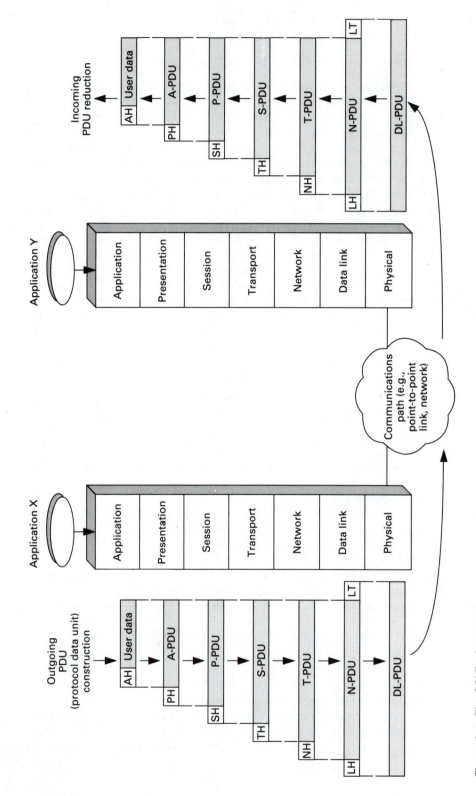

Figure A.1 The OSI Environment

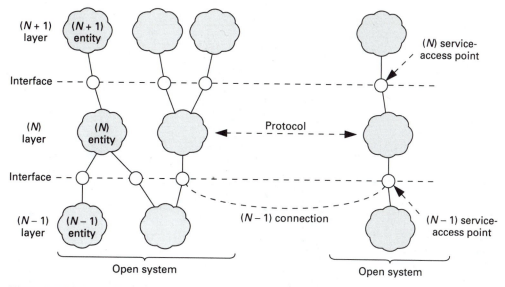

Figure A.2 The Layer Concept

may be multiple identical (N) entities if this is convenient or efficient for a given system. There might also be differing (N) entities, corresponding to different protocol standards at that level. Each entity communicates with entities in the layers above and below it across an interface. The interface is realized as one or more service-access points. Finally, two (N) entities may communicate across a logical connection provided as a service by the (N − 1) layer and known as an (N − 1) connection.

A.1.3   Standardization within the OSI Framework

The principal motivation for the development of the OSI model was to provide a framework for standardization. Within the model, one or more protocol standards can be developed at each layer. The model defines in general terms the functions to be performed at that layer and facilitates the standards-making process in two ways:

1. Since the functions of each layer are well defined, standards can be developed independently and simultaneously for each layer. This speeds up the standards-making process.
2. Since the boundaries between layers are well defined, changes in standards in one layer need not affect already-existing software in another layer. This makes it easier to introduce new standards.

Figure A.3 illustrates the use of the OSI model as such a framework. The overall communications function is decomposed into seven distinct layers, using the principles outlined in Table A.2. These principles essentially amount to using modular design. That is, the overall function is broken up into a number of modules, making the interfaces between modules as simple as possible. In addition, the design principle of information hiding is used: lower layers are concerned with greater

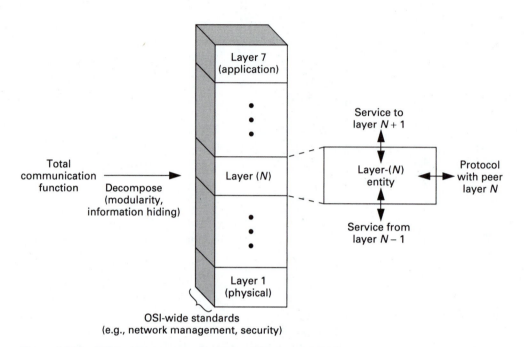

Figure A.3 The OSI Architecture as a Framework for Standardization

levels of detail; upper layers are independent of these details. Within each layer, both the service provided to the next higher layer and the protocol to the peer layer in other systems is provided.

Figure A.4 shows more specifically the nature of the standardization required at each layer. Three elements are key:

1. *Protocol specification:* Two entities at the same layer in different systems cooperate and interact by means of a protocol. Since two different open systems are involved, the protocol must be specified precisely. This includes the format of the protocol data units exchanged, the semantics of all fields, and the allowable sequence of PDUs.

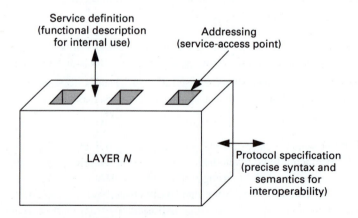

Figure A.4 Layer-Specific Standards

Table A.5 Primitive Types

Request	A primitive issued by a service user to invoke some service and to pass the parameters needed to fully specify the requested service.
Indication	A primitive issued by a service provider to do either of two things: 1. Indicate that a procedure has been invoked by the peer service user on the connection and to provide the associated parameters 2. Notify the service user of a provider-initiated action
Response	A primitive issued by a service user to acknowledge or complete some procedure previously invoked by an indication to that user.
Confirm	A primitive issued by a service provider to acknowledge or complete some procedure previously invoked by a request by the service user.

2. *Service definition:* In addition to the protocol or protocols that operate at a given layer, standards are needed for the services that each layer provides to the next higher layer. Typically, the definition of services is equivalent to a functional description that defines *what* services are provided but not *how* the services are to be provided.

3. *Addressing:* Each layer provides services to entities at the next higher layer. These entities are referenced by means of a service-access point (SAP). Thus, a network service-access point (NSAP) indicates a transport entity that is a user of the network service.

The need to provide a precise protocol specification for open systems is self-evident. The other two items in the preceding list warrant further comment. With respect to service definitions, the motivation for providing only a functional definition is as follows. First, the interaction between two adjacent layers takes place within the confines of a single open system and is not the concern of any other open system. Thus, as long as peer layers in different systems provide the same services to their next higher layers, the details of how the services are provided may differ from one system to another without loss of interoperability. Second, it will usually be the case that adjacent layers are implemented on the same processor. In that case, we would like to leave the system programmer free to exploit the hardware and operating system to provide an interface that is as efficient as possible.

The final aspect of standardization within a layer is addressing, which is explored later in this appendix.

A.1.4   Services

The services between adjacent layers in the OSI architecture are expressed in terms of primitives and parameters. A primitive specifies the function to be performed, and the parameters are used to pass data and control information. The actual form of a primitive is implementation-dependent. An example is a procedure call.

Four types of primitives are used in standards to define the interaction between adjacent layers in the architecture (X.210). These are defined in Table A.5. The layout of Figure A.5, part (a), suggests the time ordering of these events. For example, consider the transfer of data from an (N) entity to a peer (N) entity in another system. The following steps occur:

1. The source (N) entity invokes its $(N - 1)$ entity with a DATA.request primitive. Associated with the primitive are the parameters needed, such as the data to be transmitted and the destination address.

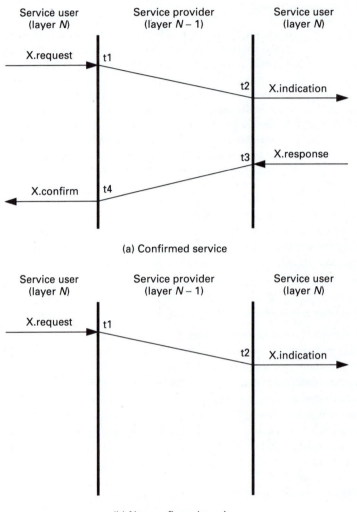

(a) Confirmed service

(b) Nonconfirmed service

Figure A.5 Time-Sequence Diagrams for Service Primitives

2.   The source $(N - 1)$ entity prepares an $(N - 1)$ PDU to be sent to its peer $(N - 1)$ entity.

3.   The destination $(N - 1)$ entity delivers the data to the appropriate destination (N) entity via a DATA.indication, which includes the data and source address as parameters.

4.   If an acknowledgment is called for, the destination (N) entity issues a DATA.response to its $(N - 1)$ entity.

5.   The $(N - 1)$ entity conveys the acknowledgment in an $(N - 1)$ PDU.

6.   The acknowledgment is delivered to the (N) entity as a DATA.confirm.

This sequence of events is referred to as a *confirmed service,* because the initiator receives confirmation that the requested service has had the desired effect at the other end. If only request and indication primitives are involved (corresponding to steps 1 through 3), then the service dialogue is a *nonconfirmed service;* the initiator receives no confirmation that the requested action has taken place (Figure A.5, part [b]).

A.1.5   Protocols

A.1.5.1   Protocol Data Units

A protocol is concerned with exchanging streams of data between two entities. Usually, the transfer can be characterized as consisting of a sequence of blocks of data of some bounded size, referred to as protocol data units (PDUs). Each PDU contains control information that is used to coordinate the joint operation of the two entities engaged in the protocol. In addition, some of the PDUs contain user data from the next higher layer.

Figure A.1 illustrates the use of PDUs in the OSI architecture. When application X has data to send to application Y, it transfers the data to an application entity in the application layer. A header consisting of the protocol-control information for the peer layer-7 entity is appended to the data, forming an application PDU. This PDU is now passed as a unit to layer 6. The presentation entity treats the whole unit as data and appends its own header. This process continues down through layer 2, which generally adds both a header and a trailer. This layer-2 PDU is then passed by the physical layer onto the transmission medium as a stream of bits. When the DL-PDU is received by the target system, the reverse process occurs. As the data ascend, each layer strips off the outermost header, acts on the protocol-control information contained therein, and passes the remainder up to the next layer.

A.1.5.2   Segmentation and Reassembly

Figure A.1 suggests a one-to-one correspondence between PDUs at adjacent layers. This is not necessarily the case. An entity in a layer may segment the PDU it receives from the next higher layer into several parts to accommodate its own requirements. These data units must then be reassembled by the corresponding peer layer on the receiving system before being passed up.

There are a number of reasons for segmentation, depending on the context. For example:

- An intervening communications subnetwork may only accept blocks of data up to a certain size. Thus, the network layer would need to break up a single transport PDU into several network PDUs.

- Error control is more efficient with a smaller PDU size. If an error is detected, only a small amount of data may need to be retransmitted if smaller PDUs are used.

- More equitable access to shared facilities, with shorter average delay, can be provided.

- A smaller PDU size may allow receiving entities to allocate smaller buffers.

There are several disadvantages to segmentation that argue for making PDUs as large as possible:

- Each PDU contains a fixed minimum of control information. Hence, the smaller the block, the greater the percentage of overhead.

- PDU arrival may generate an interrupt that must be serviced. Smaller blocks result in more interrupts.

- More time is spent processing smaller and more numerous PDUs.

All these factors must be taken into account by the protocol designer in determining minimum and maximum PDU sizes.

A.2   THE OSI LAYERS

This section provides a brief introduction to each of the seven OSI layers.

A.2.1   Physical Layer

The physical layer covers the physical interface between devices and the rules by which bits are passed from one to another. The physical layer has four important characteristics:

1. *Mechanical:* relates to the physical properties of the interface to a transmission medium. Typically, the specification is of a pluggable connector that joins one or more signal conductors, called circuits.
2. *Electrical:* Relates to the representation of bits (e.g., in terms of voltage levels) and the data-transmission rate of bits.
3. *Functional:* specifies the functions performed by individual circuits of the physical interface between a system and the transmission medium.
4. Procedural: specifies the sequence of events by which bit streams are exchanged across the physical medium.

The physical layer differs from the other OSI layers in that it cannot rely on a lower layer to transmit its PDUs. Rather, it must make use of a transmission medium whose characteristics are not part of the OSI model. There is no physical-layer PDU structure as such; no header of protocol-control information is used. The PDU simply consists of a block or stream of bits.

A.2.2   Data-Link Layer

The data-link layer must deal with both the requirements of the communications facility and the requirements of the user. Whereas the physical layer provides only a raw-bit-stream service, the data-link layer attempts to make the physical link reliable and provides the means to activate, maintain, and deactivate the link. The principal service provided by the data-link layer to higher layers is that of error detection and control. Thus, with a fully functional data-link-layer protocol, the next higher layer may assume error-free transmission over the link.

One of the best-known data-link-control-protocol standards is HDLC (high-level data-link control), developed by the ISO (ISO 4335). It is widely used for point-to-point and multidrop configurations. It is also the ancestor of a number of other data-link-control protocols, including LAPB (link-access protocol, balanced; used in packet-switching networks), LLC (logical link control; used in local area networks), and LAPD (link-access protocol, D channel; used in ISDN [integrated services digital network]).

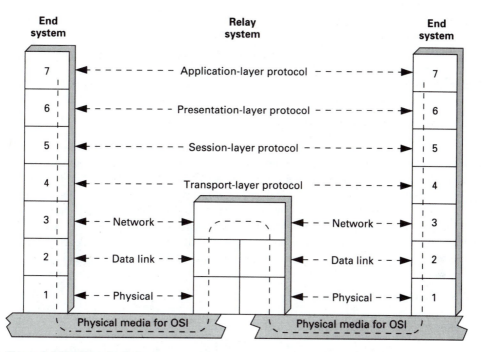

Figure A.6 The Use of a Relay

A.2.3   Network Layer

The network layer provides for the transfer of information between end systems across some sort of communications network. It relieves higher layers of the need to know anything about the underlying data-transmission and switching technologies used to connect systems. At this layer, the computer system engages in a dialogue with the network to specify the destination address and to request certain network facilities, such as priority.

There is a spectrum of possibilities for intervening communications facilities to be managed by the network layer. At one extreme, there is a direct point-to-point link between stations. In this case, there may be no need for a network layer because the data-link layer can perform the necessary function of managing the link.

Next, the systems could be connected across a single network, such as a circuit-switching or packet-switching network. As an example, the packet level of the X.25 standard is a network-layer standard for this situation. Figure A.6 shows how the presence of a network is accommodated by the OSI architecture. The lower three layers are concerned with attaching to and communicating with the network. The packets that are created by the end systems pass through one or more network nodes that act as relays between the two end systems. The network nodes implement layers 1–3 of the architecture. In the figure, two end systems are connected through a single network node. Layer 3 in the node performs a switching and routing function. Within the node, there are two data-link layers and two physical layers, corresponding to the links to the two end systems. Each data-link (and physical) layer operates independently to provide service to the network layer over its respective link. The upper four layers are "end-to-end" protocols between the attached end systems.

At the other extreme, two end systems might wish to communicate but are not even connected to the same network. Rather, they are connected to networks that, directly or indirectly, are connected to each other. This case requires the use of some sort of internetworking technique.

A.2.4   Transport Layer

The transport layer provides a mechanism for the exchange of data between end systems. The connection-oriented transport service ensures that data are delivered error-free, in sequence, with no losses or duplications. The transport layer may also be concerned with optimizing the use of network services and providing a requested quality of service to session entities. For example, the session entity may specify acceptable error rates, maximum delay, priority, and security.

The size and complexity of a transport protocol depend on how reliable or unreliable the underlying network and network-layer services are. Accordingly, the ISO has developed a family of five transport-protocol standards, each oriented toward a different underlying service.

A.2.5   Session Layer

The lowest four layers of the OSI model provide the means for the reliable exchange of data and provide an expedited data service. For many applications, this basic service is insufficient. For example, a remote-terminal-access application might require a half-duplex dialogue. A transaction-processing application might require checkpoints in the data-transfer stream to permit backup and recovery. A message-processing application might require the ability to interrupt a dialogue in order to prepare a new portion of a message and later resume the dialogue where it was left off.

All these capabilities could be embedded in specific applications at layer 7. However, since these types of dialogue-structuring tools have widespread applicability, it makes sense to organize them into a separate layer: the session layer.

The session layer provides the mechanism for controlling the dialogue between applications in end systems. In many cases, there will be little or no need for session-layer services, but for some applications, such services are used. The key services provided by the session layer include:

- *Dialogue discipline:* This can be two-way simultaneous (full-duplex) or two-way alternate (half-duplex).

- *Grouping:* The flow of data can be marked to define groups of data. For example, if a retail store is transmitting sales data to a regional office, the data can be marked to indicate the end of the sales data for each department. This would signal the host computer to finalize running totals for that department and start new running counts for the next department.

- *Recovery:* The session layer can provide a checkpointing mechanism, so that if a failure of some sort occurs between checkpoints, the session entity can retransmit all data since the last checkpoint.

The ISO has issued a standard for the session layer that includes as options services such as those just described.

A.2.6   Presentation Layer

The presentation layer defines the format of the data to be exchanged between applications and offers application programs a set of data-transformation services. The presentation layer defines the syntax used between application entities and provides for the selection and subsequent modification of the representation used. Examples of specific services that may be performed at this layer include data compression and encryption.

A.2.7   Application Layer

The application layer provides a means for application programs to access the OSI environment. This layer contains management functions and generally useful mechanisms to support distributed applications. In addition, general-purpose applications such as file transfer, electronic mail, and terminal access to remote computers are considered to reside at this layer.

A.3   ADDRESSING

This section introduces the two related concepts of service access points and network addresses.

A.3.1   Service-Access Points and Addresses

Consider the following definition from the OSI standard on addressing (ISO 7498-3):

> Within an open system, $(N+1)$ entities and (N) entities are bound together at (N) service access points $[(N)$-SAPs$]$. (N) entities provide service to $(N+1)$ entities via the exchange of service primitives at (N)-SAPs.

Thus, an $(N)-$ SAP may be considered the address that identifies an (N) entity to an $(N-1)$ entity. In the standard, reference is made to *(N) address* as being a general term that applies to a set of (N) SAPs. However, the standard also states that whether an (N) address refers to one or multiple SAPs is a matter local to that system and is not known to other systems. Hence, for all practical purposes, we can think of an SAP as providing an address for an entity.

A.3.2   Network Addresses

The network service-access point (NSAP) occupies a central point in the OSI networking scheme. The *NSAP address* is the abstract term used by OSI to refer to points where the service of the network layer is made available to its users. In practical terms, NSAPs can be considered as the addresses of open systems. The OSI standard defines three properties that NSAP addresses must possess:

1. *Global nonambiguity:* An NSAP identifies a unique open system. Synonyms are permitted. That is, an open system may have more than one NSAP address.

2. *Global applicability:* It is possible at any NSAP to identify any other NSAP, in any open system, by means of the NSAP address of the other NSAP.

3. *Route independence:* Network-service users cannot derive routing information from NSAP addresses. They cannot control the route chosen by the network service by the choice of synonym, nor can they deduce the route taken by an incoming NSDU (network-service data unit) from the source or destination NSAP address.

We also need to contrast the NSAP with another sort of address, known as a *subnetwork address.* An open system environment may consist of multiple networks, with multiple systems on each network. Each network must maintain a unique address for each host attached to that network. This allows the network to route network PDUs through the network and deliver them to the intended destination system. This is referred to as a subnetwork address. The term *subnetwork* is used to identify a physically distinct network that may be part of a complex of interconnected subnetworks to form an open systems environment.

Since the NSAP address uniquely identifies a system, why not use that for the subnetwork address as well? This is not possible since different networks use different addressing schemes, with different formats and address lengths. Thus, there must be a mapping between NSAPs and subnetwork addresses.

A.4   OSI-RELATED STANDARDS

This section provides a brief description of the way in which OSI-related standards are developed.

A.4.1   International Consultative Committee on Telegraphy and Telephony (CCITT)

The CCITT is a committee of the International Telecommunications Union (ITU), which is itself a United Nations treaty organization. Hence, the members of the CCITT are governments. The U.S. representation is housed in the Department of State. The CCITT's charter is "to study and issue recommendations on technical, operating, and tariff questions relating to telegraphy and telephony." Its primary objective is to standardize, to the extent necessary, techniques and operations in telecommunications to achieve end-to-end compatibility of international telecommunication connections, regardless of the countries of origin and destination.

The CCITT is organized into 15 study groups that prepare standards, called recommendations by the CCITT.

Work within the CCITT is conducted in four-year cycles. Every four years, a plenary assembly is held. The work program for the next four years is established at the assembly in the form of questions submitted by the various study groups, based on requests made to the study groups by their members. The assembly assesses the questions, reviews the scope of the study groups, creates new study groups or abolishes existing ones, and allocates questions to them.

Based on these questions, each study group prepares draft recommendations. Two procedures may be followed for the adoption of a new recommendation. The traditional technique is to submit all proposed recommendations to the next assembly, four years hence. A recommendation is approved if it obtains a majority of the votes. All approved recommendations are therefore published as a package of "books" once every four years.

In addition to this four-year cycle, a new method for approving recommendations was adopted at the 1988 assembly. The need for a change was dictated by two factors. First, the increasing volume of standards produced by the CCITT has made the publication process increasingly cumbersome. Many of the recommendations from the 1988 assembly, which totaled over 16,000 pages, were not finally published until 1990, and some were only published in 1991, nearly three years after approval! Second, with fast-moving areas of technology and user demand, such as broadband ISDN, a four-year gap is simply too long between updates. Accordingly, the CCITT adopted a resolution allowing for the approval of recommendations outside the four-year cycle. A study group may submit a proposed recommendation if the group's members unanimously approve. A vote of all members must be completed within four months. If 70 percent or more of the responding members approve, the recommendation is adopted.

A.4.2   International Organization for Standardization (ISO)

The ISO is an international agency for the development of standards on a wide range of subjects. It is a voluntary, nontreaty organization whose members are designated standards bodies of participating nations, plus nonvoting observer organizations. Although the ISO is not a governmental body, more than 70 percent of ISO member bodies are governmental standards institutions or organizations incorporated by public law. Most of the remainder have close links with the public administrations in their own countries. The U.S. member body is the American National Standards Institute (ANSI).

The ISO was founded in 1946 and has issued more than 7,000 standards in a broad range of areas. Its purpose is to promote the development of standardization and related activities to facilitate the international exchange of goods and services and to develop cooperation in the sphere of intellectual, scientific, technological, and economic activity. Standards have been issued to cover everything from screw threads to solar energy. One important area of standardization deals with the open systems interconnection (OSI) communications architecture and the standards at each layer of the OSI architecture.

The development of an ISO standard from first proposal to actual publication of the standard follows a seven-step process. The objective is to ensure that the final result is acceptable to as many countries as possible. The steps are briefly described in the following list. (Time limits are the minimum time in which voting could be accomplished, and amendments require extended time.)

1. A new work item is assigned to the appropriate technical committee and, within that technical committee, to the appropriate working group. The working group prepares the technical specifications for the proposed standard and publishes these as a *committee draft* (CD). The CD is circulated among interested members for balloting and technical comment. At least three months are allowed, and there may be iterations. When there is substantial agreement, the CD is sent to the ISO's administrative arm, known as the Central Secretariat.

2. The CD is registered at the Central Secretariat within two months of its final approval by the technical committee.

3. The Central Secretariat edits the document to ensure conformity with ISO practices; no technical changes are made. The edited document is then issued as a *draft international standard* (DIS).

4. The DIS is circulated for a six-month balloting period. In order to become a final standard, the DIS must receive a majority approval of the technical-committee members and 75 percent approval of all voting members. Revisions may be made to resolve any negative vote. If more than two negative votes remain, it is unlikely that the DIS will be published as a final standard.

5. The approved, possibly revised, DIS is returned within three months to the Central Secretariat for submission to the ISO Council, which acts as the ISO's board of directors.

6. The DIS is accepted by the council as an *international standard* (IS).

7. The IS is published by the ISO.

As can be seen, the process of issuing a standard is a slow one. Certainly, it would be desirable to issue standards as quickly as the technical details can be worked out, but the ISO must ensure that the standards will receive widespread support.

Within the fields of data communications and information processing, there has traditionally been a split between the interests of the CCITT and those of the ISO. The CCITT has primarily been concerned with data-transmission and communication-network issues. Roughly, these occupy the lower three layers of the OSI architecture. The ISO has traditionally been concerned with computer-communications and distributed-processing issues, which correspond roughly to layers 4 through 7. The increasing merger of the fields of data processing and data communications, however, has resulted in considerable overlap in the areas of concern of these two organizations. Fortunately, the growth of the overlap has been accompanied by a growth in cooperation, so that competing standards are not being issued.

A.4.3 International Electrotechnical Commission (IEC)

The IEC, like the ISO, is a voluntary organization composed of national members. The IEC focuses on the technical aspects of electricity. Each member is supposed to represent all the electrical interests within its country, including users, manufacturers, trade associations, government, and academic associations. Frequently, a country's representative to the IEC is the same as its representative to the ISO. The U.S. member body is the ANSI.

Procedures for the adoption of new standards are similar to those within the ISO.

A.4.4 Joint Technical Committee 1 (JTC 1)

Just as there is a growing overlap between the telecommunications concerns of the CCITT and the information-technology interests of the ISO, there is a growing overlap between the interests of the ISO and those of the IEC. Accordingly, in 1987, the ISO and the IEC formed a Joint Technical Committee on information technology. JTC 1 merges the work of ISO Technical Committee 97 on information-processing systems with related IEC technical committees. The standards resulting from JTC 1 carry the double logo of the ISO and the IEC and are published according to the procedures described earlier in this appendix for the ISO. All OSI-related standards issued by the ISO are now published through JTC 1.

Appendix **B**
The TCP/IP Protocol Suite

Based on protocol research and development conducted on its experimental packet-switched network, ARPANET, the U.S. Department of Defense (DOD) has issued a set of military standards for computer-communications protocols. Although there are five of these protocols (Table B.1), the entire set is known by the names of two of them: transmission-control protocol (TCP) and internet protocol (IP). These protocols are in widespread use within the U.S. defense community. But what is more interesting is that they have steadily built up a following in the commercial arena during a time when much attention has been focused on the international standards based on the open systems interconnection (OSI) model. There are hundreds of vendors that provide TCP/IP products, and these are the most widely available and most widely used set of standardized computer-communications protocols.

The TCP/IP architecture, like the OSI model, is layered. In the case of TCP/IP, four layers are involved: network access, internet, host-to-host, and process. This architecture is compared with that of OSI in Figure B.1. The network-access layer contains the protocols that provide access to a communications network, such as a local area network (LAN). Protocols at this layer are between a communications node and an attached host. The TCP/IP suite does not include any unique protocols at this layer. Rather, the protocol appropriate for a particular network (e.g., Ethernet, IEEE 802, X.25) is used.

The internet layer consists of the procedures required to allow data to traverse multiple networks between hosts. Thus, it must provide a routing function. This protocol is implemented within hosts and routers. A router is a processor connecting two networks, whose primary function is to relay data between networks using an internetwork protocol. The protocol at the layer is the *internet protocol*. A typical use of IP is to connect multiple LANs within the same building or to connect LANs at different sites through a wide area packet-switching network.

The host-to-host layer provides the logic for assuring that data exchanged between hosts are reliably delivered. It is also responsible for directing incoming data to the intended application. The protocol at this layer is the *transmission-control protocol*.

Finally, the process layer contains protocols for specific user applications. For each different type of application, such as file transfer, a protocol is needed that supports that application. Three such protocols are included in the TCP/IP protocol suite: SMTP, FTP, and TELNET.

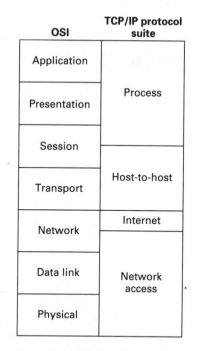

Figure B.1   A Comparison of the OSI and TCP/IP Communications Architectures

B.1   OPERATION OF TCP AND IP

Figure B.2 indicates how the TCP/IP protocols are configured for communications. To make clear that the total communications facility may consist of multiple networks, the constituent networks are usually referred to as *subnetworks*. Some sort of network-access protocol (NAP), such as the Ethernet logic, is used to connect a computer to a subnetwork. This protocol enables the host to

Table B.1 The TCP/IP Protocol Suite

MIL-STD-1777   Internet Protocol (IP)
  Provides a connectionless service for end systems to communicate across one or more networks. Does not assume the network to be reliable.
MIL-STD-1778   Transmission Control Protocol (TCP)
  A reliable end-to-end data-transfer service. Equivalent to the OSI transport protocol.
MIL-STD-1780   File Transfer Protocol (FTP)
  A simple application for the transfer of ASCII, EBCDIC, and binary files.
MIL-STD-1781   Simple Mail Transfer Protocol (SMTP)
  A simple electronic-mail facility.
MIL-STD-1782   TELNET
  Provides a remote log-on facility for simple scroll-mode terminals.

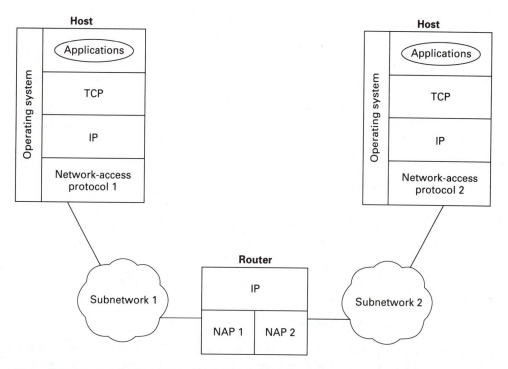

Figure B.2   Communications Using the TCP/IP Protocol Architecture

send data across the subnetwork to another host or, in the case of a host on another subnetwork, to a router. IP is implemented in all the end systems and routers. It acts as a relay to move a block of data from one host, through one or more routers, to another host. TCP is implemented only in the end systems; it keeps track of the blocks of data to assure that all are delivered reliably to the appropriate application.

For successful communication, every entity in the overall system must have a unique address. Actually, two levels of addressing are needed. Each host on a subnetwork must have a unique global internet address; this allows the data to be delivered to the proper host. Each process within a host must have an address that is unique within the host; this allows the host-to-host protocol (TCP) to deliver data to the proper process. These latter addresses are known as ports.

Let us trace a simple operation. Suppose that a process, associated with port 1 at host A, wishes to send a message to another process, associated with port 2 at host B. The process at A hands the message down to TCP with instructions to send it to host B, port 2. TCP hands the message down to IP with instructions to send it to host B. Note that IP need not be told the identity of the destination port. All it needs to know is that the data are intended for host B. Next, IP hands the message down to the network-access layer (e.g., Ethernet logic) with instructions to send it to router X (the first hop on the way to B).

To control this operation, control information as well as user data must be transmitted, as suggested in Figure B.3. Let us say that the sending process generates a block of data and passes this to TCP. TCP may break this block into smaller pieces to make it more manageable. To each

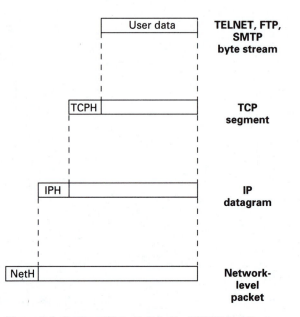

Figure B.3   Protocol Data Unit in the TCP/IP Architecture

of these pieces, TCP appends control information known as the TCP header (TCPH), forming a *TCP segment*. The control information is to be used by the peer TCP-protocol entity at host B. The following are examples of items that are included in this header:

- *Destination port:* When the TCP entity at B receives the segment, it must know to which port the data are to be delivered.

- *Sequence number:* TCP sequentially numbers the segments that it sends to a particular destination port, so that if they arrive out of order, the TCP entity at B can reorder them.

- *Checksum:* The sending TCP includes a code that is a function of the contents of the remainder of the segment. The receiving TCP performs the same calculation and compares the result with the incoming code. A discrepancy results if there has been some error in transmission.

Next, TCP hands each segment over to IP, with instructions to transmit it to B. These segments must be transmitted across one or more subnetworks and relayed through one or more intermediate routers. This operation, too, requires the use of control information. Thus, IP appends a header of control information to each segment to form an *IP datagram*. An example of an item stored in the IP header is the destination host address (in this example, B).

Finally, each IP datagram is presented to the network-access layer for transmission across the first subnetwork in its journey to the destination. The network-access layer appends its own header, creating a packet, or frame. The packet is then transmitted across subnetwork 1 to router X. The packet header contains the information that the subnetwork needs to transfer the data across the subnetwork. Examples of items that may be contained in this header include:

- *Destination subnetwork address:* The subnetwork must know to which attached device the packet is to be delivered.

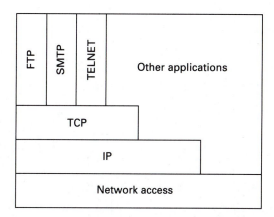

Figure B.4   TCP/IP Protocol Suite: Interfaces

- *Facilities requests:* The network-access protocol might request the use of certain subnetwork facilities, such as priority.

At router X, the packet header is stripped off and the IP header examined. On the basis of the destination-address information in the IP header, the IP module in the router directs the datagram out across subnetwork 2 to B. To do this, the datagram is again augmented with a network access-header.

When the data are received at B, the reverse process occurs. At each layer, the corresponding header is removed, and the remainder is passed on to the next higher layer, until the original user data are delivered to the destination process.

B.2   PROTOCOL INTERFACES

Each layer in the TCP/IP protocol suite interacts with its immediately adjacent layers. At the source, the process layer makes use of the services of the host-to-host layer and provides data down to that layer. A similar relationship exists at the interface of the host-to-host and internet layers and at the interface of the internet and network-access layers. At the destination, each layer delivers data up to the next higher layer.

This use of each individual layer is not required by the architecture. As Figure B.4 suggests, it is possible to develop applications that directly invoke the services of any one of the layers. Most applications require a reliable end-to-end protocol and thus make use of TCP. Some special-purpose applications do not need the services of TCP. Some of these applications, such as SNMP (simple network-management protocol), use an alternative host-to-host protocol known as the user datagram protocol (UDP); others may make use of IP directly. Applications that do not involve internetworking and that do not need TCP have been developed to invoke the network-access layer directly.

It is important to note that the TCP/IP protocol suite is not limited to the five military-standard protocols. Rather, a variety of applications and other processes may make use of this architecture. Figure B.5 shows the position of some of the key protocols commonly implemented as part of the TCP/IP protocol suite.

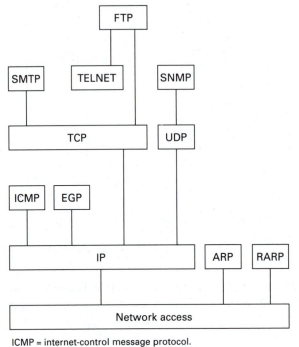

ICMP = internet-control message protocol.
EGP = external gateway protocol.
ARP = address resolution protocol
RARP = reverse address resolution protocol

Figure B.5 Protocol Dependencies

B.3 THE APPLICATIONS

The *simple mail-transfer protocol (SMTP)* provides a basic electronic-mail facility. It offers a mechanism for transferring messages among separate hosts. Features of SMTP include mailing lists, return receipts, and forwarding. The SMTP protocol does not specify how messages are to be created; some local editing or native electronic-mail facility is required. Once a message is created, SMTP accepts the message and makes use of TCP to send it to an SMTP module on another host. The target SMTP module will make use of a local electronic-mail package to store the incoming message in a user's mailbox.

The *file-transfer protocol (FTP)* is used to send files from one system to another under user command. Both text and binary files are accommodated, and the protocol provides features for controlling user access. When a user wishes to engage in file transfer, FTP sets up a TCP connection to the target system for the exchange of control messages. These allow user ID and password to be transmitted and allow the user to specify the file and file actions desired. Once a file transfer is approved, a second TCP connection is set up for the data transfer. The file is transferred over the data connection, without the overhead of any headers or control information at the application level. When the transfer is complete, the control connection is used to signal the completion and to accept new file-transfer commands.

TELNET provides a remote log-on capability, which enables a user at a terminal or personal computer to log on to a remote computer and function as if directly connected to that computer. The protocol was designed to work with simple scroll-mode terminals. TELNET is actually implemented in two modules: User TELNET interacts with the terminal I/O module to communicate with a local terminal; it converts the characteristics of real terminals to the network standard and vice versa. Server TELNET interacts with an application, acting as a surrogate terminal handler so that remote terminals appear as local to the application. Terminal traffic between user and server TELNET is carried on a TCP connection.

B.4   TCP/IP STANDARDS

As was mentioned, the five protocols that make up the core of the TCP/IP protocol suite have been issued as military standards. However, the family of protocols that make up the protocol suite extends far beyond these five core protocols. By universal agreement, an organization known as the Internet Activities Board (IAB) is responsible for the development and publication of these standards, which are published in a series of documents called requests for comments (RFCs).

This section provides a brief description of how standards for the TCP/IP protocol suite are developed.

B.4.1   The Internet and Internet Standards

The Internet is a large collection of interconnected networks, all of which use the TCP/IP protocol suite. The Internet began with the development of ARPANET and the subsequent support by the Defense Advanced Research Projects Agency (DARPA) for the development of additional networks to support military users and government contractors.

The IAB is the coordinating committee for Internet design, engineering, and management. Areas covered include the operation of the Internet itself and the standardization of protocols used by end systems on the Internet for interoperability. The IAB has two principal subsidiary task forces:

1. Internet Engineering Task Force (IETF)
2. Internet Research Task Force (IRTF)

The actual work of these task forces is carried out by working groups. Membership in a working group is voluntary; any interested party may participate.

It is the IETF that is responsible for publishing the RFCs, which are the working notes of the Internet research and development community. A document in this series may be on essentially any topic related to computer communications and may consist of anything from a meeting report to the specification of a standard.

The final decision on which RFCs become Internet standards is made by the IAB, on the recommendation of the IETF. To become a standard, a specification must meet the following criteria:

- Be stable and well understood
- Be technically competent

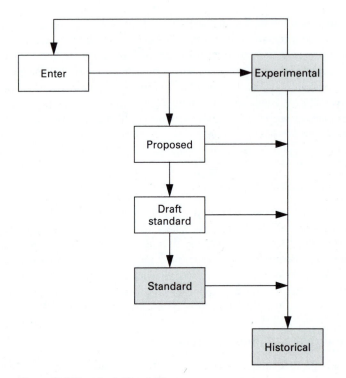

Figure B.6 Standards-Track Diagram

- Have multiple, independent, and interoperable implementations with operational experience
- Enjoy significant public support
- Be recognizably useful in some or all parts of the Internet

The key difference between these criteria and those used for international standards is the emphasis here on operational experience.

B.4.2   The Standardization Process

Figure B.6 illustrates the series of steps, called the *standards track,* through which a specification goes to become a standard. The steps involve increasing amounts of scrutiny and testing. At each step, the IETF must make a recommendation for advancement of the protocol, and the IAB must ratify it.

The white boxes in the diagram represent temporary states, which should be occupied for the minimum practical time. However, a document must remain a proposed standard for at least six months and a draft standard for at least four months to allow time for review and comment. The gray boxes represent long-term states that may be occupied for years.

A protocol or some other specification that is not considered ready for standardization may be published as an experimental RFC. After further work, the specification may be resubmitted. If the specification is generally stable, has resolved known design choices, is believed to be well understood, has received significant community review, and appears to enjoy enough community interest to be considered valuable, then the RFC will be designated a proposed standard.

For a specification to be advanced to draft-standard status, there must be at least two independent and interoperable implementations from which adequate operational experience has been obtained.

After significant implementation and operational experience has been obtained, a specification may be elevated to the status of standard. At this point, the specification is assigned an STD number as well as an RFC number.

Finally, when a protocol becomes obsolete, it is assigned to the historic state.

As of this writing, the following SNMP-related specifications are Internet standards:

Name	RFC	STD
Simple Network Management Protocol	1157	15
Structure of Management Information	1155	16
Management Information Base-II	1213	17

Appendix C
Abstract Syntax
Notation One (ASN.1)

Abstract Syntax Notation One is a formal language developed and standardized by CCITT (the International Consultative Committee on Telegraphy and Telephony; X.208) and ISO (the International Organization for Standardization; ISO 8824). ASN.1 is important for several reasons. First, it can be used to define abstract syntaxes of application data. Although any formal language could be used for this purpose, in practice ASN.1 is likely to be used almost exclusively. In addition, ASN.1 is used to define the structure of application and presentation protocol data units (PDUs). Finally, ASN.1 is used to define the management information base (MIB) for both SNMP (simple network management protocol) and OSI (open systems interconnection) systems management.

Before examining the details of ASN.1, we need to introduce the concept of an abstract syntax and discuss the three uses of ASN.1 mentioned in the preceding paragraph. Then, we will look at the fundamentals of ASN.1. Next, a special and important facility, the ASN.1 macro facility, is examined. Finally, the encoding of data whose values are defined in ASN.1 is introduced.

C.1 ABSTRACT SYNTAX

Table C.1 defines some key terms that are relevant to a discussion of ASN.1, and Figure C.1 illustrates the underlying concepts.

For purposes of this discussion, a communications architecture in an end system can be considered to have two major components. The data-transfer component is concerned with the mechanisms for the transfer of data between end systems. In the case of the TCP/IP (transmission-control protocol/internet protocol) protocol suite, this component would consist of TCP or UDP (user datagram protocol) on down. In the case of the OSI architecture, this component would consist of the session layer on down. The application component is the user of the data-transfer component and is concerned with the end user's application. In the case of the TCP/IP protocol suite, this component would consist of an application, such as SNMP, FTP (file transfer protocol), SMTP (simple mail transfer protocol), or TELNET. In the case of OSI, this component actually

Table C.1 Terms Relevant to ASN.1

Abstract syntax	Describes the generic structure of data independent of any encoding technique used to represent the data. The syntax allows data types to be defined and values of those types to be specified.
Data type	A named set of values. A type may be simple, which is defined by specifying the set of its values, or structured, which is defined in terms of other types.
Encoding	The complete sequence of octets used to represent a data value.
Encoding rules	A specification of the mapping from one syntax to another. Specifically, encoding rules determine algorithmically, for any set of data values defined in an abstract syntax, the representation of those values in a transfer syntax.
Transfer syntax	The way in which data are actually represented in terms of bit patterns while in transit between presentation entities.

consists of the application layer, which is composed of a number of application-service elements, and the presentation layer.

As we cross the boundary from the application to the data-transfer component, there is a significant change in the way in which data are viewed. For the data-transfer component, the data received from an application are specified as the binary value of a sequence of octets. This binary value can be directly assembled into service data units (SDUs) for passing between layers and into protocol data units for passing between protocol entities within a layer. The application component, however, is concerned with a user's view of data. In general, that view is one of a structured set of information, such as text in a document, a personnel file, an integrated database, or a visual display of image information. The user is primarily concerned with the semantics of data. The application component must provide a representation of these data that can be converted to binary values; that is, it must be concerned with the syntax of the data.

The approach illustrated in Figure C.1 to support application data is as follows. For the application component, information is represented in an abstract syntax that deals with data types and data values. The abstract syntax formally specifies data independently from any specific representation. Thus, an abstract syntax has many similarities to the data-type-definition aspects of conventional programming languages such as Pascal, C, and Ada and to grammars such as Backus-Naur Form (BNF). Application protocols describe their PDUs in terms of an abstract syntax.

This abstract syntax is used for the exchange of information between application components in different systems. This exchange consists of application-level PDUs, which contain protocol-control information and user data. Within a system, the information represented using an abstract syntax must be mapped into some form for presentation to the human user. Similarly, this abstract syntax must be mapped into some local format for storage. Note that such a mapping is used in the case of a management information base. However, elements within the MIB are defined using the abstract syntax. Thus, the abstract syntax notation is employed by a user to define the MIB; the application must then convert this definition to a form suitable for local storage.

The component must also translate between the abstract syntax of the application and a transfer syntax that describes the data values in a binary form, suitable for interaction with the data-

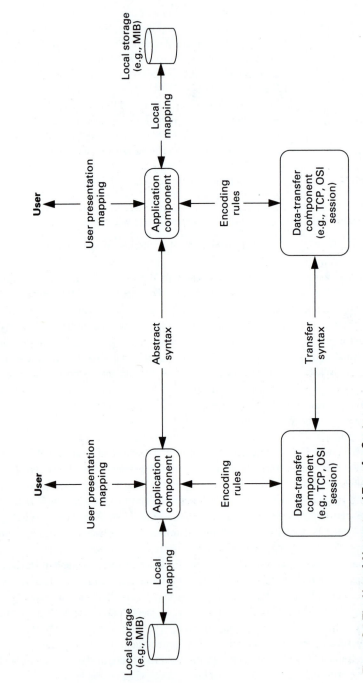

Figure C.1 The Use of Abstract and Transfer Syntaxes

transfer component. For example, an abstract syntax may include a data type of character; the transfer syntax could specify ASCII or EBCDIC encoding.

The transfer syntax thus defines the representation of the data to be exchanged between data-transfer components. The translation from the abstract syntax to the transfer syntax is accomplished by means of encoding rules that specify the representation of each data value of each data type.

This approach for the exchange of application data solves the two problems that relate to data representation in a distributed, heterogeneous environment:

1. There is a common representation for the exchange of data between differing systems.

2. Internal to a system, an application uses some particular representation of data. The abstract/transfer syntax scheme automatically resolves differences in representation between cooperating application entities.

The fundamental requirement for selection of a transfer syntax is that it support the corresponding abstract syntax. In addition, the transfer syntax may have other attributes that are not related to the abstract syntaxes that it can support. For example, an abstract syntax could be supported by any one of four transfer syntaxes, which are the same in all respects except that one provides data compression, one provides encryption, one provides both, and one provides neither. The choice of which transfer syntax to use would depend on cost and security considerations.

C.2 ASN.1 CONCEPTS

The basic building block of an ASN.1 specification is the module. We begin this section by looking at the top-level structure of the module. Then, we introduce some lexical conventions used in ASN.1 definitions. Next, the data types defined in ASN.1 are described. Finally, examples of the use of ASN.1 are given.

C.2.1 Module Definition

ASN.1 is a language that can be used to define data structures. A structure definition is in the form of a named module. The name of the module can then be used to reference the structure. For example, the module name can be used as an abstract syntax name; an application can pass this name to the presentation service to specify the abstract syntax of the APDUs (application protocol data units) that the application wishes to exchange with a peer application entity.

Modules have the following basic form:

```
<modulereference> DEFINITIONS :: =
  BEGIN
    EXPORTS
    IMPORTS
    AssignmentList
  END
```

The modulereference is a module name followed optionally by an object identifier to identify the module. The EXPORTS construct indicates which definitions in this module may be imported

```
ModuleDefinition ::= modulereference DEFINITIONS "::=" BEGIN ModuleBody END
ModuleBody ::= AssignmentList | empty
AssignmentList ::= Assignment | AssignmentList Assignment
Assignment ::= Typeassignment | Valueassignment
Typeassignment ::= typereference "::=" Type
Valueassignment ::= valuereference Type "::=" Value
Type ::= BuiltinType | DefinedType
BuiltinType ::= BooleanType | IntegerType | BitStringType | OctetStringType | NullType |
                SequenceType | SequenceOfType | SetType | SetOfType | ChoiceType |
                SelectionType | TaggedType | AnyType | ObjectIdentifierType |
                CharacterStringType | UsefulType | EnumeratedType | RealType
Value ::= BuiltinValue | DefinedValue
BuiltinValue ::= BooleanValue | IntegerValue | BitStringValue | OctetStringValue | NullValue |
                SequenceValue | SequenceOfValue | SetValue | SetOfValue | ChoiceValue |
                SelectionValue | TaggedValue | AnyValue | ObjectIdentifierValue |
                CharacterStringValue | EnumeratedValue | RealValue
DefinedValue ::= Externalvaluereference | valuereference
BooleanType ::= BOOLEAN
BooleanValue ::= TRUE | FALSE
IntegerType ::= INTEGER | INTEGER {NamedNumberList}
NamedNumberList ::= NamedNumber | NamedNumberList, NamedNumber
NamedNumber ::= identifier(SignedNumber) | identifier(DefinedValue)
SignedNumber ::= number | -number
IntegerValue ::= SignedNumber | identifier
BitStringType ::= BIT STRING | BIT STRING{NamedBitList}
NamedBitList ::= NamedBit | NamedBitList, NamedBit
NamedBit ::= identifier(number) | identifier(DefinedValue)
BitStringValue ::= bstring | hstring | {IdentifierList} | { }
IdentifierList ::= Identifier | IdentifierList, identifier
OctetStringType ::= OCTETSTRING
OctetStringValue ::= bstring | hstring
NullType ::= NULL
NullValue ::= NULL
SequenceType ::= SEQUENCE {ElementTypeList} | SEQUENCE { }
ElementTypeList ::= ElementType | ElementTypeList, ElementType
ElementType ::= NamedType | NamedTypeOPTIONAL | NamedType DEFAULT Value |
                COMPONENTS OF Type
NamedType ::= identifier Type | Type | SelectionType
SequenceValue ::= {ElementValueList } | { }
ElementValueList ::= NamedValue | ElementValueList, NamedValue
SequenceOfType ::= SEQUENCE OF Type | SEQUENCE
SequenceOfValue ::= {ValueList} | { }
SetType ::= SET{ElementTypeList} | SET{ }
SetValue ::= {ElementValueList} | { }
SetOfType ::= SET OF Type | SET
SetOfValue ::= {ValueList} | { }
```

Figure C.2 BNF Grammar for ASN.1 (ISO 8824)

by other modules. The IMPORTS construct indicates which type and value definitions from other modules are to be imported into this module. Neither the IMPORTS nor the EXPORTS construct may be included unless the object identifier for the module is included. Finally, the assignment list consists of type assignments, value assignments, and macro definitions. Macro definitions are discussed in section C.3 of this appendix. Type and value assignments have the following form:

<name> ::= <description>

```
ChoiceType ::= CHOICE {AlternativeTypeList}
AlternativeTypeList ::= NamedType | AlternativeTypeList, NamedType
ChoiceValue ::= NamedValue
SelectionType ::= identifier < Type
SelectionValue ::= NamedValue
TaggedType ::= Tag Type | Tag IMPLICIT Type
Tag ::= [Class ClassNumber]
ClassNumber ::= number | DefinedValue
Class ::= UNIVERSAL | APPLICATION | PRIVATE | empty
TaggedValue ::= Value
AnyType ::= ANY | ANY DEFINED BY identifier
AnyValue ::= Type Value
ObjectIdentifierType ::= OBJECT IDENTIFIER
ObjectIdentifierValue ::= {ObjIdComponentList} | {DefinedValue ObjIdComponent List}
ObjIdComponentList ::= ObjIdComponent | ObjIdComponent ObjIdComponentList
ObjIdComponent ::= NameForm | NumberForm | NameAndNumberForm
NameForm ::= identifier
NumberForm ::= number | DefinedValue
NameAndNumberForm ::= identifier(NumberForm)
CharacterStringType ::= typereference
CharacterStringValue ::= cstring
UsefulType ::= typereference
EnumeratedType ::= ENUMERATED {Enumeration}
Enumeration ::= NamedNumber | NamedNumber, Enumeration
EnumerationValue ::= identifier
RealType ::= REAL
RealValue ::= NumericRealValue | SpecialRealValue
NumericRealValue ::= {Mantissa, Base, Exponent} | 0
Mantissa ::= SignedNumber
Base ::= 2 | 10
Exponent ::= SignedNumber
SpecialRealValue ::= PLUS-INFINITY | MINUS-INFINITY
```

Figure C.2 BNF Grammar for ASN.1 (continued)

Figure C.2 defines the syntax for ASN.1 in Backus-Naur Form. The easiest way to describe the syntax is by example. First, we need to specify some lexical conventions.

C.2.2 Lexical Conventions

ASN.1 structures, types, and values are expressed in a notation similar to that of a programming language. The following lexical conventions are followed:

- Layout is not significant; multiple spaces and blank lines can be considered as a single space.

- Comments are delimited by pairs of hyphens (--) at the beginning and end of the comment or by a pair of hyphens at the beginning of the comment and the end of the line as the end of the comment.

- Identifiers (names of values and fields), type references (names of types), and module names consist of upper- and lowercase letters, digits, and hyphens.

- An identifier begins with a lowercase letter.

- A type reference or a module name begins with an uppercase letter.

- A built-in type consists of all capital letters. A built-in type is a commonly used type for which a standard notation is provided.

C.2.3   Abstract Data Types

ASN.1 is a notation for abstract data types and their values. A type can be viewed as a collection of values. The number of values that a type may take on may be infinite. For example, the type INTEGER has an infinite number of values.

We can classify types into four categories:

1. *Simple:* These are atomic types, with no components.

2. *Structured:* A structured type has components.

3. *Tagged:* These are types derived from other types.

4. *Other:* This category includes the CHOICE and ANY types, defined later in this subsection.

Every ASN.1 data type, with the exception of CHOICE and ANY, has an associated tag. The tag consists of a class name and a non-negative integer tag number. There are four classes of data types, or four classes of tag:

1. *UNIVERSAL:* generally useful, application-independent types and construction mechanisms; these are defined in the standard and are listed in Table C.2.

2. *APPLICATION:* relevant to a particular application; these are defined in other standards.

3. *Context-specific:* also relevant to a particular application, but applicable in a limited context.

4. *Private:* types defined by users and not covered by any standard.

A data type is uniquely identified by its tag. ASN.1 types are the same if and only if their tag numbers are the same. For example, UNIVERSAL 4 refers to OCTET STRING, which is of class UNIVERSAL and has tag number 4 within the class.

C.2.3.1   Simple Types

A simple type is one defined by directly specifying the set of its values. We may think of these as the atomic types; all other types are built up from the simple types. The simple data types in the UNIVERSAL class can be grouped into several categories, as indicated in Table C.2; these are not ''official'' categories in the standard but are used here for convenience.

The first group of simple types can be referred to, for want of a better word, as basic types. The BOOLEAN type is straightforward. The INTEGER type is the set of positive and negative integers and 0. In addition, individual integer values can be assigned names to indicate a specific meaning. The BIT STRING is an ordered set of 0 or more bits; individual bits can be assigned names. The actual value of a BIT STRING can be specified as a string of either binary or hexadecimal digits. Similarly, an OCTET STRING can be specified as a string of either binary or hexadecimal digits. The REAL data type consists of numbers expressed in scientific notation (mantissa, base, exponent); that is:

$$M \times B^E$$

Table C.2 Universal-Class Tag Assignments

Tag	Type Name	Set of Values
Basic Types		
UNIVERSAL 1	BOOLEAN	TRUE or FALSE.
UNIVERSAL 2	INTEGER	The positive and negative whole numbers, including 0.
UNIVERSAL 3	BIT STRING	A sequence of 0 or more bits.
UNIVERSAL 4	OCTET STRING	A sequence of 0 or more octets.
UNIVERSAL 9	REAL	Real numbers.
UNIVERSAL 10	ENUMERATED	An explicit list of integer values that an instance of a data type may take.
Object Types		
UNIVERSAL 6	OBJECT IDENTIFIER	The set of values associated with information objects allocated by this standard.
UNIVERSAL 7	Object descriptor	Each value is human-readable text providing a brief description of an information object.
Character String Types		
UNIVERSAL 18	NumericString	Digits 0 through 9, space.
UNIVERSAL 19	PrintableString	Printable characters.
UNIVERSAL 20	TeletexString	Character set defined by CCITT Recommendation T.61.
UNIVERSAL 21	VideotexString	Set of alphabetic and graphic characters defined by CCITT Recommendations T.100 and T.101.
UNIVERSAL 22	IA5String	International Alphabet Five (equivalent to ASCII).
UNIVERSAL 25	GraphicString	Character set defined by ISO 8824.
UNIVERSAL 26	VisibleString	Character set defined by ISO 646 (equivalent to ASCII).
UNIVERSAL 27	GeneralString	General character string.
Miscellaneous Types		
UNIVERSAL 5	NULL	The single value NULL. Commonly used where several alternatives are possible but none of them applies.
UNIVERSAL 8	EXTERNAL	A type defined in some external document. It need not be one of the valid ASN.1 types.
UNIVERSAL 23	UTCTime	Consists of the date, specified with a two-digit year, a two-digit month; and a two-digit day; followed by the time, specified

Table C.2 (*Cont.*)

Tag	Type Name	Set of Values
		Miscellaneous Types
		in hours, minutes, and optionally seconds; followed by an optional specification of the local time differential from universal time.
UNIVERSAL 24	GeneralizedTime	Consists of the date, specified with a four-digit year, a two-digit month, and a two-digit day; followed by the time, specified in hours, minutes, and optionally seconds; followed by an optional specification of the local time differential from universal time.
UNIVERSAL 11–15	Reserved	Reserved for addenda to the ASN.1 standard.
UNIVERSAL 28–	Reserved	Reserved for addenda to the ASN.1 standard.
		Structured Types
UNIVERSAL 16	SEQUENCE and SEQUENCE-OF	Sequence: defined by referencing a fixed, ordered list of types; each value is an ordered list of values, one from each component type. Sequence-of: defined by referencing a single existing type; each value is an ordered list of zero or more values of the existing type.
UNIVERSAL 17	SET and SET-OF	Set: defined by referencing a fixed, unordered list of types, some of which may be declared optional; each value is an unordered list of values, one from each component type. Set-of: defined by referencing a single existing type; each value is an unordered list of zero or more values of the existing type.

The mantissa (M) and the exponent (E) may take on any integer values, positive or negative; a base (B) of 2 or 10 may be used.

Finally, the ENUMERATED type consists of an explicitly enumerated list of integers, together with an associated name for each integer. The same functionality can be achieved with the INTEGER type by naming some of the integer values, but because of the utility of this feature, a separate type has been defined. Note, however, that although the values of the ENUMERATED type are integers, they do not have integer semantics. That is, arithmetic operations should not be performed on enumerated values.

Object types are used to name and describe information objects. Examples of information objects are standards documents, abstract and transfer syntaxes, data structures, and managed objects. In general, an information object is a class of information (e.g., a file format) rather than an instance of such a class (e.g., an individual file). An OBJECT IDENTIFIER is a unique identifier for a particular object. Its value consists of a sequence of integers. The set of defined objects has a tree structure, with the root of the tree being the object referring to the ASN.1 standard. Starting with the root of the object identifier tree, each object identifier component value identifies an arc in the tree. An OBJECT DESCRIPTOR is a human-readable description of an information object.

ASN.1 defines a number of character string types. The value of each of these types consists of a sequence of zero or more characters from a standardized character set.

There are some miscellaneous types that have also been defined in the UNIVERSAL class. The NULL type is used in places in a structure where a value may or may not be present. The NULL type is simply the alternative of no value's being present at that position in the structure. An EXTERNAL type is one whose values are unspecified in the ASN.1 standard; it is defined in some other document or standard and can be defined using any well-specified notation. UTCTime and GeneralizedTime are two different formats for expressing time. In both cases, either a universal or local time may be specified.

C.2.3.2   Structured Types

Structured types are those consisting of components. ASN.1 provides four structured types for building complex data types from simple data types:

1. SEQUENCE
2. SEQUENCE OF
3. SET
4. SET OF

The SEQUENCE and SEQUENCE OF types are used to define an ordered list of values of one or more other data types. This is analogous to the record structure found in many programming languages, such as COBOL. A SEQUENCE consists of an ordered list of elements, each specifying a type and, optionally, a name. The notation for defining the SEQUENCE type is as follows:

SequenceType ::= SEQUENCE {ElementTypeList} | SEQUENCE { }
ElementTypeList ::= ElementType | ElementTypeList, ElementType

ElementType ::=
   NamedType |
   NamedType OPTIONAL |
   NamedType DEFAULT Value |
   COMPONENTS OF Type

A NamedType is a type reference with or without a name. Each element definition may be followed by the keyword OPTIONAL or DEFAULT. The OPTIONAL keyword indicates that the component element need not be present in a SEQUENCE value. The DEFAULT keyword indicates that, if the component element is not present, then the value specified by the DEFAULT clause will be assigned. The COMPONENTS OF clause is used to define the inclusion, at this point in the ElementTypeList, of all the ElementType sequences appearing in the referenced type.

A SEQUENCE OF consists of an ordered, variable number of elements, all of one type. A SEQUENCE OF definition has the following form:

SequenceOfType :: = SEQUENCE OF Type | SEQUENCE

The notation SEQUENCE is to be interpreted as SEQUENCE OF ANY; the type ANY is explained in subsection C.2.3.4.

A SET is similar to a SEQUENCE, except that the order of the elements is not significant; the elements may be arranged in any order when they are encoded into a specific representation. A Set definition has the following form:

SetType :: = SET {ElementTypeList} | SET { }

Thus, a SET may include OPTIONAL, DEFAULT, and COMPONENTS OF clauses.

A SET OF is an unordered, variable number of elements, all of one type. A SET OF definition has the following form:

SetOfType :: = SET OF Type | SET

The notation SET is to be interpreted as SET OF ANY; the type ANY is explained in subsection C.2.3.4.

C.2.3.3   Tagged Types

The term *tagged type* is something of a misnomer, since all data types in ASN.1 have an associated tag. The ASN.1 standard defines a tagged type as follows:

A type defined by referencing a single existing type and a tag; the new type is isomorphic to the existing type, but is distinct from it. In all encoding schemes a value of the new type can be distinguished from a value of the old type.

Tagging is useful to distinguish types within an application. It may be desired to have several different type names, such as Employee_name and Customer_name, which are essentially the same type. For some structures, tagging is needed to distinguish component types within the structured type. For example, optional components of a SET or SEQUENCE type are typically given distinct context-specific tags to avoid ambiguity.

There are two categories of tagged types: implicitly tagged types and explicitly tagged types. An implicitly tagged type is derived from another type by *replacing* the tag of the old type (old class name, old tag number) with a new tag (new class name, new tag number). For purposes of encoding, only the new tag is used.

An explicitly tagged type is derived from another type by *adding* a new tag to the underlying type. In effect, an explicitly tagged type is a structured type with one component, the underlying type. For purposes of encoding, both the new and old tags must be reflected in the encoding.

An implicit tag results in shorter encodings, but an explicit tag may be necessary to avoid ambiguity if the tag of the underlying type is indeterminate (e.g., if the underlying type is CHOICE or ANY).

C.2.3.4 CHOICE and ANY Types

The CHOICE and ANY types are data types without tags. The reason for this is that when a particular value is assigned to the type, then a particular type must be assigned at the same time. Thus, the type is assigned at "run time."

The CHOICE type is a list of alternative known types. Only one of these types will actually be used to create a value. It was stated earlier that a type can be viewed as a collection of values. The CHOICE type is the union of the sets of values of all of the component types listed in the CHOICE type. This type is useful when the values to be described can be of different types depending on circumstance, and all the possible types are known in advance.

The notation for defining the CHOICE type is as follows:

ChoiceType :: = CHOICE {AlternativeTypeList}
AlternativeTypeList :: = NamedType | AlternativeTypeList, NamedType

The ANY type describes an arbitrary value of an arbitrary type. The notation is simply:

AnyType :: = ANY

This type is useful when the values to be described can be of different types, but the possible types are not known in advance.

C.2.4 Subtypes

A subtype is derived from a parent type by restricting the set of values defined for the parent type. That is, the set of values for the subtype is a subset of the set of values for the parent type. The process of subtyping can extend to more than one level; that is, a subtype may itself be a parent of an even more restricted subtype.

Six different forms of notation for designating the values of a subtype are provided in the standard. Table C.3 indicates which of these forms can be applied to particular parent types. The remainder of this subsection provides an overview of each form.

C.2.4.1 Single Value

A single-value subtype is an explicit listing of all the values that the subtype may take on. For example:

SmallPrime ::= INTEGER (2 | 3 | 5 | 7 | 11 | 13 | 17 | 19 | 23 | 29)

In this case, SmallPrime is a subtype of the built-in type INTEGER.

As another example:

Table C.3 Applicability of Subtype Value Sets

Type (or derived from such a type by tagging)	Single Value	Contained Subtype	Value Range	Permitted Alphabet	Size Constraint	Inner Subtyping
BOOLEAN	√	√				
INTEGER	√	√	√			
ENUMERATED	√	√				
REAL	√	√	√			
OBJECT IDENTIFIER	√	√				
BIT STRING	√	√			√	
OCTET STRING	√	√			√	
Character string types	√	√		√	√	
SEQUENCE	√	√				√
SEQUENCE OF	√	√			√	√
SET	√	√				√
SET OF	√	√			√	√
ANY	√	√				
CHOICE	√	√				√

```
Months :: = ENUMERATED { january (1),
                          february (2),
                          march (3),
                          april (4),
                          may (5),
                          june (6),
                          july (7),
                          august (8),
                          september (9),
                          october (10),
                          november (11),
                          december (12) }
```

First-quarter :: = Months (january | february | march)
Second-quarter :: = Months (april | may | june)

First-quarter and Second-quarter are both subtypes of the enumerated type Months.

C.2.4.2   Contained Subtype

A contained subtype is used to form new subtypes from existing subtypes. The contained subtype includes all of the values of the subtypes that it contains. For example:

First-half :: = Months (INCLUDES First-quarter | INCLUDES Second-quarter)

A contained subtype may also include a listing of explicit values:

First-third :: = Months (INCLUDES First-quarter | april)

C.2.4.3   Value Range

A value-range subtype applies only to the INTEGER and REAL types. It is specified by giving the numerical values of the end points of the range. The special values PLUS-INFINITY and MINUS-INFINITY may be used. The special values MIN and MAX may be used to indicate the minimum and maximum allowable values in the parent. Each end point of the range is either closed or open. When open, the specification of the end point includes the less-than symbol ("<"). The following are equivalent definitions:

PositiveInteger :: = INTEGER (0<..PLUS-INFINITY)
PositiveInteger :: = INTEGER (1..PLUS-INFINITY)
PositiveInteger :: = INTEGER (0<..MAX)
PositiveInteger :: = INTEGER (1..MAX)

The following are also equivalent:

NegativeInteger :: = INTEGER (MINUS-INFINITY..<0)
NegativeInteger :: = INTEGER (MINUS-INFINITY..-1)
NegativeInteger :: = INTEGER (MIN..<0)
NegativeInteger :: = INTEGER (MIN..-1)

C.2.4.4   Permitted Alphabet

The permitted-alphabet constraint may only be applied to character string types. A permitted-alphabet type consists of all values (strings) that can be constructed using a subalphabet of the parent type. Examples:

TouchToneButtons :: = IA5String (FROM
      (''0'' | ''1'' | ''2'' | ''3'' | ''4'' | ''5'' | ''6'' | ''7'' | ''8'' | ''9'' |
      ''*'' | ''#''))

DigitString :: = IA5String (FROM
      (''0'' | ''1'' | ''2'' | ''3'' | ''4'' | ''5'' | ''6'' | ''7'' | ''8'' | ''9''))

C.2.4.5   Size Constraint

A size constraint limits the number of items in a type. It can only be applied to the string types (BIT STRING, OCTET STRING, character string) and to the SEQUENCE OF and SET OF types. The item that is constrained depends on the parent type, as follows:

Type	Unit of Measure
BIT STRING	bit
OCTET STRING	octet
character string	character
SEQUENCE OF	component value
SET OF	component value

As an example of a string type, Recommendation X.121 specifies that international data numbers, which are used for addressing end systems on public data networks, including X.25 networks, should consist of at least 5 digits but not more than 14 digits. This could be specified as follows:

ItlDataNumber :: = DigitString (SIZE (5..10))

Now consider a parameter list for a message that may include up to 12 parameters:

ParameterList :: = SET SIZE (0..12) OF Parameter

C.2.4.6   Inner Subtyping

An inner type constraint can be applied to the SEQUENCE, SEQUENCE OF, SET, SET OF, and choice types. An inner subtype includes in its value set only those values from the parent type that satisfy one or more constraints on the presence and/or values of the components of the parent type. This is a rather complex subtype, and only a few examples are given here.

Consider a protocol data unit (PDU) that may have four different fields, in no particular order:

PDU :: = SET { alpha   [0]   INTEGER,
             beta   [1]   IA5String OPTIONAL,
             gamma   [2]   SEQUENCE OF Parameter,
             delta   [3]   BOOLEAN }

To specify a test that requires the Boolean to be false and the integer to be negative:

TestPDU :: = PDU (WITH COMPONENTS { ..., delta (FALSE), alpha (MIN...<0)}})

To further specify that the beta parameter is to be present and either 5 or 12 characters in length:

FurtherTestPDU :: = TestPDU (WITH COMPONENTS {..., beta (SIZE (5 | 12)) PRESENT})

As another example, consider the use of inner subtyping on a SEQUENCE OF construct:

Text-block :: = SEQUENCE OF VisibleString
Address :: = Text-block (SIZE (1..6) | WITH COMPONENT (SIZE (1..32)))

This indicates that the address consists of from one to six text blocks and that each text block is from 1 to 32 characters in length.

C.2.5   Data-Structure Example

Figure C.3, taken from the ASN.1 standard, is an example that defines the structure of a personnel record. Part (a) of the figure depicts the personnel record informally by giving an example of a specific record. Such a display might correspond to the user presentation in Figure C.1.

In part (b), we see the formal description, or abstract syntax, of the data structure. In the notation, a structure definition has the form:

<type name> :: = <type definition>

A simple example is:

SerialNumber :: = INTEGER

There are no simple types defined in the example. A similar construction is:

EmployeeNumber :: = [APPLICATION 2] IMPLICIT INTEGER

This definition makes use of the UNIVERSAL type INTEGER, but the user has chosen to give the type a new tag. The use of the term [APPLICATION 2] gives the tag (class and tag number) for this new type. Because the designation IMPLICIT is present, values of this type will be encoded only with the tag APPLICATION 2. If the designation were not present, then the values would be encoded with both the APPLICATION and UNIVERSAL tags. The use of the IMPLICIT option results in a more compact representation. In some applications, compactness may be less important than other considerations, such as the ability to carry out type checking. In the latter case, explicit tagging can be used by omitting the word IMPLICIT.

The definition of the Date type is similar to that of EmployeeNumber. In this case, the type is a character string consisting of characters from the character set defined in ISO 646, which is equivalent to ASCII. The double hyphen indicates that the rest of the line is a comment; the format of the Date type will not be checked other than to determine that the value is an ISO 646 character string.

The type of Name is the SEQUENCE type. In this case, each of the three elements in the sequence is named. ChildInformation is of the SET type. Note that no name is given to the first element of the set but that the second element is given the name dateOfBirth. The second element is the data type Date, defined elsewhere. This data type is used in two different locations, here and

Name: **John P Smith**
Title: **Director**
Employee Number: **51**
Date of Hire: **17 September 1971**
Name of Spouse: **Mary T Smith**
Number of Children: **2**

Child Information
     Name: **Ralph T Smith**
     Date of Birth: **11 November 1957**

Child Information:
     Name: **Susan B Jones**
     Date of Birth: **17 July 1959**

(a) Informal description of personnel record

PersonnelRecord ::= [APPLICATION 0] IMPLICIT SET {
        Name,
        title [0] VisibleString,
        number EmployeeNumber,
        dateOfHire [1] Date,
        nameOfSpouse [2] Name,
        children [3] IMPLICIT SEQUENCE OF ChildInformation DEFAULT {} }

ChildInformation ::= SET {
        Name,
        dateOfBirth [0] Date }

Name ::= [APPLICATION 1] IMPLICIT SEQUENCE {
        givenName VisibleString,
        initial VisibleString,
        familyName VisibleString }

EmployeeNumber ::= [APPLICATION 2] IMPLICIT INTEGER

Date ::= [APPLICATION 3] IMPLICIT VisibleString -- YYYYMMDD

(b) ASN.1 description of the record structure

```
{                         {givenName "John", initial "P", familyName "Smith"},
    title                 "Director"
    number                "51"
    dateOfHire            "19710917"
    nameOfSpouse          {givenName "Mary", initial "T", familyName "Smith"},
    children
    { {                   {givenName "Ralph", initial "T", familyName "Smith"},
      dateOfBirth         "19571111" },
      {                   {givenName "Susan", initial "B", familyName "Jones"},
      dateOfBirth         "19590717" } } }
```

(c) ASN.1 description of a record value

Figure C.3 Example of the Use of ASN.1 (ISO 8824)

in the definition of PersonnelRecord. In each location, the data type is given a name and a context-specific tag—[0] and [1], respectively. This follows the general rule that when an IMPLICIT or EXPLICIT tag is defined but only the tag number is provided, then the tag's class defaults to context-specific.

Finally, the overall structure, PersonnelRecord, is defined as a set with five elements. Associated with the last element is a default value of a null sequence, to be used if no value is supplied.

Figure C.3, part (c), is an example of a particular value for the personnel record, expressed in the abstract syntax.

C.2.6   PDU Example

As another example, consider the ASN.1 specification of the format of the protocol data units for the ROSE (remote-operations-service element) protocol (described in Appendix 12B). The specification from the standard is reproduced in Figure C.4.

One new construct in this example is the CHOICE type. This is used to describe a variable selected from a collection. Thus, any instance of the type ROSEapdus will be one of four alternative types. Note that each of the choices is labeled with a name. In the definition of RORJapdu, the CHOICE construct is used without the benefit of names.

The ROIVapdu definition is a sequence of four elements. This APDU (application protocol data unit) is used to invoke a remote operation and always includes an integer that identifies the type of APDU (invokeID) and an integer that indicates the operation invoked (OPERATION). This latter data type is defined externally. In addition, there are two optional elements to the definition. The linked-ID element is used to link this invocation to a previous one. Finally, the operation may include an argument. This definition also includes the use of the type ANY, which is the union of all defined types. A variable declared to be of type ANY may contain any value. The additional qualifier DEFINED BY provides a pointer to the semantics for this type.

The RORSapdu is used to report the result of an invoked operation. This definition gives an example of a recursive use of a structuring element. In this case, the APDU consists of a sequence of two elements, the second of which is itself a sequence of two elements. The reason that the entire structure is not defined as a simple sequence of three elements is that the last two elements, taken as a pair, are optional: either both are present or both are absent.

C.3   ASN.1 MACRO DEFINITIONS

Included in the ASN.1 specification is the ASN.1 macro notation. This notation allows the user to extend the syntax of ASN.1 to define new types and their values. The subject of ASN.1 macros is a complex one, and this section serves only to introduce the subject.

Let us begin with several observations:

- There are three levels that must be carefully distinguished:
  1. The macro notation, used for defining macros
  2. A macro definition, expressed in the macro notation and used to define a set of macro instances
  3. A macro instance, generated from a macro definition by substituting values for variables

Remote_Operations_APDUs DEFINITIONS ::= BEGIN

ROSEapdus ::= CHOICE {roiv-apdu [1] IMPLICIT ROIVapdu,
                      rors-apdu [2] IMPLICIT RORSapdu,
                      roer-apdu [3] IMPLICIT ROERapdu,
                      rorj-apdu [4] IMPLICIT RORJapdu}

ROIVapdu ::= SEQUENCE {InvokeID InvokedIDType,
                       linked-ID IMPLICIT InvokedIDType OPTIONAL,
                       operation-value OPERATION,
                       argument ANY DEFINED BY operation-value OPTIONAL}

InvokedIDType ::= INTEGER

RORSapdu ::= SEQUENCE {InvokeID InvokedIDType,
                       SEQUENCE {operation-value OPERATION,
                                 result ANY DEFINED BY operation-value
                                 }OPTIONAL}
ROERapdu ::= SEQUENCE {InvokeID InvokedIDType,
                       error-value ERROR,
                       parameter ANY DEFINED BY error-value OPTIONAL}

RORJapdu ::= SEQUENCE {InvokeID CHOICE {InvokedIDTYPE, NULL},
                       problem CHOICE {[0] IMPLICIT GeneralProblem,
                                       [1] IMPLICIT InvokeProblem,
                                       [2] IMPLICIT ReturnResultProblem,
                                       [3] IMPLICIT ReturnErrorProblem}}

GeneralProblem ::= INTEGER {unrecognizedAPDU (0),
                            mistypedAPDU (1),
                            badlyStructuredAPDU (2)}

InvokeProblem ::= INTEGER {duplicateInvocation (0),
                           unrecognizedOperation (1),
                           mistypedArgument (2),
                           resourceLimitation (3),
                           initiatorReleasing (4),
                           unrecognizedLinkedID (5),
                           linkedResponseUnexpected (6),
                           unexpectedChildOperation (7)}

ReturnResultProblem ::= INTEGER {unrecognizedInvocation (0),
                                 resultResponseUnexpected (1),
                                 mistypedResult (2)}

ReturnErrorProblem ::= INTEGER {UnrecognizedInvocation (0),
                                errorResponseUnexpected (1),
                                unrecognizedError (2),
                                unexpectedError (3),
                                mistypedParameter (4)}

END

Figure C.4 ASN.1 Abstract Syntax Specification of the ROSE Protocol (ISO 9072-1)

- A macro definition functions as a Super Type, generating a class of macro instances that function exactly like a basic ASN.1 type.[1]

- A macro definition may be viewed as a template that is used to generate a set of related types and values.

- The macro is used to extend the ASN.1 syntax but does not extend the encoding. Any type defined by means of a macro instance is simply an ASN.1 type and is encoded in the usual manner.

- In addition to the convenience of allowing a set of related types to be defined, the macro definition enables the user to include semantic information with the type.

We begin with a description of the general format of a macro definition. Then we look at an example. Finally, the overall macro definition process is defined.

C.3.1   Macro Definition Format

A macro definition has the following general form:

```
<macroname> MACRO ::=
BEGIN
    TYPE NOTATION ::= <new-type-syntax>
    VALUE NOTATION ::= <new-value-syntax>
    <supporting-productions>
END
```

The macroname is written in all uppercase letters. A new ASN.1 type is defined by writing the name of the type, which begins with a capital letter, followed by the macroname, followed by a definition of the type dictated by the form of the macro body.

The type and value notations and the supporting productions are all specified using Backus-Naur Form (BNF). The new-type-syntax describes the new type. The new-value-syntax describes the values of the new type. The supporting-productions provide any additional grammar rules for either the type or value syntax; that is, any nonterminals within the new-type-syntax and/or new-value-syntax are expanded in the supporting-productions.

When specific values are substituted for the variables or arguments of a macro definition, a macro instance is formed. This macro instance has two results. First, it generates a representation of a basic ASN.1 type, called the *returned type*. Second, it generates a representation of a generic ASN.1 value; that is, a representation of the set of values that the type may take. This generic value is called the *returned value*.

---

1. The ASN.1 standard uses the term *basic ASN.1 type* to refer to any ASN.1 type that is not a macro instance.

C.3.2   Macro Example

Now let's consider a specific instance of a macro definition.[2] Suppose we wish to represent a pair of integers and be able to refer to it as an ASN.1 type in various places within an ASN.1 module. We can define a new ASN.1 type:

Pair-integers :: = SEQUENCE (INTEGER, INTEGER)

We may also have a need for a type that represents pairs whose first member is an integer and whose second member is an octet string:

Pair-integer-octet-string :: = SEQUENCE (INTEGER, OCTET STRING)

It may happen that there is a need for a number of paired structures in our module, and a large collection of defined types is assembled:

Pair-integers, Pair-octet-strings, Pair-printable-strings, Pair-booleans,
Pair-object-identifiers, Pair-integer-octet-string, Pair-integer-character-string, Pair-reals,
  Pair-integer-real, Pair-real-integer

And so on.

We may also need pairs that contain pairs:

Pair-integer-Pair-octet-strings, Pair-integer-Pair-reals, Pair-Pair-integers-Pair-integers

If such a proliferation is occurring, much of our module definition is taken up with such definitions. It is therefore preferable to find a simple representation of the concept "pairs of types."

To begin, we need a macro name to represent this concept and choose PAIRA. By convention, macro names are in all uppercase letters; they can be used freely anywhere a basic ASN.1 type may be used. Next, we need a general format for representing types. This can simply be "PAIRA (type, type)" as the way of expressing a macro instance, with "type" being an argument for which any ASN.1 type or any macro name may be substituted. When the substitution is made, the ASN.1 type returned by the macro instance is defined to be SEQUENCE { type, type }. We also need to be able to express values for the new type, and we choose the format (value, value). For example, consider this fragment of an ASN.1 module:

SET { PAIRA (INTEGER, INTEGER), OCTET STRING }

By "executing" the macro and performing the substitution, we get the following result:

SET { SEQUENCE { INTEGER, INTEGER }, OCTET STRING }

One value of this type, written using the macro instance value representation, is:

{ (4, 20), "April 20" }

The same value using the ASN.1 value representation is:

---

2. This example is found in the ASN.1 standard. The narrative description is based on a discussion in Reinstedler (1988).

{ {4, 20}, "April 20" }

Admittedly, in this example, there is virtually no savings in using the macro definition versus directly using ASN.1 notation. We can, however, come up with a more "human-readable" form. We will call this new macro simply PAIR. The type definition format for a macro instance will be of the form:

PAIR TYPE-X = type TYPE-Y = type

with a corresponding value notation:

(X = value, Y = value)

In this case, the definition

SET { PAIR TYPE-X = INTEGER TYPE-Y = INTEGER), OCTET STRING }

yields the following type result:

{ (X = 4, Y = 20), "April 20" }

Let us look at two more macro instances from the PAIR macro:

T1 ::= PAIR   TYPE-X = INTEGER
                      TYPE-Y = BOOLEAN
T2 ::= PAIR   TYPE-X = VisibleString
                      TYPE-Y = T1

Then a value of type T1 might be:

(X = 3, Y = TRUE)

and a value of type T2 might be:

(X = "Name", Y = (X = 4, Y = FALSE))

Figure C.5 shows the macro definition for PAIR. As with all macro definitions, it has two major parts. The first part defines the *type notation*. This part simply defines the syntax for type definition to be used in a macro instance and does not define the resulting type. The production includes the following key elements:

- Character strings enclosed in quotation marks are to be reproduced exactly in the macro instance that declares a variable to be of the type of this macro.

- An argument is any nonterminal in the macro definition other than nonterminals of types local-type-reference or local-value-reference. Such terms are variables, for which a substitution is made to form the macro instance.

- The keyword type is used to specify that each macro instance contains, at this point, using standard ASN.1, some ASN.1 type name.

```
PAIR MACRO ::=
BEGIN
    TYPE NOTATION ::=
        "TYPE-X" "=" type (Local-type-1)        --Expects any ASN.1 type and assigns it
                                                 --to the variable Local-type-1
        "TYPE-Y" "=" type (Local-type-2)        --Expects a second ASN.1 type and assigns it
                                                 --to the variable Local-type-2

    VALUE NOTATION ::=
        "("
        "X" "=" value (Local-value-1 Local-type-1)   --Expects a value for the type in
                                                      --Local-type-1 and assigns it
                                                      --to the variable Local-value-1
        "Y" "=" value (Local-value-2 Local-type-2)   --Expects a value for the type in
                                                      --Local-type-2 and assigns it
                                                      --to the variable Local-value-2

        <VALUE SEQUENCE {Local-type-1, Local-type-2}
            ::= {Local-value-1, Local-value-2} >     --This "embedded definition" returns
                                                      --the final value as the value of a
                                                      --sequence of the two types
        ")"
END
```

Figure C.5 ASN.1 Macro Example (ISO 9072-1)

The second major part of the macro definition is the *value notation*. This part determines the type of the macro instance and also defines the syntax for specifying values of the macro instance. The production includes the following key elements:

- Character strings enclosed in quotation marks are to be reproduced exactly in specifying a value for a type defined by a macro instance.

- An argument is any nonterminal in the macro definition other than nonterminals of types local-type-reference or local-value-reference. Such terms are variables, for which a substitution is made to form the macro instance.

- The keyword VALUE is used to specify that each macro instance contains at this point, using standard ASN.1, some value of a type specified in the macro definition.

- The keyword VALUE is used to mark the place in the macro definition where the actual type of the macro is specified. The type appearing immediately after VALUE is the macro's returned type; that is, any value derived from the macro is encoded as a value of that type.

C.3.3   Macros versus Defined Types

The ASN.1 macro facility provides tools for:

- Defining new types
- Representing those types
- Representing values of those types
- Encoding specific values of those types

A similar capability already exists within ASN.1, which allows for the construction of defined types, either from built-in types or recursively from built-in types and defined types. The macro facility differs from the ASN.1 defined-type capability in the following respects:

- The macro facility allows the definition of a family of types. Each new type generated by a macro definition (a macro instance) is closely related to other types generated from the same macro. In contrast, there is no particular relationship between one basic ASN.1 defined type and other defined types.

- A defined type is represented in a set way from the strings symbolizing the types from which it is constructed. A macro instance is represented in whatever way the writer of the macro chooses. Thus, the syntax of a type defined via macro instance can be chosen to correspond closely to the notation used within the particular application for which the macro was written. Furthermore, the macro instance may include commentary or semantic narrative. In this way, types defined by a macro may be more readable and more writable.

- In basic ASN.1, the representation of a value of a type is derived from the representation of the type in a relatively straightforward manner. The two representations are isomorphic; that is, they have similar or identical structure. This isomorphism is not required with a macro definition. The returned type and the returned generic value may have quite different syntaxes. Again, this allows for more readable and writable values.

C.3.4   Macro Paradigm

Figure C.6 illustrates the ASN.1 macro paradigm from conception through implementation to encoding. Let us follow the steps of this diagram:

1. Starting with a concept to be represented, a set of types is chosen that adequately represents the concept. We have referred informally to this set of types as a Super Type.

2. A macro definition, which is a concrete realization of a Super Type, is written according to the rules of the ASN.1 macro definition notation.

3. The macro definition is parameterized so that any of the types in the Super Type may be generated via the substitution of arguments when writing a particular instance of the macro definition.

4. A macro instance defines an ASN.1 type, and since any ASN.1 type has a defined type representation as well as a defined generic value representation, a macro instance provides a type representation and a generic value representation for the new ASN.1 type being defined.

5. The final result of the macro instance is returned as an argument and specifies the basic ASN.1 type representation. Since this is isomorphic to the corresponding generic value representation, the latter is also implicitly returned.

6. A specific value of the type defined by the macro instance can be encoded using the equivalent ASN.1 encoding and can be represented using the basic ASN.1 value representation.

Figure C.7 illustrates the process of defining the PAIR macro.

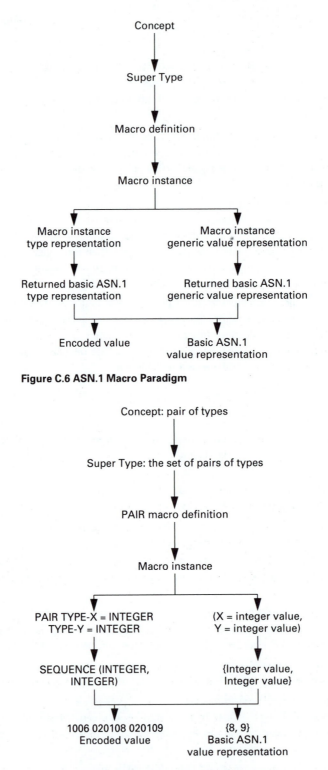

Figure C.6 ASN.1 Macro Paradigm

Figure C.7 ASN.1 Macro Paradigm Applied to PAIR

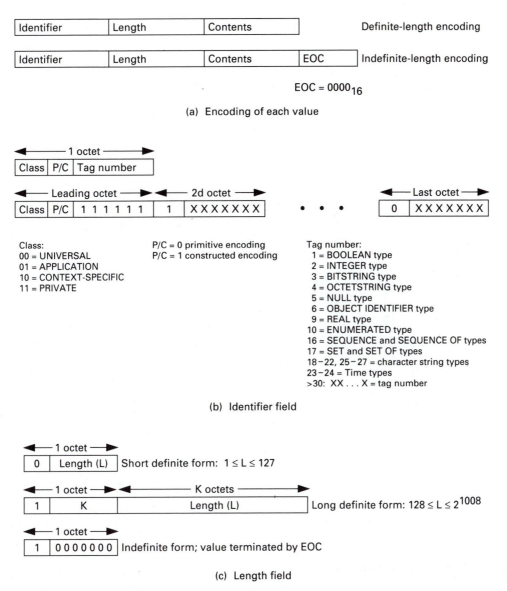

Definite-length encoding

Indefinite-length encoding

$EOC = 0000_{16}$

(a) Encoding of each value

Class:
00 = UNIVERSAL
01 = APPLICATION
10 = CONTEXT-SPECIFIC
11 = PRIVATE

P/C = 0 primitive encoding
P/C = 1 constructed encoding

Tag number:
 1 = BOOLEAN type
 2 = INTEGER type
 3 = BITSTRING type
 4 = OCTETSTRING type
 5 = NULL type
 6 = OBJECT IDENTIFIER type
 9 = REAL type
10 = ENUMERATED type
16 = SEQUENCE and SEQUENCE OF types
17 = SET and SET OF types
18−22, 25−27 = character string types
23−24 = Time types
>30: XX . . . X = tag number

(b) Identifier field

Short definite form: $1 \le L \le 127$

Long definite form: $128 \le L \le 2^{1008}$

Indefinite form; value terminated by EOC

(c) Length field

Figure C.8 BER Encoding of Values

C.4 BASIC ENCODING RULES

The basic encoding rules (BER) are an encoding specification developed and standardized by CCITT (X.209) and ISO (ISO 8825). This specification describes a method for encoding values of each ASN.1 type as a string of octets.

Personnel Record 60	Length 8185	Contents							
		Name 61	Length 10	Contents					
				Visible-String 1A	Length 04	Contents "John"			
				Visible-String 1A	Length 01	Contents "P"			
				Visible-String 1A	Length 05	Contents "Smith"			
		Title A0	Length 0A	Contents					
				Visible-String 1A	Length 08	Contents "Director"			
		Employee Number 42	Length 01	Contents 33					
		Date of Hire A1	Length 0A	Contents					
				Date 43	Length 08	Contents "19710917"			
		Name of Spouse A2	Length 12	Contents					
				Name 61	Length 10	Contents			
						Visible-String 1A	Length 04	Contents "Mary"	
						Visible-String 1A	Length 01	Contents "T"	
						Visible-String 1A	Length 05	Contents "Smith"	

Figure C.9 BER Encoding of Figure C.3, Part (c) (ISO 8825)

C.4.1 Encoding Structure

The basic encoding rules define one or more ways to encode any ASN.1 value as an octet string. The encoding is based on the use of a type-length-value (TLV) structure. That is, any ASN.1 value can be encoded as a triple with the following components:

1. *Type:* indicates the ASN.1 type, as well as the class of the type and whether the encoding is primitive or constructed, as explained later in this subsection

[3] A3	Length 42	Contents						
		Set 31	Length 1F	Contents				
				Name 61	Length 11	Contents		
						Visible- String 1A	Length 05	Contents "Ralph"
						Visible- String 1A	Length 01	Contents "T"
						Visible- String 1A	Length 05	Contents "Smith"
				Date of Birth A0	Length 0A	Contents		
						Date 43	Length 08	Contents "19571111"
		Set 31	Length 1F	Contents				
				Name 61	Length 11	Contents		
						Visible- String 16	Length 05	Contents "Susan"
						Visible- String 16	Length 01	Contents "B"
						Visible- String 1	Length 05	Contents "Jones"
				Date of Birth A0	Length 0A	Contents		
						Date 43	Length 08	Contents "19590717"

Figure C.9 BER Encoding of Figure C.3, Part (c) (ISO 8825)(cont.)

2. *Length:* indicates the length of the actual value representation

3. *Value:* the representation of the value of the ASN.1 type as a string of octets

This structure is recursive: for any ASN.1 value that consists of one or more components, the "value" portion of its TLV encoding itself consists of one or more TLV structures.

Figure C.8 illustrates the structure of the TLV encoding, and Figure C.9 illustrates its use for the example personnel record value. There are three methods for encoding an ASN.1 value:

1. Primitive, definite-length encoding

Table C.4 BER Encoding Methods

	Primitive, Definite-Length Encoding	Constructed, Definite-Length Encoding	Constructed, Indefinite-Length Encoding
Simple nonstring types	√		
Simple string types	√	√	√
Structured types		√	√
Explicit tagging		√	√

2. Constructed, definite-length encoding

3. Constructed, indefinite-length encoding

The method chosen depends on the ASN.1 type of the value to be encoded and whether or not the length of the value is known based on the type. Table C.4 summarizes the possibilities.

C.4.1.1   Primitive, Definite-Length Encoding

The primitive, definite-length encoding method can be used for simple types and types derived from simple types by implicit tagging. The BER format consists of three fields:

1. *Identifier:* This field encodes the tag (class and tag number) of the ASN.1 type of the value. The first 2 bits indicate one of the four classes. The next bit is 0 to indicate that this is a primitive encoding. The remaining 5 bits of the first octet can encode a tag number that distinguishes one data type from another within the designated class. For tags whose number is greater than or equal to 31, those 5 bits contain the binary value 11111, and the actual tag number is contained in the last 7 bits of one or more additional octets. The first bit of each additional octet is set to 1, except for the last octet, in which it is set to 0.

2. *Length:* This field specifies the length in octets of the contents field. If the length is less than 128, the length field consists of a single octet beginning with a 0. If the length is greater than 127, the first octet of the length field contains a 7-bit integer that specifies the number of additional length octets; the additional octets contain the actual length of the contents field.

3. *Contents:* This field directly represents the ASN.1 value as a string of octets. Details for particular types are given later in this section.

C.4.1.2   Constructed, Definite-Length Encoding

The constructed, definite-length encoding method can be used for simple string types, structured types (SEQUENCE, SEQUENCE OF, SET, SET OF), types derived from simple string types and structured types by implicit tagging, and any type defined by explicit tagging. This encoding method requires that the length of the value be known in advance. The BER format consists of three fields:

1. *Identifier:* as described for primitive, definite-length encoding, except that the P/C bit is set to 1 to indicate that this is constructed encoding.

2. *Length:* as described for primitive, definite-length encoding.

3. *Contents:* This field contains the concatenation of the complete BER encodings (identifier, length, contents) of the components of the value. There are three cases:

- Simple strings and types derived from simple strings by implicit tagging: the concatenation of the BER encodings of consecutive substrings of the value
- Structured types and types derived from structured types by implicit tagging: the concatenation of the BER encodings of components of the value
- Types defined by explicit tagging: the BER encoding of the underlying value

C.4.1.3 Constructed, Indefinite-Length Encoding

The constructed, indefinite-length encoding method can be used for simple string types, structured types, types derived from simple string types and structured types by implicit tagging, and any type defined by explicit tagging. This encoding method does not require that the length of the value be known in advance. The BER format consists of four fields:

1. *Identifier:* as described for constructed, indefinite-length encoding

2. *Length:* 1 octet, with the value 80_{16}

3. *Contents:* as described for constructed, indefinite-length encoding

4. *End-of-contents:* 2 octets, with the value 0000_{16}

C.4.2 Contents Encoding

Table C.5 summarizes the encoding rules for the various ASN.1 types. The table gives only a concise definition of the rules; for more detail, the reader should consult the standard.

Most of the encoding rules for ASN.1 types are relatively straightforward. For some types, a few additional comments are warranted.

C.4.2.1 Integer

Integer values are represented using two's-complement notation. This notation can be briefly summarized as follows.[3] Consider an integer in two's complement representation stored in an N-bit field. There are two cases: non-negative and negative.

Non-negative numbers are represented as follows. The leftmost (most-significant) bit is 0, and the remaining bits are the binary form of the magnitude of the number. A negative number whose magnitude is X and for which X has a value of less than or equal to 2^{N-1} is represented by calculating $2^N - X$. For all negative numbers, the leftmost bit has a value of 1. Thus, this bit functions as a sign bit.

If an N-bit sequence of binary digits $b_{N-1}b_{N-2} \ldots b_1 b_0$ is interpreted as a two's-complement representation, the value can be calculated as follows:

$$\text{Value} = -b_{N-1}2^{N-1} + \sum_{i=0}^{N-2} b_i 2^i$$

The largest negative number that can be represented is -2^{N-1}, and the largest positive integer that can be represented is $2^{N-1} - 1$. Thus, in a single octet, the range of numbers that can be represented is $-128 \leq \text{value} \leq 127$.

---

3. For a more complete discussion of two's complement representation and two's complement arithmetic, see Stallings (1993a).

Table C.5 BER Contents Encoding Rules

ASN.1 Type	BER Encoding Rules	Example Value	Encoding of Example Value*
BOOLEAN	Primitive. A single octet with a content of 0 for FALSE and a non-0 content for TRUE.	TRUE	01 01 FF
INTEGER	Primitive. Two's complement representation with the minimum number of octets.	−129	02 02 FF 7F
ENUMERATED	Same as the integer value with which it is associated.		
REAL	Primitive. If the value is 0, there are no contents octets. Otherwise, the first contents octet indicates whether the base is 10, 2, 8, or 16, or a special real value ($+\infty$, $-\infty$). If the base is 10, first contents octet also specifies one of three ISO 6093 character-encoding schemes for the remaining contents octets. If the base is 2, 8, or 16, the first contents octet also specifies length of exponent, sign of mantissa, and scaling factor to align implied decimal point of mantissa with octet boundary; following the first contents octet is 0 or 1 additional octet to specify exponent length, followed by octets for the exponent, followed by octets for the mantissa.	0	09 00

BIT STRING	Primitive or constructed. For primitive encoding, the contents consists of an initial octet followed by 0 or more subsequent octets. The actual bit string begins with the first bit of the second octet and continues through as many octets as necessary. The first octet indicates how many bits in the last octet are unused.
	
	 For constructed encoding, the bit string is broken up into substrings; each substring except the last must be a multiple of 8 bits in length. Each substring may be encoded as primitive or constructed, but usually the primitive encoding is used.
		"01011100101 110111"	Primitive:
			 03 04 06 6E 5D C0
			 Constructed:
			 23 09
			     03 03 00 6E 5D
			     03 02 06 C0

OCTET STRING	Primitive or constructed. For primitive encoding, the contents octets are identical to the value of the octet string.
	
	 For constructed encoding, the octet string is broken up into substrings; each substring may be encoded as primitive or constructed, but usually the primitive encoding is used.
		01 23 45 67	Primitive:
			 04 04 01 23 45 67
			 Constructed:
			 24 08
			     04 02 01 23
			     04 02 34 56

598

Type	Definition / Value	Encoding	Description
NULL	null	05 00	Primitive. There are no contents octets.
SEQUENCE	Definition: SEQUENCE (INTEGER, INTEGER) Value: (3,8)	30 06 02 01 03 02 01 08	Constructed. The contents octets are the concatenation of the BER encodings of the values of the components of the sequence in order of definition. If the value of a component with the OPTIONAL or DEFAULT qualifier is absent from the sequence, no encoding is included for that component. If the value of a component with the DEFAULT qualifier is the value, then encoding of that component may or may not be included.
SEQUENCE OF	Definition: SEQUENCE OF (INTEGER) Value: (3,8)	30 06 02 01 03 02 01 08	Constructed. The contents octets are the concatenation of the BER encodings of the values of the occurrences in the collection, in the order of occurrence.
SET	Definition: SET (INTEGER, INTEGER) Value: (3,8)	31 06 02 01 03 02 01 08	Constructed. The contents octets are the concatenation of the BER encodings of the values of the components of the sequence, in any order. If the value of a component with the OPTIONAL or DEFAULT qualifier is absent from the sequence, no encoding is included for that component. If the value of a component with the DEFAULT qualifier is the default value, then encoding of that component may or may not be included.
SET OF	Definition: SET OF (INTEGER) Value: (3,8)	31 06 02 01 03 02 01 08	Constructed. The contents octets are the concatenation of the BER encodings of the values of the occurrences in the collection, in any order.
CHOICE			Primitive or constructed. The encoding of the CHOICE value is the encoding of the chosen alternative.
IMPLICIT tag	Definition: [17] IMPLICIT BOOLEAN Value: TRUE	91 01 FF	Primitive or constructed. The encoding of the tag field replaces the underlying tag value. The encoding of the length and contents octets are the same as for the underlying value.
EXPLICIT tag	Definition: [17] BOOLEAN Value: TRUE	B1 03 01 01 FF	Constructed. The contents octets are the complete BER encoding of the underlying value.

Table C.5 (*Cont.*)

ASN.1 Type	BER Encoding Rules	Example Value	Encoding of Example Value*
ANY	Primitive or constructed. The encoding of the ANY value is the encoding of the actual value.		
OBJECT IDENTIFIER	Primitive. The first two components are combined using the formula $(X \times 40) + Y$ to form the first subidentifier. Each subsequent component forms the next subidentifier. Each subidentifier is encoded as a non-negative integer using as few 7-bit blocks as possible. The blocks are packed in octets with the first bit of each octet equal to 1 except for the last octet of each subidentifier.	{2 100 3}	06 03 81 34 03
Character string	Primitive or constructed. Encoded as if it had been declared [UNIVERSAL x] IMPLICIT OCTET STRING.	"Jones"	1A 05 4A 6F 6E 65 73

*All encodings are depicted using hexadecimal notation.

An important characteristic of the two's complement representation is the way in which an N-bit number is padded out to form an M-bit number, where $M > N$. For non-negative numbers, the representation is padded out by adding additional 0s to the left. For negative numbers, the representation is padded out by adding additional 1s to the left.

BER dictates that the minimum number of octets be used for representing integers. Thus, if a value is between -128 and $+127$, only a single octet is used. Note that care must be taken for unsigned variables, such as counters and gauges. If a 32-bit counter has a value of 2^{31} or greater, then 5 octets rather than 4 will be needed to encode it. For example, in the SNMP structure of management information, the counter type is defined as follows:

Counter ::= [APPLICATION 1] IMPLICIT INTEGER (0..4294967295)

This defines an unsigned 32-bit integer with a maximum value of $2^{32} - 1$.

Now consider a 32-bit counter that has its maximum value of $FFFFFFFF_{16}$. The correct encoding, in hexadecimal, is:

41 05 00 FF FF FF FF

The identifier octet specifies that this is an application class type with tag number 1. The length octet specifies that the value length is 5 octets. Because of the use of two's complement representation, the value cannot be encoded in 4 octets.

C.4.2.2 Bit, Octet, and Character Strings

For the simple string types, the encoding can be either primitive or constructed. For the constructed encoding, the string is broken up into a number of substrings, each of which is encoded using BER. Since these rules are recursive, each substring can be further subdivided into sub-substrings using the constructed encoding.

The way in which a string is broken up into substrings is arbitrary and at the convenience of the encoding process. That is, the boundaries that define the substrings are arbitrary.

C.4.2.3 Object Identifier

An object identifier consists of a sequence of integers. The BER encoding packs the first two integers into a single subidentifier. Thus, an identifier consisting of N integers has $N - 1$ subidentifiers.

The reason that the first two integers can be combined is that the first integer always takes on the value 0, 1, or 2, and the second integer must be less than 40 if the first integer is 0 or 1. The packing formula is

$$Z = (X \times 40) + Y,$$

where X is the first integer, Y is the second integer, and Z is the resulting subidentifier value. The result can be summarized as follows:

Subidentifier Value	First Integer	Second Integer
$0 \leq Z \leq 39$	0	Z
$40 \leq Z \leq 79$	1	$Z - 40$
$80 \leq Z$	2	$Z - 80$

C.5   ALTERNATIVE ENCODING RULES

BER provides options for encoding various values and does not result in a very compact representation. Currently, several new encoding rules for ASN.1 are being standardized. These rules, which will become new parts to ISO 8825 and X.208, are:

- *Packed encoding rules (PER):* This set of rules results in a very compressed encoding. Unlike BER, PER is implicitly typed, and it relies on ASN.1 subtype information to minimize the size of encodings. For example, a type defined as INTEGER (998..1001) can be encoded in PER using 2 bits.

- *Distinguished encoding rules (DER):* This set of rules is a subset of BER, which gives exactly one way to represent any ASN.1 value.

- *Canonical encoding rules (CER):* Like DER, CER is a subset of BER. Whereas DER caters to applications that have a need for a single way to encode data using definite-length encoding, CER caters to applications that have a need for a single way to encode data using indefinite-length encoding.

- *Lightweight encoding rules (LWER):* This set of rules is intended to result in faster encoding of protocol data units (PDUs) at the expense of potentially generating longer encodings.

Appendix D
Object-Oriented Design

OSI systems management relies heavily on object-oriented design principles in representing management information. This appendix provides a brief overview of these principles.

D.1 MOTIVATION

Object-oriented concepts have become quite popular in the area of computer programming, with the promise of interchangeable, reusable, easily updated, and easily interconnected software parts. More recently, database designers have begun to appreciate the advantages of an object orientation, with the result that object-oriented database-management systems (OODBMSs) are beginning to appear. It is this latter area that is of relevance to OSI systems management.

Object-oriented programming and object-oriented database-management systems are in fact different things, but they share one key concept: that software or data can be "containerized." Everything goes into a box, and there can be boxes within boxes. In the simplest conventional program, one program step equates to one instruction; in an object-oriented language, each step might equate to a whole boxful of instructions. Similarly, with an object-oriented database, one variable, instead of equating to a single data element, may equate to a whole boxful of data.

The attraction of object-oriented databases is their flexibility in representing a variety of concepts and facts. For basic text and numerical information, a conventional record-oriented database provides efficient storage, and a relational database provides simple and powerful access facilities. However, when the data are not, or cannot be, organized into neat rows and columns of words and numbers, these approaches are flawed. Here are some examples of applications that require other kinds of data representations (Garber 1992):

- A chemical or pharmaceuticals company, whose data describe the structure and properties of molecules

- An electronics shop, whose critical data are huge libraries of semiconductor designs

- A petroleum company, storing huge numbers of geophysical maps
- An ad agency, with large numbers of layouts, photographs, tapes, and films

For these applications, a database that can reflect the structure of the things that it represents is vital. The object-oriented approach provides a convenient and natural way of capturing that structure.

The object-oriented approach is well suited to representing network-management information. The resources that are to be managed can be viewed as hierarchical, interrelated objects. For example, a modem has two physical interfaces and a set of properties, such as data rate. Each interface relates the modem to another device or communications facility, each of which has its own object representation.

D.2   OBJECT-ORIENTED CONCEPTS

The central concept of object-oriented design is the *object*. An object is a distinct software unit that contains a collection of related data and procedures. Generally, these data and procedures are not directly visible outside the object. Rather, well-defined interfaces exist that allow other software to have access to the data and procedures.

D.2.1   Object Structure

The data and procedures contained in an object are generally referred to as variables and methods, respectively. Everything an object ''knows'' is expressed in its variables, and everything it can do is expressed in its methods.

The *variables* in an object are typically simple scalars or tables. Each variable has a type, possibly a set of allowable values, and may either be constant or variable (by convention, the term *variable* is used even for constants). Access restrictions may also be imposed on variables for certain users, classes of users, or situations.

The *methods* in an object are procedures that can be triggered from outside to perform certain functions. A method may change the state of the object, update some of its variables, or act on outside resources to which the object has access.

Objects interact by means of *messages*. A message includes the name of the sending object, the name of the receiving object, the name of a method in the receiving object, and any parameters needed to qualify the execution of the method. Note that the message can only be used to invoke a method within an object. The only way to access the data inside an object is by means of the object's methods. Thus, a method may cause an action to be taken, or it may cause the object's variables to be accessed, or both.

An object, then, has the property that its only interface with the outside world is by means of messages. This property is referred to as *encapsulation*. The methods and variables of an object are encapsulated and available only via message-based communication. This property offers two advantages:

1. It protects an object's variables from corruption by other objects. This may include protection from unauthorized access and protection from the types of problems that arise from concurrent access, such as deadlock and inconsistent values.

2. It hides the internal structure of the object so that interaction with the object is relatively simple and standardized. Furthermore, if the internal structure or procedures of an object are modified without changing its external functionality, other objects are unaffected.

D.2.2 Object Classes

An object in a database represents some thing, be it a physical entity, a concept, a software module, or some dynamic entity such as a virtual circuit. The values of the variables in the object express the information that is known about the thing that the object represents. The methods include procedures whose execution affects the values in the object and possibly also affects that thing being represented.

In practice, there will typically be a number of objects representing the same types of things. For example, if a virtual circuit is represented by an object, then there will be one object for each virtual circuit currently open in a system. Clearly, every such object needs its own set of variables. However, if the methods in the object are reentrant procedures, then all similar objects could share the same methods. Furthermore, it would be inefficient to redefine both methods and variables for every new but similar object.

The solution to these difficulties is to make a distinction between an object class and an object instance. An *object class* is a template that defines the methods and variables to be included in a particular type of object. An *object instance* is an actual object that includes the characteristics of the class that defines it. The instance contains values for the variables defined in the object class.

D.2.2.1 Inheritance

The concept of an object class is powerful because it allows for the creation of many object instances with a minimum of effort. This concept is made even more powerful by the use of the mechanism of inheritance.

Inheritance enables a new object class to be defined in terms of an existing class. The new class, called the *subclass,* automatically includes the methods and variable definitions in the original class, called the *superclass*. A subclass may differ from its superclass in a number of ways:

- The subclass may include additional methods and variables not found in its superclass.

- The subclass may override the definition of any method or variable in its superclass by using the same name with a new definition. This provides a simple and efficient way of handling special cases.

- The subclass may restrict a method or variable inherited from its superclass in some way.

The inheritance mechanism is recursive, allowing a subclass to become the superclass of its own subclasses. In this way, an *inheritance hierarchy* may be constructed, as illustrated in Figure D.1. Any object class inherits all the characteristics of its superclass, including those characteristics that the superclass inherited from higher up the hierarchy. For example, object class C-A2 includes all of the methods and variables in C-A that are not overridden in the definition of C-A2, and object class C-A2b includes all of the methods and variables defined in C-A that are not overridden in either C-A2 or C-A2b plus all of the methods and variables defined in C-A2 that are not overridden in C-A2b.

Conceptually, we can think of the inheritance hierarchy as defining a search technique for methods and variables. When an object receives a message to carry out a method that is not defined

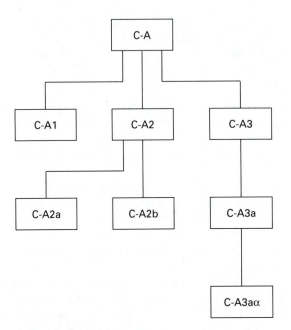

Figure D.1 An Inheritance Hierarchy of Object Classes

in its class, it automatically searches up the hierarchy until it finds the method. Similarly, if the execution of a method results in the reference to a variable not defined in that class, the object searches up the hierarchy for the variable name.

D.2.2.2   Polymorphism

Polymorphism is an intriguing and powerful characteristic that makes it possible to hide different implementations behind a common interface. Two objects that are polymorphic to each other utilize the same names for methods and present the same interface to other objects. For example, there may be a number of print objects, for different output devices, such as printDotmatrix, printLaser, printScreen, and so forth, or for different types of documents, such as printText, printDrawing, printCompound. If each such object includes a method called *print,* then any document could be printed by sending the message *print* to the appropriate object, without concern for how that method is actually carried out.

It is instructive to compare polymorphism to the usual modular programming techniques. An objective of top-down, modular design is to design lower-level modules of general utility with a fixed interface to higher-level modules. This allows the *one* lower-level module to be invoked by *many* different higher-level modules. If the internals of the lower-level module are changed without changing its interface, then none of the upper-level modules that use it is affected. By contrast, with polymorphism, we are concerned with the ability of *one* higher-level object to invoke *many* different lower-level objects using the same message format to accomplish similar functions. With polymorphism, new lower-level objects can be added with minimal changes to existing objects.

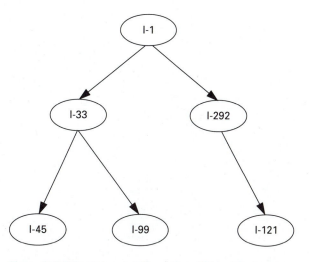

Figure D.2 A Containment Hierarchy of Object Instances

D.2.3   Containment

Object instances that contain other objects are called *composite objects*. Containment may be achieved by including the pointer to one object as a value in another object. The advantage of composite objects is that they permit the representation of complex structures. For example, an object contained in a composite object may itself be a composite object.

Typically, the structures built up from composite objects are limited to a tree topology; that is, no circular references are allowed, and each "child" object instance may have only one "parent" object instance. Figure D.2 illustrates the type of hierarchical structure that results.

It is important to be clear about the distinction between an inheritance hierarchy of object classes and a containment hierarchy of object instances. The two are not related. The use of inheritance simply allows many different object types to be defined with a minimum of effort. The use of containment allows the construction of complex data structures.

References

Aguilar, L. 1991. "Using RPC for Distributed Systems Management." *Proceedings, Second International Symposium on Integrated Network Management* (Apr.). New York: North-Holland.

Amer, P. 1982. "A Measurement Center for the NBS Local Area Computer Network." *IEEE Transactions on Computers* (Aug.).

Amer, P.; Rosenthal, R.; and Toense, R. 1983. "Measuring a Local Network's Performance." *Data Communications* (Apr.).

Aronoff, R., et al. 1989. *Management of Networks Based on Open Systems Interconnection (OSI) Standards: Functional Requirements and Analysis.* Gaithersburg, Md.: National Institute of Standards and Technology, Special Publication 500-175 (Nov.).

Bapat, S. 1991. "OSI Management Information Base Implementation." *Proceedings, Second International Symposium on Integrated Network Management* (Apr.). New York: North-Holland.

Ben-Artzi, A.; Chandna, A.; and Warrier, U. 1990. "Network Management of TCP/IP Networks: Present and Future." *IEEE Network Magazine* (July).

Black, U. 1991. *OSI: A Model for Computer Communications Standards.* Engelwood Cliffs, N.J.: Prentice-Hall.

Case, D. and Partridge, C. 1989. "Case Diagrams: A First Step to Diagrammed Management Information Bases." *Computer Communication Review,* January. Reprinted in *Connexions,* March 1989.

Cerf, V. 1988. *IAB Recommendations for the Development of Internet Management Standards.* RFC 1052 (Apr.).

Cerf, V. 1989. *Report of the Second Ad Hoc Network Management Review Group.* RFC 1109 (Aug.).

Chiu, D., and Sudama, R. 1992. *Network Monitoring Explained: Design and Application.* New York: Ellis Horwood.

Davies, D., and Price, W. 1990. *Security for Computer Networks.* New York: Wiley.

Dupuy, A., et al. 1989. "Network Fault Management: A User's View." *Proceedings, First International Symposium on Integrated Network Management* (May). New York: North-Holland.

Eckerson, W. 1992. "Net Management Traffic Can Sap Net Performance." *Network World* (May 4).

Eckerson, W., and Messmer, E. 1992. "Is OSI Dead?" *Network World* (June 15).

Feldkhun, L. 1989. "Integrated Network Management Systems (A Global Perspective on the Issue)." *Proceedings, First International Symposium on Integrated Network Management* (May). New York: North-Holland.

Fried, S., and Tjong, J. 1990. "Implementing Integrated Monitoring Systems for Heterogeneous Networks." In *Network Management and Control,* edited by A. Kershenbaum, M. Malek, and M. Wall. New York: Plenum.

Garber, J. 1992. "Here Comes OOdbms." *Forbes* (July 6).

Guynes, J. 1988. "Impact of System Response Time on State Anxiety." *Communications of the ACM* (Mar.).

Halsall, F. 1992. *Data Communications, Computer Networks, and Open Systems.* Reading, Mass.: Addison-Wesley.

Herman, J. 1992. "Distributed Network Management." *Data Communications* (June).

Horwitt, E. 1992. "Priority for Users: Easy Way to Manage Networks." *Network World* (May 25).

Johnson, J. 1985. "Universal Flow and Capacity Index Gives Picture of Network Efficiency." *Data Communications* (Feb.).

Kershenbaum, A.; Malek, M.; and Wall, M., eds. 1990. *Network Management and Control.* New York: Plenum.

Klerer, S., and Cohen, R. 1991. "Distribution of Managed Object Fragments and Managed Object Replication: The Data Distribution View of Management Information." *Proceedings, Second International Symposium on Integrated Network Management* (Apr.). New York: North-Holland.

LaBarre, L. 1991. "Management by Exception: OSI Event Generation, Reporting, and Logging." *Proceedings, Second International Symposium on Integrated Network Management* (Apr.). New York: North-Holland.

Lotter, M. 1992. *Internet Growth (1981–1991).* RFC 1296 (Jan.).

Martin, J. 1988. *Principles of Data Communication.* Englewood Cliffs, N.J.: Prentice-Hall.

Mazumdar, S., and Lazar, A. "Objective-Driven Monitoring." 1991. *Proceedings, Second International Symposium on Integrated Network Management* (Apr.). New York: North-Holland.

Mier, E. 1991a. "*Network World,* Bell Labs Evaluate SNMP on Bridges." *Network World* (Apr. 22).

———. 1991b. "*Network World,* Bell Labs Test Routers' SNMP Agents." *Network World* (July 1).

Miller, R. 1968. "Response Time in Man-Computer Conversational Transactions." *Proceedings, Spring Joint Computer Conference.*

Nechvatal, J. 1991. *Public-Key Cryptography.* Gaithersburg, Md.: National Institute of Standards and Technology, NIST Special Publication 800-2.

Partridge, C., and McCloghrie, K. 1990. "Network Management in the TCP/IP Protocol Suite." In Stallings, W. *Handbook of Computer-Communications Standards.* Stallings. Vol. 3, *The TCP/IP Protocol Suite.* 2d ed. New York: Macmillan.

Reinstedler, J. 1988. "ASN.1 Macro Facility." *Open Systems Data Transfer* (Apr.).

Schneier, B. 1991. "One-Way Hash Functions." *Dr. Dobb's Journal* (Sept.).

Shneiderman, B. 1984. "Response Time and Display Rate in Human Performance with Computers." *ACM Computing Surveys* (Sept.).

Smith, D. 1983. "Faster Is Better: A Business Case for Subsecond Response Time." *Computerworld* (Apr. 18).

Stallings, W. 1990. *Handbook of Computer-Communications Standards*, Vol. 3, *The TCP/IP Protocol Suite*. 2d. ed. New York: Macmillan.

Stallings, W. 1992. *Operating Systems*. New York: Macmillan.

Stallings, W. 1993a. *Computer Organization and Architecture*. 3d ed. New York: Macmillan.

Stallings, W. 1993b. *Local and Metropolitan Area Networks*. 4th ed. New York: Macmillan.

Stallings, W. 1993c. *Networking Standards: A Guide to OSI, ISDN, LAN, and MAN Standards*. Reading, Mass.: Addison-Wesley.

Stallings, W. 1994. *Data and Computer Communications*. 4th ed. New York: Macmillan.

Terplan, K. 1992. *Communication Networks Management*. Englewood Cliffs, N.J.: Prentice-Hall.

Thadhani, A. 1981. "Interactive User Productivity." *IBM Systems Journal*, no. 1.

Tsudik, G. 1992. "Message Authentication with One-Way Hash Functions." *Proceedings, INFOCOM '92* (May).

Waldbusser, S. 1992. "Applications Stand to Benefit from SNMP." *The Simple Times* (Sept.–Oct.).

Waldbusser, S.; Nair, M.; and Hoerth, M. 1992. "SNMP Management Goes Down to the Wire." *Data Communications* (May).

Wilkinson, S., and Capen, T. 1992. "Remote Control." *Corporate Computing* (Oct.).

Index